2020
Social Security Explained

PAYROLL MANAGEMENT PROFESSIONAL SERIES

WITHDRAWN

Wolters Kluwer

This publication is designed to provide accurate and authoritative information in regard to the subject matter covered. It is sold with the understanding that the publisher is not engaged in rendering legal, accounting, or other professional service. If legal advice or other expert assistance is required, the services of a competent professional person should be sought.

978-1-5438-1952-6

© 2020 CCH Incorporated and its affiliates. All rights reserved.

2700 Lake Cook Road
Riverwoods, IL 60015
1 866 529 6600
www.WoltersKluwerLR.com

SUSTAINABLE FORESTRY INITIATIVE   Certified Sourcing
www.sfiprogram.org
SFI-01051

Social Security Explained

SOCIAL SECURITY COST-OF-LIVING ADJUSTMENT (COLA) CHARTS

Subject to COLA[1]	2020	2019	2018
Tax rate FICA-Medicare [2]			
Employee	7.65 (6.20 OASDI, 1.45 HI)	7.65 (6.20 OASDI, 1.45 HI)	7.65 (6.20 OASDI, 1.45 HI)
Self-employed	15.30 (12.40 OASDI, 2.90 HI)	15.30 (12.40 OASDI, 2.90 HI)	15.30 (12.40 OASDI, 2.90 HI)
Taxable wage base OASDI maximum earnings taxable	137,700	$132,900	$128,400
Taxable wage base HI maximum earnings taxable [3]	unlimited	unlimited	unlimited
Quarter of coverage	$1,410	$1,360	$1,320
Retirement earnings test exempt amounts			
Earnings test [4]			
Year worker reaches full retirement age [5]	$48,600	$46,920	$45,360
Under full retirement age	$18,240	$17,640	$17,040
Maximum Social Security benefit (workers retiring at full retirement) [6]	$3,011 per mo.	$2,861 per mo.	$2,788 per mo.
Supplemental Security Income federal payment standard			
Individual	$783 per mo.	$771 per mo.	$750 per mo.
Couple	$1,175 per mo.	$1,157 per mo.	$1,125 per mo.
Supplemental Security Income resource limits			
Individual	$2,000	$2,000	$2,000
Couple	$3,000	$3,000	$3,000

[1] Sources: Social Security Administration News Release and Fact Sheet—10/10/2019.
[2] The 7.65% represents the combined Social Security and Medicare tax rate. The Social Security portion (OASDI) is 6.20% on wages up to the applicable maximum taxable amount. The Medicare portion (HI) is 1.45% on all wages. Note: A 0.9% Medicare tax is also imposed on employees who receive wages in excess of $200,000 ($250,000 for joint filers and $125,000 for married taxpayers filing separately). In addition, a 3.8% Medicare contribution tax is assessed on the lesser of (1) an individual's net investment income for the year and (2) any excess of modified adjusted gross income for the tax year over $200,000 for individuals ($250,000 for joint filers and $125,000 for married individuals filing separately).
[3] The maximum was eliminated by the Omnibus Budget Reconciliation Act of 1993 (P.L. 103-66).
[4] There is no limit on earnings beginning the month an individual attains full retirement age (66 years for retirees born in 1943-1954).
[5] Applies only to earnings for months prior to attaining full retirement age.
[6] The age at which a retiree is entitled to his or her full benefit amount—i.e., the age at which benefits are no longer reduced on account of early retirement—is gradually increasing to age 67.

ESTIMATED AVERAGE MONTHLY SOCIAL SECURITY BENEFITS (PAYABLE IN JANUARY 2020)

	2020
All retired workers	$1,503
Aged couple, both receiving benefits	$2,531
Widowed mother and two children	$2,935
Aged widow(er) alone	$1,421
Disabled worker, spouse, and children	$2,178
All disabled workers	$1,258

Due to the increase in the Consumer Price Index for Urban Wage Earners and Clerical Workers (CPI-W) from the third quarter of 2018 through the third quarter of 2019, Social Security beneficiaries and Supplemental Security Income recipients will receive a 1.6% COLA increase for benefit payments received beginning in January 2020.

OLD-AGE OR DISABILITY BENEFITS

Monthly benefits can be paid to—	If the worker—
A retired worker age 62 or over	Is fully insured.
A disabled worker under full retirement age	Would have been fully insured had he or she attained age 62 in the month the disability began and (except in the case of a person disabled because of blindness) has 20 quarters of coverage out of the 40 calendar quarters ending with the quarter in which the disability began.
A worker disabled before age 31 who does not have sufficient quarters of coverage to meet above requirement ("Special Insured" status, which allows an alternative to the "20 in 40 quarters" provision, may apply to a worker disabled after age 31 if he or she had a period of disability prior to age 31)	Has quarters of coverage in one-half of the quarters elapsing in the period after attaining age 21 and up to and including the quarter of becoming disabled, but no fewer than 6 or, if disabled in a quarter before attaining age 24, he or she has 6 quarters of coverage in the 12-calendar-quarter period immediately before he or she became disabled.

DEPENDENTS OF RETIRED OR DISABLED WORKERS

Monthly benefits can be paid to—	If the worker—
The spouse of a person entitled to disability or retirement insurance benefits, if he or she is: (a) Age 62 or over (may be divorced spouse in certain circumstances); or (b) Caring for a child who is under age 16 or disabled before age 22 and entitled to benefits	Is fully insured or insured for disability benefits, whichever is applicable, as shown above.
A dependent, unmarried child, grandchild, or stepgrandchild of a person entitled to disability or retirement insurance benefits if the child is: (a) Under age 18; or (b) Under age 19 and qualified as a full-time elementary or secondary school student; or (c) Age 18 or over and under a disability which began before the child reached age 22	Is insured for retirement or disability benefits, whichever is applicable, as shown above (and, with respect to benefits for grandchildren, if the child's natural or adoptive parents were deceased or disabled when the grandparent or stepgrandparent became entitled to benefits).

SURVIVORS BENEFITS

Monthly benefits can be paid to—	If the worker—
A widow or widower (may be surviving divorced spouse in certain circumstances) age 60 or over	Is fully insured.
A widow or widower and, under certain conditions, a surviving divorced spouse, if the widow or widower or divorced spouse is caring for a child entitled to benefits if the child is under age 16 or disabled	Is either fully or currently insured.
A disabled widow or widower (may be surviving divorced spouse in certain circumstances), age 50 or over but under age 60, whose disability began within a certain period	Is fully insured.
A dependent, unmarried child, grandchild, or stepgrandchild of a deceased worker if the child is: (a) Under age 18; or (b) Under age 19 and qualified as a full-time elementary or secondary school student; or (c) Age 18 or over and under a disability which began before the child reached age 22	Is either fully or currently insured (and, with respect to benefits for grandchildren, if the child's natural or adoptive parents were deceased or disabled when the grandparent or stepgrandparent became entitled to benefits).
The dependent parents, age 62 or over, of the deceased worker	Is fully insured.

LUMP-SUM DEATH PAYMENT

The lump-sum death payment will be paid in the following order of priority to—	If the worker—
(a) The widow(er) of the deceased wage earner who was living in the same household as the deceased wage earner at the time of death;	Is either fully or currently insured.
(b) The widow(er) (excluding a divorced spouse) who is eligible for or entitled to benefits based on the deceased wage earner's record for the month of death;	
(c) Children who are eligible for or entitled to benefits based on the deceased wage earner's record for the month of death	
If no surviving widow(er) or child as defined above survives, no lump sum is payable	

QUICK TAX AND BENEFITS FACTS

To contact a Wolters Kluwer Legal & Regulatory US Sales Representative, please call 1-800-638-8437

Preface

A central pillar of the post-employment retirement system in the United States is Social Security. Most Americans have protection under the Social Security System, either because they have worked in jobs covered by the system or because they have the required family relationship with a person who has worked in the system. This book provides a concise explanation of the federal old-age, survivors, and disability insurance (OASDI) program under Title II of the Social Security Act—the program most people refer to simply as "Social Security." While explaining the nuances of the governing law, the book also provides detailed information on the benefit computation process so that individuals may calculate the amount of benefits to which they may be entitled under the current program and make basic decisions such as whether or not to retire early or delay retirement. The explanatory text is supplemented by examples that not only illustrate the rules, but will enable employees to better plan for retirement.

Major developments that will impact Social Security benefits in 2020 include:

1.6% COLA for 2020. There will be a 1.6% cost-of-living increase for the coming year. The Social Security Act provides for a cost-of-living adjustment, or COLA, based on changes in the Consumer Price Index for Urban Wage Earners and Clerical Workers (CPI-W) from the third quarter of one year to the third quarter of the next year, but only if the adjustment is a positive one (Act §215(i)). The increase in the index from the third quarter of 2018 to the third quarter of 2019 means that benefits will increase by a small amount in 2020.

Maximum amount of earnings subject to Social Security tax increases in 2020. The maximum amount of earnings subject to Social Security tax is $137,700 in 2020. Social Security beneficiaries will see an estimated average monthly benefit of $1,503 for all retired workers in 2020.

Full retirement age at 66. The full retirement age has been adjusted from 65 to 66. Pursuant to this change, workers who attain age 65 in 2020 will have to wait until 2021 to retire if they wish to receive full retirement benefits. The only individuals attaining full retirement age in 2020 will be those attaining age 66 (i.e., individuals born January 2, 1954, through January 1, 1955). The maximum possible benefit for such individuals will be $3,011 per month.

Note: The full retirement age will eventually increase to 67.

A note about the citations in the text

Throughout the text, statements are documented by citations to the law, regulations, congressional committee reports, administrative rulings, agency manuals, etc. Generally, only the highest authority for a statement is given, but in some instances, only the most widely available source is cited. References to the "Social Security Handbook" throughout the text refer to the online version at *https://www.ssa.gov/OP_Home/handbook/handbook.html*.

Other available products

Detailed coverage of this material is available in UNEMPLOYMENT INSURANCE REPORTS WITH SOCIAL SECURITY. This product is available on the Internet. Note that Medicare is treated in a separate book titled "Medicare Explained" and in the MEDICARE AND MEDICAID GUIDE, a product that is available in print and on the Internet.

Contents

The Social Security System

¶101   In General

The purpose of the Social Security Act, stated in its broadest terms, is to "provide for the general welfare." To this end, the Act covers a wide range of programs, including retirement (old-age) insurance, survivor's insurance, disability insurance, hospital and medical insurance for the aged and disabled, black lung benefits, supplemental security income, unemployment insurance, and a variety of public assistance and "welfare" services.

The benefit portions of the Social Security Act discussed in this book are those dealing with what most people mean when they refer to "Social Security." Accordingly, the book discusses the old-age, survivor's, and disability insurance program for insured workers under Title II of the Social Security Act, rather than any of the other social insurance programs.

¶102   The Social Security Administration

The Social Security Administration is an independent agency in the executive branch of the federal government that is responsible for administering the Old-Age, Survivors, and Disability Insurance (OASDI) and Supplemental Security Income (SSI) programs, and programs providing health benefits (including Black Lung benefits to coal industry workers). [Soc. Sec. Act §701.]

The Social Security Administration is headed by a Commissioner of Social Security appointed by the President, with the advice and consent of the Senate, to serve a six-year term. The Commissioner is responsible for the exercise of all powers and the discharge of all duties of the Administration, and has authority and control over all personnel and activities thereof. The Commissioner may prescribe rules and regulations (subject to established rulemaking procedures) to carry out the functions of the agency. [Soc. Sec. Act §§702(a), 704(a).]

A seven-member Social Security Advisory Board advises the Commissioner on policies related to the OASDI and SSI programs. The Board meets at least quarterly, serves without pay, and is nominally bipartisan. Three Board members are chosen by the President, with no more than two from the same political party. The remaining four members of the Board are appointed by Congress: two by the Speaker of the House, in consultation with the chairman and ranking member of the minority party on the House Ways and Means Committee, and two others by the President Pro Tempore of the Senate. [Soc. Sec. Act §703.]

¶103   Financing the Social Security Program

The old-age, survivors, and disability insurance system and hospital insurance benefits for the aged and disabled are largely financed out of taxes paid by employers, employees, and the self-employed under the provisions of the Federal Insurance Contributions Act and the Self-Employment Contributions Act. That is, a portion of the revenues from these taxes is used to fund current benefit payments, rather than saved and invested to fund the benefits to be claimed by current workers when they retire. These taxes are collected by the Internal Revenue Service and paid into the United States Treasury as internal revenue collections. Amounts collected are appropriated to the Federal Old-Age and Survivors Insurance (OASI) Trust Fund, the Federal Disability Insurance (DI) Trust Fund, and the Federal Hospital Insurance (HI) Trust Fund. There is also a Federal Supplementary Medical Insurance (SMI) Trust Fund, which consists primarily of the premiums and matching payments made under the SMI program. [Soc. Sec. Act §§201(a), 201(b), 201(c), 201(g), 709, and 710.] In the case of each of these funds, portions of the funds not needed for current withdrawals are invested in special issue U. S. Treasury notes, which, in turn, earn interest for the trust funds. [Soc. Sec. Act §201(a), (d).]

The Social Security Disability Income (DI) program faced the most imminent financing shortfall of the separate trust funds. In order to bolster the financial security of the DI funds, a portion of the OASI tax is allocated to the DI funds. [Soc. Sec. Act §201(b)(1).] The 2019 Annual Report of the Board of Trustees of the Federal Old-Age and Survivors Insurance (OASI) and Federal Disability Insurance (DI) Trust Funds ("2019 Trustees' Report") reported that the DI Trust Fund was projected to be depleted of funds by 2052, extended 20 years from the previous year's estimate of 2032.

Reallocation of payroll tax revenue. The Social Security Benefit Protection and Opportunity Enhancement Act of 2015 reallocated an additional 0.57 percentage points of payroll tax revenue from the OASI Trust Fund to the DI Trust Fund (for a total of 2.37 percentage points of the total combined 12.4 percent payroll tax) in 2016, 2017, and 2018. The total tax rate did not change. [Social Security Benefit Protection and Opportunity Enhancement Act of 2015 (P.L. 114-74), Act Sec. 833.]

The OASI Trust Fund will have sufficient reserves to pay full benefits on time until 2034. However, the Trustees estimate that Social Security costs will exceed income throughout the 75-year projection period.

The total annual cost of the program is projected to exceed total annual income in 2020 for the first time since 1982. As a result, asset reserves are expected to decline during 2020.

Treasury will redeem trust fund asset reserves to the extent that program costs exceed tax revenue and interest earnings until depletion of total trust fund reserves. Thereafter, tax income would be sufficient to pay about three-quarters of scheduled benefits through 2093.

The projected 75-year actuarial deficit for the combined OASDI Trust Funds is 2.78 percent of taxable payroll (down from 2.84 percent projected in the 2018 report).

2035 projected depletion date for combined trust funds. The *combined* OASDI trust funds have a projected depletion date of 2035 (one year later than projected in the 2018 report). Once reserves are depleted, the Trustees advise that continuing tax income would be sufficient to pay 80 percent of scheduled benefits in 2035.

Deficit as percentage of payroll. An instructive way in which to demonstrate the financial shortfall is as a percentage of taxable payroll. The 75-year projection for the deficit changed from 2.22% of taxable payroll in the 2011 report, to 2.67% of taxable payroll in the 2012 report, to 2.72% of payroll in the 2013 report, to 2.88% in the 2014 report, to 2.68% in the 2015 report, to 2.66% in the 2016 report, to 2.83% in the 2017 report, to 2.84% in the 2018 report, and to 2.78% in the 2019 report. Social Security costs are projected to grow from 13.91% of taxable payroll in 2019 to 17.47% in 2093.

A summary of how these solvency projections have changed in the Trustees' reports over the past years appears in the following table:

History of Trustees' Reports' Insolvency Projections

	Year in which costs exceed FICA/SECA tax revenue	Year costs exceed tax revenue and interest	Year in which Social Security (OASDI) trust fund assets are exhausted	Long-term deficit as a percentage of taxable payroll
2000 report	2015	2025	2037	1.89%
2001 report	2016	2025	2038	1.86%
2002 report	2017	2027	2041	1.87%
2003 report	2018	2028	2042	1.92%
2004 report	2018	2028	2042	1.89%
2005 report	2017	2027	2041	1.92%
2006 report	2017	2027	2040	2.02%
2007 report	2017	2027	2041	1.95%
2008 report	2017	2027	2041	1.70%
2009 report	2016	2024	2037	2.00%
2010 report	2015	2025	2037	1.92%
2011 report	2010	2023	2036	2.22%
2012 report	2010	2021	2033	2.67%
2013 report	2010	2022	2033	2.72%
2014 report	2010	2020	2033	2.88%
2015 report	2010	2020	2034	2.68%
2016 report	2010	2020	2034	2.66%
2017 report	2010	2022	2034	2.83%
2018 report	2010	2018	2034	2.84%
2019 report	2010	2020	2035	2.78%

Legislative means of maintaining solvency. The Trustees stress that the deficits at the end of the 75-year projection period indicate that sustained solvency would require payroll tax rate increases or benefit reductions (or a combination thereof) by the end of the period that are larger than those needed on average for the long-range period (2019-93).

Specifically, in order for the combined OASI and DI Trust Funds to remain solvent throughout the 75-year projection period, the Trustees note that: (1) revenues would need to increase by an amount equivalent to an immediate and permanent payroll tax rate increase of 2.70 percentage points (from its current level of 12.40 percent to 15.10 percent); (2) scheduled benefits during the period would need to be reduced by an amount equivalent to an immediate and permanent reduction of about 17 percent applied to all current and future beneficiaries, or about 20 percent if the reductions were applied only to those who become initially eligible for benefits in 2019 or later; or (3) some combination of the two approaches would need to be implemented.

In order for benefits to be financed fully for each year starting in 2035, revenues would need to increase by an amount equivalent to a payroll tax rate increase of about 3.65 percentage points (yielding a total payroll tax rate of 16.05 percent) at the point of trust fund reserve depletion.

Alternatively, solvency could be maintained if benefits were reduced to the level that would be payable with scheduled tax rates and earnings subject to tax in each year beginning in 2035. At the point of trust fund reserve depletion in 2035, this level would require a reduction in all scheduled benefits of 23 percent.

The Trustees caution that some strategies for achieving solvency would not be feasible if delayed until trust fund reserve depletion in 2035. Finally, the Trustees recommend that lawmakers phase in any changes gradually in order to give workers and benefit recipients time to adjust.

¶104   Account Numbers and Identification Numbers

Every employee and every self-employed worker covered by the Social Security Act must have a Social Security account number, which is used to maintain the individual's earnings record. The earnings credited to the individual's account are used to determine whether the worker is insured under the Social Security system and the amount of benefits that might be payable to the worker and/or his or her dependents or survivors based on the worker's old-age, disability, or death. The earnings credited to the account are also used in determining entitlement to hospital insurance benefits. The same number should be used for an individual's entire life. If the worker loses the original Social Security card, he or she should obtain a duplicate card, with the same number. If a worker's name is changed—for example, upon marriage—the Social Security office should be asked for a new card showing the same account number. [Soc. Sec. Act §205(c)(2); IRS Reg. §31.6011(b)-2(a).]

Even if a person's work is not covered by Social Security, a Social Security number may be needed as a taxpayer identification number (TIN) for income tax purposes, or in connection with an application for supplemental security income, for hospital or medical insurance, or for certain state-run programs, including tax programs, driver's license and motor vehicle registration, and public assistance. [Soc. Sec. Handbook, February 2, 2006, §1401.4.]

A victim of domestic violence may obtain a new Social Security number by showing corroborating evidence from a third party, such as a local shelter, treating physician, or law enforcement official, of the abuse. Victims are not required to provide proof that their abuser had misused their Social Security number or could be expected to misuse it to locate the victim. [See the Social Security Administration's website at *http://www.ssa.gov/pubs/10093.html*.]

A TIN is required for any individual, regardless of age, claimed as a dependent on a federal income tax return. [IRC §151(e).] However, for tax years beginning in 1995 or 1996, the requirement was waived for children born in November or December 1995 or December 1996, respectively. [P.L. 103-465, §742(a), (b), amending IRC §§32(c)(3)(D)(i), 6109(e).]

The Commissioner is authorized to facilitate the issuance of Social Security numbers (1) to children who are below school age at the request of their parents or guardians, (2) to children of school age at the time of their first enrollment in school, and (3) to aliens at the time of their admission to the

U.S. under conditions that would permit them to work. A person who may not legally work when admitted to the U.S. may be issued a number after investigation proves that the person's status has changed. In addition, numbers will be issued to persons who do not have them at the time they apply for benefits under any federally financed program. [Soc. Sec. Act §205(c).]

Applying for a Social Security number

An individual needing a Social Security number may apply for one by completing a prescribed application and submitting the required evidence. [Reg. §422.103.] Applicants must establish age, identity and U.S. citizenship or lawful alien status.

2015 changes. In order to support the development of electronic service delivery options, the Social Security Administration updated its application regulations to remove references to Form SS-5 and replaced it with the term "prescribed application." [80 *Fed. Reg.* 47831, Aug. 10, 2015; amending Regs. §422.103 and §422.110.] Also, the word "documentary" was removed from the description of certain evidence requirements. [80 *Fed. Reg.* 47831, Aug. 10, 2015; amending Reg. §422.107.] These changes will provide more flexibility in the ways in which the public may request SSN cards and allow the Social Security Administration to implement an online Social Security number replacement card application system. [See the Social Security Administration's website at *https://www.ssa.gov/ssnumber.*]

Age may be established by submitting a birth certificate, a religious record made before the age of five showing date of birth, a hospital record of birth, adoption record, or a passport.

Identity may be established with a driver's license, identity card, school record, medical record, marriage record, passport, Department of Homeland Security (DHS) document, or other similar evidence. Birth records may not be used to establish identity. In addition, an in-person interview requirement applies to children age 12 and older. [Reg. §422.107.]

U.S. citizenship may be established with a birth certificate, or other evidence, as described above, showing a U.S. place of birth. Foreign-born applicants claiming U.S. citizenship must present documentary evidence of citizenship, such as a certificate of naturalization, certificate of citizenship, U.S. passport, U.S. citizen identification card (DHS Form I-179 or I-197), consular report of birth, or other verification from the DHS, U.S. Department of State, or Federal or State court records confirming citizenship. Note that for this purpose, foreign adopted children who receive automatic citizenship status by virtue of the Child Citizenship Act of 2000, P.L. 106-395, 8 U.S.C. §1431, are still required to present documentary evidence of citizenship in the form of a passport or certificate of naturalization or citizenship. Until such evidence is presented, foreign adopted children who have lawful alien status will be regarded as legal aliens by the Social Security Administration.

Evidence of alien status must be shown by any person who is not a U.S. citizen. This may be established with current DHS documents showing lawful admission into the United States, either for permanent residence or under authority of law permitting him or her to work. The only valid non-work purpose for which a Social Security number will be issued to an alien will be satisfaction of a federal, state or local law that requires the alien to have the Social Security number in order to receive a benefit. Earnings reported to the Social Security Administration on a Social Security number issued for a valid non-work purpose will be reported to Department of Homeland Security. [Reg. §422.104.] The Social Security Administration now also requires that foreign academic students (*i.e.,* students with Bureau of Citizenship and Immigration Services classification status F-1) applying for a Social Security number must present evidence that employment has been secured and that the student's school has authorized the student to be employed prior to assignment of a Social Security number. For purposes of these requirements, evidence of a formal job offer, a promise of a job, or evidence that the student is in fact engaged in that job will be considered "secured" employment. [69 *Fed. Reg.* 55065, Sept. 13, 2004; amending Regs. §422.105 and §422.107.]

All documents submitted must be originals or certified copies. The prescribed application must be signed by applicants age 18 and older and may be mailed to any Social Security office unless the applicant is age 12 or older and has never previously been assigned a number. [Soc. Sec. Act §205(c), Reg. §422.107; Instructions, Form SS-5, rev. August 2011.]

Requesting a replacement card

There are limits on the number of replacement cards that individuals are allowed to obtain. An individual may obtain no more than three cards per year and ten cards during his or her lifetime. However, the Administration may make "reasonable exceptions" in compelling circumstances on a case-by-case basis if an individual provides evidence that a hardship would result if he or she does not receive a new card.

Based on a person's immigration status, a restrictive legend may appear on the face of a SSN card to indicate that work is either not authorized or that work may be performed only with the Department of Homeland Security (DHS) authorization. This restrictive legend appears on the card above the individual's name and Social Security number. Replacement cards that are required because of a name change or change in alien status that result in a necessary change to a card's restrictive legend do not count toward the three-per-year limit. However, cards issued because of name changes will only be approved by the Administration if the change can be verified through a legal process. [Reg. §§ 422.103(e)(2), 422.110 (a).]

Criminal penalties are provided for (1) knowingly and willfully using a Social Security number that was obtained with false information, (2) using someone else's Social Security number, (3) disclosing or compelling the disclosure of someone else's Social Security number, (4) altering, buying, selling or counterfeiting Social Security cards, or (5) possessing a regular or counterfeit card with intent to sell or alter it. The penalty involves a fine of up to $25,000 or imprisonment for up to five years or both. [Soc. Sec. Act §208.] Use of a Social Security number to accomplish identity theft may also result in the imposition of even harsher penalties under the Identity Theft and Assumption Deterrence Act of 1998, which provides for fines and/or imprisonment of up to 20 years, as well as forfeiture of property. [18 U.S.C. §1028, as amended by P.L. 105-318, Nov. 2, 1998.]

Applying for an employer identification number

Every employer of one or more individuals subject to the Federal Insurance Contributions Act must have an identification number. You, as an employer, should have only one identification number. If you have more than one and have not been advised which to use, contact the IRS office where your returns are filed. Do not confuse your employer identification number (EIN) with your Social Security number, which takes the form 000-00-0000. Social Security numbers are used to identify individual persons and estates of decedents.

You must apply for an employer identification number, if you have not done so previously, on Form SS-4, Application for Employer Identification Number. You should apply for an EIN early enough to receive the number by the time you must file a return or statement or make a tax deposit. If you apply online, you can get an EIN immediately. If you apply by mail, file Form SS-4 at least four to five weeks before you need an EIN. The form, together with any supplementary statement, must be prepared and filed in accordance with the form, instructions, and regulations, and must set forth fully and clearly the data called for on the form.

EIN applicant's responsible party. An individual may be authorized to act on an EIN applicant's behalf for purposes of obtaining the EIN. However, effective January 1, 2014, Form SS-4 has been revised to require disclosure of the EIN applicant's "responsible party" and the party's identifying number. The identifying number refers to the party who has control over the business, whether that is a corporate principal officer, a general partner, or the owner of a disregarded entity. [IRS Reg. 301.6109-1(d); 78 *Fed. Reg.* 26244, May 16, 2013.]

One EIN issuance per party per day. The IRS limits EIN issuance to one responsible party per day. The limitation is applicable to all requests for EINs whether online, by fax, or mail.

Only one application is required and only one identification number will be assigned, regardless of how many *establishments* a particular employer may have. This rule applies even if business may be conducted under more than one business or trade name. However, each corporation of an *affiliated group* must be treated separately and each, therefore, must have its own identification number. Third parties can receive an EIN on a client's behalf by completing the new "Third Party Designee" section and obtaining the client's signature on Form SS-4.

Employer identification numbers may be assigned by fax. EINs can be assigned by completing Form SS-4 and faxing it to the IRS for processing. Fax requests for an EIN 24 hours-a-day/7 days-a-week by dialing the fax number (855) 641-6935. Taxpayers located outside the U. S. will fax to (304) 707-9471. Taxpayers also can mail Form SS-4 to get an EIN. The instructions on the form provide the correct address.

IRS website offers EINs for businesses. The IRS allows businesses to obtain identification numbers directly from its website. After the employer completes an application form online, the system issues an EIN that may be used immediately.

This online process eliminates the need to send paperwork to the IRS as well as the delay in issuing a number that may result from an incomplete application form. Once an employer has its EIN, it can file tax returns and may enroll in the Electronic Federal Tax Payment System (EFTPS) to handle its payments most efficiently.

Employers do not need to pre-register before requesting an EIN. The number issued is the permanent EIN for the employer, unless the IRS finds that it has already issued an EIN for that employer or if the principal officer's name and Social Security number do not match social security records. In such cases, the IRS will void the number issued through the website and notify the employer.

An accountant or tax preparer may use the website at www.irs.gov to request EINs on behalf of clients. The online application process is not available to some EIN requestors, including federal, state, or local government agencies, Indian tribal governments, real estate mortgage investment conduits, and taxpayers with addresses outside the 50 states.

Internet is preferred method. The IRS states that the internet is the preferred method to use when applying for an EIN. If you apply online, you will not need a Form SS-4. [See the IRS website at *www.irs.gov* (keyword "EIN" for the online EIN application.]

Apply for new number if business is sold or transferred. If a business is sold or otherwise transferred and the new owner does not have an identification number, the new owner should **not** use the number assigned to the former owner, but should file an application for its own number unless the new owner became the owner of a corporation by acquiring its stock.

Electronic Federal Tax Payment System. All businesses receiving a new EIN that have a federal tax obligation will automatically be pre-enrolled in the Electronic Federal Tax Payment System (EFTPS) for paying federal taxes electronically. When businesses receive their EINs, they will also receive a separate mailing containing an EFTPS PIN (personal identification number) and instructions for activating their enrollment. [IRS Pub. 4275, Oct. 2007.] See ¶223.1 regarding EFTPS.

Privacy

Confidentiality of Social Security numbers and records is safeguarded under the Social Security Act, the Privacy Act, and the Freedom of Information Act, all of which protect personal information from disclosure. Disclosure is, however, permitted under a number of circumstances, mostly involving the administration of other state and federal programs (*e.g.,* VA benefits), including the collection of other federal debts (see ¶568). In addition, a claimant may authorize disclosure of Social Security records to his or her legal representative. [Soc. Sec. Act §§205(c), 1106.]

The permissible use of Social Security numbers has been expanded in select cases: state and federal courts may use Social Security numbers to eliminate duplications in jury lists; the Department of Labor and the Department of Agriculture may use Social Security numbers in programs for preventing fraud and abuse of other federal laws; and the Social Security Administration may reveal whether an individual is dead or alive for epidemiologic research purposes. [P.L. 103-296 (Social Security Independence and Program Improvement Act of 1994) §§304, 311, 316, 318.)]

However, beginning December 18, 2013, federal, state, or local agencies are prohibited from displaying the Social Security account number of any individual, or any derivative of such number, on any check issued for any payment by the agency. The agencies have also been prohibited, since December 2011, from employing, or entering into a contract for the use or employment of, prisoners in any capacity that would allow them access to the Social Security account numbers of other individuals. [Soc. Sec. Act §205(c)(2)(C), as amended by the Social Security Number Protection Act of 2010, P.L. 111-318.]

Beginning in 2022, no agency of the federal government may include Social Security numbers on documents sent by mail unless the head of the agency determines inclusion of the number is necessary. Each agency, including the Social Security Administration, is required to issue regulations specifying the circumstances under which inclusion of the Social Security numbers is necessary on a mailed document. [Social Security Number Fraud Prevention Act of 2017, P.L. 115-59.]

Federal, state, and local prisons are monetarily incented to enter into agreements with the Commissioner of Social Security to provide the names, Social Security account numbers, confinement dates, and dates of birth of residents who receive Social Security benefits. [Soc. Sec. Act §§202(x)(3), 1611(e)(1)(I), and Title 5 U.S.C. 552a(a)(8)(B), as amended by P.L. 106-170, §402.]

Access to records: Individuals, including minors, may obtain access to their records, including medical records, in the files of the Social Security Administration by visiting a local Social Security office or by writing to the manager of the Social Security Administration system of records in which the record is filed. The names and addresses of managers for various record systems are published in the *Federal Register.* [Reg. §401.40.] An individual seeking access to his or her own medical records in Social Security Administration files must name a physician, other health professional, or other responsible individual who will be willing to review the record with the individual seeking the records. Representatives who receive medical records from the Social Security Administration are required to release those records to the person on whose behalf the request was made or, in the case of a minor, to that person's parent or legal guardian. However, if a representative is not named, the Administration may decline to release the medical information. [Reg. §401.55.] The regulations set forth procedures for appealing refusals to correct or allow access to records. [Reg. §401.70.] A subpoena is not considered to be a court order unless signed by a federal judge. However, at its discretion the Administration may decide to honor subpoenas from state courts, as well as from court clerks and attorneys representing parties to a proceeding. [Reg. §401.180.]

Computer matching: The Social Security Administration, together with other Federal agencies, routinely matches computer data to reduce fraud, collect debts, and insure a beneficiary's compliance with Federal law and regulations. The Social Security Administration has in place programs that match Social Security data with data from a number of agencies, including the Office of Personnel Management, the Department of Labor, the Internal Revenue Service, the Center for Medicare and Medicaid Services, the Railroad Retirement Board, and the Bureau of Public Debt. For example, pursuant to the computer matching program with the IRS, SSA will disclose certain information to the IRS on aged, blind, or disabled individuals who are applicants for or recipients of SSA benefits and/or federally-administered state supplementary payments. IRS will match SSA's information with its Information Return Master File (IRMF) and disclose to SSA return information with respect to the unearned income of applicants or recipients identified by SSA. The information IRS discloses to SSA, however, will be limited to unearned income reported on information returns. [Social Security Notice, 78 *Fed. Reg.* 51264, August 20, 2013.]

Death Master File. The Death Master File (DMF) is a publicly accessible data base maintained by SSA that contains death notices for individuals enrolled in the United States Social Security program since 1936. The Master File contains identifying information (*e.g.*, date of birth, date of death) about each individual to whom SSA has assigned a Social Security Number.

The DMF is used by other federal agencies to alert them to deceased benefit recipients. Six federal agencies have full access to the DMF. Other agencies have partial access to the DMF.

The Bipartisan Budget Act of 2013 created a program under which the Secretary of Commerce will restrict access to information contained in the DMF for a three-year period beginning on the date of an individual's death. Each improper disclosure or misuse of information obtained from the DMF would be subject to a penalty. [Bipartisan Budget Act of 2013 (H.J. Res. 59), Act Sec. 203.]

Social Security and Hospital Insurance Taxes

TAX RATES

¶201   Employer and Employee Tax Rates

Old-age, survivors, disability, and hospital insurance taxes imposed by the Federal Insurance Contributions Act are paid by both the employer and the employee. Until 2011, the rate was the same for both; however, for 2011 and 2012, only, the rate was reduced by two percentage points for employees. [The Tax Relief, Unemployment Insurance Reauthorization, and Job Creation Act of 2010 (P.L. 111-312), §601, as amended by The Middle Class Tax Relief and Job Creation Act of 2012 (P.L. 112-96), §1001.] The payroll tax holiday expired at the end of 2012. Accordingly, the 7.65% tax rate is again in effect. The following table indicates annual rates as a percentage of wages:

Social Security and Hospital Insurance Rates*
[P.L. 95-216; IRC §§3101, 3111.]

Calendar Year	Social Security Rate	Hospital Insurance Rate	Combined Rate
1937–1949	1.0%		
1950–1953	1.5%		
1954–1956	2.0%		
1957–1958	2.25%		
1959	2.5%		
1960–1961	3.0%		
1962	3.125%		
1963–1965	3.625%		
1966	3.85%	0.35%	4.2%
1967	3.9%	0.5%	4.4%
1968	3.8%	0.6%	4.4%
1969–1970	4.2%	0.6%	4.8%
1971–1972	4.6%	0.6%	5.2%
1973	4.85%	1.0%	5.85%
1974–1977	4.95%	0.90%	5.85%
1978	5.05%	1.00%	6.05%
1979–1980	5.08%	1.05%	6.13%
1981	5.35%	1.30%	6.65%
1982–1983	5.40%	1.30%	6.70%
1984 (employee rate)	5.40%	1.30%	6.70%
1984 (employer rate)	5.70%	1.30%	7.00%
1985	5.70%	1.35%	7.05%
1986–1987	5.70%	1.45%	7.15%
1988–1989	6.06%	1.45%	7.51%
1990–2010	6.20%	1.45%	7.65%
2011–2012 (employer rate)	6.20%	1.45%	7.65%
2011–2012 (employee rate)	4.20%	1.45%	5.65%
2013 and thereafter (under current law)	6.20%	1.45%**	7.65%

*Note: For the maximum amount of annual earnings taxable under the law, see ¶208
**An additional Medicare tax applies to high wage earners and for certain investment income. See text.

Both the old-age, survivors, and disability insurance taxes—called "Social Security taxes"—and the hospital insurance taxes are levied by the Federal Insurance Contributions Act, which is part of the Internal Revenue Code. Although the rates are levied by different subsections of the Code, the Internal Revenue Service, for the sake of convenience, requires the combining of the two rates in withholding employee taxes and in paying employer and employee taxes.

The applicable employee tax rate is that in effect at the time the wages are received. [IRC §3101.] The employer tax rate is that in effect at the time such wages are paid. [Reg. §31.3111-3.]

> **Example:** In 2012, Ernie performed services for his employer that constituted employment covered by the law. In 2013, Ernie received from his employer $1,000 as remuneration for such services. The tax is payable at the combined Social Security and hospital insurance rate of 7.65% in effect for calendar year 2013 (the year in which the wages were received) and not at the rate that was in effect for calendar year 2012 (the year in which the services were performed).

This situation would not apply if services had been performed in 2013, given the expiration of the payroll tax holiday.

"Wages" subject to Social Security tax are discussed in detail beginning at ¶206.

The maximum amount of wages subject to employment tax in a year (*i.e.*, wage base) is discussed at ¶208.

ADDITIONAL MEDICARE TAX

Tax on wages

In addition to the 1.45% employee portion of the HI (Medicare) tax imposed on wages, a 0.9% Medicare tax is imposed on every taxpayer (other than a corporation, estate or trust) who receives wages with respect to employment during any tax year *beginning after December 31, 2012*, in excess of $200,000 ($250,000 in the case of a joint return, $125,000 in the case of a married taxpayer filing separately). Note, these amounts are not indexed for inflation.

The additional tax is imposed on employees only and means that employees will pay a total Medicare tax of 2.35% on the portion of wages received in connection with employment in excess of the threshold. The total of the employee and employer Medicare rates on income in excess of the threshold is 3.8%. [IRC §3101(b)(2), as added and amended by Secs. 9015 and 10906 of the Patient Protection and Affordable Care Act (the Affordable Care Act) (P.L. 111-148), and amended by Sec. 1402(b) of the

Health Care and Education Reconciliation Act of 2010 (P.L. 111-152); IRS Reg. §31.3101-2(b)(2).]

Unlike the general 1.45% Medicare tax on wages, the additional 0.9% tax is on the combined wages of the employee and the employee's spouse, in the case of a joint return. [Joint Committee on Taxation, Technical Explanation of the Revenue Provisions of the "Reconciliation Act of 2010," as amended, in combination with the "Affordable Care Act" (JCX-18-10), March 21, 2010.]

The obligation to withhold the additional Medicare tax is only imposed on an employer if the employee receives wages from the employer in excess of $200,000. [IRC §3102(f)(1), as added by the Affordable Care Act]. The employer is permitted to disregard the amount of wages received by the taxpayer's spouse (or from self-employment income or wages received from another employer).

Reporting requirements. Individuals are required to report Additional Medicare Tax on Form 1040, U.S. Individual Income Tax Return. Taxpayers may claim credit for any withheld Additional Medicare Tax on Form 1040 and must pay any tax due not paid through withholding or estimated tax payments.

Note, an employee may not request an employer to deduct and withhold Additional Medicare Tax on wages of $200,000 or less. The employee, however, may request additional income tax withholding, which will be applied against all taxes shown on the individual's return, including any liability for Additional Medical Tax.

Correcting employer over/underpayments. In order to correct an overpayment of Additional Medicare Tax, an employer may make an adjustment only if it repays or reimburses the employee prior to the end of the calendar year in which the wages/compensation was paid. In order to correct an underpayment of Additional Medicare Tax, an employer may make an interest-free adjustment only if the error is ascertained within the calendar year in which the compensation was paid.

Note, an employer may not make an adjustment or file a claim for refund for Additional Medicare Tax withholding when there is a repayment of wages received by an employee in a prior year. [IRS Reg. 31.6402(a)-2.] The employee, however, may be able to file an amended return (Form 1040X) claiming a refund of Additional Medicare Tax.

Employer liability. If an employer deducts less than the correct amount of Additional Medicare Tax, the employer is liable for the correct amount of tax, unless and until the employee pays the tax. [IRC §3102(f)(3).] Under proposed regulations, the tax would not be collected from the employer if the employee paid the tax that the employer failed to deduct. Final regulations issued in November 2013 clarify that the employer is not relieved of its liability for payment of any Additional Medicare Tax required to be withheld unless the employer can show the employee paid the tax. [IRS Reg. §31.3102-4(c) and 31.3201-(g)(3).]

Tax on investment income

A separate additional 3.8% Medicare contribution tax is imposed on the lesser of: (1) an individual's net investment income for the tax year, or (2) any excess of modified adjusted gross income (AGI) for the tax year over a threshold amount that is $250,000 for joint filers, $125,000 for married individuals filing separately, and $200,000 for all other individuals. [IRC §1411(a)(1), as added by the Health Care Reconciliation Act of 2010 (P.L. 111-152).]

The operation of the applicable employment taxes is illustrated at ¶208.

¶202   Self-Employment Tax Rates

The Self-Employment Contributions Act (SECA) imposes two taxes, OASDI (Old Age, Survivors, and Disability Insurance, also known as "Social Security") and hospital insurance (Medicare), on the self-employed. Pursuant to the Social Security Amendments of 1983, both the Social Security and hospital insurance taxes of the self-employed were increased to equal the combined employer-employee rates, beginning in 1984. For a tax year that began in 2011 or 2012, a self-employed person received a two percentage-point reduction in employment taxes, paying a Social Security tax of 10.4% (down from 12.4%) and a hospital insurance (Medicare) tax of 2.9% for a combined rate of 13.3%. This reduced rate applied only with respect to a tax year that began in 2011 or 2012. [The Tax Relief, Unemployment Insurance Reauthorization, and Job Creation Act of 2010 (P.L. 111-312), §601.] With the expiration of the tax break after 2012, self-employed persons will be subject to combined tax rate of 15.3%.

The Additional Medicare Tax discussed in ¶201 also applies with respect to self-employment income, *beginning in 2013*. Thus, a 0.9% Medicare tax is imposed on every taxpayer (other than a corporation, estate or trust) who receives wages with respect to employment during any tax year *beginning after December 31, 2012*, in excess of $200,000 ($250,000 for a joint return, $125,000 for a married taxpayer filing separately). [IRC §1401(b)(2), as amended by the Affordable Care Act (P.L. 111-148), §§9015(b)(1)(B) and 10906(b).]

The following system was designed to achieve parity between employees and the self-employed:

(a) *Determination of net earnings from self-employment (NESE).* A self-employed individual is entitled to a deduction in computing net earnings from self-employment to reflect the fact that employees do not pay FICA tax on the value of the employer's FICA tax. Thus, when determining the amount of earnings that are "net earnings from self-employment," a self-employed person may deduct from net earnings from self-employment (as determined prior to any deduction for amounts paid under SECA) an amount equal to one-half of the self-employment tax rate multiplied by the individual's net earnings from self-employment. For 2020, this deduction is 7.65% of the net earnings from self-employment (prior to any deduction for amounts paid under SECA).

(b) *Deductible business expense.* In addition to the self-employment tax deduction allowed when determining the amount of earnings that are "net earnings from self-employment," the self-employed person can deduct the employer-equivalent portion of the self-employment tax (i.e., one-half of the total Social Security tax) as a business expense in calculating adjusted gross income. This deduction reflects the fact that employees do not pay income tax on the value of the employer's FICA tax. [IRC §164(f).] Note, in order to deduct the tax, enter on Form 1040 the amount shown on the deduction for the employer-equivalent portion of self-employment tax line of Schedule SE.

The following table shows the tax rates for the self-employed:

Social Security and Hospital Insurance Rates
[IRC §1401.]

Calendar Year	Social Security Rate	Hospital Insurance Rate	Combined Rate
1951–1953	2.25%		
1954–1956	3.0%		
1957–1958	3.375%		
1959	3.75%		
1960–1961	4.5%		
1962	4.7%		
1963–1965	5.4%		
1966	5.8%	0.35%	6.15%
1967	5.9%	0.5%	6.4%
1968	5.8%	0.6%	6.4%
1969–1970	6.3%	0.6%	6.9%
1971–1972	6.9%	0.6%	7.5%
1973	7.0%	1.0%	8.0%
1974–1977	7.0%	0.90%	7.90%
1978	7.10%	1.00%	8.10%
1979–1980	7.05%	1.05%	8.10%
1981	8.00%	1.30%	9.30%
1982–1983	8.05%	1.30%	9.35%
1984 *	11.40%	2.60%	14.00%
1985 *	11.40%	2.70%	14.10%
1986–1987 *	11.40%	2.90%	14.30%
1988–1989 *	12.12%	2.90%	15.02%
1990–2010 *	12.40%	2.90%	15.30%
2011–2012 *	10.40%	2.90%	13.30%
2013 and thereafter (under current law) *	12.40%	2.90%**	15.30%

* **Note:** Rates shown do not reflect the credits discussed in the preceding paragraphs. For the maximum amount of annual self-employment income taxable under the law, see ¶404.
** An increased Medicare tax applies to high wage earners and for certain investment income. See text.

Note that if a self-employed person reports earnings on a fiscal-year basis, the tax rate to be used is the one that applies to the calendar year in which the fiscal year began. [IRC §1401.]

The maximum amount of earnings subject to Social Security tax is capped ($137,700 for 2020). The HI tax applies to all earnings.

Taxation and coverage of self-employed workers is discussed in detail in Chapter 4.

AVOIDING TAX SCAMS

¶203   Common Tax Scams

The IRS has targeted tax scams in promotions targeted to small business owners. Despite the IRS's attempts to educate business owners about employment tax scams, some taxpayers are still buying into them. More often than not, the alleged tax evader does not start out intending to avoid payment of federal employment taxes. After a business suffers a downturn, the owner may miss a federal tax deposit deadline. After missing one deadline, it becomes easier to miss more and, in a short time, the owner may find himself or herself with a significant employment tax liability. The Internal Revenue Service has identified the following common scams.

- **Pyramiding** is a scam where a business withholds employment taxes but fails to remit them to the IRS. The employer uses the withheld funds to pay other liabilities. Businesses involved in pyramiding frequently shut down or file for bankruptcy, then start up under a different name and begin the cycle again.

- **Unreliable third-party payers.** Two categories of third-party payers are payroll service providers and professional employer organizations. Payroll service providers are hired by employers to file returns and make employment tax payments. Professional employer organizations offer employee leasing, handling administrative, personnel, and payroll functions for employees who have been leased to other companies. Sometimes, third-party payers fail to remit employment taxes, leaving millions in employment tax unpaid.

- **Frivolous arguments.** A variety of false or misleading arguments have been raised for not paying employment taxes. These are based on incorrect interpretations of Code Sec. 861 and the improper use of Form 941c, Supporting Statement to Correct Information on Form 941, to try to secure a refund of employment taxes.

- **Offshore employee leasing.** This scheme misuses employee leasing. An individual appears to resign from his or her current employer and signs an employment contract with an offshore employee leasing company. The offshore company leases the individual back to the original employer using a domestic leasing company as an intermediary. The individual performs the same services, but compensation is labeled as "deferred compensation," and sent offshore. The "deferred" compensation is then paid to the individual as a "loan" or ends up in an account under the individual's control for which scheme promoters claim no current tax is due. The IRS has identified this scam as a "listed transaction" under the tax shelter rules. Individuals, promoters and businesses must disclose their participation in this activity.

- **Misclassification of worker status.** Some employers incorrectly treat employees as independent contractors to avoid paying employment taxes. Employers, however, are liable for employment taxes on wages paid to misclassified workers and risk penalties. A joint effort between the IRS and state employment officials, the Questionable Employment Tax Practice (QETP) Initiative, allows the agencies to combine resources to help reduce fraud and ensure proper worker classification. [IR 2007-184, Nov. 6, 2007.]

- **Paying employees in cash.** Employment taxes are owed regardless of how employees are paid. The IRS will build its case using all available information even if there are no payroll records or checks and the employee is paid "under the table."

- **Filing false payroll returns.** One common tactic to evade payroll taxes is to intentionally understate wages on which taxes are owed or fail to file returns.

- **S Corp officer compensation treated as corporate distributions.** In an effort to avoid employment taxes, some S Corporations are improperly treating officer compensation as a corporate distribution instead of wages or salary. By law, officers are employees for employment tax purposes and the compensation they receive for their services is subject to employment taxes. See ¶302.2.

EMPLOYEE TAXES

¶204 Employer Withholding of Employee Taxes

Employers collect the employee taxes from each of their employees by deducting the taxes from the employee's wages as and when paid. [IRC §3102(a), (b).]

With respect to remuneration paid to an employee for domestic service, for service not in the course of the employer's trade or business, for agricultural labor, or for industrial homework, the employer may deduct an amount equivalent to the employee taxes, even though at the time of payment the employer cannot be certain that the test for liability for the taxes will be met. This is also true as to tips of less than $20 reported during a month to an employer by an employee. [IRC §3102(a), (b).] See ¶204.1, below.

In collecting employee taxes, the employer disregards any fractional part of a cent unless it amounts to one-half cent or more, in which case it is increased to one cent. The employer is liable for the employee taxes with respect to all wages paid to each of his or her employees whether or not the taxes are collected from the employee. If, for example, the employer deducts less than the correct amount, or if he or she fails to deduct any part of the taxes, the employer is nevertheless liable for the correct amount. Until collected from the employee, the employee also is liable for the employee taxes with respect to all the taxable wages he or she has received. [Reg. §31.3102-1(c).]

Special rules apply in the case of tips or life insurance; see ¶204.1 and 204.2, respectively.

Severe penalties are provided for a willful failure to pay, collect or truthfully account for and pay over the employee taxes, or for a willful attempt in any manner to evade or defeat the taxes. Additions to the tax may also be imposed in the case of failure to file a tax return or to pay the taxes. See ¶227.1.

¶204.1 Tip Reporting

Cash tips received by an employee in the course of employment must be reported by the employee to the employer on or before the tenth day of the month following the month in which the tips are received. No report is required for any month in which the tips were less than $20. An employee must furnish the employer with a written statement of tips showing (a) his or her name, address and Social Security number, (b) the name and address of the employer, (c) the calendar month or period for which the statement is furnished, and (d) the total amount of tips. [IRC §6053; IRS Reg. §31.6053-1.] Form 4070 may be used by employees for reporting tips and is available in Pub. 1244, Employee's Daily Record of Tips and Report to Employer.

Tips paid in any medium other than cash are not taxable. Amounts designated as tips by a customer who uses a credit card to pay the bill are included as cash. [IRC §3121(a)(12); IRS Reg. §31.3121(a)(12)-1.]

In the case of a large food or beverage establishment that normally employs more than 10 employees on a typical business day (not counting an individual who owns 50% or more in value of the stock of a corporation operating the establishment), the employer must file a separate calendar year information return, Form 8027, reporting employees' tip income. Note, filings on magnetic media are no longer being accepted.

Employers that file 250 or more Forms 8027 are required to file the returns electronically using the FIRE System. To connect to the FIRE (Filing Information Returns Electronically) System, access this website: *IRS.gov/ FIRE*. The due date for electronically filed forms is March 31, 2020. Each employee must also be furnished by the employer with a statement of the amount allocated to the employee for all payroll periods ending within the calendar year. [IRC §6053(c); Pub. 1239, Specifications for Electronic Filing of Form 8027, Employer's Annual Information Return of Tip Income and Allocated Tips.]

If additional time is required to report tip income, one must submit Form 8809, Application for Extension of Time to File Information Returns. It may be filed electronically and is available as a fill-in form on the FIRE System. The IRS encourages its use there in place of the filing of a paper application. [Rev. Proc. 2008-34.] Failure to make a timely report of tip income to the employer subjects the employee to a penalty equal to 50% of the tax due on the unreported income. The penalty will not apply, however, if it is shown that the failure to report was due to reasonable cause and not to willful neglect. [IRC §6652(b).]

An employer must collect the employee tax on tips reported by the employee from wages due the employee or from other funds that the employee makes available, but taxes need not be withheld on tips that are merely allocated. Operators of food or beverage establishments with more than ten employees must allocate to tipped employees the excess of 8% (or as little as 2% upon petition by the employer or a majority of employees) of gross receipts over the tips reported by the employees to the employer. However, allocation of the 8% amount is not required if employees voluntarily report aggregate tips equal to at least 8% of gross receipts.

Compliance in tip reporting is a severe problem for the IRS. An employee who reports less than the allocated amount of tips must be able to substantiate this reporting position with adequate books and records. However, the allocated tip income does not necessarily reflect the amount actually reportable by the employee as gross income. Employees who directly receive tips are required to report the full amount of the tips received. Thus, the amount of tips reported by employees should be greater than the charged tips reported by the employer. [IRC §§3102(c), 6053.]

Tip jars: Amounts placed in "tip jars" at stores are to be treated as tips under IRC §3121(q) and not as wages subject to FICA withholding. An employer is ordinarily required to withhold and pay over the employee portion of the FICA tax. However, that withholding requirement applies only to tips that are included in a written statement furnished to the employer (Form 4070), and only to the extent that collection can be made by the employer by deducting the amount of the tax from wages paid to the employee, including tips. An employer is required to deduct and withhold the tax on tips constituting wages only for those tips the employee reports to the employer in a written statement. If the tips are not reported, or the reporting is incomplete or inaccurate, the tips are considered to be paid on the date that the IRS makes notice and demand for the taxes to the employer. Consequently, the amounts placed in tip jars are not subject to the employer share of FICA tax until the IRS files a notice and demand for the taxes from the taxpayer. [IRC §3121(q); Chief Counsel Advice (CCA) 200929004.]

Employees may use IRS Forms 4070 or 4070-A to report tips, or an employer may establish an electronic system that their employees may use for reporting their tips. If an electronic system is used, IRS regulations require that certain safeguards be in place to ensure the integrity of the system and the privacy of individual employees. Employees are deemed to maintain sufficient evidence to establish the amount of tip income received during a calendar month through a daily record if they report tips on a daily basis through an electronic system that meets the substantiation requirements of the regulations and receive a hard copy of a daily record based on those entries from the employer. [IRS Reg. §31.6053-1.]

Collection of the employee tax should be discontinued when the employee's combined wages and tips total the taxable wage bases for the year in question (see ¶208). The employer's liability for employer tax on wages also continues until the wages and tips total the taxable wage bases for the year. [Reg. §31.3121(a)(1)-1.]

Tip credit. A business tax credit is available for food or beverage establishments in an amount equal to the employer's FICA tax obligation (7.65%) attributable to reported tips in excess of those treated as wages for purposes of satisfying the minimum wage requirements of the Fair Labor Standards Act. [OBRA '93 §13433(a), (b).] Although the federal minimum wage is $7.25 per hour, employers should continue to compute the amount of tip credit based on the federal minimum wage that was in effect on January 7, 2007 (*i.e.*, $5.15/hour). This requirement, included in the Small Business and Work Opportunity Tax Act of 2007, allows for a higher tip credit for employers. In addition, taxpayers may claim the FICA tip credit against the Alternative Minimum Tax. [P.L. 110-28, May 25, 2007.]

> **Example:** Laura averages $7.00 an hour in tips. This amount is added to her cash wage of $2.13 an hour. That equals $9.13. The federal minimum wage is subtracted from this amount. Using the tip credit, her employer subtracts the old minimum wage of $5.15 an hour ($9.13 - $5.15 = $3.98). The resultant sum of $3.98 is multiplied by the employer FICA tax rate to yield a tip tax credit of $0.304 an hour for the employee.

If, by the tenth day of the month following the month in which an employee's (tips) report was received, an employer has not had available sufficient employee funds to permit deduction of the employee tax, the employer is no longer liable for the collection of the tax. [IRC §3102(c).] The employer must show on Form W-2 the amount of the uncollected tax. See ¶205.

In making deductions of taxes on tips, employers are permitted to estimate the amounts of tips that will be reported by an employee during any year, and to spread the deductions over the wage payments made during the year. If the estimated tips are less than the actual tips reported to the employer, the additional tax due may be deducted from payments of wages (other than tips) made to the employee during the year and within the first 30 days thereafter. [IRC §3102(c).] If the employer collects more than the correct amount of tax on tips, the overcollection should be repaid to the employee. [IRS Reg. §31.6413(a)-1.]

Whether the IRS may assess an employer-only FICA tax on the aggregate estimate of allegedly unreported tips of employees had been the subject of litigation. However, the U.S. Supreme Court has held that the IRS does not have the obligation to audit each employee it suspects is underreporting his or her tips before it is able to assess the employer-restaurant for its share of total FICA taxes due. [*U.S. v. Fior D'Italia, Inc.*, 536 US 238, 2002-1 USTC ¶50,459 (2002).]

As a result of the Court's decision, whenever employees are suspected of underreporting cash tips, the IRS can go directly to the employer and collect the employer's share of the FICA tax using an aggregate estimate based on tips reported on credit card receipts. The IRS need not first estimate each individual employee's tip income separately and then add the individual estimates together to calculate the total FICA liability of the employer. However, penalties will not attach and interest will not accrue until the IRS actually demands the extra payment and the employer refuses to pay in a timely fashion.

All industries in which tipping is a customary practice may participate in the Internal Revenue Service's voluntary tip compliance programs. In exchange for employer participation in the program, the IRS agrees to refrain from tip examinations of the employer.

TRDA

Under the Tip Rate Determination Agreement (TRDA), an employer and the IRS determine the amount of tips that employees receive and the amount that should be reported to the IRS.

TRAC

Under the Tip Reporting Alternative Commitment (TRAC), an employer agrees to educate employees about the tax consequences of tip income and to establish tip reporting procedures. Employers in the food and beverage industry that have employees who receive both cash and charged tips may design their own TRAC program, subject to IRS approval. In 2003, the IRS expanded a new tip compliance agreement nationwide to the gaming industry. Under the agreement, as long as tips are reported at or above the established tip rate, the IRS is generally prohibited from auditing the employees' tip income. [Rev. Proc. 2003-35; *www.irs.gov/pub/irs-drop/rp-03-35.pdf.*] Pro forma TRDAs, TRAC agreements, and approval request letters can be obtained from the IRS website (*www.irs.gov*). The IRS announced that it was indefinitely extending these voluntary tip compliance programs, which were set to expire in 2005. With the indefinite extension of the tip program, existing tip agreements will be administered without the need for employers to re-sign agreements. [IRS News Release 2004-117, Sept. 16, 2004.]

¶204.2 Group-Term Life Insurance Premiums

In the event an employer continues to provide taxable group-term life insurance (*i.e.*, coverage exceeding $50,000) to an individual who has left his or her employment, the former employee is required to pay the employee portion of the FICA tax directly. To facilitate this the employer is required to list on the former employee's W-2 each year both the amount of the employer's payment for taxable group-term life insurance and the amount of the employee FICA tax imposed on it. Instructions on Form 1040 then direct the employee to add this amount to his or her individual tax liability. [IRC §§3102(d), 3121(a)(2)(C).]

¶205 Employees' Receipts—Forms W-2 and W-3

The employer must furnish to each of his or her employees a written statement with respect to the wages paid (including tips reported by the employee) during the calendar year. If an employee gives consent (see below), this statement may be furnished electronically. The statement must be furnished on or before January 31 of the year succeeding such calendar year. However, as to an employee whose employment is terminated before the close of the calendar year, the statement may be given to the worker at any time after the termination of employment, but no later than January 31 of the following calendar year. However, if there is no reasonable expectation on the part of both employer and employee of further employment during the calendar year, and if the employee requests that the statement be furnished at an earlier time, the statement must be furnished within 30 days of the request or 30 days after the last payment of wages, whichever is later. [IRC §6051; IRS Reg. §31.6051-1(d).]

Form W-2, Wage and Tax Statement, is designed for use in meeting the requirements relative to furnishing employee receipts under both the Federal Insurance Contributions Act and the income tax statutes. By furnishing their employees with copies of this form, properly filled in, employers satisfy the requirements of both statutes relative to the furnishing of employee statements. In this respect, no other statements are required. As a general rule, an employer must furnish Form W-2 to each employee, whether or not the wages specified on the statement are subject to income tax withholding. [IRS Reg. §31.6051-1(a).] Copies B and C of Form W-2 generally should be given to the employee. Copy A goes to the Social Security Administration, which forwards the income tax information to the Internal Revenue Service. See "Filing Forms W-2 and W-3," below.

If an employer pays an employee wages not subject to income tax withholding, he still must furnish to the employee the tax return copy and the employee's copy of a statement on Form W-2 for the calendar year. The statement must show the following: (a) name and address of the employer, (b) name, address, and Social Security account number of the employee, (c) total amount of taxable wages paid during the calendar year, (d) amount of employee tax deducted from the employee's wages, and (e) the proportion of the amount of withheld FICA taxes that represents the tax for hospital insurance benefits. [IRS Reg. §31.6051-1(b)(1).] Form W-2 requires employers to report separately the amounts withheld for the old-age, survivors and disability insurance (OASDI) portion and the Medicare portion of the FICA tax. [IRS *2019 Instructions for Forms W-2 and W-3*.]

Effective December 18, 2015, the requirement to include a Social Security number on a Form W-2 was replaced with the requirement to use an identifying number. [IRC §6051(a)(2), as amended by the Protecting Americans from Tax Hikes (PATH) Act of 2015 (P.L. 114-113).] This change permitted the Department of the Treasury to promulgate regulations requiring or permitting a truncated Social Security number on Form W-2. The IRS issued final regulations in July 2019 that allow employers to truncate employees' Social Security numbers on copies of Forms W-2 (and W-2c) that are furnished to employees, but not on a copy that is filed with the SSA. The regulations are effective for statements required to be furnished to employees after December 31, 2020. [IRS Reg. §§31.6051-1 and 31.6051-2.]

Advance payments of the earned income credit must be reported on Form W-2. [Reg. §31.6051-1(b)(1).] Regarding earned income credits in general, see ¶229.

Tips reported by an employee to an employer must be reflected on Form W-2, even if the employer did not have sufficient funds to collect the Social Security or Medicare tax. The total reported in Boxes 3 and 7 should not exceed the applicable wage base ($137,700 for 2020). In addition, the employer must show on Box 12 (Codes A and B) the Social Security and Medicare tax that could not be collected because the employee did not have sufficient funds from which to deduct the required amounts. [*2019 Instructions for Forms W-2 and W-3.*]

An exception is made to the requirement that all employees' wage and tax statements must be made on Form W-2 in cases in which a composite return on electronic or other approved media is used by the employer. In such cases, the requirement is satisfied if, in lieu of Form W-2, the employee is provided with a statement on a form that contains all of the information required to be shown on Form W-2. [Reg. §31.6051-1(g).]

If after reasonable effort the employer is unable to deliver Form W-2 to an employee, the employer is required to retain the form (the employee copy and the IRS copy) for a period of four years. [Reg. §31.6051-1(a)(3).]

If it becomes necessary to correct a Form W-2 after it has been given to an employee, a corrected statement must be issued to the employee. Corrected statements should be clearly marked "Corrected by Employer." [Reg. §31.6051-1(c).]

An employer that willfully fails to furnish an employee with an annual receipt showing the amount of employee taxes deducted under the Federal Insurance Contributions Act and the amount of income tax withheld, together with the amount of wages subject to such taxes, or who willfully furnishes a fraudulent receipt, will, for each such failure, upon conviction thereof, be fined not more than $1,000, or imprisoned for not more than one year, or both. [IRC §7204.] In addition, the employer is liable for a $50 civil penalty, which will be assessed and collected in the same manner as the employer's taxes under the Federal Insurance Contributions Act. [IRC §6674.] Employers may also be subject to a penalty for failure to file, or a fraudulent filing of, tip information returns, as noted at ¶204, above.

Amounts exempted from tax under "totalization agreements" (see ¶330) with foreign governments are not required to be shown on employee receipts. [IRC §6051(a).]

Electronic Furnishing of Form W-2

Employers that are required to furnish a W-2 form to an employee may furnish the W-2 in an electronic format instead of a paper format if the employee consents to receive it in electronic form (69 *Fed. Reg.* 7567, Feb. 18, 2004). For example, the W-2 can be made available through a company website or the website of a payroll outsourcer. However, the employer must provide adequate notification of the statement's availability (Reg. §31.6051-1(j)).

Consent. The employee must affirmatively consent to receive the Form W-2 in an electronic format. There are two ways in which consent may be made. Consent may be made in a paper document, if it is confirmed electronically, or the employee may consent electronically in any manner that reasonably demonstrates that the employee can access the W-2 in the electronic format in which it will be furnished to the recipient. The consent requirement is not satisfied if the employee withdraws consent and the withdrawal becomes effective prior to the time the W-2 is furnished. The employer may provide that a withdrawal of consent takes effect either on the date it is received by the employer or on a subsequent date. In addition, the employer may provide that a request for a paper statement will be treated as a withdrawal of consent [Reg. §31.6051-1(j)(2).]

Required disclosures. The employer must provide the employee with a disclosure statement, either before consent, or at the time of consent, addressing the following:

(1) the scope and duration of the consent;
(2) that a paper form will be furnished, if consent is not given;
(3) the procedure for obtaining a paper copy of the form, after consent is given, to furnish the form electronically;
(4) the procedures for withdrawal of consent;
(5) the conditions under which an employer will cease furnishing electronic statements;

(6) the procedures for updating the information provided to the employer for contacting the recipient;

(7) a description of the hardware and software required to access, print, and retain the form; and

(8) the date on which the form will no longer be available on the website. [Reg. §31.6051-1(j)(3).]

Notice requirements. If the statement is furnished on a website, the employer must notify the employee that the statement is posted on the website. The notice may be delivered by regular mail, e-mail, or in person. It must include instructions on accessing and printing the statement and must include the following statement in capital letters, "IMPORTANT TAX RETURN DOCUMENT AVAILABLE." If the notice is sent by e-mail, the foregoing statement must appear on the e-mail's subject line. If the e-mail notice is returned as undeliverable, and a correct e-mail address cannot be obtained, a notice must be delivered by mail or in person within 30 days after the e-mail was returned. [Reg. §31.6051-1(j)(5).]

Access period. All W-2 forms that are required to be furnished on a website, must be retained on the website through October 15 of the year following the calendar year to which the forms relate. In the event October 15 falls on a Saturday, Sunday, or legal holiday, the retention period is the first business day after October 15. Corrected forms posted to a website must be retained until the later of:

(1) October 15 of the year following the calendar year to which the forms relate;

(2) the first business day after October 15, if October 15 falls on a Saturday, Sunday, or legal holiday; or

(3) the date 90 days after the corrected form is posted. [Reg. §31.6051-1(j)(6).]

See ¶223 for information about filing Form W-2 with the Social Security Administration.

Filing Forms W-2 and W-3

Employers must file with the Social Security Administration a copy of Form W-2 for wages paid to each employee from whom income, Social Security, or Medicare tax was withheld or income tax would have been withheld if the employee claimed no more than one withholding allowance or had not claimed exemption from withholding for Form W-4, Employee's Withholding Allowance Certificate. Also, every employer engaged in a trade or business that pays remuneration for services performed by an employee, including non cash payments must file a W-2 for each employee even if the employee is related to the employer. Household employers, even those with only one household employee, must file Form W-3 if filing a paper Form W-2. Anyone required to file Form W-2 must file Form W-3 to transmit Copy A of Form W-2. Employers should keep a copy of Form W-3 and Copy D of Form W-2 for four years.

Form W-3 and Copy A of Form W-2 should be sent to: Social Security Administration; Direct Operations Center; Wilkes-Barre, PA 18769-0001. For certified mail, change the zip code to "18769-0002." If an IRS-approved delivery service is used (see ¶223.5), add "ATTN: W-2 Process, 1150 E. Mountain Dr." to the address and change the zip code to "18702-7997."

Filing due date for 2019 forms W-2 and W-3. The due date for filing 2019 Forms W-2 and W-3 with the Social Security Administration is January 31, 2020, whether employers file using paper or electronically. [Reg. §31.6051-2; *2019 Instructions for Forms W-2 and W-3.*] See below for discussion of filing date extensions.

Employers filing paper forms must use either an official IRS form or a substitute form that exactly meets the IRS's specifications. The IRS will answer questions about substitute forms via e-mail. Taxpayers may direct questions about red-ink Forms W-2 (Copy A) and Forms W-3 to substituteforms@irs.gov and indicate "substitute forms" on the subject line. [Rev. Proc. 2017-42, IRS Pub. 1141.]

Electronic reporting: Forms W-2 and W-2c may be submitted electronically or on paper. However, employers that file at least 250 returns annually are required to electronically file.

All employers, even those that do not meet these requirements, are encouraged to file electronically. However, employers can request a waiver from the requirement to file electronically by submitting Form 8508 (Request for Waiver From Filing Information Returns Electronically) at least 45 days before the due date of Form W-2 or 45 days before the filing of the first Form W-2c. [*Instructions for Forms W-2 and W-3.*]

Business Services Online. Employers or third-party preparers filing wage reports electronically must use the Social Security Administration's Business Services Online, a suite of Internet services for companies to conduct business with the Social Security Administration. [SSA Notice, 69 *Fed. Reg.* 33691, June 16, 2004; SSA/IRS Reporter, Winter 2005; *www.ssa.gov/bso/bsowelcome.htm.*]

The Business Services Online can be utilized to file Form W-2, W-2c, and W-3, as well as to check on the status of previously submitted wage reports. At the Business Services Online website, *www.ssa.gov/bso/bsowelcome.htm*, employers may file Forms W-2c and W-3c electronically. Employers can upload the EFW2 software to create "fill-in" versions of the forms. This format allows employers to print out copies to file with state and local governments, distribute to employees, and retain for internal records. As an alternative, employers can also complete up to 50 W-2 and 25 W-2c forms at the SSA website without uploading the additional software. [Rev. Proc. 2009-48.] Additionally, the Social Security Number Verification Service will allow employers to verify the accuracy of Social Security numbers reported by their employees.

To register for e-filing, go to *www.ssa.gov/bso/bsowelcome.htm*, select "Register" and follow the prompts. A User Identification Number (User ID) will be issued immediately, on-screen, and the applicant will be able to immediately create a password. The User ID will no longer be deactivated after 365 days of non-use. Passwords will expire after 90 days; a user will be prompted to change his or her password upon logging on after it has expired in order to access BSO services. If an employer is already registered but has forgotten its User ID or password, the employer should call 1-800-772-6270. The Business Services Online Handbook provides detailed information about how to register, use the site, report wages to the Social Security Administration, and view the processing status of wage files and/or reports that the employer has filed.

Waiver and Extensions

If an employer is unable to file with the IRS the required Forms W-2 by the deadline, the employer should request an extension. The preferred method of filing an extension request is electronically through IRS' "Filing Information Returns Electronically (FIRE)" system. See *www.irs.gov/taxtopics/tc803.html* for additional information. An employer must request the extension before the due date of the report using IRS Form 8809 (Application for Extension of Time to File Information Returns). Note, employers that request an extension of time to file the 2019 Form W-2 must still furnish the form to their employees by January 31, 2020.

Effective for filings due on or after January 1, 2017, extensions of time to file Form W-2 with the Social Security Administration will no longer be automatic. Employers may request one 30-day extension to file Form W-2. [80 *Fed. Reg.* 48433, Aug. 13, 2015.]

An employer may also request an extension of time to furnish forms W-2 to employees by sending a letter to: Internal Revenue Service, Mail Stop 4360, Attn: Extension of Time Coordinator, 240 Murall Drive, Kearneysville, WV 25430. The letter must be mailed on or before the due date for furnishing Form W-2 to employees and indicate the reason for delay, the employer's name, address and EIN, and a statement that an extension is being requested, and the signature of the employer or its authorized agent.

The IRS may waive the electronic filing requirement for an employer that can show hardship. To request a waiver, an employer must apply 45 days before the due date of the report using IRS Form 8508.

WAGES

¶206   What Are Wages?

The two kinds of employment taxes under the Federal Insurance Contributions Act (old-age, survivors, and disability insurance taxes and hospital insurance taxes) are measured by the amount of wages paid by an employer to employees during the calendar year. [IRC §3101.] An employee and an employer must each pay Social Security and hospital insurance tax on the employee's wages. However, only wages earned by an employee or income of a self-employed person are subject to tax.

Wages include all remuneration that is currently includible in income for income tax purposes (e.g., salaries, fees, bonuses, sales commissions, and cash tips of at least $20 a month). Wages for purposes of Social Security also include elective deferrals to 401(k) plans, vacation pay, termination pay, and fringe benefits other than those specially excluded.

Note, however, for FICA purposes, the term "wages" generally is not limited to actual money received, but includes the cash value of remuneration, including benefits, paid in any medium other than cash, such as room and board. The name by which the remuneration is designated is immaterial. Salaries, commissions, and bonuses constitute "wages" if paid by an employer to an employee with respect to employment covered by the statute. Also, the basis upon which the remuneration is paid is generally immaterial. For example, it may be paid on the basis of piecework or a percentage of profits, and it may be paid hourly, daily, weekly, monthly, or annually. [IRC §3121; IRS Reg. §31.3121(a)(1).]

As to those instances when remuneration for services paid in a medium other than cash is excluded from the definition of "wages," see ¶209–210.

Certain other forms of remuneration are also excluded from the term "wages," *e.g.*, certain medical, hospitalization, or death benefits (see ¶211), certain retirement benefits (see ¶212), payment of an employee's taxes without deduction from the employee's wages (see ¶215), payments to disabled former employees or to the survivor or estate of a former employee (see ¶222.1), payments to retired judges, and income from protected Indian fishing rights. The status of other forms of remuneration is discussed at ¶216–222.

¶206.1   Members of the Uniformed Services

Members of the uniformed services are covered while on active duty, while training for active duty, or while in inactive duty training. [IRC §3121(m).] Contributions and benefits are computed on members' basic pay, subject, of course, to the taxable-wage limitations discussed at ¶208, below. A member of the uniformed service, as employee, and the United States, as employer, pay taxes on the service member's basic pay or compensation for inactive duty training. [IRC §3121(i).]

Basic pay does not include such items as the value of food, shelter, clothing, allowances, allotments, special pay, or incentive pay. However, the wage credit that was available prior to 2002 to members of the uniformed services on active duty to reflect the cash value of wages-in-kind as food and shelter is no longer available. See ¶534.1.

Employers that continue to pay an employee's full salary or the difference between the regular salary and the amount received from the military must be aware that the employment relationship between the employee and the employer is considered terminated when the worker is called up for active military service with the U.S. government or for active service with his or her state's National Guard.

Regarding *differential pay*, the payments made by an employer to a former employee to cover the difference between the employee's (higher) civilian pay and (lower) military pay while he or she is in military service with the U.S. government or state National Guard, see ¶316.

¶206.2 Peace Corps Volunteers

Services performed by an individual as a "volunteer" or "volunteer leader" within the meaning of the Peace Corps Act are, generally, covered. However, only amounts paid pursuant to section 5(c) or 6(l) of the Peace Corps Act are counted as wages. These sections refer to termination payments to volunteers and volunteer leaders. [IRC §3121(i).] See also ¶312.1.

¶207   Taxes Attach When Wages "Paid"

Employer taxes attach at the time that the wages are "paid" by the employer, and employee taxes attach at the time they are received by the employee (see ¶201), *i.e.*, at the time they are paid by the employer to the employee. Wages are considered paid by an employer at the time that they are actually or constructively paid. [IRS Reg. §31.3121(a)-2(a).]

Wages are *constructively* paid when they are credited to the account of or set apart for an employee so that they may be drawn upon by the employee at any time although not then actually reduced to possession. To constitute payment in such cases the wages must be credited to or set apart for the employee without any substantial limitation or restriction as to the time or manner of payment or condition upon which payment is to be made, and must be made available to him or her so that they may be drawn upon at any time, and their payment brought within his or her own control and disposition. [IRS Reg. §31.3121(a)-2(b).]

Cash tips totaling $20 or more a month received by an employee in the course of employment for one employer are deemed to be remuneration paid at the time the employee furnishes to the employer a written statement regarding the tips. If the statement is not furnished, the tips are deemed paid at the time they were received. [IRC §3121(q).] See, further, ¶204.1.

Back Pay/Front Pay

For purposes of the Federal Insurance Contribution Act (FICA) and the Federal Unemployment Tax Act (FUTA), the U.S. Supreme Court upheld IRS practice that treats a back wages settlement awarded to employees as being taxable in the year the wages are in fact paid. *U.S. v. Cleveland Indians Baseball Company*, U.S. Sup. Ct., 121 Sup.Ct. 1433, U.S. Tax Cases ¶50,341 (2001). However, the court reaffirmed its prior decision in *Social Security Bd. v. Nierotko*, 327 U.S. 358 (1946), that for purposes of the Social Security "earnings" or "retirement" test, back wages are assigned to the period within which they *should* have been paid.

Back pay claims are generally awarded for illegal termination or illegal failure to hire. Thus, back pay may relate to periods when no services were performed. Similarly, front pay is paid when it is impractical to place an employee in a job. Although back pay is not a tort-like remedy and is generally taxable, lost wages and attorneys' fees paid because of physical injury can be excluded. Employment taxes are calculated for the year of actual payment. However for determining Social Security benefits, back pay awards are allocated to the periods for which the amounts were awarded. [Program Manager Technical Advice (PMTA), Chief Counsel's Office, 2009-035, Oct. 28, 2008.]

Employers may be required to withhold employment taxes from settlement proceeds allocated to an employee's back and front pay claims. In *Josifovich v. Secure Computing Corp.*, D. N.J., 2009-2 USTC ¶50,543, the court held that such amounts are "wages" on which withholding is required even though the claims were not in exchange for work actually performed. Services performed are only a component of wages that are subject to withholding; wages encompass the entire employee-employer relationship and are not restricted to work actually performed.

¶208 Amount Subject to Taxes

There is a limit on the amount of earnings subject to FICA (and SECA) taxes each year. For 2020, earnings in excess of $137,700 are excluded from taxable wages for purposes of the old-age, survivors, and disability insurance (OASDI) portion of the FICA tax. Since 1994 there has been no limit on the amount of earnings subject to the Medicare hospital insurance portion of the FICA tax.

The maximum amount of wages counted for tax and benefit purposes has been increased numerous times since the enactment of the Social Security program, as shown in the following table:

1937-1950	$3,000	1992	$55,500*
1951-1954	3,600	1993	57,600*
1955-1958	4,200	1994	60,600*
1959-1965	4,800	1995	61,200*
1966-1967	6,600	1996	62,700*
1968-1971	7,800	1997	65,400*
1972	9,000	1998	68,400*
1973	10,800	1999	72,600*
1974	13,200	2000	76,200*
1975	14,100	2001	80,400*
1976	15,300	2002	84,900*
1977	16,500	2003-2004	87,000*
1978	17,700	2005	90,000*
1979	22,900	2006	94,200*
1980	25,900	2007	97,500*
1981	29,700	2008	102,000*
1982	32,400	2009-2011	106,800*
1983	35,700	2012	110,100*
1984	37,800	2013	113,700*
1985	39,600	2014	117,000*
1986	42,000	2015-2016	118,500*
1987	43,800	2017	127,200*
1988	45,000	2018	128,400*
1989	48,000	2019	132,900*
1990	51,300	2020	137,700*
1991	53,400*		

* Amounts shown for years after 1990 are the maximum amount of wages subject to FICA taxation under the OASDI portion of the wage tax only.

There is an automatic escalator in the law (see ¶541) that increases the tax and earnings bases annually, following an increase in benefits under the cost-of-living escalator. The amount of increase in the tax and earnings bases depends on the rate of increase in average total wages, and is generally announced in October of the year prior to the year in which the increase is to occur. [Soc. Sec. Act §230(a).] However, if there is no increase in the cost of living from the third quarter of the prior year to the third quarter of the current year, and thus, no increase in the cost of living pursuant to SSA §215(i), then there can be no increase in the tax and earnings base. [SSA §230(a).]

Note, an employer must determine the wage base to be used for the current year in January of that year.

Under the tax rates in effect for 2020 (6.2% for employers and 6.2% for employees), the maximum Social Security tax will be $17,074.80 (*i.e.*, 6.2% of $137,700 plus 6.2% of $137,700).

There is no limit on the amount of wages on which the employer and the employee each would pay the 1.45% hospital insurance tax. Thus, an individual earning $140,000 in 2020 will pay $8,537.40 in OASDI taxes (*i.e.*, 6.2% of $137,700) and $2,030 in HI taxes (*i.e.*, 1.45% of $140,000) for a total tax liability of $10,567.40.

Individuals may also be subject to an additional 0.9% Medicare tax on wages in excess of $200,000 ($250,000 for joint filers and $125,000 for married taxpayers filing separately) (see ¶201). The tax is assessed on employees only and will result in individuals paying a total Medicare tax of 2.35% on wages in excess of the applicable threshold. In addition, note, the tax is assessed on the *combined* wages of an employee and his or her spouse, in the case of a joint return.

Pursuant to the added tax, an individual earning $210,000 would be subject to $8,537.40 in OASDI tax (6.2% of $137,700) plus $3,045 in HI taxes (1.45% of $210,000) plus $235 in additional Medicare taxes (2.35% of $10,000) for a total employment tax liability of $11,817.40. Alternatively, assume the individual is married and his spouse earns $30,000. Their combined income would be under the $250,000 threshold and, thus, not subject to the 0.9% Medicare tax.

High earning individuals are also subject to a separate 3.8% Medicare tax on investment income (see ¶201). The tax is imposed on the lesser of: (1) the individual's net investment income for the year, or (2) any excess of modified adjusted gross income for the tax year over $200,000 ($250,000 for joint filers and $125,000 for married taxpayers filing separately). Note, the tax would be assessed in addition to the applicable capital gains tax.

Accordingly, an individual with investment income of $225,000 would be subject to an additional Medicare tax of $8,550 (3.8% of $225,000). If the individual is married, however, the 3.8% tax would not apply as combined net investment income of the couple is below $250,000.

Application of Limit

Wages in excess of the limits are not taxable under the OASDI portion of the FICA tax. However, all wages are subject to the 1.45% Hospital Insurance (Medicare) portion of the tax. If an employee, by reason of working for more than one employer during a calendar year, pays taxes on wages in excess of one or both of the limits (*e.g.*, Social Security tax in 2020 in excess of $8,537.40 (6.2% of $137,700)), he or she is entitled to a credit or refund. See ¶230. As for employers, however, the limits apply to the wages paid by each employer. The employer is liable for the taxes on all wages within the taxable wage limits that he or she pays to an employee during a calendar year, without regard to any wages received by the employee during the same calendar year from other employers. [IRC §3121(a); IRS Reg. §31.3121(a)(1)-1(a).] Accordingly, an employment services provider could not aggregate employee wages to calculate FICA and FUTA wage bases. The taxpayer provided design and production workers to motion picture and television companies. Although the companies reimbursed the taxpayer for the payroll costs and paid a fee for the taxpayer's services, for FICA and FUTA purposes, the taxpayer treated itself, rather than the motion picture and television producers, as the employer of the workers. However, because the production companies, and not the taxpayer, controlled the payment of wages, the IRS determined that the production companies were the common law employers of the workers and aggregation was therefore improper. [*Cencast Services L.P. v. U.S.*, 62 Fed. Cl. 159 (2004), *aff'd* CA-FC (2013) Nos. 2012-5142, 2012-5143, 2012-5144, 2012-5145, 2012-5146, 2012-5147, 2012-5148, 2012-5149, 2012-5150, 2012-5151.]

Alternatively, where an employer acquires the trade or business of another employer during a year, the successor may count the wages paid to an employee during the same year by the predecessor for purposes of the annual tax base. The method of acquisition is immaterial, but the successor must have acquired substantially all the property used in the trade or business. [IRC §3121(a)(1); IRS Reg. §31.3121(a)(1)-1(b).]

Concurrent Employment/Common Paymaster

When an individual is concurrently employed by two or more related corporations and is compensated by a common paymaster that is one of the corporations, the group of corporations is treated as a single employer for employer tax purposes. That is, each of the corporations is considered to have paid as remuneration to the individual only amounts it paid to the individual, and is not considered to have paid amounts that were disbursed to the individual by another of the corporations. [IRC §3121(s); IRS Reg. §31.3121(s)-1.]

This rule applies whether the remuneration was paid with respect to the employment relationship of the individual with the disbursing corporation or on behalf of another related corporation. Accordingly, if all of the remuneration to the individual from the related corporations is disbursed through the common paymaster, the total amount of taxes imposed is determined as though the individual had only one employer (the common paymaster). The common paymaster is responsible for filing information and tax returns and issuing Forms W-2 with respect to wages that it is considered to have paid in this manner. [Reg. §31.3121(s)-1(a).]

The common paymaster has the primary responsibility for remitting taxes with respect to the remuneration it disburses. If taxes due are not remitted, the common paymaster remains liable for the full amount of the unpaid taxes, and each of the other related corporations using the common paymaster is jointly and severally liable for its appropriate share of these taxes. [Reg. §31.3121(s)-1(c).]

State university faculty members concurrently employed both as health care professionals at the medical school and under a tax-exempt faculty practice plan are treated as having a common paymaster, provided that 30% or more of the plan employees are concurrently employed by the medical school. [P.L. 98-21, §125.] In a private letter ruling, the IRS determined that employees of a single-member limited liability company (LLC) should not be included in applying the common paymaster rules. The IRS treated the single-member LLC as a corporation, distinct from its owner. The taxpayer, a 501(c)(3) corporation, was the sole member of an LLC. The taxpayer was set up to absorb private physician groups and university faculty. Some of these entities employed non-physicians as well as physicians. The non-physicians were to be employed by the LLC. They would continue in their job roles unchanged from previous years. The LLC planned to maintain a separate payroll for the non-physician employees and would provide their services through a services agreement. The IRS determined that the LLC was a separate corporation, distinct from the taxpayer. Therefore, the non-physician individuals employed by the LLC were solely employees of the LLC. The IRS concluded that the LLC's employees should not be counted as employees of the faculty practice plan. This allowed the faculty practice plan to satisfy the 30 percent test. [IRS Letter Ruling 200944016.]

¶209   Noncash Remuneration Excepted from Wages

With certain exceptions, remuneration for employment, including benefits, paid in any medium other than cash constitutes "wages," and therefore such remuneration is subject to taxes. The term "cash" includes checks and other monetary media of exchange. [IRC §3121(a).] Exceptions to this rule are discussed below.

¶209.1 Remuneration Paid to Farm Workers

Farm workers are covered if their annual cash remuneration from one employer amounts to at least $150 or if the employer's expenditures for agricultural labor in the year equal or exceed $2,500. See also ¶307. Only their cash remuneration is taxable, and then only if it amounts to at least $150 a year or if the $2,500 annual payroll test is met. [IRC §3121(a)(8).]

The cash-remuneration test applies with respect to the remuneration received by the employee from each employer during the calendar year. If an employee receives cash remuneration in any one year from more than one employer, the test must be applied separately to each employer. [IRS Reg. §31.3121(a)(8)-1(d)(3).]

For special provisions with respect to crew leaders, sharecroppers, temporary farm workers from foreign countries, and some seasonal piece-rate hand-harvest workers, see ¶307.

¶209.2 Remuneration Paid to Domestic Workers

In 2020, domestic workers in private homes are covered during any calendar year in which they are paid cash wages of at least $2,200 annually. [IRC §3121(x); 84 *Fed Reg.* 56515, Oct. 22, 2019.] Only cash remuneration is subject to the tax, and then, only if the worker is age 18 or older. Workers under age 18 are subject to the tax only if the service is the worker's principal occupation; however, being a student is considered an occupation for purposes of this test. [IRC §3121(b)(21).]

The Social Security Domestic Employment Reform Act of 1994 (P.L. 103-387, the "Nanny Tax Act") significantly increased the threshold for withholding and paying Social Security taxes on domestic service over the $50 per quarter threshold that previously had been in effect. The threshold for current and prior years is shown below. Thus, for 2020, an employer may pay a domestic worker up to $2,200 without withholding FICA tax.

Calendar Year	Threshold	Source	Calendar Year	Threshold	Source
Prior to 1994	$ 50/quarter		2007	1,500	71 FR 62636
1994	1,000	P.L. 103-387, §2(a)	2008	1,600	72 FR 60703
1995	1,000	P.L. 103-387, §2(a)	2009	1,700	73 FR 64651
1996	1,000	60 FR 54751	2010	1,700	74 FR 55614
1997	1,000	61 FR 55346	2011	1,700	75 FR 74123
1998	1,100	62 FR 58762	2012	1,800	76 FR 66111
1999	1,100	63 FR 58446	2013	1,800	77 FR 65754
2000	1,200	64 FR 57506	2014	1,900	78 FR 66413
2001	1,300	65 FR 63663	2015	1,900	79 FR 64455
2002	1,300	66 FR 54047	2016	2,000	80 FR 66963
2003	1,400	67 FR 65620	2017	2,000	81 FR 74854
2004	$ 1,400	68 FR 60437	2018	2,100	82 FR 59937
2005	$ 1,400	69 FR 62497	2019	2,100	83 FR 53702
2006	1,500	70 FR 61677	2020	2,200	84 FR 56515

In the future, the limit is subject to increase to account for the rise in national average wages. [IRC §3121(x).] If an employer elects to pay the worker's portion of FICA taxes, this amount is not considered additional taxable income for FICA or FUTA purposes [IRC §3121 (a)(7)], but the worker may have to pay additional federal income tax on the amount of FICA tax paid on his or her behalf.

An employer may deduct FICA taxes from each paycheck, even if it is uncertain that the $2,200 cash-payment test will be met for the year. If the employer deducts too little, he or she is liable to the IRS for any shortfall and should correct the error by deducting it from a later payment to the worker. If too much is deducted or if it becomes obvious that the $2,200 threshold will not be met by the end of the year, the employer should repay the amount withheld. However, an employer that has paid FICA taxes for a domestic worker who earned less than the applicable threshold for the year is entitled to a refund from the IRS.

An employer may elect to compute to the nearest dollar any payment of cash wages for domestic service. If the employer elects to do this, the payment of any fractional part of a dollar is disregarded, unless it amounts to 50¢ or more, in which case it is increased to the next higher whole-dollar amount. If this method is used with respect to one domestic worker, then it must be used for all other domestics employed by the same employer, and whole-dollar amounts are then used for other purposes of the law, such as determining whether the payments constitute taxable wages, computing the taxes, record-keeping, and reporting and paying the taxes. [Reg. §31.3121(i)-1.]

Note that domestic service performed for family members is excluded in many cases (see ¶310). A general discussion of domestic service as "employment" appears at ¶309. The filing requirements for employers of household workers are discussed at ¶223.3.

¶209.3 Remuneration Paid to Casual Workers

Individuals engaged in performing service that is not in the course of the employer's trade or business are covered if they can meet a cash-pay test of $100 in cash wages received in a calendar year. Remuneration paid in any medium other than cash is not counted. [IRC §3121(a)(7)(C); IRS Reg. §31.3121(a)(7)-1(b).]

The cash-pay test applies with respect to the remuneration received by the employee from each employer during the period. If an employee receives cash remuneration in any period from more than one employer, the test must be applied separately to the remuneration received from each employer. [Reg. §31.3121(a)(7)-1(c).]

¶209.4 Payments by Tax-Exempt Organizations

Annual remuneration of less than $100 paid by an organization exempt from income tax under Sec. 501(a) and (c)(3) of the Internal Revenue Code is excluded from the definition of "wages." [IRC §3121(a)(16); Soc. Sec. Act §209(a)(14).] Such tax-exempt organizations include certain nonprofit organizations, trusts, agricultural or horticultural organizations, etc.

¶209.5 Certain Fringe Benefits

An employee's gross income does not include certain fringe benefits provided by an employer as long as the benefit qualifies as a no-additional-cost service, a qualified employee discount, a working condition fringe, a *de minimis* fringe, or an employer-operated athletic facility provided to employees.

In order to qualify, fringe benefits available to favored groups must meet certain *nondiscrimination* requirements. For example, the benefit must be available on substantially the same basis to each person in a group of employees that does not discriminate in favor of officers, owners, or highly compensated employees. However, the nondiscrimination rules do not apply to working condition fringes or *de minimis* fringes (other than subsidized eating facilities). Thus, if for valid business reasons an employer makes a bodyguard available only to its executives, the working condition fringe exclusion would apply, even though the availability of the benefit would not satisfy the nondiscrimination rules.

The following are excluded from "wages":

(1) The value of *no-additional-cost services* provided to employees or their spouses or dependent children by employers is excluded from the definition of income as long as the service is available on a nondiscriminatory basis, the employer does not incur any significant costs in providing the service to the employee, and the service is offered for sale to customers in the ordinary course of the employer's business for which the employee is working. For example, free flights to airline employees could be excluded. This exclusion applies whether the service is provided directly for no charge, at a reduced price, or through a cash rebate.

The exclusion may also apply to a no-additional-cost service provided by an unrelated employer if the service otherwise qualifies under the no-additional-cost service exclusion and is offered pursuant to a written reciprocal agreement with the employee's employer. For example, free travel on a standby basis pursuant to a qualifying agreement for employees of airline A on airline B may be excluded.

(2) *Certain employee discounts on the selling price of qualified property or services* are excluded from income if available on a nondiscriminatory basis. Qualified property or services includes property, other than real property and other personal property of a kind held for investment, and services offered for sale to nonemployee customers in the ordinary course of the employer's line of business. The discount can be excluded only to the extent that it does not exceed the gross profit percentage of the price at which the property is offered by the employer to customers or, in the case of a qualified service, more than 20 percent of the price at which the service is offered in the ordinary course of the employer's business.

(3) The fair market value of any property or service provided to an employee by an employer as a *working condition fringe benefit* is excluded to the extent that the costs of the property or service would be deductible by the employee as an ordinary and necessary business expense (expenses under IRC §162) if the employee had paid for such property or service. The nondiscrimination rules do not apply as a condition for exclusion of a working condition fringe. The following benefits are among those that may be excluded: employee parking facilities, the value of a company car used for business purposes, or subscriptions to business periodicals.

(4) If the value of any property or service provided to an employee is so minimal that accounting for the property or service would be unreasonable or administratively impractical, it is a *de minimis* fringe benefit that is excluded. The typing of personal letters by a company secretary, occasional personal use of a company copying machine, and coffee and doughnuts furnished to employees may be excluded.

An eating facility operated by an employer for the benefit of employees is treated as a *de minimis* fringe benefit as long as it is located on or near the business premises of the employer, the revenue normally equals or exceeds the direct operating costs of the facility, and the nondiscrimination rules are satisfied.

(5) *Athletic facilities* located on the employer's premises, operated by the employer, and run substantially for the use of employees, their spouses, or their dependent children may be excludable. Examples of qualifying facilities are swimming pools, gymnasiums, tennis courts, and golf courses. [IRC §§132(a), 3121(a)(20); Soc. Sec. Act §209(a)(17); Deficit Reduction Act of 1984 (P.L. 98-369), §531; H.R. 4170 and Conference Committee Reports, June 22, 1984.]

The taxability of employer-provided meals or lodging is discussed below at ¶218.

¶209.6 Employer-Provided Parking and Transportation

The amounts excludable from income in 2020 will be: (1) $270 per month for qualified parking and (2) $270 per month for combined highway vehicle transportation and transit passes. [Rev. Proc. 2019-44, I.R.B. 2019-47, Nov. 18, 2019.]

The excludable amounts for parking and mass transit passes for current and prior years are shown below:

Qualified Transportation Fringe Benefits Amounts
Excludable from Income

Year	Parking	Commuter vehicle / transit pass	Source
1994	$155	$60	Rev. Proc. 93-49, 1993-2 CB 581
1995	160	60	Rev. Proc. 94-72, 1994-2 CB 811
1996	165	65	Rev. Proc. 95-53, 1995-2 CB 445
1997	170	65	Rev. Proc. 96-59, 1996-2 CB 392
1998	175	65	Rev. Proc. 97-57, 1997-2 CB 584
1999	175	65	IRC §132(f)(2)
2000	175	65	Rev. Proc. 99-42, I.R.B. 1999-46, 568
2001	180	65	Rev. Proc. 2001-13, I.R.B. 2001-3,337
2002	185	100	Rev. Proc. 2001-59, I.R.B. 2001-52, 623
2003	190	100	Rev. Proc. 2002-70, I.R.B. 2002-46
2004	195	100	Rev. Proc. 2003-85, I.R.B. 2003-49
2005	200	105	Rev. Proc. 2004-71, I.R.B. 2004-50
2006	205	105	Rev. Proc. 2005-70, I.R.B. 2005-47
2007	215	110	Rev. Proc. 2006-53, I.R.B. 2006-48
2008	220	115	Rev. Proc. 2007-66, I.R.B. 2007-45
2009	230	120/230*	Rev. Proc. 2008-66, I.R.B. 2008-45
2010	230	230	Rev. Proc. 2009-50, I.R.B. 2009-45
2011	230	230	Rev. Proc. 2011-12, I.R.B. 2011-2
2012	240	240	Rev. Proc. 2011-52, I.R.B. 2011-45
2013	245	245	Rev. Proc. 2013-5, I.R.B. 2013-5
2014	250	130	Pub 15-B
2015	250	130 /250*	Pub 15-B
2016	255	255	Pub 15-B
2017	255	255	Pub 15-B
2018	260	260	Rev. Proc. 2017-58, I.R.B. 2017-45
2019	265	265	Rev. Proc. 2018-57, I.R.B. 2018-49
2020	270	270	Rev. Proc. 2019-44, I.R.B. 2019-47

* The Consolidated Appropriations Act, 2016 (P.L. 114-113) created parity for periods after December 31, 2014. See IRS Notice for 2016-06 for guidance and procedures on retroactive parity for transit and parking benefits.

These rules have applied since 1998 even if a cash option is offered. However, if the employee chooses the cash, the cash counts as wages.

The limits are subject to indexing for inflation in future years. An employee may receive advance transit passes for more than one month, but only if the value of the pass does not exceed the monthly limit times the number of months for which the pass is applicable. However, if an employee with an advance pass terminates employment before the pass has expired, the employer must include in the employee's wages for employment tax (as well as income tax) purposes the value of the pass provided for those months beginning after the termination to the extent the employer does not recover either the transit pass or value. [IRC §132(f)(2) and (4), IRS Rev. Procs. 2001-13 and 2001-59, Reg. §1.132-9.]

Bicycle commuting. Reimbursement for reasonable expenses incurred for bicycle commuting, including the purchase, repair, and storage of a bicycle, may be excluded from wages as long as the bicycle is regularly used for travel between the employee's residence and place of employment. There is a limit of $20 for every "qualified bicycle commuting month" for any calendar year. "Qualified bicycle commuting month" refers to any month during which an employee regularly uses a bike for a substantial portion of travel between the employee's residence and place of employment and the employee did not receive any other transportation fringe benefit. [IRC §132(f)(5)(F), as added by the Emergency Economic Stabilization Act of 2008, P.L.110-343, Div. B, §211(e).]

Suspension of exclusion. Pursuant to legislation signed into law by President Trump in December 2017, the exclusion for qualified bicycle commuting reimbursements will not apply to any taxable year beginning after December 31, 2017, and before January 1, 2026. [IRC §132(f)(8), as added by the Tax Cuts and Jobs Act of 2017, P.L. 115-97.]

¶210   Remuneration Paid to Homeworkers

If a homeworker is an "employee" as defined in the Federal Insurance Contributions Act (see ¶303.4) and if the remuneration paid to the homeworker amounts to at least $100 in cash per calendar year, such remuneration, including remuneration paid in any medium other than cash, is subject to tax. If the cash-pay test is not met, then none of the remuneration, whether in cash or in any medium other than cash, is taxable. [IRC §3121(a)(10).]

The cash-remuneration test applies with respect to the remuneration received by the employee from each employer during the period. If an employee receives cash remuneration in a period from more than one employer, the test must be applied separately to the remuneration received from each employer. [IRS Reg. §31.3121(a)(10)-1(c).]

The above exclusion from wages does not apply to remuneration paid to homeworkers who are employees under common-law rules for determining who is an employer or employee. It applies only to remuneration paid to homeworkers who are covered under the special provisions discussed at ¶303.4.

¶211   Medical Payments and Death Payments

Payments made to or on behalf of an employee or any of the employee's dependents for sickness or disability are generally included as wages for FICA purposes. However, specifically *excluded* from the definition of wages under FICA are the following:

(1) Employer payments (including any amount paid for the insurance or annuities, or into a fund, to provide for any such payment) made from the employer's own funds to, or on behalf of, an employee or any of the employee's dependents under a "qualifying" plan or system in the following categories: (a) on account of sickness or accident disability, whether made by the employer or a third party, but only if paid under a worker's compensation law, or (b) for medical or hospitalization expenses in connection with sickness or accident disability. This includes both employer payments for insurance or annuities or into a fund to provide for such payments and any payments for such expenses under the plan, or (c) on account of death, except payments

for group-term life insurance to the extent that the payment is includible in the gross income of the employee (see, further, below). Whether or not the benefit payments are considered in arriving at the amount of the employee's pay or are required by the employment agreement does not alter the exclusion of such employer payments under a qualifying plan or system. [IRC §3121(a) (2); IRS Reg. §31.3121(a)(2)-(1)(d); Soc. Sec. Act §209(a)(2).] Note that if the employer subsequently reimburses the employee for salary reduction amounts used to pay for health insurance premiums, the reimbursement payments are not excludable from gross income under IRC §106 or IRC §105 and are therefore subject to FICA tax. [Rev. Rul. 2002-3.]

(2) Coverage and reimbursements under an employer-provided accident and health plan for employees generally and their dependents. No age limit, residency, support, or other test applies for these purposes. Thus, coverage and reimbursements under a plan for employees and their dependents that are provided for an employee's child under age 27 are not wages for FICA or FUTA purposes. [IRC §§ 3121(a)(2) and 3306(b)(2); IRS Notice 2010-38, IRB 2010-30, May 17, 2010.]

(3) Payments made after six calendar months. Sickness and accident disability payments, or medical or hospitalization expenses in connection with sickness or accident disability, whether or not under a plan or system, that were made by the employer more than six calendar months after the calendar month in which the employee last worked for the employer are not wages if the employee does not actually perform services for the employer during the requisite period. (Payments for sickness and accident disability are counted as "wages" for Social Security purposes if paid before the end of six calendar months after the last month in which the employee worked.) [IRC §3121(a) (4); Soc. Sec. Act §209(a)(3).]

(4) Payments attributable to employee's contribution. Any portion of sick pay paid by a third party or under a state disability law that is attributable to the employee's own contribution is not wages since this is not remuneration for employment but a return on the employee's premium contributions. [Conference Report No. 97-409 (CB 1982-1, 315) accompanying P.L. 97-123, §3.]

(5) Payments on account of retirement for disability or death (see below). Payments on account of termination of employment are not wages if made because of death or retirement for disability, under a "qualified plan," and if the payments would not have been made if the employee's employment relationship had not been so terminated. [IRC §3121(a)(13) and 14; Soc. Sec. Act §209(a)(11) and (12).]

(6) Concurrent entitlement to Social Security disability payments. Payments by an employer to an employee who became entitled to disability insurance benefits under Section 223(a) of the Social Security Act prior to the

calendar year in which the payment is made are not wages if the employee did not perform any services for the employer during the period for which the payment is made. [IRC §3121(a)(15); Soc. Sec. Act §209(a)(13).]

(7) Employer payments into a plan or system for insurance premiums or into a fund to provide sick payments to employees continue to be excluded from wages even though the actual sick payments are not. [SSA POMS §RS 01402.090 (TN 19 11/97).]

Payments because of termination under a plan or system established solely for the dependents of the employees are not within the exclusion from wages. [Reg. §31.3121(a)(13)-1(b).]

Included in the definition of wages under the Social Security and Federal Insurance Contributions Acts are the following: (A) Payments by a third party under a sick pay plan to an employee or any of the employee's dependents on account of the employee's illness, unless paid more than six months after the last month the employee worked [IRC §3121(a); Soc. Sec. Act §209(a)(3)]; and (B) Payments made under a state temporary disability insurance law during the first six months of absence from work. However, any portion of these payments attributable to the claimant's own contribution is not wages. [P.L. 97-123, §3(e).] Also included as wages, subject to taxation under the FICA are an employer's "advance reimbursements" or "loans" to purportedly reimburse employees for uninsured medical expenses. [Rev. Rul. 2002-80.]

Regarding the qualifying conditions that must be met for an employer's plan, see ¶212 below.

Payments Made on or After Death

Payments made on account of death.—Payments (including any amount paid by an employer for insurance or annuities, or into a fund, to provide for any such payment) to or on behalf of an employee or any dependents under a plan or system established by the employer on account of the employee's death are excluded from the definition of wages, except for an employer payment under a plan or system to provide to or on behalf of an employee a group term life insurance policy, to the extent that such a payment is includible in the gross income of the employee. "Group-term life insurance" policies are permitted to include some "permanent benefits," but if they do, the cost of the permanent benefits as determined under the regulations is included in the employee's gross income. Also included as "wages" is an employer's payment under such a plan or system for a whole life insurance policy, since this type of policy can normally be surrendered for cash before the employee's death. [IRC §§79, 3121(a)(2)(C); Soc. Sec. Act §209(a)(2); IRS Reg. §§1.61-2(d)(2)(ii)(*a*) and 1.79-1(d).]

Payments made in or after the year of death.—Wages earned before the wage earner died and paid after death to a survivor or to the wage earner's estate are wages provided they are paid in the year of death. Any payments made by an employer to a survivor or to the estate of a former employee after the calendar year in which the employee died are not wages for Social Security purposes and are not subject to FICA contributions. [IRC §3121(a)(14); Soc. Sec. Act §209(a)(12).]

Disaster relief payments.—Certain relief payments made to victims and their families on account of losses arising from a "qualified" disaster are exempt from taxation under FICA and SECA, beginning with taxable years ending on or after September 11, 2001. See ¶211.1.

Payments made upon or after death.—Payments made upon termination of employment because of death are also excluded from wages if (1) the payment would not have been made unless the termination of the employment was due to death, and (2) the payment was made under a qualified plan. [IRC §3121(a)(13); Soc. Sec. Act §209(a)(11).]

> **Examples:** (1) John was injured on February 15 in an accident occurring in the employer's plant. He was in the hospital until May 30; after that he convalesced at home through September. He returned to work October 1. During John's absence from work, his employer paid him sick pay equal to his regular salary and also paid his hospitalization and medical expenses. Payments made to John from February 15 through August 31 are wages. The payments after August are not wages as more than six calendar months had elapsed since February when John last worked for his employer.
>
> (2) Fred suffered a heart attack at work on February 15 and was hospitalized until the end of June. He convalesced at home through October, and returned to work on November 1. At least once a month during his period of convalescence Fred went to work and at other times gave advice to his employer over the phone. The employer, during the entire period of Fred's illness, paid Fred's salary as sick pay, and also paid Fred's medical and hospital expenses. None of these payments was made under a plan or system. All of the payments from February 15 through October 31 are wages. Although Fred was sick for eight months, there were only four consecutive months in which he did not work for his employer. [Former SSA POMS §RS 01402.041 (8/83), which has since been replaced.]

¶211.1 Disaster Relief Payments

"Qualified disaster relief payments" are exempt from taxation under FICA or SECA. These are payments that reimburse reasonable and necessary personal, family, living, or funeral expenses incurred as a result of a qualified disaster, or, which reimburse or pay for the repair or rehabilitation of a personal residence or its contents on account of a qualified disaster. Payments by a common carrier, such as an airline, as a result of death or injuries suffered in the wake of a disaster involving the carrier, and payments by a governmental body in connection with a qualified disaster are also exempt from employment taxes, as are payments made from a major disaster leave sharing plan. [I.R.B. 2006-28, IRS Notice 2006-59, July, 10 2006.] A "qualified" disaster is any one of the following:

- a disaster resulting from a terrorist or military action;
- a presidentially declared disaster;
- a disaster that results from an accident involving a common carrier or from any other catastrophic event as determined by the Secretary of the Treasury;
- a disaster determined by a governmental body to warrant its assistance.

The law applies to taxable years ending on or after September 11, 2001. [IRC §139, as amended by the Victims of Terrorism Tax Relief Act of 2001, P.L. 107-134, §111; Jan. 23, 2002.]

¶211.3   Employee Donations to Leave Bank

Employers may maintain leave banks that allow employees to surrender accrued paid leave for use by other employees who need additional time off. If the time off can be used only by employees who need the leave for a qualified medical emergency, (*i.e.*, to care for a spouse or child in a medical emergency or following the death of a parent, spouse or child), it will qualify as a bona fide employer sponsored medical leave sharing plan. The amounts paid to an employee are wages, includible in gross income and subject to withholding, but the donor is not subject to income or withholding taxes. [Rev. Rul. 90-29, April, 9, 1990.] If the time off is used for purposes related to recovering after a major disaster in cases where the President has declared a "major disaster," the plan will qualify as a major disaster leave sharing plan. These plans are subject to the same withholding rules described above. [IRS Notice 2006-59; I.R.B. 2006-28, July 10, 2006.] However, the IRS has made clear that a "hybrid" leave bank that allows employees to donate leave both for qualified medical emergencies and for "catastrophic casualty losses," will not qualify as a leave sharing plan. Because the leave is not limited to a qualified medical emergency, the plan cannot qualify as a medical leave sharing plan. Additionally, a plan that allows employees to use the leave for "catastrophic casualty losses" without a requirement that the President declare a "major disaster," will not qualify as a major disaster leave sharing plan. [IRS Letter Ruling 200720017, Feb. 9, 2007.]

¶212   Retirement and Employer Payments

Pensions and retirement payments and employer contributions into plans to provide for such payments are excluded from wages *only* if paid pursuant to a qualified plan. Amounts voluntarily excluded from wages by the employee pursuant to some arrangement, plan, or annuity are not excludable from Social Security base income. [IRC §3121(a)(5); Soc. Sec. Act §209(a)(4).]

Payments excluded from wage base

Payments made to or on behalf of an employee are *excludable* from the definition of wages if made:

(1) from or to a trust that forms part of a *qualified pension, profit-sharing, or stock bonus plan*, as defined in IRC §401(a), if, at the time of payment (for payments made after 1954), the trust is exempt from tax under IRC §501(a), unless the payment is made to an employee of the trust as remuneration for services as an employee of the trust, and not as a beneficiary of the trust [IRC §3121(a)(5)(A); Soc. Sec. Act §209(a)(4)(A)];

(2) under or to an *IRC §403(a) annuity plan* after 1962 [IRC §3121(a)(5) (B); Soc. Sec. Act §209(a)(4)(C)];

(3) under an *IRC §408(k)(1) simplified employee pension (SEP)* plan, other than any contributions made pursuant to a salary reduction agreement, as described at IRC §408(k)(6) prior to its repeal [IRC §3121(a)(5)(C); Soc. Sec. Act §209(a)(4)(H)];

(4) under or to an *IRC §403(b) annuity contract,* other than a payment for the purchase of such contract that is made by reason of a salary reduction agreement [IRC §3121(a)(5)(D); Soc. Sec. Act §209(a)(4)(E)];

(5) under or to an *exempt governmental deferred compensation plan* [IRC §§3121(a)(5)(E), 3121(v); Soc. Sec. Act §209(a)(4)(F)];

(6) to *supplement pension benefits* under a plan or trust as described above to take into account some portion or all of the cost-of-living increases since retirement [IRC §3121(a)(5)(F); Soc. Sec. Act §209(a)(4)(G)];

(7) under a *cafeteria plan* within the meaning of IRC §125 (note that a plan is not a cafeteria plan unless it meets the detailed requirement set forth in IRC §125) [IRC §3121(a)(5)(G); Soc. Sec. Act §209(a)(4)(I)];

(8) under a SIMPLE plan as described in IRC §408(p) other than elective employee contributions under IRC §408(p)(2)(A)(i) [Soc. Sec. Act §209(a)(4)(J); see below];

(9) under a plan as described in IRC §457(e)(11)(A)(ii), which pays length of service awards of $3,000 or less to volunteers on account of their performance in firefighting, emergency medical, or ambulance services [Soc. Sec. Act §209(a)(4)(K)]; and

(10) upon or after termination of the employee's employment because of *death or retirement for disability,* as long as the payment would not have been made if the employment relationship had not so terminated and the

payment is made under a plan established by the employer that makes provision for the employees generally or a class or classes of employees (or for such employees or class or classes of employees and their dependents). [IRC §3121(a)(2), (13); Soc. Sec. Act §209(a)(2) and (11).]

Trusts. Payments made after 1954 to or on behalf of an employee or employee's beneficiary are not wages if they are made from or to a trust that is exempt from tax under IRC §§401 and 501(a) at the time of payment. [IRC §3121(a)(5)(A); Soc. Sec. Act §209(a)(4)(A).]

A trust is exempt from tax if the IRS has ruled that the trust is tax-exempt. If the IRS has ruled that the trust is not tax-exempt, or if the IRS has not made a ruling, the payments are wages. [SSA POMS §RS 01402.140 (TN 10 9/90).]

Payments under a qualified cash or deferred arrangement (any arrangement which is part of a profit-sharing, stock bonus, pre-ERISA money purchase, or rural cooperative plan that meet the requirements of IRC §401(k)(2)) are wages if the employee could have elected to receive cash in lieu of the contributions and the amounts were not included in the gross income by reason of IRC §402(a)(8). The contributions are counted as wages at the time the distributions are paid to the trust. [*Soc. Sec. Handbook,* March 2001, §1313. Reg. §404.1049(c)(1).]

Non-exempt employee's trust. In cases where an employer contributes to a non-exempt employee's trust on the behalf of highly compensated individuals, the employer's responsibility for FICA and FUTA taxation on the contributions depends on when the employee's interest in the trust and distributions occurs. Thus, if the employee is vested in the plan at the time of the contribution is made, the employer is liable for FICA and FUTA taxes at that time. However, if there is a waiting period, and the employee does not become vested in the plan for a period of time, the contributions and earnings on the contributions, are subject to FICA and FUTA at the time the employee becomes vested. At that point, the trust is considered the "employer," and is responsible for FICA and FUTA taxation. [Rev. Rul. 2007-48; I.R.B. 2007-30, July 23, 2007.]

Simplified employee pension. Employer payments made to, or on behalf of, an employee or employee's beneficiary under a simplified employee pension (defined at IRC §408(k)), other than contributions under a salary reduction SEP agreement (SARSEP), as provided for in IRC §408(k) prior to its repeal by the Small Business Job Protection Act of 1996 (P.L. 104-188, §1421), are excluded from wages for both Social Security tax and coverage purposes. [IRC §3121(a)(5)(C); Soc. Sec. Act §209(a)(4)(H).]

The provision for excluding elective deferrals (IRC §408(k)(6)) for income tax purposes does not exclude such deferrals from the definition of wages for employment tax purposes. Nor does this exclusion apply after 1983 to an employee's contribution to an IRA. [SSA POMS §RS 01402.125

and .130 (TN 10 9/90).] After 1996, an employer is no longer allowed to establish a SARSEP. Participants in a SARSEP that was established before 1997 may continue to elect to have their employer contribute part of their pay to the plan.

Savings incentive match plans for employees (SIMPLE) plans. An employee's elective contributions to a SIMPLE account will be treated as wages for purposes of employment tax. However, employer matching or nonelective contributions to the SIMPLE account will not be viewed as wages. [Soc. Sec. Act §209(a)(4)(J) and (K); IRC §408(p)(8).] Small businesses that normally employ 100 or fewer employees, paid them at least $5,000 in compensation in the preceding year, and do not maintain another plan may establish a SIMPLE retirement plans for years beginning after 1996. [Small Business Job Protection Act of 1996, P.L. 104-188, §1421(a), amending IRC §408(p).]

Employer payments to or from exempt governmental deferred compensation plans are excluded from the definition of wages after 1983. [IRC §3121(v)(3); Soc. Sec. Act §209(a)(4)(F); SSA POMS §RS 01402.115 (TN 10 9/90).]

An exempt governmental deferred compensation plan is a plan providing for deferred compensation established and maintained for its employees by the U.S., by a state or political subdivision thereof, or by an agency or instrumentality of any of these. This term *does not* include:

(1) contributions that are made when services are performed or when there is no substantial risk of forfeiture of the employee's right to the amount within the meaning of IRC §83;

(2) contributions to non-exempt trusts, within the meaning of IRC §402(b);

(3) premiums paid by an employer for a nonqualified annuity contract, within the meaning of IRC §403(c);

(4) amounts deferred under an eligible state deferred compensation plan and any income attributable thereto, but only for the taxable year when paid or made available to the participant or participant's beneficiary, as described at IRC §457(a);

(5) compensation from a state deferred compensation plan that is not an eligible plan for the first taxable year in which there is no substantial risk of forfeiture of the rights to that compensation, as described at IRC §457(f)(1);

(6) premiums for a tax-sheltered annuity described at IRC §403(b) [IRC §3121(v)(3)]; or

(7) the Thrift Savings Fund (within the meaning of subchapter III of chapter 84 of title 5, United States Code). [IRC §3121(v)(3).]

Tax-sheltered annuities. Amounts paid by certain nonprofit charitable, religious, educational, etc., organizations (described at IRC §501(c)(3)) and by state and local educational institutions for employees under or to an IRC §403(b) annuity contract are not subject to employment tax, as long as the annuity contract is not made by reason of a salary reduction agreement (whether evidenced by written instrument or otherwise). [IRC §3121(a)(5) (D); Soc. Sec. Act §209(a)(4)(E).]

Supplemental pension benefit (cost-of-living adjustment). Payments made to supplement pension benefits under a plan or trust described in any of the subsections of IRC §3121(a)(5) (see above) by means of some portion or all of the cost-of-living increase since retirement (as determined by the Secretary of Labor) are excluded from wages but only if the plan is treated as a welfare plan under §3(2) (B)(ii) of the Employee Retirement Income Security Act of 1974. [IRC §3121(a) (5)(F); P.L. 98-21,§324(a)(2); *Soc. Sec. Handbook*, March 2001, §1319.]

Cafeteria plans. Under a *cafeteria plan* an employee is offered a choice between cash and one or more qualified benefits. Cafeteria plan payments are excluded if the payments would not be treated as wages if provided outside the plan, and if it is reasonable to believe that (if IRC §125 applied for FICA taxes) IRC §125 would not treat any wages as constructively received. The fact that cash has been offered as an option in a cafeteria plan, but not selected, does not constitute constructive payment for Social Security and FICA purposes. However, when cash in lieu of qualified benefits is selected, such payments are wages. The Social Security tax status of each noncash benefit selected is determined separately. [IRC §3121(a)(5)(G); SSA POMS §RS 01402.036(B)(2) (TN10 9/90).]

To eliminate any implication that a taxable benefit provided through a cafeteria plan is nontaxable, and to clarify that certain taxable benefits permitted under Treasury regulations can be provided in a cafeteria plan, the Tax Reform Act of 1986 changed the reference in the law to permissible cafeteria plan benefits from "nontaxable benefits" to "qualified benefits." Qualified benefits are any benefits that are not includible in the income of an employee by reason of an express provision of the Code. [Committee Reports accompanying P.L. 99-514, §§1151, 1853(g); SSA POMS §RS 01402.036(B)(2) (TN10 9/90).]

A *qualifying plan or system* is one established by an employer that makes provision from the employer's own funds (as distinguished from a deduction from the employee's salary) for all employees and/or their dependents, generally, or for a class(es) of employees and their dependents. The following features must be incorporated as part of the written plan: (1) a definite basis for determining who is eligible, such as length of service, occupation, classification, or salary; (2) a definite standard for determining the minimum duration of payment; and (3) a formula for determining the minimum amount to be paid to an eligible employee. Furthermore, the employer must communicate the terms and conditions of the plan to all of the employees or the class affected. [IRC §3121(a)(2); SSA POMS §RS 01402.005 (TN23 6/10).]

Payments included in wage base

The following amounts are *includible in the FICA wage base:*

Amounts deferred under nonqualified deferred compensation plans, which are plans other than those identified at (2) through (10), above, are included in the employee's FICA wage base, beginning in 1984, when services are performed or, if later, when there is no substantial risk of forfeiture (within the meaning of IRC §83) of the employee's right to those amounts. Under this special "timing rule," if an employee has a vested right to benefits in a nonqualified plan, FICA (and FUTA) taxes are applicable each year to plan contributions, even if the benefits are not actually distributed. [IRC §3121(v)(2).]

Section 885 of the American Jobs Creation Act of 2004 (P.L. 108-357) added IRC §409A, which provides that all amounts deferred under a nonqualified deferred compensation (NQDC) plan for all tax years are currently includible in gross income (to the extent not subject to a substantial risk of forfeiture and not previously included in gross income) and subject to additional taxes, unless certain requirements are met pertaining to, among other things, elections to defer compensation and distributions under a NQDC plan. Although employers must withhold federal income tax on any amount includible in gross income under Section 409A, *the procedures do not affect the application or reporting of Social Security, Medicare or FUTA taxes.* [IRS Notice 2006-100, IRB. 2006-51 (Dec. 18, 2006); Notice 2007-86, IRB 2007-46; 2008-115, IRB 2008-52; IRS *Pub. 15-A, Supp. to Circ. E,* Rev. Jan. 2012, p. 14.]

Determination of amount deferred. Amounts deferred under a nonqualified compensation plan include not only the principal amounts credited to an individual account for an employee, but also the income attributable to that amount through the date the amount is required to be taken into account as FICA wages or the present value of the additional future payments to which the employee has acquired a legally binding right. The present value of a benefit does not need to be included in FICA wages until it becomes reasonably ascertainable.

Account balance and non-account balance plans. IRS Reg. §31.3121(v)(2)-1(c) distinguishes between *account balance and non-account balance plans.* The amount deferred under an *account balance plan* generally is based on the principal amount credited to the account, increased or decreased by any income that is attributable to the principal amount through the date the principal amount is required to be taken into account as wages (*i.e.,* the later of the date on which services creating the right to the deferred amount are performed or the date on which the right to the amount is no longer subject to a substantial risk of forfeiture). Under a *non-account balance plan,* the amount deferred for a period and, thus, the amount subject to FICA and FUTA tax, is the present value of the additional future payments to which the employee has obtained a legally binding right under the plan during that period. The present value of the additional future payments must be determined as of the later of the date on which the services creating the right to the deferred amounts are performed, or the date on which the right to the amount deferred is no longer subject to a substantial risk of forfeiture.

Withholding rules. An amount deferred under a nonqualified deferred compensation plan is generally treated, for purposes of withholding and depositing FICA and FUTA taxes, as wages paid by the employer and received by the employee at the time it is taken into account under IRC §3121(v)(2) and IRS Reg. §31.3121(v)(2)-1(e). However, because some employers may be unable to readily calculate the amount deferred for a given year by December 31 of that year, two alternative methods, (a) the *estimated method* and (b) the *lag method,* are provided for determining the withholding and depositing of FICA and FUTA tax. [IRS Reg. §31.3121(v)(2)-1(f)(1).] The methods may be used as of any date during the year and whether or not the amount deferred may be readily calculated.

Estimated method. Under the estimated method, an employer may make a reasonable estimate of the amount deferred as of the date that the amount deferred is required to be taken into account. The estimated amount is taken into account as wages paid by the employer and received by the employee on the estimate date for purposes of withholding and depositing FICA and FUTA tax. If the employer *underestimates* the deferred amount that should have been taken into account and, therefore, deposits less FICA and FUTA tax than the amount due, the employer may treat the shortfall as wages either on the estimate date or on any date that is no later than three months after the estimate date. An employer that makes this election must take the shortfall into account as wages for the date that is no later than three months after the estimate date for purposes of FICA and FUTA tax. In the event that the employer *overestimates* the amount deferred that should have been taken into account as wages on the estimate date, and deposits more than the amount required, the employer may claim a refund or credit. An employer that treats any shortfall as wages on the estimate date or overestimates the amount deferred on the estimate date, must correct any previously reported wage information.

Lag method. The lag method enables an employer to treat the amount deferred, plus interest, as wages paid on any date that is no later than three months after the date the amount is required to be taken into account. Under the lag method, an employer may calculate the FICA or FUTA tax due by using a fixed rate of interest that is not less than the applicable federal rate (mid-term applicable federal rate) for January 1 of the calendar year. Accordingly, an employer is not required to calculate FICA and FUTA tax dues on the basis of income under the plan. [IRS Reg. §31.3121(v)(2)-(1)(f).]

Rule of administrative convenience. An employer may treat a deferred amount as required to be taken into account on any date that is later than, but within the same calendar year, as the actual date on which the deferred amount must otherwise be taken into account, provided that income attributable to the deferred amount through that date is included. Accordingly, the present value of amounts deferred throughout a year under a nonaccount balance plan may be determined as of the end of the year, based on the employee's age and appropriate actuarial assumptions at the end of the year. [Preamble to IRS Reg. §31.3121(v)(2)-1, 64 *Federal Register* 4542, Jan. 29, 1999.]

Time for deducting payroll tax liabilities. The time for taking a deduction under the accrual method is generally determined under the "all events test." For employers using the accrual method, the IRS has issued specific rules for determining the year in which payroll tax liabilities can be deducted. These rules may allow payroll tax liabilities to be deducted in an earlier year than the year in which the related wages are paid or deferred compensation can be deducted. Under the all events test and the recurring item exception, a tax liability can be treated as incurred for a tax year if: (1) at the end of the tax year, all events have occurred that establish the fact of the liability and the amount can be determined with reasonable accuracy; (2) economic performance occurs on or before the earlier of (a) the date that the taxpayer timely files a return, including extensions for the tax year, or (b) the 15th day of the ninth calendar month after the close of the tax year; and (3) the liability is recurring in nature. Based on these principles, the IRS developed a rule for accrual-method employers that incur a liability for FICA and FUTA taxes imposed on year-end wages. Such employers may deduct the payroll taxes in the year that the wages are properly accrued, even though the wages are not paid until the following year, as long as the employer satisfies the requirements of the all events test and the recurring item exception with respect to the taxes. [Rev. Rul. 96-51, 1996-2 CB 36.] The IRS has now expanded this rule to cover deferred compensation that is deductible under IRC §404. If the all events test and recurring item exception are met, an accrual-method employer may treat its payroll tax liability as incurred in one year, even if the compensation to which the liability relates is deferred compensation that is not deductible under IRC §404 until the following year. [Rev. Rul. 2007-12, 2007-11 I.R.B. 685.] Employers that want to change their treatment of payroll taxes associated with deferred compensation to follow this IRS ruling must obtain the consent of the IRS before making the change.

Nonduplication rule. Under this rule, once an amount deferred under a nonqualified deferred compensation plan is treated as wages for FICA and FUTA tax purposes, neither that amount nor the income attributable to that amount may be treated as FICA or FUTA wages again. Accordingly, benefit payments under a nonqualified deferred compensation plan are not subject to FICA or FUTA tax when they are actually or constructively paid, if the benefit payments consist of amounts deferred under the plan that were previously treated as wages for FICA and FUTA tax purposes. Of course, benefits under a nonqualified deferred compensation plan will be subject to FICA and FUTA tax when they are actually or constructively paid, to the extent the benefits relate to a deferred amount that was not previously treated as FICA or FUTA wages under the timing rule. [IRC §3121(v)(2)(B) and §3306(r)(2)(B); IRS Reg. §31.3121(v)(2)-1(a)(2)(iii) and §31.3306(r)(2)-1.]

Salary reduction agreements. Employee-elected contributions to deferred compensation salary reduction arrangements, such as 401(k) plans, are treated as wages for Social Security purposes, although they are not subject to income tax until distribution. The amount of the salary reduction is contributed by the employer to a plan. [SSA POMS §RS 01402.010 (TN 23 6/10).] IRS regulations broadly define these agreements as including elections that are required as a condition of employment as well as voluntary elections. Although the use of the term "agreement" in the relevant Code section suggests that the provision is intended to only apply to voluntarily negotiated agreements, the Seventh Circuit, in *University of Chicago v. USA*, 547 F3d 773 (7th Cir. 2008), ruled that Congress intended to include mandatory employee contributions to a 403(b) plan under a salary reduction agreement as wages subject to FICA under IRC §3121(a)(5)(D) just as voluntary contributions are included. Thus, the employer was required to have withheld FICA taxes on its employees' salary reduction contributions and was subject to failure-to-deposit and failure-to-pay penalties.

Employer contributions to 401(k) plans that are not made under salary reduction agreements (*i.e.*, nonelective and employer matching contributions) are also not subject to FICA and FUTA taxes. [IRC §3121(a)(5); IRS *Circular E*, Pub. 15, p. 42, Dec. 23, 2019.]

State and local government pick-up plans.—The term "pick-up plan" refers to a plan under IRC §414(h)(2) in which the employer pays, on behalf of the employee, contributions to a state or local government retirement system. Payments under such plans may be excluded under IRC §3121(v) and Soc. Sec. Act §209(a)(4)(F) as payments to an exempt governmental deferred compensation plan provided they are made from the employer's own funds and not pursuant to a salary reduction agreement. [IRC §3121(v)(1) and (3); Soc. Sec. Act §209.]

See, also, ¶222, regarding pay after termination of employment.

Refunds on FICA tax paid for unpaid plan benefits. Retired taxpayers are not entitled to a refund of FICA taxes paid by their employer on their behalf on the reasonably ascertainable value of nonqualified deferred compensation plan benefits. The fact that a portion of the valued benefits would never be distributed to such employees due to the plan's termination did not create the right to a refund. In a matter considered by the IRS chief counsel involving a bankrupt company, the fact that an employee later receives less than the amount originally deferred as a result of an employer's bankruptcy does not give rise to a refund of the FICA taxes paid on amounts deferred, according to Chief Counsel. [Chief Counsel Advice 200823001.]

¶213 Exercise of Statutory and Nonstatutory Stock Options

A stock option is an offer made to an employee by a corporation, or by its parent or subsidiary corporation, to sell stock of any such corporations at a stated or determinable price, with the offer continuing for a stated period of time and the employee being under no obligation to purchase the stock. There are two general types of employee stock options—statutory and nonstatutory, also called "qualified" and "nonqualified", options. Qualified stock options, which include incentive stock options (ISOs) [IRC §422] and employee stock purchase plans (ESPPs) [IRC §423], offer tax advantages over nonqualified options. [IRS Reg. §1.421-1.] Nonstatutory stock options refer to those options that do not qualify for the favorable tax treatment accorded options that are covered by a specific code provision. Generally, if an employee acquires stock under a statutory option arrangement, the employee is taxed only when he or she disposes of the stock. However, if an option was acquired under a nonstatutory program, the employee may be taxed,

(1) when the option is granted,
(2) when the employee exercises the option,
(3) when the employee sells or otherwise disposes of the option, or
(4) when restrictions on disposition of the option-acquired stock lapse [IRS Reg. §1.83-7(a).]

The income that the employee must recognize is considered compensation and, thus, is taxed at ordinary income rates.

ISOs and ESPPs are subject to a variety of definitional requirements as well as requirements regarding holding periods and employment. If the definitional requirements are satisfied, but the holding periods and employment requirements are not satisfied, sale of the stock will be treated as a disqualifying disposition. As a result, the employee recognizes a gain in the tax year of disposition that will be treated as compensation. [IRC §421(b).] Unlike ISOs, which must have an exercise price at least equal to the fair market value of the stock when the option is granted, options granted under an ESPP can have an exercise price as low as 85% of the fair market value of the stock. The difference between the option price and 100% of the actual value of the stock at the time the option was granted (or the amount received in a disposition, if lower) is treated as compensation upon disposition of the stock. The balance of any gain is treated as capital gain. [IRC §423(c).]

Statutory stock options

Employment taxes do not apply to statutory stock options. Wages for FICA tax purposes do not include remuneration on account of a transfer of a share of stock pursuant to an exercise of an ISO or ESPP option, or on account of a disposition of stock acquired through such an exercise. [IRC §3121(a), as amended by JOBS Act §251(a)(2); IRC §3306(b) as amended by JOBS Act §251(a)(3).] Although withholding is not required, employers must still report such payments on Form W-2, and individuals must still include compensation in income upon a disposition of stock acquired through the exercise of a statutory stock option. [IRC §423(c); IRS Reg. §1.6041-2(a)(1); IRS Notice 2002-47.]

Nonstatutory stock options

Nonstatutory stock options are subject to FICA and FUTA taxation. However, these options rarely are subject to tax on the date of grant, and taxation at grant typically occurs only if an option is actively traded on an established securities market on that date or, if not so traded, has a readily ascertainable fair market value. [IRC §83(a) and (e), and IRS Reg. §1.83-7(a) and (b).] A non-publicly traded nonstatutory stock option is considered to have a readily ascertainable fair market value on the grant date only if, on that date, it satisfies four conditions: (1) the option is transferable; (2) the option is exercisable immediately in full by the optionee; (3) the option or the property subject to the option is not subject to any restriction or condition which has a significant effect upon the fair market value of the option; and (4) the fair market value of the option privilege is readily ascertainable. [IRS Reg. §1.83-7(b); IRS Notice 2004-28, April 19, 2004.]

When a nonstatutory stock option is exercised by an employee the spread (difference between the exercise price and fair market value of the stock at the time of exercise) is generally included in wage income [IRS Reg. §1.83-7] and is subject to income tax withholding. This wage income is also subject to FICA and FUTA tax when the option is exercised. Consequently, Social Security and Medicare withholding is also required. [IRS Pub. 15-B, "Employer's Tax Guide to Fringe Benefits", p. 12, Dec. 26, 2019.]

In the case of a nonemployee (*i.e.*, independent contractor), the spread is not wage income subject to withholding. Instead, it should be reported on a Form 1099. In the case of an employee, the spread may be included in total wages for purposes of withholding or the spread may be treated as a supplemental wage payment. [Act Sec. 13273 of the Revenue Reconciliation Act of 1993 (P. L. 103-66), as amended by the Economic Growth and Tax Relief Reconciliation Act 2001 (P. L. 107-16), and the Jobs and Growth Tax Relief Reconciliation Act of 2003 (P.L. 108-27).]

Withholding from nonmonetary wages. Under IRS Reg. §31.3402(a)-1(c), an employer is required to deduct and withhold tax notwithstanding that the wages are paid in something other than money (for example, wages paid in stock or bonds) and to pay over the tax in money. If the wages are paid in property other than money, the employer should make necessary arrangements to insure that the amount of the tax required to be withheld is available for payment in money.

Reimbursement by employee of employer payment of withholding taxes. The employer is required to deposit all withholding taxes even if it cannot collect them from the former employee. To avoid this situation (a problem which is more likely if the option is exercised by a former employee), a stock option agreement should require the employee or former employee to reimburse the employer for the payment of withholding taxes. The agreement will typically allow an employer to sell a sufficient number of shares when a nonstatutory option is exercised to cover commission costs and pay for state, local, federal, and foreign withholding taxes (this is commonly referred to as a cashless exercise).

Employer payment of employee's taxes. If an employer pays the income tax withholding and employee's or former employee's share of Social Security and Medicare taxes (*i.e.*, FICA taxes), these amounts are included in wage income for income tax withholding and Social Security, Medicare, and FUTA taxes. This increases the additional taxes that must be withheld and deposited. This in turn is considered wage income subject to income tax withholding and FICA and FUTA taxes. A special formula must be used to determine the proper amount to include in wage income. [See IRS Pub. 15-A, rev'd Dec. 23, 2019, p. 22.] Note that this does not apply to household and agricultural employers. See ¶215.

Nonstatutory options transferred incident to a divorce. When a nonstatutory stock option is transferred incident to a divorce by an employee [Rev. Rul. 2002-22, 2002-1 CB 849], the income is recognized by the transferee spouse (former spouse) when the former spouse exercises the option. The income is reported by the employer on Form 1099-MISC (box 3) and the withheld income tax is reported in box 4. The supplemental wage withholding rate may be used to determine the amount of income tax withholding. The former spouse is entitled to the credit allowable for the income tax withheld at the source on these wages.

The fact that payments are includible in the gross income of an individual other than an employee does not remove the payments from FICA wages. Nonstatutory stock options are subject to FICA and FUTA taxes at the time of exercise by the former spouse to the same extent as if the options had been retained by the employee spouse and exercised by the employee spouse. Although the employee does not recognize income upon the transfer, to the extent FICA and FUTA taxation apply, the wages are the wages of the employee spouse according to Revenue Ruling 2004-60. The employee portion of the FICA taxes, however, should be deducted from the payment to the nonemployee spouse. The Social Security wages, Medicare wages, Social Security taxes withheld, and Medicare taxes withheld, if applicable, are reportable on the employee spouse's Form W-2. However, no amount is includible in Box 1 (wages) and Box 2 (income tax withholding) of the Form W-2.

New deferral election option. Legislation signed into law by President Trump in December 2017, generally effective with respect to stock attributable to options exercised, or restricted stock units settled, after December 31, 2017, provides a "qualified employee" with a new option to elect to defer, for income tax purposes, the inclusion in income of the amount of income attributable to "qualified stock" transferred to the employee by the employer. The election to defer income for up to five years, however, is not available to certain executives, highly compensated employees, and 1-percent owners. The inclusion deferral election applies only for income tax purposes. The application of FICA and FUTA taxes is not affected. [IRC §83(i), as added by the Tax Cuts and Jobs Act of 2017, P.L. 115-97.]

¶214 Standby Payments

Payments made by an employer to an employee after the employee attains the age of 62, and with the expectation that the employee will subsequently render services, are not excluded from wages. [IRC §3121(a)(13); SSA POMS §RS 01402.290 (TN 13 6/92); see P.L. 98-21 §324(a)(3).] Regarding sick pay, see ¶211; regarding vacation pay, see ¶219.

¶215 Payment by Employer of Employee Tax

Excluded from the definition of "wages" paid by the employer for domestic service in the employer's private home or for agricultural labor are: (a) payments of the employee's Social Security or hospital insurance tax, and (b) a payment required from an employee under a state unemployment compensation law. However, the payment by the employer must be made without deduction from the remuneration of an employee, or other reimbursement. [IRC §3121(a)(6).]

¶216 Bonuses, Commissions, Expenses, Benefits

Bonuses and commissions on sales are ordinarily "wages." The fact that such payments are not designated as "wages," but bonuses and commissions, is immaterial. So long as the amounts are paid as compensation for employment, they are taxable. [Reg. §31.3121(a)-1(c).]

By contrast, amounts paid either as advances or reimbursements for traveling or other bona fide ordinary and necessary expenses incurred or reasonably expected to be incurred in the business of the employer are not taxable. These payments include *reasonable* per diem advance allowances paid by an airline to its pilots and flight attendants. [*United Air Lines, Inc. v. U.S.*, 51 Fed. Cl. 722, 2001-2 USTC ¶50,577, UNEMPL. INS. REP. ¶16,625B, Aug. 10, 2001.]

Note, however, that an airline may not avoid payment of employment taxes on travel, lodging and per diem amounts that it pays to an employee where such payments are in effect, commuter expenses. [*Jordan v. U.S.*, 490 F3d 677 (8th Cir. 2007), 2007-2 USTC ¶50,603.] Traveling and other reimbursed expenses must be identified either by making a separate payment or by specifying the separate amounts when both wages and expense allowances are combined in a single payment. [Reg. §§31.3121(a)-1(h); 31.3121(a)-3.]

If an employer pays expense allowances that exceed the federal per diem rates, the excess amounts are subject to income tax and employment tax unless the employee repays or substantiates the excess expenses. A per diem allowance arrangement that fails to track these excess amounts and does not include the unsubstantiated or excess payments in the employee's income and wages will be viewed by the IRS as a pattern of abuse. If an arrangement is found to be abusive, all the allowances paid to the employee - not just the excess amounts - are subject to income tax and employment tax. [IRS Rev. Rul. 2006-56, I.R.B. 2006-46; IR 2006-175 (Nov. 9, 2006).] Auditors will determine whether a plan is abusive by looking at the extent of the excess payments and whether the employer has a system in place. If the employer's system fails to track the excess payments properly, the employer will not be found to be abusive. [IRS Small Business/Self Employed Division Memo SBSE-04-1106-049, Jan 14, 2008.]

Moving expenses. Amounts received by an employee as reimbursement of moving expenses incurred in connection with commencement of work at a new principal place of work are excluded from "wages," if the expenses are "reasonably expected" to be deductible for income tax purposes. [IRC §§217, 3121(a)(11); IRS Reg. §31.3121(a)(11)-1.] Reimbursements are deductible if the new job location is at least 50 miles farther from the employee's former home than the old job location; if the employee works full time for at least 39 weeks during the first 12 months after arriving in the new location. Self-employed individuals must work for at least 78 weeks in the new locations. Only reasonable expenses of moving household goods and personal effects and of traveling from the former residence (including lodging costs) are deductible and thus excluded from wages.

Suspension of exclusion. Pursuant to legislation signed into law by President Trump in December 2017, the exclusion for qualified moving expense reimbursements is suspended (except in the case of a member of the Armed Forces of the U.S. on active duty, who moves pursuant to a military order), effective for tax years beginning after December 31, 2017, and before January 1, 2026. [IRC §132(g), as amended by the Tax Cuts and Jobs Act of 2017, P.L. 115-97.]

Ratification and signing bonuses. Bonuses paid for signing an employment contract or ratifying a collective bargaining agreement are treated as wages for employment tax and income tax withholding purposes. Where a baseball club enters into a contract with a baseball player that provides that the player will receive a signing bonus if he reports for spring training at the proper time and location, the bonus is treated as remuneration for employment even though it is not contingent on the performance of future services. Since the player receives the signing bonus in connection with establishing the employer-employee relationship and does not provide separate consideration for the payment, the bonus is treated as wages for purposes of employment taxes and income tax withholding.

Where an employer negotiates a collective bargaining agreement with a union that will take effect on the date that it is ratified by a majority of the union members covered by the agreement, bonuses paid upon ratification are treated as remuneration for employment even though they are the same in amount, are not based on seniority or position, and are not contingent on the performance of future services. Since the employees receive the bonus payments as part of the collective bargaining agreement that establishes the terms and conditions of the employment relationship and the employees do not provide separate consideration for the payments that are not dependent on the employer-employee relationship, the payments are treated as wages for purposes of employment taxes and income tax withholding.

¶216.1   Educational Assistance

Up to $5,250 in educational assistance provided by an employer may be excluded from the definition of "wages." [IRC §§127, 3121(a)(18); Soc. Sec. Act §209(a)(15).] The exclusion, which includes graduate level course, applies regardless of whether the education is job-related.

Qualifying educational assistance to employees covers tuition, fees, and similar payments, as well as the cost of books, supplies, and equipment paid for, or provided by, the employer as long as the assistance program does not discriminate in favor of highly compensated employees (i.e., 5% owners or employees receiving over $130,000 (for 2020; $125,000 for 2019) in pay for the preceding year) or their dependents. Included as "employees" for purposes of the exclusion are retired, disabled, or laid-off employees, employees on leave, and individuals who are self-employed. While the covered education is not limited to courses that are part of a degree program, the exclusion does not extend to tools or supplies provided by the employer that the employee is permitted to retain or to courses involving sports, games, or hobbies. [IRC §§127, 3121(a)(18).]

Education expense reimbursement as a fringe benefit. Apart from the exclusion allowed under IRC §127, reimbursement for educational expenses may be excluded under IRC §132 as a working condition fringe benefit if the expense is work-related. As a general rule, the expense qualifies if the education is undertaken for the purposes of maintaining or improving skills required in the taxpayer's employment or other trade or business, or meeting legal, regulatory, or employer-established requirements that are a condition of employment. There is no cap on the allowable amount. [IRC §132(d), 162; IRS Reg. §1.162-5; Soc. Sec. Act §209(a)(17).]

Qualified tuition reductions to employees of educational institutions are excluded from gross income, if certain conditions are met. Scholarships and fellowship grants are also specifically excluded from the definition of "wages" for FICA purposes. [IRC §§117, 3121(a)(20); P.L. 98-369, §532.]

¶216.2 Dependent Care Assistance

Dependent care assistance furnished by the employer pursuant to a qualified program is excluded from "wages" for FICA purposes, so long as "it is reasonable to believe that the employee will be able to exclude such payment or benefit from income" for income tax purposes. To qualify for the FICA exclusion, the program must be a written nondiscriminatory plan. The amount excluded may not be more than the employee's earned income or $5,000 ($2,500 in the case of a married individual filing separately).

The exclusion does not apply if the money for the care is being paid to a dependent of the employee or the employee's spouse, or a child of the employee under 19. In addition, the exclusion is not available to employees covered by a collective bargaining agreement if dependent care benefits were the subject of good-faith bargaining. [IRC §§129, 3121(a)(18).]

¶216.3 Adoption Assistance Programs

Amounts that an employee receives under an employer's adoption assistance program pursuant to Code Sec. are excludable from income tax, but remain subject to Social Security and Medicare taxes, FUTA tax, and railroad retirement withholding. [IRS Notice 97-9, December 31, 1996, 1997-1 CB 365; modified by IRS Notice 97-70, November 24, 1997, 1997-2 CB 332; Form 8839 (Qualified Adoption Expenses) Instructions.]

¶216.4 Certain Below-Market-Rate Loans

The benefit derived from term or demand below-market-rate loans that are gift loans, compensation-related loans, corporation-shareholder loans, or tax-avoidance loans in the form of "foregone interest" or a savings on interest is generally treated as cash or as income received. "Foregone interest" with respect to any period during which the loan is outstanding means (1) the amount of interest that would have been payable on the loan for the period if interest accrued at the applicable federal rate and was payable annually on the last day of the calendar year, over (2) any interest payable on the loan properly allocable to such period.

De minimis *exception for gift loans between individuals:* Unless the loan is directly attributable to the purchase or carrying of income-producing assets, no amount is treated as transferred by the lender to the borrower, or retransferred by the borrower to the lender, for any day during which the aggregate outstanding amount of loans does not exceed $10,000. This *de minimis* rule does not apply, however, if a principal purpose of the interest arrangement is the avoidance of any federal tax.

Additional exceptions to the operation of this provision may be provided for in regulations exempting from these provisions any class of transactions in which the interest arrangements do not have a significant effect on the tax liability of the borrower or the lender, such as employee-relocation loans. [IRC §7872.]

¶216.5   Flexible Spending Arrangements

A flexible spending arrangement (FSA) is an employer-sponsored benefit program that is offered as part of a cafeteria plan and designed to provide covered employees with a method of paying for certain covered expenses (*e.g.*, medical or dependent care) with pre-tax dollars. Generally, a covered employee makes contributions through payroll deductions to a health or a dependent care FSA. Because contributions to a FSA reduce an employee's gross income, these amounts, though compensatory in nature, are not subject to federal income tax or to FICA and FUTA. However, a cafeteria plan may not allow an employee to request salary reduction contributions for a health FSA in excess of $2,750 (for 2020).

Amounts selected, but unused by the employee at the end of the plan year, are forfeited under the "use it or lose it" rule. The maximum amount of reimbursement paid to the employee may not be greater than 500% of the premium for the participant's coverage. Health FSA's must qualify as accident or health plans under IRC §105 and provide at least 12 months of coverage. Employees must elect to participate prior to the beginning of the plan year. [IRS Proposed Reg. §1.125-2, Q&A-7.]

¶216.6   Health Savings Accounts

A Health Savings Account (HSA) is a tax-exempt trust or custodial account established exclusively to pay qualified medical expenses of the account beneficiary who, for the months for which contributions are made to an HSA, is covered under a high-deductible health plan (HDHP) that satisfies certain requirements concerning deductibles and out-of-pocket expenses. HSA funds can be used to cover health insurance deductibles and any co-payments for medical services, prescriptions or products; they can also be used to purchase both over-the-counter drugs and long-term care insurance and to pay health insurance premiums during any period of unemployment. However, distributions that are not used for qualified expenses will be taxable, and a 10 percent penalty will be imposed to deter the use of the HSA for nonmedical purposes.

HSA contributions may be made in the following ways: (1) the individual and family members can make tax deductible HSA contributions even if the individual does not itemize deductions; (2) the individual's employer can make contributions that are not taxed to either the employer or the employee; and (3) employers with cafeteria plans can allow employees to contribute untaxed salary through a salary reduction plan. HSA distributions are not subject to tax if they are used to pay qualifying medical expenses.

The maximum annual contribution limit is determined only by the indexed statutory amounts. [Rev. Proc. 2019-25; I.R.B. 2019-22, May 28, 2019.] The following shows the maximum limits for the current and prior years:

Maximum Annual Contribution Rates

Year	Self-only coverage	Family coverage
2005	The lesser of the annual deduction under the HDHP or $2,650	The lesser of the annual deduction under the HDHP or $5,250
2006	The lesser of the annual deduction under the HDHP or $2,700	The lesser of the annual deduction under the HDHP or $5,450
2007	$2,850	$5,650
2008	$2,900	$5,800
2009	$3,000	$5,950
2010	$3,050	$6,150
2011	$3,050	$6,150
2012	$3,100	$6,250
2013	$3,250	$6,450
2014	$3,300	$6,550
2015	$3,350	$6,650
2016	$3,350	$6,750
2017	$3,400	$6,750
2018	$3,450	$6,850
2019	$3,500	$7,000
2020	$3,550	$7,100

For 2020, a "high deductible health plan" must have an annual deductible that is not less than $1,400 for self coverage or $2,800 for family coverage, and must limit the annual out-of-pocket expenses (deductions, co-pays and other amounts, but not premiums) to $6,900 for self-only coverage or $13,800 for family coverage. [IRC §223(c)(2)(A); Rev. Proc. 2019-25, I.R.B. 2019-22, May 28, 2019.]

In order to encourage saving for health expenses after retirement, HSA owners 55 and older can make additional catch-up contributions of up to $1,000 to their HSAs. [IRC §223(b)(3)(B); IRS Notice 2004-2; Rev. Proc. 2012-26; IRS Pub. 15-B.]

¶216.6

Employer contributions to employee HSAs are excluded from wage withholding, FICA, and FUTA, but must be reported on the employee's W-2 form. [IRC §223, as added by the Medicare Prescription Drug, Improvement, and Modernization Act of 2003, P.L. 108-173; IRS Notice 2004-2.]

¶217   Supplemental Unemployment Benefit Payments

Supplemental unemployment benefit (SUB) payments are excludable from the definition of wages for FICA purposes only if the benefits are linked to the receipt of state unemployment compensation payments and are not received in a lump sum. [Rev. Rul. 90-72.] Contributions by a corporation to a trust under the terms of a plan to supplement unemployment compensation benefits are not treated as wages for FICA purposes [IRS Letter Ruling 9525054, Mar. 27, 1995]. However, where payments to employee-beneficiaries were derived from a liquidated SUB trust fund, they were wages because the payments were derived solely from employer contributions and were contingent on work requirements. [*Sheet Metal Workers Local 141 SUB Trust Fund v. U.S.*, 64 F3d 245 (6th Cir. 1996), Unempl. Ins. Rptr. ¶14,792B.]

Note that payments made by a company to eligible employees under a negotiated preretirement leave benefit plan that (1) was adopted to offset layoffs resulting from periodic slack seasons, (2) provides benefits whether or not an actual need for a layoff ever occurs, and (3) guarantees benefits at the time leave is scheduled are wages for Social Security tax purposes since they are not part of a supplemental unemployment benefit plan. [Rev. Rul. 80-124; IRS Letter Rul. 200322012.]

¶218   Facilities or Privileges

Ordinarily, facilities or privileges (such as entertainment, medical services, or so-called "courtesy" discounts on purchases), furnished or offered by an employer to the employees generally, are not considered as remuneration for employment if such facilities or privileges are of relatively small value and are offered or furnished by the employer merely as a means of promoting the health, good will, contentment, or efficiency of the employees. The term "facilities or privileges" does not ordinarily include the value of meals or lodging furnished, for example, to restaurant or hotel employees, or to crew members or other employees aboard vessels, on the rationale that generally these items constitute an appreciable part of the total remuneration of such employees [Reg. §31.3121(a)-1(f)], making meals and lodging generally taxable for FICA purposes. Under a separate provision, lodging stipends provided to federal employees temporarily assigned to foreign posts are excluded from "gross income" and thus, are not subject to FICA taxes. [IRC §912(1).]

¶219   Vacation Allowances

Amounts of so-called vacation allowances or vacation pay paid to an employee constitute wages. Thus, the salary of an employee on vacation, paid notwithstanding absence from work, constitutes wages. [Reg. §31.3121(a)-1(g).]

¶220   Dismissal, Buy-out and Separation Payments

Historically, the Social Security Administration has held that dismissal payments made by an employer to an employee whose services are ended independently of the employee's will or wishes are counted as wages for Social Security purposes. [SSA POMS §RS 1401.180 (TN 8 11/93); *Soc. Sec. Handbook,* Nov. 18, 2010, §1324.] However, there has been much discussion as to whether such payments should be treated as wages subject to FICA. The Internal Revenue Service and a number of courts have weighed in on the issue.

The issue, in many cases, hinges on whether the payments were made on the account of involuntary or voluntary separations. In IRC §3402(o)(2), Congress identified employer payments due to "an employee's involuntary separation from employment" as non-wages (*i.e.*, payments occurring outside of the employment relationship). Such payments are "supplemental unemployment compensation benefits" and are not subject to FICA. However, as previously discussed (¶217), Rev. Rul. 90-72 sets limiting parameters for considering such payments as qualifying for exclusion from FICA tax.

The contingency of FICA liability hinging on a distinction between voluntary and involuntary separation payments was removed by the Federal Circuit Court of Appeals in 2008, which held that all such payments were subject to FICA. The court further ruled that payments made to employees whose full-time positions were eliminated but who continued to be employed by the company on an as-needed basis were also wages and subject to employment tax. [*CSX v. US,* 518 F3d 1328 (Fed Cir. 2008), 2008-1 USTC ¶50,218, rev'g, *CSX v. US,* 52 Fed. Cl. 208, 2003-1 USTC ¶50,337, UNEMP. INS. REP. ¶22,277, April 1, 2002 and *CSX v. US,* 71 Fed. Cl. 630, 2006-2 USTC ¶50,377 UNEMP. INS. REP. ¶17,769B, June 27, 2006.]

Supreme Court decision. In 2014, the U.S. Supreme Court took up the issue of whether severance payments made to terminated employees are wages for FICA tax purposes.

Pointing to the broad definition of "wages" under FICA and the Act's history, the Supreme Court held that severance payments made to employees who were laid off when the employer ceased doing business were taxable under FICA as payment for "service." Reversing a Sixth Circuit ruling to the contrary, the High Court noted that the employer varied the amount of severance based on an employee's function and seniority, confirming that "service" means not only work actually done but the entire employer-employee relationship for which compensation is paid. The Court also rejected the contention that the analysis was changed by an Internal Revenue Code provision stating that "any supplemental unemployment compensation benefit paid" shall be treated "as if" it were a payment of wages for income tax purposes. [*United States v. Quality Stores, Inc.*, Dkt. No. 12-1406, UNEMP. INS. REP. ¶15,227C, March 25, 2014.]

Quality Stores was subject to involuntary bankruptcy in 2001, eventually closing all stores and terminating all employees. The company paid severance under two plans, neither of which was tied to the receipt of state unemployment benefits. The pre-petition severance plan based the pay on job grade and management level.

Quality Stores reported the severance as wages and withheld federal income tax. It also paid FICA tax, but disagreed with the IRS position that the payments were wages under FICA. The company argued the payments were supplemental unemployment compensation benefits (SUB payments) not taxable under FICA and sought a refund. When the refund was denied, Quality Stores filed an adversary action in bankruptcy court. The bankruptcy court granted summary judgment for Quality Stores and the district court and Sixth Circuit affirmed. The Sixth Circuit ruled that severance payments to employees whose employment ended involuntarily due to business cessation constituted SUB payments not taxable as wages under FICA. This decision stood in stark contrast to both IRS revenue rulings and a 2008 decision from the Federal Circuit, *CSX Corp v United States*.

Reversing, the Supreme Court noted that FICA defines wages broadly as "all remuneration for employment," and as a matter of plain meaning, severance payments fit this definition. They are a form of remuneration made only to employees in consideration for "employment," which is defined in IRC §3121(b) as "any service" performed by an employee for an employer. Here, Quality Stores varied the amount of severance based on an employee's function and seniority, confirming that "service" means not only work actually done but the entire employer-employee relationship for which compensation is paid.

The High Court also noted that the broad definition was reinforced by the specificity of FICA's lengthy list of exemptions. Indeed, the exemption for severance payments "because of . . . retirement for disability" would be unnecessary were severance payments generally not considered wages. FICA's statutory history further confirmed this reading of the statute because an exception for "[d]ismissal payments" from the definition of wages was repealed in 1950 and FICA has contained no general exception for severance payments since then.

Quality Stores argued that the Internal Revenue Code indicates that the definition of wages for income tax withholding does not cover severance payments. Specifically, IRC §3402(o) on the extension of withholding to "certain payments other than wages" states a general rule that "any supplemental unemployment compensation benefit paid to an individual . . . shall be treated as if it were a payment of wages by an employer to an employee for a payroll period." Quality Stores contended that the instruction that SUBs be treated "as if" they were wages for purposes of income tax withholding was an indirect means of stating that the definition of wages did not cover severance payments and, by extension, severance payments would not be covered under FICA's similar definition of wages.

The High Court disagreed. The "as if" language in the IRC did not mean that severance pay falls outside the definition of wages for income tax withholding and, in turn, is not covered by FICA's definition. In the Court's view, IRC §3402(o) must be understood in light of the regulatory background existing when it was enacted. In the 1950s and 1960s, because some states provided unemployment only to terminated employees not earning wages, IRS rulings took the position that severance payments tied to the receipt of state benefits were not wages. To address the problem that severance payments were still considered taxable income, which could lead to a large year-end tax liability for unemployed workers, Congress enacted IRC §3402(o), treating both SUBs and severance payments the IRS considered wages "as if" they were wages subject to withholding. By extending this treatment to all SUBs, Congress avoided potential problems should the IRS decide that SUBs, besides severance payments linked to state benefits, should be exempt. Considering this background, the assumption that Congress meant to exclude all SUBs from the definition of wages was unsustainable, concluded the High Court.

Finally, because the severance payments here were not tied to state unemployment benefits, the Court declined to address whether IRS Revenue Rulings providing a FICA exemption for payments tied to unemployment benefits were consistent with FICA's broad definition of wages.

IRS guidance. In February 2015, the IRS released guidance on the application of the decision in *United States v. Quality Stores, Inc.,* to claims for refund of employment taxes paid with respect to severance payments. During the years prior to the decision, the IRS received over 3,000 refund claims for FICA, Railroad Retirement Tax Act (RRTA), and Federal Unemployment Tax Act (FUTA) taxes paid with respect to severance payments. These claims were disallowed by the IRS, prompting a number of taxpayer appeals, which were suspended pending the outcome of the *Quality Stores* litigation.

Under Rev. Rul. 90-72, 1990-2 CB 211, supplemental unemployment compensation benefits that are linked to the receipt of state unemployment compensation, and that satisfy certain other requirements, are excludable from wages for

FICA, FUTA, and income tax withholding purposes, and are excludable from compensation for RRTA tax purposes. In *Quality Stores*, the parties agreed that the payments at issue did not satisfy the requirements for the narrow exclusion from FICA tax contained in Rev. Rul. 90-72. Accordingly, the Supreme Court did not address whether the exclusion from FICA taxes set forth in the Revenue Ruling for certain payments linked to state unemployment benefits was consistent with the definition of wages under FICA. Rev. Rul. 90-72 remains effective.

As a result of the Supreme Court's holding in *Quality Stores*, the IRS will disallow all claims for refund of FICA, RRTA, or FUTA taxes paid with respect to severance payments that do not fall within the narrow exclusion under Rev. Rul. 90-72. [*IRS Announcement 2015-08*, February 10, 2015.]

¶221   Tips or Gratuities

Under specified conditions, tips received by employees are "wages" for purposes of employee and employer FICA taxes. Tips are deemed to be paid when the employee submits a timely written statement identifying them to the employer pursuant to IRC §6053(a). If no statement is furnished to the employer, tips are deemed paid at the time they are received. Tips are subject to employee taxes if they are paid in cash, amount to at least $20 in a calendar month, and are received by an employee in the course of employment with a single employer. [IRC §§3121(a)(12), 3121(q); Soc. Sec. Act §209(f).]

Tips are considered to be received by an employee in the course of employment for an employer regardless of whether the tips are received by the employee from a person other than the employer or are paid to the employee by the employer. However, only those tips that are received by an employee on his or her own behalf (as distinguished from tips received on behalf of another employee) are considered as remuneration paid to the employee. Thus, where employees practice tip splitting (for example, where servers pay a portion of the tips received by them to the bussers), each employee who receives a portion of the tip left by a customer of the employer is considered to have received tips in the course of employment. [Reg. §31.3121(q)-1(c).]

Service charges added on to the regular charges for food or beverages, which are later distributed to the employees, are not tips but are the same as other cash wages paid by the employer. [*Soc. Sec. Handbook,* March 2001, §1329.]

For the rules on reporting tips, see ¶204.1.

¶222   Payments After Termination of Employment

Remuneration for employment, unless such remuneration is specifically excepted, constitutes wages even if at the time paid the relationship of employer and employee no longer exists between the person in whose employ the services were performed and the individual who performed them. [Rev. Rul. 57-92.]

See ¶211, with respect to payments after death, and ¶212, with respect to retirement pay.

¶222.1 Payments to Disabled Former Employee

Payments made to an employee entitled to Social Security disability insurance benefits are excluded from the definition of "wages" and, therefore, may not be taxed. However, the exclusion applies only if the employee became entitled to the benefits prior to the calendar year in which the payment is made and the employee did not perform any services for the employer during the period for which payment is made. [IRC §3121(a)(15).] Also, payments made to an employee's estate or survivor after the year in which the employee died are excluded from the definition of "wages" and may not be taxed. For example, commissions of deceased life insurance salespersons paid after the year of their death do not constitute taxable wages. [IRC §3121(a)(14).]

¶222.2 Compensation for Lost Income

Generally, a payment to an individual to compensate for lost wages will not be wages for purposes of the Social Security tax and Medicare tax because it is not an actual payment for employment within the meaning of the law. However, if the payment is made by an employer to its own employees, or by a third party to employees of another employer in satisfaction of an obligation of that employer to its employees, the payment may be subject to social security tax, Medicare tax, and income tax withholding.

Accordingly, compensation for lost wages, lost income, and profits arising from the Deepwater Horizon oil rig explosion and the resulting oil spill in the Gulf of Mexico, must be included in gross income. However, these payments may or may not be subject to employment tax, depending upon who makes the payment and whether or not the recipient is an employee or self-employed.

A self-employed individual who receives a payment that represents compensation for lost income of the individual's trade or business should include the amount of the payment in net earnings from self-employment for purposes of the self-employment tax under SECA. [*IRS Gulf Oil Spill: Questions and Answers*, June 25, 2010.]

RETURNS AND PAYMENT OF TAXES

¶223   Reporting Taxes Under the FICA

A quarterly return of withheld income and Social Security (FICA) taxes must be filed by employers that are subject to these taxes. The form used is Form 941, except with respect to:

- the wages of household employees (for which Schedule H is used, but see ¶223.3);
- the wages of agricultural employees (for which Form 943 is used);
- the wages of employees in American Samoa, Guam, the Northern Mariana Islands, or the Virgin Islands not subject to U.S. income tax withholding (for which Form 941-SS is used);
- the wages of Puerto Rican employees (for which Form 941-PR is used); and
- employers with an annual estimated employment tax liability of $1,000 or less (for which Form 944 is used).

Quarterly Reporting

Only one calendar quarter is reported on Form 941 for quarterly returns. In the usual case, a preaddressed form is provided; but if the employer does not have a preaddressed form, he or she is directed by the IRS to "get one from any IRS office in time to file the return when due." Forms may be ordered online at *www.irs.gov/orderforms*.

If the employer stops paying wages temporarily, he or she should file a return for each quarter even though there are no taxes to report. Seasonal employers no longer file for quarters in which they regularly have no tax liability because they paid no wages, provided they checked the "Seasonal Employer" box on line 18 of their previous Form 941. [IRS *Circular E*, Pub. 15, rev. Dec. 23, 2019, §12.]

IRC §501(c)(3) nonprofit organizations must also report FICA taxes and withheld income taxes on Form 941. Regarding reports of the wages of household and agricultural employees, see ¶223.2 and ¶223.3, below.

If an employer goes out of business, or stops paying wages, a final return must be filed for the last quarter in which wages are paid. An employer going out of business must also furnish Form W-2 to its employees by the due date of the final Form 941. Forms W-2 and W-3 must be filed with the Social Security Administration by the last day of the month following the due date of the final Form 941 (two months after the end of the quarter). [Reg. §§31.6011(a)-6, 31.6051-1(d)(1)(ii), 31.6071(a)-1(a)(3).] Regarding the filing of Forms 941 and W-2 by predecessor, merged and acquired employers, see the discussion at the end of this section.

Form 941 and most of its variants are due quarterly on or before the last day of the month immediately following the calendar quarter covered by the return. Thus, the return for the first quarter of the year (Jan.–Mar.) is due April 30; the return for the second quarter (Apr.–June) is due July 31; the return for the third quarter (July–Sept.) is due October 31; and the return for the fourth quarter (Oct.–Dec.) is due January 31. However, the employer that deposits all taxes when due for the quarter has until the 10th day of the second month following the quarter to file the return. [Reg. §31.6071(a)-1.]

Form 941 may be filed on paper or electronically. Paper forms are filed with the Internal Revenue Service at the addresses listed in the instructions for the form. See Rev. Proc. 2011-39 for specifications for reproducing paper and computer-generated paper substitutes for Form 941 and Schedule B (Form 941).

For electronic filing, the Employment Tax e-file System was designed to replace all previous electronic filing options for returns in the 940 and 941 families. Previous e-file formats were maintained in order to allow for transition to the XML based system. XML is the only acceptable format for electronically transmitting Forms 940, 941 and 944. Publication 3823, The Employment Tax e-file System Implementation and User Guide, contains the procedural guidelines and validation criteria for the Employment Tax e-file System. The IRS no longer processes magnetic tape for Forms 940 and 941. [IRS Notice, July 31, 2003.]

Form 941 e-file: The Form 941 e-file program allows a taxpayer, a transmitter, or reporting agent to electronically file Form 941 using a personal computer, modem, and commercial tax preparation software. The forms must be submitted in the Extensible Markup Language (XML). In order to participate in the program, transmitters, reporting agents, and software developers must complete an IRS e-file application at *https://www.irs.gov.* Publication 3112 has instructions for completing this form and is available on line at *www.irs.gov/pub/irs-pdf/p3112.pdf.* Business taxpayers currently using software to prepare Form 941 should ask their software provider when they will offer the employment tax e-file program or check the list of approved IRS e-file providers.

Reporting agents must also submit Form 8655, Reporting Agent Authorization, to the IRS prior to or at the same time they complete the e-file application. For additional information, see: Pub. 3823, Employment Tax E-File Implementation and User Guide; IRS Circular E, Pub. 15, Sec. 12; and IRS Supplement to Circular E, Pub. 15A, Sec. 7.

Many employers are required to make deposits of the taxes due, some as often as eight or more times a month; see ¶223.1. Employers that do not accumulate enough tax to be subject to the deposit rules pay the tax along with the quarterly return (Annual Return for Small Employers (Form 944)). Small businesses, with annual tax liability of less than $1,000, may be invited by the IRS to file—or voluntarily pay their tax with—annual form 944. An employer may elect out of filing Form 944 if it either: (1) anticipates that its income tax liability for the year will be over $1,000, or (2) it wants to electronically file quarterly Form 941 for the year. Employers eligible to file Form 944 will be required to pay employment taxes once a year when the form is filed. Form 944 and the employment taxes are due on January 31 of the year after the tax year for which the return is filed.

Returns of self-employed persons are discussed at ¶413–¶415.

"E-Services" and Electronic Filing

The Internal Revenue Service and the Social Security Administration provide online tools under the moniker "E-Services" that allow tax professionals and payers to conduct business with the IRS and SSA electronically. Sole proprietors, businesses and other organizations may become authorized e-file providers. This status allows taxpayers to file returns faster and with fewer errors and to pay taxes by debit or credit. The procedures for e-file applications are found in Publication 3112, *IRS e-file Application and Participation.* Specific information about the electronic filing and payment options for employment taxes is available at *http://www.irs.gov* and from the e-help Desk toll-free number (866) 255-0654.

Before becoming authorized e-file providers, taxpayers must first complete an e-file application and identify themselves as one or more of the following:

- **Electronic Return Originators (ERO)** who originate the electronic submission of income tax returns to the IRS.
- **Intermediate Service Providers** who receive tax information from EROs or from taxpayers who file electronically, process it and forward it to a transmitter or back to the EROs or taxpayers.
- **Transmitters** who send prepared returns to the IRS and are able to connect to IRS computers.
- **Software developers** who write programs to IRS specifications.
- **Reporting Agents** who are accounting services, franchisers, banks or other persons who are authorized to e-file Form 940/941 on behalf of taxpayers.
- **Large taxpayers** with assets of $10 million or more or a partnership with more than 100 partners.
- **Online providers.**
- **Affordable Care Act (ACA) providers.**

All Authorized IRS e-file Providers, except those that function solely as Software Developers, must pass a suitability check on the firm as well as on all Principals and Responsible Officials of the firm prior to acceptance to participate in IRS e-file. Principals and responsible officials of their firms may have to submit to a background check and provide fingerprints or evidence of their professional status. If all individuals pass the background check, the IRS will issue an Electronic Filing Identification Number (EFIN) and an acceptance letter. Authorized e-file providers that obtain taxpayer information via the Internet directly or through third parties to file returns must submit an Excel spreadsheet with the relevant URLs of websites used in the preparation and filing of returns.

All authorized e-file providers are eligible to:

- **Register online** and select a username, password and PIN;
- Obtain a **preparer tax identification number** (PTIN) that may be used in place of the practitioner's Social Security number on returns they prepare for clients; and
- Use an **online e-file application**.

Authorized e-file providers who have e-filed five or more accepted returns and attorneys, CPAs, enrolled agents and other persons qualified to represent taxpayers before the IRS per Treasury Department Circular 230 (Rev. June 2014) are eligible to use the following electronic services:

- **Disclosure Authorization (DA).** Eligible tax professionals may complete authorization forms, view and modify existing forms, and receive acknowledgement of accepted submissions immediately— all online. Disclosure

Authorization allows tax professionals to electronically submit Form 2848, *Power of Attorney and Declaration of Representative* and Form 8821, *Tax Information Authorization*. This e-service expedites processing and issues a real-time acknowledgment of accepted submissions.

- **Electronic Account Resolution (EAR)** allows tax professionals to expedite closure on a client's account problems by electronically sending/receiving account related inquiries. Tax professionals may inquire about individual or business account problems, refunds, installment agreements, missing payments or notices. Tax professionals must have a power of attorney on file before accessing a client's account. The IRS response is delivered to an electronic secure mailbox within three business days.

- **Transcript Delivery System (TDS).** Eligible tax professionals may use Transcript Delivery System to request and receive account transcripts, wage and income documents, tax return transcripts, and verification of non-filing letters. A new product (the Record of Account) combines both the Return Transcript and Account Transcript in one product. Tax Professionals can request the products for both individual and business taxpayers. The TDS application may be used to resolve a client's need for return and account information quickly, in a secure, online session. Tax professionals must have a Power of Attorney authorization on file with the IRS before accessing a client's account (or use Disclosure Authorization to file an authorization on a new client and obtain TDS information immediately).

Reporting Agents who are accepted participants have access to TDS and EAR products that are tailored to meet their needs.

Business Services Online

The Social Security Administration's portal for employers and third parties for electronic wage reporting purposes and for verifying Social Security numbers for such purposes is at Business Services Online, *http://www.ssa.gov/bso/bsowelcome.htm*. Registration is required to access services. Once the employer registers and receives a user ID and password, the employer must return to *www.ssa.gov/bso/bsowelcome.htm*, login with the user ID and password, and select "Request Access and Activation Code." An activation code will then be sent to the address listed on the company's Form 941. Within 60 days the account must be activated or the activation code will expire.

The expiration of a password does not deactivate a user ID. However, passwords must now be changed every 90 days for security purposes. A user who forgets to change the password within 90 days can still log in, but will be instructed to change it at that time.

The Business Services Online tutorial is updated annually and provides the latest instructions and screen shots of the various programs. In addition, the tutorial explains how Forms W-2s/W-3s can be reported electronically to the agency. The tutorial, which may be accessed at *https://www.ssa.gov/employer/bsotut.htm,* offers step-by-step instructions for BSO services, including:

- Business Services Online registration;
- How to submit a wage file;
- W-2 and W-2c Online; and
- Access to the Social Security Number Verification Service for wage reporting purposes.

SSN Verification Services. The Social Security Administration can post employee wages correctly only when employers and submitters report employee wages under the correct name and Social Security Number. Recording names and SSNs correctly will save the employer administrative processing costs and allow the SSA to properly credit employee earnings records which will help ensure that an eligible employee receives the correct amount of benefits. The SSA offers several ways in which an employer (and third parties acting on its behalf) may verify that the payroll record of employee names and Social Security numbers match the Social Security Administration's records: the online Social Security Number Verification Service (SSNVS), the Telephone Number Employer Verification (TNEV), E-Verify, and Consent-Based Social Security Number Verification Service (CBSV).

SSNVS: To be able to use the SSNVS, an employer must register for the SSA's Business Services Online (BSO) at *http://www.ssa.gov/bso/bsowelcome.htm* and request SSNVS. Note, every BSO user must register separately (i.e., a person may not register on behalf of another party. (See also the SSNVS Handbook, rev'd June 2015, at *http://www.ssa.gov/employer/ssnvs_handbk.htm*). If the employer already has a user ID and password it can directly sign up for the SSNVS at the BSO welcome webpage. There are no fees for using SSNVS (unlike the Consent-Based Social Security Number Verification Service (see below)) and the signed consent of the number holder is not needed.

If the employee's Social Security number matches SSA's records, the employer will receive the given name and the last four digits of the individual's Social Security number. For mismatches, SSA will notify the employer of the reason, or if it was "unable to verify." If an employee's name and number do not match, the employer should ask to see the employee's Social Security card and determine whether the name and number on the card are the same as those it submitted to the SSNVS. If they are the same, (*e.g.,* there were no "typos"), the employer should ask the employee to contact the SSA to fix the discrepancy.

¶223

An employer can also: submit a paper listing of 50 or fewer names and SSNs to their local Social Security office. Instructions for submitting paper listings are found in the SSNVS Handbook. Note, SSA will verify SSNs and names solely to ensure that the records of current or former employees are correct for Form W-2 reporting purposes. An employer may not use SSNVS to verify the SSNs of potential new hires or contractors or in the preparation of tax returns. More information about SSNVS is available at *http://www.ssa.gov/employer/ssnv.htm.*

TNEV: TNEV was an automated telephone service that through FY 2012 allowed registered employers (and third parties acting on their behalf) to verify employee Social Security numbers for wage reporting purposes. TNEV allowed registered users to verify up to 10 employee names and SSNs at one time without having to speak to a Social Security representative.

The TNEV program ended in FY 2012. However, acknowledging that registered SSNVS users may occasionally need to perform verification when the users do not have online access, SSA is allowing registered users to call an employer 800 number (800-772-6270) to secure name and SSN verification.

E-Verify: The E-Verify program is operated by the U.S. Department of Homeland Security's U.S. Citizenship and Immigration Service in partnership with the Social Security Administration. E-Verify was established as part of the Illegal Immigration Reform and Immigrant Responsibility Act (IIRIRA) of 1996 to verify the employment eligibility of both U.S. citizens and noncitizens at no charge to the employer. [*https://www.uscis.gov/e-verify.*] All federal agencies are required to use E-Verify for their new hires and certain federal contractors and subcontractors are required to use the system for newly hired employees working in the United States as well as existing employees working directly under a contract. To enroll in E-Verify, an employer should go to the webpage at *https://www.uscis.gov/e-verify.*

Employees had received a Tentative Nonconfirmation Notice (TNC) in the event of a record mismatch that needed to be resolved with Homeland Security or SSA before E-Verify confirmed work authorization. A Further Action Notice will inform employees of the occurrence of a TNC, provide the option of contesting it with Homeland Security or SSA, and explain the steps that must be taken to resolve the record mismatch.

Once an employer refers a case to Homeland Security or SSA, a one page Referral Date Confirmation (RDC) will be generated for the employer to provide the employee. The RDC will disclose the deadline by which the employee must contest the case.

The U.S. Citizenship and Immigration Services (USCIS) Department will further lock in Social Security Numbers in E-Verify that appear to have been used fraudulently. USCIS will use a combination of algorithms, detection reports, and analysis to identify patterns of fraudulent Social Security Number use and then lock the number in E-Verify. If an employee attempts to use a locked Social Security Number, E-Verify will generate a TNC.

Consent-Based Social Security Number Verification Service (CBSV): CBSV is a fee and consent-based Social Security number (SSN) verification service available to enrolled private companies and federal, state and local government agencies. It provides instant, automated verification and it easily handles large volume requests. Using CBSV, participating companies can verify the SSNs of their prospective hires, customers and clients. A company must have an Employer Identification Number (EIN) to enroll.

CBSV requires the written consent of the SSN holder and the verification results may only be used for the reason specified by the number holder. CBSV is fee-based. To use CBSV, a company must pay a one-time non-refundable enrollment fee of $5,000 and then pay a transaction fee per SSN verification request. The transaction fee must be paid in advance. The transaction fee can change at any time. [*http://www.ssa.gov/cbsv.*] Note, CBSV does not verify identity, citizenship, or employment eligibility. Nor does it interface with the Department of Homeland Security Verification System.

Self-Check

Self-Check is a voluntary service that allows individuals to check their employment status. If any mismatches are found between the information an individual provides and that individual's Department of Homeland Security or Social Security Administration records, Self Check will inform the individual of how to correct those mismatches. In 2012, the U.S. Citizenship and Immigration Services expanded the availability of Self-Check to all 50 states, the District of Columbia, Guam, Puerto Rico, the U.S. Virgin Islands, and the Commonwealth of the Northern Mariana Islands. [USCIS News Release, Feb. 9, 2012.] To use Self-Check, an individual should go to the webpage at *https://www.uscis.gov/mye-verify/self-check.*

Validating incorrect SSN

Recipients of interest, dividends, wages and other reportable amounts who receive a second notice from a payor, pursuant to IRC §3406(a)(1)(B), that the SSN furnished by the payee is incorrect will need to validate their SSNs.

This can be done by contacting the local SSA office, providing a copy of the notice to the office, and requesting a Social Security number printout. This printout is sufficient for SSN validation purposes. The SSA no longer issues Form SSA-7028 for this purpose. [IRS Announcement 2010-41, June 21, 2010, IRB 2010-25.]

Predecessor, Merged, and Acquired Employers

In the event an employer is acquired by a successor employer, the IRS has provided standard and alternative procedures for preparing and filing employment tax returns. Schedule D (Form 941) (Report of Discrepancies Caused by Acquisition, Statutory Mergers or Consolidations) is to be used by employers to provide the IRS with information about employment tax discrepancies created by an acquisition, statutory merger or consolidation. If an acquisition, statutory merger or consolidation creates a discrepancy between what was reported to the IRS on Form W-2, Wage and Tax Statement, and what was reported on Form 941, Employer's Quarterly Federal Tax Return, the employer can use Schedule D (Form 941) to explain the discrepancy, even if the employer e-filed its employment tax returns. Only employers that experience a statutory merger or consolidation or an acquisition that satisfies the requirements for predecessor-successor status should use Schedule D (Form 941).

Standard procedure: Generally, under the standard procedure, the acquired employer reports all of the wages and compensation it pays by filing Form 941 and furnishing and filing Forms W-2. However, after an acquisition, the acquired employer may go out of business, in which case it must file a final Form 941 for the quarter of the acquisition. Moreover, if the acquired employer goes out of business, it must furnish and file Forms W-2 on an expedited basis. Additionally, the acquired employer must keep all records, including Forms W-4, Employee's Withholding Allowance Certificate, and W-5, Earned Income Credit Advance Payment Certificate, for all its employees, even those who transfer employment to the acquiring employer. Employees who transfer employment to the acquiring employer must provide new Forms W-4 and W-5. The acquiring employer now becomes responsible for deducting and withholding tax from wages paid to those employees as well as reporting all of the wages and compensation that it pays to them.

Alternate procedure: Under the alternate procedure, the acquiring employer becomes responsible for filing and furnishing all employment-related tax forms. If the acquiring employer assumes this obligation, the Forms W-2 furnished to the acquired employees must include wages paid and taxes withheld by both the acquired and acquiring employer. However, the acquired employer must provide and file Forms W-2 on an expedited basis to any employees who are not employed by the acquiring employer. Thus, there may be differences between the Forms W-2 (Copy A) filed by the acquired employer and the amount shown on its Form 941. In this case, the acquired employer would use Schedule D to report and explain the discrepancies. Similarly, the acquiring employer should use Schedule D to report and explain discrepancies between its Forms W-2 (Copy A) and Form 941. Schedule D should be filed with the first quarter return for the year after the calendar year of the acquisition.

Facsimile Signatures

Any form required to be made to the IRS must be signed. Employment tax returns must be signed by the individual who is required to submit the form. [IRC §6061(a).] IRC §6061(b) authorizes the IRS to develop acceptable methods for electronic or digital signatures. Corporate officers or duly authorized agents may use a facsimile signature in filing Forms 940, 941, and 943. Under prior procedures, a facsimile signature could only be used if the forms were accompanied by a letter signed by the person authorized to sign the returns declaring, under penalties of perjury, that the facsimile signature appearing on the returns was the signature adopted by him or her to sign the returns. The letter was also to list each return by name and identifying number. However, the IRS no longer requires that the taxpayer include a letter authenticating the facsimile signature when filing the return (unless specifically requested). Instead, the person responsible for filing the return must retain such a letter for four years from the due date of the return or the date on which the tax related to the return is paid. The letter must affirm that the signature was used at the direction of the officer or agent, and that it is affirmed under penalties of perjury because the officer or agent is personally responsible for ensuring their facsimile signature is affixed to the returns. The IRS has also expanded the employment-related returns that may be filed with the use of facsimile signatures to include any variant of the Form 940X series. [Rev. Proc. 2005-39; IRS News Release IR-2005-73, July 12, 2005.]

¶223.1   Deposits

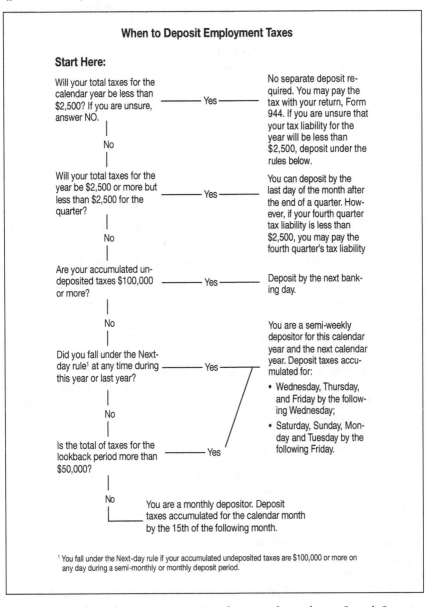

When to Deposit Employment Taxes

Start Here:

Will your total taxes for the calendar year be less than $2,500? If you are unsure, answer NO. ——— Yes ——— No separate deposit required. You may pay the tax with your return, Form 944. If you are unsure that your tax liability for the year will be less than $2,500, deposit under the rules below.

No

Will your total taxes for the year be $2,500 or more but less than $2,500 for the quarter? ——— Yes ——— You can deposit by the last day of the month after the end of a quarter. However, if your fourth quarter tax liability is less than $2,500, you may pay the fourth quarter's tax liability

No

Are your accumulated undeposited taxes $100,000 or more? ——— Yes ——— Deposit by the next banking day.

No

Did you fall under the Next-day rule[1] at any time during this year or last year? ——— Yes ———

No

Is the total of taxes for the lookback period more than $50,000? ——— Yes ———

You are a semi-weekly depositor for this calendar year and the next calendar year. Deposit taxes accumulated for:

- Wednesday, Thursday, and Friday by the following Wednesday;
- Saturday, Sunday, Monday and Tuesday by the following Friday.

No

You are a monthly depositor. Deposit taxes accumulated for the calendar month by the 15th of the following month.

[1] You fall under the Next-day rule if your accumulated undeposited taxes are $100,000 or more on any day during a semi-monthly or monthly deposit period.

Deposits of employment taxes (employer and employee Social Security and Medicare taxes) are generally made by the employer on a monthly or semi-weekly schedule. An employer's status as a monthly depositor or semi-weekly depositor is known before the beginning of each calendar year and is determined annually based on employer's employment tax history over a

12-month lookback period ending the preceding June 30. The IRS informs employers by November of each year which schedule they will need to follow for the upcoming year. [IRS Reg. 31.6302-1(a) and (b).]

All federal tax deposits must be made by using the Electronic Federal Tax Payment System (EFTPS). However, employers with a deposit liability of less than $2,500 for either the current quarter or the preceding quarter (and who do not incur a $100,000 next day deposit obligation during the current quarter) may remit their employment taxes with a quarterly (Form 941) or annual return (Forms 943 and 944) (see ¶223.2).

The above rules generally apply also with respect to taxes reportable for agricultural workers except that, since the agricultural employer's tax return is filed annually rather than quarterly, if the total undeposited taxes are less than $2,500 at the end of any month, the taxes carry over to the following month. If, at the end of December, total undeposited taxes are less than $2,500, the accumulated liability may be paid by the following January 31 with Form 943. [IRS Reg. §31.6302-1(a)(4), (g); IRS *Circular A*, Pub. 51, §7, rev. Dec. 19, 2019.]

Tax reportable on quarterly return: Separate deposits of any taxes reportable on a quarterly return must be made for each type of tax. When preparing a quarterly return, all deposits must be listed for that quarter, including any overpayments or underpayments applied from prior quarters. Supporting information regarding prior period adjustments must be reported on Form 941-X or on an attached statement and filed together with Form 941. [IRS *Circular E*, Pub. 15, §11 and §13, rev. Dec. 23, 2019; Instructions, Form 941.] See ¶228 regarding correcting mistakes and reporting adjustments.

When to Deposit and the Lookback Period

An employer will deposit employment taxes under a monthly or semiweekly schedule. Under the governing payroll tax deposit rules an employer's deposit requirement is based on the employer's tax liabilities (and not by how often the employer pays its employees or makes deposits) during the *lookback period,* which is the 12-month period beginning July 1 and ending the preceding June 30. The lookback period for 2020 is the period from July 1, 2018, to June 30, 2019, for filers of Form 941. However, for filers of annual Form 944 there is a different lookback period. **For either of the preceding two years**, the deposit schedule is determined from the total taxes (that is, Social Security, Medicare, and Federal Income Tax Withholding, not reduced by any advance Earned Income Credit payments) reported during the second preceding calendar year. For example, the lookback period for 2020 for a Form 944 filer is calendar year 2018. [Reg. §31.6302-1, Pub. 15, Instructions for Form 944.]

Reg. §31.6302-1 specifies that the lookback period is the second preceding calendar year for employers who filed Form 944 **for either of the two previous calendar years**, not just the first previous calendar year because an employer would not have filed the requisite quarterly returns to use the other lookback period (12-month period ending June 30) if the employer filed Form 944 in either of the prior years. For example, if an employer filed Form 944 in 2017 but not in 2018, the lookback period for 2019 would be 2017, because they would not have filed quarterly returns for July through December 2017 and, thus, it would be impossible to use July 2017 – June 2018 as the lookback period.

The amount of tax reported during the lookback period is determined without regard to the employer's filing requirement. In other words, in the preceding example, if an employer is required to file Form 941 for 2013 but filed Form 944 for the lookback period (2017), the amount of employment tax liability reported for the lookback period would be the amount of employment tax the employer reported on its Form 944 for 2017 even though the employer will file Forms 941 to report its 2019 liability. The reverse also is true. The employment tax liability reported for the lookback period (2017 for an employer required to file Form 944 for 2019) would be the sum of the liabilities it reported on its four Forms 941 for 2016. [Reg. §31.6302-1.]

New employers are treated as having no tax liability during quarters for which there were no employees. Accordingly, new employers are considered to be monthly depositors for the first calendar year of the business. For wages reportable on Form 943, the tax return for agricultural employees, the lookback period is the calendar year preceding the calendar year just ended. Thus, the lookback period for 2019 for employers of agricultural workers is calendar year 2017. If an employer pays wages to both farm and non-farm workers, the rules must be applied separately for Form 941 and Form 943, and separate deposits must be made for each category. [Reg. §31.6302-1(a), (b), and (g)(4).]

Monthly and semi-weekly depositors. An employer is either a monthly or semi-weekly depositor, unless invited by the IRS to become an annual depositor (see below). An employer is a monthly depositor for a calendar year if total taxes (reported on Form 941, Line 10) for the four quarters in the lookback period are $50,000 or less. Taxes accumulated during each month of a quarter must be deposited by the 15th day of the following month.

An employer is a semi-weekly depositor if the total accumulated taxes (reported on Form 941, Line 10) for the lookback period are more than $50,000. Taxes accumulated for Wednesday, Thursday, and/or Friday paydays must be deposited by the following Wednesday. Taxes accumulated for Saturday, Sunday, Monday, and/or Tuesday paydays must be deposited by the following Friday. [IRS Reg. §31.6302-1(c).]

Semi-weekly depositors must complete Schedule B (Report of Tax Liability for Semi-weekly Schedule Depositors) and submit the Schedule with Form 941. Semi-weekly depositors that file Form 944 must submit Form 945A (Annual Record of Federal Tax Liability) instead of Schedule B.

Next-day depositors. Employers with accumulated liability of $100,000 within a monthly or semi-weekly deposit period must deposit accumulated taxes on the *first* business day after the day on which the employer has accumulated $100,000 or more of such taxes (*i.e.*, "one day rule"). [Reg. §31.6302-1(c)(3).]

Employers that accumulate liability of less than $2,500 during a return period (quarterly or annually), must deposit or remit taxes with Form 941. [Reg. §31.6302-1(f)(4).]

Advance earned income credit. In the case of employers paying advanced earned income credit amounts (¶229), the amount of total accumulated taxes during a lookback period is not reduced by any advance earned income credit payments when determining an employer's deposit schedule. However, the next-day deposit rule is not triggered unless a tax liability of $100,000 or more is accumulated *after* reduction for advance amounts paid to employees. [Reg. §31.3507-1(c)(1)(i)(C).]

The safe harbor (accuracy of deposits) rule. Employers are required to deposit 100% of their tax liability on or before the deposit due date. However, an employer will be considered to have satisfied its deposit requirements if any shortfall does not exceed the greater of $100 or 2% of the taxes otherwise required to be deposited, and the shortfall is deposited by the shortfall makeup date.

Specifically, a *monthly depositor* may deposit the shortfall or pay the amount with the return by the due date of the return for the period in which the shortfall occurred (even if $2,500 or more). A *semi-weekly depositor* may deposit the amount by the earlier of the first Wednesday or Friday on or after the 15th day of the month following the month in which the deposit was required to be made, or, if earlier, the due date of Form 941. [IRS Reg. §31.6302-1(f).] Even if the safe harbor rule is not met, employers that deposit less than the full amount of their deposit obligation can have penalties abated under IRC §6656 if they show that their failure was due to reasonable cause.

States and local governments are subject to the same depository requirements as private-sector employers. [P.L. 99-509, §9002(c)(1).]

Special Safe Harbor Rule For Quarterly Filers

In addition to the safe harbor rules noted above, an alternate method for determining whether the employer's employment tax obligations are *de minimis*, based on the employment taxes due for the prior return period, is available. The safe harbor helps small employers that file Form 941 and have an unexpected increase in their deposit liability for a quarterly return period. This special rule applies only to employers filing quarterly tax returns and, therefore, does not apply to employers that file Form 944.

Employers may pay their employment taxes when they timely file their quarterly returns and be deemed to have timely deposited if the amount of the taxes due for the current quarter *or for the prior quarter* is less than $2,500. The change should prevent employers from risking a failure to file penalty, the IRS has predicted. [Reg. §31.6302-1(f)(4)(i) and (ii).]

Annual Returns for Small Employers (Form 944)

To alleviate the reporting burdens on small employers, an employer with estimated annual tax liability of $1,000 or less for the tax year may file an annual employment tax return on Form 944 (Annual Employer's Tax Return Program) rather than the quarterly return. Form 944 will generally be due January 31 of the year following the year for which the return is filed.

Small employers are not required to file Form 944. In addition, procedures are provided for opting out of the program, as well as opting in.

Opting out procedures. Qualifying employers are no longer required to file Form 944. An employer may opt out of filing Form 944 for any reason as follows: [Rev. Proc 2009-51, I.R.B. 2009-45; IRS Reg. 31.6011(a) (76 FR 77672, Dec. 14, 2011).]

- *Employers that have previously filed Form 941 or Form 944 or the related Spanish-language returns or returns for U.S. possessions:* Employers that want to call to opt out of filing Form 944 must call the IRS on or before April 1 of the current year. Employers that want to write to opt out of filing Form 944 must have their written correspondence postmarked on or before March 15 of the current year.

- *New employers:* Businesses that recently received an employer identification number or had an employer identification number but were not previously required to file Form 941 or Form 944 or the related Spanish-language returns or returns for U.S. possessions that want to call to opt out must call the IRS on or before the first day of the month that their first required Form 941 is due. Employers that want to write to opt out of filing Form 944 must have their written correspondence postmarked on or before the 15th day of the month before their first required Form 941 is due. For any due date that falls on a Saturday, Sunday, or legal holiday in the District of Columbia, the last day employers may call the IRS or have their written correspondence postmarked is the next business day following that Saturday, Sunday, or legal holiday in the District of Columbia.

Employers in the United States, including Puerto Rico and the Virgin Islands can call 800-829-4933. Employers in Guam, American Samoa, the Commonwealth of the Northern Mariana Islands, and international callers should call 01-215-516-2000 or the nearest IRS office. Employers who prefer to opt out in writing should use one of the following two addresses: Department of Treasury, Internal Revenue Service, Ogden, Utah 84201-0038 or Department of Treasury, Internal Revenue Service, Cincinnati, Ohio 45999-0038. [Rev. Proc. 2009-51, IRB 2009-45, Nov. 9, 2009.]

Confirmation of opt-out of filing Form 944: The IRS will send written confirmation to employers that their filing requirement was changed to Form 941. Employers that are notified to file Form 944 and are not notified that their filing requirement was changed to Form 941 must file Form 944 rather than Form 941.

Opting in procedure: The IRS will send notification of eligibility to file Form 944 only upon request by the qualified employer. Employers may request to receive such notification by calling the IRS at the telephone numbers identified above by the due dates indicated. Employers that previously received notification of their qualification to file Form 944 must continue to file Form 944 unless they opt out consistent with the procedures described above. New employers should also contact the IRS if they anticipate that their annual employment tax liability will be $1,000 or less. The IRS estimates that only employers paying approximately $4,000 or less in annual wages will qualify. New employers are eligible for the Form 944 program in addition to already established employers. New employers should indicate their estimated liability on Form SS-4, Application for Employer Identification Number.

Payment/filing dates: Employers that file Form 941 must remit employment taxes to the IRS on a monthly or semi-weekly basis. However, employers eligible to file Form 944 will only have to pay employment taxes once a year when the form is filed. Form 944 and the employment taxes are due on January 31 of the year after the tax year for which the return is filed. However, if the employer has paid all accumulated employment taxes by that date, the employer will have 10 extra calendar days to file the form. Payment of the balance due on Form 944 may be paid by credit card; however, credit card payments for federal tax deposits are not allowed.

Agricultural and domestic employers: Form 944 completely replaces Form 941 for program participants. However, Form 944 will not replace Form 943 for agricultural employers or Schedule H, Form 1040 for employees with only household employees.

Reporting agents: Reporting agents are now able to be authorized to sign, file and make deposits and payments reported on Form 944. Employers that wish to authorize an agent may do so by using Form 8655, Reporting Agent Authorization. [Rev. Proc. 2012-32.]

Lookback period: For most employers, the lookback period is the 12-month period ending on the preceding June 30. For employers in the Form 944 Program during the current or either of the two preceding calendar years, the lookback period for determining whether an employer is a monthly or semi-weekly depositor is the second calendar year preceding the current calendar year. For instance, the lookback period for 2020 is calendar year 2018. A participating employer may not realize that its annual employment tax liability exceeded $1,000 until it files its Form 944 on January 31 of the following year. These employers can avoid the penalty for failing to make a timely monthly deposit of their January taxes as long as they fully pay those taxes by March 15. [Reg. §31.6302-1(c)(6).]

> **Example:** Employer Acme Corp. participates in the Form 944 Program for 2020. When Acme files its Form 944 at the end of January 2020, it discovers that its employment tax liability for 2019 was $4,000. Acme is not eligible for the Form 944 Program in 2020, and must make monthly deposits of its employment taxes. Acme will need to deposit its January 2020 employment taxes by March 16, 2020.

De minimis rules: An employer that files Form 944 whose employment tax liability for the year equals or exceeds $2,500 but whose employment tax liability for a quarter of the year is less than $2,500 will be deemed to have timely deposited the employment taxes due for that quarter if the employer fully deposits the employment taxes accumulated during the quarter by the last day of the month following the close of that quarter. Employment taxes accumulated during the fourth quarter can be either deposited by January 31 or remitted with a timely filed return for the return period.

> **Example:** Harvey, a monthly depositor, was notified to file Form 944 to report his employment tax liabilities for the 2012 calendar year. In the first quarter of 2012, Harvey accumulates employment taxes in the amount of $1,000. On April 28, 2013, Harvey deposits the $1,000 of employment taxes accumulated in the 1st quarter. Harvey accumulates another $1,000 of employment taxes during the second quarter of 2013 and makes a timely deposit on July 31, 2013. Harvey's business grows and accumulates $1,500 in employment taxes during the third quarter of 2013, which he timely deposits. Harvey accumulates another $2,000 in employment taxes during the fourth quarter and files Form 944 on January 31, 2014, reporting a total employment tax liability for 2013 of $5,500. Harvey submits a check for the remaining $2,000 of employment taxes with the return. Harvey will be deemed to have timely deposited the employment taxes due for all of 2013,

because he complied with the *de minimis* deposit rule that requires deposit by January 31 or payment with a timely filed final return. Therefore, the IRS will not impose a failure-to-deposit penalty under Code Sec. 6656 for any month of the year. Under this *de minimis* deposit rule, as Harvey was required to file Form 944 for calendar year 2013, if his employment tax liability for a quarter is *de minimis*, he may deposit that quarter's liability by the last day of the month following the close of the quarter. This rule allows Harvey to have the benefit of the same quarterly *de minimis* amount that he would have received if he filed Form 941 each quarter instead of Form 944 annually. Thus, as Harvey's employment tax liability for each quarter was *de minimis*, he could deposit quarterly.

Payment of Deposits: Electronic Federal Tax Deposit System

Federal tax deposits must be made using the Electronic Federal Tax Deposit System (EFTPS). This requirement, however, does not change the deposit requirements or thresholds. Taxpayers that owe minimal amounts and are not subject to the tax rules will continue to be permitted to make payment with the filed tax return, Form 941, 943, or 944.

For deposits made by EFTPS to be on time, a taxpayer must initiate the deposit by 8 p.m. Eastern time the day before the date the deposit is due. Third parties that are used to making a deposit may have a different cutoff time. [IRS *Circular E*, Pub. 15, §11.]

The above rules generally apply also with respect to taxes reportable for agricultural workers except that, since the agricultural employer's tax return is filed annually rather than quarterly, if the total undeposited taxes are less than $2,500 at the end of any month, the taxes carry over to the following month. If, at the end of December, total undeposited taxes are less than $2,500, the accumulated liability may be paid by the following January 31 with Form 943. [IRS Reg. §31.6302-1(f)(4), (g); IRS *Circular A*, Pub. 51, §7.]

Tax reportable on quarterly return: Separate deposits of any taxes reportable on a quarterly return must be made for each type of tax. When preparing a quarterly return, Form 941, all deposits must be listed for that quarter, including any overpayments or underpayments for that quarter. Prior period adjustments must be reported on Form 941X . [IRS *Circular E*, Pub. 15, §11 and §13; Instructions, Form 941.] See ¶228 regarding correcting mistakes and reporting adjustments.

Electronic funds transfer: Unless reasonable cause is established, a taxpayer is subject to the failure-to-deposit penalty if the taxpayer is required to deposit its taxes using EFT and instead makes the deposit with a quarterly or annual return. The IRS may also waive penalties if a taxpayer inadvertently fails to deposit in the first quarter the taxpayer was required to deposit any employment tax. A taxpayer that deposits the taxes 16 or more days late is subject to a 10% penalty rate. A 5% rate applies if the EFT deposit is made within five days but not more than 15 days after the regular due date. A 2% penalty applies if the EFT deposit is made within five days after the regular due date. [Rev. Rul. 95-68; IRS Notice 99-20, IRB 1999-17, Apr. 26, 1999.]

Enrollment: All taxpayers—individuals and businesses—regardless of the size of their deposits, can make payments through the online version of EFTPS, located at *www.eftps.gov.* To encourage the use of EFTPS, all taxpayers using FTD coupons are to be pre-enrolled in the EFTPS. Upon receipt of notification of pre-enrollment, a taxpayer can use the phone or Internet to activate their Personal Indentification Number (PIN), enter their financial account information, and begin scheduling payments on the same day. To set up electronic payments, a taxpayer may enroll online or call EFTPS Customer Service at (800) 555-4477 (for business payments). [75 *Federal Register* 75897, December 27, 2010; IRS EFTPS webpage, *http://www.eftps.gov.*]

To encourage new businesses to use the EFTPS system, all businesses requesting a new EIN that have a federal tax obligation will be automatically pre-enrolled in EFTPS to make all their federal tax deposits. When the businesses receive their EINs, they will also receive a separate mailing containing an EFTPS PIN and instructions for activating their enrollment. New business taxpayers will be able to activate their enrollment by calling an 800-number, entering their banking information, and completing an authorization for EFTPS to transfer funds from their account to Treasury's account for tax payments per the instructions. Although EFTPS is offered to both businesses and individuals, Express Enrollment is available only to business taxpayers requesting a new EIN that have federal tax obligations. When business taxpayers complete Form SS-4, Request for Employer Identification Number, by phone, online or through the mail, they indicate that they will have employees, and therefore federal deposit requirements. These are the businesses that will be pre-enrolled in EFTPS through this program. [IRS News Release 2004-10; IRS Pub. 4274, Jan. 2004; IRS Pub. 4725, Jan. 2008.]

Business days and legal holidays: If a deposit is required to be made on a day that is not a business day, the deposit is considered timely if it is made by the close of the next business day. Every calendar day that is not a Saturday, Sunday, or legal holiday under IRC §7503 is a "business day." The term "banking day" is no longer used. Additionally, because EFTPS is available 24 hours a day, seven days a week, the regulations provide that, consistent with IRC §7503, the term "legal holiday" for FTD purposes includes only those legal holidays in the District of Columbia. Thus, a statewide legal holiday will no longer be considered a legal holiday unless the holiday coincides with a legal holiday in the District of Columbia. The following days are currently legal holidays in the District of Columbia: New Year's Day, Birthday of Martin Luther King, Jr., Washington's Birthday, District of Columbia Emancipation Day, Memorial Day, Independence Day, Labor Day, Columbus Day, Veteran's Day, Thanksgiving Day, Christmas Day, and the day of the inauguration of the President, in every fourth year. [Reg. §31.6302-1(c)(4).]

Semiweekly depositors will always have three business days after the end of a semi-weekly period in which to make a deposit. Thus, if any of the three week days after the end of a semi-weekly period is a legal holiday, an employer will have an additional business day in which to deposit. [IRS Reg. §31.6302-1(c)(2)(iii).]

If the employer makes timely deposits sufficient to pay the full tax liability on the quarterly return on Form 941, he or she is allowed 10 additional days for filing the return beyond the due date for employers generally. [IRS Reg. §31.6071(a)-1(a)(1).]

Note that taxes on household employees are not subject to these deposit rules, but that taxes on agricultural employees are subject to basically the same deposit rules; see ¶223.2 and 223.3, respectively.

The penalties assessed for failure to comply with deposit requirements are discussed ¶227.1.

Payment With Return

An employer may make a payment with Form 941 or Form 944 instead of depositing, without incurring a penalty, if one of the following applies:

- An employer reports less than a $2,500 tax liability for the quarter on line 10 of Form 941 (or for the year on line 9 of Form 944). However, if an employer is unsure that it will report less than $2,500, it should deposit under the appropriate rules so that it will not be subject to failure-to-deposit penalties.

- An employer is a monthly schedule depositor (see above) and makes a payment in accordance with the safe harbor rule, described above. The rule relates to how shortfalls of limited amounts may be paid without incurring a penalty. This payment may be $2,500 or more.

¶223.2 Returns of Agricultural Employers

Every employer that employs one or more covered agricultural workers (see ¶307) must make an annual return on Form 943. [Reg. §31.6011(a)-1(a) (2)(ii).] The return, together with payment of any taxes due, should be sent to the District Director not later than January 31 following the year for which the return is made. However, an employer that makes timely deposits sufficient to pay the full tax liability on the return for the year is allowed 10 additional days for filing the return beyond the January 31 due date. In that case, the return for a calendar year would be due on or before the following February 10. [IRS Reg. §31.6071(a)-1(a)(1).]

The tax deposit rules for agricultural employers, including the requirements for deposit by electronic funds transfer, are basically the same as those applicable to employers reporting on Form 941. If wages are subject to Social Security and Medicare taxes, they are also subject to income tax withholding. Note, however, Social Security and Medicare taxes do not apply to wages paid to share farmers or to alien workers admitted under Section 101(a)(15) of the Immigration and Nationality Act on a temporary basis (H-2(A) workers). [IRC §§3121(b)(16) and (19), IRS *Circular A*, Pub. 51, §3, rev. Dec. 21, 2016.]

The deposit system of employment taxes for agricultural employers is determined on an annual rather than quarterly basis. However, the lookback period is the second calendar year preceding the current calendar year. [IRS *Circular A*, Pub. 51, §7, rev. Dec. 19, 2019.] For example, the lookback period for calendar year 2020 is calendar year 2018.

Agricultural employers are classified as either monthly or semi-weekly depositors based on an accumulated level of $50,000 or less during the base period.

For deposits made by EFTPS to be on time, a taxpayer must initiate the deposit by 8 p.m. Eastern time the day before the date a deposit is due. If a taxpayer uses a third party to make a deposit on its behalf, the third party may have different cutoff times. If a taxpayer fails to initiate a deposit transaction on EFTPS by 8 p.m. Eastern time the day before the date a deposit is due, the taxpayer can still make a deposit on time by using the Federal Tax Collection Service (FTCS). To learn more about the information one will need to provide to a financial institution to make a same-day wire payment, visit *www.irs.gov/SameDayWire.* [IRC §7502(e); IRS *Circular A*, Pub. 51, §7, p. 19, rev. Dec. 19, 2019.]

An agricultural employer may also be liable for self-employment taxes. See ¶411. Employers with both agricultural and nonagricultural workers will need to file special returns. See ¶223.4.

¶223.3   Returns of Employers of Domestic Workers

Individuals who pay $2,200 or more in cash wages to domestic workers in 2020 (see ¶309 for prior year thresholds) must report at the end of the year any FICA taxes due on Schedule H, to be filed with the employer's individual income tax return, Form 1040. [IRC §3510(a).] Employers will still need to file the annual W-2 for each domestic employee with the Social Security Administration. Form W-2 Copy A must be filed by the end of February of the year following the year of employment. Sole proprietors who employ both domestic and non-domestic workers may continue to report both types of workers on the employer's quarterly Form 941. Farm owners are no longer required to report domestic wages on their Form 943; they may use the same FICA form used by other employers of domestics.

An employer that expects to pay at least $2,200 to a domestic employee in 2020 should withhold 7.65% from each payment made to the employee, even if the employer is not sure that the $2,200 cash-payment test will be met for the year. If too little is withheld from a payment, the employer should correct the error by deducting it from a later payment. If too much is deducted or it becomes obvious that the $2,200 threshold will not be reached by the end of the year, the employer should repay the amount withheld. [IRC §3101.]

Estimate tax. Employers will need to estimate at the beginning of the year the total amount of FICA (as well as FUTA and federal income) taxes that will be owed on any domestic worker in his or her employ during the year and have this amount withheld from the employee's paycheck or added to the employer's quarterly estimated income tax payments. [IRC §§3510(a), 3510(b)(4).] The amount, which includes both the employer's half and the employee's half of the FICA tax, must be added to the amount withheld from the employee's paycheck or to the employer's quarterly estimated payments.

Voluntary withholding. Withholding of income taxes for domestic workers is done on the basis of a completely voluntary agreement between the worker and the employer. [IRC §3402(p).] Domestic workers may request voluntary withholding by filing a Form W-4, "Employee's Withholding Allowance Certificate," with the employer. Either party may end the agreement by letting the other know in writing. The agreement becomes effective when the employer accepts it by beginning the withholding. [Reg. §31.3402(p)-1; IRS Pub. 926, *Household Employer's Tax Guide*, p. 9, rev. Dec. 17, 2019.]

Tax agents for individuals employing home care providers. Any person, in addition to the actual employer, who pays or controls the payment of wages may obtain authorization to act as the agent of the employer for purposes of withholding income taxes and paying employment taxes. [IRC §3504.] To the extent that an agent is authorized to act on behalf of the employer, it is subject to all laws (including penalties) that apply to the employer. Thus, both the employer and the agent are liable for the employment tax and penalties related to the employer's employment tax obligations that the agent performs. [IRS Reg. 31.3504-1(a).] However, an agent is only liable for acts that the IRS has authorized the agent to perform on behalf of the employer. The agent is not liable for all of an employer's employment tax liabilities.

Home care services recipients. A home care services recipient may designate an agent to report, file and pay all employment taxes, including taxes imposed under the Federal Unemployment Tax Act (FUTA). [Reg. §31.3504-1(b).] Thus, an intermediary may file a single income tax, withholding FICA or FUTA return on behalf of multiple home care service recipients.

A home care services recipient is defined as an individual who is an enrolled participant in a program administered by a federal, state or local government agency that provides federal, state or local government funds to pay, in whole or in part, for the provision of home care services to individuals with physical, intellectual, or developmental disabilities. A participant qualifies as a home care recipient while enrolled in a program and until the end of the calendar year in which the participant ceases to be enrolled in the program. [Reg. §31.3504-1(b)(3).] However, services provided outside of a home care service recipient's private home may qualify as home care services, even if the services do not qualify as domestic services under Code Sec. 3121(a)(7), 3306(c), and 3401(a)(3).

File Form 2678. An employer must submit a properly executed Form 2678, Employer/Payer Appointment of Agent, to the person it wishes to appoint as agent, indicating the acts for which it seeks to appoint the agent and whether the agent will be appointed with regard to some or all of the employer's employees. If the employer anticipates paying any wages (such as taxable noncash fringe benefits or bonuses) to any of its employees, the employer must indicate on Form 2678 that the appointment of the agent is only for some of its employees. To accept the appointment, the agent files Form 2678 with the IRS as provided in the Form's instructions. If either the employer or the person the employer wishes to appoint as agent has not obtained an EIN prior to the filing of the Form 2678, the agent must include a properly executed Form SS-4, Application for Employer Identification Number, with the Form 2678 to request an EIN for the employer or agent as necessary. If the IRS approves the request, the IRS sends a letter of approval to the agent and the employer. [Rev. Proc. 2013-39, I.R.B. 2013-5, December 11, 2013.]

State agents. Special rules apply to a state or local government agency acting as a 3504 agent. A state agent may request authorization without filing Form 2678 on behalf of each home care service recipient for whom the state seeks to act. In lieu of Form 2678, the state agent may solicit approval by each recipient on the forms the individual must complete in order to enroll in the program administered by the state agent. However, each recipient must obtain an EIN so that the state agent can fulfill its reporting obligations to the IRS. [Rev. Proc. 2013-39.]

¶223.4   Employers of Both Agricultural and Nonagricultural Labor

If both agricultural labor, whose wages are reportable on Form 943, and nonagricultural labor, whose wages are reportable on Form 941 or Form 944, are employed, the taxes reportable on both returns are not combined for purposes of applying any of the deposit schedule rules. Separate tax forms must be used with each type of deposit. [IRS *Circular A*, Pub. 51, §7, p. 21, rev. Dec. 19, 2019.]

¶223.5   Timely Filing Requirement

In general, a return or petition, including a claim for credit or refund made on a late-filed original tax return, is filed on the day it is *received*. However, if the requirements of IRC §7502 are met (*i.e.*, the item is postmarked within the prescribed filing period, the postage is prepaid, the item is properly addressed, and the item is mailed within the United States), a return, petition, claim for credit or refund, or other document will be regarded as having been filed on the date it was *mailed*. [IRC §7502, Reg. §301.7502-1.]

In addition to the U. S. Postal Service, the IRS has designated specific private delivery services that can be relied on for purposes of the timely-mailing-is-timely-filing rule. Documents and payments sent by one of the specified services will be considered filed as of the date mailed. The rule applies only with respect to the specific types of delivery services listed. Go to *www.irs.gov/PDS* for a list of IRS-approved private delivery services. [IRS Notice 2016-30, May 2, 2016, IRB 2016-18.]

Electronic postmarks. The date of an electronic postmark, which is a record of the date and time that an authorized return transmitter receives the transmission of a document on the transmitter's host system, is the filing date so long as it is before the filing deadline. [Reg. §301.7502-1(d)(1).]

Proof of delivery: In the absence of direct proof of actual delivery, the exclusive means to establish prima facie evidence of the delivery of federal tax documents to the IRS and the United States Tax Court is to prove the use of registered or certified mail if mailed through the U.S. Postal Service, or to prove use of a designated private delivery service. No other evidence of a postmark or of mailing will be *prima facie* evidence of delivery or raise a presumption that the document was delivered. This rule is effective for all documents mailed after September 20, 2004. [IRS Reg. §301.7502-1, 76 Fed. Reg. 52561, Aug. 23, 2011.]

"Mailbox rule" vs. §7502: The U.S. Circuit Courts of Appeals have split over whether proof that a taxpayer has mailed a properly addressed and postaged document through the U.S. Postal Service before the filing deadline can establish that the document was timely filed when there is no direct proof that the document was postmarked on or before the filing deadline through the use of registered or certified mail. Prior to the enactment of Internal Revenue Code (IRC) §7502 in 1954, all documents mailed to the IRS were considered to have been filed at the time of actual receipt. The appellate courts have reached different conclusions over the question of whether IRC §7502 effectively repealed the presumption of delivery or whether the presumption of delivery continues to exist and is merely supplemented by a safe harbor provided by IRC §7502. The Eighth and Ninth Circuits which were joined by the Tenth Circuit, continue to presume that a properly mailed document was delivered in the normal course, even without the documentation that accompanies registered or certified mail, because Congress evidenced no intent to abolish the common law rule. On the other hand, in the Second and Sixth Circuits the only exceptions to the rule that filing occurs at delivery are if: (1) the IRS acknowledges receipt of the document with a postmark that is not later than the filing deadline or (2) the document is sent by registered mail and the date of registration, which is equated by IRC §7502 with the postmark date, is not later than the filing deadline. [*See, Est. of L.A. Wood v. Commr. of IRS.*, 909 F.2d 1155 (8th Cir. 1990), 90-2 USTC ¶50,488; *Anderson v. USA*, 966 F.2d 487 (9th Cir. 1992), 92-1 USTC ¶50,308; and *Sorrentino v. IRS*, 383 F.3d 1187 (10th Cir. 2004), 2004-2 USTC ¶50,372; and *see Deutsch v. Commr. IRS*, 599 F.2d 44 (2nd Cir. 1979), 79-1 USTC ¶9407; *Miller v. U.S*, 784 F.2d 728 (6th Cir. 1986), 86-1 USTC 9261; and *Surowka v. USA*, 909 F.2d 148 (6th Cir. 1990), 90-2 USTC 50,410.]

¶224   Self-Employment Tax Returns

Returns of individuals liable for the tax imposed by the Self-Employment Contributions Act are made as a part of the regular income tax return. See ¶413.

¶225   Information Returns

The Commissioner of Social Security (or the Secretary of the Railroad Retirement Board) is required to report to the Treasury (1) the aggregate amount of benefits paid with respect to any individual during any calendar year; (2) the aggregate amount of benefits repaid by the individual during the calendar year; (3) aggregate reductions in benefits otherwise payable due to the receipt of worker's compensation benefits; and (4) the name and address of the individual with respect to whom benefits are paid. Each individual receiving Social Security or railroad retirement benefits must be furnished with a written statement showing the aggregate amount of payments, repayments, and reductions made by the agency. [IRC §6050F.] Tip information returns may also be required. [IRC §6053(c).]

¶226   Extensions of Time

No extensions of time are granted for payment of the tax. [Reg. §31.6161(a)(1)-1.] However, extensions of time for filing returns are granted in limited circumstances. For example an extension is authorized for information returns of employers required to file monthly, but not beyond the last day of the calendar month in which the information return is due. An extension of up to 30 days may also be granted for filing copies of withholding statements (Form W-2) and the accompanying transmittal form (Form W-3) that constitute an information return. [Reg. §31.6081(a)-1.] Good cause must be shown.

¶227   Interest on Underpayments

If taxes are not paid to the District Director of Internal Revenue when due, or if an underpayment of tax is made, interest will accrue at a specified percentage per annum, as periodically adjusted, from the last date prescribed for payment (without regard to any extension of time) until the date when finally paid. [IRC §6601.] The interest on tax underpayments, compounded daily [IRC §6622], accrues at the rate of three percentage points above the federal short-term rate (rounded to the nearest full percentage point). The rates are determined during the first month of a calendar quarter and become effective for the following calendar quarter. Thus, for example, the rates that are determined during January are effective for the following April through June. For the quarter beginning January 1, 2020, the general interest rate is 5%.

The interest rate applicable to "large corporate underpayments" is five, rather than three, percentage points greater than the federal short-term rate. Thus, for the quarter beginning January 1, 2020, the interest rate for large corporate underpayments is 7%. The term "large corporate underpayment" means an underpayment exceeding $100,000 (excluding interest or penalties) by a C corporation. Interest accrues at this higher rate beginning on the 30th day after a taxpayer is sent a deficiency notice or a first letter of proposed deficiency allowing the taxpayer an opportunity for IRS administrative review.

[IRC §6621(c).] For recent quarters, the rates are:

Period:	General Rate:	Rate For Corporate Underpayments > $100,000:
Apr. 1, 1999—Mar. 31, 2000	8%	10%
Apr. 1, 2000—Mar. 31, 2001	9%	11%
Apr. 1, 2001—June 30, 2001	8%	10%
July 1, 2001—Dec. 31, 2001	7%	9%
Jan. 1, 2002—Dec. 31, 2002	6%	8%
Jan. 1, 2003—Sept. 30, 2003	5%	7%
Oct. 1, 2003—Mar. 31, 2004	4%	6%
Apr. 1, 2004—June 30, 2004	5%	7%
July 1, 2004—Sept. 30, 2004	4%	6%
Oct. 1, 2004—Mar. 31, 2005	5%	7%
Apr. 1, 2005—Sept. 30, 2005	6%	8%
Oct. 1, 2005—June 30, 2006	7%	9%
July 1, 2006—Dec. 31, 2007	8%	10%
Jan. 1, 2008—Mar. 31, 2008	7%	9%
Apr. 1, 2008—June 30, 2008	6%	8%
July 1, 2008—Sept. 30, 2008	5%	7%
Oct. 1, 2008—Dec. 31, 2008	6%	8%
Jan. 1, 2009—Mar. 31, 2009	5%	7%
Apr. 1, 2009—Dec. 31, 2010	4%	6%
Jan. 1, 2011—Mar. 31, 2011	3%	5%
Apr. 1, 2011—Sept. 30, 2011	4%	6%
Oct. 1, 2011—Mar. 31, 2013	3%	5%
Oct. 1, 2011—Mar. 31, 2014	3%	5%
Oct. 1, 2014—Mar. 31, 2015	3%	5%
Apr. 1, 2015—Mar. 31, 2016	3%	5%
Apr. 1, 2016—Mar. 31, 2017	4%	6%
Apr. 1, 2017—Mar. 31, 2018	4%	6%
Apr. 1, 2018—Dec. 31, 2018	5%	7%
Jan. 1, 2019—June 30, 2019	6%	8%
July 1, 2019—Mar. 31, 2020	5%	7%

[IRC §§6601, 6621; Rev. Rul. 2019-28, I.R.B. 2019-52.]

¶227.1   Penalties—Failure to Comply with Procedures

Any person who is required to collect, truthfully account for, and pay over any tax but fails to do so, or who willfully attempts in any manner to evade or defeat any such tax, is subject to a penalty equal to the total amount of tax payable. [IRC §6672(a); IRS Reg. §301.6672-1.] Collection can be stayed, however, if, within 30 days after the day demand for the penalty is made, the taxpayer (a) pays an amount which is not less than the minimum amount required to begin court proceedings, (b) files a claim for refund, and (c) furnishes a bond equal to one and one-half times the amount of the excess of the penalty assessed over the amount described in (a), above. [IRC §6672(c).]

Effective for tax years beginning in 2020, the penalty for failure to file an income tax return within 60 days (including extensions) of the prescribed date may not be less than $435 or 100% of the amount of tax shown on the return under a minimum penalty provision, unless such failure was due to reasonable cause. [IRC §6651(a).]

The penalty for failure to timely file returns required by other chapters of the Code, in the absence of a showing of reasonable cause, accrues at the rate of 5% per month up to an aggregate of 25% of the tax due. [IRC §6651(a)(1).]

The penalty for failure to pay any amount of tax shown (or required to be shown) on the return is 0.5% of the amount of tax due per month up to an aggregate of 25% of the tax due. The penalty, however, may be abated if the failure is due to reasonable cause and not willful neglect. [IRC §6651(a)(2), (3).] Note, the penalty is not deductible.

The penalty for failure to pay taxes increases from 0.5% to 1% per month (up to the 25% limit) if the taxpayer has been notified that the IRS will levy upon the taxpayer's assets to collect past due taxes. [IRC 6651(d).]

The penalty for underpayment of a mandatory deposit ranges from 2% if the underpayment is paid five days late to 10% if it is paid more than 15 days late, unless the taxpayer shows that the underpayment or overstatement was due to reasonable cause. [IRC §6656(a), (b).]

An employer that fails to pay over employee tax or income tax withheld from wages may be required to make special deposits and to file monthly tax returns. [IRC §7512(b); IRS Reg. §§31.6011(a)-5, 31.6071(a)-1(a)(2).]

In addition to the civil penalties, there are criminal penalties that may be imposed for the above actions. [IRC §§7201-7342.]

An employee's failure to report cash tips to the employer, as discussed at ¶204.1, will render the employee liable for the employee tax on such tips and for a penalty amount equal to 50% of the amount of employee tax due on such tips, unless the employee can show that such failure was due to reasonable cause and not to willful neglect. [Reg. §31.6652(c)-1(a).]

Suspension of reporting agents: An agent may be suspended from the reporting agent program if he or she fails to perform his or her authorized duties; submits payment information on behalf of taxpayers without authorization; fails to comply with the rules and regulations relating to reporting agents; fails to cooperate with the IRS's efforts to monitor agents and investigate abuse; or if the IRS receives significant complaints about the agent. [Rev. Proc. 2007-28, IRB 2007-25, June 18, 2007.]

Reliance on a third party does not establish reasonable cause for failure: Generally, a taxpayer will be excused for failing to timely pay taxes if the failure did not result from willful neglect and was due to reasonable cause. Willful neglect is a conscious, intentional failure or reckless indifference. Reasonable cause exists if the taxpayer exercised ordinary business care and prudence, but nevertheless was unable to pay within the prescribed time.

Employers should be cautioned that courts have held that reliance on an agent is not reasonable cause and does not excuse a taxpayer's failure to timely file a tax return. For example, a taxpayer utilized a payroll agent for its accounting needs, including the making of payroll taxes. However, that agent embezzled the money into a personal account while submitting documents to the taxpayer that reflected that the taxes were paid. In addressing whether the circumstances justified an employer's failure to file, the federal trial court noted that, while an employer may designate agents to pay payroll taxes, the form that the taxpayer uses to authorize an agent, specifically provides that the taxpayer is responsible to "ensure that all returns are filed and that deposits and payments are made." (23 U.S.C. 3504, Tax Form 8655, Reporting Agent Authorization). In rejecting the employer's position, the court distinguished the case from one where the failure to pay was caused by a company officer who had final control over the taxpayer's withholding responsibilities. These individuals are not supervised and thus their misconduct would disable the company from paying its taxes. [*Pediatric Affiliates, P.A. v. U.S.*, 2006-1 USTC ¶50,201 (DC N.J. 2006), *aff'd,* 230 Fed. Appx167 (3d Cir. 2007), 2007-1 USTC ¶50,477, UNEMPL. INS. REP. ¶14,018C.]

Notice requirements: The IRS is required to notify a taxpayer of its proposed assessment of the trust fund recovery penalty. The "trust fund recovery penalty" refers to assessments made against any person required to collect, truthfully account for and pay over any tax imposed by the Internal Revenue Code who willfully fails to collect, or truthfully account for and pay over the tax, or who willfully attempts in any manner to evade or defeat the tax. See ¶227.2 regarding the term "person." The IRS must include on each penalty notice the name of the penalty, the Code section that authorizes the penalty, and the computation that results in the penalty. (A similar requirement will also apply to notices of interest assessments.) The notice must provide the taxpayer with the opportunity to (1) sign a form agreeing to the proposed assessment, or (2) appeal the proposed assessment within 60 days of the date on the notice (75 days if the notice is addressed to a taxpayer outside the United States). If the taxpayer fails to sign an agreement form or appeal the proposed assessment, the IRS will assess the penalty. [Rev. Proc. 2005-34, June 13, 2005.] Also, a penalty will not be imposed without supervisory approval unless the penalty is for a failure to file or pay tax under IRC §6651, a failure to pay estimated tax, or any other penalty that is automatically computed. [IRC §6751.]

An employer's failure to actually receive notice of the intent of the IRS to assess a penalty will not relieve an employer of liability where the IRS sends notice by certified letter to the employer's last known address and the letter is returned to the IRS undelivered and marked "unclaimed." [*M.M. Mason v. Commissioner*, 132 T.C. No. 14, CCH Dec. ¶57,807 (May 6, 2009).]

Appeal procedures: A taxpayer may appeal a proposed assessment of $25,000 or less by submitting two copies of a written appeal request that includes: (1)

a copy of the proposed assessment, or the date and number of the notice, and the taxpayer's name and Social Security number (and any other information that would assist the IRS in locating the correct file); (2) a statement that the taxpayer is requesting an Appeals conference; and (3) a list of the issues the taxpayer is contesting and an explanation of the basis for the taxpayer's disagreement. More formal appeal procedures apply to proposed assessments exceeding $25,000. In this situation, taxpayers must submit a formal written request that includes the information described above and the tax periods involved, a list of the findings the taxpayer is contesting and a statement of facts. The formal written request must be signed under penalty of perjury. A taxpayer may represent himself/herself at the Appeals conference or be represented by an individual authorized to represent taxpayers under Circular 230. If an authorized representative attends the Appeals conference without the taxpayer, then the representative must have power of attorney. [Rev. Proc. 2005-34, June 13, 2005.]

Limitations period: Generally, the IRS has three years to make an assessment after a return has been filed. A taxpayer may agree to extend the period of assessment, and this waiver can be valid even if it is executed outside of the original three-year assessment period. Thus, where the IRS issues a notice of proposed assessment which automatically extends the three-year statute of limitations for an additional 90 days, an agreement made with a taxpayer during that time is valid and enforceable. [IRS Chief Counsel Advice 200637001, May 31, 2006.]

In addition, there are many exceptions to the three-year limitations period. [IRC §6501(a).] In the case of a fraudulent return, tax may be assessed at any time. Tax may also be assessed at any time in the case of a willful attempt to evade taxation and if a return is required but not filed. [IRC §6501(c).] According to the IRS Chief Counsel, the open assessment periods under IRC §6501(c) also apply to trust fund recovery penalty cases in cases where the same circumstances of fraud, tax evasion and failure to file exist. Where the statute of limitations on assessment is open indefinitely as to the employer's employment tax liability under Code Sections 6501(c)(1), (2) or (3), the responsible person is likewise subject to the same unlimited period of limitations for assessment of the trust fund recovery penalty. The trust fund recovery penalty does not create a liability that is separate and distinct from the underlying employment tax liability. Therefore, if the statute of limitations on assessment of the employment tax is still open because of fraud, the statute of limitations for the trust fund recovery penalty is also open. The same is true if the statute of limitations on assessment of the employment tax is still open because of willful attempt to evade tax or failure to file a return. It does not matter if the fraud, willful attempt to evade tax or failure to file is the fault of the employer, the responsible person, or the return preparer. In addition, the focus of the exceptions under Code Sec. 6501(c) is the filing or non-filing of the return and not who was responsible for the filing or non-filing. [IRS Chief Counsel Advice 200532046, June 30, 2005; *Allen v. IRS*, 128 TC 37 (2007).]

The statute of limitations on assessments of the penalty does not expire before the later of (1) 90 days after the date on which the notice was mailed (or delivered in person), or (2) 30 days after the IRS makes a final administrative determination on the protest if there is a timely protest of the proposed assessment. Within the 30-day period between notice and assessment, a stay on collection will be issued provided the taxpayer posts a bond equal to one and one-half times the amount of the claimed penalty, pays the minimum amount required to commence a court proceeding on the penalty and files a claim for refund of that amount. [Rev. Proc. 2005-34, June 13, 2005.]

Mitigation of penalty: The IRS automatically applies deposits to the most recent period to which the deposit relates, unless, within 90 days of the date of the penalty notice, the taxpayer requests otherwise by calling the toll-free number shown on the penalty notice or writing (including a revised schedule of deposits) to the Accounts Management Unit at the address of the IRS's Account Management site shown on the penalty notice. This avoids the phenomenon of "cascading penalties" in which, in the event of a missed or underdeposit, later timely deposits are applied to an earlier missed deposit, causing shortfalls for the later deposits. [IRC §6656(e); Rev. Proc. 2001-58, Dec. 10, 2001.]

Waiver of penalties for first-time depositors: The IRS will waive the penalty for failure to deposit employment taxes if (1) the failure was inadvertent; (2) the employer meets the net worth requirements for awards of attorney's fees ($2 million for individuals and $7 million for corporations); (3) the failure occurred either (a) during the first quarter that the employer was required to deposit any employment tax or (b) with respect to the first deposit a taxpayer is required to make after the taxpayer is required to change its frequency of payroll deposits; and (4) the employment tax return was filed on or before the due date. [IRC §6656(c).]

¶227.2   Responsible Person

In order to establish liability under IRC §6672, the government must show that a responsible person has willfully failed to collect and/or pay over withholding taxes. The withheld sums are commonly referred to as "trust fund taxes" and refer only to the amounts that an employer is required to withhold from its employees. The penalty may be assessed against the employer, but it is most often levied on at least one "responsible person," usually an individual within the organization who had the authority to pay over the withheld taxes. In a typical situation, a struggling business that has fallen behind in its bills pays other creditors before the IRS to assure a continued supply of needed goods and services. Those responsible for paying the bills may hope that, by the time the IRS catches up with the delinquency, the business will again have sufficient funds to satisfy employment tax liabilities. Alternatively, such persons may hope that, if the business goes bankrupt, the employment tax debt will be discharged. In fact, the business's liabilities gain a measure of priority in bankruptcy (11 U.S.C. §507 and §724(b)), and the persons responsible for paying business creditors in preference to the government may be personally liable for 100% of the unpaid trust fund taxes. Furthermore, this personal liability is neither dischargeable in bankruptcy nor deductible as a business expense or bad debt. However, for penalties assessed after July 30, 1996, a responsible person who pays the penalty has a right of contribution against other responsible persons. [IRC §6672(d).]

The personal liability created under Code §6672 is separate and distinct from that imposed upon the employer corporation, and the government need not attempt to collect from the corporation before making an assessment against an officer thereof. [*Datlof v. U.S.*, 370 F.2d 655 (3d Cir. 1966); cert. den., 387 U.S. 906 (1967).] Given a broad interpretation by the courts, the term "responsible person" may include an individual who possesses the actual or effective power to pay taxes, the ultimate authority for payment decisions, the authority to direct payment of creditors, or significant control over the business entity's general finances or decision making. Corporate officers are generally regarded as responsible persons, unless they can show otherwise.

Liability for the 100% penalty arises only if the responsible person's failure to collect, account for, and pay over trust fund taxes was "willful." It has been held, however, that a responsible person does not violate §6672 by willfully using employer funds for purposes other than satisfaction of the trust fund tax claims of the United States when at the time the individual assumed control there were no funds with which to satisfy the tax obligation and the funds thereafter generated are not directly traceable to collected taxes referred to by the Code. [*Slodov v. U.S.*, 436 U.S. 238 (1978).]

A determination of responsible person status does not depend upon exclusive authority or control over the entity's financial affairs. Instead, *significant* authority or control shared with others is sufficient to confer responsible person status. [*Barnett v. IRS*, 988 F.2d 1449 (5th Cir. 1993), 93-1 USTC ¶50,269, and *Finley v. USA*, DC Kan., 839 F.Supp. 1484 (1994), 94-1 USTC ¶50,012.] Thus, there may be more than one responsible person for any quarter. The primary factors considered in determining responsibility is the control of funds, the authority to sign or co-sign checks and the actual signing or co-signing of checks. Delegation of the authority to sign checks or to pay employment taxes seldom relieves a responsible person from liability for the trust fund recovery penalty. However, the fact that an employee has signed or co-signed a check does not in itself establish responsibility.

Responsibility is also examined in terms of management authority or the extent to which an individual participated in the day-to-day control of the business. Thus, a spouse was liable, as a company's sole shareholder and chairman, for a trust fund recovery penalty, even though she had delegated authority for day-to-day operations, to her husband. The wife had effective control of the company and retained the nondelegable duty to maintain the company's finances. [*Johnson v. United States*, (4th Cir 2013), No. 12-1739, Unempl. Ins. Reptr ¶15,189C.] Similarly, former corporate officers were found to be responsible persons where the former CEO was deeply involved in the day-to-day management of the corporation, was a signatory on the bank accounts, regularly signed checks, and was authorized to sign financial obligations up to $100,000 without a second signature. Likewise, the former CFO was a signatory on two of the corporation's principal accounts, had check-signing authority up to $75,000 without a second signature, and had access to all the corporation's financial records. Moreover, he decided which outstanding bills to pay. The status of the former corporate officers demonstrated that they were both responsible persons during the relevant time period. [*Schiffmann v. United States,* (1st Cir 2016), No. 14-2179, Unempl. Ins. Reptr ¶15,468C.] By contrast, an officer-stockholder with check signing authority who was not involved in the daily operations of the corporation and did not make decisions regarding the disbursement of funds and payment of creditors was not a responsible person. [*Pototzky v. U.S.*, 8 Cls Ct 308 (1985), 85-1 USTC ¶9438.] Neither was a chief financial officer of a bankrupt company a responsible person where, even though he had check-signing authority, the company's president maintained absolute control of all finances of the employer. [*J.D. Salzillo v. U.S.*, FedCl, 2005-1 USTC ¶50,324.]

Even where a clerk fails to mail checks that a CEO regularly signed and gave to the clerk, a CEO is not necessarily liable where "wilfulness" cannot be shown. In one decision, a court found that this set of facts evidenced that the CEO either considered the taxes to be paid or, at worst, was negligent in failing to realize that the payroll clerk was not mailing the checks. In either case, his behavior may have been negligent, but did not rise to the level of willful. "Willfulness" requires a showing that the responsible person clearly ought to have known of a grave risk that the withholding taxes were not being paid, the court observed. [*Kilraine v. U.S.A.*, D. N.J., 2010-1 USTC ¶50,196, Unempl. Ins. Reptr ¶14,499C.]

Note, however, a member (or the chairperson) of an organization's board of directors can be held responsible for employment taxes, even though he or she was not an officer or high-ranking employee and did not manage the organization's day-to-day operations. In 2009, an appellate court affirmed a decision by a federal district court upholding the responsible person status of a hospital's board chairperson under IRC § 6672. Since the individual willfully failed to account for over $400,000 of the hospital's unpaid employment taxes, he was liable for the trust fund recovery penalty. The district court cited a number of factors showing willfulness: (1) the taxpayer was aware of the hospital's recent failure to pay the taxes and the hospital's deteriorating finances, but took no steps to guard against future nonpayment; (2) he knew or should have known that the hospital was not current on its obligations in the last half of 2001; (3) he implemented financial controls over his personal financial affairs but neglected to exercise such care with respect to the hospital; and (4) he did not qualify for the exception for voluntary board members of tax-exempt organizations, as he was not serving solely in an honorary capacity, and he played an active role in the management of the hospital. The Fifth Circuit looked at both the individual's activities and authority as a board member in upholding the determination of responsible person status. [*Verret v. United States of America*, 312 Fed. Appx. 615 (5th Cir. 2009), 2009-1 USTC ¶50,248.]

A stay of collection of the 100% penalty may be granted if within 30 days after notice and demand of such penalty against any person, such person (1) pays at least the minimum amount required to commence a court proceeding with respect to liability for the penalty, (2) files a claim for refund of the amount so paid, and (3) furnishes a bond which meets requirements prescribed by regulations of the Secretary of the Treasury. Note that, in addition to this so-called "100% penalty," IRC §7201, §7202, and §7203 contain criminal penalties for willful attempts to evade or defeat tax, willful failures to collect, account for, or pay over tax, and willful failures to file returns, supply information, or pay tax.

Statute of limitations: A person responsible for paying employment taxes is subject to the same assessment period that applies to his or her employer's return. See ¶227.1.

Professional Employment Organizations: The IRS has ruled that it can assert the trust fund recovery penalty for failure to pay employment taxes against an officer of a professional employment organization (PEO) that failed to remit its clients' taxes to the IRS when the PEO filed the clients' employment tax returns under the PEO's name. Small businesses often contract with employee leasing companies (also known as PEOs) to ensure compliance with workplace laws. In a typical contract between a PEO and business, the PEO becomes the "co-employer" of the businesses' employees. Courts have held that an officer of a PEO can be liable for the trust fund recovery penalty for failure to remit its clients' employment taxes for leased employees (see *P. Thosteson v. United States*, CA-11, 2002-2 USTC ¶50,649). Thus, if the courts can rule that a PEO can be the employer of leased employees for payroll purposes, they will likely uphold the penalty against an officer of a PEO that self-assesses a clients' employment tax liabilities against itself. [CCA 200916024.]

Partners and partnership liability: A partnership's delegation of responsibility to an employee who is hired to perform all bookkeeping and tax functions does not constitute reasonable cause to abate the penalty assessments. [*McGrath v. USA*, D. DC, Ore., 2004-2 USTC ¶50,409.] Note that the individual liability of partners under IRC §6672 for partnership debts does not apparently require the IRS to separately assess individual partners in order to collect partnership debts from them within the 10-years period allowed for collection after assessment. So long as proper assessment is made against the partnership, that will suffice to extend the 10-years limitations period for collection against individual partners. [*U.S. v. Abel Cosmo Galletti, et al.*, USSCt, 124 SCt 1548 (2004).]

Limited liability companies: The IRS has ruled that if members of the Limited Liability Company (LLC) are not liable for the LLC's debts under state law, then despite the classification of an LLC as a partnership for federal tax purposes, it cannot collect the LLC's federal employment tax liabilities from the LLC's members as if they were general partners of a partnership. For federal tax purposes, a multi-member domestic LLC is an eligible entity that is classified by default as a partnership under IRS Reg. §301.7701-1. According to the laws of those states that permit LLCs, members of an LLC are generally not liable for the LLC's debts, with some exceptions. Because members of an LLC generally are not liable for the LLC's debts, the IRS cannot levy upon LLC member's property or rights to property. However, special circumstances, such as a fraudulent transfer of assets from the LLC to its members, might cause a change in treatment and expose the members to liability. [Rev. Rul. 2004-41, I.R.B. 2004-18, 845, May 3, 2004.]

Note that the owner of a single-member LLC will not be held liable for employment taxes from the LLC's previous multi-member existence. The LLC itself, however, remains liable for the unpaid taxes, and its property is subject to levy. [Field Attorney Advice (FAA) 200093701F, Sept. 17, 2009.]

Disregarded entities: Disregarded entities must pay their own employment taxes and file tax reports. As such, these entities will need an employer identification number (EIN). In effect, the disregarded entity (such as a single-member limited liability corporation disregarded as an entity separate from its owner or a qualified subchapter S corporation—"Q-Subs") is treated as a separate corporation for employment tax purposes, but continues to be treated as a disregarded entity for all other tax purposes. [IRS Reg. §301.7701-2(a); (c)(2)(iv) and (v).] See also ¶409.

Treating disregarded entities as a corporation for the purpose of employment taxes, however, effectively removed the operation of the family and religious FICA exception found in IRC §§ 3121(b)(3), 3127 and 3306(c)(5) when a disregarded entity is involved. Ordinarily, under these exceptions, payments for the services of a child under age 18 who works for his or her parent in a trade or business are not subject to Social Security and Medicare taxes if the trade or business is a sole proprietorship or a partnership in which each partner is a parent of the child. Additionally, service performed by an individual under the age of 21 employed by his father or mother, or performed by an individual employed by his spouse or son or daughter (subject to certain conditions) for domestic service in a private home of the employer is not considered employment for FICA purposes. However, wages for all these services are subject to Social Security and Medicare if the family member works for a corporation, even if it is controlled by another otherwise qualifying member of the immediate family, *i.e.*, a parent, spouse, or child. Similarly, wages are not subject to Social Security tax when paid to an employee who is a member of a recognized religious group by an employer who is also a member of a recognized religious group opposed to participation in the Social Security Act. (The employer and the employee must have filed and had approved an application certifying that they are members of a qualifying religious sect though.) However, this exemption does not apply where the employer is a corporation. A 2011 rule change restored the operation of both the family member and religious group exemptions when disregarded entities are involved by stating that for the purpose of the exemptions the owner of a disregarded entity will be treated as the employer and the employee will be considered to be an employee of the owner. [IRS Reg. §§31.3121(b)(3)-1T(d), 31.3127-1T(c), 31.3306(c)(5)-1T(d), 301.7701-2T, as amended by *76 Fed. Reg.* 67363, November 1, 2011.]

¶227.3   Tax Debt Collections

Collections after assessment: The IRS generally has 10 years from the date of assessment to collect a tax liability. Extension agreements entered into after January 1, 2000, are allowed only if the agreement is executed at the time an installment agreement is entered into or prior to the release of a levy of the taxpayer's property if the release occurs after the expiration of the original period of limitations on collection. [IRS Restructuring and Reform Act of 1998 (P.L.105-296); Reg. §301.6502-1, as amended (Sept. 6, 2006).]

In cases where the IRS has imposed an assessment and then erroneously abated it, the assessment will be reinstated even after the statutory period ended if the taxpayer fails to show reasonable and detrimental reliance on the erroneous abatement. In a representative case, a taxpayer paid part of an assessment, but through a clerical error, the form was processed as if the entire payment had been made. The taxpayer was orally informed of the mistake before the three-year period had run and could not show evidence of detrimental reliance on the abatement. [*Stuart Becker v. IRS*, 407 F.3d 89 (2nd Cir. 2005), 2005-1 U.S.T.C. ¶50,337.] Another court reached a similar result, finding that "an unauthorized and accidental abatement of an entire assessment in contravention of section 6404(a)(1) is not effective." [*Bugge v. U.S.*, 99 F.3d 740 (5th Cir. 1996), 96-2 U.S.T.C. ¶ 50,629.]

CDPs and DETLs: Ordinarily, no levy may be made on any property or right to property of any person unless the IRS has notified the person in writing of the right to a collection due process (CDP) hearing before the levy is made. [IRC §6330; Reg. §301.6330-1(a)(1).] However, taxpayers are not entitled to a pre-levy CDP notice or hearing for levies issued after September 22, 2007, if the IRS serves a disqualified employment tax levy. A disqualified employment tax levy (DETL) is a levy to collect an employment tax liability owed by a taxpayer (or predecessor) if the taxpayer (or predecessor) had previously requested a collection due process (CDP) hearing under IRC §6330 for unpaid employment taxes arising in the two-year period before the period for which the DETL is served. A taxpayer subject to a DETL must have an opportunity for a post-levy CDP hearing within a reasonable time after the levy. The taxpayer may also seek judicial review in the Tax Court of a CDP determination resulting from a post-levy hearing under IRC §6330(f). [IRC §6330(f) and (h); Reg. §301.6330-1(a)(2).] Neither the statute nor the procedures define a "reasonable time" for holding the post-levy hearing.

In the event that a collection agency purporting to be representing the IRS in a tax collection matter contacts a taxpayer concerning a federal tax debt, the taxpayer should notify the Treasury Inspector General for Tax Administration (TIGTA) immediately by calling toll free: 1-800-366-4484.

¶228   Correcting Mistakes on Tax Returns

Errors in Social Security taxes reported on an earlier return or errors in credits for overpayments of penalty or interest paid on tax for an earlier quarter may generally be corrected with the 94X series of forms, 941X, 943X, and 944X. (See ¶229 for further discussion about the changes.) Each form corresponds to, and relates line-by-line with, the employment tax return it is correcting. For example, an employer that discovers an underpayment or overpayment error on a previously filed Form 941, Employer's Quarterly Federal Tax Return, will use Form 941X, Adjusted Employer's Quarterly Federal Tax Return or Claim for Refund, to make a correction. Unlike the Form 941c, Supporting Statement to Correct Information, that was previously used, each new dual-purpose form will stand alone and will not need to be attached to an employment tax return. Employers and payers can file the "X" form as soon as they discover an error, rather than having to wait to file it with the next employment tax return that is due. Form 941c is now obsolete.

If, in any quarter, more than the correct amount of tax is deducted from any wage payment, the overcollection should be repaid to the employee. The employer must obtain and keep as part of his or her records a written receipt from the employee showing the date and amount of the repayment. Every overcollection not repaid and receipted for by the employee must be reported and paid to the IRS on the return for the return period in which the overcollection is made. [Reg. §31.6413(a)-1.]

Process for 941-X

Form 941-X must be used to correct errors on a previously filed Form 941. A separate Form 941-X must be filed for each Form 941 that is being corrected. Unlike Form 941c, Form 941-X must be filed separately. Form 941 no longer provides adjustment lines for correcting prior quarter errors. However, current quarter adjustments may still be reported on Form 941. Form 941-X is used to report errors in reported wages, tips, and other compensation; income tax withheld from wages, tips, and other compensation; taxable Social Security and Medicare wages and tips; and advance earned income credit payments made to employees.

Due Dates: The due date is dependent on the type of error and whether a credit or claim is being made in the case of overreported tax. For purposes of the period of limitations, Forms 941 for a calendar year are considered filed on April 15 of the succeeding year if filed before that date.

- *Underreported tax:* File Form 941 by the due date of the return for the return period in which the error was discovered and pay the amount owed when filing. Doing so will generally ensure that the correction is interest free and not subject to failure-to-pay penalties. For each of the four quarterly return periods, the due dates are April 30, July 31, October 31, and January 31, respectively. An employer may correct underreported taxes on a previously filed Form 941 if it files Form 941-X within three years of the date the Form 941 was filed.

- *Overreported tax—credit:* If tax is overreported, and an employer chooses to apply the credit to Form 941, the employer should file Form 941-X soon after the error is discovered but more than 90 days before the period of limitations on credit or refund for Form 941 expires. That period is within three years of the date Form 941 was filed or two years from the date the tax was paid as reported on Form 941, whichever is later. The IRS urges employers that wish to make an overreporting adjustment to correct the overreported amount in the first two months of a quarter. This will ensure that the IRS has sufficient time to process and post the credit before Form 941 is filed for that quarter and avoid receipt of an erroneous balance due notice from the IRS.

> **Example:** ABC filed and paid its 2010 fourth quarter Form 941 on January 31, 2011. On January 2, 2014, ABC discovers that it overreported tax on the 2010 fourth quarter Form 941. ABC files Form 941-X on January 13, 2014. The IRS treats the credit as a tax deposit made on January 1, 2014. When the 2014 first quarter Form 941 is filed, the amount from Form 941-X should be reported on your first quarter Form 941.

- *Overreported tax—claim:* An employer that overreports tax, may choose to file a claim for refund or abatement on Form 941-X any time before the period of limitations on credit or refund expires. Only the claims process can be used to correct overreported amounts in the last 90 days of a period of limitations. (If the employer needs to correct any underreported amounts, it must file another Form 941-X reporting only corrections to the underreported amounts.)

> **Example:** Ed files the 2013 fourth quarter Form 941 on January 27, 2014, and payments were timely made. The IRS treats the return as if it were filed on April 15, 2014. On January 10, 2017, Ed discovers that he overreported Social Security and Medicare wages on that form by $350. To correct the error Ed must file Form 941-X by April 18, 2017, which is the end of the period of limitations, and use the claim process.

If you discovered an error on or before December 31, 2008, but did not report it as a line adjustment on Form 941 for any quarter ended before 2009 and did not file a claim (Form 843), you may use Form 941-X to correct the error. File Form 941-X for the quarter in which you made the error. [Instructions, Form 941-X, rev. Apr. 24, 2017.]

IRS Revenue Ruling 2009-39 (IRB 2009-52, Dec. 10, 2009) reviews ten different situations in which errors occurred and explains how corrections should be made. The situations reviewed are the following:

- Underpayment of FICA tax and income tax withholding when the error is not ascertained in the year the wages were paid;
- Overpayment of income tax withholding when the error is ascertained in the same year the wages were paid;

- Both an overpayment and an underpayment of FICA tax for the same tax period;
- Underpayment of FICA tax when the employer's filing requirement has changed;
- Underpayment of FICA tax due to failure to treat workers as employees;
- Overpayment of FICA tax on wages paid to a household employee;
- Overpayment of FICA tax when the error is ascertained close to the expiration of the period of limitations on credit or refund;
- Underpayment of FICA tax and income tax withholding ascertained in the course of an employment tax examination; and
- Underpayment of FICA tax and income tax withholding ascertained in the course of the appeals process.

> **Example:** ABC Co. timely filed its 2014 fourth quarter Form 941 on January 10, 2015, and timely paid all employment tax reported on the return. On February 9, 2015, ABC Co. ascertains that it underwithheld and underpaid FICA tax and income tax with respect to its employees' wages in the fourth quarter. ABC Co. now must file Form 941-X by the due date of the return for the return period in which it ascertained the error and pay the amount owed by the time it files Form 941-X for an interest-free adjustment.

Where to file

A claim for credit or refund needs to be filed with the IRS Service Center serving the Internal Revenue District in which the tax was paid. Regulations clarify that taxpayers should file a claim for credit or refund with the same IRS Service Center where the taxpayer files a return for the type of tax to which the claim relates. Claims for refunds or credits should not be filed at a different location where the tax was paid or was required to have been paid. Additionally, note that when filing a claim for employment taxes, a separate claim must be made for each tax period. [IRS Reg. §301.6402-2(a)(2), 80 *Fed. Reg.* 43949, July 24, 2015.]

¶229 Employers' Refunds and Adjustments

An employer that makes, or has made, an undercollection or underpayment of employment taxes must correct the error by reporting an adjustment. An employer that pays more than the correct amount of an employee or employer tax may file a claim for refund of the overpayment, or may claim credit for such overpayment.

Adjustment of underpayments: If an employer collects less than the correct amount of employee FICA or RRTA (Railroad Retirement Tax Act) tax from an employee and the employer discovers the error *before filing the return* on which the tax is required to be reported, the employer must report on the return and pay to the IRS the correct amount of tax. If the employer, under these circumstances fails to report the correct amount of tax, the employer will not be allowed to later correct the error through an interest-free adjustment. [Reg. 31.6205-1(b)(1).]

If a return is filed and less than the correct amount of FICA tax or RRTA tax is reported, and the employer discovers the error *after filing the return*, the employer may adjust the resulting underpayment of tax by reporting the additional amount due on an adjusted return for the return period in which the compensation was paid. The adjustment must be made by the due date of the return for the return period in which the error was discovered and the amount of the underpayment must be paid by the time the adjustment is made, or interest will begin to accrue from that date. An underpayment adjustment may only be made within the period of limitations for assessment—three years, three months, and fifteen days after the calendar year for which the return was filed (see ¶228 regarding the limitations period). [Reg. 31.6205-1(b)(2).]

Employer responsible for underpayment: If no tax, or less than the correct amount of tax (other than the tax on tips), is deducted from any wage payment, the employer is authorized to deduct the amount of the undercollection from later payments to the employee. However, the employer is liable for any underpayment. Reimbursement is a matter for settlement between the employer and the employee. [Reg. §31.6205-1(d).]

Note that an accuracy-related penalty does not preclude interest-free adjustment for underpayment of employment taxes. [Chief Counsel Advice 200846022.]

Overpayments: If an employer discovers an overpayment error within the applicable period of limitations on credit/refund, the employer is required to reimburse its employees for their portion of the over-collected FICA or RRTA tax prior to the expiration of the applicable period of limitations on credit or refund. If the overpayment is discovered during the return period in which the overpayment was made, the employer must repay the employee within that period. In this circumstance, the employer should not report on any return or pay to the IRS the amount of the overcollection. However, if the overpayment is discovered after the return is filed, the employer has until the expiration of the limitations period to repay the employee, but only if the employer is able to locate the employee with reasonable effort. In all instances where repayment is made, the employer is required to obtain a receipt from the employee showing the date and the amount of payment.

Where an employer cannot locate an employee, after reasonable efforts, the reimbursement requirement does not apply and the employer may make an interest-free adjustment for only its portion of FICA or RRTA tax. The adjustment will be permitted if the overpayment is reported on an adjusted return filed before the 90th day prior to expiration of the period of limitations on credit or refund. The adjustment may not be made once a claim for refund has been filed. [Reg. §31.6413(a)-1(a) (repayments to employees) and §31.6413(a)-2(a) (adjustment of overpayments).]

Employer refunds: Instead of making an interest-free adjustment for an overpayment, employers may file a claim for refund under IRC §6402 on Form 843 for the amount of overpaid FICA and RRTA taxes. An employer must certify as part of the refund claim process that it has reimbursed the employee for his or her share of FICA or RRTA tax or has secured the written consent of the employee to allowance of the refund or credit. [Reg. §31.6402(a)-2.]

The IRS explains that Code Sec. 6402(a) authorizes the credit of overpaid tax against any tax liability "on the part of the person who made the overpayment." Accordingly, if an employer has separate tax liability, unrelated to the employee for whom it was claiming a refund of overpaid FICA taxes, the employee's refund may not be used to offset the employer's tax liability. [IRS Chief Counsel Advice Memorandum 201307006.] In the event such an offset did occur, the IRS will reverse the overpayment credit with respect to the employee's share of the refund.

The IRS released guidance to employers on the requirements for employee consents used by an employer to support a claim for refund of over-collected Social Security and Medicare taxes. The notice and proposed revenue procedure clarify the basic requirements for a request for a consent and for the employee consent itself, and permits a consent to be requested, furnished, and retained in an electronic format as an alternative to a paper format. The notice also contains guidance concerning what constitutes "reasonable efforts" if a consent is not secured to permit the employer to claim a refund of the employer share of over-collected Social Security and Medicare taxes. [IRS Notice 2015-15, I.R.B. 2015-9, February 13, 2015.]

Payment of advance earned income credits: In the case of employers paying advance earned income credits to eligible employees, payment is credited on a dollar-for-dollar basis against the employer's liability for income tax withholding and FICA taxes. For eligible employees subject to income tax withholding, the advance payment is based on the amount of wages subject to withholding; for employees not subject to withholding, but subject to FICA taxes, the payment is based on the amount of wages subject to FICA taxes (see ¶208). If advance payments exceed the employer's liability for the payroll period, the employer may either ratably reduce each advance amount paid or elect to pay the full advance amounts, with the excess amount treated as an advance payment of the employer's liability for income tax withholding, employee FICA taxes and employer FICA taxes, in that order of priority. The employer takes any advance earned income amounts into account on its Form 941, or 943. For details concerning earned income credits, see CCH's STANDARD FEDERAL TAX REPORTS and PAYROLL MANAGEMENT GUIDE.

Credit for repayment of tax: In lieu of refunding an overpayment of tax under the Federal Insurance Contributions Act, a District Director may, in his or her discretion, credit the overpayment against any other tax due from the taxpayer. [Reg. §301.6402-1.] Overpayments may also be credited against past-due child support, past-due, legally enforceable debt owed to a federal agency, future liability for federal tax, and, beginning in the year 2000, past-due legally enforceable state income tax debt. [IRC §6402(e)-(k).]

Several employers have tried to argue that payroll tax payments become overpayments merely because the IRS failed to assess liability until after the statute of limitations expired. However, appeals courts have rejected this argument. For examples, the Eleventh Circuit has held that a late assessment of taxes, properly paid within the statutory period for assessment, does not create an overpayment. [*Williams-Russell & Johnson, Inc. v. USA*, 371 F.3d 1350, 2004-1 USTC ¶50,266.]

¶230   Employees' Refunds

An employee may file a claim for refund or credit of an overpayment of Social Security and hospital insurance taxes if: (1) the employer collects more than the correct amount from the employee and pays it to the District Director of Internal Revenue, (2) the employee has not claimed reimbursement through credit against, or refund of, income tax, and (3) the employee does not receive reimbursement in any manner from the employer and does not authorize the employer to file a claim and receive refund or credit. [Reg. §31.6402(a)-2(b).] The employee may file a claim for a refund of the overpayment on Form 943.

Overpayment from work for multiple employers. Since, generally, each employer is required to deduct employee taxes on a specifically limited amount (see ¶208) of wages paid to an employee, an employee may in some cases pay taxes on more than the amount of remuneration subject to the taxes. An employee who has paid taxes on wages over the taxable limit because he or she worked for *more than one* employer during a calendar year is entitled to a "special refund" of the overpayment. [Reg. §31.6413(c)-1.]

The amount of the special refund to which an employee is entitled with respect to a year should be credited against the employee's federal income tax for that year. If the amount of such special refund when added to amounts deducted and withheld as income tax exceeds the total taxes due, the amount of the excess constitutes an overpayment of income tax. Thus, the Social

Security and hospital insurance taxes to be refunded are treated as an over-payment of income tax. [Reg. §31.6413(c)-1.]

Note, if the employee is not required to file an income tax return, a claim for refund should be filed on Form 843. However, the excess amount should be reported on Line 69 of Form 1040 or Line 41 of Form 104A.

The provision allowing employees to credit these overpayments against their income tax applies only to those cases where the overpayment was caused by an employee having worked for more than one employer during the calendar year. Other overpayments by an employee may not be credited against his or her federal income tax. [Reg. §31.6413(c)-1.] That is, if an employee works for only one employer in a given year, and more than the maximum Social Security tax is withheld from the employee's wages, the excess may not be claimed as a credit against the employee's income tax. An adjustment in such cases should be obtained from the employer. [IRS Pub. 505 §3, *Excess Social Security or RR Retirement Tax Withholding.*]

Refunds of self-employment tax. Refunds of self-employment tax may be offset with un-assessed employment taxes, but only with respect to the employee portion of the employment taxes. [IRS Chief Counsel Advice Memorandum 201315023, March 7, 2013.] This situation typically arises when self-employed workers are reclassified as employees and seek the refund of self-employment taxes they have erroneously paid. Code Sec. 6521 authorizes the offset of refunds of self-employment tax. However, the offset is limited to the employee portion of the employment taxes. Thus, the IRS may offset a refund of self-employment tax only with the employee's portion of un-assessed employment taxes. [*Beane v. Commissioner*, TC.Memo 2009-152, CCH Dec. ¶57,870M.]

See ¶212 regarding refunds for taxes paid on unpaid benefits under a terminated deferred compensation plan.

¶231   Interest on Overpayments

In the case of an overpayment of taxes by *non-corporate* taxpayers, the amount of interest owed by the Treasury is equal to the federal short-term rate plus three percentage points. Prior to 1999, the rate had been equal to the federal short-term rate plus two percentage points. For amounts owed by the Treasury to corporate taxpayers, the spread above the short-term rate has not changed and remains at two percentage points.

Reduced rate for large corporate overpayments after 1994: The rate of interest paid by the IRS to corporate taxpayers on overpayments of tax is reduced to the sum of the federal short-term rate plus one-half of one percentage point for any portion of overpaid tax that exceeds $10,000. This rate is equal to 1½ percentage points below the standard overpayment rates. [IRC §6621(a)(1), as amended by P.L. 103-645, §713(a).]

For recent periods, the rates are:

Period:	General Rate:	Corporate Rate:	Rate for Corporate Overpayment > $10,000:
Apr. 1, 1999—Mar. 31, 2000	8%	7%	5.5%
Apr. 1, 2000—Mar. 31, 2001	9%	8%	6.5%
Apr. 1, 2001—June 30, 2001	8%	7%	5.5%
July 1, 2001—Dec. 31, 2001	7%	6%	4.5%
Jan. 1, 2002—Dec. 31, 2002	6%	5%	3.5%
Jan. 1, 2003—Sept. 30, 2003	5%	4%	2.5%
Oct. 1, 2003—Mar. 31, 2004	4%	3%	1.5%
Apr. 1, 2004—June 30, 2004	5%	4%	2.5%
July 1, 2004—Sept. 30, 2004	4%	3%	1.5%
Oct. 1, 2004—Mar. 31, 2005	5%	4%	2.5%
Apr. 1, 2005—Sept. 30, 2005	6%	5%	3.5%
Oct. 1, 2005—June 30, 2006	7%	6%	4.5%
July 1, 2006—Dec. 31, 2007	8%	7%	5.5%
Jan. 1, 2008—Mar. 31, 2008	7%	6%	4.5%
Apr. 1, 2008—June. 30, 2008	6%	5%	3.5%
July 1, 2008—Sept. 30, 2008	5%	4%	2.5%
Oct. 1, 2008—Dec. 31, 2008	6%	5%	3.5%
Jan. 1, 2009—Mar. 31, 2009	5%	4%	2.5%
Apr. 1, 2009—Dec. 31, 2010	4%	3%	1.5%
Jan. 1, 2011—Mar. 31, 2011	3%	2%	0.5%
Apr. 1, 2011—Sept. 30, 2011	4%	3%	1.5%
Oct. 1, 2011—Mar. 31, 2014	3%	2%	0.5%
Oct. 1, 2014—Mar. 31, 2016	3%	2%	0.5%
Apr. 1, 2016—Mar. 31, 2017	4%	3%	1.5%
Apr. 1, 2017—Mar. 31, 2018	4%	3%	1.5%
Apr. 1, 2018—Dec. 31, 2018	5%	4%	2.5%
Jan. 1, 2019—June 30, 2019	6%	5%	3.5%
July 1, 2019—Mar. 31, 2020	5%	4%	2.5%

[IRC §§6601, 6621; Rev. Rul. 2019-28, I.R.B. 2019-52.]

Interest netting: Prior to 1999, taxpayers had paid higher interest rates on tax underpayments than the IRS has paid on tax overpayments. Congress subsequently eliminated the interest differential, equalizing the interest rate for overpayments and underpayments for any period of mutual indebtedness between a taxpayer and the IRS. No interest will be imposed to the extent that underpayment and overpayment interest run simultaneously on equal amounts. [IRC §§6601(f), 6621(d), amended by the IRS Restructuring and Reform Act of 1998, §3301.]

Taxpayers should request the zero net interest rate or request that the IRS recalculate a rate computation. To request interest netting, a taxpayer must file IRS Form 843, Claim for Refund and Request for Abatement. The IRS advises taxpayers to label the top of the form "Request for Net Interest Rate of Zero Under Rev. Proc. 2000-26." Taxpayers should send Form 843 to the IRS Service Center where they filed their most recent income tax return.

On Form 843, a taxpayer must identify the taxable period for which it overpaid and underpaid its tax liability. More than one period may be identified on the same form. If the underpayment is satisfied, the taxpayer must identify when it paid the tax. Likewise, if the taxpayer received a refund, it must identify when it received the refund. Background information, such as copies of examination reports and notices, should be attached to the form. A taxpayer also must calculate, to the extent possible, the amount of interest to be credited, refunded or abated to generate a net interest rate of zero for the periods of overlap.

Federal Income Taxability of Benefits

¶250   Income Tax on Social Security Benefits

Social Security benefits may be taxable. The extent to which Social Security benefits are subject to tax is a function of a recipient's total income and marital status. Generally, however, if a recipient's only income consists of Social Security benefits, the benefits will not be taxable and the recipient will not be required to file a federal income tax return. In addition, most people affected by the tax will not pay tax on more than 50% of their benefits, although some individuals may be subject to a tax on 85% of their benefits.

In determining whether benefits (as reflected on Form SSA-1099) are taxable, a recipient will need to compare the base amount (see below) for the recipient's filing status with the total of:

1.   one-half of the benefits, plus

2.   all non-Social Security incomes (*e.g.*, wages, income from self-employment, tax exempt interest, dividends) and other exclusions from income (*e.g.*, interest from qualifying U.S. savings bonds).

Combine spousal income. Married individuals filing a joint return must combine their income and benefits to determine whether any of the combined benefits are taxable. The IRS further cautions that spousal income must be added to a recipient's income, even if the spouse did not receive benefits, in order to ascertain whether any of the recipient's benefits are taxable.

¶252   Taxation of U.S. Citizens Residing Abroad

U.S. citizens residing in the following countries are exempt from U.S. tax on their Social Security benefits: Canada, Egypt, Germany, Ireland, Israel, Italy (but only for those who are also citizens of Italy), Romania and the United Kingdom. [IRS Pub. 915, 2019 returns, rev. Jan. 10, 2020.]

¶253   Taxation of Nonresident Aliens

Special rules apply to nonresident aliens. A nonresident alien, *i.e.*, an individual who is not a citizen or resident of the United States, is subject to a flat 30% tax on eighty-five percent of his or her social security benefits. However, residents of the following countries are exempt from U.S. tax on their benefits: Canada, Egypt, Germany, Ireland, Israel, Italy, Japan, Romania, and the United Kingdom. Residents and nationals of India are exempt if the benefits are for services performed for the United States or state or local government. Residents of Switzerland are taxed on 100% of their benefits at a 15% rate. [IRC §871(a)(3); IRS Pub. 915, 2019 returns, rev. Jan. 10, 2020.]

¶254   Taxation of Lawful Permanent Residents

Lawful permanent residents (*i.e.*, "green card holders") are considered resident aliens until their lawful permanent resident status is either removed or is administratively or judicially determined to have been abandoned. Social Security benefits paid to a green card holder are not subject to 30% withholding. In the event tax was erroneously withheld on the Social Security benefits of a lawful permanent resident with a foreign address, the withheld tax is refundable by the SSA or the IRS. [IRS Pub. 915, 2019 returns, rev. Jan. 10, 2020.]

¶255   Computation of Benefit Income

Generally, up to one-half of the Social Security benefits of an individual with modified AGI over a threshold amount may be subject to income tax. The test is whether the individual's adjusted gross income combined with 50% of his or her Social Security benefits plus any (1) tax-exempt interest, (2) foreign earned income, (3) income from U.S. possessions, (4) income from Puerto Rico by Puerto Rican residents, and (5) amounts received under an adoption assistance program of the employer exceeds a base amount. [IRC 86(a).]

The base amount is:

1. $25,000 for single persons, heads of household, qualified widow(er)s with a dependent child, or married individuals filing separately who did not live with their spouse at any time during the year;

2. $32,000 for married couples filing jointly; and

3. $0 for married persons who lived together during the year but file separately. [IRS 86(c)(1).]

Accordingly, if a recipient files a federal tax return as an individual and his or her combined income (AGI plus nontaxable interest plus one half of the recipient's Social Security benefits) is between $25,000 and $34,000, the recipient will be subject to tax on 50% of the benefits.

85% tax rate for high income individuals. For individuals whose combined income exceeds a higher *adjusted* base amount ($34,000 for single individuals; $44,000 for a married couple filing a joint return), the amount of benefits that will be included in taxable income for a tax year is the lesser of (A) 85 percent of the benefits or (B) 85 percent of the excess of the taxpayer's combined income over the adjusted base amount plus the lesser of (1) one-half the benefits or (2) $4,500 ($6,000 for married couples). [IRC 86(a)(2) and (c)(2).]

Estranged married couples. For purposes of IRC §86, an estranged couple, filing separately, but living in the same residence, will not necessarily be considered to be living apart. In a case where a taxpayer and his wife lived at the same residence, but maintained separate bedrooms, and were neither legally separated or divorced, the Tax Court rejected the taxpayer's arguments that because he and his wife maintained separate bedrooms and because he merely visited intermittently (although some visits were over 30 days in length), they were "living apart." [*McAdams v. Commr.*, 118 T.C. 373, UNEMPL. INS. REPTR. ¶16,726B (2002).]

Married joint filers combine SS benefits. If a taxpayer is married and files a joint income tax return, the taxpayer and his or her spouse must combine their incomes and Social Security benefits in determining tax liability, even if the spouse did not receive any benefits. [IRC §86(b), (c).]

For example, Tom and Tina, a married couple, file a joint return, reporting combined income between $32,000 and $44,000. Tom may be required to pay income tax on up to 50% of his benefits. By contrast, if the combined income of Tom and Tina exceeded $44,000, up to 85% of Tom's benefits would be taxable.

Note: Individuals who are married and file separate tax returns will generally be subject to tax on their Social Security benefits.

Impact of working spouse on benefits. Be aware that where one spouse works and the other is drawing benefits, the base amount can easily be exceeded.

Example: Don and Patty Smith received $30,000 in pension income, $6,000 in interest and dividend payments, $3,500 in interest from tax-exempt municipal bonds, and $11,000 in Social Security benefits. Their combined income would be $45,000 ($30,000 + $6,000 +$3,500 + $5,500 (1/2 Social Security benefits.)

As the Smiths have combined income over $44,000, 85% of their benefits are subject to tax. The amount of benefits actually taxable can be determined as follows.

(1) $45,000 (combined income) - $32,000 base amount = $13,000

(2)   ½ of $13,000 = $6,500

(3)   Lesser of ½ of their benefits or $5,500 = $5,500

(4)   Adjusted base amount = $44,000

(5)   Difference between combined income and adjusted base amount = $1,000

(6)   85% of $1,000 = $850

(7)   ½ of adjusted base amount – base amount ($12,000) = $6,000

(8)   Lesser of line 3 or line 7 = $5,500

(9)   Line 6 + Line 8 = $6,350

(10) 85% of benefits = $9,350

(11) Actual taxable benefits = $6,350

Modified adjusted gross income. "Modified adjusted gross income" is the taxpayer's adjusted gross income with the following modifications [IRC §86(b), (c)]:

(1) The taxpayer must add back any exclusion taken for the following: interest exclusion that applied to savings bonds used to finance education [IRC §135], foreign earned income, foreign housing [IRC §911], U.S. possessions source income [IRC §931], if the taxpayer is a bona fide resident of Puerto Rico, Puerto Rican source income [IRC §933], amounts paid under an adoption assistance program of the employer [IRC §137], and, interest on qualified education loans [IRC §§86(b)(2)(A) and 221].

(2) The taxpayer must include all tax-exempt interest, such as tax-exempt interest received on municipal bonds, that he or she received or accrued during the tax year. [IRC §86(b)(2)(B).]

Calculating taxable benefits. The following examples illustrate the calculation of taxable benefits.

> **Examples:** (1) Tom, a single retired individual, has an adjusted gross income of $12,000, receives Social Security benefits of $7,000 a year, and has $1,500 of tax-exempt interest from a mutual fund. Tom must add his $1,500 of tax-exempt interest to his $12,000 adjusted gross income to arrive at a modified adjusted gross income of $13,500. He then adds $3,500 (one-half of his Social Security benefits) to his modified adjusted gross income to arrive at a provisional income of $17,000. Since Tom's $17,000 provisional income does not exceed his $25,000 base amount, none of Tom's Social Security benefits is includible in his gross income.
>
> (2) John and Jane, who are married, have an adjusted gross income of $24,000. John, who is retired, receives Social Security benefits of $7,200 per year. The couple also receives $6,000 a year from a mutual fund that invests solely in tax-exempt municipal bonds. On their joint return, John and Jane

would make the following computation to determine how much (if any) of John's Social Security benefits must be included in their gross income.

(1)	Adjusted gross income	$24,000
(2)	Plus: All tax-exempt interest	6,000
(3)	Modified adjusted gross income	$30,000
(4)	Plus: One-half of Social Security benefits	3,600
(5)	Provisional income	$33,600
(6)	Less: Base amount	32,000
(7)	Excess above base amount	$1,600
(8)	One-half of excess above base amount	$800
(9)	One-half of Social Security benefits	3,600
(10)	Amount includible in gross income (lesser of (8) or (9))	$800

(3) Marcia, who is single, receives $10,000 in Social Security benefits and has $70,000 in modified adjusted gross income. Marcia's provisional income (the amount determined under IRC §86(b)(1)(A)) of $75,000 exceeds the threshold amount for single individuals, $34,000. Thus, Marcia must compute the amount of her Social Security benefit that is includible in gross income as follows (IRC §86(a)(2)):

(1)	Provisional income	$75,000
(2)	Threshold amount	$34,000
(3)	Excess of (1) over (2)	$41,000
(4)	85% of amount in (3)	$34,850
(5)	Amount includible under IRC §86(a)(1)	$5,000
(6)	Amount determined under IRC §86(a)(2)(A)(ii)	$4,500
(7)	Lesser of (5) or (6)	$4,500
(8)	Sum of amounts shown in (4) and (7)	$39,350
(9)	85% of Social Security benefits	$8,500
(10)	Lesser of (8) or (9)	$8,500

Payment of tax. Income tax due on Social Security benefits may be paid through quarterly estimated tax payments. Alternatively, a recipient may choose to have federal tax withheld from benefits by completing Form W-4V (Voluntary Withholding Request).

Social Security earnings may not be gross income. Earnings for purposes of the retirement test (see ¶551) and "income" for federal tax purposes are not the same. For example, most pensions, for example, are not counted in the retirement test, but are included in gross income.

When determining what to count as Social Security benefits for income tax purposes, count benefits actually received (after reductions for early retirement, or because of the family maximum or the retirement test). Amounts deducted from disability benefits under the worker's compensation offset are included as benefits received for purposes of income tax. Benefits are included in the taxable income of the person who has the legal right to receive them. A child's benefits, for example, are added to the *child's* other income (if any) to determine taxability.

Accounting for repayment of benefits. Taxpayers who are required to repay a portion of their Social Security or railroad retirement benefits to the government (for example, the taxpayer is rendered ineligible for benefits for a portion of the year), should reduce annual benefits by the amount of the benefits repaid. Such reduction is to be made whether or not the repayment pertains to benefits received in the current or previous tax year. [IRC §86(d)(2)(A).]

If during the current tax year a taxpayer repays benefits that were included in gross income in a previous tax year, the taxpayer should reduce the benefits received during the current tax year by the amount of the repayment. If the repayment exceeds the taxpayer's benefits for the current year, he or she may take such excess repayment amount as an itemized deduction for income tax purposes. [IRC §86(d)(2)(B).]

¶260   Voluntary Tax Withholding

Taxpayers who receive certain federal payments, including Social Security OASDI benefits and Tier I railroad retirement benefits, are given the option of requesting that the payor withhold federal income taxes. [P.L. 103-465, §702(a), amending IRC §3402(p).] Withholding may be desirable for some beneficiaries whose benefits exceed certain thresholds that make them subject to federal income taxation. Without such withholding, a beneficiary whose benefits are subject to taxation must pay income taxes either through quarterly payment of estimated taxes or with a U.S. Form 1040 tax return. However, without paying estimated taxes, a taxpayer may be subject to payment of a penalty for not having paid enough tax prior to the end of the tax year. The Social Security Act's prohibition against assignment of benefits, including assignment to the federal government, precluded implementation of voluntary withholding until an amendment to the Act in 1998 exempted the federal government from the anti-assignment provision. [Soc. Sec. Act §207(c), added by the Tax and Trade Relief Extension Act of 1998, §4005.]

Benefits may be withheld at one of the following rates: 7%, 10%, 12%, and 22%. No other percentages or flat dollar amounts are acceptable. To arrange for withholding, a taxpayer must complete IRS Form W-4V—Voluntary Withholding Request, and submit it to the beneficiary's payer. [IRS Pub. 915, 2019 returns, rev. Jan. 10, 2020.]

Coverage

¶301 Introduction

Whether an individual is "covered" for Social Security purposes depends on (1) whether the individual is an "employee," (2) whether the services that the individual renders are in an "employment capacity," and (3) whether the compensation received constitutes "wages" within the meaning of the law. All three of these factors must be present before an individual is "covered." For example, an individual may be what the law considers an "employee" working in qualifying "employment," but unless the individual is also compensated by what the law defines as "wages," the work is not "covered" by the Social Security system and, therefore, cannot provide insurance for future benefits. What constitutes "wages" is discussed at ¶206 *et seq.*

Social Security coverage of the self-employed is discussed beginning at ¶401.

EMPLOYEES

¶302 General Definition of "Employee"

Every individual is an "employee" if the relationship between him or her and the person for whom he or she performs services is the common-law relationship of employer and employee. Generally, that relationship exists when the person for whom services are performed has the right to control and direct the individual who performs the services, not only as to the result to be accomplished by the work but also as to the details and means by which that result is to be accomplished. That is, an employee is subject to the will and control of the employer not only as to *what* shall be done but also as to *how* it shall be done. In this connection, it is not necessary that the employer actually direct or control the manner in which the services are performed; it is sufficient that the employer has the right to do so. [IRS Reg. §31.3121(d)-1(c).] Following are some of the factors, sometimes referred to as the IRS' "20-factor test," that may be considered in determining whether or not sufficient control is exercised over a worker to indicate employee status. [Rev. Rul. 87-41, 1987-1, C.B. 296; see also *Soc. Sec. Handbook,* Sept. 1, 2009, §802; March 2001, Nov. 16, 2010, §§803-823]:

(1) A person who is required to comply with instructions about when, where, and how to work is ordinarily an employee. The control factor is present if the employer has the right to instruct.

(2) Training by an experienced employee is a factor of control because it is an indication that the employer wants the services performed by a particular method or in a particular manner.

(3) Integration of the person's services in the business operation generally shows that the person is subject to direction and control.

(4) If the services must be rendered personally, it is taken as an indication that the employer is interested in methods as well as results.

(5) Hiring, supervising, and payment of assistants by the employer generally shows control over all of the workers on the job. Where one worker hires, supervises, and pays other workers, under a contract providing that the worker furnish labor and materials and that he or she will be responsible only for the attainment of a result, the worker is an independent contractor.

(6) The existence of a continuing relationship between an individual and the person for whom the individual performs services is a factor tending to indicate the existence of an employer-employee relationship.

(7) The establishment of set hours of work by the employer is a factor indicative of control.

(8) If the worker is required to devote full time to the business of the employer, the worker is implicitly restricted from doing other gainful work; whereas an independent contractor may choose for whom and when to work.

(9) Doing the work on the employer's premises is not control in itself, but it does imply that the employer has control.

(10) If the person must perform services in the order or sequence set by the employer, it shows that the worker may be subject to control, although the fact that the employer retains the right to order the work may also show control.

(11) If regular oral or written reports must be submitted to the employer, this shows control.

(12) Employees are usually paid by the hour, week, or month; payment on a commission or job basis is customary when the worker is an independent contractor. A guarantee of a minimum salary or the granting of a drawing account at stated intervals with no requirement of repayment of excess over earnings tends to indicate an employer-employee relationship.

(13) Payment by the employer of the worker's business or travelling expenses is a factor indicating control.

(14) The furnishing of tools, materials, etc., by the employer is indicative of control.

(15) A significant investment by a worker in facilities used in performing services tends to show independent status, while the furnishing of all necessary facilities by the employer tends to indicate employee status for the worker.

(16) Individuals who are in a position to realize a profit or suffer a loss as a result of their services are generally independent contractors.

(17) If a person works for a number of employers or firms at the same time it usually indicates an independent status.

(18) Workers who make their services available to the general public are usually independent contractors.

(19) The right to discharge is an important factor in indicating that the person possessing the right is an employer, even if the right is somewhat restricted by a union contract.

(20) Employees have the right to end the relationship with an employer at any time the employee wishes without incurring liability, as distinguished from independent contractors, who usually agree to complete a specific job and are responsible for its satisfactory completion or are legally obligated to make good for failure to complete the job.

Independent contractors are not employees. In general, if an individual is subject to the control or direction of another merely as to the result to be accomplished by the work and not as to the means and methods for accomplishing the result, the individual is an independent contractor, rather than an employee. [Reg. §31.3121(d)-(1)(C).] For example, house cleaners sent by an agency are probably not domestic employees if the agency sets and collects the fee, pays the cleaners, provides cleaning supplies, requires regular reports, and exercises control over the cleaners' appearance and conduct. However, if the agency merely provides a list of house cleaners from which the homeowner may choose and does not prescribe hours, pay, or work standards, the cleaners may be domestic employees.

The distinction is important because an employer is not required to withhold or pay tax on payments made to an independent contractor. If the relationship of employer and employee exists, the designation or description of the relationship by the parties as anything other than that of employer and employee is immaterial. Thus, if such a relationship exists, it is of no consequence that the employee is designated as a partner, co-adventurer, agent, independent contractor, or the like. [Reg. §31.3121(d)-1(a)(3).] Rather, a business must base its determination as to whether a worker is an employee or an independent contractor on all of the facts and circumstances of its relationship with the worker. Businesses can use Form SS-8, "Determination of Worker Status for Purposes of Federal Employment Taxes and Income Tax Withholding" to have the IRS make the determination.

Certain individuals are considered employees whether or not they are employees under common-law rules. See ¶303.

The distinction between employee and independent contractor status is not always clear cut and different outcomes can occur in the same industry. For example, the Tax Court has come to opposite conclusions in separate cases featuring employment contracts that contained language designating drivers as "independent contractors." In one case, the court found that the facts demonstrated that the drivers were employees. While the company did not control the manner in which the drivers performed their work, such control was not necessary because this type of work requires little supervision. Further, the drivers assumed no risk of loss, did not contribute to the cost of operating the trucks and performed work that was an integral part of the employer's business. [*Peno Trucking, Inc v. IRS.*, TC Memo 2007-66, (2007), UNEMPL. INS. REPTR. ¶14,094C.] By contrast, the Tax Court also ruled that, even though a driver's job was an integral part of the business, he was self-employed and liable for self employment tax. The court noted that the driver leased his truck, and thus had a financial investment which caused him to risk a net loss if he did not earn sufficient funds making deliveries. [*Byers v. IRS*, TC Memo 2007-331, (2007).]

Workers hired under federal contracts. To determine if a worker hired by a federal agency through a service contract is an independent contractor or an employee for employment tax purposes, the specific facts and circumstances surrounding the worker's employment should be applied to the Internal Revenue Code's common law test. [IRS Advice Memorandum AM 2009-002.] The IRS has had several disputes with federal agencies over the status of workers hired under personal service contracts. Typically the agency takes the position that the workers are independent contractors for all purposes, while the IRS takes the position that at least some of the workers are employees, and the agency has withholding requirements with respect to them.

The federal authorizing statute under which a worker is hired should be analyzed first to determine whether it addresses the worker's tax treatment or otherwise specifies how workers hired under the authorized personal service contracts are to be classified for federal tax purposes.

If the authorizing statute (or another federal statute) does not specify the federal tax status of the worker, the Code's common law test applies to determine whether the worker is an employee or independent contractor. Under the common law test, an initial determination must be made to determine if the services contract is personal or nonpersonal, with most service contracts acquired by an agency being nonpersonal. In determining whether a services contract is personal or nonpersonal, each contract arrangement is judged in the light of its own facts and circumstances. The key question is whether the federal agency will exercise relatively continuous supervision and control over the performance of services by the contractor. In a typical case, the work is not subject to supervision or control by the agency to the extent usually found in relationships between the government and its employees.

S Corp. employers. The Tax Court has rejected an S corporation's claim that the president, associate attorneys and law clerk of the S corporation, which was doing business as a law firm, enjoyed sufficient control over their work to be treated as independent contractors. The president made all the decisions for the corporation, such as hiring. Thus, he was a statutory employee of the S corp. for employment tax purposes. The associate attorneys all had some independence over the preparation of their cases, but the president did assign all of them and also reviewed the pleadings and correspondence prepared by them. He also provided all of the office tools and furnishings. The law clerk had considerable flexibility regarding the hours and location of work. However, he received all of his assignments from the president and associates and, therefore, was also found to be an employee. Safe haven relief under IRC §530 was not available because the corporation president failed to investigate whether the associate attorneys and the law clerk were employees or independent contractors. Instead he relied on the advice of a tax professional. The court found this reliance misplaced and upheld a penalty under IRC §6656. [*Cave, et al, v. Commissioner*, T.C. Memo 2011-48 (2011), 101 TCM 1224, UNEMPL. INS. REPTR. ¶14,773C.]

Correction of Misclassification Errors

A worker who is determined to be an employee, but is treated by his or her employer as an independent contractor, may file Form 8919, Uncollected Social Security and Medicare Tax on Wages. This form allows the taxpayer to pay only his or her share of FICA and Medicare taxes. In order to use Form 8919, a worker, must meet at least one of the following criteria:

- receipt of a determination letter or other correspondence from the IRS stating the worker is an employee;
- filing of a Form SS-8, Determination of Worker Status for Purposes of Federal Employment Taxes and Income Tax Withholding, by the individual and no receipt of a reply; or
- receipt of a Form W-2 and a Form 1099-MISC and the amount on Form 1099-MISC should have been included as wages on Form W-2.

Course of action following reclassification as an employee

The proper course of action depends on whether or not the taxpayer has filed a return reporting the income earned, as well as on how the income was reported. The taxpayer may be owed a refund, or may reduce an existing tax liability, or may be found to owe additional tax as a result of the change in status to "employee." It is not necessary for the taxpayer to wait for corrected pay documents from his or her employer before filing or amending the return to reflect the taxpayer's status as employee. Different steps should be taken based on what documents the employee has already filed with the IRS.

1. *Return not yet filed.* If the taxpayer has not yet filed a federal tax return, he or she must file Form 1040 for the relevant tax years, reporting the income that had been reported by the employer on Form 1099-MISC. Because no Social Security or FICA tax was withheld from these wages, the taxpayer must compute and pay the employee portion of those taxes with the return. Form 8919 should be used to compute FICA tax. If the returns are late and tax is due, penalties and interest will apply.

2. *Return filed, but 1099-MISC income not reported.* In some cases, the taxpayer will have filed an income tax return, but will have omitted reporting the income that was received and listed on the taxpayer's Form 1099-MISC. In this case, the taxpayer must file Form 1040X, an amended tax return, for the relevant year to include the additional income as wages, and must then recompute the federal income received. The taxpayer must also determine his or her portion of FICA taxes on this income using Form 8919.

3. *Return filed, income reported, but FICA tax not properly computed.* In a case where the taxpayer has filed a return and properly reported the income received as wages, but has not computed the FICA tax on the income, the taxpayer must file Form 1040X, the amended tax return, and use Form 8919 for the relevant tax years in order to compute the FICA tax due on this income.

4. *Return filed, 1099-MISC income reported as self-employment income instead of wages.* If the taxpayer has filed a tax return and reported the income received as self-employment income instead of wages, he or she must file a

Form 1040A for the relevant tax years. The taxpayer will not owe self-employment tax, but must compute and pay the employee's portion of FICA tax on the income using Form 8919.

5. *Taxpayer has already paid his or her portion of FICA tax with the original return using Form 4137 or Form 8919.* If the taxpayer has already reported the income on his or her tax return and computed the proper FICA tax using Form 4137, Social Security and Medicare Tax on Unreported Tip Income, or Form 8919, it is not necessary for the taxpayer to amend the return as a result of the determination changing the taxpayer's status to employee. The taxpayer should retain the determination letter with tax records to substantiate the way the return was filed.

6. *Taxpayer has already reported Form 1099-MISC income on Schedule C and claimed expenses.* Schedule C cannot be used to report the taxpayer's income since wages earned by an employee are reported on line 7 of Form 1040. The taxpayer must file an amended return to reflect the correct amount of tax on his or her wages. When the taxpayer originally filed, if he or she reduced income by claiming expenses, the change to employee status may increase the tax because the taxpayer will now compute FICA tax on gross wages instead of computing self-employment tax on the net income. Furthermore, the expenses the taxpayer deducted from the income on Schedule C must now be deducted as miscellaneous itemized deductions on Schedule A, subject to a limitation. Some of the expenses may no longer be deductible.

Self-employed individuals are also allowed a deduction on Form 1040 in an amount equal to one-half of SE tax paid. As an employee, the taxpayer will lose this deduction and any other deduction he or she was allowed due to treating himself or herself as self-employed, such as the self-employed health insurance deduction and the deduction for contributions to a Keogh-type retirement plan. The taxpayer's taxable income is affected by these changes, and as a result, the income tax due is adjusted.

7. *Employer provides the taxpayer with a corrected Form W-2 reflecting payment of the proper portion of FICA tax.* If the employer pays the taxpayer's portion of FICA tax on the income, that additional amount becomes income to the taxpayer in the year it is paid. If the taxpayer already paid FICA tax on the income, he or she can amend the return to request a refund of the FICA tax at that time. If the taxpayer does not receive a Form W-2 from the employer, the taxpayer can assume that the employer did not pay the taxpayer's portion of the FICA tax, and the taxpayer remains responsible for it.

Time limit for filing an amended return. Generally, a taxpayer must file Form 1040X within three years following the date the taxpayer filed the original return, or within two years after the date the taxpayer paid the tax, whichever is later, if the amended return will decrease the tax owed. A taxpayer generally has three years after the date the original return was filed if the amended return will increase the tax owed. A return filed before the due date is considered to have been filed on the due date. If an amended return is received after the statutory time limit for filing it has expired, the amended return will be rejected.

Refunds subsequent to filing of return. The taxpayer must file Form 1040X to receive a refund or credit toward any unpaid taxes. Generally, a refund is only possible if the taxpayer initially calculated and paid self-employment tax on the income or if the employer issued a corrected Form W-2 to the taxpayer showing the employer paid the FICA tax. [IRS Notice 989, Rev. July 2009.]

Assessment of liability through mitigation rules:

Under IRC §6521, certain types of errors involving FICA or self-employment taxes may be corrected by the IRS even though the statute of limitations has expired. Specifically, the IRS may assess the taxes when the taxpayer's employment status is erroneously classified and either self-employment income incorrectly classified as wages and FICA taxes are paid, or wages are incorrectly classified as self-employment income and self-employment taxes are paid.

The IRS Chief Counsel has ruled that the mitigation provisions under IRC §6521 may not be used by the IRS to assess unpaid FICA taxes against individuals treated as independent contractors and not as employees when the taxpayers have not paid the FICA taxes or paid self-employment taxes and the statute of limitations for the assessment of the FICA taxes has otherwise expired. [CCA 200918021, Mar. 24, 2009.] Accordingly, if a classification matter is before the Tax Court, and the statute of limitations for assessment of FICA taxes has already expired, the case can still proceed with respect to the issue of whether the individuals are employees or independent contractors. If the individuals lose and they are classified as independent contractors, they would be obligated to pay the SECA taxes. However, if they win and are classified as employees, they would not be required to pay FICA taxes since the statute of limitations has run. The individuals may enter into a closing agreement with the IRS to pay their share of FICA taxes if they want the Social Security credit for that period, but the employer might not agree to a closing agreement to pay the employer's share of FICA.

Status Controversies; Safe Haven

An individual who has consistently not been treated as a common-law employee by a taxpayer will not be deemed a common-law employee as long as the taxpayer filed all required federal tax returns with respect to such individual, unless the taxpayer had no reasonable basis for not treating the individual as such. This relieves taxpayers of potential liabilities based on erroneous employment status classifications. However, Section 530 is generally not applied in the case of certain technical personnel; see ¶302.1 below. [P.L. 95-600 (Revenue Act of 1978), §530; P.L. 97-248, §269.]

"Reasonable basis" standards include reasonable reliance on judicial precedent, published rulings, technical advice, a past IRS audit, or long-standing, recognized practices of a significant segment of the industry in which the individual, whose status is at issue, was engaged. [P.L. 95-600, §530; P.L. 97-248, §269.] However, industry practice will not necessarily shield a professional from employee status where the professional forms a corporation for which he provides professional services that are the backbone of the corporation when the corporation is, in fact, a separate entity. See ¶302.2. A reasonable basis for not withholding taxes was also not shown where the taxpayer's failure to withhold or pay FICA taxes was based on the fact that the alien workers were illegally present in the U.S., and not on a belief that they were independent contractors rather than employees. [Rev. Rul. 82-116 (CB 1982-1, 152).]

An industry practice need not have continued for more than ten years to be considered long standing and it need not have been exercised by more than 25% of the industry for it to have been exercised by a "significant segment." This latter provision is intended to be a safe harbor; depending upon the particular facts and circumstances, a lower percentage may suffice. [Revenue Act of 1978 (P.L. 95-600), §530(e)(2)(B)(C), as amended by the Small Business Job Protection Act of 1996 (P.L. 104-188), §1122(a).] The consistency requirement is retrospective only. An employer may reclassify a worker as an employee without compromising its independent classification for prior years. [P.L. 95-600, §530(e)(5), as amended by P.L. 104-188, §1122(b).]

It is not necessary that a worker be first determined to be an employee of a taxpayer under the common-law rules in order for Section 530 safe-haven protection to apply. [P.L. 95-600, §530(e)(3), as amended by P.L. 104-188, §1122(a).] Once a taxpayer establishes a prima facie case that it was reasonable not to treat a worker as an employee for purposes of Section 530, the burden of proof shifts to the IRS with respect to such treatment. [P.L. 95-600 (The Revenue Act of 1978), §530(e)(4), as amended by P.L. 104-188, §1122(b).]

An employer must demonstrate actual and reasonable reliance prior to the period for which employment decisions are made. The employer may be permitted to satisfy the reasonable basis requirement by establishing that it actually and reasonably relied upon the asserted basis *prior to* making the employment decisions regarding the workers' status for later periods. However, employers cannot offer ex post facto justification for prior treatment. [Program Manager's Technical Advice (PMTA) 2011-15.]

Regarding the employment status of salespersons who are licensed real estate agents and direct sellers, see ¶401.5.

Voluntary Classification Settlement Program

The Internal Revenue Service maintains a voluntary program for employers that have erroneously classified workers as independent contractors in the past but agree to reclassify them as employees. Under the program, eligible employers can obtain substantial relief from federal payroll taxes they may have owed for those past workers if they prospectively treat them as employees. The Voluntary Classification Settlement Program (VCSP) will enable employers to resolve past worker classification issues and also to achieve certainty under the tax law at a low cost by voluntarily reclassifying their workers, according to the IRS. [IRS Announcement 2012-45.]

The program gives employers the chance to be in compliance by paying 10% of the employment tax liability under IRC §3509 that may have been due on worker compensation paid for the most recent tax year (this amounts to just over one percent of the wages paid to the reclassified worker for the past year), rather than waiting for an IRS audit. Once the taxpayer has been approved to participate in the VCSP, it will enter into a closing agreement with the IRS, pursuant to which it will prospectively treat the class or classes of workers as employees in future tax periods.

The program is designed to increase tax compliance and reduce the burden on employers by providing greater certainty for employers, workers and the government. No interest or penalties will be due, and the employers will not be audited on payroll taxes related to these workers for prior years. Participating employers will no longer be subject to a special six-year statute of limitations, rather than the usual three years that generally applies to payroll taxes.

The VCSP is available to many businesses, tax-exempt organizations and government entities. To be eligible, an employer must:

- Consistently have treated the workers in the past as nonemployees; and
- Have filed all required Forms 1099 for the workers for the previous three years.

IRS audit does not preclude eligibility. As initially drafted, VCSP was restricted to taxpayers who were not currently under audit by the IRS, Department of Labor or a state agency with respect to worker classifications. The IRS subsequently modified the VCSP to permit a taxpayer under IRS audit, *other than an employment tax audit*, to be eligible to participate in the program. [IRS Announcement 2012-45.] In addition, the IRS clarified that: (1) a taxpayer that is member of an affiliated group is not eligible to participate in the VCSP if any member of the affiliated group is under an employment tax audit; and (2) a taxpayer is not eligible to participate in the VCSP if the taxpayer is contesting in court the classification of the class or classes of workers from a previous audit by the IRS or DOL. However, the IRS eliminated the requirement that a taxpayer agree to extend the period of limitation on the assessment of employment taxes as part of the VCSP closing agreement with the IRS.

Application for VCSP. Interested employers can apply for the program by filing Form 8952, "Application for Voluntary Classification Settlement Program," at least 60 days before they want to begin treating their workers as employees. IRS rejection of this form will not automatically trigger initiation of an audit.

Effect of reclassification. All workers do not have to be reclassified as employees. The VCSP permits taxpayers to reclassify some or all of their workers. However, once a taxpayer chooses to reclassify certain of its workers as employees, all workers in the same class must be treated as employees for employment tax purposes. [IRS Announcement 2011-64, I.R.B. 2011-41, Sept. 21, 2011, modified by IRS Announcement 2012-45, I.R.B. 2012-5, Dec. 18, 2012.]

Status Controversies: Procedure

Either a worker or an employer may file Form SS-8 with the IRS to request a determination or ruling letter regarding a worker's status for federal employment tax purposes. If the IRS determines that the worker is an employee, the employer will generally be liable for any resulting underpayment of employment taxes. At any time, including throughout the determination process, the employer may reclassify a worker as an employee and resolve any resulting employment tax liability with the IRS.

Under the governing procedures, the taxpayer, prior to an assessment of employment taxes, will receive a Notice of Determination of Worker Classification (NDWC). The mailing of the NDWC suspends the period of limitations for assessment of taxes attributable to the worker classification issues for a 90-day period. During this time, the taxpayer can file a petition with the Tax Court and preclude the IRS from assessing the taxes identified in the NDWC prior to the expiration of the 90 days. If the IRS erroneously makes an assessment of taxes attributable to the worker classification issues without first either issuing a NDWC or obtaining a waiver of restrictions on assessment from the taxpayer, the taxpayer is entitled to an automatic abatement of the assessment.

¶302

Under IRC §6020, if a taxpayer fails to make a required return, an IRS agent is authorized to make a Substitute for Return (SFR) from his or her own knowledge and from such information as can be obtained through testimony or otherwise.

If these procedures are not followed, there can be no assessment of taxes under IRC §7436. However, the IRS Chief Counsel has determined that such procedural missteps will not be fatal if the agent takes corrective measures and reassesses as if the abated assessment had not occurred. The IRS Chief Counsel has also determined that because the agent failed to meet the procedure requirements, an assessment of employment taxes based on the SFR was improper. However, the Chief Counsel concluded that the government was not required to concede the case. Once procedural defects are corrected and the requirements are satisfied, employment taxes could be assessed. [CCA 200822026, Feb. 26, 2008.]

Private claims for tax fraud. According to at least one court, an individual who believes that his or her employer has fraudulently reported the individual's income as payments to an independent contractor rather than as wages subject to FICA does not, however, have a private attorney general claim for tax fraud against the employer. The court held that the Internal Revenue Code does not indicate that Congress intended to enforce the tax laws by creating civil causes of action or authorizing private attorneys general. Although the plaintiffs had no success bringing a private attorney general claim or civil cause of action against their former employers, they may have been able to bring a whistleblower claim with the IRS under IRC §7623. Irrespective, any argument that they were employees and not independent contractors, in order to reduce their share of Social Security taxes and allow them to share in tax-favored employee benefits, had to be made directly either in response to an IRS notice of deficiency against them for unpaid payroll taxes, or against the employer under an ERISA action. They could not act as a surrogate for the IRS against the employer (*United States of America, ex rel. Ellsworth et al. v. United Business Brokers of Utah*, U.S.D.C. (Utah), 2011-1 USTC ¶50,119 (2010), Unempl. Ins. Reptr. ¶14,767C).

Reduced rates. Reduced rates of tax may apply under IRC §3509 for employers in certain situations involving misclassification of workers. To be eligible, the employer must have treated the worker (without intentional disregard) as a nonemployee for purposes of both income tax withholding and FICA tax. The employer must also have treated the worker as a nonemployee for purposes of information reporting.

Under IRC §3509, the employer's liability is generally reduced to 1.5% of wages for federal income tax withholding, and 20% of the employee's portion of the FICA tax. If the employer failed to file Form 1099-MISC for the worker, the percentages are doubled. The employer remains liable for the full amount of its share of FICA taxes.

IRC §3509 and its legislative history are silent as to whether the reduced rates apply only if the reclassification occurs pursuant to an audit by the IRS and only to a prior tax year. In response, the IRS has held that if an employer meets the requirements of IRC §3509, the reduced rates may be used where the employer has become aware of a misclassification after receiving a determination letter from the IRS through the Form SS-8 process. However, the reduced rates may only be used to correct a failure to withhold employment taxes for a prior year. They do not apply where the employer discovers a misclassification during the calendar year. This is because the employer can remedy the failure before the year ends.

Adjustments to pay. IRC §6205 and its accompanying regulations permit an employer to correct their employment tax underpayments without incurring any interest, if the error is timely reported and the tax is timely paid. Like IRC §3509, however, nothing limits employers to making interest-free adjustments solely in the context of an audit. As a result, the IRS has held that if an employer meets the requirements of IRC §3509, the employer is eligible to make an interest-free adjustment in paying its employee FICA tax and federal income tax withholding liability for prior years, as determined using the reduced rates, when the employer is reclassifying the worker after receiving an IRS SS-8 determination letter. [IRS CCA 200825043, May 13, 2008.] Revised regulations that were released subsequent to the issuance of the IRS Chief Counsel ruling, detail the procedures for correcting the misclassification through an interest-free adjustment if the error is determined after the due date of the return. The employer is required to file an original return for the return period for which the return had not been filed, along with an adjusted return. The adjusted return must include a detailed explanation of the amount being reported. These returns must be filed by the due date for the period in which the error is discovered. The due date is determined by reference to the return being corrected. Thus, if the error was on a quarterly report, even if the employer is currently filing annually, the return is due by the current due date for quarterly returns. [Reg. §31.6205-1(b)(3), effective Jan. 1, 2009.]

Tax Court Jurisdiction

In all cases, tax court jurisdiction is extended only if the employer files an appeal with the court within 90 days after the IRS mails a Notice of Determination to the taxpayer. Taxpayers filing late may still obtain judicial review by paying the tax and filing a claim for refund. Only the employer may seek tax court review of an IRS determination. [IRS Notice 98-43, July 31, 1998.] The employer may change the employment tax treatment of the individual while the matter is pending in court without any adverse inference being drawn from the change. A claim for a refund following a favorable ruling by the court must be filed on or before the last day of the second calendar year after the calendar year in which the determination becomes final. [P.L. 105-34, §1454, amending IRC §§6511(d)(7), 7421(a), 7436, 7437, 7453, and 7481(b); Community Renewal Tax Relief Act of 2000, P.L. 106-554, §314(f), amending IRC §7436(a).]

Interest accrual during tax court action. Generally, interest-free adjustments may be made to employment tax returns before assessment of any tax. Because assessment is barred when a dispute is in litigation before the Tax Court, regulations finalized in 2001 clarified that a taxpayer will not be able to extend the time to make interest-free adjustments by filing for relief in Tax Court. Rather, the period for adjustment of employment tax underpayments is until a notice of determination from the IRS is received. In order for taxpayers to make a remittance to stop the accrual of interest, still receive a Notice of Determination, and retain the right to petition the Tax Court, the regulations provide that prior to receipt of a notice, a taxpayer may make a cash bond deposit in lieu of making a payment. That deposit will have the effect of stopping the accrual of interest but will not deprive the taxpayer of the right to receive a Notice of Determination. [Reg. §31.6205-1(a).]

¶302.1   Technical Personnel

Consistently not treating a worker performing technical services as an employee will not automatically create nonemployee status. An employment status determination must be made for an individual performing technical services whose service as an engineer, designer, drafter, computer programmer, systems analyst, or other similarly skilled work for another organization is provided pursuant to an arrangement between the taxpayer (*e.g.*, a technical services firm) and the other organization. A technical service specialist who was treated as an independent contractor for employment tax purposes before the enactment of Section 1706 of the Tax Reform Act of 1986 will continue to be treated as an independent contractor after 1986 only if he or she is an independent contractor under the common-law standards. [P.L. 95-600, §530; P.L. 99-514, §1706; IRS Notice 87-19.] For example, an engineer retained by a technical services firm to provide services to a manufacturer cannot avoid the 1986 amendment by organizing a corporation that he or she controls and then claim to provide service as an employee of that corporation. [SSA POMS §RS 02101.808 (6/25/08).]

¶302.1A Independent Contractors

Independent contractors are generally covered as self-employed individuals unless they are included in the occupational groups discussed at ¶303. The rules for determining whether an individual is an employee or an independent contractor are set forth at ¶302. Self-employment is discussed in detail in Chapter 4 (¶401, *et seq.*).

¶302.2 Officers and Directors of Corporations

The term "employee" ordinarily includes an officer of a corporation. [IRC §3121(d)(1).] However, an officer of a corporation who, as such, does not perform any services or performs only minor services and who neither receives nor is entitled to receive, directly or indirectly, any remuneration is considered not to be an employee of the corporation. [Reg. §31.3121(d)-1(b).]

A director of a corporation is not an employee of the corporation with regard to any services performed as a director. However, any nondirectorial services performed under the control of the board of directors are performed as an employee of the corporation. [*Soc. Sec. Handbook,* March 2001, §824.] With respect to self-employment coverage of directors of corporations, see ¶401.2.

Note that in the case of a professional practice in which services are the backbone of the business, the owner can rarely argue successfully that the corporation should be ignored for tax purposes. Although Section 530 of the 1978 Revenue Act generally provides relief from employment tax liability in situations in which a worker has historically been treated as an independent contractor (*see* "Status Controversies" at ¶302), where the corporation is a separate entity and pays the owner for his or her services, the owner is an employee and the corporation is liable, as employer, for the employee's employment taxes. However, if the corporation is merely an agent for the professional employee or is merely a shell, then the corporate entity may be disregarded. [*Dennis Katz, DDS, PC v. Commr,* TC Memo 2002-118, 83 TCM 1629 (2002).]

Based on these principles, a personal services corporation providing legal services through the work of an attorney, the corporation's sole shareholder, owed back employment taxes on compensation paid to the lawyer. The lawyer had been making cash withdrawals from corporate funds to cover business and personal expenses, without receiving any salary checks from the corporation on a regular basis. The corporation classified these withdrawals as "loans" on its ledgers and did not file Form 1099-MISC. The Tax Court found that the attorney was a "statutory employee" under IRC §3121(d). The attorney was an officer of the corporation and performed substantial services for the corporation. As such, he was a statutory employee to which FICA and FUTA taxes attached. Safe haven relief under IRC §530 was not available because the corporation had failed to file the required information returns (Form 1099-MISC) to report compensation paid to the attorney consistent with any misinterpreted status as an independent contractor and, it had previously treated the attorney as an employee when, three years earlier, its board of directors voted to pay the attorney a substantial salary at that time and issued a Form W-2. [*Western Management, Inc. v. Commr.*, TC Memo 2003-162, 85 TCM 1442, CCH Dec. 55,177(M) (2003), affirmed in part, remanded in part (on another issue), 9th Cir., 2006-1 USTC ¶50,267 (2006).]

The term "corporation" includes an association of several persons engaged in a joint business undertaking without a corporate charter, provided the association meets the following conditions: (a) there is centralized management and control vested in a certain number of the associates who act as a board of directors for the association in the conduct of its business, (b) the organization is not ended or interrupted by the death of one of the owners or by a change in share ownership, (c) the members have the absolute right to dispose of their interests in the organization, (d) the object of the organization is to continue as a going business, and (e) in some associations no associate is personally liable for debts incurred by the association in excess of its assets. When an association is classifiable as a corporation under these conditions, members who perform duties similar to those of officers of a corporation are employees. [*Soc. Sec. Handbook,* Apr. 5, 2012, §825.]

S-Corporations

Compensation paid to S corporation shareholders who are officers of or otherwise perform services for their corporations are subject to income tax withholding and FICA and FUTA taxes to the same extent as compensation paid to other employees. The difference in the employment tax treatment of compensation versus dividends paid to S corporation shareholders may make it more desirable to pay dividends to shareholder-employees for their services rather than compensation because the compensation is subject to all of the employment taxes while the dividends are not. Therefore, in some instances, S corporations have paid little or no compensation to S corporation shareholders—employees who served as officers or performed other substantial services, and have paid them dividends instead, to minimize employment tax withholding and payments. However, this strategy has been increasingly scrutinized by the IRS. The view of the IRS is that when little or no compensation is paid and instead, dividends are paid to S corporation shareholder-employees, the dividends should be recharacterized as compensation and subject to income tax withholding and FICA and FUTA taxes. [Rev. Rul. 74-44; *J. Radtke v. U.S.,* 895 F.2d 1196 (7th Cir. 1990); *Dunn & Clarke, P.A. v Commr.,* 853 F. Supp. 365 (D. Id. 1994), 94-2 USTC ¶50,447, aff'd, 9th Cir., No. 94-35562, June 8, 1995 (unpublished memorandum), 95-2 USTC ¶50,383; *Nu-Look Design, Inc. v. Commr. of IRS,* 356 F.3d 290 (3d Cir. 2004), 2004-1 USTC ¶50,138.]

¶302.3 Partners

Partners generally are not employees either of the partnership or of the other partners with regard to partnership business. If, however, a partnership functions as an association classifiable as a corporation under the conditions described in ¶302.2, above, any partner who performs services comparable to those of corporate officers would be an employee. [*Soc. Sec. Handbook,* Apr. 5, 2012, §825.2.] With regard to the coverage of partners as self-employed individuals and the exclusion for limited partnerships, see ¶401, *et seq.*, below. See ¶227.2 regarding the liability of partners for non-payment of employment taxes.

¶303 Special Classes Deemed Employees

The definition of "employee" includes full-time life insurance salespersons, agent-drivers and commission-drivers, traveling and city salespersons, and homeworkers because, while members of these groups may not be employees under the usual common-law rules, they occupy substantially the same status as those who are. [Reg. §31.3121(d)-1(d)(1).] The mere fact that an individual falls within one of these groups, however, does not of itself make such an individual an "employee," unless (1) the contract of service contemplates that substantially all of the services are to be performed personally by the individual, (2) there is no substantial investment by the individual in facilities (other than those for transportation) used in connection with the performance of the services, and (3) the services are part of a continuing relationship with the person for whom the services are performed and are not in the nature of a single transaction. [Reg. §31.3121(d)-1(d)(4)(i).]

The contract of service may be formal or informal but the worker may not have the authority to delegate a substantial part of the work to any other person. [Reg. §31.3121(d)-1(d)(4)(ii).] However, a salesperson could hire a chauffeur without affecting the personal service requirement since the chauffeur's services would be merely incidental to the selling activity. Similarly, a worker could hire a substitute or an assistant occasionally and still be an employee under this test. The important thing is that the parties intended that the worker perform the essential services of the job. [*Soc. Sec. Handbook,* Sept. 1, 2009, §826.]

Facilities include such items as office furniture and fixtures, premises, and machinery. A salesperson maintaining an office in his or her home may not have a substantial investment; but a salesperson maintaining an office outside the home frequently does have a substantial investment in facilities. Facilities do not include education, training, experience, tools, instruments, or clothing commonly or frequently provided by employees, and do not include a vehicle used for the worker's own transportation, or for carrying the goods or commodities sold, or for supplying laundry or dry cleaning service. [Reg. §31.3121(d)-1(d)(4)(iii); *Soc. Sec. Handbook,* Sept. 1, 2009, §826.]

If the services are not performed as part of a continuing relationship with the person for whom the services are performed, but are in the nature of a single transaction, the individual performing such services is not an employee of such person. The fact that the services are not performed on consecutive workdays does not indicate that the services are not performed as part of a continuing relationship. [Reg. §31.3121(d)-1(d)(4)(iv).]

See, further, ¶303.1–303.4, below.

¶303.1   Agent- or Commission-Drivers

Provided that the test described at ¶303 is met, an agent-driver or commission-driver who distributes, for a principal, meat or meat products, vegetables or vegetable products, fruit or fruit products, bakery products, beverages other than milk, or laundry or dry cleaning services is an employee. Agent-drivers or commission drivers include individuals who operate their own trucks or the trucks of the persons for whom they perform services and who serve customers designated by the principals as well as those solicited on their own. They may sell at wholesale or retail, and their manner of compensation is immaterial. They may distribute other products if the handling of the additional products is incidental to the handling of the specified items. If the distribution of other products is not incidental to the handling of the specific items listed above, the workers are not employees under this test. [Reg. §31.3121(d)-1(d)(3)(i); *Soc. Sec. Handbook,* March 2001, §827.]

Note that the worker must perform the services for the person engaging him or her; if the worker buys merchandise on his or her own account and sells it or furnishes services to the public as part of his or her own independent business, the worker is not an employee under this test. [*Soc. Sec. Handbook,* March 2001, §827.]

¶303.2   Life Insurance Salespersons

Provided that the test described in ¶303 is met, any individual, although not an employee under the usual common-law rules, whose entire or principal business activity is devoted to the solicitation of life insurance and/or annuity contracts primarily for one life insurance company, is an employee. [Reg. §31.3121(d)-1(d)(3)(ii).]

These salespersons are usually furnished with office space, stenographic help, telephone facilities, forms, rate books, and advertising materials by the company or its general agent. They may be employees of either the company or its general agent. [Reg. §31.3121(d)-1(d)(3)(ii).]

Generally, the contract of employment reflects the intention of the salesperson and the company in regard to full-time activity. The intention of the salesperson and the company (as shown by the contract) and their mutual performance in fact, not the time devoted to the work, govern in determining whether or not the individual is a full-time or part-time salesperson. Thus, the "entire business activity" referred to above may or may not be full time: an individual may work regularly only a few hours each day and still qualify as a full-time life insurance salesperson. A "principal business activity" is one that takes the major part of the salesperson's working time and attention.

The salesperson's efforts must be devoted to the solicitation of life insurance or annuity contracts. While occasional or incidental sales of other types of insurance for the employer, or the occasional placing of surplus-line insurance, will not affect this requirement, the salesperson who is required to devote efforts to selling applications for insurance contracts other than life insurance (for example, health and accident, fire, automobile, etc.) does not meet the requirement. [Reg. §31.3121(d)-1(d)(3)(ii); *Soc. Sec. Handbook,* March 2001, §828.] Regarding termination payments received by retired insurance salespersons, see ¶410.

¶303.3   Traveling and City Salespersons Soliciting Orders from Wholesalers, Retailers, etc.

Provided that they meet the test described in ¶303, full-time traveling or city salespersons, other than agent-drivers or commission-drivers, are employees if they have as their entire or principal activity the solicitation of orders for merchandise on behalf of their principal and transmit the orders to their principal, and obtain their orders from wholesalers, retailers, contractors, or operators of hotels or restaurants or other similar establishments for merchandise or resale of supplies for use in their business operations. "Full time" refers to an exclusive or principal business activity for a single firm or person, and not to time spent on the job. [Reg. §31.3121(d)-1(d)(3)(iv).]

Manufacturer's representatives who hold themselves out as independent business persons and serve the public through their connection with a number of firms are not included in this category. Multiple-line salespersons are generally not employees under this test because they usually solicit orders for more than one principal. However, the salespersons who solicit orders primarily for one principal can be employees of that principal even though they carry on incidental sideline activities on behalf of other persons or firms. [*Soc. Sec. Handbook,* March 2001, §829.]

¶303.4   Homeworkers

Provided that they meet the test described in ¶303, homeworkers are included in the term "employee" if they perform work according to specifications of the persons for whom the services are performed on materials or goods furnished by such persons that are required to be returned to them or persons designated by them. It is immaterial whether the employer calls for the work or the worker delivers it. [Reg. §31.3121(d)-1(d)(3)(iii); *Soc. Sec. Handbook,* March 2001, §830.]

The pay received by a homeworker in this category from any one employer is not counted for Social Security benefits for any calendar quarter in which that employer pays the homeworker *cash wages* of less than $100 in a calendar year. However, all pay, cash and noncash, is counted in applying the annual earnings test to a beneficiary even if the cash-pay test is not met. If the cash-pay test is met, then all pay, cash and noncash, from that employer is counted for benefits, as well as for the annual earnings test. [Reg. §31.3121(a)(10)-1; *Soc. Sec. Handbook,* March 2001, §830.]

The cash-pay test is applicable only to homeworkers who are not employees under the common-law rules of employer and employee. If a homeworker is an employee under these rules, the amount of remuneration paid to him or her during a particular period is immaterial. [Reg. §31.3121(a)(10)-1.]

¶303.5   Retail Securities Brokers

Although the IRS ordinarily uses the fact that instructions are provided by a business to its worker as an indication that the worker is an employee, in the case of a broker-dealer, no weight may be given to such instructions when determining a broker-dealer's employment status if the instructions are given only in compliance with investor protection standards imposed by the state or federal governments. Although this applies to services performed after December 31, 1997, pursuant to the Taxpayer Relief Act of 1997, prior treatment of instructions to securities brokers in the same manner was not necessarily contrary to law. [P.L. 105-34, §921.]

EMPLOYERS

¶304   General Definition of Employer

The liability of an employing unit for employment taxes is generally arrived at through determinations of who are "employees," what are "wages," and what constitutes "employment." In fact, there is no statutory definition of the term "employer" in the Federal Insurance Contributions Act. An employer may be an individual, corporation, partnership, trust, estate, joint-stock company, association, or a syndicate, group, pool, joint venture, or other unincorporated group or entity. A trust or estate, rather than the fiduciary acting for or on behalf of the trust or estate, is generally the employer. [Reg. §31.3121(d)-2.]

An "employer" is one who pays "wages" to at least one "employee" in "employment" not exempt from coverage. The amount of wages, the number of employees, and the length of employment are generally immaterial in the matter of determining employer liability. [Reg. §31.3121(d)-2(a).] The place of performance of service is, however, crucial in some cases. Generally, the service must be performed within the United States; see ¶305 for exceptions. In some cases, employers that would not otherwise be liable become covered as a consequence of an election of coverage; see ¶321, *et seq.*

Regarding the responsibility of certain individuals or entities to pay employment tax and file returns see ¶227.2 and ¶409.

EMPLOYMENT

¶305 General Definition of Employment

The term "employment" generally means any service performed by an employee for the person employing him, irrespective of the citizenship or residence of either. [IRC §3121(b); IRS Reg. §31.3121(b)-3.] For categories of service that are specifically excepted from or included in the term "employment," see ¶306-320.1.

The term "employment" includes [IRC §3121(b); Soc. Sec. Act §210(a)]:

(1) Service performed within the United States;

(2) Service performed on or in connection with an American vessel or American aircraft if (a) the employee is also employed on or in connection with such vessel or aircraft when outside the United States, and (b) the services are performed under a contract of service which is entered into within the United States or the vessel or aircraft touches at a port within the United States during the performance of the contract and while the employee is employed thereon;

(3) Service performed by American citizens employed by American employers on vessels or aircraft of foreign registry, whether the services of such citizens are performed here or abroad;

(4) Service performed outside the U.S. by a citizen or resident of the U.S. as an employee of an American employer; and

(5) Services designated as employment under an international Social Security agreement.

Note that "employment" for Social Security coverage purposes also includes certain classes of services that would otherwise be excluded, once each class has elected coverage, as discussed at ¶321, *et seq.*

The terms "State" and "United States" include the District of Columbia, the Commonwealth of Puerto Rico, the Virgin Islands, Guam, American Samoa, the Northern Mariana Islands, or the territorial waters of any of these places. [Reg. §31.3121(e)-1; *Soc. Sec. Handbook,* June 30, 2004, §961.] Filipino workers who come to Guam under contracts to work temporarily are excluded from coverage. [Reg. §31.3121(b)(18)-1.] Coverage of government workers in Guam and American Samoa is discussed at ¶314.1.

The term "American employer" means an employer that is (1) the United States or any instrumentality thereof, (2) an individual who is a resident of the United States, (3) a partnership, if ⅔ or more of the partners are residents of the United States, (4) a trust, if all of the trustees are residents of the United States, or (5) a corporation organized under the laws of the United States or of any state. [IRC §3121(h); Soc. Sec. Act §210(e).]

For a discussion of "totalization agreements" with foreign governments for coverage of persons subject to the laws of more than one country, see ¶330.

¶305.1   Service for Communist Organizations

Communist organizations are not exempt for purposes of the Federal Insurance Contributions Act. [IRC §3121(b)(17); P.L. 90-237, Jan. 2, 1968.]

¶305.2   Aliens and Nonresidents

Generally speaking, the term "employment" includes all service performed in the United States by an employee for the person employing him, irrespective of the citizenship or residence of either the employee or employer (see ¶305). Therefore, the services of an alien or nonresident are covered, if performed within the United States, unless specifically exempted by another provision of law. See, for example *Zheng v. United States,* 89 FedCl 263 (2009), which held that taxes under FICA apply to wages paid to nonresident aliens working in the Commonwealth of the Northern Mariana Islands (See, also, ¶305, above, with respect to services performed on or in connection with an American vessel or aircraft.)

However, service performed by a nonresident alien for the period he or she is temporarily present in the United States as a nonimmigrant under subparagraph (F), (J), (M), or (Q) of Sec. 101(a)(15) of the Immigration and Nationality Act, and which is performed to carry out the purpose specified in the subparagraph, is exempt. [Reg. §31.3121(b)(19)-1.] Work by a student or exchange visitor other than that performed to carry out the purpose for which he or she was admitted is not excluded from Social Security coverage. However, if the foreign nonresident has received special permission to work, then his or her services may be excluded from coverage. In the case of a student, special permission may be granted by the Department of Homeland Security and, in the case of an exchange visitor, by the sponsor. [*Soc. Sec. Handbook,* Jan. 25, 2007, §939.1.] The specified subparagraphs of the Immigration and Nationality Act refer to foreign students and exchange program participants performing services to carry out the purposes for which they were admitted to the United States, such as studying, teaching, or conducting research. If they are employed for other purposes, however, their services are not exempt. Work performed by the spouse or child of an exchange visitor is covered under the Social Security program. [*Soc. Sec. Handbook,* Jan. 25, 2007, §939.3.]

Special treatment is accorded to foreign service performed by United States citizens or residents in countries with which the U.S. has "totalization agreements." See ¶330.

See ¶410.1 regarding the self-employment tax treatment of work performed by aliens and nonresident aliens.

¶306   Included and Excluded Services

The only services that are not covered are those that are specifically exempted. However, if a portion of the services performed by an employee for an employer during a pay period constitutes employment, and the remainder does not constitute employment, all the services performed by the employee for the employer during the period are treated alike, that is, either all as included or all as excluded. If the services performed during one-half or more of a pay period (not more than 31 consecutive days) by an employee for an employer constitute covered employment, all the services of the individual for such period will be considered to be covered employment. On the other hand, if services performed during more than one-half of a pay period do not constitute covered employment, then all of the services for such period will be excluded. [Reg. §31.3121(c)-1.]

The classes of service described in the following sections will be specifically defined as to the extent to which they qualify as "covered" or "exempt" employment, as the case may be.

¶307   Agricultural Labor

To be covered, an agricultural laborer must either (1) receive cash wages of at least $150 from one employer for agricultural labor during a calendar year, or (2) perform agricultural labor during the year for an employer whose expenditures for agricultural labor in the year equal or exceed $2,500. Thus, if cash remuneration of $150 or more is paid by an employer in a calendar year to an employee for agricultural labor, such employee is covered regardless of the rate, basis, or unit of payment. Cash remuneration for seasonal hand-harvest workers can be excluded from wages after 1987, even if the employer's labor expenses equal or exceed $2,500 a year, if the worker is a hand-harvest laborer who is paid on a piece-rate basis in accordance with regional custom, commutes daily from his or her permanent residence to the farm on which he or she is employed, and has been employed in agricultural labor less than 13 weeks during the preceding calendar year. The exception does not apply, however, to wages of $150 or more. [IRC §3121(a)(8); IRS Reg. §31.3121(a)(8)-1.] See also ¶209.1.

Share farmers, variously called "sharecroppers," "renters," "croppers," "tenants," and "lessees," who operate farms under share-farming arrangements made with the owners or tenants of these farms, are considered self-employed individuals, see ¶402 and ¶410.

A crew leader who furnishes workers to perform agricultural labor for another person (usually a farm operator) and who pays the workers (either for himself or for the farm operator) is the employer of the workers. The leader is self-employed (see Chapter 4), and is responsible for the payment of employment taxes and for reporting the workers for Social Security and hospital insurance purposes. However, if the crew leader has entered into a written agreement with the farm operator whereby the crew leader is designated the employee of the farm operator, then the crew leader and all the members of the crew will be employees of the farm operator. If there is no written agreement and the crew leader does not pay the crew members, then the common-law test is applied in determining the identity of the employer of the workers and the status of the crew leader. [IRC §3121(o).]

The employer of an agricultural laborer is permitted, but not required, to make deductions for employee Social Security and hospital insurance taxes from the employee's wages even though such wages are less than $150 and the employer's expenditures for agricultural labor have not yet equaled $2,500. [IRC §3121(a)(8); IRS Reg. §31.3102-1(b).] See ¶204. For the tax returns required of agricultural employers, see ¶223.2.

As to the method of computing quarters of coverage for farm workers under the benefit provisions, see ¶504.

All agricultural labor performed by foreign agricultural workers lawfully admitted from any foreign country or its possessions on a temporary basis for the purpose of performing agricultural service is excluded from coverage. Temporary agricultural labor performed by foreign workers who have entered this country illegally is not excluded from coverage. [Reg. §31.3121(b)(1)-1; Rev. Rul. 77-140 (CB 1977-1, 301).]

Meaning of "Agricultural Labor"

"Agricultural labor" includes [IRC §3121(g); IRS Reg. §31.3121(g)-1; *Soc. Sec. Handbook,* March 2001 and June 30, 2004, §§904-913.3]:

(1) Service performed on a farm, in the employ of any person, in connection with cultivating the soil or in connection with raising or harvesting any agricultural or horticultural commodity, including the raising, shearing, feeding, caring for, training, and/or management of livestock, bees, poultry, and fur-bearing animals and wildlife. *Cultivating, raising, and harvesting* may include connected activities such as irrigating growing crops, cutting of top soil, spraying, or dusting. *Raising* does not include the care of nursery stock bought for resale unless it is kept long enough to grow appreciably.

(2) Service performed in the employ of the owner, tenant, or other operator of a farm in connection with the operation, management, conservation, improvement, or maintenance of such farm and its tools and equipment, or in salvaging timber or clearing land of brush and other debris left on a farm by a hurricane.

(3) Service performed in connection with the production or harvesting of any commodity defined as an agricultural commodity in section 15(g) of the Agricultural Marketing Act. Agricultural or horticultural commodities include food crops such as nuts, fruits, mushrooms, vegetables, and grain; flowers, cut flowers, trees, and shrubbery; animal feed or bedding; grass, vegetable, and cereal seed; and such other crops as flax, cotton, tobacco, tung nuts, and medicinal herbs raised for sale or for home use.

(4) Service performed in the employ of the operator of a farm in handling, planting, drying, packing, packaging, processing, freezing, grading, storing, or delivering to storage or to market or to a carrier for transportation to market, any agricultural or horticultural commodity in its unmanufactured state, but only if such operator produced more than half of the commodity. (Service performed in connection with commercial canning or commercial freezing or in connection with any agricultural or horticultural commodity after its delivery to a terminal market for distribution for consumption does not constitute "agricultural labor.")

¶307

(5) Service performed on a farm operated for profit if such service is not in the course of the employer's trade or business or is domestic service in a private home of the employer.

The term "farm" includes stock, dairy, poultry, fruit, fur-bearing animal, and truck farms, plantations, ranches, nurseries, ranges, greenhouses or other similar structures used primarily for the raising of agricultural or horticultural commodities, and orchards. [IRC §3121(g); IRS Reg. §31.3121(g)-1.]

The type of services described in paragraph (4), above, also constitutes "agricultural labor" if performed in the employ of a group of operators (other than a cooperative organization), but only if such operators produce all of the commodity with respect to which such services are performed. An unincorporated group of more than 20 operators is deemed to be a cooperative. [IRC §3121(g)(4)(B).]

¶308   Casual Labor

Service that is not in the course of an employer's trade or business is commonly known as "casual labor." As used in the statutes, the term "service not in the course of the employer's trade or business" includes only services that do not promote or advance the trade or business of the employer. The term does not include services performed for a corporation. [Reg. §31.3121(a)(7)-1.]

The test for determining whether or not a casual worker is covered is based solely on the amount of cash remuneration paid to the worker during a calendar year. Only cash pay for this type of work may be counted for Social Security and only if the employee is paid at least $100 in a calendar year. [IRC §3121(a)(7); IRS Reg. §31.3121(a)(7)-1.] See ¶209.3. The employer of such an employee is authorized to make deductions for employee taxes from the employee's wages in anticipation of the employee's attainment of the specified amount of wages. See ¶204. If such services are performed on a farm operated for profit, the rules applicable to farm workers are used in determining the status of such services (see ¶307). [Reg. §31.3121(g)-1(f).]

The term "cash remuneration" includes checks and other monetary media of exchange, but not compensation in the form of food or lodging. [Reg. §31.3121(a)(7)-1(b).]

¶309   Domestic Workers

Coverage of a worker engaged in domestic service is determined on the basis of a cash pay test. A domestic worker is covered in 2020 if he or she receives at least $2,200 from an employer during the calendar year. Thus, earnings under the threshold are not subject to Social Security tax. However, such earnings also do not count towards future benefits.

The threshold amount is subject to upward adjustment in the future as national average wages increase. The annual thresholds have been as follows:

1994–1997	$1,000
1998–1999	1,100
2000	1,200
2001–2002	1,300
2003–2005	1,400
2006–2007	1,500
2008	1,600
2009–2011	1,700
2012–2013	1,800
2014–2015	1,900
2016–2017	2,000
2018–2019	2,100
2020	2,200

Where a worker performs domestic service for more than one employer, the cash-pay test applies separately to each employer. [*Soc. Sec. Handbook,* Nov. 13, 2015, §915.4.]

Domestic service by someone under the age of 18 is exempt from coverage unless it is the worker's principal occupation. [IRC §3121(b)(21), Soc. Sec. Act §210(a)(21).]

Prior to 1995, if domestic service was performed on a farm operated for profit, the rules applicable to farmworkers were used in determining the status of such service (see ¶307). Domestic employees on a farm operated for profit are now subject to the new domestic threshold. [Reg. §31.3121(g)-1(f)1; *Social Security Handbook,* Nov. 13, 2015, §915.5.]

Domestic service. Domestic service means work ordinarily performed as an integral part of household duties that contributes to the maintenance of the employer's residence or administers to the personal wants and comforts of the employer, other members of the household, and guests. In general, this includes work performed by cooks, waiters, waitresses, butlers, housepersons, security guards, governesses, maids, companions, nursemaids, valets, babysitters, janitors, laundresses, furnacemen, caretakers, gardeners, footmen, grooms, seamstresses, handymen, and chauffeurs of family automobiles. [Reg. §31.3121(a)(7)-1(a)(2).]

A "private home" is the fixed abode of one or more persons. Any shelter used as a dwelling may be considered as a private home, for example, a tent, boat, trailer, or a room or a suite in a hospital, hotel, sanatorium, or nursing home. A co-operative boarding and lodging facility may be a private home; however, company-operated facilities are not private homes. In an apartment house, each apartment together with its private stairways, halls, porches, etc., is a private home, but any part of the premises devoted to common use is not. If a house is used mainly as a commercial rooming house or boarding house, only that part of the house used as the operator's living quarters is considered to be a private home. [Reg. §31.3121(a)(7)-1; *Soc. Sec. Handbook,* July 7, 2004, §917.3.]

Domestic workers employed by landlords or rental agencies to do work in or about property being rented as a private home are not performing work in the private home of the employer. [*Soc. Sec. Handbook,* July 7, 2004, §917.4.] Domestic services performed in a local college club, or local chapter of a college fraternity or sorority, by a student who is enrolled and is regularly attending classes at a school, college, or university, are exempt. [Reg. §31.3121(b)(2)-1.]

A person engaged in the trade or business of putting sitters in touch with individuals who wish to employ them is not treated as the employer of the sitters, and the sitters are not treated as the employees of that person, if the person does not pay or receive (directly or through an agent) the wages of the sitters and is compensated solely on a fee basis by the sitters or the individuals for whom the sitting is performed. The term "sitters" is defined in the law as individuals who furnish personal attendance, companionship, or household care services to children or to individuals who are elderly or disabled. Any individual who is deemed not to be the employee of a companion sitting placement service is deemed self-employed for purposes of the tax on self-employment income. [IRC §3506; IRS Reg. §31.3506-1.]

Employer withholding requirements. Employers are required to increase their quarterly estimated tax payments or income tax withholding from their own wages to account for the employment taxes owed on domestic workers. Thus, employers may not pay domestic employment taxes (or unemployment taxes) in a lump-sum when they file their own tax returns.

¶310   Family Employment

For Social Security purposes, the definition of "employment" does not include service performed by a child under the age of 18 for his or her parent. Service performed by a child age 18, 19, or 20 in the employ of his or her parent is also generally excluded from coverage if such work is not performed in the course of the parent's trade or business. [IRC §3121(b)(3); Soc. Sec. Act §210(a)(3).]

Most services performed by a parent in the employ of a child or a spouse are covered. However, services not in the course of the employer's business, and (except as noted below) domestic service in the employer's home, when performed by an individual in the employ of a spouse or child, continue to be excluded. [Reg. §31.3121(b)(3)-1.]

Domestic service in a private home of the employer performed by an individual in the employ of a son or daughter is covered under Social Security if, during the calendar quarter in which the individual performs the domestic service, (a) the employer has living at home at least one son or daughter (including an adopted son or daughter or a stepson or stepdaughter) who is under the age of 18 or who has a mental or physical condition that requires the personal care and supervision of an adult for at least four continuous weeks in such calendar quarter and (b) the employer is a surviving spouse or a divorced individual who has not remarried or has a spouse living in the home who has a mental or physical condition that results in the spouse's being incapable of caring for the child for at least four continuous weeks in such calendar quarter. [IRC §3121(b)(3); Soc. Sec. Act §210(a)(3).]

Services performed in the employ of a corporation are not within the exclusion. Nor are services performed in the employ of a partnership unless the requisite family relationship exists between the employee and each of the partners comprising the partnership. [Reg. §31.3121(b)(3)-1(c).] However, beginning November 1, 2011, if the corporation is a "disregarded entity" (see ¶227.2), such as a single member limited liability corporation or a subchapter S corporation, the owner of the disregarded entity will be treated as the employer and the employee will be considered to be an employee of the owner so as to allow a family member to be excluded from coverage. [IRS Reg. §§31.3121(b)(3)-1T(d), 31.3306(c)(5)-1T(d), 301.7701-2T, as amended by 76 *Fed. Reg.* 67363, November 1, 2011.]

¶311   Fishing and Related Activities

While services performed in the fishing industry are generally not exempt, crewmembers performing services on small boats engaged in catching fish may be treated as self-employed for purposes of the Federal Insurance Contributions Act and for self-employment tax purposes under the following conditions: (1) the services must be performed on a boat under an arrangement with the boat owner pursuant to which the individual does not receive any cash remuneration but instead receives a share of the catch or of the proceeds from the sale of the catch, and the amount of the crewmember's share depends on the amount of the boat's catch; and (2) the operating crew of the boat is generally fewer than 10 individuals. [IRC §§3121(b)(20), 6050A.] The boat operator uses Form 1099-MISC for reporting such payments.

After 1994, a crew member may receive cash payments of $100 or less per trip, contingent on a minimum catch, and if paid solely for additional duties (*e.g.*, as mate, engineer, or cook), for which payment is customarily made. This provision also applies between 1985 and 1995 unless such payments were treated as subject to FICA at the time of payment. [P.L. 104-188, §1116(a).]

See the following chapter for a detailed discussion of self-employment coverage.

¶312 Government Employees—Federal

Newly hired and certain current federal employees covered under the Social Security Act include the following:

(1) all federal employees hired on or after January 1, 1984, including those with previous periods of federal service, unless the period of separation from federal employment does not exceed 365 consecutive days;

(2) all legislative branch employees on the same basis, as well as current employees of the legislative branch who were not participating in the Civil Service Retirement System as of December 31, 1983;

(3) all current and future Members of Congress, the President and Vice-President;

(4) all sitting federal judges, magistrates, bankruptcy judges and referees in bankruptcy, except federal judges who took office prior to 1983 (*U.S. v. Hatter*, 121 S. Ct. 1782 (2001));

(5) all executive level and senior executive service political appointees [Soc. Sec. Act §210(a)(5)]; or

(6) certain federal employees who, although subject to the Civil Service Retirement System, elect to become subject to the Federal Employee's Retirement System under chapter 84, Title 5 of the U.S. Code, or who elect to become subject to the Foreign Service Pension System provided under the Foreign Service Act of 1980. [IRC §3121(b)(5); Soc. Sec. Act §210(a)(5)(H).]

Federal employees have been subject to the hospital insurance portion of the FICA tax since the beginning of 1983.

These coverage provisions do not have the effect of reducing accrued entitlement under any federal retirement program. [P.L. 98-21, §101(e).]

Excluded Services

Specifically excluded from coverage under the Act is federal employment or service for any U.S. instrumentality if performed:

(A) by an inmate of a penal institution;

(B) by an individual as an employee included under 5 U.S.C. §5351(2), relating to certain interns, student nurses, and other student employees of hospitals of the federal government, other than as medical or dental interns or residents in training;

(C) by temporary employees serving in case of emergencies such as fires, storms, earthquakes, or floods;

(D) by individuals in the employ of the U.S. or any U.S. instrumentality since December 31, 1983, or who return to such employment as long as the period of separation from federal service does not exceed 365 consecutive days [Soc. Sec. Act §210(a)(6)]; or

(E) by certain retired federal judges actively performing judicial duties. [IRC §3121(i)(5).]

Prior to 1984, the employment of all civilians employed by the U.S. Government or its instrumentalities was excluded from coverage if (a) the employment came under a retirement system established by a law of the U.S. (see the following paragraph), (b) the service was performed for certain U.S. instrumentalities that were exempt from tax in 1950, and was one for which the instrumentality had established a retirement system, or (c) the service was performed by certain specific individuals or groups, such as the President of the U.S., a member of Congress, an inmate of a penal institution, etc. [IRC §3121(b)(6); Soc. Sec. Act §210(a).]

¶312.1   U.S. Instrumentality; Peace Corps

Federal workers employed by an instrumentality of the U.S. are covered under the Act unless their work is excluded under category (A), (B), (C), (D), or (E), as noted above at ¶312. [IRC §3121(b)(6); Soc. Sec. Act §210(a).]

Work as a volunteer or volunteer leader in the Peace Corps by a citizen or national of the U.S. is covered by Social Security. [IRC §3121(i)(3); *Soc. Sec. Handbook,* June 30, 2004, §943.]

With respect to the limitation on amounts paid to such individuals as "wages," see ¶206.2.

¶313   Government Employees—Foreign

Services performed by an employee in the employ of a foreign government are excepted from coverage. The exception applies not only to services performed by ambassadors, ministers, and other diplomatic officers and employees but also to services performed as a consul or other officer or employee of a foreign government, or as a nondiplomatic representative thereof. For purposes of this exception, the citizenship or residence of the employee is immaterial. [Reg. §31.3121(b)(11)-1.] Regarding "totalization agreements" with other governments, see ¶330.

Certain services performed in the employ of instrumentalities wholly owned by foreign governments are likewise excepted. [Reg. §31.3121(b)(12)-1.]

The family members of a diplomatic agent, as well as the members of the administrative, technical, and service staff of a foreign mission, are excepted from coverage and exempt from taxation with respect to services rendered for a foreign government that has ratified the Vienna Convention on Diplomatic Relations. [Articles 33 and 37 of the Convention, entered into force with respect to the U.S., Dec. 13, 1972.]

However, self-employment coverage is provided for services performed by citizens of the United States in the United States (which includes the Virgin Islands, Puerto Rico, Guam, American Samoa, and the Commonwealth of the Northern Mariana Islands) in the employ of a foreign government, in the employ of an instrumentality wholly owned by a foreign government, or in the employ of an international organization as described at ¶314, below. [IRC §1402(c)(2)(C); SSA Reg. §404.1096.] For further discussion, see ¶402.

¶314   Government Employees—International

Services performed in the employ of international organizations that come under the International Organizations Immunities Act (such as the United Nations, World Health Organization, etc.) are exempt [Reg. §31.3121(b) (15)-1]; however, as noted at ¶313, above, self-employment coverage is provided for certain services performed for an organization of this type. Further discussion of this coverage appears at ¶402.

¶314.1   Government Employees—State

Service in the employ of a state or any of its political subdivisions, or any instrumentality of a state or any of its political subdivisions, is excluded, with the exceptions listed below. [Reg. §31.3121(b)(7)-1.]

For employees of state and local governments, coverage may be elected; see ¶321.2. However, as discussed below at ¶321.2, no state coverage agreement may be terminated after April 20, 1983, the date of enactment of the 1983 Amendments. [Soc. Sec. Act §218(f).]

Service performed by an employee of a state (other than the District of Columbia, Guam, the Commonwealth of the Northern Mariana Islands, or American Samoa) or local government is compulsorily included as covered employment if the employee is not actually participating in a retirement system of the state or unit of local government. [SSA Reg. §404.1200.] This extension of coverage does not apply to individuals employed to relieve them from unemployment; to patients or inmates in hospitals, homes, or other institutions; to employees serving on a temporary basis in case of fire, storm, snow, earthquake, flood, or other similar emergency; to election officials or election workers paid less than the threshold amount (see below); or to employees compensated solely on a fee basis (see ¶321.2 and ¶420, below) who are treated as engaged in self-employment under §1402(c)(2)(E).

Election workers: The annual exclusion for election workers in 2020 is $1,900. In prior years, the exclusion has been as follows:

Prior to 1995	$ 100
1995–1999	1,000
2000–2001	1,100
2002–2005	1,200
2006–2007	1,300
2008	1,400
2009–2012	1,500
2013–2015	1,600
2016	1,700
2017–2019	1,800
2020	1,900

The exclusion for election workers is indexed to wage increases in the economy. [IRC §3121(b)(7)(F), as amended by the Social Security Independence and Program Improvements Act of 1994, P.L. 103-296, §303(a)(2); 84 *FedReg* 56515, Oct. 22, 2019 and prior annual announcements.]

Service performed in the employ of the District of Columbia, or any wholly owned instrumentality thereof, is included as employment if such service is not covered by a retirement system established by a law of the United States, except that the extension of coverage may not apply to service performed: (1) in a hospital or penal institution by a patient or inmate thereof; (2) in a hospital of the District of Columbia by student nurses and certain other student employees (other than as a medical or dental intern or as a medical or dental resident-in-training); (3) on a temporary basis in certain emergencies; or (4) as a member of a board, committee, or council of the District of Columbia paid on a per diem, meeting, or other fee basis. [IRC §3121(b)(7)(C).]

Coverage is provided on a compulsory basis to officers and employees or members of the legislatures of the governments, political subdivisions, or instrumentalities of Guam and American Samoa. The two places are included in the definition of "state" for purposes of the law. [IRC §3121(b)(7)(B); IRS Reg. §31.3121(b)(7)-1; SSA Reg. §404.1004.]

Coverage is provided for service performed in the employ of the government of Guam, or any wholly owned instrumentality thereof, by an employee properly classified as a temporary or intermittent employee whose services are not covered under a retirement system established by a law of Guam. However, service performed by an elected official or member of the legislature or by a patient or inmate of a hospital or penal institution is specifically excluded from coverage. [IRC §3121(b)(7)(D); SSA Reg. §404.1022.]

The wages of the state and local government employees are generally subject to the hospital insurance portion of the FICA tax and the affected employees are provided with hospital insurance coverage, effective with respect to employees hired after March 31, 1986. This coverage was made optional for existing staff. Not covered are individuals employed to relieve them from unemployment, patients or inmates in a hospital, home, or other institution, employees serving on a temporary basis in case of fire, storm, snow, earthquake, flood, or other similar emergency, and interns (other than medical or dental interns or medical or dental residents in training), student nurses, and other student employees of hospitals of the District of Columbia, election workers receiving less than the applicable threshold and employees compensated solely on a fee basis [IRC §3121(u).]

Questions on state and local coverage issues, in general, may be directed to specialists in each of the ten regional offices of the Social Security Administration. Their contact information is located at *www.ssa.gov/slge/specialists.htm.*

Emergency response personnel. Qualified state and local tax benefits and qualified payments provided by a state or local government to a member of a qualified volunteer emergency response organization that are excludable from the volunteer's gross income under Code Sec.139B are not "wages" for employment tax purposes. A qualified benefit under Code Sec. 139B is any reduction or rebate of a state or local real property, personal property, or income tax, on account of services performed as a member of a volunteer emergency response organization that provides firefighting or emergency medical services in tax years after 2007 and before 2011. [IRC §3121(a) (23); SSA §209(a)(20).]

¶315   Publicly Owned Transportation Systems

All service connected with the operation of a public transportation system is covered provided that: (1) substantially all such service is not subject to a general retirement system protected by a state constitution; and (2) all or any part of the system was acquired from private ownership after 1936 and prior to 1951; or (3) if a transportation system is acquired after 1950, such a system was not operated by the state or political subdivision prior to 1951. [Reg. §31.3121(b)(7)-1.]

Service for a public transportation system that is not subject to compulsory coverage may be subject to voluntary coverage; see ¶321.2.

¶316   Members of the Uniformed Services

Service performed by an individual as a member of a uniformed service on active duty, while training for active duty, or while in inactive duty training is covered. [IRC §3121(m).] See ¶534.1. "Member of a uniformed service" includes appointed, enlisted, inducted, or retired members of the Army, Navy, Air Force, Marine Corps and the Coast Guard and includes reserve components of such branches of the Armed Forces with the exception of temporary members of the Coast Guard Reserve. [IRC §3121(n).] The employer taxes are paid by the Federal Government from appropriations available for the pay of the members of the uniformed services, and the employee taxes are deducted from the member's pay. The tax rates are the same as those for civilian employers and employees subject to the taxes, computed on the same taxable wage base. See ¶206.1, 534.1.

As to the benefit provisions applicable to members of the uniformed services, including the special noncontributory wage credits they received until 2002, see ¶534.2.

Military differential pay: Differential pay is an amount paid by a civilian employer to its former employee that is on active military duty and is the difference between the worker's civilian and military pay. These payments are taxable to the employee and subject to income tax withholding but are not subject to FICA or FUTA tax. [Rev. Rul 69-136, 1969-1 CB 252; Rev. Rul. 2009-11. IRB 2009-18, May 4, 2009. IRC §3401(h)(1), as added by P.L. 110-245, §105(a)(1), Heroes Earnings Assistance and Relief Tax Act of 2008.]

¶317   Newspaper Distributors

Congress has granted direct-seller status, a type of statutory nonemployee status, to certain newspaper carriers and distributors. Under Sec. 1118 of the Small Business Job Protection Act (P.L. 104-188), those carriers and distributors whose remuneration is directly related to sales rather than to the number of hours worked are considered to be direct sellers for employment tax purposes. In addition, the worker must sign a contract stating that the worker will not be treated as an employee for federal tax purposes. IRC §3508(b)(2)(A)(iii) applies under either a buy-sell distribution system (where newspapers are purchased from the publisher) or an agency distribution system (where the pay is based on the number of papers delivered), according to the legislative history. The net profit of direct sellers is subject to self-employment tax. Carriers and distributors not covered by the new law will be subject to existing common law or special provisions.

The provision did not however, amend Soc. Sec. Act §210(a)(14), which excludes from "employment" (1) newspaper carriers and distributors under age 18, but only if they do not deliver or distribute newspapers and shopping news to any point for subsequent distribution, and (2) carriers and distributors over age 18 if the magazines or newspapers are sold under a buy-sell distribution system where they are sold to the ultimate consumer at an arranged fixed price, and the employee's pay is the difference between the fixed selling price and the amount at which they are charged to him or her, whether or not the worker is guaranteed a minimum wage or is entitled to be credited with any unsold newspapers or magazines turned back. If the employee is age 18 or over, the work is covered as self-employment under a special provision of the law (see ¶402). If a person under age 18 performs the work in an independent capacity and not as an employee, the work may be covered as self-employment. [Reg. §3121(b)14-1(b); *Soc. Sec. Handbook,* June 30, 2004, §1123.]

"Newspaper or shopping news" includes shopping guides, handbills, or other types of advertising material. "Delivery or distribution" means retail sale, house-to-house delivery, or the passing out of handbills on the street. [Reg. §31.3121(b)(14)-1(a).]

¶318   Railroad Employees

Services performed by railroad employees subject to the Railroad Retirement Act are exempt from Social Security coverage. [IRC §3121(b)(9).]

¶319   Students and Student Nurses

Services performed by a student who is enrolled and regularly attending classes at a school, college, or university are exempt if performed (a) in the employ of the institution at which the student is enrolled and regularly attending classes, or (b) as domestic service in a local college club or local chapter of a college fraternity or sorority. [IRC §3121(b)(2), (10).]

The exclusion of student services from coverage under FICA is governed by amended regulations that specify that whether an organization is considered a school, college or university is determined based on the primary function of that organization. Whether an employee is a student for purposes of the exclusion is determined by examining the individual's relationship with the employer to determine if employment or education is predominant in the relationship.

Who qualifies as a "student?" In order to be defined as a student, an employee's services must be incidental to and for the purpose of a course of study. A "career employee" is an individual whose service dominates the employer-employee relationship and, thus, cannot be said to provide services incident to and for the purpose of a course of study. The final rules provide that in determining whether an employee is a student, the educational and service aspects of the employer-employee relationship are evaluated based on all the relevant facts and circumstances, including whether services were regularly performed for 40 or more hours per week, if the employee is a professional, and if the employee received employment benefits and was required to be licensed. However, if an employee is a full-time "employee," then the employee's services are not incident to or for the purpose of pursuing a course of study.

Treatment of graduate assistants: Graduate research and teaching assistants are not automatically ineligible for the student FICA exception, even though their work may be described under the standard for professional employees. A "professional employee" is an employee who performs work that requires "knowledge of an advanced type in a field of science or learning." However, if an employee has "professional" status, that only suggests that the service aspect of the employee's relationship with the employer is predominant. Whether a professional employee is a student "will depend," says the preamble to the regulations, "upon all the facts and circumstances." If an employee is licensed and/or receives benefits, then that will further suggest the predominance of the service aspect of the empoyee's relationship with the employer. [IRS Reg. §31.3121(b)(2)-1 and IRS Reg. §31.3121(b)(10)-2, as amended by 69 *FedReg* 76404, Dec. 21, 2004.]

Safe harbor: The student exception to FICA applies with respect to services performed by a half-time undergraduate, graduate or professional student for an institution of higher education. An institution of higher education is defined as a public or private nonprofit school, college or university, or affiliated private foundations under IRC §509(a)(3). The safe harbor does not apply to: full-time employees; professional employees; employees eligible to receive vacation, sick leave or paid holiday benefits; employees eligible to participate in a qualified pension, profit-sharing or stock bonus plan under IRC §401(a), or to receive employer contributions; employees eligible to receive an annual deferral of nonelective employer contributions pursuant to a deferred compensation plan under IRC §457(b); employees eligible for reduced tuition due to their employment; or employees eligible to receive life insurance, qualified educational assistance, dependent care assistance or adoption assistance. An employee will not be ineligible under the safe harbor if receipt of employment benefits is mandated by state or local law. The safe harbor also does not apply to postdoctoral students and fellows, medical residents or medical interns. Services performed by these employees cannot be assumed to be incident to and for the course of study. These standards, however, do not constitute the exclusive method for determining whether or not the student exception to FICA applies. Where the safe harbor does not apply, qualification for the student exception to FICA for services performed for a school, college or university is determined based on all the facts and circumstances. [Rev. Proc. 2005-11, replacing Rev. Proc. 98-16, with respect to services performed on or after April 1, 2005.]

Services performed by students who are enrolled and regularly attending classes at a school, college, or university are also excluded from coverage if such service is performed in the employ of an auxiliary organization described in Section 509(a)(3) of the Internal Revenue Code of 1986 (describing certain nonprofit organizations with tax-exempt status), and if such organization is organized and operated exclusively for the benefit of, to perform the functions of, or to carry out the purposes of the school, college, or university, and is operated, supervised, or controlled by or in connection with such school, college, or university. Examples of enterprises operated by such auxiliary nonprofit organizations might be a bookstore, housing, publishing or food service. The exclusion from coverage does not apply if the school, college, or university is an instrumentality of a state or political subdivision thereof, and the services performed by a student in its employ are covered under Social Security pursuant to a state coverage agreement (a "Section 218" agreement) with the Commissioner of Social Security. [IRC §3121(b)(10)(B).]

Most states opted to exclude students from the coverage under the state's Section 218 Agreement. Some states elected to provide Social Security and Medicare coverage to services performed by students in certain schools. The following states have statewide student exclusion: Arizona, California, Colorado, Delaware, Georgia, Hawaii, Idaho, Illinois, Iowa, Kansas, Maine, Maryland, Mississippi, Missouri, Montana, Nebraska, New Hampshire, New Jersey, New Mexico, New York, North Carolina, North Dakota, Oregon, Puerto Rico, South Carolina, South Dakota, Utah, Virginia, Washington, West Virginia, Wisconsin, Wyoming. States with limited student coverage include: Alabama, Alaska, Arkansas, Connecticut, Florida, Indiana, Kentucky, Louisiana, Michigan, Minnesota, Oklahoma, Pennsylvania, Rhode Island, Tennessee, Texas, Vermont, Virgin Islands. Massachusetts, Nevada and Ohio have virtually no Section 218 coverage. Therefore, the rules for mandatory FICA apply. [*http://www.ssa.gov/slge/ student_coverage_chart.htm.*]

Interested individuals in states with limited coverage may determine which students are specifically covered by contacting the state Social Security Administrator—not the Social Security Administration—for their state. [P.L. 105-277, Div. J, §2023; communication from Soc. Sec. Admn., July 19, 1999.] In general, the state Social Security Administrator is the main resource for information about coverage and reporting issues for state and local governments under a state's Section 218 agreement. A list providing contact information for each state's Social Security Administrator may be found at the website of the National Conference of State Social Security Administrators (NCSSA): *www.ncsssa.org/statessadminmenu.html.* Questions on state and local coverage issues, in general, may be directed to specialists in each of the ten regional offices of the Social Security Administration. Their contact information is located at *www.ssa.gov/slge/specialists.htm.*

Student nurses: Service performed as a student nurse in the employ of a hospital or a nurses' training school by an individual who is enrolled and is regularly attending classes in a nurses' training school chartered or approved pursuant to state law is exempt. [IRC §3121(b)(13).] This work is excluded even though the work of other employees of the hospital or nurses' training school is covered. [*Soc. Sec. Handbook,* Sept. 24, 2007, §922.]

¶319

¶320   Hospital Interns and Residents

Work as an intern for a hospital is covered by Social Security as follows: (1) if performed for a privately owned and operated hospital, coverage is compulsory; (2) if performed for a federal hospital, the work is covered on the same basis as the work of other federal employees (see ¶312); and (3) if performed for a state or local government hospital, coverage depends on whether the position is in a group covered under the federal-state agreement (see ¶321.2) or whether the individual is covered by a state or local retirement program (see ¶314.1). [*Soc. Sec. Handbook,* June 30, 2004, §923.] After July 1, 1991, medical residents and interns performing services for a state or local government not participating in a retirement system of the state are mandatorily covered, according to the *Handbook for State Social Security Administrators, SSA Informational Release,* No. 107, April 24, 1992.

Medical residents working at least 40 hours per weeks in any facility are covered under FICA and are ineligible to be exempt as a student. [Reg. §31.3121(b)(10)–2; *Mayo Foundation for Medical Education and Research v. United States,* 131 S. Ct. 704 (2011), 2011-1 USTC ¶50,143, UNEMPL. INS. RPTR ¶14,691C.] For tax periods ending prior to April 1, 2005, the IRS will, however, accept claims that medical residents qualify under the student FICA exception and will issue refunds for previously paid FICA (Social Security) taxes. [IR-2010-25, March 2, 2010.]

University hospitals and the IRS have litigated this issue since the 1990s. Generally, the courts upheld the employer's position that medical residents were not subject to FICA taxes because their services were incident to and for the purpose of pursuing an educational course of study. Following an adverse decision in 2003, [*U.S. v. Mayo Foundation for Medical Education,* 282 FSupp 2d 997 (D. Minn. 2003); 2003-2 USTC ¶50,615; *further proceedings at* 503 FSupp 2d 1164 (D. Minn. 2007); 2007-2 USTC ¶50,577; UNEMPL. INS. REPTR ¶14,099C] the IRS amended the FICA regs [69 *Federal Register* 76404 (Dec. 21, 2004).]

Under the revised regulations, an organization qualifies as a "school" only if its "primary function" is the presentation of formal instruction. Additionally, full-time employees (working at least 40 hours) are not entitled to the student exception, regardless of their student status [Reg §31.3121(b)(10)–2]. In 2011, the U.S. Supreme Court upheld these regulations, affirming the Eighth Circuit's decision and resolving a long-standing issue between the IRS and teaching hospitals. [See *Mayo Foundation for Medical Education and Research v. United States, supra,* reversing *Mayo Clinic, University of Minnesota v. U.S.,* 2009-1 USTC ¶50,432.]

¶320.1   Religious, Charitable, & Nonprofit Organizations

Services performed by employees of §501(c)(3) nonprofit organizations who receive remuneration of $100 or more from the organization during the calendar year are, generally, covered by Social Security. This coverage extends to employees of organizations that have terminated coverage as well as to those who have never before been covered. [IRC §3121(a)(16); P.L. 98-21, §102.]

Nonprofit organization employees over the age of 55 are deemed to be fully insured for Social Security benefits if they acquire, after 1983, a given number of quarters of coverage, according to a sliding scale. Twenty quarters are required for persons age 55 or 56 on January 1, 1984, ranging down to six quarters for those age 60 and over on that date. See ¶505 for a schedule of quarters of coverage required.

Note that employees of nonprofit organizations who are covered on a mandatory basis by the Civil Service Retirement System, such as Legal Service Corporation employees, are to be treated as federal employees for Social Security purposes from 1984. They are, therefore, covered as federal employees by Social Security if newly hired after 1983, or if they had a break in their federal service lasting more than 365 days. [P.L. 98-369, §2601(e).] See, also, ¶312.

Regarding the exemption of certain services performed in the employ of a church or qualified church-controlled organization, see discussion at ¶321.3.

ELECTION OF COVERAGE OR EXEMPTION

¶321   In General

Coverage can be extended to certain classes of services that would otherwise be excluded. The classes involved are certain state and local governmental employees, the lay employees of certain churches and church-controlled organizations, members of religious orders under a vow of poverty, and United States citizens employed abroad by foreign affiliates of American employers. Each class has a different method of obtaining coverage. The following sections involve a discussion of the election requirements in these special classes of services.

¶321.1   Employment by Foreign Affiliate

Citizens or residents of the U.S. employed outside the U.S. by foreign affiliates of an American employer can be covered if the American employer and the Secretary of the Treasury enter into an agreement for the payment of Social Security taxes for such employees. All employees who are citizens or residents of the U.S. and employed by a given affiliate must be included under such agreements if any are to be covered. [IRC §3121(l)(1); Soc. Sec. Act §210(a).]

An American employer may enter into a coverage agreement if it has at least a 10% interest in the employing foreign affiliate (either directly or through one or more entities), with such interest existing in the voting stock thereof in the case of a corporation and in the profits thereof in the case of any other entity. [IRC §3121(l)(6).]

A standard form of agreement (Form 2032) has been provided for American employers wishing to enter into such coverage agreements and may be obtained at the office of any District Director of Internal Revenue or online at *www.irs.gov*. [Reg. §36.3121(l)(1)-1.]

Foreign subsidiaries of American companies performing services under a U.S. government contract are treated as American employers for employment tax purposes. Under the statute, the domestic parent is jointly liable for employment taxes imposed on the foreign subsidiary. The provision does not apply, however, to wages subjected to a foreign country's social security system by a totalization agreement (see ¶330), nor does it apply to services of an employee that are covered by a Section 3121(l) agreement. [IRC §3121(z) and SSA §210(e), as added and amended by the Heroes Earnings Assistance and Relief Tax Act of 2008, P.L. 110-245, §302.]

¶321.2   Government Employees—State and Local

Service in the employ of a state, or any political subdivision thereof, or any instrumentality that is wholly owned by one or more states or political subdivisions, is excluded from coverage, with several important exceptions (see ¶314.1). [IRC §3121(b)(7).] However, provision is made for voluntary agreements for coverage of most employees of state and local governments, other than transportation workers, and for compulsory coverage of transportation workers. [Soc. Sec. Act §218(a).]

Where a voluntary agreement is entered into by a state or local government with the Commissioner of Social Security, each such state or local government must file returns with the IRS and deposit FICA taxes through the Federal Tax Deposit System. [IRC §3126.]

All states have entered into agreements ("Section 218 agreements"), some having provided coverage for most employees and some having provided coverage for only a few employees. Each state has designated an administrator who deals with the Social Security Administration in all matters relating to the agreement. [*Soc. Sec. Handbook,* Oct. 11, 2005, §1000.] See *www.ncsssa.org* for a list with contact information for each state's administrator.

Once an agreement has been entered into with a state, employees of the state and its political subdivisions are brought under the agreement in groups known as "coverage groups." There are two basic types of coverage groups [Soc. Sec. Act §218(b), (c)(4)]:

A. Groups composed of employees of the state or one of its political subdivisions whose positions are not under a state or local retirement system; and

B. Retirement system coverage groups, which are groups composed of employees whose positions are covered by a state or local retirement system.

The Social Security Act gives each state the right to decide which coverage groups are to be included under its agreement. A state may permit its political subdivisions to decide whether to include the subdivisions' employees under the agreement. A state includes additional coverage groups by modifying its agreement.

A *"state"* for the purpose of coverage agreements includes the 50 states, Puerto Rico, the Virgin Islands, and interstate instrumentalities but does not include the District of Columbia, Guam, the Northern Mariana Islands, or American Samoa. [Soc. Sec. Act §218(b)(1); SSA Reg. §404.1200.]

A *"political subdivision"* ordinarily includes a county, city, town, village, or school district, and in many states, depending upon the manner in which such entities are created under state law, includes a sanitation, utility, reclamation, improvement, drainage, irrigation, flood control, or similar district. A political subdivision also includes an instrumentality of a state, or of one or more political subdivisions of a state, or of a state and one or more of its political subdivisions.

An *"interstate instrumentality"* is an independent legal entity organized by two or more states to carry out some function of government, *e.g.*, regional transportation systems. For purposes of a Section 218 agreement, an interstate instrumentality has the status of a state under the Social Security Act. [Soc. Sec. Act §218(g); *Soc. Sec. Handbook,* Jul. 8, 2004, §1002.3.]

Positions Not Covered by Retirement System

A coverage group composed of employees whose positions are not covered by a retirement system may consist of any of the following groupings of employees or political subdivisions: all employees of the state or political subdivision who are performing services in connection with governmental functions; all employees of the state or political subdivision performing services in connection with a single proprietary, or nongovernmental, function; civilian employees of a state's National Guard units; or inspectors of agricultural products employed pursuant to an agreement between the state and the Department of Agriculture under the Agricultural Marketing Act (7 U.S.C. 1624) or the Perishable Agricultural Commodities Act (7 U.S.C. 499n). [Soc. Sec. Act §218(b)(5).]

Coverage is provided for all present and future employees in the group unless one of the mandatory exclusions described below applies. [Soc. Sec. Act §218(c)(2).]

A state can cover, as part of any one of these groups, employees whose positions are under a retirement system but who are personally ineligible to become members of the system. [Soc. Sec. Act §218(c).]

Mandatory Exclusions

Services that *must be* excluded from any group to which coverage is extended are those performed by [Soc. Sec. Act §218(c)(6), (d)(5)(A)]:

(1) employees engaged in work relief projects;

(2) patients or inmates working in hospitals or institutions;

(3) transportation workers covered under the provisions discussed at ¶315;

(4) workers performing service (except agricultural and student work) that is not "employment" as defined in the law;

(5) service performed by an individual as an employee serving on a temporary basis in case of fire, storm, snow, earthquake, flood, or other similar emergency; and

(6) state and local government workers who are compulsorily covered by Social Security (*i.e.*, most workers who are not members of a state or local retirement system as of July 1, 1991).

Work in connection with a public transportation system operated by a state or political subdivision of a state can be included in a federal-state agreement as part of a "coverage group" if the work is not covered by Social Security on a compulsory basis. [Soc. Sec. Act §218(c).] Generally, the work is compulsorily covered where the transportation system was acquired from private ownership after 1950 if no general retirement system became applicable to the employees at the time it was acquired. See ¶315.

Optional Exclusions

Public employees performing the following types of services can be included or excluded at the option of the state [Soc. Sec. Act §218(c)]:

(1) services in elective positions;

(2) services in part-time positions;

(3) services in positions paid for on a fee basis (see, however, below for coverage of such services under the self-employment provisions);

(4) services performed by a student for a school he is attending (students are excluded in at least 30 states; see ¶319, above;

(5) services performed by an agricultural laborer who receives cash wages of less than $150 in a calendar year from one employer, or who performs services for any employer whose expenditures for agricultural labor during the year are less than $2,500;

(6) election officials or election workers who are paid less than a specified amount in a calendar year ($1,900 for 2020); and

(7) police officers and firefighters (see below).

These exclusions may be taken by the state in any combination it wishes with respect to each separate coverage group. Any services that a state chooses to exclude may be included later if state law and the general terms of the state's agreement permit it. If one of the types of work listed above has been included with respect to a coverage group, it cannot later be removed from coverage. [Soc. Sec. Act §218(c)(4).]

Police officers and firefighters: Police officers and firefighters who participate in a public retirement system may be covered under a Section 218 agreement, subject to a majority vote by all current members of the retirement system not already covered.

Police officers and firefighters not covered by a retirement system are generally covered when a Section 218 agreement, or a modification to such an agreement is made applicable to the absolute coverage group of which they are a part in the same manner as services performed by other noncovered employees. [*Soc. Sec. Handbook,* Oct. 17, 2005, §§1007, 1016.]

Retroactive Coverage

Any agreements or modifications entered into by any state for extending coverage to current employees may be effective as early as the last day of the sixth calendar year preceding the year in which the agreement or modification is mailed or delivered to the Commissioner. States may also retroactively cover an individual who leaves the employ of a state or locality (because he died, retired, or for other reasons) during the period when a coverage agreement between the state and the Commissioner of Social Security is in the process of being negotiated or executed. Accordingly, states may obtain retroactive coverage, within the general time limits applying to state and local employment, for individuals who are employees on any state-specified date that is (1) not earlier than the date the state mails or otherwise delivers its agreement or modification to the Commissioner of Social Security and (2) not later than the date the agreement is executed by the Commissioner. If an individual is in the employ of the state or local government on the date specified by the state, the employee would be covered for whatever retroactive period is provided for the employment group, even though the employment is terminated before the agreement is executed. States are permitted to extend such retroactive coverage to former employees of the coverage group to which the agreement applies whose earnings had been erroneously reported and not refunded. [Soc. Sec. Act §218(e).]

State or Local Retirement Systems

A state can bring members of a state or local retirement system under its federal-state agreement if a referendum by secret written ballot is held among the members of the system and a majority of the members of the system eligible to vote in the referendum vote in favor of coverage. This action can be taken without dissolving the retirement system. [Soc. Sec. Act §218(d)(3).]

A retirement system means a pension, annuity, retirement, or similar fund or system established by a state or political subdivision thereof. [Soc. Sec. Act §218(b)(4).] The system need not have been created by legislative action of the state or political subdivision nor does it have to be one providing for benefits guaranteed by the state constitution. Ordinarily, the plan is "established" by the state or political subdivision if the state, political subdivision, or instrumentality pays part of the cost of the retirement plan or has established the plan under its authority. [*Soc. Sec. Handbook*, Oct. 11, 2005, §1005.]

Whether or not an individual is a member of a retirement system is a matter for determination by the state under applicable state law. Generally, a worker is a member of a retirement system if his or her relationship to the retirement system would serve as a basis for qualifying for retirement benefits or would count toward added benefits after first qualification. [*Soc. Sec. Handbook*, Oct. 11, 2005, §1005.2.]

Ordinarily, only individuals in an employment relationship on a specific date, set out in the agreement, can obtain retroactive coverage for services. However, under certain conditions, a State may consider former employees, whose earnings were incorrectly reported to the Social Security Administration and to the Internal Revenue Service, to be in the coverage group for the period of retroactive coverage. [*Soc. Sec. Handbook*, Aug. 25, 2009, §1011.]

A retirement system coverage group for referendum and coverage purposes may, at the option of the state, consist of: (1) all employees in positions under the system; (2) only employees of the state in positions under the system; (3) all employees of one or more political subdivisions in positions under the system; (4) any combination of the groups referred to in (2) and (3); or (5) all employees of each institution of "higher learning" or of any hospital that is not a political subdivision in itself. Institutions of higher learning include colleges, junior colleges, and teachers' colleges. [Soc. Sec. Act §218(d)(6); *Soc. Sec. Handbook*, Jan. 25, 2007, §1006.]

A referendum must be held under the supervision of the particular state concerned. Not less than ninety days' notice of the referendum must be given to all eligible employees. (It should be noted that only those eligible employees who are given ninety days' notice are also eligible to elect coverage for themselves under the referendum.) The state, before holding the referendum, must decide which classes of positions (such as agricultural labor), if any, are to be excluded from participation in the referendum. The state also has the option of excluding from the agreement specifically designated positions within the coverage group. The referendum itself must be held within two years of a relevant agreement; and no two referendums with respect to the same retirement system can be held within a year's time. Additional provision is made for those employees whose positions are covered by a retirement system, but who are not themselves

¶321.2

eligible for membership in the system. Such employees may obtain coverage without means of a referendum; however, despite the fact that they cannot vote in a referendum as members of a retirement system, such employees could also be covered along with the system members if the referendum were favorable to coverage. When a retirement system covers positions of employees of more than one institution of higher learning, the employees of each such public institution of higher learning may, if the state so desires, be considered as having a separate retirement system. [Soc. Sec. Act §218(d)(3).]

All members of a retirement system (with certain minor exceptions) must be treated as a single group for purposes of coverage. Thus, all members of a retirement system must be covered if any are covered. However, some states are permitted to divide a state or local government retirement system into two parts for purposes of coverage, one part to consist of the positions of members who desire coverage and the other to consist of the positions of members who do not desire coverage. Services performed by the members in the part consisting of positions of members who desire coverage may then be covered under the regular referendum procedure. Once this is done, the services of all persons who in the future become members of the retirement system must also be covered. [Soc. Sec. Act §218(d)(6).]

An individual who is in a position covered under a divided retirement system and who is not a member of such system but who is eligible to become a member thereof is considered to be a member of the system. However, a state is permitted, if it so desires, to modify its agreement to include persons in positions covered by the system but ineligible to join under the separate retirement system consisting of the positions of members of the group electing to be covered under Social Security. [Soc. Sec. Act §218(d)(6)(E).]

The list of the states (including political subdivisions within such states) permitted to split a retirement system as expanded by amendments to the Act includes Alaska, California, Connecticut, Florida, Georgia, Hawaii, Illinois, Kentucky, Louisiana, Massachusetts, Minnesota, Nevada, New Jersey, New Mexico, New York, North Dakota, Pennsylvania, Rhode Island, Tennessee, Texas, Vermont, Washington, and Wisconsin. It is possible to extend coverage, without a regular coverage referendum, to those retirement system members who choose to be included in that part of the retirement system made up of the positions of members desiring coverage, provided certain safeguards are observed in the division of the system into two parts. [Soc. Sec. Act §218(d)(6)(C).]

In the case of state and local government employees who are compensated solely on a fee basis (such as constables and justices of the peace), fees received directly from the public (and not from government funds) that are not covered under a state agreement are covered under the self-employment provisions of law (see ¶402, below). However, a state can modify its coverage agreement to provide coverage for fee-basis employees as employees. States are permitted to remove from coverage under an agreement classes of persons who are compensated solely on a fee basis. However, once a modification of this nature is made, the agreement cannot be further modified to again provide coverage for these fee-based employees. [Soc. Sec. Act §218(m).]

Notice Requirement: Effect of Noncovered Employment

State and local government employers are required to disclose to new employees who will be working in noncovered employment that their entitlement to Social Security benefits, either on their own earnings record, or on the earnings record of a spouse or former spouse will be reduced by any pension they may receive from the noncovered employment. The Social Security Administration has prescribed Form SSA-1945 for this purpose. This notice, which may be downloaded from the internet at *www.ssa.gov/forms/ssa-1945.pdf*, must be provided to the new employee before employment begins. The employee must sign the form, which the employer must then forward to the pension-paying agency.

Specifically, the notice explains to new noncovered employees that earnings from the position are not covered by Social Security and that when the individual retires or becomes disabled, they may receive a pension from their work in noncovered employment. However, if so, and if the worker is also entitled to a Social Security benefit based on their own work, then, under the Windfall Elimination Provision (see ¶512), their benefit is figured under a modified formula that will reduce their Social Security benefit.

Termination of Coverage—the "Drop-Out"

A federal-state Social Security coverage agreement can no longer be terminated in its entirety or with respect to any coverage group on or after April 20, 1983, the date of enactment of the Social Security Act Amendments of 1983. [Soc. Sec. Act §218(f).]

¶321.3   Religious, Charitable, and Other Nonprofit Organizations

Churches or qualified church-controlled tax-exempt organizations are afforded the option of making an election to exclude from the FICA tax base remuneration for all services performed for the organization, other than in an unrelated trade or business. The employees of organizations so electing will then be liable for self-employment (SECA) taxes with respect to the excluded services unless they claim a religious exemption from SECA. See ¶401.4. [IRC §3121(w); IRS Reg. §301.9100-6T(c).]

For employees of electing organizations, wages of less than $100 per calendar year are not subject to SECA taxes and the SECA tax base is generally conformed to the applicable FICA rules. Remuneration that actually may be received before the SECA tax is imposed is $108.28. See ¶410. [IRC §§1402(a)(12); 3121(a)(16); IRS Reg. §301.9100-6T(c)(1).] Electing organizations remain subject to income tax withholding and reporting requirements with respect to all employees. [IRS Pub. 15-A, *Supplement to Pub. 15, Employer's Tax Guide,* §3, p. 10 (rev. Dec. 23, 2019).]

Revocation of election: Either the electing church or the Internal Revenue Service may revoke this election. A church or organization may revoke its election under IRC §3121(w) to exclude the payment of employment and Social Security taxes by filing Form 941 (Employer's Quarterly Federal Tax Return) and paying Social Security and Medicare taxes in full for the first quarter for which the revocation is to be effective. [IRC §3121(w)(2); IRS Reg. §301.9100-7T(i)(2).] Once an election is revoked, a new election to exclude the payment of employment and Social Security taxes may not be made. [Reg. §301.9100-7T(i)(3).] The Treasury Department will permanently revoke an election if the electing organization fails to provide the required information for a period of two years or more regarding the wages paid to each employee. The revocation is effective from the first year of the two-year period for which there was a failure to furnish such information. [IRC §3121(w)(2); IRS Reg. §301.9100-6T(c)(5).]

An organization is *eligible to make an election* if it states that it is opposed for religious reasons to the payment of Social Security taxes and if the organization is (1) a church (including conventions or associations of churches), (2) an elementary or secondary school controlled, operated, or principally supported by churches (or conventions or associations of churches), or (3) a church-controlled tax-exempt organization under IRC §501(c)(3). However, such an organization, although otherwise tax-exempt, does not qualify if (A) it offers goods, services, or facilities for sale to the general public (*i.e.,* to persons who are not church members), other than on an incidental basis and other than at a nominal charge, and, also, (B) it normally receives more than 25 percent of its support from the sum of (a) governmental sources, and (b) receipts from admissions, sales of merchandise, performance of services or furnishing of facilities other than in unrelated trades or businesses. [IRC §3121(w)(1), (3).]

When to file: An organization must file an application for exemption prior to the first date on which a quarterly employment tax return would otherwise be due from the electing organization. [IRS Form 8274; IRC §3121(w)(2).]

The remuneration subject to SECA tax is discussed at ¶410.

Regarding the status of ministers, Christian Science practitioners, and members of religious orders, other than those under a vow of poverty or in the employ of such a religious, charitable, or other organization, see ¶401.1.

Members of Religious Orders Under Vow of Poverty

If an individual is a member of a religious order and has taken a vow of poverty, he is automatically exempt from the self-employment tax for any amount received while working for his church or an agency of such church (the last sentence of Code Sec. 1402(c)). No exemption application need be filed. However, if the individual works for an outside organization, the exemption from the self-employment tax does not extend to the amount earned from the outside employment. [IRS Reg. §1.1402(c)-5(d).] The law has long provided that services are covered if the order, or an autonomous subdivision thereof, elects coverage for its entire active membership by filing a certificate of election (Form SS-16) with the Internal Revenue Service. [IRC §3121(r); IRS Reg. §31.3121(r)-1(a).] A member of a religious order is any individual who is subject to a vow of poverty as a member of the order, who performs tasks usually required (and to the extent usually required) of an active member of the order, and who is not considered retired because of old age or disability. [IRS Reg. §31.3121(r)-1(b).]

The certificate of election must specify: (1) that the election of coverage will be irrevocable; (2) that the coverage will apply to all current and future members of the order or subdivision; (3) that all services performed by a member in the exercise of the duties required will be deemed to have been performed as an employee of the order or subdivision; and (4) that the order or subdivision will pay the tax imposed on employees and employers with respect to the wages of each active member. [Reg. §31.3121(r)-1(c).]

The order or subdivision may elect to have the coverage begin on the first day of the calendar quarter in which the certificate of election is filed, or the first day of the following quarter, or the first day of any of the 20 quarters preceding the quarter in which the certificate of election is filed. If the order or subdivision elects an effective date earlier than the first day of the quarter in which the election is filed, the coverage can apply only to services performed during the retroactive period by a person who was an active member when the services were performed, and who is alive on the first day of the quarter in which the certificate of election is filed. The date for filing FICA returns and paying the taxes for quarters in the retroactive period without incurring penalties and interest is the last day of the month following the quarter in which the certificate of election is filed, and the period for assessing taxes does not expire before the end of the three years after that last day. [IRS Reg. §31.3121(r)-1(d).]

The wages of a member of a religious order for which a certificate of election of coverage may be in effect includes the fair market value (but not less than

$100 a month) of any board, lodging, clothing, and other perquisites furnished to the member by the order or subdivision, or by any person or organization under an agreement with the order or subdivision. [IRS Reg. §31.3121(i)-4.]

¶321.4 Religious Objectors to Social Security

An exemption is provided for the employer and employee portion of the FICA tax where both the employer and the employee are members of a recognized religious sect that has been in existence since December 31, 1950, has established tenets and teachings in opposition to insurance benefits, and generally provides for its own dependent members. As adherents of the sect, the employer and employee must be conscientiously opposed to receipt of private or public insurance benefits, must file applications for exemption from the tax as required for an exemption from SECA tax under IRC §1402(g), and must waive the right to receive Social Security benefits pursuant to Soc. Sec. Act §202(v). This exemption is also available to employees of partnerships in which each partner holds a religious exemption from Social Security coverage. [IRC §3127.]

Services performed in the employ of a corporation are not within the exception. However, if the corporation is a "disregarded entity" (see ¶227.2), such as a single member limited liability corporation or a subchapter S corporation, the owner of the disregarded entity will be treated as the employer and the employee will be considered to be an employee of the owner so as to allow a religious objector to Social Security to be excluded from coverage. [IRS Regs. §31.3127-1T(c) and §301.7701-2T, as amended by 76 *Fed. Reg.* 67363, November 1, 2011.]

See ¶401.4 regarding the filing for an exemption from tax on religious grounds under SECA.

TOTALIZATION AGREEMENTS

¶330   Totalization Agreements

The President of the United States is authorized to enter into bilateral arrangements, generally known as "totalization agreements," with foreign countries in order to prevent double Social Security taxation of U.S. citizens employed abroad and to assure continuity of coverage for those U.S. citizens who divide their working careers between work covered by the U.S. Social Security system and work covered under a foreign social insurance or pension system of general application that provides for payment of benefits based on old age, death, or disability. [Soc. Sec. Act §233.]

The agreements cover all types of retirement, survivor and disability insurance benefits (except benefits paid to the transitionally insured and payments under either the U.S. Medicare or Supplemental Security Income (SSI) programs). [SSA POMS §GN 01701.135 (TN 10 3/04).]

The purpose of a totalization agreement is to eliminate dual coverage and dual employee and employer taxation for the same work. Since the individual cannot receive credit under both systems, he or she does not have to pay Social Security taxes under both systems. Under the territoriality rule, the employee will generally only be subject to Social Security taxes of the country where he or she is working. However, see discussion of an exception under the "detached worker rule" below.

A certificate of coverage (see below) must be obtained in order to avoid paying taxes to both countries. If the individual works in either country and his or her work is covered under only one Social Security system, the individual must pay taxes only to that system. No certificate of coverage is necessary. Note, also, that foreign coverage can be used to establish an earlier month of entitlement for workers fully insured with U.S. coverage only. [Soc. Sec. Act §233(c).]

Note, totalization agreements do not allow directly covered workers to elect the system to which they will contribute. Nor do the agreements change the basic coverage provisions of participating countries' Social Security laws (*e.g.*, definition of covered earnings). The agreements merely exempt workers from coverage under the system of one country or the other where workers would otherwise be covered under both systems.

Coverage

The *country of coverage* is usually specified by the terms of the agreement. Generally, a worker will be covered by the country in which he or she is working, although an agreement may provide for coverage by the country to which the worker has the greater attachment. [Reg. §404.1913.]

Certificate of coverage. Employees (including self-employed workers) who are exempt from U.S. or foreign Social Security taxes under a totalization agreement must document the exemption by obtaining a Certificate of Coverage from the country that will continue to provide coverage. Thus, U.S. employees sent on temporary assignment to the United Kingdom must obtain a Certificate of Coverage from the Social Security Administration in order to establish the exemption from paying U.K. Social Security tax. Similarly a U.K.-based employee working temporarily in the United States must obtain a certificate from the U.K. documenting the exemption from U.S. Social Security tax.

Each certificate will indicate the period of time for which it is valid. The certificate is accepted by the other country as evidence that the employment or self-employment is exempt from coverage by that country. Certificates from the

U.S. will be issued by the Division of International Program Policy and Agreements, Office of International Policy, to whom requests for certificates should be addressed at P.O. Box 17741, Baltimore, Maryland 21235. Requests for certificates of coverage may also be submitted by fax to 410-966-1861 and online at *https://opts.ssa.gov.* [Reg. §404.1914.]

To avoid difficulties, certificates should be requested as soon as possible, preferably before the work in the other country begins. Once the certificate is issued, indicating that a U.S. employee is covered by a foreign system, the employer can immediately stop withholding and paying U.S. Social Security tax on the employee's earnings. Note, employers generally require certificates for employees that have transferred abroad. Self-employed persons must request their own certificate.

Certificates of coverage issued by a foreign country should be retained by the employer in the United States in the event of an audit by the IRS. No copy should be sent to the IRS unless specifically requested. [SSA POMS §RS 02001.005 (TN 17 6/97).] Self-employed U.S. citizens or residents (see below) must attach a photocopy of the foreign certificate to their U.S. tax returns.

If the individual works in either country and the work is covered under only one Social Security system, he or she must pay taxes only to that system. No certificate of coverage is necessary.

The effective date of a coverage exemption is the date shown on the certificate of coverage received from the other country. Generally, this will be the date the period of work began, but may be no earlier than the effective date of the totalization agreement. It is the responsibility of the individual who has been issued a certificate of coverage by the U.S. to present the certificate to the other government authorities. [Reg. §404.1914.]

Minimum coverage requirement. The wage earner must have a minimum amount of coverage, ranging from one year to 18 months, in order to be eligible to have the U.S. and foreign credits combined. A minimum of six quarters of coverage from covered work under Title II is required in the U.S. to have foreign coverage considered in determining a worker's entitlement to or amount of a Title II benefit. [Reg. §404.1908.]

If the minimum coverage requirement is met, work credits from the other country may be added to determine if the wage earner is insured for benefits. Generally, one U. S. quarter of coverage will be credited for every three months of foreign coverage without regard to the usual earnings criteria for crediting quarters of coverage. However, if the foreign country credits coverage on a weekly basis, one U.S. quarter of coverage will be credited for every 13 weeks or fraction thereof of foreign employment. Similarly, if the foreign country credits on an annual basis, four U.S. quarters will be credited for each year of foreign coverage. [SSA POMS GN 01701.125 (TN 10 3/04).]

> **Example:** An employee files for benefits from the U.S. and has at least six U.S. quarters of coverage but not enough to qualify for a regular benefit. Swiss coverage may be counted. Alternatively, if the employee applies for benefits from Switzerland and has at least one year of Swiss coverage, U.S. coverage can be counted.

Self-employed. Social Security coverage extends to self-employed U.S. citizens and residents even if they work in another country. Thus, self-employed employees and residents are generally dually covered when they work outside the United States, as the host country will also typically provide coverage. However, most U.S. agreements eliminate dual coverage for the self-employed by assigning coverage to the worker's country of residence. For example, a covered self-employed U.S. citizen living in Sweden is covered by the Swedish system, but excluded from U.S. coverage.

Totalization Benefits

If the claimant is applying for totalization benefits from the U.S., he or she must also file the regular Title II applications for benefits required without regard to totalization unless the individual is already receiving regular Title II benefits. A special application for totalization benefits, which is unique for each agreement, is also required. Generally, only one totalization agreement is required to protect the rights of all persons entitled to Title II benefits. [Reg. §404.1925; SSA POMS §GN 01702.105 (TN 2 3/04).]

The Application for Benefits Under a U.S. International Social Security Agreement (Form SSA-2490-BK) is a multipurpose form that may be used to claim totalization benefits from the U.S., foreign benefits from another country (under specified agreements), or both U.S. and foreign benefits. A separate special form is used to claim Canadian benefits, CDN-USA 1, or if the applicant last resided in Quebec, QUE/USA-1. [SSA POMS §GN 01715.220 (TN 7 6/04).] Form D/USA is used to claim German retirement and disability benefits. Form D/USA 2 is used to claim German survivor benefits. Form US/Italy1 is used for claims for benefits from Italy.

Each country determines eligibility for benefits under its own laws and pays its benefits independently of the other. A claim for benefits under an agreement may result in: (a) both countries paying totalization benefits based on combined periods of coverage; (b) one country paying regular (nontotalization) benefits (if the worker is insured under its system) and the other paying totalization benefits based on combined periods of coverage; (c) both countries paying regular (nontotalization) benefits; or (d) one or both countries denying the claim. U.S. payments are made by the U.S. Department of the Treasury early each month and cover benefits for the preceding month. [SSA POMS §GN 01701.100 (TN 10 3/04).]

A claimant, for example, filing for disability benefits under the U.S. and Italian agreements may be found not disabled and, therefore, denied benefits under the U.S. law, yet found disabled and entitled to benefits under the Italian law, in which case Italy would pay a proportionate benefit based on Italian earnings while the U.S. would pay nothing.

Limit on totalized benefits. U.S. periods of coverage may be combined with coverage from only one foreign system at a time to determine eligibility for any U.S. totalization benefit. If, for example, an individual is eligible for a totalized benefit under the U.S.-Italian agreement and the U.S.-German agreement, benefits will be paid only under one of the agreements.

No dual Social Security coverage. Benefits will be awarded under the agreement resulting in the highest benefit amount. Work performed prior to the effective date of a totalization agreement may generally be applied to establish entitlement, but there can be no entitlement for months preceding the effective date of the agreement. [Reg. §404.1910.]

Benefit amount (Relative Earnings Position (REP) method). To determine the benefit payable under a totalization agreement, unless the agreement provides otherwise, a theoretical earnings record is created using the worker's actual earnings under the U.S. system and the national average of earnings by year under the U.S. system. (Information concerning foreign earnings is not required. Only foreign coverage information to determine eligibility must be submitted.) Once this theoretical earnings record has been created, a theoretical primary insurance amount (PIA) will be determined using one of the regular computation methods. The theoretical PIA is then prorated to reflect the proportion of a coverage lifetime actually completed under the U.S. program. A coverage lifetime is defined in the revised regulations as the number of the worker's benefit computation years, *i.e.*, the years that must be used in determining a worker's average earnings under the regular U.S. computation method. The theoretical PIA is multiplied by a pro rata fraction that is equal to the actual number of U.S. quarters of coverage earned multiplied by three and then divided by the number of divisor months in the computation period. The divisor months are the months in the worker's computation base years (post-age-22) (see ¶507.5 regarding "computation base years").

To ensure that the totalization benefit payable will not in any case be higher than the benefit that could be payable if the beneficiary were eligible without totalization, the REP rules contain a "cap" equal to the nontotalization (national law) benefit. Thus, if the pro rata PIA should be higher than the nontotalizaton benefit amount, the nontotalization amount will be paid. [Reg. §404.1918(a)(4); SSA POMS GN 01701.146E.]

If a claimant does not agree with a determination of rights based on a claim filed under a totalization agreement, he or she may file a written request for reconsideration, hearing, or appeal under the same conditions as ordinarily apply under each country's Social Security laws. Only one request is necessary, even when independent decisions by both countries are questioned, and the date of filing with one country will be recognized as the date of filing with the other. [Reg. §404.1927.]

After U.S. totalization benefits have been awarded, recomputations to include additional U.S. earnings will be done without the need for a written request. Recomputations to include additional foreign earnings, when appropriate, will be done only upon written request. [Reg. §404.1919.]

General questions about international Social Security agreements (but not about individual claims) may be directed to the Office of International Programs at 410-965-7306. Individuals outside the United States with questions about pending or existing claims, or other non-claim matters may contact the Social Security Administration by fax or voice telephone at one of several numbers, depending upon the claim status and the last two digits of a claimant's or beneficiary's Social Security Number. A directory of these numbers is available online at *www.ssa.gov/foreign/phones.html.*

Tax Rules

A totalization agreement effectively limits an employee's liability for Social Security taxes to the country in which the employee is actually working.

Detached worker rule. Totalization agreements (except with Italy), however, contain a "detached worker rule," pursuant to which an employee who has been stationed in a foreign country for less than five years will be subject to the Social Security taxes of the employee's home country. In the event the employee is permanently located in the foreign country, the employee will be subject to the Social Security taxes of that country, and not to U.S. Social Security tax. [IRS Chief Counsel Advice 201214023, April 6, 2012.]

3121(l) agreements. The advantage of totalization agreements to employers is that, because a worker in a foreign country is subject only to the Social Security taxes of that country, the employer is not required to pay U.S. Social Security taxes for that employee. U.S. employers, however, may enter into 3121(l) agreements with the U.S. Treasury, pursuant to which U.S. Social Security coverage may be provided to U.S. citizens or resident employees of a foreign affiliate of the employer outside the United States. U.S. coverage will not continue in the event a transferred employee works for a foreign affiliate, absent a 3121(l) agreement. The IRS has ruled, however, that, in the event a U.S. citizen is permanently transferred to the foreign country, the employee will be subject to the Social Security taxes of the foreign nation, irrespective of any 3121(l) agreement. [Ibid.]

Agreements in Effect

The complete text of each agreement, as well as information that explains how an employer can request the documentation needed to avoid Social Security taxes in a foreign country under an agreement, is available online from the Social Security Administration at *www.ssa.gov/international/totalization_agreements.html.*

The following summary, prepared by the Social Security Administration, lists the status of totalization agreements as of January 10, 2020 [*http://www.ssa.gov/international/agreements_overview.html,* visited Jan. 10, 2020]:

☐ *Australia:* The U.S.-Australian Social Security agreement was signed at a ceremony in Canberra, Australia, on September 27, 2001, and entered into force on October 1, 2002.

☐ *Austria:* The U.S.-Austrian Social Security agreement was signed on July 13, 1990, and entered into force on November 1, 1991. A supplementary agreement dealing primarily with Austrian benefits was signed on October 5, 1995, and transmitted to Congress on May 17, 1996. It entered into force on January 1, 1997.

☐ *Belgium:* The U.S.-Belgian Social Security agreement was signed on February 19, 1982, with an additional protocol signed on November 23, 1982. Both entered into force on July 1, 1984.

☐ *Brazil:* The U.S.-Brazilian Social Security agreement was signed on June 30, 2015, and entered into force on October 1, 2018.

☐ *Canada:* The U.S.-Canadian Social Security agreement was signed on March 11, 1981 and a supplemental agreement was signed on May 22, 1981. A U.S.-Quebec understanding to extend the agreement to Quebec's provincial-level Social Security program was signed on March 30, 1983. All of these agreements entered into force on August 1, 1984. A draft supplementary agreement primarily intended to authorize U.S. and Canadian Social Security agencies to assist each other in administering their respective programs was signed on May 28, 1996, and entered into force on October 1, 1997.

Note that the Tax Court has ruled that a citizen and resident of the United States who worked as a consultant in Canada had income subject to self-employment tax in the United States even though the Canadian authorities incorrectly required his employer to withhold taxes from his compensation. Under the totalization agreement, a tie-breaker rule applies when a taxpayer is subject to employment taxes in both countries if he is treated by the United States as self-employed and by Canada as an employee. The rule grants the IRS the exclusive right to tax the taxpayer as a self-employed person residing in the United States. [*R.L.Rusten,* TC Summary Opinion 2008-16.]

☐ *Chile:* The U.S.-Chilean agreement was signed on February 16, 2000, in Santiago and entered into force on December 1, 2001.

☐ *Czech Republic:* The U.S.-Czech agreement was signed in Prague on September 7, 2007, and entered into force on January 1, 2009. A supplementary agreement that exempts a worker subject exclusively to U.S. laws from contributing to the Czech health insurance system entered into force on May 1, 2016.

☐ *Denmark:* The U.S.-Danish agreement was signed in Copenhagen on June 13, 2007, and entered into force on October 1, 2008.

☐ *Finland:* The U.S.-Finnish agreement was signed on June 3, 1991, and entered into force on November 1, 1992.

☐ *France:* The U.S.-French Social Security agreement was signed on March 2, 1987, and entered into force on July 1, 1988.

☐ *Germany:* The U.S.-German agreement was signed on January 7, 1976, and entered into force on December 1, 1979. A supplementary agreement intended primarily to simplify the method used by the United States to compute benefits under the agreement was signed on October 2, 1986, and entered into force on March 1, 1988. Reunification extended application of the agreement to former East German territory, effective October 3, 1990. A second supplementary agreement permits certain ethnic German Jews who fled Nazi Europe and are now residing in the United States to make retroactive voluntary contributions to the German social security system. German benefits based on these contributions are retroactive to July 1990 and will usually exceed the amount of voluntary contributions due. The agreement was signed in Bonn on March 6, 1995, and entered into force on May 1, 1996. [SSA POMS GN §01707.036 (TN 4 7/96).]

☐ *Greece:* The U.S.-Greek Social Security agreement was signed on June 22, 1993, and entered into force on September 1, 1994.

☐ *Hungary:* The U.S.-Hungarian agreement was signed on February 3, 2015, and entered into force on September 1, 2016.

☐ *Iceland:* The U.S.-Icelandic agreement was signed on September 27, 2016, and entered into force on March 1, 2019.

☐ *Ireland:* The U.S.-Irish agreement was signed on April 14, 1992, and entered into force on September 1, 1993.

☐ *Italy:* The U.S.-Italian agreement was signed on May 23, 1973 and an administrative protocol was signed on November 22, 1977. Both entered into force on November 1, 1978. A supplementary agreement, which simplifies certain provisions of the original agreement and authorizes the United States to use a simplified method of computing benefits under the agreement, was signed on April 17, 1984, and entered into force on January 1, 1986. Note, the agreement with Italy does not include a detached worker provision. Coverage for expatriate workers is based principally on the worker's nationality.

☐ *Japan:* The U.S.-Japan agreement was signed on February 19, 2004, in Washington, D.C. and entered into force October 1, 2005.

☐ *Luxembourg:* The U.S.-Luxembourg agreement was signed on February 12, 1992, and entered into force on November 1, 1993.

☐ *Netherlands:* The U.S.-Netherlands agreement was signed on December 8, 1987. A supplementary protocol to clarify one of the provisions of the agreement concerning Netherlands benefits was signed on December 7, 1989. Both the agreement and the protocol entered into force on November 1, 1990. A supplementary protocol to allow payment of Netherlands child allowances to beneficiaries in the United States was signed on August 30, 2001, and entered into force on May 1, 2003. The primary purpose of the supplementary protocol is to permit payment of the Netherlands children's allowance while the qualified recipient or the child lives in or visits the United States.

☐ *Norway:* The U.S.-Norwegian agreement was signed on January 13, 1983, and entered into force on July 1, 1984. A new agreement replacing the original agreement was signed on November 30, 2001. The new agreement, which entered into force on September 1, 2003, will improve Norwegian benefit rights and update and clarify several provisions in the original agreement. In particular, it will permit U.S. citizens who have lived in Norway to receive full credit for their periods of residence under Norway's Social Security system and to increase thereby the amount of their Norwegian benefits. The new agreement also improves disability and survivors benefit protection under the Norwegian system for people who have worked in both countries.

☐ *Poland:* The U.S.-Poland Social Security agreement was signed on April 1, 2008, and entered into force on March 1, 2009.

☐ *Portugal:* The U.S.-Portuguese Social Security agreement was signed on March 30, 1988, and entered into force on August 1, 1989.

☐ *Slovak Republic:* The U.S.-Slovak Republic agreement was signed on December 10, 2012, and entered into force on May 1, 2014.

☐ *Slovenia:* The U.S.-Slovenian Social Security agreement was signed on January 17, 2017, and entered into force on February 1, 2019.

☐ *South Korea:* The U.S.-South Korean agreement was signed on March 13, 2000, along with a related administrative arrangement and entered into force April 1, 2001.

☐ *Spain:* The U.S.-Spanish agreement was signed on September 30, 1986, and entered into force on April 1, 1988.

☐ *Sweden:* The U.S.-Swedish Social Security agreement was signed on May 27, 1985, and entered into force on January 1, 1987. A supplementary agreement amending the U.S.-Swedish agreement to take into account recent major reforms in Swedish Social Security law was signed on June 22, 2004. It became effective November 1, 2007.

☐ *Switzerland:* A new agreement, signed on December 3, 2012, and entered into force on August 1, 2014, replaced the original U.S.-Swiss agreement in effect since November 1, 1980.

☐ *United Kingdom:* The U.S.-U.K. agreement was signed on February 13, 1984. The provisions of the agreement to eliminate double Social Security taxation became effective January 1, 1985. The provisions that permit persons who meet certain conditions to use their work in both countries to qualify for benefits became effective January 1, 1988. A supplementary agreement dealing primarily with U.K. disability benefits was signed on June 6, 1996, and, entered into force on September 1, 1997.

☐ *Uruguay:* The U.S.-Uruguayan Social Security agreement was signed on January 10, 2017, and entered into force on November 1, 2018.

Other countries: There have also been discussions or correspondence on proposed agreements with the following countries:

☐ *Argentina:* Negotiations were held in June 1997 in Buenos Aires, but a second planned meeting was postponed and has not been rescheduled.

☐ *Mexico:* The U.S.-Mexico agreement was signed on June 29, 2004, in Guadalajara, Mexico. The agreement is not yet in effect.

Coverage of Self-Employed Persons

INTRODUCTION

¶401   Introduction—Coverage of Self-Employed Workers

Coverage under the Social Security system was first extended to the self-employed in 1951, but at that time many professional groups were specifically exempted from coverage under the system. Then, effective beginning in 1955, coverage was extended to self-employed farm operators (see ¶411, below), architects, professional engineers, funeral directors, certified, licensed, and full-time practicing public accountants, and (on an elective basis) clergy. Effective beginning in 1956, coverage was further extended to include self-employed lawyers, dentists, osteopaths, veterinarians, naturopaths, chiropractors, and optometrists. For 1966 and thereafter, coverage was extended to self-employed doctors of medicine (¶401.3) and, under certain circumstances and for the limited purposes of hospital insurance taxes only, to employee representatives normally covered under the railroad retirement tax and benefits system. In 1967, coverage was made compulsory for clergy unless they file for an exemption on religious or conscientious grounds (see ¶401.1).

The taxes levied under the Self-Employment Contributions Act, and the amount of income that may be credited toward old-age, survivors, and disability insurance benefits or hospital insurance coverage, are based on an individual's "self-employment income" (see ¶404, below). In general, self-employment income consists of the net earnings derived by an individual (other than a nonresident alien) from a trade or business carried on as sole proprietor or by a partnership of which the individual is a member. The term "trade or business" as defined in the law is discussed at ¶402, below. Since self-employment income is, in turn, defined in terms of "net earnings from self-employment," an individual may not be covered under the system if his or her income is exempted by the definition of this latter term (see ¶408–411, below).

¶401.1   Ministers, Christian Science Practitioners, and Members of Religious Orders

Services performed by a duly ordained, commissioned, or licensed minister of a church, a member of a religious order (other than one who has taken a vow of poverty—see below), or a Christian Science practitioner are covered under the Self-Employment Contributions Act unless the minister, member, or practitioner files an application together with a statement that he or she is either conscientiously opposed to, or because of religious principles is opposed to, the acceptance of any public insurance that makes payments in the event of death, disability, old age, or retirement or makes payments toward the cost of, or provides services for, medical care (including benefits of any insurance system established by the Social Security Act). [IRC §1402(a)(14), (c), (e)(1); IRS Reg. §1.1402(e)-2A.] The individual must also inform the ordaining, commissioning, or licensing body of the church or order that he or she is opposed to such insurance with respect to applications filed after 1986. Furthermore, an application for exemption may be approved after 1986 only if the Commissioner has verified that the individual applying for an exemption is aware of the grounds on which an exemption is granted and sought the exemption on such grounds. [IRC §1402(e)(1), (2).]

Whether the services performed by the minister, member, or practitioner are performed as an employee or as a self-employed person, in either case the earnings will be considered as self-employment income and, unless an exemption has been granted, taxed as such. [IRC §1402(c).] Note, however, that the rental value of any parsonage or any parsonage allowance provided after a minister retires, or any other retirement benefit that the minister may receive from a church plan is not subject to Social Security taxes and is not to be treated as self-employment for the purpose of acquiring insured status and calculating Social Security benefit amounts. [SSA §211(a)(7), as amended by P.L. 108-203, §422; Reg. §404.1091.]

Members of religious orders who have taken a vow of poverty: If an individual is a member of a religious order and has taken a vow of poverty, he is automatically exempt from the self-employment tax for any amount received while working for his church or an agency of such church (the last sentence of Code Sec. 1402(c)). No exemption application need be filed. However, if the individual works for an outside organization, the exemption from the self-employment tax does not extend to the amount earned from the outside employment. [IRS Reg. §1.1402(c)-5(d).]

Exemption application: A minister, a member of a religious order, or a Christian Science practitioner seeking exemption from self-employment tax must file an exemption application (Form 4361, Application for Exemption from Self-Employment Tax for Use by Ministers, Members of Religious Orders and

Christian Science Practitioners) (Reg. §1.1402(e)-2A(a), Reg. §1.1402(e)-5A(a), and Reg. §1.1402(e)-5A(b)). The application is to be filed by the due date (including extensions) for filing the individual's income tax return for the second tax year in which the individual has $400 or more of net earnings from self-employment, some of which were earnings from services performed in the exercise of his duties as a minister, a member of a religious order or as a Christian Science practitioner. [Reg. §1.1402(e)-3A(a).]

On Form 4361, the individual must certify a statement proclaiming his religious or conscientious opposition, and a statement that he has not previously elected Social Security coverage by filing a Form 2031 (Waiver Certificate for Use by Ministers, Certain Members of Religious Orders, and Christian Science Practitioners Electing Coverage Under the Social Security Act). An exemption must be approved by the IRS before it is effective. [Reg. §1.1402(e)-2A(a)(2) and Reg. §1.1402(e)-2A(c).] A minister or member of a religious order, but not Christian Science practitioners, must include with Form 4361 a statement that he has informed the ordaining, commissioning, or licensing body of the church or order of his opposition. Applications cannot be approved by the IRS unless it has verified that the applicant (including Christian Science practitioners) is aware of the grounds on which he may receive an exemption and that the applicant, indeed, seeks an exemption on such grounds. To verify the exemption application, the IRS will mail to the applicant a statement describing the grounds on which an individual may obtain an exemption, and the applicant must sign the certification contained on the statement and mail the signed copy to the IRS Service Center from which the statement was issued within 90 days after its issuance. [Reg. §1.1402(e)-5A(b) and Reg. §1.1402(e)-5A(c).]

If a duly ordained minister seeks an exemption based on a change of faith, and, as a result, now opposes the acceptance of public insurance, the minister must provide a statement using language that meets the requirements of IRC 1402(a). However, according to the Chief Counsel of the IRS, this requirement is satisfied by signing Form 4361. [IRS Chief Counsel Advice 200404048, Dec. 16, 2003.]

¶401.2   Directors of Corporations

The Internal Revenue Service has held that directors' fees and other remuneration received by a director of a corporation for performance of services as such constitute self-employment income whether received for attending directors' meetings or for serving on committees. [Rev. Ruls. 68-595, 72-86.] Between January 1, 1988, and January 1, 1991, earnings attributable to a corporate director's services were taxable when the services were performed, regardless of when actually paid. Beginning in 1991, directors' earnings are treated as received in the year that the relevant services are performed only for purposes of the Social Security retirement test. [IRC §1402(a); Soc. Sec. Act §§203(f)(5)(E), 211(a).] Concerning the "employee" status of certain officers as directors of corporations, see ¶302.2, *ante*.

¶401.3   Doctors of Medicine

The services of self-employed persons in the practice of their profession as doctors of medicine, either as individuals or as members of a partnership, are included in the term "trade or business" and are, thus, covered under the Self-Employment Contributions Act. [IRC §1402(c); IRS Reg. §31.3401(c)-1(c).]

¶401.4   Members of Religious Groups Opposed to Insurance

Self-employment services performed by individuals who have conscientious objections to insurance (including Social Security) by reason of their adherence to established tenets or teachings of a religious sect (or division thereof) of which they are members do not constitute a trade or business. [IRC §1402(g).]

The sect (or division thereof) must be one that has been in existence at all times since December 31, 1950, and has for a substantial period of time been making reasonable provision for its dependent members. To qualify as grounds for the tax exemption, the objections of the individual and the sect (or division thereof) to insurance must include objections to acceptance of the benefits of any private or public insurance that makes payments in the event of death, disability, old-age or retirement or makes payments toward the cost of, or provides services for, medical care (including the benefits of any insurance system established by the Social Security Act). Before an individual can be granted exemption he or she is required to waive all benefits and other payments under any insurance system established by the Social Security Act on the basis of his or her own earnings as well as all such benefits and other payments based on the earnings of any other person. The exemption cannot be granted to any person to whom the Social Security benefits claimed to be waived became payable at or before the time of the filing of the waiver (or would have been payable but for a reduction of the benefits or deduction thereof on account of a refusal to accept rehabilitation services). An individual's exemption (and the waiver of Social Security benefits) will be terminated if, and as of the time, the conditions under which the exemption was granted are no longer met, and an exemption will not again be granted. [IRC §1402(g); IRS Reg. §1.1402(h)-1.] Generally, an application for this exemption must be filed on or before the due date of the return for the first taxable year in which the individual has self-employment income. [Reg. §1.1402(h)-1(c).]

The exemption is also available to members of religious faiths opposed to insurance who are employees of a church or church-controlled organization, where that body has elected to treat the employees as self-employed for FICA tax purposes. See ¶321.3. [IRC §1402(g)(3).]

¶401.5   Statutory Nonemployees

Two categories of statutory nonemployees have been established—salespersons who are licensed real estate agents and individuals who are direct sellers. They are to be treated as self-employed where substantially all the remuneration paid for their services is directly related to sales or other output and where such services are performed pursuant to a written contract providing that they will not be treated as employees for federal tax purposes. [IRC §3508.]

¶402   "Trade or Business" Defined

With certain exceptions noted below, the self-employed person must be engaged in carrying on a "trade or business," either personally or through agents or employees, or as a member of a partnership, before he or she can be covered under the self-employment provisions of the Social Security and hospital insurance system. [IRC §1402(a).] The term "trade or business," with the exceptions listed below, has the same meaning when used with reference to self-employment income or net earnings from self-employment as when used in Section 162 of the 1986 Internal Revenue Code, relating to trade or business expenses for income tax purposes. [IRC §1402(c).] The exceptions to this rule are as follows:

1. The performance of the functions of a public office does not constitute a trade or business, other than the functions of a public office of a state or local government in positions that are compensated solely on a fee basis (such as constables and justices of the peace) if the fees are received in a period in which the position is not covered under a state Social Security coverage agreement (see ¶321.2, *ante,* for state Social Security coverage agreements). [IRC §1402(c)(1).]

2. The performance of service by an individual as an "employee" as defined in the Federal Insurance Contributions Act (see ¶302, *ante*) does not constitute a trade or business. [IRC §1402(c)(2).] There are, however, exceptions to this general rule. Thus, the following services are not excepted from the term "trade or business" as used in the Self- Employment Contributions Act or Title II of the Social Security Act, even though performed under circumstances which would ordinarily make the individual an "employee" and not a self-employed person:

    (a) Service performed by an individual who has attained the age of 18 in and at the time of the sale of newspapers or magazines to ultimate consumers under an arrangement whereby they are to be sold by the individual at a fixed price, with compensation being based on the retention of the excess of such price over the amount at which the newspapers or magazines are charged to him or her (see, further, ¶317, *ante*) [IRC §1402(c)(2)(A)];

(b) Service performed by a "share farmer" as defined in the Federal Insurance Contributions Act (see ¶307, *ante,* and ¶410, below) [IRC §1402(c)(2)(B)];

(c) Service performed in the United States (or in Puerto Rico, the Virgin Islands, Guam, the Northern Mariana Islands, or American Samoa) by a citizen of the United States in the employ of a foreign government, certain service performed for an instrumentality wholly owned by a foreign government, and service performed in the employ of an international organization, but only where the employment is pursuant to a transfer of the individual from covered employment with a Federal agency [IRC §1402(c)(2)(C) and §3121(y); SSA Reg. §404.1022];

(d) Service performed by a duly ordained, commissioned, or licensed minister of a church or by a member of a religious order (other than one who has taken a vow of poverty) unless the affected individual applies for an exemption (see ¶401.1, above) [IRC §1402(c)(2)(D), (e)];

(e) Service performed by an individual as an employee of a state or local government in a position compensated solely on a fee basis (such as constables and justices of the peace) with respect to fees received directly from the public in a period in which the service is not covered under a state Social Security coverage agreement (see ¶321.2, *ante*) [IRC §1402(c)(2)(E)]; except that, beginning January 1, 1992, when a public official receives payment for services from government funds and no portion of the monies collected from the public belongs to or can be retained by him or her as compensation, the payment will not be treated as a fee [SSA Informational Release No. 106, 12/31/91];

(f) Service performed by members of a fishing boat crew working on a share-of-the-catch basis (see ¶311) [IRC §1402(c)(2)(F)]; and

(g) Service performed in the employ of a church or qualified church-controlled organization, if such church or organization is otherwise exempt from liability for the payment of FICA taxes, unless such service is unrelated to the trade or business carried on by such organization. [IRC §1402(c)(2)(G).]

3. The performance of service by an individual as an employee or employee representative under the railroad retirement system does not constitute a trade or business for Social Security purposes. [IRC §1402(c)(3).]

4. Service performed by a Christian Science practitioner in the exercise of his or her profession constitutes a trade or business unless the practitioner applies for an exemption (see ¶401.1, above). [IRC §1402(c)(5), (e).]

5. Members of certain religious groups who are opposed to insurance may elect not to be covered. See ¶401.4.

The trade or business must be carried on by the individual either personally or through agents or employees in order for the income to be included in net earnings from self-employment. [IRC §1402(a); IRS Reg. §1.1402(a)-2(b).] Accordingly, income derived from a trade or business carried on by an estate or trust is not included in determining net earnings from self-employment of its individual beneficiaries. [Reg. §1.1402(a)-2(b).]

An individual may be engaged in more than one trade or business. If so, the net earnings from self-employment are the aggregate of the net earnings from self-employment derived from each trade or business carried on by the individual. Thus, a loss sustained in one trade or business will operate to reduce the income derived from another. [Reg. §1.1402(a)-2(c).]

SELF-EMPLOYMENT INCOME AND TAXES

¶403   Rates of Taxes

The self-employment tax rate (Social Security and Hospital Insurance) for the 2020 tax year is 15.3%. A self-employed person pays the combined employee and employer OASDI rate (12.4%) and the 2.9% HI rate.

Note, the tax rate applicable in the 2011 and 2012 tax years was 13.30%. The reduced rate reflected a reduction in the Social Security portion of the tax from 12.40% to 10.40%. This paralleled the reduction of the employee Social Security tax rate (but not the employer tax rate) for 2011 and 2012 from 6.2% to 4.2%. The reduced tax rate expired at the end of 2012.

¶404   Self-Employment Income Subject to Taxes

As in the case of wages, there is a limit on the amount of self-employment earnings subject to the SECA tax and creditable towards a worker's Social Security earnings record. For 2020, $137,700 is the maximum amount to which the OASDI portion of the SECA tax applies. Since January 1, 1994, there has been no limit on the amount of earnings subject to the Medicare hospital insurance portion of the tax. The SECA tax and coverage limits are the same as the FICA tax and wage base (see ¶208). However, in computing the amount of self-employment income subject to tax, any wages paid during the taxable year are taken into consideration. Thus, the amount of self-employment income taxable is limited to the stated amounts, *minus* the amount of "wages" received during the taxable year. [IRC §1402(b).]

For 1991–1993, separate taxable wage bases for the Social Security and Medicare portions of the tax (12.04% and 2.90%, respectively) were in effect as follows:

Calendar Year:	Maximum Amount Subject to OASDI Tax:	Maximum Amount Subject to HI Tax:
1991	$53,400	$125,000
1992	55,500	130,200
1993	57,600	135,000

Under pre-1991 law there was a single earnings cap that applied for both portions of the SECA tax. The maximum amount of earnings counted for tax and benefit purposes has been increased numerous times since the enactment of the Social Security program, as shown in the following table:

1951-1954	$3,600		1993	$57,600*
1955-1958	4,200		1994	60,600*
1959-1965	4,800		1995	61,200*
1966-1967	6,600		1996	62,700*
1968-1971	7,800		1997	65,400*
1972	9,000		1998	68,400*
1973	10,800		1999	72,600*
1974	13,200		2000	76,200*
1975	14,100		2001	80,400*
1976	15,300		2002	84,900*
1977	16,500		2003	87,000*
1978	17,700		2004	87,900*
1979	22,900		2005	90,000*
1980	25,900		2006	94,200*
1981	29,700		2007	97,500*
1982	32,400		2008	102,000*
1983	35,700		2009-2011	106,800*
1984	37,800		2012	110,100*
1985	39,600		2013	113,700*
1986	42,000		2014	117,000*
1987	43,800		2015-2016	118,500*
1988	45,000		2017	127,200*
1989	48,000		2018	128,400*
1990	51,300		2019	132,900*
1991	53,400*		2020	137,700*
1992	55,500*			

* Amounts shown for years after 1990 are the maximum amount of earnings subject to SECA taxation under the OASDI portion of the wage tax only.

Wages include wages paid to an employee covered under a voluntary agreement providing for bringing employees of state and local governments, or employees of foreign affiliates of American employers, under coverage. See ¶321.1 and ¶321.2, *ante*. The term "wages" also includes (but solely with respect to the payment of the hospital insurance tax) compensation subject to the Railroad Retirement Tax Act. See ¶318, *ante*. [IRC §§1402(b), 7701(a)(23).]

It should be noted, however, that the term "wages" refers to wages paid for "employment"; consequently, the citizenship or residence of either the employee or employer is immaterial if the work is performed within the United States (see ¶305.2, *ante*). This is not true of self-employment income, since the net earnings from self-employment of nonresident aliens are excluded unless otherwise provided for by international agreement. See ¶330. However, an individual who is not a citizen of the United States but who is a resident of Puerto Rico, the Virgin Islands, Guam, the Northern Mariana Islands, or American Samoa is not considered to be a nonresident alien. [IRC §1402(b); SSA Reg. §404.1096.]

A resident of Puerto Rico computes net earnings from self-employment in the same manner as a citizen of the United States without regard to Section 933 of the Code relating to income from sources within Puerto Rico. [IRC §1402(a)(6).]

Exclusion for earnings under $400. The term "self-employment income" as defined in the Self-Employment Contributions Act and Title II of the Social Security Act excludes net earnings from self-employment in any taxable year if such earnings are less than $400. [IRC §1402(b)(2); Soc. Sec. Act §211(b)(2).] An individual whose net earnings from self-employment for the taxable year are less than $400, therefore, has no self-employment income for such year that is taxable or creditable (see ¶411, below, with respect to an optional method that may be used in reporting income from self-employment).

In determining the amount of tax due on self-employment income, any *wages* paid during the taxable year are taken into account.

> **Example:** Mr. King, who is a member of a partnership, reported his net earnings from self-employment on a fiscal-year basis. He reported $132,900 for the taxable year ending October 31, 2019, the maximum taxable at the time (since the applicable base is that for the calendar year in which the taxable year begins), and paid the self-employment taxes due thereon. However, the partnership became a corporation on November 1, 2019, and King, as an employee thereof, received wages for services rendered to the corporation for the remainder of the calendar year totaling $12,000. Taxes were due from both King and his corporate employer on the $12,000, and neither King nor his employer was entitled to a refund.

The amount of self-employment taxes due is computed without regard to the number of income tax exemptions an individual might have or whether any income tax would be due. [Reg. §1.1402(a)-10.] Concerning the filing of returns and payment of the self-employment taxes, see ¶413–415, below.

¶405   Taxable Year

Since the taxes on self-employment income are imposed as one of the income taxes under Subtitle A of the 1986 Internal Revenue Code, the "taxable year" for purposes of computing the taxes on self-employment income is the same as the "taxable year" used for income tax purposes. [Soc. Sec. Act §211(e); IRS Reg. §1.1402(a)-2.] The term "taxable year" is defined in the income tax provisions as—

(1) The taxpayer's annual accounting period, if it is a calendar year or a fiscal year;

(2) The calendar year, if, except for returns for a period of less than 12 months, (a) the taxpayer keeps no books, (b) the taxpayer does not have an annual accounting period, or (c) the taxpayer has an annual accounting period but such period does not qualify as a fiscal year; or

(3) The period for which the return is made, if a return is made for a period of less than 12 months. [IRC §441(b).]

In the case of partnership income, if the taxable year of a partner does not correspond with that of the partnership, the partner is required to base his or her distributive share on the ordinary income or loss of the partnership for any taxable year ending with or within the partner's taxable year. [Reg. §1.1402(a)-2(e).] See, further, the discussion of net earnings from self-employment at ¶408–411, below.

NET EARNINGS FROM SELF-EMPLOYMENT

¶408   Definition

Self-employment taxes are ultimately based upon net earnings from self-employment. "Net earnings from self-employment" means the sum of:

(1) the gross income derived by an individual from any trade or business he or she carries on, less allowable deductions attributable to such trade or business, and

(2) the individual's distributive share (whether or not distributed) of the ordinary net income or loss from any trade or business carried on by a partnership of which he or she is a member. [IRC §1402(a).]

But this definition is subject to the exclusion of certain trades and businesses (see ¶402, above) and to certain special rules for computing gross income and deductions and the distributive share of partnership ordinary net income or loss (see ¶409–411, below).

An individual may be engaged in more than one trade or business. If so, net earnings from self-employment are the aggregate of the net earnings from self-employment in each trade or business he or she carries on. Thus, a loss sustained in one trade or business of an individual will operate to reduce the income derived from another trade or business of such individual. [Reg. §1.1402(a)-2(c).] The trade or business must be "carried on" by the individual, either personally or through agents or employees, in order for the income to be included in net earnings from self-employment. [Reg. §1.1402(a)-2(b).] The gross income and deductions attributable to a trade or business are to be determined by reference to the applicable income tax provisions of the Internal Revenue Code. [Reg. §1.1402(a)-2(a).]

The rules applicable in computing net income for income tax purposes must be applied in determining, for purposes of computing net earnings from self-employment, the taxable year in which items of gross income are to be included and the taxable year for which deductions shall be taken (see, also, ¶405, above). If an individual uses the accrual method of accounting in computing net income from a trade or business for income tax purposes, he or she must use the same method in computing the gross income and deductions for self-employment tax purposes. Likewise, if the taxpayer is engaged in the trade or business of selling property on the installment plan and elects to use the installment method of computing income for income tax purposes, the same basis must be used to compute the gross income and deductions attributable to such trade or business for self-employment tax purposes. [Reg. §1.1402(a)-2(a).]

¶409   Partnership Income

Net earnings from self-employment are, with certain exceptions, computed in the same fashion as is adjusted gross income for income tax purposes. When more than one business is involved, net earnings (or losses) from the several businesses are combined. An individual's net earnings also include the distributive share or shares of ordinary net taxable income (or loss) from all partnerships of which he or she is a member. [Soc. Sec. Act §211(a); *Soc. Sec. Handbook,* July 20, 2006, §1200; IRS Reg. §1.1402(a)-2(d).] Only a partnership recognized as such for income tax purposes is treated as a partnership for the purpose of determining the net earnings from self-employment of the partner. [Reg. §1.1402(a)-2(f).] An individual's distributive share of such income or loss of a partnership is determined as provided in Section 704 of the Internal Revenue Code. [Reg. §1.1402(a)-2(d).] Consequently, only the ordinary net income or loss derived by the partnership from carrying on a trade or business is taken into account. Any ordinary net income or loss of the partnership derived from sources clearly unrelated to the trade or business carried on by it is excluded in determining the net earnings from self-employment of the partners. [Reg. §1.1402(a)-2(g).]

Partners are individually liable for partnership debt and so long as assessment is made against the partnership, that will suffice to extend the 10-year limitations period for collection against individual partners. *See* ¶227.2. Regarding partnership retirement payments, see item 6 at ¶410.

Limited Partners

The distributive share of income or loss received by a limited partner from the trade or business of a limited partnership is excluded in determining net earnings from self-employment. However, this exclusion does not extend to guaranteed payments described in Section 707(c) of the Internal Revenue Code, such as a salary or professional fees received for services actually performed by a limited partner for the partnership. If a person is both a limited partner and a general partner in the same partnership, the distributive share received as a general partner will continue to be covered. [IRC §1402(a)(13).]

When the taxable year of a partner does not correspond with that of the partnership, the partner is required to base the distributive share on the ordinary income or loss of the partnership for any taxable year of the partnership ending with or within the partner's taxable year. [Reg. §1.1402(a)-2(e).] However, if, as a result of a partner's death, his or her taxable year ends within (but not with) the taxable year of the partnership, there will be included in computing net earnings from self-employment for the taxable year ending with the partner's death so much of his or her share of the partnership's ordinary income or loss for the partnership taxable year as is not attributable to an interest in the partnership during any period beginning on or after the first day of the first calendar month following the month in which the partner died. In other words, a deceased partner's distributive share of partnership income is included in computing net earnings from self-employment for the year of death. [Reg. §1.1402(f)-1.]

Limited Liability Companies

A limited liability company (LLC) is an entity created by state statute. The IRS does not have a tax classification for the LLC, but instead uses the tax entity classifications it has always had for business taxpayers: corporation, partnership, or sole proprietor. An LLC is always classified by the IRS as one of these types of taxable entities.

A multi-member LLC can be either a partnership or a corporation, including an S corporation. To be treated as a corporation, an LLC has to "check the box" on Form 8832, *Entity Classification Election* (*www.irs.gov/pub/irs-pdf/f8832.pdf*), and elect to be taxed as a corporation. A multi-member LLC that does not so elect will be classified by the IRS as a partnership. A single member LLC (SMLLC) can be either a corporation or a single member "disregarded entity." Again, to be treated by the IRS as a corporation, the SMLLC has to check the appropriate box on Form 8832. An SMLLC that does not elect to be a corporation will be classified by the IRS as a disregarded entity which is taxed as a sole proprietor for **income taxes**.

In determining **employment tax** requirements for an SMLLC that is a disregarded entity, the SMLLC had two options prior to 2009 for reporting and paying employment taxes: Using the name and EIN assigned to the LLC; or using the name and EIN of the single member owner. Even if the employment tax obligations are reported using the SMLLC's name and employer identification number, the single member owner retains ultimate responsibility for collecting, reporting and paying the employment taxes. The first method merely allows the owner to pay the LLC's tax through a separate calculation. [IRS Notice 99-6, 1999-3 I.R.B. 12, Jan. 19, 1999.]

A SMLLC must be treated as the taxpayer for employment tax and excise tax obligations. Thus, the SMLLC will be treated as a corporation for employment tax purposes except (starting November 1, 2011) for purposes of applying the family member and religious objector exceptions allowed by IRC §3121(b)(3) and §3127(b) as explained in ¶227.2. The single member owner is no longer personally liable for the LLC's employment tax liability unless the owner "checks the box." The change is designed as a way to simplify compliance for taxpayers. In addition, because most states recognize disregarded entities as employers, the regulations are intended to more closely align federal and state reporting, payment and collection of employment taxes. The regulation obsoleted Notice 99-6. [Reg. §301.7701-2(a), (c)(2)(iv) and (v); 72 *Federal Register* 45,891 (August 16, 2007).]

Three court cases raised the issue of whether the taxpayer's limited liability status under state law would limit his or her liability from employment taxes as an individual. The courts unanimously rejected the argument that the IRS must recognize the separate existence of the LLC as a matter of state law. The courts noted that while state laws of incorporation may affect federal tax provisions they do not control tax law. The courts concluded that the government could disregard the state classifications for federal tax purposes. [*McNamee v. IRS*, 488 F.3d 100 (2d Cir. 2007); 2007-1 USTC ¶50,515; UNEMPL. INS. REPTR ¶14,097C; *Stearn and Company, LLC v. USA*, 499 F. Supp. 2d (ED Mich. 2007); 2007-2 USTC ¶50,676; UNEMPL. INS. REPTR ¶14,098C; *Littriello v. USA*, 484 F.3d 372 (6th Cir. 2007); 2007-1 USTC 50,426.] *Medical Practice Solutions, LLC,* above, also addressed this issue, and reached the same conclusion.

A member of an LLC that has elected to be (or is otherwise) taxed as a corporation (association) is subject to employment taxes on his or her salary, but not on dividends or distributions. [IRC §1402(a).]

Note, however, that the IRS, as a general matter, cannot collect the LLC's employment tax liability from the members if the LLC member is not liable under state law for the LLC's debts. *See* ¶227.2.

¶410   What Are Net Earnings from Self-Employment

Income, or loss, from the following sources, and deductions attributable thereto, are not, with certain exceptions, taken into account in computing net earnings from self-employment:

1. *Real Estate Rentals—Income of Landowners.*—Rentals from real estate and from personal property leased with the real estate (including rentals paid in crop shares) are excluded, unless the rentals are received in the course of a trade or business as a real estate dealer. [IRC §1402(a)(1).] In general, an individual who is engaged in the business of selling real estate to customers with a view to the gains and profits that may be derived therefrom is a real estate dealer. On the other hand, an individual who merely holds real estate for investment and speculation and receives rentals therefrom is not considered

a real estate dealer. Where a real estate dealer holds real estate for investment or speculation in addition to real estate held for sale to customers in the ordinary course of a trade or business as a real estate dealer, only the rentals from the real estate held for sale to customers in the ordinary course of the trade or business as a real estate dealer, and the deductions attributable thereto, are included in determining net earnings from self-employment; the rentals from real estate held for investment or speculation, and the deductions attributable thereto, are excluded. [Reg. §1.1402(a)-4(a).]

Payments for the use or occupancy of an entire private residence or living quarters in duplex or multiple-housing units are generally rentals from real estate and, except in the case of real estate dealers, are therefore excluded in determining net earnings from self-employment, even though such payments are in part attributable to personal property furnished under the lease. However, payments for the use or occupancy of rooms or space where services are also rendered to the occupant do not constitute rentals from real estate and are consequently included in determining net earnings from self-employment. [Reg. §1.1402(a)-4(c).]

Payments for the use or occupancy of rooms or other space are not rentals from real estate and are usually considered to be self-employment income where services are also rendered to the occupant for the use or occupancy of rooms or other quarters in hotels, boarding houses, or apartment houses furnishing hotel services; or the use or occupancy of space in parking lots, warehouses, or storage garages. This rule applies when the services rendered are of such a substantial nature as to affect materially the amount charged for the premises and facilities, are primarily for the convenience of the occupant, and are not primarily for the protection or maintenance of the property. [SSA POMS §RS 01803.624 (TN 9 2/98).]

The following are kinds of services furnished primarily for the convenience of the occupant: making beds, furnishing linens and towels, dusting and cleaning the space and its furnishings and providing swimming pools and tennis courts. The following are kinds of services furnished for the protection or maintenance of property: furnishing heat, light and water, painting, collecting trash and garbage, and cleaning common areas. [SSA POMS §RS 01803.624 (TN 9 2/98).]

Qualified Joint Ventures: If rental real estate income is otherwise excludable from net earnings from self-employment (NESE) under IRC §1402(a), it does not become self-employment income merely because it is held in a qualified joint venture. In general, an individual with income from a rental real estate business is not subject to self-employment tax on such income because it is excluded from NESE under IRC §1402(a)(1). IRC §761(f), as added by the

Small Business and Work Opportunity Tax Act of 2007, provides that a qualified joint venture (QJV) will not be treated as a partnership for federal tax purposes. According to the IRS the purpose of IRC §761(f) was to eliminate the reporting burden stemming from the filing of a partnership income tax return in addition to the spouses' joint income tax return. It was not to convert income otherwise excludable from self-employment income into income subject to self-employment tax. Accordingly, a husband and wife who elect QJV status for a rental real estate business may exclude QJV income from self-employment income pursuant to the IRC §1402(a)(1) exclusion. [IRS Chief Counsel Advice 200816030, Mar. 18, 2008.]

Farm rental income: The general exclusion of real estate rentals does not apply to farm rental income if there is "material participation" by the owner or tenant. Whether or not "material participation" has occurred is determined without regard to any activities of an agent of the owner or tenant, so that an individual landowner or tenant who enters into an agreement with a person to manage a farm will not have rental income under the agreement counted as income for Social Security purposes, provided that the landowner or tenant does not personally participate in the management or production of the farmland. [IRC §1402(a)(1).]

The factors to be weighed in determining whether a farm landlord is materially participating are included in the following four tests. Where any one of these tests is met, the landlord is materially participating [SSA POMS §RS 01803.700 *et seq.* (TN 7 6/90)]:

Test No. 1. A landlord materially participates where at least three of the following elements exist: periodic advice and consultation; periodic inspection; furnishing a substantial portion of machinery, equipment, and livestock; or assuming responsibility for a substantial portion of the production expenses.

Test No. 2. A landlord materially participates if the landlord's decisions have a significant effect or contribution to the success of the farm. However, this test is not met if the tenant has the right to make the final decision. Some examples of management decisions are land use, crops to plant, when to plant, and when to market the harvested crop.

Test No. 3. A landlord materially participates if he or she performs a significant amount of physical labor in the production of the commodity. Physical labor is always significant if the landlord performs at least 100 hours of physical labor in five or more different weeks during the year. Lesser amounts of work may also meet the requirement depending on other circumstances.

Test No. 4. Even if a landlord does not meet tests 1, 2, or 3, he or she may be found to be materially participating if the landlord does things that, when considered in their total effect, show material and significant involvement in activities related to the crop production.

2. *Interest and Dividends.*—Dividends on shares of stock, and interest on bonds, debentures, notes, certificates, or other evidences of indebtedness, is-sued with interest coupons or in registered form by a corporation, or by a government or political subdivision thereof, are excluded, unless received in the course of a trade or business as a dealer in stocks or securities. Other forms of interest, such as interest received by a merchant on accounts or notes re-ceivable, are not excluded in computing net earnings from self-employment. [Reg. §1.1402(a)-5.]

3. *Property Gains or Losses.*—The following kinds of gain or loss sustained in the disposition of property are excluded in determining net earnings from self-employment:

(a) gain or loss from the sale or exchange of a capital asset;

(b) gain or loss from the cutting of timber, or the disposal of timber, coal, or iron ore, if Section 631 of the Internal Revenue Code is applicable;

(c) gain or loss from the sale, exchange, involuntary conversion, or other dis-position of property if the property is neither (1) stock in trade or other property which would properly be includible in inventory if on hand at the close of the taxable year, nor (2) property held primarily for sale to custom-ers in the ordinary course of the trade or business. [Reg. §1.1402(a)-6.]

The general effect of these provisions is to exclude from the computation of net earnings from self-employment all gains or losses that are treated as capital gains or losses, as well as gains or losses arising from the disposition or conversion of property that is not "stock in trade," etc., or property held primarily for sale to customers in the ordinary course of a trade or business. In the case of timber, coal, or iron ore, gain or loss is excluded if Section 631 of the Internal Revenue Code is applicable, although these items may be held primarily for sale to customers. [Reg. §1.1402(a)-6.]

4. *Net Operating Losses.*—No deductions for net operating losses of other years are permitted in determining net earnings from self-employment. [Reg. §1.1402(a)-7.]

5. *Community Income.*—The community property law, as of this writing, pro-vides that all community income from a trade or business is to be considered the income of the husband unless the wife exercises substantially all the management and control of the trade or business, in which case it will be considered the in-come of the wife. [Soc. Sec. Act §211(a)(5)(A); IRS Reg. §1.1402(a)-8.] Pend-ing modification of the law, the I.R.S. and Social Security Administration have

acquiesced, however, to court decisions declaring the current provision unconstitutional on grounds of sex discrimination. The announced rule in community property states will be the same as in non-community property states, *i.e.,* only the spouse carrying on the trade or business will be subject to the self-employment tax. [Rev. Rul. 82-39 (CB 1982-1, 119); SSR 81-18C (SSR CB 1981, 48); SSA POMS §RS 01802.400, *et seq.* (TN 17 9/06); 46 *Federal Register* 55709.]

The following states have community property laws: Arizona, California, Idaho, Louisiana, Nevada, New Mexico, Texas, Washington, and Wisconsin. So, too, does the Commonwealth of Puerto Rico. The court decisions and rulings affect only federal Social Security coverage. The state laws themselves were not declared unconstitutional.

6. *Partnership Retirement Income.*—Certain periodic payments made by a partnership to a retired partner on account of retirement pursuant to a written plan of the partnership are excluded from net earnings from self-employment. If the exclusion is to be effective, the following conditions must be fulfilled: (1) the plan meets such requirements as are prescribed by the Internal Revenue Service; (2) the plan provides for periodic payments that are to continue at least until the partner's death and that are made on account of retirement to partners generally or to a class or classes of partners; (3) the retired partner renders no services in any trade or business conducted by the partnership (or its successors) during the taxable year of such partnership (or its successors) which ends within or with the taxable year of the retired partner in which such amounts were received; (4) at the end of such partnership's taxable year there is no obligation from the other partners in the partnership to the retired partner other than to make retirement payments or other benefits paid due to medical expenses or death under the partnership plan; and (5) at the end of the taxable year the retired partner's share in the capital of the partnership has been paid to him in full. [IRC §1402(a)(10); IRS Reg. §1.1402(a)-17(c)(i) and (ii).] Note that if a "retired" partner served "of counsel" or continued to participate in the firm's investment, retirement payments would not be excluded from self-employment income. [IRS Letter Rul. 200403056, Sept. 29, 2003.]

7. *Foreign Earned Income of US Citizens or Residents.*—In the belief that there is no reason to distinguish between citizens who qualify as residents of a foreign country for a year and U.S. citizens who are physically present in a foreign country for 11 months of the year, all U.S. citizens working abroad are to be treated in a consistent manner with respect to self-employment taxes. Self-employment income for Social Security purposes is, thus, computed without regard to the exclusion of foreign earned income, regardless of whether a U.S. citizen qualifies as a *bona fide* resident of a foreign country or satisfies the physical presence test. [IRC §1402(a)(11); Soc. Sec. Act §211(a)(10); P.L. 98-21, §323(b)(2)(B).]

Example: Jan, who is self-employed, works in Saudi Arabia during all of 2020 and receives $110,000 as compensation. While $107,600 of that compensation is excluded under the foreign earned income exclusion for income tax purposes for 2020 (the excludable amount is indexed to inflation), none is excluded for self-employment tax purposes.

8. *Foreign Missionaries.*—In order to remove any question as to the Social Security coverage of U.S. citizens who are priests serving foreign congregations outside the United States and who do not maintain a residence in the United States, a minister or member of a religious order with earned income abroad is no longer required to have been either an employee of an American employer or serve a congregation which is composed predominantly of U.S. citizens in order to compute income for Social Security purposes without regard to the annual exclusion. [IRC §1402(a)(8).] See ¶330 regarding totalization agreements with foreign governments.

9. *Ministers.*—A covered minister must, in determining net earnings from self-employment, include the rental value of a parsonage (or allowance for the rental value of a parsonage) and the value of meals and lodging furnished to him or her for the convenience of the employer. [IRC §1402(a)(8).] Not affected by this provision is the traditional tax-exempt status of such remuneration accorded ministers for income tax purposes. Retirement benefits received from a church plan after a minister retires and the rental value or allowance of a parsonage, including utilities, are exempt from self-employment taxes. [IRC §1402(a)(8), as amended by The Small Business Job Protection Act of 1996, P.L. 104-188, §1456, effective beginning before, on, or after December 31, 1994.] Under prior law, these benefits were subject to self-employment tax.

10. *The remuneration of employees of electing churches or qualified church-controlled tax-exempt organizations* subject to self-employment tax is generally the same as the amount that would have been subject to FICA tax if that individual had continued to be treated as an employee. Thus, business expenses are subtracted from self-employment income and the $400 threshold on self-employment income does not apply. However, if the employee's remuneration from such an employer is less than $100 for the taxable year, it is not includable in self-employment income. Church employees are actually not subject to self-employment tax on church employee income unless they receive remuneration from the church of $108.28 or more because church employee income equals wages for services performed for the church less the deduction for ½ of self-employment taxes paid. The $100 ($108.28) threshold amount for paying self-employment tax from church employee income is computed separately from the $400 threshold applicable to other self-employment income, and church employee income is not taken into account for purposes

of determining whether the $400 threshold has been reached with respect to other self-employment income. [IRC §1402(a)(12) and (j); IRS Pub. 517, for 2019 returns, Jan. 7, 2020.]

11. *Dealers in options and commodities* may treat as net earnings from self-employment gains and losses derived in the ordinary course of dealing or trading in "IRC §1256" contracts or property related to such contracts, such as stock used to hedge options. Accordingly, such earnings are subject to self-employment tax. However, no inference should be drawn as to whether option and commodity dealers are to be viewed as engaged in a trade or business in connection with their transactions in IRC §1256 contracts as a result of the application of the self-employment tax. [IRC §1402(i); Soc. Sec. Act §211(h); Deficit Reduction Act of 1984, P.L. 98-369, §102.]

12. *Termination payments received by former insurance salespersons* are excludable from net earnings from self-employment starting in 1998. The exclusion, added by the Taxpayer Relief Act of 1997, and codifying recent court decisions, applies if the amount is received after the individual retires, the individual performs no services for the company after termination and before the end of the tax year, the salesperson agrees not to compete with the company for at least one year, and the amount of payment depends on the number of policies sold during the last year and/or the extent to which the policies remain in force. [P.L. 105-34 §922, adding IRC §1402(k) and Soc. Sec. Act §211(j).]

13. *Agricultural program payments:*

Wheat and cotton payments: Wheat and cotton payments and similar government payments received by a farm landlord who materially participates count for Social Security, just as they do for farm operators. When the landlord does not materially participate such payments do not count. However, these payments must be included in earnings for income tax purposes whether or not they count for Social Security. [SSA POMS §01803.210 (TN11 12/08).]

Conservation Reserve Program: The Conservation Reserve Program is a voluntary program operated by the U.S. Department of Agriculture (USDA). Under this program, the USDA makes annual payments to farm owners and operators who agree to perform certain activities (such as establishing vegetative cover, preventing grazing and controlling pests and weeds) on environmentally sensitive cropland for 10 to 15 years. Although the IRS has attempted to treat CRP payments as being subject to SECA, such payments remain excluded from SECA, provided that the recipient is also receiving Social Security benefit payments under SSA §202 (retirement and survivor benefits) or SSA §223 (disability benefits). The CRP benefit payments will also not reduce regular benefits from Social Security for those who retire before full retirement age, or Social Security disability payments for those who would otherwise exceed the threshold for substantial gainful activity. [IRC §402(a)(1) and SSA §211(a)(1), as amended by P.L. 110-234, The Heartland, Habitat, Harvest, and Horticulture Act of 2008, §15301(c).]

14. *Health Insurance premiums.* Self-employed individuals are able to deduct the costs of health insurance for themselves and for members of their immediate family, including any child of the taxpayer under age 27, when determining an individual's net earnings from self-employment for employment tax purposes. Ordinarily, such expenses are deductible for income tax purposes only, but not for determining the amount of income subject to employment taxes. [IRC §162(l)(4), as amended by the Creating Small Business Jobs Act of 2010 (P.L. 111-240), §2042(a).]

¶410.1   Self-Employment Earnings of Resident and Nonresident Aliens

The rules applicable to U.S. citizens or residents with respect to self-employment tax are generally the same whether the individual is living in the United States or abroad. Nonresident aliens are not subject to self-employment tax. However, self-employment income received while a resident alien is subject to self-employment tax even if it was paid for services performed as a nonresident alien.

> **Example:** Gabriel is an author engaged in the business of writing books. He has several books published in a foreign country while a citizen and resident of that country. During 2019, Gabriel enters the United States as a resident alien. After becoming a U.S. resident, he continues to receive royalties from his foreign publisher. He reports income and expenses on the cash basis (income is reported on the tax return when received and expenses deducted when paid). Gabriel's 2019 self-employment income includes the royalties received after he became a U.S. resident, even though the books on which the royalties were based were published while he was a nonresident alien. This royalty income is subject to self-employment tax in 2019.

> [International Tax Gap Series, *www.irs.gov.*]

¶411   Optional Methods re: Self-Employment Earnings

Optional methods of computing net earnings from self-employment are available to individuals engaged in farm self-employment, nonfarm self-employment, or both, so long as certain requirements are met. [IRC §1402(a).] The purpose of the optional methods of computation is to enable a self-employed individual to maintain Social Security coverage for years during which he or she has very low net earnings or a net loss by allowing such individuals to report more than the actual amount of earnings as self-employment income in order to receive greater credit towards Social Security benefits. [*Soc. Sec. Handbook,* March 2001, §1233.] The earnings thresholds below which the optional methods may be used have been increased. The thresholds have also been indexed to inflation so that the self-employed with low net earnings will be able to secure at least four quarters of Social Security coverage. See discussion of "Quarters of coverage" at ¶504.

Payment thresholds are increased and indexed for farm and nonfarm optional methods of computing net earnings from self-employment.

Farm Method:

A farmer who is a sole proprietor, or partner, may elect to report as net earnings from self-employment.

(1) two-thirds of his gross income from farming, if his gross income from farming operations is not more than 150% of the sum of the minimum earnings required for a quarter of coverage under the SSA for each quarter of the tax year; or

(2) the sum of the minimum earnings required for a quarter of coverage under the SSA for each quarter of the tax year, if his gross income from farming operations is more than 150% of that amount and his actual net earnings from such operations are less than that amount. [IRC §1402(a) and (l) and SSA §211(a) and (k), as amended and added by the Heartland, Habitat, Harvest, and Horticulture Act of 2008 (P.L. 110-246), §15352.]

In 2020, the minimum amount of earnings that will provide an individual with a quarter of Social Security coverage is $1,410 ($1,360 in 2019). Therefore, a self-employed farmer in 2020 can elect to report as net earnings from self-employment two-thirds of his gross income from farming as long as that gross income is not more than $8,460 (150% × $1,410 × 4). If his gross income from farming exceeds $8,460 but his actual net earnings from such operations are less than $5,640 ($1,410 × 4), he can report $5,640 as his net earnings from self-employment.

Non-Farm Method:

(1) If a self-employed individual (sole proprietor or partner) has gross nonfarm income of not more than 150% of the sum of the minimum earnings required for a quarter of coverage under the SSA for each quarter of the tax year, she can report two-thirds of her gross nonfarm income as net earnings from self-employment.

(2) If the individual's gross nonfarm income is more than 150% of the sum of the minimum earnings required for a quarter of coverage under the

SSA for each quarter of the tax year, she can report the sum of the minimum earnings required for a quarter of coverage under the SSA for each quarter of the tax year as her net earnings from self-employment.

[IRC §1402(a) and (l) and SSA §211(a) and (k), as amended and added by the Heartland, Habitat, Harvest, and Horticulture Act of 2008 (P.L. 110-246), §15352.]

Since the minimum earnings that will provide an individual with a quarter of Social Security coverage in 2020 is $1,410, a self-employed individual who has gross nonfarm income of $8,460 (150% × $1,410 × 4) or less in 2020 can report two-thirds of her gross nonfarm income as net earnings from self-employment. If her gross nonfarm income exceeds $8,460, she can report $5,640 ($1,410 × 4) as net earnings from self-employment.

The self-employed individual with nonfarm income must still meet the general requirements for using the nonfarm optional method of computing net earnings from self-employment. Specifically: (1) the individual must be self-employed on a regular basis (net earnings from self-employment of $400 or more in two of the three preceding tax years), and (2) in the election tax year, actual net earnings from nonfarm self-employment must be: (a) less than the sum of the minimum earnings required for a quarter of coverage under the SSA for each quarter of the tax year (the sum for 2020, based on a quarter-of-coverage amount of $1,410, is $5,640); and (b) less than two-thirds of total gross income from nonfarm self-employment. The nonfarm optional method has a lifetime limit of five years and cannot be used to report an amount less than actual net earnings from self-employment. [IRC §1402(a).]

Annual threshold increase:

Section 213(d) of the SSA provides the formula for computing the amount of earnings required to qualify for a quarter of Social Security credit. The formula provides for automatic annual increases to account for increases in average annual wages. Since the thresholds for computing net earnings from self-employment under the optional methods are now based on the Social Security earnings requirement under SSA §213(d), the thresholds will change annually. Self-employed individuals who qualify and choose to elect one of the optional methods for computing net earnings from self-employment can accrue four quarters of Social Security coverage. This will allow more self-employed individuals to accrue the necessary quarters of coverage for Social Security retirement, disability, and survivor benefits.

RETURNS AND PAYMENT OF TAXES UNDER SECA

¶413   Returns

An individual reports self-employment income by transferring certain information from the appropriate schedule of the income tax return (Form 1040) to a Social Security schedule on the same return. If a self-employed person is not required to file an income tax return, a separate return will be required for purposes of the tax under the Self-Employment Contributions Act (SECA). If the individual's net earnings from self-employment amount to less than $400 in any taxable year, he or she will pay no self-employment tax on such income and will receive no credit toward Social Security or hospital insurance coverage. [IRC §6017.] This procedure avoids collection of self-employment tax from persons whose self-employment is of a casual nature. See, however, ¶411, above, with respect to farm operators.

If a husband and wife file a joint return, Schedule SE of Form 1040 should show the name of the one with self-employment income. If the husband and wife each have self-employment income, separate Schedules SE must be filed by each. [IRC §6017.]

¶414   Assessment and Collection of Taxes

Self-employment taxes are levied, assessed, and collected as part of the income tax. [IRC §1401.] In most instances, items which require adjustments in self-employment income for self-employment tax purposes also require adjustments in income for income tax purposes. Except as otherwise provided, self-employment taxes are included with the normal tax and surtax under Chapter 1 of the Internal Revenue Code in computing any overpayment or deficiency in tax and in computing interest and any additions to such overpayment, deficiency, or tax.

¶415   Time for Payment of Taxes

There are no special provisions governing collection and payment of the Social Security and hospital insurance taxes levied under the Self-Employment Contributions Act, since these taxes are imposed as an income tax under Chapter 2 of the Internal Revenue Code. Note, however, the Tenth Circuit has held that under IRC §1401, a cash-basis taxpayer must pay SECA taxes on income received in the current year, even though the income was attributable to a prior year. [*Walker (Floyd) v. U.S.*, 202 F.3d 1290 (10th Cir. 2000); 2000-1 USTC ¶50,201.]

A portion of the tax that is paid under SECA is deductible as discussed at ¶202.

BENEFITS

¶418   Eligibility

Old-age, survivors, and disability insurance benefits, and hospital insurance benefits, are payable to the self-employed and their dependents or survivors under the same conditions as to wage earners and their dependents or survivors. The provisions concerning eligibility for, and computation of, benefits are discussed in the following chapter.

¶419   Crediting of Self-Employment Income to Calendar Quarters

Self-employment income must be credited to calendar quarters in order to make possible computations of an individual's Social Security benefits. For taxable years beginning before 1978 where the taxable year coincides with the calendar year, the individual's self-employment income is credited equally to each quarter of the calendar year. For taxable years beginning before 1978 that are other than a calendar year, the individual's self-employment income is credited equally to the calendar quarter in which the taxable year ends and to each of the next three or fewer preceding quarters any part of which is in the taxable year. [Soc. Sec. Act §212(a).]

In the case of self-employment income derived in a taxable year that begins after 1977 and that coincides with the calendar year or is included within a calendar year, the individual's self-employment income is credited to that calendar year. In the case of a taxable year that straddles two calendar years, the individual's self-employment income is allocated proportionately to the two calendar years involved on the basis of the number of months in each such year that are included completely within the taxable year. The calendar month in which a taxable year ends is treated as included completely within that calendar year. [Soc. Sec. Act §212(b).] See also ¶504.

¶420   Retirement Test for the Self-Employed

The Social Security retirement test is applied on a taxable year basis for both wages and self-employment earnings, and the two types of income are combined for purposes of determining an individual's total earnings.

See ¶551 for a detailed discussion of this test. Note that, in the case of the self-employed, excess earnings under this test cannot be charged to any month in a grace year in which the individual does not render "substantial services" in his or her trade or business. [Soc. Sec. Act §203(f).] The meaning of "substantial services" is discussed below at ¶420.1, and exceptions to the annual earnings test and a definition of "grace year" are noted at ¶551.

¶420.1   Substantial Services in Self-Employment

Since a self-employed individual's monthly work activity usually cannot be gauged accurately in terms of monthly earnings, as is done with employed workers, the services are measured by considering whether they are substantial. In general, the substantial services test is one of whether, in view of all services rendered in all trades or businesses by the individual and the surrounding circumstances, he or she can reasonably be considered retired in the month in question. Even though the individual performs some trade or business in a month, the services will not be considered substantial if the evidence establishes to the satisfaction of the Administration that he or she may be reasonably considered retired in that month. While no single rule can be stated for determining whether or not a beneficiary has rendered substantial services in self-employment during a particular month, the following factors are considered [Reg. §404.446]:

(1) The amount of time the individual devoted to all trades and businesses (see further below);

(2) The nature of the services rendered by the individual;

(3) The extent and nature of the activity performed by the individual before allegedly retiring as compared with that performed thereafter;

(4) The presence or absence of an adequately qualified paid manager, partner, or family member who manages the business;

(5) The type of business establishment involved;

(6) The amount of capital invested in the trade or business; and

(7) The seasonal nature of the trade or business.

An individual who alleges that no substantial services were rendered in any month must submit detailed information about the operation of the trades or businesses, including activities in connection therewith and other evidence the Administration may consider necessary for a proper determination. Failure of the individual to submit the requested statements, information and other evidence is regarded as a sufficient basis for a determination that he or she rendered substantial services in self-employment during the period in question. [Reg. §404.446(c).]

The amount of time devoted to trades or businesses, the net income or loss of which is includible in computing an individual's earnings, is the first consideration when determining whether services performed were substantial. Time devoted to a trade or business includes all the time spent by the individual in any activity, whether physical or mental, at the place of business or elsewhere in furtherance of the trade(s) or business(es). All time at the place of business that cannot reasonably be considered completely separate from business activities will be found to be time devoted to business.

Any form of service is not substantial if it is rendered for less than 15 hours per month. Services rendered for more than 45 hours per month are considered substantial unless the individual could reasonably be found to be retired in that month. Services rendered between 15 and 45 hours per month will be considered substantial for purposes of determining whether the individual is retired only if other factors, such as the nature, complexity or importance of the services rendered, warrant a determination that an individual is not retired. [Reg. §404.447(a).]

The nature of services rendered, including the regularity with which such services are rendered, is then considered. Services are evaluated in relation to the technical and management needs of the business in which they are rendered. Therefore, the more highly skilled and valuable the services in self-employment, the more likely the individual rendering the services will not be considered retired. [Reg. §404.447(b).]

A comparison of services before and after retirement is then made if consideration of time spent and nature of services rendered is insufficient to establish whether services performed were substantial. While the absence of a significant reduction in services performed tends to indicate that the individual is not retired and a significant reduction tends to show retirement, the presumption of retirement based on a significant reduction in services may be overcome by an evaluation of how highly skilled and valuable these services are. [Reg. §404.447(c).]

If consideration of amount of time spent, nature of services rendered, and comparison of services rendered before and after retirement is not sufficient, all other factors are considered. These include the presence or absence of a capable manager, the kind and size of the business, the amount of capital invested, and whether the business is seasonal. [Reg. §404.447(d).]

For a special provision applicable to work performed outside the United States, see ¶551.

Social Security Benefits

INTRODUCTION

¶501   Introduction

Although there are several different kinds of benefits payable under the various titles of the Social Security Act, chances are that when someone uses the phrase "Social Security benefits," he or she means old-age, survivors, or disability insurance benefits. It is these benefits—also called "OASDI benefits" or "Title II benefits"—that are discussed in this chapter. The benefits are paid to workers, their spouses, children, and parents, and to widows, widowers, and divorced persons. A table showing all of the various categories of benefits under Title II is set out at ¶502, below.

Benefits cannot be paid to a claimant under Title II unless the claimant, or the worker on whose account the claim is based, is insured under Title II. The requirements for being insured under Title II are discussed at ¶504–¶506.5, below. An individual who is disabled, blind, or age 65 or older who fails to meet the insured status requirements under Title II may be able to obtain benefits under Title XVI, otherwise known as "Supplemental Security Income" (SSI). However, benefits under Title XVI are means tested: a claimant must meet certain low income and asset limitations set forth in the law and regulations. Generally, individuals may not have more than $2,000 and couples may not have more than $3,000 in countable assets in order to be eligible for SSI benefits. A discussion of the asset and income limitations and exclusions under Title XVI is beyond the scope of this publication. Additional information regarding Title XVI may be obtained at the Social Security Administration's SSI home page, *www.ssa.gov/ssi/*.

Old-age, survivors, and disability insurance benefits are paid under Title II of the Social Security Act. The money for payment of the benefits comes, for the most part, from taxes collected from employers, employees, and the self-employed under the Federal Insurance and Self-Employment Contributions Acts, although certain special benefits are paid out of general revenues. [IRC §§1401(a), 3101(a), 3111(a); Soc. Sec. Act §228(g).] The "wages" or "self-employment income" on which the taxes are based is the same as that used to compute benefits, so that if an individual and an employer paid tax on (for example) $70,000 of the worker's wages in 2020, that same $70,000 will eventually be used (after indexing for subsequent increases in national average wages) in the computation of the worker's benefit. [IRC §§1402(b), 3121(a); Soc. Sec. Act §§209(a), 211(b).]

Nearly all of these Social Security benefits are based on what is called the "primary insurance amount," determined as described in the following pages. [Soc. Sec. Act §215(a).] Those whose benefits are based on a worker's entitlement receive some percentage of the worker's primary insurance amount; a wife, for example, can receive a benefit that is the equivalent of half of her worker-husband's primary insurance amount. [Soc. Sec. Act §202(b).]

A benefit may be subject to reduction, most commonly when the individual decides to begin drawing benefits early. For example, workers age 62 who elect to apply for retirement benefits at age 62 will receive a reduced benefit. Workers born on January 1 will have a slightly lower monthly reduction for those years in which retirement age increases from year to year. [Soc. Sec. Act §202(q).]

Benefits begin with the month in which the individual meets the conditions of entitlement and end with the month preceding the month in which occurs an event that causes the cessation of entitlement; for example, if a beneficiary dies in February, benefit entitlement ends with the preceding January. [Soc. Sec. Act §202.]

One feature of the Social Security law that is of concern to many people is the "retirement test" (also called the "annual earnings test"). Stated simply, an individual is allowed to earn up to a specified amount with no effect on the worker's own benefit or dependents' benefits, but if the worker earns more than that amount, there will be a reduction or loss of benefits. The test ceases to apply after a worker reaches "full retirement age" (age 66 and six months for individuals whose date of birth is from January 2, 1957, through January 1, 1958, etc.—see ¶518 and Reg. §404.409.) Previously, the test ceased to apply after the worker reached age 70. The test is discussed at ¶551.

The disability insurance provisions of Title II give five general types of protection. First, there are monthly cash benefits for a disabled worker and his or her family. Second, the worker's wage record can be protected during a period of disability, so as to minimize the detrimental effects of disability on his or her earnings record. Third, monthly cash benefits are provided for severely disabled widows or widowers and surviving divorced spouses age 50 and over. Fourth, monthly cash benefits are provided for a disabled child beneficiary age 18 or older. Fifth, vocational rehabilitation services are provided for disability beneficiaries capable of being restored to productive activity. The main discussion of disability benefits begins at ¶520.

For estimated future benefits, see the Benefit Projections Tables at ¶519.

¶502   Kinds of Benefits

The benefits payable under Title II may be divided into four basic types: (1) old-age or disability benefits paid to the worker, (2) benefits for dependents of retired or disabled workers, (3) benefits for surviving family members of a deceased worker, and (4) lump-sum death payments. [Soc. Sec. Act §202.] All of these benefits are based on the earnings record of a worker who is insured for Social Security coverage. [Soc. Sec. Act §§213, 228(h).] A worker may be fully insured, currently insured, and/or insured for disability benefits; see ¶505–¶506, below.

The following table shows the kind of insured status required for the various types of Social Security benefits.

Insured Status and Benefit Table

OLD-AGE OR DISABILITY BENEFITS

Monthly benefits can be paid to—	If the worker—
A retired worker age 62 or over	Is fully insured.
A disabled worker under full retirement age	Would have been fully insured had he or she attained age 62 in the month the disability began and (except in the case of a person disabled because of blindness as described in ¶520.1) has 20 quarters of coverage out of the 40 calendar quarters ending with the quarter in which the disability began.
A worker disabled before age 31 who does not have sufficient quarters of coverage to meet above requirement ("Special Insured" status, which allows an alternative to the "20 in 40 quarters" provision, may apply to a worker disabled after age 31 if he or she had a period of disability prior to age 31. See ¶505.5.)	Has quarters of coverage in one-half of the quarters elapsing in the period after attaining age 21 and up to and including the quarter of becoming disabled, but no fewer than 6 (see ¶505.5), or, if disabled in a quarter before attaining age 24, he or she has 6 quarters of coverage in the 12 calendar-quarter period immediately before he or she became disabled.

DEPENDENTS OF RETIRED OR DISABLED WORKERS

Monthly benefits can be paid to—	If the worker—
The spouse of a person entitled to disability or retirement insurance benefits, if he or she is: (a) Age 62 or over (may be divorced spouse in certain circumstances; see ¶522.5); or (b) Caring for a child who is under age 16 or disabled before age 22 and entitled to benefits	Is fully insured or insured for disability benefits, whichever is applicable, as shown above.
A dependent, unmarried child, grandchild, or stepgrandchild of a person entitled to disability or retirement insurance benefits if the child is: (a) Under age 18; or (b) Under age 19 and qualified as a full-time elementary or secondary school student as described in ¶524; or (c) Age 18 or over and under a disability which began before the child reached age 22	Is insured for retirement or disability benefits, whichever is applicable, as shown above (and, with respect to benefits for grandchildren, if the child's natural or adoptive parents were deceased or disabled when the grandparent or stepgrandparent became entitled to benefits).

SURVIVORS BENEFITS

Monthly benefits can be paid to—	*If the worker—*
A widow or widower (may be surviving divorced spouse in certain circumstances) age 60 or over	Is fully insured.
A widow or widower and, under certain conditions, a surviving divorced spouse, if the widow or widower or divorced spouse is caring for a child entitled to benefits if the child is under age 16 or disabled	Is either fully or currently insured.
A disabled widow or widower (may be surviving divorced spouse in certain circumstances; see ¶525.1), age 50 or over but under age 60, whose disability began within a certain period (see ¶525.2)	Is fully insured.
A dependent, unmarried child, grandchild, or stepgrandchild of a deceased worker if the child is: (a) Under age 18; or (b) Under age 19 and qualified as a full-time elementary or secondary school student as described in ¶524; or (c) Age 18 or over and under a disability which began before the child reached age 22	Is either fully or currently insured (and, with respect to benefits for grandchildren, if the child's natural or adoptive parents were deceased or disabled when the grandparent or stepgrandparent became entitled to benefits).
The dependent parents, age 62 or over, of the deceased worker	Is fully insured.

LUMP-SUM DEATH PAYMENT

The lump-sum death payment will be paid in the following order of priority to—	*If the worker—*
(a) The widow(er) of the deceased wage earner who was living in the same household as the deceased wage earner at the time of death; (b) The widow(er) (excluding a divorced spouse) who is eligible for or entitled to benefits based on the deceased wage earner's record for the month of death; (c) Children who are eligible for or entitled to benefits based on the deceased wage earner's record for the month of death. If no surviving widow(er) or child as defined above survives, no lump sum is payable.	Is either fully or currently insured.

INSURED STATUS REQUIREMENTS

¶504   Quarters of Coverage

An individual must meet certain "insured status" requirements before Social Security benefits may be paid to the individual or to his or her family. The measure of insured status is the number of "quarters of coverage" acquired.

Quarters of coverage are credited on the basis of annual earnings, without regard to the actual calendar quarters in which the amounts were earned. [Soc. Sec. Act §213(a).] Thus, a specified amount of earnings (wages, farm wages, or self-employment income) in a given year will entitle the worker to a quarter of coverage, up to a maximum of four quarters for any year. The specified amount of earnings for 2020 is $1,410 ($1,360 in 2019), so that a worker who earns at least $5,640 in 2020 ($5,440 in 2019) will be credited with four quarters of coverage. However, because a quarter of coverage cannot be credited to a calendar quarter prior to the beginning of that quarter, a worker cannot be credited with four quarters of coverage for 2020 until October 1, 2020.

In addition, an employee cannot earn more than four quarters of coverage in a year, regardless of the amount of earnings.

The Tests for a Quarter of Coverage

The following may be counted as quarters of coverage [Soc. Sec. Act §213(a)]:

(1) For years before 1978, either (a) a calendar quarter in which the individual has been paid $50 or more in wages for employment covered under the law, or (b) a calendar quarter after 1954 in which the individual has been credited with $100 or more cash wages paid for agricultural labor (see "Farm Workers," below);

(2) For years before 1978, a calendar quarter in which the individual has been credited with $100 or more in self-employment income. A worker must have at least $400 in net earnings from self-employment in a taxable year beginning after 1950 before any quarters in the taxable year can be credited with self-employment income;

(3) For 1978, workers receive one quarter of coverage (up to a total of four) for each $250 of earnings in the calendar year. [Soc. Sec. Act §213(d).] Beginning with 1978, wages can be added to any creditable self-employment income

to determine the number of quarters of coverage to be credited. A self-employed person, however, will still be required to have at least $400 in net earnings from self-employment for any taxable year after 1950 before any quarters of coverage in the taxable year can be credited with self-employment income.

(4) For 1979 and subsequent years, the earnings requirement for a quarter of coverage is subject to automatic annual increases to account for increases in average annual wages. The amount required for a quarter of coverage for any calendar year after 1978 is the larger of (a) the amount in effect in the calendar year prior to the year for which the determination is made, or (b) the amount determined by multiplying $250 by the ratio of (1) the average amount, per employee, of the wages of all employees reported for the second calendar year before the year for which the determination is made, to (2) the average of the total wages reported for 1976, with the final product rounded to the nearest multiple of $10. This computation yields the following amounts:

Year	Amount Required for Quarter of Coverage	Year	Amount Required for Quarter of Coverage
1979	$ 260	2000	$ 780
1980	290	2001	830
1981	310	2002	870
1982	340	2003	890
1983	370	2004	900
1984	390	2005	920
1985	410	2006	970
1986	440	2007	1,000
1987	460	2008	1,050
1988	470	2009	1,090
1989	500	2010	1,120
1990	520	2011	1,120
1991	540	2012	1,130
1992	570	2013	1,160
1993	590	2014	1.200
1994	620	2015	1,220
1995	630	2016	1,260
1996	640	2017	1,300
1997	670	2018	1,320
1998	700	2019	1,360
1999	$ 740	2020	1,410

The requirement that a self-employed person have at least $400 in net earnings from self-employment in the taxable year before any quarters of coverage in the taxable year can be credited with self-employment income remains unchanged. As noted above, combined wages and self-employment income may be used to determine creditable quarters of coverage.

(5) Each calendar quarter during a year in which the worker has been credited with the maximum amount of earnings subject to the FICA or SECA tax (see ¶208 and ¶404) for that year.

¶504

Self-Employment

Quarters of coverage may be based on self-employment income derived in taxable years beginning after 1950. There are special rules to be followed in the allocation of self-employment income to calendar quarters. The individual's net earnings from covered self-employment must amount to at least $400 for the taxable year. [Soc. Sec. Act §211(b).] However, a self-employed farmer with actual net earnings of less than $400 still may be credited with quarters of coverage if his or her gross earnings amounted to at least $600 and the "optional method" of reporting farm earnings is used (see ¶411); similarly, self-employed persons can elect to report two-thirds of their gross income from nonfarm self-employment. [Soc. Sec. Act §211(a).] In the case of nonfarm self-employment, there is a regularity-of-coverage requirement, and the option cannot be used more than five times by any individual; see, further, ¶411.

Self-employment income derived after 1977 during any taxable year that begins and ends with or during a calendar year will be allocated to that calendar year. In the case of any other taxable year after 1977, income will be allocated proportionately to the two calendar years, portions of which are included within the taxable year, on the basis of the number of months in each calendar year that are included completely within the taxable year. Before 1978, self-employment income derived during a taxable year that was a calendar year would be credited equally to each calendar quarter or, in the case of any other taxable year, would be credited equally to the calendar quarter in which the taxable year ends and to each of the next three or fewer preceding quarters, any part of which was in the taxable year. [Soc. Sec. Act §212.]

For years before 1978, a person was credited with one quarter of coverage for each calendar quarter to which $100 or more in self-employment income was allocated. For 1978 and subsequent years, the amount of income required for a quarter of coverage is the same for the self-employed as for employees (see above). Note that in a taxable year before 1978 in which a person's self-employment income (or self-employment income plus any wages paid during that taxable year) equaled the maximum amount of income creditable during a taxable year, a quarter of coverage would be counted for each calendar quarter wholly or partly in that taxable year, whether or not self-employment income was allocated to each quarter. [Soc. Sec. Act §213(a)(2).]

¶505   Fully Insured

It is a condition of eligibility for most benefits that a worker be "fully insured," *i.e.*, that he or she have somewhere between six and 40 quarters of coverage. [Soc. Sec. Act §214(a).] Special rules apply to employees of nonprofit organizations, to whom mandatory coverage was extended under the Social Security Act Amendments of 1983, as explained below.

How many quarters a given individual needs depends on when he or she reaches a specified age or dies, as described below. Because 40 quarters of coverage will fully insure any worker for life, anyone who has 10 years (*i.e.*, 40 quarters) of Social Security coverage need not bother making the count unless applying for disability benefits (see ¶505.5, below). For those who need to make the count, however, this is how it is done [Soc. Sec. Act §214(a)]:

Step 1

Men born in 1913 or later and all women: Count the number of years after the year in which you reached age 21 and before the year in which you reach age 62. If you were born before 1930, begin the count with 1951 and end it with the year before the one in which you reach age 62. If you die before you reach age 62, the count will stop with the year before the one in which you die. In making the count, do not include any year of which all or any part was included in a period of disability for disability benefits purposes.

Men born before 1913: The 1972 Amendments phased out the use of different calculations for men and women and required 24 years for men born in 1910, 1911, or 1912. Men born before 1910 were required to count the number of years after 1950 and before the year in which they reached age 65 or died, whichever first occurred. As above, do not include years involving a period of disability.

Step 2

Men and women: If the number of quarters of coverage you have is at least equal to the number you obtained in Step 1, you are fully insured. Note that all of the quarters of coverage credited to an individual's Social Security record are counted in determining whether he or she has the required number, even those that are not within the elapsed period used to determine the required number.

Note that under the law in effect prior to the 1972 Amendments, the age used in figuring insured status for men (65) was different than for women (62). Thus, in determining whether a man who applied for reduced old-age benefits at 62 was "fully insured," years before the year in which he attained 65 had to be counted, regardless of the fact that he became entitled to benefits before reaching age 65. In the case of women, only years before the one in which age 62 was reached were counted both under prior law and the 1972 Amendments. [Soc. Sec. Act §214(a)(1).]

A minimum of six quarters of coverage is required for fully insured status. [Soc. Sec. Act §214(a)(1).]

As noted above, the rules for determining insured status for disability benefits are somewhat different; see ¶505.5.

Employees of Nonprofit Organizations

Participation in the Social Security system is mandatory for all employees of nonprofit organizations (see ¶321.3). So that older employees with little or no covered employment might be able to reap some benefit from being lately included in the Social Security system, nonprofit organization employees age 55 or older who were brought into the system under the 1983 Amendments were deemed fully insured for Social Security benefits after acquiring a given number of quarters of coverage, according to the following sliding scale [P.L. 98-21, §102]:

If on January 1, 1984, the person is—	The number of quarters needed is
Age 60 or over	6
Age 59	8
Age 58	12
Age 57	16
Age 55-56	20

¶505.5 Insured Status for Disability Benefits

In order to be eligible for disability insurance benefits, a worker must not only be determined to be disabled, but also must meet certain insured status requirements. The special insured status requirements to qualify for disability benefits are satisfied if the worker (1) would have been fully insured had he or she attained age 62 and applied for old-age benefits when the disability began (see ¶505), and (2) has either 20 quarters of coverage during the 40-quarter period ending with such quarter (not counting as part of the 40-quarter period any quarter any part of which was included in a prior period of disability, unless it was a quarter of coverage), *or*, if disabled before the quarter in which the applicant attains (or would attain) age 31, earned quarters of coverage for not less than one-half and not less than six of the quarters during the period beginning with the quarter after the quarter in which the applicant attained age 21 and ending with the quarter in which he or she became disabled, except in the case of a worker disabled because of blindness, who need not meet requirement (2) at all. [Soc. Sec. Act §§214(a)(1), 216(i)(3), 223(c)(1).]

The exception applicable to the blind exempts them from the requirement of recent attachment to covered work. Thus, a blind worker will meet the test by acquiring quarters of coverage, at any time, equal to the number of years elapsed after 1950 (or the year he or she reached age 21, if later) and up to the year in which the disability began, subject to the limitation that no less than six and no more than 40 quarters are required. [Soc. Sec. Act §§216(i)(3), 223(c)(1).]

A worker who had a period of disability that began before age 31, from which he or she recovered, and who is subsequently disabled at age 31 or later may again be insured for disability benefits if he or she earned quarters of coverage in half the calendar quarters after age 21 and through the quarter in which the later disability begins (up to a maximum of 20 out of 40 quarters). If there are fewer than 12 calendar quarters in such period, a minimum of six quarters of coverage will be needed for reentitlement. [Soc. Sec. Act §216(i)(3)(B)(iii).]

In computing disability insured status, when the number of quarters in any period is an odd number, it is reduced to the next-lower even number; and a quarter may not be counted as part of any period if any part of the quarter was included in a prior period of disability unless the quarter was a quarter of coverage. However, a minimum of six quarters of coverage is required. Thus, if a worker became disabled before the quarter in which he or she attained age 24, six quarters of coverage must have been earned in the 12-quarter period ending with the quarter in which disability began. [Soc. Sec. Act §223(c)(1).]

Here is a simplified discussion of the requirements for insured status for disability benefits:

A worker who becomes severely disabled will be eligible for monthly benefits if the worker has worked under Social Security long enough and recently enough. The amount of work a worker will need depends on the age when the worker becomes disabled:

Before 24: A worker needs credit for 1½ years of work in the three-year period ending when the disability begins.

24 through 30: A worker needs credit for having worked half the time between 21 and the time the worker becomes disabled.

31 or older: All workers disabled at 31 or older—except the blind— need the amount of credit shown in the chart below:

Work credit for disability benefits		
Born after 1929, became disabled at	Born before 1930, became disabled before 62 in	Years you need
42 or younger	1971	5
44	1973	5 ½
46	1975	6
48	1977	6 ½
50	1979	7
52	1981	7 ½
54	1983	8
56	1985	8 ½
58	1987	9
60	1989	9 ½
62 or older	1991 or later	10

Five years of this credit must have been earned in the 10 years ending when the worker became disabled. The years need not be continuous or in units of full years. [*Soc. Sec. Handbook,* Aug. 9, 2005, §207.]

¶506   Currently Insured

To be currently insured a worker must have not less than six quarters of coverage during the 13-quarter period ending with the quarter in which the worker dies, becomes entitled to old-age insurance benefits, or most recently became entitled to disability benefits. However, any quarter, any part of which was included in a period of disability, will not be counted in this 13-quarter period unless it was a quarter of coverage (see ¶504). [Soc Sec. Act 214(b)).] Old age benefits and benefits for dependents of retired workers generally are payable only if the worker is fully insured, but lump-sum benefits and certain survivor benefits are payable if the worker is only currently insured. See ¶502. For the benefits payable on the basis of transitional insured status, see ¶513.

In order to be eligible for disability benefits, the individual must meet the insured requirements discussed at ¶505.5. Note, "disability benefits" as used here do not include the benefits payable to disabled widows or widowers (¶525.2)

¶506.5 Insured Status Required

The table below shows the insured status required of a worker in order to receive a specified type of benefit.

Retirement Benefits

- *Retired Worker*, 62 or over—Fully insured
- *Spouse, or divorced spouse*, 62 or over—Fully insured
- *Spouse*, any age, if caring for child entitled to benefits—Fully insured
- *Child, or grandchild*, under age 18 (under age 19 for full-time elementary or secondary school student), or any age if disabled, but only if the disability began before age 22—Fully insured

Survivors Benefits

- *Widow, widower, or divorced person*, 60 or over, or 50-59 and disabled—Fully insured
- *Widow, divorced parent of deceased worker's child, or widower*, any age, caring for a young child entitled to benefits—Either fully or currently insured
- *Child, or grandchild*, under 18 (under 19 if student), or any age if disabled, but only if the disability began before age 22—Either fully or currently insured
- *Dependent parent*, 62 or over—Fully insured

Disability Benefits

- *Disabled worker* (except one who is blind)—Fully insured and insured for disability

Lump-Sum Payments

- *Widow or widower, or eligible child*—Either fully or currently insured

COMPUTING AVERAGES OF EARNINGS

¶507   Benefit Computation

Computing a Social Security benefit is a complicated matter, requiring detailed information about the worker's earnings record, age, and date of retirement, disability, or death. Whether the benefit is for the worker or for a spouse, child, or other relative, it is necessary to compute a "primary insurance amount" that is based on the worker's earnings averaged over much of his or her career (average indexed monthly earnings (AIME)).

This chapter details the manner in which the benefits computation is made for workers who are currently becoming eligible for benefits. The computation requires that the worker's actual earnings be mathematically "indexed" to national average earnings. The adjustment reflects the change in general wage levels that occurred during the worker's years of employment. The indexing ensures that a worker's future benefits reflect the general rise in the standard of living that occurred during his or her entire working lifetime.

A formula is applied to the average indexed monthly earnings to determine the primary insurance amount (PIA). This "PIA" is then converted to the actual benefit. Note that persons who first became eligible before 1983 may use other computations.

¶507.3   Elapsed Years

The first step in ascertaining the number of years to be used in computing an individual's average earnings is to determine the amount of the worker's "elapsed years."

Retirement benefits: For workers born after 1929, count the number of calendar years after the year of attainment of age 21 and prior to the year of attainment of age 62. For workers born before 1930, count the number of calendar years after 1950 and before either 1961 or the year in which the worker attained or will attain age 62, whichever is later. If, however, the count is being made for a male worker who attained age 62 before 1975, count the number of years after 1950 and before (a) the year the worker attained or would attain age 65, or (b) 1975, whichever is earlier.

Survivors benefits: Count the number of calendar years after 1950 (or after the year in which the worker reached age 21, if later) and before the year in which the worker died. However, if the worker dies after the ending point described for retirement benefits, above, the count is ended as if a retirement benefit were being computed.

Disability benefits: The count for a disabled worker is made as described above for retirement benefits as if the worker had attained age 62 in the first month of his or her waiting period (see ¶520.2) or, if he or she is entitled to disability benefits for a second or subsequent period of disability and can meet the requirements for not serving a waiting period, as though the appropriate age had been attained in the first month in which he or she became entitled to disability benefits. [Soc. Sec. Act §223(a)(2).]

In the case of an individual who actually attained age 62 in 1975 or thereafter and in or before the month used for determining his or her primary insurance amount, the elapsed years may not include the year in which he or she reached age 62 or any year thereafter. [Soc. Sec. Act §223(a)(2).]

Any year for which any part of that year was included in a period of disability is not included in determining the number of elapsed years. [Soc. Sec. Act §215(b)(2)(B)(iii).]

¶507.4   Eligibility Year

The year the worker reaches age 62, dies, or becomes disabled (i.e., the eligibility year) is important in benefit computation. A worker's PIA is computed under the AIME-PIA formula for his or her eligibility year (see ¶512). For old-age benefits, the eligibility year is the year the worker attains age 62. For disability benefits, the eligibility year is either the year the disability begins or the year the worker attains age 62, whichever is earlier. For survivors benefits, the eligibility year is the earlier of the year of the worker's death or the year of attainment of age 62.

¶507.5   Base Years

Base years are the available earnings years from which the benefit computation years will ultimately be selected to compute the primary insurance amount. Computation base years are the years occurring (1) after 1950 and (2) before the earlier of either (a) the year in which the worker first became entitled to old-age or disability benefits (including retroactive entitlement), or (b) the year following the one in which the worker dies. Years wholly within a period of disability are excluded, but years partially within a period of disability are included. If the period of disability was not excluded in counting elapsed years, it cannot be excluded from base years. [Soc. Sec. Act §215(b)(2)(B)(ii).]

Note that while actual earnings in each base year are used for computations using the old average monthly wage method, actual earnings must be indexed (*i.e.*, updated to reflect increases in the average of total wages nationwide) for each base year if the average indexed monthly earnings computation method is used. See ¶510 below.

¶507.7   Benefit Computation Years

Benefit computation years are selected from those base years in which total earnings (after indexing, if computing the AIME) from wages and/or self-employment are greatest. The quotient obtained by dividing the total earnings in the benefit computation years by the number of months in those years is the worker's average monthly wage or average indexed monthly earnings. [Soc. Sec. Act §215(b)(1).]

Benefit computation years are in most cases equal in number to elapsed years minus five, although a minimum of two computation years is required in every case and a special rule applies in the case of younger disabled workers. [Soc. Sec. Act §215(b)(2)(A).]

For purposes of computing the primary insurance amounts of younger workers who first become entitled to disability benefits after June 1980 based on eligibility after 1978, the number of elapsed years that may be excluded in selecting benefit computation years is limited. Under the "1 for 5 rule," the number of dropout years to be excluded equals the number of elapsed years divided by five, disregarding any fraction, with a maximum quotient of five. Thus, a disabled worker under age 27 is no longer able to exclude any years of low or no earnings. A disabled worker age 27 through 31 may exclude one year; a worker age 32 through 36, two years; a worker 37 through 41, three years; a worker 42 through 46, four years; and a disabled worker 47 or older may exclude five years. This provision continues to apply to a worker until death unless, before age 62, he or she ceases to be entitled to disability benefits for 12 continuous months. This provision also allows a disabled worker to drop out additional years if there was a child of the worker (or of his or her spouse) under age three living in the same household substantially throughout each such year and the worker did not engage in any employment in each such year. The combined number of child care and regular disability dropout years may not exceed three, and a minimum of two computation years is required in every case. [Soc. Sec. Act §215(b)(2)(A)(ii).]

In summary, remember that a determination of elapsed years reveals only the *number* of years to be considered, a determination of base years reveals years of *earnings* that may be considered in the average earnings computation, and a determination of benefit computation years reveals the actual *computation* years for which earnings will be averaged, equal in number to the number of elapsed years, reduced as described above, and chosen from the base years in which earnings were greatest.

¶508   Amount of Earnings Counted

Only wages up to a prescribed amount may be used in determining the average monthly wage or average indexed monthly earnings [Soc. Sec. Act §§215(e), 230]:

1937-1950	$ 3,000	1994	60,600
1951-1954	3,600	1995	61,200
1955-1958	4,200	1996	62,700
1959-1965	4,800	1997	65,400
1966-1967	6,600	1998	68,400
1968-1971	7,800	1999	72,600
1972	9,000	2000	76,200
1973	10,800	2001	80,400
1974	13,200	2002	84,900
1975	14,100	2003	87,000
1976	15,300	2004	87,900
1977	16,500	2005	90,000
1978	17,700	2006	94,200
1979	22,900	2007	97,500
1980	25,900	2008	102,000
1981	29,700	2009	106,800
1982	32,400	2010	106,800
1983	35,700	2011	106,800
1984	37,800	2012	110,100
1985	39,600	2013	113,700
1986	42,000	2014	117,000
1987	43,800	2015	118,500
1988	45,000	2016	118,500
1989	48,000	2017	127,200
1990	51,300	2018	128,400
1991	53,400	2019	132,900
1992	55,500	2020	137,700
1993	$ 57,600		

Self-employment income credited to any year after 1950 is also included in computing the average monthly wage or average indexed monthly earnings (see ¶419, above). If an individual has both self-employment income and wages during a year, the average is figured on the basis of combined earnings, limited to the same amounts as those shown above. [Soc. Sec. Act §215(e)(1).]

¶508.1   Earnings After Attainment of Age 62

For workers whose primary insurance amount must be based on an average monthly wage, computation base years after attainment of age 62 may be used as benefit computation years if it is advantageous to do so. Workers who reach age 62 after 1978 and before 1984 and, accordingly, to whom the transitional guarantee applies (see ¶511), are allowed to use earnings in the year of attainment of age 62 and thereafter only under the wage-indexing computation. [Soc. Sec. Act §215(b)(4).] Earnings in or after the indexing year (*i.e.*, the second year prior to the year of attainment of age 62) are not indexed, but rather are used at their actual dollar amounts. [Soc. Sec. Act §215(b)(3)(B).]

¶509   Average Monthly Wage Computation

The average monthly wage computation applies to individuals age 99 or older in 2020 (effective dates and applicability are discussed at ¶511 and ¶513). For most persons who use the old method of establishing a primary insurance amount, the computation is simple: total earnings in the benefit computation years divided by the number of months in those years (and disregarding any fraction of a dollar) equals the average monthly wage, from which the primary insurance amount is identified. [Soc. Sec. Act §215(b)(1).] For those who must determine average indexed monthly earnings, an additional step—indexing—is required before average earnings can be converted to a primary insurance amount.

¶510   Average Indexed Monthly Earnings Computation

For workers whose eligibility year is 1984 or later, the primary insurance amount will be computed on the basis of "average indexed monthly earnings" (AIME). The average summarizes up to 35 years of a worker's indexed earnings (generally, the highest 35 years of earnings).

In determining AIME, first figure the number of "elapsed years" as described above. Next, deduct five from this number to determine "computation years," unless a disability benefit is being computed for a worker under age 47, in which case deduct four years if the worker is age 42 through 46, three if age 37 through 41, two if age 32 through 36, one if the worker is age 27 through age 31, and none if the worker is under age 27 (but if the number of years to be deducted is less than three, it may be raised to not more than three by adding one year for each year the disabled person did not work and had a child or children under age three in care). In any case, two computation years is the minimum.

Now, make a list of "base years" and the worker's earnings in those years beginning with 1951 and ending with the year *before* the one in which benefits will begin. List only the worker's earnings covered by Social Security. (For survivors benefits, include the year of death.)

However, no matter how much the worker earned in any year, no more than the maximum creditable amount ($137,700 in 2020) may be listed (see ¶508).

Indexing earnings. The worker's earnings next must be mathematically related ("indexed") to national average earnings over the same period. Such indexation ensures that a worker's future benefits reflect the general rise in the standard of living that occurred during his or her lifetime.

The formula for indexing uses the worker's creditable earnings for a given year, national average earnings in the "indexing year" (which is the second year before the "eligibility year"), and national average earnings in the year being indexed, as follows:

$$\text{Worker's Creditable Earnings} \times \frac{\text{Average Earnings in Indexing Year}}{\text{Average Earnings in Year Being Indexed}} = \text{Worker's Indexed Earnings}$$

For example, suppose a worker reaches age 62 and retires in 2020. In 1980, he had $6,000 in earnings credited to his Social Security record. Average annual wages in 2018 (his "indexing year") were $52,145.80, and average annual wages in 1980 (the year being indexed) were $$12,513.46. The formula is applied as follows:

$$\$6,000 \times \frac{\$52,145.80}{\$12,513.46} = \$25,003.06$$

Alternatively, assume a worker reaches age 66 and retires at full retirement age in 2020. This worker, like the 62-year-old in the example above, had $6,000 credited to his earnings record in 1980. Average annual wages in his indexing year, 2014, were $46,481.52. The formula applies as follows:

$$\$6,000 \times \frac{\$46,481.52}{\$12,513.46} = \$22,287.13$$

In this manner, using the indexing year appropriate to the worker, index the earnings for each of the worker's base years (rounded to the nearest penny). Do not index earnings for the years after the indexing year; these are allowed to remain unchanged. The next step is to reduce the list to a number of years that is equal to the number of computation years. Eliminate the years with the lowest earnings (or no earnings at all) until the number of years remaining on the list equals the number of computation years. Then, add up the earnings entries for the years that remain on the list. Divide the result by the number of months in the computation years (that is, divide by computation years times 12) and drop any fraction of a dollar, rounding down to the next dollar amount.

The result is the worker's average indexed monthly earnings. This amount is then converted to a primary insurance amount as described at ¶512, below.

The table below shows average earnings in each year beginning with 1951. [20 C.F.R. Part 404, Subpart C, Appendix I.]

Table of Averages of Total Wages

Year	Average Earnings	Year	Average Earnings	Year	Average Earnings
1951	$ 2,799.16	1974	8,030.76	1996	25,913.90
1952	2,973.32	1975	8,630.92	1997	27,426.00
1953	3,139.44	1976	9,226.48	1998	28,861.44
1954	3,155.64	1977	9,779.44	1999	30,469.84
1955	3,301.44	1978	10,556.03	2000	32,154.82
1956	3,532.36	1979	11,479.46	2001	32,921.92
1957	3,641.72	1980	12,513.46	2002	33,252.09
1958	3,673.80	1981	13,773.10	2003	34,064.95
1959	3,855.80	1982	14,531.34	2004	35,648.55
1960	4,007.12	1983	15,239.24	2005	36,952.94
1961	4,086.76	1984	16,135.07	2006	38,651.41
1962	4,291.40	1985	16,822.51	2007	40,405.48
1963	4,396.64	1986	17,321.82	2008	41,334.97
1964	4,576.32	1987	18,426.51	2009	40,711.61
1965	4,658.72	1988	19,334.04	2010	41,673.83
1966	4,938.36	1989	20,099.55	2011	42,979.61
1967	5,213.44	1990	21,027.98	2012	44,321.67
1968	5,571.76	1991	21,811.60	2013	44,888.16
1969	5,893.76	1992	22,935.42	2014	46,481.52
1970	6,186.24	1993	23,132.67	2015	48,098.63
1971	6,497.08	1994	23,753.53	2016	48,642.15
1972	7,133.80	1994	23,753.53	2017	50,321.89
1973	$ 7,580.16	1995	$ 24,705.66	2018	52,145.80

COMPUTING THE PRIMARY INSURANCE AMOUNT

¶511   Introduction

Virtually all Social Security benefits are based on a percentage of the insured worker's primary insurance amount (PIA). The PIA is the benefit an employee would receive if he or she began receiving retirement benefits at retirement age. Note, at this age the benefit is not reduced for early retirement or increased for delayed retirement.

PIA is a function of AIME and is determined by applying a PIA formula to AIME. Generally, PIA is the sum of three separate percentages of portions of AIME. The portions depend on the year in which a worker attains age 62, becomes disabled before age 62, or dies before attaining age 62.

The percentages used in the PIA formula are fixed by law. However, the dollar amounts in the formula are adjusted to reflect changes in the national average wage index. The dollar amounts are referred to as "bend points."

Old AMW PIA method.—For years prior to 1979, the system of determining a primary insurance amount involved primarily the "old" method, based on the worker's average monthly wage (AMW), as described at ¶513.

New AIME PIA method.—Under the "new" computation system prescribed by the 1977 Amendments, benefits for workers who first become eligible after 1978 are separated—"decoupled"—from those of persons already receiving benefits, and automatic cost-of-living increases (see ¶541) do not apply until the year of first eligibility (see ¶512).

Designed to stabilize future replacement rates (benefits as a percentage of earnings) in relation to future wage levels, major provisions of the revised benefit structure provided for (1) indexing of wages and the benefit formula to reflect changes in wage levels up to the time of eligibility in order to assure that future replacement rates will be relatively constant, and (2) lower replacement rates than those that had been expected to apply in years after 1978 while guaranteeing that workers approaching retirement when the amendments were enacted would receive as much as would have been payable under the 1978 benefit table (see ¶537). Computation of the AIME PIA is described at ¶512.

Transitional guarantee.—In order to protect the benefit rights and expectations of persons approaching retirement when the benefit system was restructured by the 1977 Amendments, a transitional guarantee in the amendments allowed workers (and their dependents or survivors) who first became eligible for retirement benefits within the period 1979-1983 to receive an initial benefit that was the higher of either a benefit derived under the new AIME PIA formula or a benefit derived under a somewhat modified version of the method in effect before January 1979, the general effective date of the restructured benefit system.

PIA of disabled workers.—The primary insurance amount of an insured worker who becomes disabled is computed as though he or she had attained age 62 in the first month of his or her waiting period (see ¶520.2) or, if he or she becomes entitled to disability benefits for a second or subsequent disability and can meet the requirements for not serving a waiting period, as though the appropriate age had been attained in the first month of entitlement to disability benefits. The computation is made as though the worker had become entitled to old-age benefits in the month in which the application for disability benefits was filed and as though the worker was entitled to an old-age benefit for each month for which he or she applied and was entitled to disability benefits. [Soc. Sec. Act §223(a)(2).]

¶512   Primary Insurance Amount Based on Average Indexed Monthly Earnings (AIME PIA)

The primary insurance amounts of virtually all workers who reach age 62, become disabled, or die (before age 62) are derived from a formula applied to the worker's average indexed monthly earnings (see ¶510), except that a worker who reached age 62 before 1984 may use the old average monthly wage PIA computation method if it will be to his or her advantage to do so.

PIA formula based on first eligibility year. The AIME PIA is determined by factoring the worker's AIME into the PIA formula that applies with respect to the worker's eligibility year, (i.e., the year in which he or she attains age 62). The eligibility year formula continues to apply even if the worker delays retirement (and, therefore, entitlement) to a later year. Even though the eligibility year formula continues to apply to a worker who delays retirement, the benefit he or she eventually receives will be increased by any cost-of-living "escalator" increases that occur in or after the initial year of eligibility, regardless of when entitlement to benefits is established (see ¶541) as well as by any delayed retirement credits due to retirement after full retirement age (see ¶539). [Soc. Sec. Act §215(a)(1)(A).]

Bend points. The percentages used in the PIA formula are set by law and remain constant. However, the formula dollar brackets, or "bend points," are annually adjusted to wages by multiplying them by the ratio of average wages for the second year before the year for which the determination is made to average wages in 1977. [Soc. Sec. Act §215(a)(1)(B)(ii).] Bend points for the AIME PIA formula for each year since 1979 are as follows:

	90%	32%	15%	
1979	$180	$180.01—1,085	over	$1,085
1980	194	194.01—1,171	over	1,171
1981	211	211.01—1,274	over	1,274
1982	230	230.01—1,388	over	1,388
1983	254	254.01—1,528	over	1,528
1984	267	267.01—1,612	over	1,612
1985	280	280.01—1,691	over	1,691
1986	297	297.01—1,790	over	1,790
1987	310	310.01—1,866	over	1,866
1988	319	319.01—1,922	over	1,922
1989	339	339.01—2,044	over	2,044
1990	356	356.01—2,145	over	2,145
1991	370	370.01—2,230	over	2,230
1992	387	387.01—2,333	over	2,333
1993	401	401.01—2,420	over	2,420
1994	422	422.01—2,545	over	2,545
1995	426	426.01—2,567	over	2,567
1996	437	437.01—2,635	over	2,635
1997	455	455.01—2,741	over	2,741
1998	477	477.01—2,875	over	2,875
1999	505	505.01—3,043	over	3,043
2000	531	531.01—3,202	over	3,202
2001	561	561.01—3,381	over	3,381
2002	592	592.01—3,567	over	3,567
2003	606	606.01—3,653	over	3,653
2004	612	612.01—3,689	over	3,689
2005	627	627.01—3,779	over	3,779
2006	656	656.01—3,955	over	3,955
2007	680	680.01—4,100	over	4,100
2008	711	711.01—4,288	over	4,288
2009	744	744.01—4,483	over	4,483
2010	761	761.01—4,586	over	4,586
2011	749	749.01—4,517	over	4,517
2012	767	767.01—4,624	over	4,624
2013	791	791.01—4,768	over	4,768
2014	816	816.01—4,917	over	4,917
2015	826	826.01—4,980	over	4,980
2016	856	856.01—5,157	over	5,157
2017	885	885.01—5,336	over	5,336
2018	895	895.01—5,397	over	5,397
2019	926	926.01—5,583	over	5,583
2020	960	960.01—5,785	over	5,785

The bend points for the 2020 PIA formula ($960 and $5,785) apply for workers becoming eligible in 2020. Thus, for a worker who first becomes eligible for old age insurance or disability benefits in 2020, the Average Indexed Monthly Earnings are converted to a PIA by adding:

90% of the first $960 or less of AIME
32% of any AIME above $960 through $5,785
15% of any AIME above $5,785

PIAs determined under the AIME PIA method are rounded to the next-lower multiple of 10 cents, if not already a multiple of 10 cents, but intermediate steps in the computation are not rounded. [Soc. Sec. Act §215(a)(1)(A).]

Note: Monthly benefits derived from PIA may be higher or lower than PIA depending on whether an employee retires before normal retirement age or elects to delay retirement.

Special Rule Regarding Public Pensioners—WEP

Employees who have worked for employers that did not withhold Social Security tax from their salary (e.g., federal or state civil service employers) may be subject to a reduction in Social Security benefits under the Windfall Elimination Provision (WEP). Enacted in 1983, WEP is intended to redress the windfall allowed under the generally applicable Social Security benefits formula (which replaces a greater proportion of wages for lower earners than for higher earners) to workers who spent most of their careers in uncovered employment and, thus, were treated, for purposes of benefits calculations, as being long-term, lower-wage earners. Absent adjustment, such workers would receive a Social Security benefit representing a higher percentage of their earnings, plus a pension for service during which they did not pay Social Security taxes.

Under the benefits formula, as modified by WEP, the first figure in the PIA formula is decreased (thus lowering the final benefit) depending on how many years of Social Security coverage the individual has in a job that paid "substantial earnings." Substantial earnings for WEP purposes varies from year to year as follows:

1951-54	$ 900	1985	$ 7,425	2002	$ 5,750
1955-58	1,050	1986	7,875	2003	16,125
1959-65	1,200	1987	8,175	2004	16,275
1966-67	1,650	1988	8,400	2005	16,725
1968-71	1,950	1989	8,925	2006	17,475
1972	2,250	1990	9,525	2007	18,150
1973	2,700	1991	9,900	2008	18,975
1974	3,300	1992	10,350	2009-11	19,800
1975	3,525	1993	10,725	2012	20,475
1976	3,825	1994	11,250	2013	21,075
1977	4,125	1995	11,325	2014	21,750
1978	4,425	1996	11,625	2015-16	22,050
1979	4,725	1997	12,150	2017	23,625
1980	5,100	1998	12,675	2018	23,850
1981	5,550	1999	13,425	2019	24,675
1982	6,075	2000	14,175	2020	25,575
1983	6,675	2001	$ 14,925		
1984	7,050				

If the individual has 20 or fewer years of coverage, the first figure in the PIA formula (90%) is reduced to 40%. With 21 years of coverage, the number is 45%; with 22 years, the number is 50%; with 23 years, 55%; with 24 years, 60%; with 25 years, 65%; with 26 years, 70%; with 27 years, 75%, with 28 years, 80%; with 29 years, 85%; and with 30 or more years, the full 90% is used in the PIA formula.

The amount of the reduction may be substantial, especially for employees with significantly fewer than 30 years of substantial earnings. For example, the maximum monthly amount by which a benefit can be reduced in 2020 for a worker with 20 years or less of substantial earnings is $463 (subject to protection for low earners). See www.ssa.gov/retire2/wep-chart.htm.

Lower earners protected. Workers with relatively low pensions are shielded from the harshest effects of WEP. The reduction in Social Security benefits may not exceed one-half of the worker's pension that is based on earnings after 1956 on which Social Security taxes were not paid.

Exceptions to WEP. As noted above, WEP does not apply to workers who have 30 years or more of substantial earnings under Social Security. In addition, WEP does not apply to federal workers first hired after December 31, 1983; individuals employed on December 31, 1983 by non-profit organizations that did not initially withhold Social Security taxes, but subsequently began withholding; workers whose only pension is based on railroad employment; and workers whose only experience working a job on which they did not pay Social Security taxes was before 1957.

Survivors benefits. WEP does not apply to survivors benefits. However, the benefits of a widow or widower may be subject to reduction.

Cost-of-living increases

Cost-of-living increases for the eligibility year and years thereafter are added to primary insurance amounts. Social Security beneficiaries will receive a cost-of-living adjustment (COLA) in their benefits for 2020 of 1.6% based on the change in the CPI-W from the third quarter of 2018 to the third quarter of 2019.

Applying cost-of-living adjustment. A worker reaching age 66 in 2020 increases his or her PIA by 0.3% for 2016, 2.0% in 2017, 2.8% in 2018, and 1.6% for 2019. Workers reaching age 62 in 2020 do not receive these prior-year increases, but they will benefit from any later increases. A worker reaching age 63 and retiring in 2020 would add only the 2019 increase to his or her PIA (plus any later increases in subsequent years).

Amounts not even multiples of 10 cents are rounded *down* at each step of the computation process (after the AIME computation), and the final benefit amount is rounded down to the next-lower dollar. When a Medicare Part B premium is involved, the rounding to the next-lower dollar occurs after the premium is deducted.

Converting a PIA to a benefit

Once the PIA has been computed, including cost-of-living increases, the actual benefit that will be paid to the worker or to his or her survivors or dependents can be determined.

The amount of retirement benefits paid depends on a person's age when he or she begins receiving benefits. Benefits taken before a person attains full retirement age are reduced, while benefits taken after full retirement age are increased.

The old-age benefit of a worker who has reached full retirement age (age 66 if you were born January 2, 1943–January 1, 1955) will be approximately the same as his or her PIA, but the benefit will be reduced for every month for which benefits are paid prior to full retirement age. The only individuals attaining full retirement age in 2020 will be individuals attaining age 66, i.e., individuals born January 2, 1954, through January 1, 1955. For such individuals, the maximum possible monthly benefit is $3,011.

Currently, the old-age benefit may be reduced to 75.4167% (*i.e.*, a 24.5833% reduction) of the PIA for most retirees exactly age 62 at retirement. For retirees born on the second day of the month and retiring at exactly age 62, the reduction is slightly more, 25.00%, reducing their benefit to 75.00% of their PIA, but they will have one additional month of benefits before reaching full retirement age.

A wife's, husband's, child's, or other dependent's benefit is also derived from the PIA. A wife's or husband's basic benefit, for example, is equal to half of the PIA of the spouse upon whose earnings record the benefit is based. Note that some benefits may be reduced because of age, the limitation on maximum family benefits or because of excess income.

If the worker delays retirement past full retirement age, the benefit amount of the worker and for the worker's surviving spouse may be higher than the primary insurance amount because of the delayed retirement credit.

The actual benefit check will be reduced if the recipient is eligible for Medicare because of the Part B premium ($144.60/month in 2020), for most enrollees. Higher amounts for individuals with high incomes will ordinarily be deducted each month.

The final benefit payment, after all of these alterations and computations, is reduced to round the sum to the next-lower multiple of one dollar, if it is not already a multiple of one dollar.

¶513　Primary Insurance Amount Based on Average Monthly Wage (AMW PIA)

In the case of insured persons born before 1917 and other beneficiaries initially eligible before 1979, the primary insurance amount was generally computed on the basis of the worker's actual, unindexed, average monthly wage under the old "AMW PIA" (Average Monthly Wage PIA) method. For insured persons born after 1916 and others initially eligible after 1978, the new "AIME PIA" method is used, although a "transitional guarantee" permits persons initially eligible during the period 1979–1983 to compute their PIAs under either a version of the old method or the new method, whichever will produce the higher benefit. This "notch," which shifts the PIA computation from the old to the new method, can cause benefits payable to persons born in 1917 or later to be substantially less than benefits payable to persons with similar earnings records born in 1916 or earlier. A Congressional commission concluded, however, that the "notch babies" had not been treated unfairly. Rather, unduly large benefits were paid to those born 1910–1916 as a result of a flaw in the prior benefit computation method that was corrected by 1977 legislation that created the AIME PIA method.

RETIREMENT BENEFITS

¶517   Retired Worker's Benefit

The amount payable each month to a retired individual on the basis of his or her earnings from employment or self-employment covered by the old-age, survivors, and disability (OASDI) system is called an "old-age insurance benefit," or, perhaps more flatteringly, a retirement benefit.

A worker is entitled to a monthly old-age benefit if he or she is fully insured (see ¶505), has reached age 62, and has filed an application for old-age benefits. [Soc. Sec. Act §202(a).]

Although a worker may become eligible for retirement benefits at age 62, such early retirement will result in the reduction of his or her monthly benefits, based on the number of months remaining before the worker attains "retirement age," which is the age at which a fully insured worker becomes eligible for a monthly old-age benefit equal to his or her primary insurance amount. Age 65 had long been the "full" retirement age. However, since 2000, full retirement age has been gradually increasing and will continue to increase until it reaches age 67. "Early" retirement age will remain at 62.

The monthly benefit of a worker who becomes entitled to old-age benefits at full retirement age will equal his or her primary insurance amount. An individual who becomes entitled to old-age benefits between ages 62 and full retirement age will receive an actuarially reduced benefit, as discussed at ¶535.1, whereas an individual who postpones entitlement by working beyond full retirement age will receive an increased benefit as a result of the delayed retirement credit, as discussed at ¶539. [Soc. Sec. Act §202(a).]

Benefits for workers (and their dependents) retiring at age 62 begin with the first month throughout all of which the worker meets all the requirements for eligibility (*i.e.*, the month after the month in which the worker attains age 62, in the usual case). For workers retiring after the month of attainment of age 62, benefits begin with the month in which the conditions of entitlement are met. In either case, benefits end with the month before the month in which the individual dies. Benefits may be terminated earlier in cases of entitlement to a federal benefit based on military service, and in cases of entitlement to benefits under the Railroad Retirement Act. [Soc. Sec. Act §202(a).]

Note that, for Social Security purposes, an individual is deemed to have attained a given age on the first moment of the day *before* the anniversary of his or her birth. [20 C.F.R. §404.2(c)(4).] Accordingly, individuals born on the first of the month are deemed to have attained retirement age on the last day of the preceding month. These individuals therefore become eligible for retirement benefits in the month of their 62nd birthday. Similarly, individuals born on the second day of the month are deemed to have attained retirement age on the first of the month and, thus, also become eligible to receive retirement benefits in the month of their 62nd birthday.

Even though an individual is entitled to old-age benefits, benefits may not be payable for certain months or may be payable only in part because of deductions under the retirement test, deportation, etc. See ¶550, *et seq.*

Finally, note the benefits of a beneficiary will be automatically recomputed each year to reflect earnings that would increase the amount of benefits. The recomputation, however, may not decrease the primary insurance amount or benefits. See ¶565.

¶518   Increased Retirement Age

The age at which a retiree is entitled to his or her full benefit amount—*i.e.*, the age at which benefits are no longer reduced on account of early retirement—is increasing to 67. However the change is being phased in gradually and does not affect individuals born in 1937 or earlier.

The retirement age was first raised to 66 by increasing the age for full benefits by two months per year for six years, effective beginning with workers who reached age 62 in 2000, so that the full retirement age was set at 66 for workers reaching age 62 in 2005. Beginning in 2017, the retirement age will again be raised, again in two-month increments over a six-year period, so that the full retirement age will be set at 67 for workers reaching 62 in 2022 (67 in 2027). [Soc. Sec. Act §216(l).]

The 1983 Amendments did not alter the provisions permitting early retirement at age 62. However, employees who retire at age 62 in the year 2022 or later will receive 70% of their full benefit, rather than 80%, as the reduction period will increase in stages between 2002 and 2022 (see ¶535.1).

The following table shows how the full retirement age—*i.e.*, the age at which a beneficiary is entitled to unreduced benefits (see ¶535.1)— will be increased under the 1983 Amendments:

Year of attainment of age 62		Retirement age		
Years through	1999	65		
	2000	65 +	2 months	
	2001	65 +	4 months	
	2002	65 +	6 months	
	2003	65 +	8 months	
	2004	65 +	10 months	
2005 through	2016	66		
	2017	66 +	2 months	
	2018	66 +	4 months	
	2019	66 +	6 months	
	2020	66 +	8 months	
	2021	66 +	10 months	
2022 and beyond		67		

As explained above, individuals born on January 1 of any given year are deemed to have attained age 62 on the last day of the preceding year. Thus, while the 62nd birthday of an individual born January 1, 1958, would occur on January 1, 2020, because this person would have *attained* age 62 on December 31, 2019, the individual would reach full retirement at age 66 and six months.

¶519   Estimating the Benefit Amount

Individuals may estimate retirement benefits using the Social Security Administration's online "Retirement Estimator" at *www.ssa.gov/retire/estimator/html.* The Retirement Estimator is available for persons who have earned enough Social Security credits to qualify for benefits. In addition, you may not be: currently receiving benefits on your own Social Security record; waiting for a decision about your application for benefits or Medicare; age 62 or older and receiving benefits on another Social Security record; or eligible for a pension based on work not covered by Social Security. However, if you are currently receiving only Medicare benefits, you may still receive an estimate.

This estimator will initially provide, based on your earnings history, an estimate of retirement benefits at age 62, at full retirement age, and at age 70. You may also specify at what age you intend to retire.

Note that the Social Security Administration will not calculate your actual benefit until you actually apply for benefits. The actual amount of your benefit also may differ from the estimated benefit because: your earnings may increase or decrease in the future; benefits will be adjusted for cost-of-living increases; or your benefit amount may be affected by military service, railroad employment, or pensions earned from work on which you did not pay Social Security taxes. In addition, the law governing benefit amounts may change because (under current law) by 2033, payroll taxes will only cover about 75 cents for every dollar of scheduled benefits.

Be further cautioned that unlike the earnings statement, the estimator will not provide an estimate for disability benefits, nor will it provide an earnings history that allows you to compare your records with Social Security Administration records. For that you need to go to a local Social Security office and declare that you have an "urgent need" for the information. You are not required to prove that the need is urgent, however. The information will be provided using an online query system at the Social Security office.

Estimating benefits with scaled earnings. You can make a rough estimate of your future benefits by applying "scaled" earnings levels. Scaled earnings reflect realistic lifetime fluctuations in income. Specifically, scaled earnings assume lower earnings levels for younger workers, with the earnings levels increasing until reaching a peak sometime in mid-career, and then gradually decreasing again until retirement.

Actuarial tables available from the Social Security Administration show projected *annual* benefits in the average and maximum income categories, expressed both in the actual dollar amount that is expected to be paid, and in an amount that is the equivalent of the benefit as if it were being paid in current dollars. While it is assumed that the worker's annual earnings will keep pace with moderate increases in national average wages, and that there will be annual increases in the cost of living, the exact amount of any benefit will depend on the worker's individual earnings and on the course of the economy.

The following table, from the 2019 Annual Report of the Federal Old-Age and Survivors Insurance and Federal Disability Insurance Trust Funds, reveals the annual scheduled benefit amounts for retired workers with various pre-retirement earnings patterns based on the intermediate assumptions.

Table V.C7.—Annual Scheduled Benefit Amounts for Retired Workers With Various Pre-Retirement Earnings Patterns Based on Intermediate Assumptions, Calendar Years 2019-2095

		BENEFITS IN 2019 DOLLARS[a] WITH RETIREMENT AT NORMAL RETIREMENT AGE					
YEAR ATTAIN AGE 65[b]	AGE AT RETIREMENT	SCALED VERY LOW EARNINGS[c]	SCALED LOW EARNINGS[d]	SCALED MEDIUM EARNINGS[e]	SCALED HIGH EARNINGS[f]	STEADY MAXIMUM EARNINGS[g]	NATIONAL AVERAGE WAGE INDEX IN 2019 DOLLARS[h]
2019	66:0	$10,125	$13,243	$21,843	$28,934	$35,355	$53,864
2020	66:2	10,451	13,671	22,545	29,867	36,513	54,951
2025	67:0	10,917	14,294	23,586	31,212	38,428	59,454
2030	67:0	11,807	15,466	25,516	33,757	41,601	63,817
2035	67:0	12,672	16,595	27,366	36,220	44,642	67,950
2040	67:0	13,497	17,668	29,133	38,560	47,493	72,155
2045	67:0	14,327	18,756	30,933	40,947	50,445	76,437
2050	67:0	15,183	19,873	32,773	43,384	53,389	81,136
2055	67:0	16,119	21,097	34,796	46,051	56,568	86,237
2060	67:0	17,129	22,424	36,984	48,949	60,058	91,656
2065	67:0	18,208	23,833	39,305	52,024	63,786	97,297
2070	67:0	19,327	25,299	41,721	55,221	67,711	103,121
2075	67:0	20,486	26,812	44,216	58,527	71,769	109,179
2080	67:0	21,688	28,386	46,813	61,963	75,991	115,493
2085	67:0	22,942	30,028	49,517	65,543	80,390	122,122
2090	67:0	24,258	31,753	52,360	69,308	85,012	129,158
2095	67:0	25,657	33,584	55,380	73,302	89,920	136,637
		BENEFITS IN 2019 DOLLARS[a] WITH RETIREMENT AT AGE 65					
2019	65:0	9,518	12,451	20,538	27,208	33,134	53,864
2020	65:0	9,621	12,598	20,766	27,515	33,539	54,951
2025	65:0	9,461	12,378	20,427	27,034	33,043	59,454
2030	65:0	10,234	13,398	22,092	29,244	35,789	63,817
2035	65:0	10,979	14,375	23,705	31,382	38,423	67,950
2040	65:0	11,691	15,302	25,240	33,416	40,878	72,155
2045	65:0	12,416	16,253	26,801	35,480	43,425	76,437
2050	65:0	13,156	17,220	28,396	37,592	45,958	81,136
2055	65:0	13,963	18,281	30,144	39,902	48,692	86,237
2060	65:0	14,845	19,429	32,041	42,412	51,700	91,656
2065	65:0	15,778	20,651	34,055	45,078	54,912	97,297
2070	65:0	16,748	21,920	36,145	47,850	58,296	103,121
2075	65:0	17,749	23,233	38,309	50,714	61,792	109,179
2080	65:0	18,792	24,597	40,560	53,692	65,428	115,493
2085	65:0	19,880	26,020	42,904	56,796	69,217	122,122
2090	65:0	21,022	27,513	45,367	60,058	73,195	129,158
2095	65:0	22,233	29,099	47,982	63,519	77,422	136,637

[a] Annual amounts are the total for the 12-month period starting with the month of retirement, adjusted to be in 2019 dollars by using the CPI indexing series from table VI.G6.

[b] Attains age 65 on January 1 of the year.

[c] Career-average earnings at about 25 percent of the AWI.

[d] Career-average earnings at about 45 percent of the AWI.

[e] Career-average earnings at about 100 percent of the AWI. Such a worker would have career-average earnings at approximately the 56th percentile of all new retired-worker beneficiaries.

[f] Career-average earnings at about 160 percent of the AWI.

[g] Earnings for each year at or above the contribution and benefit base.

[h] Average Wage Index from table VI.G6, adjusted to be in 2019 dollars by using the CPI indexing series from table VI.G6.

Note: Benefits shown at age 65 reflect adjustments for early retirement. For early retirement as early as age 62, the benefit amount is reduced 5/9 of one percent for each month before normal retirement age, up to 36 months. If the number of months exceeds 36, then the benefit is further reduced 5/12 of one percent per month. For example, if the number of reduction months is 60 (the maximum number for retirement at 62 when normal retirement age is 67), then the benefit is reduced by 30 percent. *Delayed retirement credit* is generally given for retirement after the normal retirement age. The delayed retirement credit is 2/3 of one percent per month for persons born in 1943 and later. No credit is given for delaying benefits after attaining age 70. See table V.C3 for additional details, including adjustments applying to other birth years.

DISABILITY

¶520   Introduction

The program of social insurance that is now called "Social Security" was originally envisioned to provide financial security against the economic uncertainties of unemployment and old age. [Franklin Delano Roosevelt, address to Congress, June 8, 1934.] Benefits for disabled workers were not added to the Social Security Act until 1956. Over the years, Congress has expanded certain aspects of the program while also "tightening up" certain of the benefit requirements. Some of the major changes are briefly outlined below, while details of the disability program are discussed in the sections that immediately follow.

Historical Overview

Over the past five decades, amendments have extended benefits to spouses and children of disabled workers, removed the restriction that limited payment of benefits to persons age 50 or older, eliminated the requirement that an impairment be of "long-continued and indefinite duration," extended benefits to disabled widows and widowers at age 50, liberalized entitlement for the blind, reduced the waiting period for disability benefits, allowed the filing of claims after the death of the insured, restricted payments somewhat for younger disabled workers, limited the maximum benefit that could be paid to all family members (the "family maximum") based on disability, liberalized the provisions on vocational rehabilitation and trial work, tightened the standards for determining disability, and set in place a process for expedited consideration of claims for those individuals with certain debilitating or terminal diseases.

The Disability Benefits Reform Act of 1984 provided stricter prerequisites for terminating disability benefits and provided for continued payment of benefits pending appeal. The Omnibus Budget Reconciliation Act of 1990 removed the stricter standard of disability that formerly required disabled widows to establish an inability to engage in any gainful activity. The Social Security Independence and Program Improvements Act of 1994 placed limits on the payment of disability benefits to substance abusers. The definition of childhood disability under Title XVI was narrowed by the Personal Responsibility and Work Opportunity Act of 1996 to require marked or severe functional limitations and imposed new criteria with respect to redeterminations. The Ticket to Work and Work Incentives Improvement Act of 1999 expanded the availability of health care coverage for working individuals with disabilities and provided such individuals with expanded opportunities to return to work, including monetary incentives to the states for assisting with a disabled person's vocational rehabilitation.

Programatic Overview

For a discussion of the definition of "disability" for Social Security purposes and the conditions of entitlement to benefits based on disability, see ¶520.1 and ¶520.2, respectively. The disability "freeze," pursuant to which a worker may have his or her earnings record frozen so that benefit rights will not be unduly impaired because of disability is discussed at ¶520.3. The special insured status requirements that apply to workers applying for disability benefits are explained at ¶505.5.

Disability determinations are generally made by appropriate state agencies, as discussed at ¶520.4, and state agencies are likewise responsible for providing vocational rehabilitation services (see ¶520.6).

Once a disability benefit has been granted, a beneficiary may still be subject to continuing review of his eligibility (see ¶520.5). Programs designed to encourage disabled beneficiaries to return to work are covered at ¶520.6.

Various factors, such as receipt of disability benefits from another source or engaging in substantial gainful activity during a period of alleged disability, can cause a reduction or loss of benefits. The applicable rules are addressed at ¶520.7–¶520.9.

¶520.1   "Disability" Defined

Disability (with the exception of blindness) is generally defined under the Social Security Act as an inability to engage in any substantial gainful activity by reason of any medically determinable physical or mental impairment which can be expected to result in death or which has lasted or can be expected to last for a continuous period of not less than 12 months." [Soc. Sec. Act §§216(i), 223(d)(1).] Thus, it is not sufficient for a disability claimant to merely establish an impairment lasting at least 12 months or to show an inability to perform his or her usual work. In order to meet the statutory definition of disability, a claimant must further establish the existence of a severe impairment resulting in the inability to engage in previous work or in any other substantial gainful activity that exists in the national economy.

The U.S. Supreme Court has endorsed the Social Security Administration's position that disability benefits require a claimant to establish the inability to engage in substantial gainful activity by reason of the impairment for at least 12 months. [*Barnhart v. Walton*, 535 U.S. 212, 122 S.Ct. 1265, 152 L.Ed.2d 330 (2002); Soc. Sec. Ruling 82-52.] The Court also endorsed the SSA's opposition to the granting of a "trial-work period" (see ¶520.6) and the allowance of a benefit to individuals who have performed any substantial gainful activity prior to the conclusion of a 12-month period following the date of disability onset.

Substantial gainful activity. "Substantial gainful activity" has a specialized meaning for purposes of the Social Security disability program. Specifically, substantial gainful activity refers to work that requires significant and productive physical or mental duties and that is undertaken for pay or profit, regardless of whether a profit is actually realized. Work may be considered substantial gainful activity even if it is performed on a part-time basis or if it involves less work, less pay, or less responsibility than work the claimant has performed in the past. While activities such as taking care of oneself, household tasks, hobbies, therapy, school attendance, and club activities or social programs may be indicative of residual functional capacity for various types of work, such activities are not considered to be substantial gainful activity. [Reg. §§404.1510, 404.1572.] Other types of work that are excluded from the meaning of "substantial gainful activity," as well as the earnings levels that give rise to a presumption that a worker is engaged in substantial gainful activity, are discussed further below in this section under "Sequential Evaluation Process" in Step 1.

Work that exists in the national economy means work existing in significant numbers in the region where the claimant lives or in several regions of the country, regardless of whether such work exists in the immediate area in which the claimant lives, whether a specific job vacancy exists, or whether the claimant would be hired if he or she applied for work. [Soc. Sec. Act. §§216(i)(1), 223(d)(2).]

In assessing a claimant's ability to engage in any substantial gainful activity, evidence of vocational factors, including age, education, and work experience, will be evaluated, in that order and in light of the individual's impairment(s), in order to determine the claimant's residual functional capacity for other work. [Soc. Sec. Act §223(d)(2).]

Consider combined impact of impairments. In determining whether an individual's physical or mental impairments are of sufficient medical severity to provide the basis for entitlement, the Commissioner is required to consider the combined effect of all the individual's impairments without regard to whether any such impairment, if considered separately, would be of disabling severity. If the Commissioner does find a medically severe combination of impairments, the combined impact of the impairments is considered throughout the disability determination process. [Soc. Sec. Act §223(d)(2)(C).]

A "physical or mental impairment" is one that results from anatomical, physiological, or psychological abnormalities that are demonstrable by medically acceptable clinical and laboratory diagnostic techniques. Criteria are prescribed for determining when services performed or earnings derived from services demonstrate an individual's ability to engage in substantial gainful activity. An individual whose work or earnings meet these criteria will be found not to be disabled. [Soc. Sec. Act §223(d)(3), (4).]

Any physical or mental impairment arising in connection with or aggravated by the commission of a felony will not be considered in determining whether an applicant is disabled. Nor will any impairment arising during the individual's confinement for having committed such a felony be considered when assessing disability during confinement. [Soc. Sec. Act §223(d)(6).]

Drug addiction and alcoholism. Legislation enacted in 1996 ended entitlement to disability benefits if drug addiction or alcoholism are the contributing factors material to the determination of disability. [Senior Citizens' Right to Work Act, Title I of The Contract With America Advancement Act, P.L. 104-121, §105(a)(1) and (b)(1), amending Soc. Sec. Act §§223(d)(2) and 1614(a) (3), respectively.] Moreover, a person who is determined to be disabled based on an impairment other than drug addiction or alcoholism must have his or her benefits paid to a representative payee if the SSA determines that such payment would serve the person's interests because he or she also has an alcoholism or drug addiction condition and is incapable of managing his or her benefits. [Soc. Sec. Act §205(j).] In addition, such an individual must be referred to the appropriate state agency for substance abuse treatment. [P.L. 104-121, §105(a)(3) and (b)(3), amending Soc. Sec. Act §§222(e) and 1636, respectively.]

The SSA policies for determining whether drug addiction or alcoholism is material to a determination of disability are set forth in Social Security Ruling (SSR) 13-2p (78 *Fed. Reg.* 11939, February 20, 2013).

Blindness. Blindness is defined as central visual acuity of 20/200 or less in the better eye with the use of correcting lenses, or visual acuity greater than 20/200 if accompanied by a limitation in the field of vision such that the widest diameter of the visual field subtends an angle no greater than 20 degrees. An individual will satisfy the definition of disability for benefit purposes if he or she has attained the age of 55 and is unable, by reason of blindness, to engage in substantial gainful activity requiring skills or abilities comparable to those of any gainful activity previously performed with some regularity over a substantial period of time. [Soc. Sec. Act §§216(i)(1)(B), 223(d)(1)(B); Reg. §§404.1583–.1584.]

Disabled survivor benefits. Widows, widowers, and surviving divorced spouses who are disabled may receive disabled widow(er)'s benefits on the account of an insured spouse. The statutory standard for secondary disability benefits for a widow, widower, or surviving divorced spouse is the same as the disability standard for a worker seeking disability benefits on his or her own account. Thus, an applicant must be unable to engage in *substantial* gainful activity, rather than *any* gainful activity. [Soc. Sec. Act §223(d)(2)(B), prior to amendment by P.L. 101-508, §5103.]

Sequential Evaluation Process

In determining whether an individual is disabled, a sequential evaluation process is followed whereby current work activity, severity and duration of the impairment(s), ability to engage in former types of work, and vocational factors are considered in light of all the material facts of the case. In following this sequential evaluation process, whenever a determination that an individual is or is not disabled can be made at any step, further evaluation is not necessary. [Reg. §404.1520(a).]

Step one: Substantial gainful activity—

If a claimant is working and the work meets the specialized definition of "substantial gainful activity" (SGA), disability benefits will be denied, regardless of the claimant's medical condition or age, education, and work experience.

The amount of money a claimant earns from work activities may give rise to a presumption that he or she is engaged in substantial gainful activity, even if the work is performed sporadically or only part time. Average monthly earnings greater than an upper threshold will trigger a presumption that the claimant is engaged in substantial gainful activity. Earnings equal to or below that threshold will give rise to a presumption that the claimant is not engaged in substantial gainful activity. This presumption is rebuttable, however, if circumstances indicate that the individual may be engaging in substantial gainful activity or might be in a position to defer or suppress earnings. The threshold amount is subject to annual adjustment for people with impairments other than blindness (see below regarding the special threshold for blind individuals), based on increases in the national average wage index. [Regs. §§404.1574(b), 416.974(b); 71 *Fed. Reg.* 66845, Nov. 17, 2006.]

In 2020, the amount of average monthly earnings that is ordinarily indicative of substantial gainful activity is $1,260 (up from $1,220 in 2019). The threshold for blind individuals is higher, as discussed further in this section. Thresholds for prior years appear in the chart, below.

Substantial Gainful Activity Thresholds for Non-Blind Individuals
(Step 1 of the 5-part Test to Establish Disability)

Year		Lower Threshold	Upper Threshold
1980-1989		$190	$ 300
1990-June 1999		300	500
July 1999-Dec. 2000		300	700

Year	Threshold	Year	Threshold
2001*	$ 740	2012	$ 1,010
2002	780	2013	1,040
2003	800	2014	1,070
2004	810	2015	1,090
2005	830	2016	1,130
2006	860	2017	1,170
2007	900	2018	1,180
2008	940	2019	1,220
2009	980	2020	1,260
2010–2011	1,980		

* Lower threshold eliminated in 2001.

[Reg. §404.1574, as amended by 65 *Fed. Reg.* 82905, Dec. 29, 2000; 66 *Fed. Reg.* 54047, Oct. 25, 2001; 67 *Fed. Reg.* 65620, Oct. 25, 2002, 68 *Fed. Reg.* 60437, Oct. 22, 2003, 69 *Fed. Reg.* 62497, Oct. 26, 2004; 70 *Fed. Reg.* 61677, Oct. 25, 2005; 71 *Fed. Reg.* 62636, Oct. 26, 2006; 72 *Fed. Reg.* 60703, Oct. 25, 2007; 73 *Fed. Reg.* 64651, Oct. 30, 2008; 74 *Fed. Reg.* 55614, Oct. 28, 2009; 75 *Fed. Reg.* 74123, Nov. 30, 2010; 76 *Fed. Reg.* 66111, Oct. 25, 2011; 77 *Fed. Reg.* 65754, Oct. 30, 2012; 78 *Fed Reg.* 66413, Nov. 5, 2013; 79 *Fed. Reg.* 64455, October 29, 2014; 80 *Fed. Reg.* 66963, October 30, 2015; 81 *Fed. Reg.* 74854, October 27, 2016; 82 *Fed. Reg.* 59937, December 15, 2017; 83 *Fed. Reg.* 53702, October 24, 2018; 84 *Fed. Reg.* 56515, October 22, 2019.]

Treatment of earnings derived from services. Note that when a disability beneficiary works, the SSA must consider which month the income was earned in determining whether the individual's earnings exceed the SGA amount. Under the Social Security Benefit Protection and Opportunity Enhancement Act of 2015, the SSA now will be permitted to streamline the process of evaluating a beneficiary's earnings by presuming that wages and salaries were earned when paid, unless information is available to the SSA that shows when the income was earned. Beneficiaries would receive a notification when such presumption is made, and afforded an opportunity to provide additional wage information regarding when the services were performed. [Soc. Sec. Act §223(d)(4), as amended.]

Self-employment. While the same levels of earnings may give rise to a presumption of substantial gainful activity by self-employed individuals, earnings alone are not determinative since the amount of income a self-employed person receives may depend on other factors such as capital investment, profit-sharing arrangements, etc. Work activities in self-employment will be evaluated on the basis of their value to the business. A self-employed person will be considered to have engaged in substantial gainful activity if his or her work activity, in terms of factors such as hours, skills, energy, output, efficiency, duties, and responsibilities, is comparable to that of unimpaired individuals involved in the same or similar work. [Reg. §404.1575.]

Evaluation of work attempts. Effective November 16, 2016, the SSA issued final rules that remove the additional conditions the agency used when it evaluated a work attempt in employment or self-employment that lasted between three and six months and use instead the current three-month standard for all work attempts that are six months or less. Under these new rules, ordinarily, work an individual has done will not show that the individual is able to do substantial gainful activity if, after the individual has worked for a period of six months or less, his or her impairment forces the individual to stop working or to reduce the amount of work he or she is doing so that earnings from such work fall below the substantial gainful activity level. [Regs. §404.1574(c) and §404.1575(d).]

Illegal acts. The Commissioner is required to consider illegal, as well as legal, activity in determining whether an individual alleging disability is engaging in substantial gainful activity. [Soc. Sec. Act §223(4)(B).] However, work performed under special circumstances (*e.g.* assistance from other employees, permission to take frequent breaks, work tailored to accommodate an impairment, work performed at a substandard level, or work provided because of a special relationship with an employer) may not necessarily be evidence of substantial gainful activity. [Reg. §404.1573(c).] Also excluded is work performed in certain federal volunteer programs and services during a trial-work period (see ¶520.6 regarding trial work programs). [Reg. §404.1574(d).]

Higher income threshold for blind. There is a separate, higher threshold for blind individuals. A blind individual age 55 or older who earns less than an annual exempt amount will not be regarded as having demonstrated an ability to engage in substantial gainful activity. The monthly exempt amounts for blind individuals have been:

1996	$ 960		2007	$ 1,500
1997	1,000		2008	1,570
1998	1,050		2009–2011	1,640
1999	1,110		2012	1,690
2000	1,170		2013	1,740
2001	1,240		2014	1,800
2002	1,300		2015–2016	1,820
2003	1,330		2017	1,950
2004	1,350		2018	1,970
2005	1,380		2019	2,040
2006	1,450		2020	2,110

[Soc. Sec. Act §§203(f)(8), 223(d)(4)(A).]

Blind self-employed. In determining whether work performed by blind self-employed persons is substantial gainful activity, the SSA will evaluate self-employment work activity based on whether the blind person has received a substantial income from the business and rendered significant services to the business. The SSA will ascertain the blind person's countable income in the same manner as it determines the countable income of non-blind persons, determining gross income, deductions, and net income from self-employment. The reasonable value of any significant amount of unpaid help furnished by the person's spouse, children, or others; impairment-related work expenses; and unincurred business expenses are deducted. The income remaining after all applicable deductions are made represents the actual value of work performed and is the amount the SSA uses to determine whether the person has engaged in SGA. This amount is referred to as the blind person's countable income. [20 CFR §404.1575(c) and §404.1584(d).] The SSA then compares the individual's countable income from the business with the dollar amounts in its published SGA earnings guidelines for persons who are blind.

If the average monthly countable income of a self-employed blind person exceeds the SGA earnings guidelines for the applicable year, the SSA will consider the person's work activity to be SGA, unless he or she has not rendered significant services to the business. If the blind person operates a business alone, the SSA considers any services rendered to be significant to the business. However, if the business involves the services of more than one person, the SSA evaluates the actual services rendered by the blind person to determine whether they are significant. It will consider services significant if the blind person provides more than half the total time needed to manage the business, or more than 45 hours a month regardless of the total management time the business required.

If the average monthly countable income of the blind person is equal to or less than the SGA earnings guidelines for the applicable year, the SSA will not consider his or her work activity to be SGA. Special provisions apply to farm landlords. [Social Security Ruling (SSR) 12-1p (77 *Fed Reg.* 58604, Sept. 21, 2012).]

Deduction for impairment-related work expenses. The earnings of an impaired individual are reduced, however, prior to evaluation, by the amount of any impairment-related work expenses, attendant care costs, and the cost of medical devices, equipment, prosthetic devices, and certain essential non-medical appliances and equipment. The costs of installing, maintaining, and repairing deductible items also will be considered. Furthermore, the costs of drugs and medical services, including diagnostic procedures, may be deducted if they are prescribed or utilized to reduce or eliminate the symptoms of an impairment or to slow down its progression. Only the costs of drugs or services directly related to the impairment will be deducted. In addition, if the claimant's impairment requires a vehicle that has structural or operational modifications in order to get to work, the costs of the modifications or the cost of hiring such a vehicle will be deducted, as well as a mileage allowance

¶520.1

for the extra costs involved in operating such a vehicle. [Soc. Sec. Act §223(d)
(4); Reg. §404.1576.] Subsidies above the value of the actual work performed
are also not included in the amount of earnings used to assess whether substantial gainful activity has been performed. [Reg. §404.1574(a).]

Step two: Severity of impairment—

If a determination of disability cannot be based on current work activity, then
the Commissioner will consider the severity of the claimant's impairment,
i.e., whether the individual's impairment or combination of impairments significantly limits his or her physical or mental ability to do basic work activities, without consideration of age, education, and work experience. An impairment is not considered severe if it is a slight abnormality or combination
of slight abnormalities that would have no more than a minimal effect on an
individual's ability to perform basic work activities. [Reg. §404.1520(b), (c).]

However, when mental impairments are present, a psychiatric review technique (PRT) is mandatory and must be documented in the ALJ's written decision, including the findings and conclusions based on the PRT. Accordingly,
a PRT was required for a claimant who had dementia with impaired memory,
concentration, and motor functions, as well as a mood disorder. The Step 4
determination that the claim was not credible was negated by the failure to
perform the PRT at Step 2. [*Cuthrell v. Astrue,* No. 12-2329 (CA-8, 2013).]

Step three: Listed impairment—

If the claimant establishes the presence of a severe impairment and it meets the
12-month duration requirement, the Commissioner continues the sequential
evaluation process and determines whether the impairment is listed in the Listing of Impairments in Appendix 1 of the disability regulations [20 C.F.R. Part
404, Subpart P] or is equal to a listed impairment, in which case the individual
is found disabled without considering age, education, and work experience.

The Listing of Impairments describes, for each of the major body systems,
impairments that are considered severe enough to prevent a person from engaging in any gainful activity. Most of the listed impairments are permanent
or expected to result in death, or a specific statement of duration is made.
Note that where the criteria in the appendix to the Social Security disability
regulations do not give appropriate consideration to particular disease processes in childhood, an evaluation may be made under the supplemental appendix containing a separate listing of impairments applicable to children
under age 18. [Reg. §§404.1520(d), 404.1525.]

The Listing of Impairments applicable to adults is organized in 14 sections, as follows:

1.00	**Musculoskeletal System.** Musculoskeletal impairments include major dysfunction of one or more joints due to any cause; reconstructive surgery of a major weight bearing joint where return to ambulation did not occur; disorders of the spine; amputation; and certain fractures and soft tissue injuries.
2.00	**Special Senses and Speech.** This category includes: ophthalmological disorders such as loss of central visual acuity, visual efficiency, or muscle function; statutory blindness; severe hearing impairments; vertigo; and organic loss of speech.
3.00	**Respiratory System.** Listed respiratory impairments include: chronic pulmonary insufficiency; asthma; pneumoconiosis; bronchiectasis; and mycobacterial or mycotic infections of the lungs.
4.00	**Cardiovascular System.** Disabling conditions may include: severe cardiac impairments; congestive heart disease; hypertensive vascular disease; ischemic heart disease; recurrent arrhythmias; myocardiopathies; chronic venous insufficiency; and peripheral arterial disease.
5.00	**Digestive System.** Category includes: recurrent upper gastrointestinal hemorrhage; stenosis or obstruction of the esophagus; peptic ulcer disease; chronic liver disease such as chronic active hepatitis and cirrhosis; chronic colitis; enteritis; and weight loss due to persisting gastrointestinal disorder.
6.00	**Genitourinary System.** Severe impairment of renal (kidney) function and other disorders are listed.
7.00	**Hematological Disorders.** This listing includes: chronic anemia; sickle cell disease; leukemia; lymphomas; and other disorders of the blood.
8.00	**Skin.** Ichthyosis (noninflammatory scaling of the skin), bullous disease, chronic infections of the skin or mucous, dermatitis (inlcuding psoriasis and allergic contact) hidradenitis suppurativa, photosensitivity disorders (including xeroderma pigmentosum), and burns are some of the conditions that may be disabling under the criteria set forth in Sec. 8.00 of the Listing of Impairments. A corresponding listing for childhood skin disorders, 108.00, also includes erythropoietic porphyrias and hemangiomas.
9.00	**Endocrine System.** Thyroid disorders, adrenal hyperfunction, certain types of diabetes, and other impairments caused by hormonal disorders are listed in this category.
10.00	**Congenital Disorders that Affect Multiple Body Systems.** Down syndrome. Abnormalities that affect multiple body systems, such as trisomy X syndrome, fragile X syndrome, phenylketonuria (PKU), caudal regression syndrome, and fetal alcohol syndrome.
11.00	**Neurological.** Epilepsy and other convulsive disorders, brain tumors, persistent disorganization of motor function, multiple sclerosis, cerebral palsy, amyotrophic lateral sclerosis, myasthenia gravis, and muscular dystrophy are among the disabling neurological impairments.
12.00	**Mental Disorders.** Listed impairments include: organic mental disorders; schizophrenic, paranoid, and other psychotic disorders; affective disorders; intellectual disability (formerly mental retardation); anxiety-related, somatoform, and personality disorders; substance addiction disorders; and autistic and other developmental disorders.
13.00	**Cancer.** Malignant tumors, sarcomas, melanomas, lymphomas (including Hodgkin's disease), and many other types of cancers are included.
14.00	**Immune System.** Systemic lupus, vasculitis, sclerosis and scleroderma, HIV infection, connective tissue disorders, inflammatory arthritis, and other deficiencies of the immune system are listed.

Chronology of rule changes

If a claim is pending before the SSA when new criteria set forth in the Listing of Impairments take effect, the agency may choose to evaluate the claim under the revised criteria.

2017: The SSA has revised its rules regarding medical evidence. The revisions include redefining several key terms related to evidence, revising the rules about acceptable medical sources, revising how the SSA articulates its consideration of medical opinions and prior administrative medical findings, revising the rules about medical consultants and treating sources, and reorganizing the evidence regulations for ease of use (82 *Fed. Reg.* 5844, January 18, 2017).

The SSA has issued SSR 17-1p, which explains how the agency will apply its reopening rules when it has applied a federal or state law to a claim for benefits that the U.S. Supreme Court later determines to be unconstitutional and the SSA finds the application of that law was material to the determination or decision. The agency expects that the ruling will clarify SSA policy in light of recent questions that it has received on this issue. SSR 17-1p became effective on March 1, 2017 (82 *Fed. Reg.* 12270, March 1, 2017).

On July 1, 2016, the SSA published a final rule entitled "Revised Medical Criteria for Evaluating Neurological Disorders," in which it incorporated those portions of SSR 87-6 that continue to be relevant regarding the treatment of epilepsy (81 *Fed. Reg.* 43048). The rule became effective on September 29, 2016. Consequently, the SSA has rescinded SSR 87-6 as obsolete (82 *Fed. Reg.* 12485. March 3, 2017).

On December 2, 2016, the SSA published a final rule entitled "Revised Medical Criteria for Evaluating Human Immunodeficiency Virus (HIV) Infection and for Evaluating Functional Limitations in Immune System Disorders" (81 *Fed. Reg.* 86915). The final rule revises the listing criterial under which the agency evaluates impairments related to HIV infection. At the time the SSA published SSR 93-2p, which provides guidance about evaluating duration in cases meeting or equaling HIV infection listings, medical outcomes for individuals infected with HIV were sufficiently unfavorable that the SSA could reasonably assume that all such impairments either were permanent or would result in death. However, that is no longer a proper assumption for the SSA to make so the agency is rescinding SSR 93-2p as obsolete.

The SSA has issued SSR 17-2p, which provides guidance as to how adjudicators at the hearing and Appeals Council levels of the administrative review process should make findings about medical equivalence in disability claims under Titles II and XVI of the Social Security Act. It became effective on March 27, 2017 (82 *Fed. Reg.*15263, March 15, 2017).

Effective March 27, 2017, the SSA rescinded SSRs 96-2p, 96-5p, and 06-3p regarding medical source opinions. The three SSRs are inconsistent or unnecessarily duplicative with the SSA's final rules entitled "Revisions to Rules Regarding the Evaluation of Medical Evidence," which were published on January 18, 2017 (82 *Fed. Reg.* 5844).

The SSA has rescinded SSR 91-3p as obsolete because a new application for disabled widow(er)'s benefits cannot establish entitlement to these benefits prior to January 1991, and the agency has no pending applications that involve entitlement to disabled widow(er)'s benefits for months prior to that date. The rescission was effective on May 30, 2017 (82 *Fed. Reg.* 24769, May 30, 2017).

The SSA has issued SSR 17-3p, which provides guidance on Sickle Cell Disease (SCD) and how the SSA evaluates SCD in disability claims under Titles II and XVI of the Social Security Act. Information is provided in a "question and answer" format that explains how to consider evidence regarding the impairment (82 *Fed. Reg.* 43442, September 15, 2017).

On October 30, 2017, the SSA announced a new disability program demonstration project: Promoting Opportunity Demonstration (POD). Under this project the agency will modify program rules applied to beneficiaries who work and receive Title II disability benefits. The project is scheduled to begin in November 2017 and end in June 2021 (82 *Fed. Reg.* 50214, October 30, 2017).

The SSA has issued SSR 17-4p, which clarifies the agency's responsibilities as well as the responsibilities of the claimant and a claimant's representative to develop evidence and other information in disability and blindness claims. The ruling applies at all levels of the administrative review process (82 Fed. Reg. 46339, October 4, 2017).

The SSA has issued a final rule extending the expiration dates of the following body systems in the Listing of Impairments in its regulations: Musculoskeletal System, Cardiovascular System, Digestive System, and Skin Disorders. The rule extended the expiration dates for all four systems from January 26, 2018, to January 27, 2020 (82 *Fed. Reg.* 59514, December 15, 2017).

2018: The SSA extended the expiration dates of the following two body systems in the Listing of Impairments in its regulations: Special Senses and Speech and Congenital Disorders That Affect Multiple Body Systems. The final rule became effective on April 2, 2018. The new expiration date for the Special Senses and Speech body system is April 24, 2020, and the new expiration date for the Congenital Disorders That Affect Multiple Body Systems body system is April 3, 2020 (83 *Fed. Reg.* 13863, April 2, 2018).

The SSA proposes to revise the criteria in the Listing of Impairments that the agency uses to evaluate claims involving musculoskeletal disorders in adults and children under Titles II and XVI of the Social Security Act. These proposed revisions reflect the adjudicative experience, advances in medical knowledge and treatment of musculoskeletal disorders, and recommendations from medical experts (83 *Fed. Reg.* 20646, May 7, 2018).

The SSA has removed from the Code of Federal Regulations (CFR) its "Special Payments at Age 72" rules because they are obsolete. The agency is removing these rules in accordance with the requirements of Executive Order 13777. The removal became effective on May 10, 2018 (83 Fed. Reg. 21707, May 10, 2018).

The SSA has extended the expiration date of the Endocrine Disorders body system in the Listing of Impairments in its regulations. The extension ensures that the SSA will continue to have the criteria it needs to evaluate impairments in the affected body system at step three of the sequential evaluation processes for initial claims and continuing disability reviews. The final rule became effective on May 22, 2018. The new expiration date for the body system is June 26, 2020 (83 *Fed. Reg.* 23579, May 22, 2018).

On February 28, 2005, the SSA published Social Security Ruling (SSR) 05-02, which provides guidance about determining whether substantial work activity that is discontinued or reduced below a specified level may be considered an unsuccessful work attempt (UWA) under the disability provisions of the law. SSR 05-02 explains the policies and procedures for evaluating a work effort of three months or less and work efforts between three and six months.

On October 17, 2016, the SSA published final rules, Unsuccessful Work Attempts and Expedited Reinstatement Eligibility, in the *Federal Register* at 81 *Fed. Reg.* 71367. These rules, among other things, removed some of the requirements for evaluation of an UWA that lasts between three and six months. Specifically, the rules removed the additional conditions that the SSA used when it evaluated a work attempt in employment or self-employment that lasted between three and six months and provided that the agency now uses one standard for work attempts lasting six months or less.

Due to these final rules and the resulting simplification of SSA policies, SSR 05-02 is no longer correct. The final rules at 20 CFR 404.1574(c), 404.1575(d), 416.974(c), and 416.975(d) (unsuccessful work attempts) were effective November 16, 2016. Consequently, the agency rescinded SSR 05-02 as obsolete, effective May 14, 2018 (83 *Fed. Reg.* 22308, May 14, 2018).

The SSA has rescinded SSR 96-3p, Titles II and XVI: Considering Allegations of Pain and Other Symptoms in Determining Whether a Medically Determinable Impairment is Severe, and 96-4p, Titles II and XVI: Symptoms, Medically Determinable Physical and Mental Impairments, and Exertional and Nonexertional Limitations as unnecessarily duplicative." The recessions were applicable on June 14, 2018 (83 *Fed. Reg.* 27816, June 14, 2018).

The SSA has revised its rules of conduct and standards of responsibility for representative payees. The agency also is updating and clarifying the procedures it uses when it brings charges against a representative for violating these rules and standards. The changes are necessary to better protect the integrity of the SSA's administrative process and to further clarify representatives' existing responsibilities in their conduct with the agency. The revisions should not be interpreted to suggest that any specific conduct was permissible under

¶520.1

its rules prior to these changes; instead, the SSA seeks to ensure that its rules of conduct and standards of responsibility are clearer as a whole and directly address a broader range of inappropriate conduct. The final rules became effective on August 1, 2018 (83 *Fed. Reg.* 30849, July 2, 2018).

The Acting Commissioner of Social Security has given notice of the rescission of Social Security Ruling (SSR) 82-53: Titles II and XVI: Basic Disability Evaluation Guides. The rescission became effective on August 29, 2018. SSR 82-53 provided an overview and an explanation of the definitions and terms contained in the disability provisions of Titles II and XVI of the Social Security Act (Act) and implementing regulations. The information in the SSR duplicates information available in the Act, regulations, and other subregulatory policy documents. For example, the definitions of "disability" and "blindness" already appear in those documents (83 *Fed. Reg.* 44119, August 29, 2018).

Nancy A. Berryhill, the Acting Commissioner of Social Security, has given notice of the rescission of Social Security Rulings (SSR): SSR 62-47; SSR 65-33c; SSR 66-19c; SSR 67-54c; SSR 68-47c; SSR 71-23c; SSR 72-14c; SSR 72-31c; SSR 82-19c; and SSR 86-10c. These rescissions became effective on September 14, 2018. The SSA is rescinding the SSRs, which address due process rights to counsel; fees for representational services; and judicial review of representative fees, because the information provided therein either reflects well-established legal principles and is already reflected clearly in the Social Security Act or regulations, or has since been clarified in agency regulations and subregulatory guidance (83 *Fed. Reg.* 46771, September 14, 2018).

The SSA has issued notice of SSR 18-01p, "Titles II and XVI: Determining the Established Onset Date (EOD) in Disability Claims," which rescinds and replaces SSR 83-20, "Titles II and XVI: Onset of Disability," except as noted below. Specifically, SSR 18-01p addresses how the SSA determines the EOD in claims that involve traumatic, non-traumatic, and exacerbating and remitting impairments. The ruling also addresses special considerations related to the EOD, such as work activity and previously adjudicated periods. Additionally, the SSR clarifies that an administrative law judge may, but is not required to, call upon the services of a medical expert to assist with inferring the date that the claimant first met the statutory definition of disability.

The SSA concurrently has published a separate ruling, SSR 18-02p, "Titles II and XVI: Determining the Established Onset Date (EOD) in Blindness Claims," to discuss how it determines the EOD in statutory blindness claims.

SSR 18-02p rescinds and replaces two parts of SSR 83-20. Specifically, it rescinds and replaces the subsection, "Title II: Blindness Cases," under the section, "Technical Requirements and Onset of Disability"; and the subsection, "Title XVI—-Specific Onset is Necessary," which is also under the section "Technical Requirements and Onset of Disability," as it applies to statutory blindness claims. Therefore, SSR 83-20 is completely rescinded and replaced by SSR 18-01p and SSR 18-02p. Both SSRs became applicable on October 2, 2018 (83 *Fed. Reg.* 49613, October 2, 2018, and 83 *Fed. Reg.* 49621, October 2, 2018).

The SSA has provided notice of SSR 18-3p. The ruling provides guidance as to how the agency applies its failure to follow prescribed treatment policy in disability and blindness claims under Titles II and XVI of the Social Security Act. The SSA will apply this notice effective on October 29, 2018 (83 *Fed. Reg.* 49616, October 2, 2018).

The SSA proposes to amend its regulations to prohibit persons convicted of certain crimes from serving as representative payees under the Social Security Act. The agency is proposing these revisions because of changes to the Act made by the Strengthening Protections for Social Security Beneficiaries Act of 2018 (83 *Fed. Reg.* 51400, October 11, 2018).

The SSA is proposing to revise its rules to explain that the agency retains the right to determine how parties and witnesses will appear at a hearing before an administrative law judge (ALJ) at the hearing level of its administrative review process. The SSA also will set the time and place for each hearing. In addition, the agency proposes to revise its rules to explain that the state agency or the Associate Commissioner for Disability Determinations, or his or her delegate, will determine how parties and witnesses will appear, and will set the time and place for a hearing, before a disability hearing officer (DHO) at the reconsideration level in continuing disability review (CDR) cases. At both levels, the SSA proposes to schedule the parties to a hearing to appear by video teleconference (VTC), in person, or, in limited circumstances, by telephone. The agency proposes that parties to a hearing will not have the option to opt out of appearing by the manner of hearing it chooses. The SSA also proposes rules that explain how it will determine the manner of a party's or a witness's appearance (83 *Fed. Reg.* 57368, November 15, 2018).

2019: The SSA is proposing to eliminate the education category "inability to communicate in English" when it evaluates disability claims for adults under Titles II and XVI of the Social Security Act. Changes in the national workforce since the agency added this category to its rules in 1978 demonstrate that this education category is no longer a reliable indicator of an individual's educational attainment or the vocational impact of an individual's education. The proposed revisions reflect research and data related to English language proficiency, work, and education; expansion of the international reach of the SSA's disability programs; and audit findings by the Office of the Inspector General (OIG). The proposed revisions also would help the SSA better assess the vocational impact of education in the disability determination process (84 *Fed. Reg.* 1006, February 1, 2019).

The SSA has issued notice of SSR 19-1p. This ruling explains how the agency will adjudicate cases pending at the Appeals Council in which the claimant has raised a timely challenge to the appointment of an Administrative Law Judge (ALJ) under the Appointments Clause of the United States Constitution in light of the Supreme Court's 2018 decision in *Lucia v. SEC.* The SSA will apply the notice effective March 15, 2019 (84 *Fed. Reg.* 9582, March 15, 2019).

In a unanimous decision, the U.S. Supreme Court in *Smith v. Berryhill,* No. 17-1606 (2019), found that the Appeals Council's (AC) dismissal of a SSI claimant's request for review on timeliness grounds, after the claimant had a hearing before an Administrative Law Judge (ALJ), qualified as a "final decision" made after a hearing for purposes of allowing judicial review within the context of 42 U.S.C. §405(g). The holding reversed the decision of the Sixth Circuit Court of Appeals, which maintained that there had been no "final decision" (No. 17-1606 (2019)).

The SSA is proposing to revise the criteria in the Listing of Impairments that it uses to evaluate claims involving digestive and skin disorders in adults and children under Titles II and XVI of the Social Security Act. The proposed revisions reflect the agency's adjudicative experience, advances in medical knowledge, and comments the SSA received from experts and the public in response to two previous advance notices of proposed rulemaking (ANPRM). The SSA last published final rules revising the digestive disorders listing on October 19, 2007. The skin disorders listing was last revised on June 9, 2004 (84 *Fed. Reg.* 35936, July 25, 2019).

The SSA has issued notice of SSR 19-3p. This SSR explains the two options available to claimants appealing the agency's determinations that they are not disabled based on medical factors. In this SSR, the SSA explains both the paper and electronic appeal options for requesting reconsideration of a hearing by an administrative law judge (ALJ), and the similarities and differences between these two options. The agency explains these options to help claimants make informed decisions when deciding whether to use the paper appeal or electronic appeal option to request reconsideration of a hearing.

SSR 19-3p became applicable on August 14, 2019 (84 *Fed. Reg.* 40467, August 14, 2019).

The SSA has issued notice of SSR 19-4p, which provides guidance on how the agency establishes that a person has a medically determinable impairment (MDI) of a primary headache disorder and how it evaluates primary headache disorders in disability claims under Titles II and XVI of the Social Security Act. The notice became effective on August 26, 2019 (84 *Fed. Reg.* 44667, August 26, 2019).

Obesity

Obesity is no longer listed as a separate impairment, having been removed in 1999. A sharply divided Sixth Circuit, sitting *en banc*, concluded in 2006 that the Social Security Administration's decision to delete obesity (Listing §9.09) from the Listing of Impairments while the claimant's disability claim was being administratively adjudicated, and to base the adjudication on the Listing of Impairments, as amended, did not have an impermissible retroactive effect. A thin majority held that the presumption of disability created by Listing §9.09 was a rule that governed adjudicatory conduct, and the adjudication took place years after the listing was deleted. Accordingly, there was no impermissible retroactive effect, according to the court, because the effect of the regulatory change took place at the time of adjudication. [*Combs v. Commissioner of Social Security*, 459 F3d 640 (Sixth Cir. 2006).]

On May 20, 2019, the SSA issued SSR 19-2p, which provides guidance on how the agency establishes that a person has a medically determinable impairment (MDI) of obesity and how the SSA evaluates obesity in disability claims under Titles II and XVI of the Social Security Act. This SSR rescinds and replaces SSR 02-1p: Titles II and XVI: Evaluation of Obesity (84 *Fed. Reg.* 22924).

Chronic Fatigue Syndrome

Chronic Fatigue Syndrome (CFS) is a medically determinable impairment that can provide the basis for a finding of disability. SSR 99-2p (64 *Fed. Reg.* 23380, April 30, 1999) lists examples of signs and laboratory findings that will establish the existence of a medically determinable impairment.

On April 3, 2014, the SSA issued a new ruling, SSR 14-1p, providing guidance on how the agency develops evidence to establish that a person has a medically determinable impairment of chronic fatigue syndrome (79 *Fed. Reg.* 18750, Apr. 3, 2014).

Fibromyalgia

Fibromyalgia is not a listed impairment. However, the SSA has issued guidance, effective July 25, 2012, on the development of evidence necessary to establish that a person has a medically determinable impairment (MDI) of fibromyalgia. [SSR 12-2p.]

Generally, an MDI of fibromyalgia can be established through evidence provided by "an acceptable medical source," *i.e.,* a physician or osteopath, applying specified criteria. However, the SSA will not rely on a diagnosis without evidence. The evidence must document that the physician reviewed the person's medical history and conducted a physical examination.

The Social Security Administration will generally request documentation for the 12-month period that precedes the application date. Evidence may also be considered from medical sources who are not "acceptable medical sources," such as psychologists, as well as from nonmedical sources such as neighbors, friends, employers, rehab counselors, teachers, and SSA personnel who have interviewed the claimant. If the evidence is insufficient, the SSA may purchase a consultative examination.

Once an MDI of fibromyalgia is established, it will then be considered in the five-step sequential evaluation process. At step two, when determining severity, the ruling states, "If the person's pain or other symptoms cause a limitation or restriction that has more than a minimal effect on the ability to perform basic work activities, we will find that the person has a severe impairment(s)." Because fibromyalgia is not a listed impairment, the SSA at step three, will determine whether FM medically equals a listing (for example, listing Sec. 14.09D in the listing for inflammatory arthritis), or whether it medically equals a listing in combination with at least one other medically determinable impairment.

In *Revels v. Commissioner*, the Ninth Circuit reversed the decision of the district court, which had affirmed both the ALJ and Appeals Council, and determined that they all failed to follow the guidelines set forth in SSR 12-2p, which provided guidelines for the proper evaluation of fibromyalgia (No. 15-16477, October 26, 2017).

Medical equivalence

An individual's impairment or impairments will be determined to be medically the equivalent of an impairment listed in Appendix 1 only if the medical findings with respect thereto are at least equivalent in severity and duration to those described in the appendix, based on medical evidence demonstrated by medically accepted clinical and laboratory diagnostic techniques, including a medical judgment furnished by one or more physicians designated by the Commissioner (which may include a physician employed by, or engaged for the purpose by, the SSA or a state agency authorized to make determinations of disability).

All relevant evidence other than the vocational factors of age, education, and work experience, will be considered when making medical equivalency findings. Accordingly, lay testimony may be used to establish (or rebut) equivalency. [Regs. §§404.1526 and 416.926.]

Mental disorders

Mental disorders listing pre-January 17, 2017. The evaluation of mental disorders requires for all but mental retardation (Listing §12.05) and substance addiction (§12.09) substantiation of the criteria set forth in paragraph A of Listing §12.00—a set of medical findings, as well as the criteria in either paragraph B (impairment-related functional criteria) or paragraph C (additional functional criteria for organic mental disorders (§12.02), psychotic disorders (§12.03), affective disorders (§12.04), and anxiety related disorders (§12.06)).

Intellectual disability. The SSA, effective September 3, 2013, replaced the term "mental retardation" with "intellectual disability" in the Listing of Impairments. [78 *Fed. Reg.* 46499, Aug. 1, 2013, amending Reg. §§404.1513, 404.2045, 416.645, and 416.913.]

The change reflects widespread adoption of the term "intellectual disability" by Congress, government agencies, and various public and private organizations. However, note, an individual who has a medically determinable intellectual impairment, including an intellectual disability, would not be considered disabled for SSA purposes, absent a determination by the agency that the impairment has resulted in an inability to perform any substantial gainful activity or, with respect to a child under Title XVI, resulted in marked and severe limitations. Thus, the use of the term "intellectual disability" would not guarantee that the SSA has found an individual to be disabled within the meaning of the Social Security Act.

The listing for intellectual disability, §12.05, has an introductory paragraph and four sets of functional criteria. An impairment will be found to meet the listing if it satisfies the diagnostic description in the introductory paragraph and any one of the four sets of criteria: (A) mental incapacity; (B) a verbal performance or full scale IQ less than 60; (C) an IQ of 60 through 70 and a physical or other mental impairment imposing an additional and significant work-related limitation of function; or (D) an IQ of 60 through 70 resulting in at least two of the criteria set forth under paragraph B of the other mental criteria.

Listing of Impairments. The SSA includes mental disorders in the Listing of Impairments (§§12.00 and 112.00). The expiration date of the mental disorders body system impairment has been extended to January 17, 2022.

Note that new rules go into effect on January 17, 2017, and expire on January 17, 2022.

Mental disorders listing post-January 17, 2017. The SSA issued final rules on September 26, 2016, which revised both the content and structure of the adult and childhood mental disorders listings (81 *Fed. Reg.* 66137, September 26, 2016).

Evidence from medical and non-medical sources

Only acceptable medical sources may render medical opinions and be considered as treating sources entitled to controlling weight. "Acceptable medical sources" refers only to medical or osteopathic physicians, psychologists, optometrists and podiatrists, all of whom must be licensed, and qualified speech-language pathologists. Optometrists (other than those in the Virgin Islands) also may be considered an acceptable medical source for all visual disorders, and not just the measurement of visual acuity and visual fields.

In resolving conflicting opinions between medical professionals, the "treating physician rule" requires that the opinion of the medical source who has examined a claimant be given more weight than the opinion of a source who has not performed an examination. Similarly, the opinion of a medical source who regularly treats the claimant is to be afforded more weight than that of a source who has examined the claimant, but does not have an ongoing relationship with the party. The medical opinion of the treating source will be accorded controlling weight if it is well supported by medically acceptable clinical and laboratory diagnostic techniques and is not inconsistent with other substantive evidence in the case. [*Gayheart v. Commissioner*, No. 12-3553 (Sixth Cir. 2013).]

Evidence from medical sources that are not acceptable. Evidence from other health care providers who are not "acceptable" medical sources, such as nurse practitioners, physician assistants, licensed clinical social workers, naturopaths, chiropractors, audiologists and therapists, as well as other non-medical sources, may be used to show the severity of a claimant's impairment and how it affects his or her ability to function. [Regs. §404.1513(a), (d) and §416.913(a), (d); 72 *Fed. Reg.* 9239, March 1, 2007.]

In addition, although medical opinions from an acceptable medical source may be accorded greater weight, an opinion from a medical source who is not an acceptable medical source may, depending on the applicable facts, outweigh the opinion of an acceptable medical source, including the opinion of a treating source, says SSR 06-30. This scenario could arise where the "not acceptable" medical source has seen the claimant more often than the treating source or has provided a better explanation for his opinion. For similar reasons, the ruling also states that an opinion from a nonmedical source who has seen the claimant in his or her professional capacity, such as a teacher, may properly be determined to outweigh the opinion from a medical source, including a treating source. [SSR 06-30, 71 *Fed. Reg.* 45593, Aug. 9, 2006.] See, for example, *Popa v. Commissioner*, CA-9, 15-16848, August 18, 2017).

Exclusion of certain medical sources of evidence. Effective after November 2, 2016, the Social Security Benefit Protection and Opportunity Enhancement Act of 2015, prevents evidence submitted by unlicensed or sanctioned physicians and health care providers from being considered when determining disability. [Soc. Sec. Act §223(d)(5), as amended.]

Note that in accordance with §812 of the Bipartisan Budget Act of 2015 (BBA §812), the SSA has issued final rules to explain how the agency will address evidence furnished by medical sources that meet one of BBA §812's exclusionary categories (excluded medical sources of evidence). Under the new rules, the SSA will not consider evidence furnished by an excluded medical source of evidence unless it finds good cause to do so. The SSA identifies five circumstances in which it may find good cause. In addition, the rules also require excluded medical sources of evidence to notify the SSA of their excluded status under §223(d)(5)(C)(i) of the Social Security Act, in writing, each time they furnish evidence to the agency that relates to a claim for initial or continuing benefits under Titles II or XVI. These final rules became effective on November 2, 2016 (81 *Fed. Reg.* 37138, June 9, 2016).

The SSA also has revised its rules regarding medical evidence. The revisions include redefining several key terms related to evidence, revising the rules about acceptable medical sources (AMS), revising how the SSA considers and articulates its consideration of medical opinions and prior administrative medical findings, revising the rules about medical consultants (MC) and psychological consultants (PC), revising the rules about treating sources, and reorganizing the evidence regulations for ease of use (82 *Fed. Reg.* 5844, January 18, 2017; technical corrections made in 82 *Fed. Reg.* 15132, March 27, 2017).

Resolution of medical record conflicts. Whenever there is insufficient evidence to determine if a claimant for disability benefits is disabled, or when a report from a medical source contains a conflict or ambiguity that must be resolved, the SSA was required to seek additional evidence or clarification from the claimant's medical source, such as a treating physician. [Reg. §§404.1512e) and 416.912(e).]. If the information needed was not readily available from that source, the SSA could request additional medical records, ask the claimant to undergo a consultative examination at the agency's expense, or ask others for more information. Effective March 26, 2012, the SSA eliminated the requirement to recontact a medical source. [Reg §404.1520b (§416.920b for SSI claims) (77 *Fed. Reg.* 10651, Feb. 23, 2012).]

In the event evidence is insufficient or inconsistent, the SSA will "determine the best way to resolve the inconsistency or insufficiency." While one option would be for the adjudicator to recontact a claimant's treating physician, psychologist, or other medical source, the new rules also give the adjudicator the discretion to bypass this step and, instead, either (1) require the claimant to undergo a consultative examination, (2) seek additional records, or (3) ask the claimant or others for more information. Under the new rules, if the adjudicator determines that he or she is unable to resolve the inconsistency despite his or her best efforts to obtain additional evidence, the adjudicator will be able to make a decision or determination based on the evidence already in the record.

Obtaining evidence beyond the current "special arrangement sources." The SSA has issued interim final rules amending its regulations to state that the agency now will obtain evidence from any appropriate source. Previous regulations provide that the SSA will obtain information from "special arrangement sources" for those infrequent situations when it is in a better position than its state agency partners to obtain evidence. Due to improved evidence collection through the increased use of health information technology (health IT), the SSA is obtaining evidence electronically with increasing frequency. The agency expects that, over time, the electronic exchange of medical records will become its primary means for obtaining medical evidence. Accordingly, as the SSA increases its use of health IT, the designation of "special arrangement sources" no longer will adequately describe from whom it collects evidence. The interim final rules became effective on June 12, 2014.

Step four: Past relevant work: Residual functional capacity—

If the Commissioner cannot make a decision based on current work activity or on medical facts alone, and the individual has a severe impairment(s), then the Commissioner will review the individual's residual functional capacity ("RFC"—the most that a claimant can do despite his or her limitations) and the physical and mental demands of the work the individual performed within the past 15 years. [Regs. §§404.1512, 404.1545, and 404.1560.]

In order to make a proper evaluation, the SSA needs information about each of the claimant's jobs during that period, including information about job duties, tools, or machinery used; the amount of physical exertion required in terms of the amount of walking, standing, lifting and carrying during the workday; the length of time that a claimant worked each job; and the physical and mental demands of the job. With this information, the SSA compares the claimant's RFC to the physical and mental demands of the past relevant jobs to determine if the claimant can still perform any of them. If so, the claimant is found to be not disabled. This rule applies even if a claimant's past relevant work no longer exists in the national economy. [*Barnhart v. Thomas*, 124 SCt 376 (2003); SSR 05-1c, 70 *Fed. Reg.* 7787, Feb. 15, 2005.] However, if the claimant is unable to perform any past relevant work, the adjudicator will proceed to Step five.

The ALJ, the Tenth Circuit advised, must make specific findings with respect to the physical and mental demands of the claimant's past jobs. The ALJ cannot neglect to make such findings in addressing the larger issue of the claimant's ability to perform past relevant work. [*Villabos v. Colvin*, No. 13-2005 (Tenth Cir. 2013).]

Evidence and burden of proof: An individual claimant must present evidence of an impairment and its effect on the claimant's functioning [Reg. §404.1545], although the SSA will make the actual RFC assessment (to be used at both steps four and five) [Reg. §404.1546.] Evidence from both medical and non-medical sources may be used at this step. (See Step three, above, regarding the use of evidence from medical and non-medical sources.) [68 *Fed. Reg.* 51153 at 51155, Aug. 26, 2003, citing *Bowen v. Yuckert*, 482 U.S. 137, 146 n.5 (1987).]

Note, on April 20, 2015, final rules went into effect that clarify SSA regulations to require claimants to inform the agency about or submit all evidence known to that claimant that relates to his or her disability claim, subject to two exceptions for certain privileged communications. This requirement includes the duty to submit all evidence that relates to a disability claim received from any source in its entirety, unless the claimant previously submitted the same evidence to the SSA or the agency instructs the claimant otherwise. The SSA is also requiring the claimant's representative to help him or her obtain the information or evidence that it requires the claimant to submit under the regulations. These modifications to the regulations will better describe a claimant's duty to submit all evidence that relates to the disability claim and enable the SSA to have more complete case records on which to make more accurate disability determinations and decisions (80 *Fed. Reg.* 14828, Mar. 20, 2015).

In addition, the SSA has revised its rules regarding medical evidence. The revisions include redefining several key terms related to evidence, revising the rules about acceptable medical sources (AMS), revising how the SSA considers and articulates its consideration of medical opinions and prior administrative medical findings, revising the rules about medical consultants (MC) and psychological consultants (PC), revising the rules about treating sources, and reorganizing the evidence regulations for ease of use (82 *Fed. Reg.* 5844, January 18, 2017; technical corrections made in 82 *Fed. Reg.* 15132, March 27, 2017).

Consider all medically determinative impairments in RFC assessment. The ALJ is required to consider the combined effects of all of the claimant's medically determinable impairments, whether severe or not, in making the RFC assessment. The ALJ, the Tenth Circuit advises, may not rely on a finding of non-severity as a substitute for a proper and complete RFC analysis. In addition, the ALJ is required to provide a narrative discussion, describing how each conclusion is supported by specific evidence. [*Wells v. Commissioner,* No. 12-6234 (Tenth Cir. 2013).]

Weighing multiple RFC assessments. The Seventh Circuit has explained that an ALJ is not required to weigh all RFC assessments by medical professionals equally, as long as the assessment justifying the denial of benefits is supported by substantial evidence. [*Schomas v. Colvin,* No. 13-1197 (Seventh Cir. 2013).]

Function-by-function analysis. The Second Circuit has declined to adopt a per se rule requiring an ALJ, in making a RFC determination, to engage in a specific function-by-function analysis. The substantial evidence supporting an RFC determination does not require a specific function-by-function assessment of a claimant's limitations, the court explained. [*Cichocki v. Colvin,* No. 12-3343-cv (Second Cir. 2013).]

Explanation for conflict between VE, DOT must be elicited. Noting long-standing precedent, the U.S. Court of Appeals for the 8th Circuit in *Thomas v. Commissioner,* No. 16-4559, February 5, 2018, ruled that an ALJ was required to elicit from a vocational expert (VE) an explanation for an apparent conflict that existed between the expert's testimony and a job description in the Dictionary of Occupational Titles (DOT). An ALJ may not rely on unexplained VE testimony that a claimant with a particular residual functional capacity (RFC) is qualified to do a job that the DOT describes differently. Because the ALJ failed to elicit from the VE an opinion on whether a reasonable explanation existed for the conflict, the VE's testimony did not constitute substantial evidence that the claimant could perform a certain job and was, therefore, not disabled. The decision of the district court affirming the benefits denial was reversed and the case was remanded to the agency for a new five-step determination. [*Thomas v. Commissioner,* No. 16-4559 (Eighth Cir. 2018).]

Expedited sequential evaluation process allows for bypassing Step four. Because it can be time-consuming to gather all of the necessary information regarding the claimant's work history during the 15-year period that precedes the alleged disability onset date, disability determinations are often delayed. Accordingly, the SSA has amended the process for evaluating a disability claim to allow adjudicators the discretion to bypass Step four and proceed directly to Step five when the SSA does not have sufficient information about a claimant's work history to make the findings required by Step four. By going directly to Step five, a determination can be expedited if it is found that a claimant is not disabled under the criteria for Step five. At Step five the adjudicator would consider if the claimant is disabled based on (1) the special medical-vocational profiles set forth at Reg. §404.1562; (2) the Medical-Vocational Guidelines (Appendix 2 to 20 CFR, Part 404, Subpart P), whether directly or as a framework, or (3) an inability to meet the mental demands of unskilled work. If application of the Step five rules indicates that a claimant may be disabled or if the adjudicator has any doubt whether the claimant can perform other work existing in significant numbers in the economy, the adjudicator must return to Step four since the Social Security Act requires the SSA to make a finding about a claimant's ability to do past relevant work before a determination is made that a claimant is disabled at Step five. [Regs. §404.1520 and §416.920 (77 *Fed. Reg.* 43492, July 23, 2012.]

Note, the expedited process has already been used for the past 12 years in 10 "prototype" states. These states are Alabama, Alaska, California (Los Angeles North and Los Angles West Branches), Colorado, Louisiana, Michigan, Missouri, New Hampshire, New York, and Pennsylvania. This expedited process will eventually be used in all disability evaluations except for childhood disability claims under Title XVI, since those claims do not use vocational criteria.

Step five: Vocational adjustment to other work—

Finally, if it is established that the claimant cannot perform his or her past relevant work, the disability evaluation process turns to an evaluation of the claimant's ability to do other work. At this stage, the interaction of residual functional capacity with other factors affecting vocational adaptability, *i.e.*, age, education, and work experience, are given emphasis. If the claimant's remaining physical and mental capacities are sufficient to meet the demands of a significant number of jobs in the national economy, and the claimant has the vocational capabilities to make an adjustment to work different from that performed in the past, a determination of nondisability is indicated. [Reg. §404.1520(e), (f).]

Acceptable medical evidence of impairments includes medical sources such as licensed physicians, osteopaths, optometrists, and licensed or certified psychologists, and reports sent by authorized persons from medical health facilities. The medical reports should include the following: a medical history; clinical and laboratory findings; a diagnosis; the treatment prescribed with response and prognosis; and, except in statutory blindness claims and disability claims for widows and widowers and surviving divorced spouses, a medical assessment describing the person's ability to do work-related activities such as sitting, standing, moving about, lifting, carrying, handling objects, hearing, speaking, and traveling; and in cases of mental impairment, the individual's ability to reason or make occupational, personal, or social adjustments. Information from other sources including public and private social welfare agencies, observations by nonmedical sources, and other practitioners such as naturopaths, chiropractors, and audiologists may also be presented in support of a disability claim. [Reg. §404.1513.]

Evidence and burden of proof. If the SSA decides at Step five that a claimant is not disabled, the SSA is responsible for providing evidence of other work that the claimant can perform (consistent with Reg. §404.1512(g)). However, the agency is not responsible for providing additional evidence of RFC or for making another RFC assessment at Step five. The SSA will use the same RFC assessment at Step five that was made at Step four, where the claimant has the burdens of production and persuasion. [Reg. §404.1560.] Accordingly, the SSA does not have the burden at Step five of proving that a claimant has the RFC to perform other work, since it will disclaim any burden of proving the RFC of a claimant.

Disabled Child's Benefits

A disabled child may be entitled to disability benefits under the Social Security Act through one of two programs. Benefits are available under Title XVI if:

1. the child is under age 18;

2. the child has an impairment or combination of impairments that meet the definition of disability for children (see below);

3. the child is not engaged in any substantial gainful activity (less than $1,260/mo. in 2020—see above); and

4. the income and resources of the child and others living in the same household are within the allowed limits. [SSA §1614(a)(3)(C).]

Benefits are available under Title II if:

1. the individual is a "child" of an individual insured under Title II, and that individual is receiving retirement or disability benefits or is deceased (see ¶524 regarding the definition of "child" for Title II purposes);

2. the child is age 18 or older (of course, a child under age 18 of an insured individual who is disabled, retired or deceased is eligible regardless of the child's disability status);

3. the child has an impairment or combination of impairments that meet the definition of disability for adults (see above);

4. the disability began before age 22; and

5. the child is unmarried. [SSA §202(d)(1); Reg. §404.350.]

The statutory standard for childhood disability benefits under Title II is the same as that for adults. Thus, the disabled child of a retired or disabled wage earner must establish an inability to engage in any substantial gainful activity by reason of any medically determinable physical or mental impairment that can be expected to result in death or that has lasted or can be expected to last for a continuous period of at least 12 months. [Soc. Sec. Act §202(d)(1).]

Historical background for Title XVI definition of childhood disability

Prior to the U.S. Supreme Court's 1990 decision in *Sullivan v. Zebley* (110 S. Ct. 885), analysis of childhood disability claims under the SSI program did not go beyond step three of the sequential evaluation process. After the threshold determinations that the claimant was not working and had an impairment of the required duration that significantly limited ability to work, the third step required evaluation under the Listing of Impairments. Children's claims were evaluated under both the general listings, *i.e.*, Part A, and a special Part B listing of medical criteria for the evaluation of impairments of children under age 18 where criteria in Part A of the Listing of Impairments do not give appropriate consideration to the particular disease process in children. The *Zebley* court invalidated the use of the listings-only approach and required the use of an individualized functional assessment of children whose impairments did not meet or equal the severity of those set forth in the Listing of Impairments.

As a result of *Zebley*, if a child's medically determinable impairments did not functionally equal the criteria of the Listing of Impairments, the next step of the inquiry was to determine whether the child's impairments so limited the ability to function in an age-appropriate manner that the limitations were comparable in severity to those that would disable an adult. Where the usual vocational factors, such as education and work experience, were not appropriate in making individualized functional assessments of children, consideration would be given to the child's ability to engage in activities appropriate for children at his or her age level; activities of daily living; developmental milestones; and domains of development or functioning, including cognition, communication, motor abilities, social abilities, behavioral patterns, and task completion. [Reg. §416.924, *et seq.*]

The Personal Responsibility and Work Opportunity Act of 1996 repealed the comparable severity standard and established a new definition of childhood disability for SSI (Title XVI) eligibility that requires a physical or mental impairment to result in marked and severe functional limitations that can be expected to result in death or last for at least 12 months. Although the SSA uses the term "severe" to often mean "other than minor," the House-Senate conference agreement accompanying the legislation stated that it was the conferees' intention that only needy children with severe disabilities be eligible for SSI, "severe" being understood by its common-sense meaning. Use of the Individualized Functional Assessment for children set forth in the regulations at 20 CFR §§416.924d and 416.924e was discontinued and references in the Listing of Impairments at §§112.00C.2. and 112.02B.2.c.(2) to maladaptive behavior among the medical criteria for evaluation of mental and emotional disorders in the domain of personal/behavioral function were also eliminated. However, the SSA continues to ensure that the combined effects of all physical and mental impairments of an individual under 18 are taken into account, and also continues to use criteria in the Listing of Impairments and in the application of other determination procedures, such as functional equivalence (see below), when making a determination regarding childhood disability.

¶520.1

Redeterminations based on the new criteria are to be made: (1) every three years for any child qualifying for SSI benefits whose impairment is likely to improve; (2) within one year of the birth of any child who receives benefits on the basis of low birth weight; and (3) within one year after any child receiving benefits becomes 18 years of age. The amendments apply to any applicant whose benefits are finally adjudicated on or after August 22, 1996. All current beneficiaries as of August 22, 1996, were to have been re-evaluated under the new criteria by February 22, 1998, but the reevaluations were to have only been applicable to benefits for months beginning July 1, 1997, or the date of the redetermination, whichever was later. [P.L. 104-193, §§211 and 212, amending Soc. Sec. Act §§1614(a)(3) and (4); further amended by P.L. 105-33, §5101.]

New regulations for determining disability in children were finalized in 2000. These amendments implemented changes, outlined above, required by the Personal Responsibility and Work Opportunity Reconciliation Act of 1996 (P.L. 104-193), as well as those suggested by studies and consultants. Some of the changes listed below had been long-standing policy of the SSA prior to 2000, but until then, had not been codified in the regulations.

Current law

Under current rules, the SSA considers at Step two of the sequential evaluation process both whether a child has a medically determinable impairment and whether any impairment, or combination of impairments, that a child has is severe. [Reg. §416.924(c).] In determining whether a child is disabled, the SSA considers evidence not only from traditional medical professionals, but also from other medical sources such as speech-language pathologists and physical and occupational therapists, and from non-medical sources such as parents and teachers. [Reg. §416.924a.] If a child has a functional limitation because of an impairment, the SSA considers the child's functioning in relation to other children of the same age who do not have the impairment. [Reg. §416.924a(b)(3).] An important indication of the severity of a child's impairment is the amount of effort that must be made to help the child function. This includes help from parents, teachers, medical personnel, and special equipment, devices, or medication. [Reg. §416.924a(b)(5).]

Functional equivalence

If a child's impairment does not meet or equal a listing, the SSA will then decide if the impairment results in limitations that are functionally equivalent to a listed impairment. Functional limitations are assessed in six broad areas or "domains": acquiring and using information, attending and completing tasks, interacting with others, moving about and manipulating objects, self-care, and health and physical well-being. An impairment must result in marked limitations in two domains of functioning or extreme limitation in one domain of functioning to be of listing-level severity. The regulations provide examples for evaluating limitations in each of the domains. [Reg. §416.926a, and generally, Regs. §§416.924–416.926a, as amended by 65 *Fed. Reg.* 54747, Sept. 11, 2000.] A series of SSRs issued in 2009 provide guidance on how the SSA evaluates limitations with respect to each functional domain (see below).

Evaluation of functional equivalence in a child begins with consideration of the child's functioning without considering the domains or individual impairments. After identifying which of a child's activities are limited, the SSA will determine which domains are involved in those activities. Finally, the agency will rate the severity of the limitations in each affected domain. [Reg. §416.926a(b) and §416.926a(c).]

Whole child approach. The SSA evaluates the "whole child" when it makes a finding regarding functional equivalence unless it can make a fully favorable determination or decision without having to do so. To accomplish this, the SSA will consider the following questions for each claim:

1. How does the child function? This refers to a child's activities, both at home as well as at school and in the community, including, but not limited to everyday activities like getting dressed, playing with friends, and doing class assignments.

2. Which domains are involved in performing the activities? Many activities may require abilities present in more than one domain and could be affected by problems evaluated in the sixth domain.

3. Could the child's medically determinable impairment(s) account for limitations in the child's activities?

4. To what degree does the impairment(s) limit the child's ability to function age-appropriately in each domain?

The "whole-child" approach recognizes that many activities require the use of more than one of the abilities described in the first five domains and that they also may be affected by a problem that the agency considers in the sixth domain. The SSA notes that it is:

> "incorrect to assume that the effects of a particular medical impairment must be rated in only one domain or that a combination of impairments must always be rated in several. Rather, adjudicators must consider the particular effects of a child's impairment(s) on the child's activities in any and all of the domains that the child uses to do those activities, based on the evidence in the case record."

[SSR 09-1p.]

Note, the Second Circuit has held that there is no requirement to add together less-than-"marked" limitations from two or more separate domains of function so as to increase the limitation level in another domain based on limitations in other domains. [*Encarnacion v. Astrue*, 568 F3d 72 (2nd Cir. 2009).] In addition, although SSR 09-6p requires that an ALJ or the Appeals Council obtain an updated medical expert opinion before making a decision of disability based on *medical* equivalence, there is no such requirement for decisions of disability based on *functional* equivalence. [SSR 09-1p, 74 *Fed. Reg.* 7527, Feb. 17, 2009.]

Documenting a child's impairment-related limitations

The evidence used to evaluate a childhood disability claim must be sufficient to evaluate a child's limitations over a period of time, *i.e.*, a longitudinal analysis. The evidence also must allow the SSA to determine what activities the child can and cannot do, which activities are limited in comparison to other children of the same age, where the child has difficulties, and how much help the child needs to perform various activities.

The evidence must enable the adjudicator to have a clear picture as to how the child functions in each domain. The SSA emphasizes that "the critical element in evaluating the severity of a child's limitations is how appropriately, effectively, and independently the child performs age-appropriate activities." Adjudicators are instructed that a child who is having significant, but unexplained problems may have an impairment that has not yet been diagnosed or may have a diagnosed impairment for which it lacks evidence. [SSR 09-2p, 74 *Fed. Reg.* 7625, Feb. 18, 2009.] Adjudicators are required to pursue indications that one or more impairments may be present if that fact may be material to the determination or adjudication.

There are a number of sources from which evidence should be obtained. Evidence from "acceptable" medical sources (listed in Reg. §404.913(a)) may establish that the child has a medically determinable impairment and can also provide information about how an impairment affects a child's everyday activities. By contrast, evidence from other medical sources who are not acceptable medical sources, such as occupational and physical therapists, audiologists, etc., may not be used to establish that a child has a medically determinable impairment. However, such evidence may be used to illustrate the severity of an impairment.

Evidence from nonmedical sources, such as neighbors, caregivers, clergy, teachers, etc., will also be considered when the SSA evaluates the severity of the impairment and how the child functions in comparison to other children within the same age group.

Adjudicators are required to try and get early intervention (EI) and school records when needed to make a decision. Individualized Family Service Plans (IFSPs) and Individualized Education Programs (IEPs) are also considered to be important sources of information that "provide valuable information about the various kinds and levels of support a child receives." SSR 09-2p explains in detail how it uses the information provided by these sources of information to assess a claim of childhood disability.

Functional domains

The SSA evaluates limitations with respect to each functional domain as described below.

Acquiring and using information. In the domain of acquiring and using information, the SSA considers a child's ability to learn information and to think about and use the information. However, the agency does not consider limitations that are associated with academic underachievement by a student who does not have a physical or mental impairment. [SSR 09-3p, 74 *Fed. Reg.* 7511, Feb. 17, 2009.]

Attending and completing tasks. This domain refers to a child's ability to focus and maintain attention, and to begin, carry through, and finish activities or tasks. The SSA will consider the child's ability to

> "initiate and maintain attention, including the child's alertness and ability to focus on an activity or task despite distractions, and to perform tasks at an appropriate pace. [The SSA] consider[s] the child's ability to focus on an activity or task despite distractions, and to perform tasks at an appropriate pace. [The SSA] also consider[s] the child's ability to change focus after completing a task and to avoid impulsive thinking and acting. Finally, [the SSA] evaluate[s] a child's ability to organize, plan ahead, prioritize completing tasks, and manage time."

Limitations in this domain are more often associated with mental impairments, but physical impairments can also affect a child's mental ability to attend and to complete tasks. For example, pain can interfere with an ability to concentrate. [SSR 09-4p, 74 *Fed. Reg.* 7630, Feb. 18, 2009.]

Interacting and relating with others. SSR 09-5p states that the SSA will consider

> "a child's ability to initiate and respond to exchanges with other people, and to form and sustain relationships with family members, friends, and others. This domain includes all aspects of social interaction with individuals and groups at home, at school, and in the community. Important aspects of both interacting and relating are the child's response to persons in authority, compliance with rules, and regard for the possessions of others. In addition, because communication is essential to both interacting and relating, [the SSA will] consider in this domain the speech and language skills children need to speak intelligibly and to understand and use the language of their community."

Children with limitations in this domain may or may not necessarily be disruptive and both physical as well as mental impairments can affect a child's ability to relate to others. [SSR 09-5p, 74 *Fed. Reg.* 7515, Feb. 17, 2009.]

Moving about and manipulating objects. In this domain, the SSA considers the physical ability to move from one place to another and to move and manipulate things at both the gross and/or fine motor skill levels. Both physical as well as mental impairments can affect a child's ability to move and manipulate objects. Medications can also impact a child's ability in this area. [SSR 09-6p, 74 *Fed. Reg.* 7518, Feb. 17, 2009.]

Caring for oneself. In this domain, the SSA considers a child's ability to maintain a healthy physical and emotional state. This includes how a child obtains his or her emotional or physical desires in appropriate ways; how a child copes with stress; and how a child takes care of his or her own health, possessions, and living area. The SSR identifies age-appropriate ways in which a child may self-regulate or return to a state of emotional equilibrium after experiencing any emotion and gives examples as to some of the inappropriate ways in which a child with anxiety disorder or hyperactivity disorder might behave. [SSR 09-7p, 74 *Fed. Reg.* 7521, Feb. 17, 2009.]

Health and physical well-being. In this domain, the SSA will not address typical functioning. Rather, the SSA considers the "cumulative physical effects of physical and mental impairments and their associated treatments on a child's health and functioning." The domain addresses how such things as recurrent illness, the side effects of medication and the need for ongoing treatment affect a child's body (i.e., the child's health and sense of physical well-being). In this domain, the SSA will also consider the cumulative effects of physical and mental impairments and their associated treatments or therapies not addressed in other domains. [SSR 09-8p, 74 *Fed. Reg.* 7524, Feb. 17, 2009.]

Continuing disability reviews for child disability beneficiaries under age 18

In SSR 05-3p, the SSA set forth its policies for evaluating a child's continuing disability under the Medical Improvement Review Standard Sequential Evaluation Process for children under age 18. The ruling focuses on Step 2 of the medical improvement review standard, which relates to determinations of whether the impairments that were present at the time of the most recent favorable determination still meet or are functionally equivalent to the severity of the listed impairment that was previously considered. [70 *Fed. Reg.* 21833, Apr. 27, 2005.]

Waiting period and back benefits

Disability benefits based on eligibility as a child or disabled adult child are not (unlike the benefits of a disabled surviving spouse (see ¶520.2 and ¶525.2) subject to a waiting period, as these benefits are paid as child insurance benefits. [Soc. Sec. Act §202(d)(1).] However, such benefits may only be paid for up to six months prior to the month in which the application is filed unless the claim is filed on the earnings record of a person who is entitled to disability benefits. In this latter case, benefits are payable to the child for up to 12 months prior to the month in which the child's application is filed. [Reg. §404.621(a)(1) and (2).]

Evaluation by pediatric specialist

There has been disagreement as to whether the SSA is required to obtain pediatric review in childhood disability determinations under Title XVI. Although SSA §1614(a)(3)(I) requires that when making any child disability determination under Title XVI, there must be an evaluation by a "qualified physician or other individual who specializes in a field of medicine appropriate to the disability of the individual," the SSA maintains that the requirement refers only to the initial determination made by a state agency. The U.S. Court of Appeals for the Ninth Circuit, however, has held that in child disability cases under Title XVI, the statutory provision requires the SSA to make a reasonable effort to obtain review by a pediatrician or other specialist trained in a field of medicine relevant to the claim. [*Wolff v. Barnhart*, 341 F.3d 1006 (9th Cir. 2003).] The SSA has acquiesced to this holding. [AR 04-1(9), Apr. 26, 2004, 69 *Fed. Reg.* 22578, Apr. 26, 2004.]

Children of military parents assigned overseas

Blind or disabled children living outside of the United States, who are citizens of the United States and are living with a parent who was assigned to permanent duty outside of the United States, or are living outside of the United States because their parent was assigned to permanent duty outside of the United States, are eligible to receive Title XVI disability benefits. The child is not required to have been eligible for an SSI benefit for the month before the parent reported for military assignment. [P.L. 108-203 (Social Security Protection Act of 2004), §434; Soc. Sec. Act §1614(a)(1)(B)(ii); Reg. §416.216.]

Termination of children's disability benefits

Disabled child's benefits end:

1. with the second month following the month in which the disability ceases, unless in such month the child beneficiary is under age 19 and is a full-time student [Soc. Sec. Act §202(d)(1)(E); Reg. §404.352(b)(1) and (2)];

2. when a disabled child 18 or older marries, unless the child marries a Social Security beneficiary other than: a child beneficiary under age 18, or a child age 18 or 19 who is entitled to benefits as a full-time student [Soc. Sec. Act §202(d)(5), §202(s); Reg. §404.352(b)(4)];

3. when the insured's entitlement to disability benefits terminates for a reason other than death or attainment of retirement age [Soc. Sec. Act §202(d)(1); Reg §404.352(b)(5)];

4. death of the disabled child [Soc. Sec. Act §202(d)(1)(D); Reg. §404.352(b)(6)]; and

5. for those age 18 and over whose disability is based on a finding that drug addiction or alcoholism was a contributing factor material to the determination of disability, disabled child's benefits will also terminate in:

    a. the month following the twelfth consecutive month of a benefits suspension for failure to comply with treatment, or

    b. the month following receipt of 36 months of benefit payments regardless of the number of entitlement periods.

However, children's benefits will continue if disability can be otherwise established without regard to drug addiction or alcoholism [§404.352(c)].

Reentitlement to children's benefits

An individual can become reentitled to childhood disability benefits at any time if prior entitlement was terminated due to the performance of substantial gainful activity. [Soc. Sec. Act §202(d)(6)(B) as amended by the Social Security Protection Act of 2004, P.L. 108-203, §420A; Reg. §404.351(d).]

SSI Payments for Institutionalized Children

Residents of public institutions are ordinarily ineligible to receive SSI payments. However, if the institution is a medical treatment facility and if Medicaid pays for more than 50% of a resident's care, the resident may receive a reduced benefit of $30 per month.

In addition, if the resident's physician certifies that the resident is not likely to be in the institution for more than three months, then the resident may continue to receive payment of the full SSI benefit if he or she needs the funds in order to continue to maintain the home to which he or she may return. Note that if the resident is a child under the age of 18, these provisions apply so long as the institution: (1) receives on the child's behalf payments under a health insurance policy issued by a private provider or (2) a combination of Medicaid and private health insurance pays more than 50% of the cost of the child's care. [Soc. Sec. Act §1611(e)(1)(B), (G); Reg. §416.212.] Thus, when a child who is receiving SSI while living at home goes into a medical treatment facility, and private insurance through the parent's employment pays for more than 50% of the cost of care, the child can continue to receive SSI benefits during a temporary institutionalization of up to three months.

Disability in Young Adults

When evaluating disability in young adults under Titles II or XVI, the SSA considers that the abilities, skills, and behaviors that young adults use are "essentially the same" as those that older adolescents use for age-appropriate activities. Thus, the evidence that the agency considers when making disability determinations for young adults is generally the same as, or similar to, the evidence it considers for making disability determinations for older adolescents under Title XVI.

Evidence may come from "acceptable" as well as nonacceptable medical sources such as physical therapists, occupational therapists, and social workers. While evidence from the latter group cannot be used to establish a medically determinable impairment, it can be used to determine the severity of the impairment and how it affects a young adult's ability to perform work-related activities. Nonmedical sources such as family members, educational personnel, and private social welfare agency staff may also be consulted.

Another source of information is evidence from school programs, such as an Individualized Education Program (IEP). The IEP will describe a student's levels of functioning and the kinds of vocational and living skills the young adult needs to develop in order to function independently as an adult. A claimant's achievement of an IEP's goals may or may not demonstrate that the claimant has limitations. However, a young adult who does not achieve a goal likely has an impairment-related limitation. [SSR 11-2p, 76 *Fed. Reg.* 56263, Sept. 12, 2011.]

Evaluation of limitations

When evaluating a young adult's limitations, the SSA determines the severity of the limitation, whether the impairment meets or equals a listed impairment, and the claimant's residual functional capacity (RFC). To accomplish this evaluation, the agency will look at how the claimant functioned in school, as well as community experiences such as on-the-job training, community-based instruction, and work experience. The SSA also will examine what type of psycho-social supports the young adult has, how structured their setting is, and what extra help and accommodations the young adult has received. In addition, it will look at the effects of treatment including medication and any work-related stress. [SSR 11-2p.]

Insured status

The Social Security Act considers that the disability insured status requirements (see ¶505.5) are met for young adults aged 21 up to age 24 if claimants have six quarters of coverage in a 12-quarter period ending with the quarter in which the disability began. Although there is no comparable provision for young adults under the age of 21, SSR 11-2p establishes that the SSA will apply the same requirements to such individuals.

Determination of disability

As with older adults, the SSA will determine whether a young adult is disabled by examining the claimant's work activity, whether he or she has a medically determinable impairment, the claimant's ability to perform past relevant work, and his or her ability to adjust to other work. Many young adults whose impairments arose during military service continue on active duty and receive full pay while in treatment. Active duty status or receipt of pay by a member of the military does not, however, indicate by itself that the service person has demonstrated the ability to perform substantial gainful activity. Additionally, the payments received for volunteer service in government-sponsored programs, such as VISTA, do not count as earnings.

When a young adult has previously been found disabled as a child under Part B of a listing, the impairment will often meet or medically equal a Part A listing at age 18 unless the impairment(s) has medically improved. The broad domains of functioning used to evaluate a child's impairment-related limitations also may provide guidance about a young adult's RFC. [SSR 11-2p.]

Vocational rehabilitation and IEPs

As with adults, a young adult who participates in a Ticket to Work program or another vocational rehabilitation program will be allowed to receive benefits during his or her participation in those programs. In addition, when a young adult participates in an Individualized Education Program (IEP), the SSA will continue benefit payments until the IEP is completed or the person stops participating in it. [SSR 11-2p.]

¶520.2 Disability Insurance Benefits

Monthly disability insurance benefits are payable, upon the filing of an application (see ¶575), to an individual who is insured for disability benefits (see ¶505.5, above) and who has not attained retirement age. The amount of the disability insurance benefits is equal to the insured individual's primary insurance amount, except in the relatively uncommon case where an actuarial reduction applies (¶520.8). The benefit is payable beginning with the first month after the "waiting period" in which the individual becomes entitled to benefits and ending with the month preceding whichever of the following months is the earliest: the month in which the individual dies, the month in which he or she attains retirement age, or the third month following the month in which disability ceases. An individual may also become entitled to disability insurance benefits for the first month throughout which he or she is under a disability and insured, without fulfilling a "waiting period," provided the individual was entitled to disability insurance benefits that terminated, or had a prior period of disability (disability "freeze") that ceased, not more than 60 months before such first month. [Soc. Sec. Act §223(a).]

Substantial gainful activity by blind. Individuals who meet the definition of disability as a result of the provisions relating to blindness will not be paid disability benefits for any month in which they engage in substantial gainful activity (see ¶520.1). Similarly, no wife's, husband's, or child's benefits may be paid on the basis of wages or self-employment income of such individuals. [Soc. Sec. Act §223(a).]

Waiting period. The term "waiting period" means the earliest period of five consecutive calendar months throughout which the individual has been under a disability. However, the waiting period cannot begin more than 17 months before the month in which an application for disability insurance benefits is filed. If the individual is insured for disability insurance benefits in such month, the waiting period begins with that month. If he or she is not insured in that month, the waiting period begins with the first month thereafter in which the individual is insured for disability benefits. [Soc. Sec. Act §223(c)(2).]

Timely application for benefits. An application for disability insurance benefits filed before the first month in which the applicant satisfies the requirements for disability benefits is valid only if the applicant satisfies the requirements before the Commissioner makes a final decision on the application and no request under Soc. Sec. Act 205(b) for notice and opportunity for a hearing with respect to the decision is made. In the event such a request is made, the application must be filed before a decision based on the evidence adduced at the hearing is made. [Soc. Sec. Act §§205(b), 223(b).] If the applicant is found to satisfy the requirements, the application is deemed to have been filed in the first month in which the requirements were satisfied.

Retroactively effective applications. An application for disability benefits may be made retroactively effective for as many as 12 months before the one in which the application is filed. [Soc. Sec. Act §223(b).] It is possible to file a claim within three months after the month of the death of a disabled worker. The intent of this provision is to avoid situations in which a disabled worker, who would have been eligible for benefits, dies without filing a claim, thereby losing benefit rights. [Soc. Sec. Act §223(a)(1).]

Prior entitlement to old age benefits. An individual who has not attained retirement age may become entitled to disability benefits after having become entitled to old-age, wife's, husband's, widow's, widower's, or parent's insurance benefits. If the old-age benefit was a reduced benefit, the disability benefit is subject to a reduction (see ¶520.8). [Soc. Sec. Act §§202(q)(3), 223(a)(1).] An important feature of this provision is that a wife who is at full retirement age or over and whose husband is between the ages of 62 and full retirement age and insured can qualify for hospital insurance, provided her husband files for reduced old-age insurance benefits. The husband may be working full time and not receive any of the old-age benefits.

Report improved condition. A recipient of disability benefits is required to report to the SSA any of the following: 1. an improvement in condition, 2. return to work, 3. increase in the amount of work, and 4. any increase in earnings. See ¶557, regarding penalties for nondisclosure. [Regs. §§404.1588 and 416.708.]

¶520.3   Period of Disability (Disability "Freeze")

It is important to determine an individual's period of disability. As noted at ¶504–506, certain quarters or years contained wholly or partially in a period of disability are "frozen," *i.e.*, not counted, in determining the number of quarters of coverage needed for insured status. Similarly, any year any part of which was included in a period of disability, is not included in determining an individual's "elapsed years" in computing his or her average monthly earnings (see ¶507.3).

Individual under disability. A period of disability is a continuous period, beginning and ending as described below, during which an individual was under a disability (defined at ¶520.1). The period must last for at least five full calendar months or the individual must have been entitled to disability insurance benefits for one or more months in the period.

Application for benefits. No period of disability can begin unless the individual files a timely application for a disability determination. Ordinarily, the application must be filed within 12 months after the month in which a period of disability ends. However, the period is extended for an additional 24 months where the disabled individual's failure to file within the 12-month period is due to mental or physical incapacity to execute such an application. Note, that retroactive payment of benefits is not extended beyond the normal 12-month period. [Soc. Sec. Act §216(i)(2).]

Beginning of disability period. If an individual can satisfy the coverage requirements to be eligible for a period of disability as discussed above at ¶505.5, the period of disability will begin on the day the disability began. If the individual cannot satisfy the coverage requirements on the day referred to in the preceding sentence, then the period of disability will begin on the first day of the first quarter thereafter in which those requirements are satisfied. [Soc. Sec. Act §216(i)(2)(C).]

End of disability period. A period of disability ends no later than the month preceding the month in which the individual attains retirement age. Where disability ceases prior to the attainment of retirement age, the period of disability ends with the month preceding the termination month, *i.e.,* the third month following the month in which the disability ceases, unless the individual has engaged in a trial-work period, or if earlier, the first month for which no benefits are payable following the trial-work period. Note that the requirement that a decision to terminate benefits on the basis of cessation of disability generally be supported by substantial evidence of medical improvement to the point where the individual is able to engage in substantial gainful activity applies in the same manner and to the same extent with respect to determinations of whether a period of disability has ended. [Soc. Sec. Act §216(i)(2)(D); Reg. §404.321.] See ¶520.6, below, for a discussion of the trial-work period.

¶520.4   Disability Claims Applications, Determinations, and Appeals

A disability claim may begin with a call to a Social Security office (1-800-772-1213) or with the filing of a disability claim form, SSA 16-F6, which may be filed online. When the Social Security Administration is contacted, it will set up a time and date for a full interview. If you file online, your application will be processed and a decision will be mailed to you. For more detailed information about the claims filing process, see ¶575, below.

The Determination Process and Appeals

The administrative determination process following the filing of a claim can be resolved in as little as three to six months (even shorter in cases of obvious, terminal disability), or it can drag on for years, depending upon the complexity of the claim and the extent to which adverse determinations are appealed. This section focuses on the administrative determination process. For a discussion of the judicial review process at the federal courts level after exhaustion of administrative review, see ¶586, "Review and Appeal of Administrative Decisions."

There are four steps to the administrative determination process: (1) initial determination by a state agency that has contracted with the Social Security Administration, (2) reconsideration by the Social Security Administration, (3) hearing before an Administrative Law Judge, and (4) review by the Social Security Administration's Appeals Council in Washington, D.C. [Regs. §§404.907; 404.929; and 404.967.] Only after this administrative process is exhausted may an appeal be filed in a U.S. District Court. [Soc. Sec. Act §205(g)].

Initial determinations:

State agency determination: Disability determinations, including the beginning and ending dates of periods of disability, are generally made by appropriate state agencies. Those state agencies that enter into agreements with the SSA are required to make decisions in accordance with the law and regulations and other written guidelines of the agency pertaining to disability determinations.

A state agency may only make a determination based on the evidence in its files. Disability determinations may be made by either a disability hearing officer or a disability examiner. However, except in Quick Disability Process and Compassionate Allowance cases (see below), the disability examiner cannot make a determination without a medical or psychological consultant, unless: (1) there is no medical evidence to be evaluated or (2) the state agency is unable to obtain any medical evidence that does exist and the claimant fails or refuses, without good reason, to attend a consultative examination. [Regs. §404.1615 and §416.1015.]

Any state agency found to be in noncompliance with the SSA's regulations and guidelines will be subject to an investigation. Twenty-one days following the receipt of information that an agency is not in compliance, the SSA will issue a preliminary finding, and the state agency will have 21 days from the date of the preliminary finding to provide assurances that it is in compliance. If the SSA determines that the agency is still not in compliance, it will make the necessary disability determinations itself. [Soc. Sec. Act §221(a), (b).]

Notices of denials of disability claims are required to contain a statement of the case, a discussion of the evidence, the reasons for the administrative decision in clear and simple language, and the telephone number and address of the local Social Security office. In addition, upon a written request from an individual whose rights may be prejudiced by a denial of benefits, the Commissioner will provide the individual with notice and an opportunity for a hearing. [Soc. Sec. Act §205(b).]

Requirement for medical review. The Social Security Benefit Protection and Opportunity Enhancement Act of 2015, requires the Commissioner, in order to make an initial determination of disability, to make every reasonable effort to ensure that a qualified physician, psychiatrist or psychologist has completed the medical portion of the case review. [Soc. Sec. Act §221(h), as amended.]

Expedited determination processes. The Social Security Administration maintains two programs designed to expedite the processing of claims that are likely to receive a favorable determination, the *Quick Disability Determination Process (QDD)* and *Compassionate Allowances (CAL).* These programs allow a state agency disability examiner alone to make a fully favorable determination for adult cases without medical or psychological consultant approval. However, the examiner may use a consultant when deemed necessary. [Regs. §404.1615(c)(3) and §416.1015(c), 75 *Fed. Reg.* 62676, Oct. 13, 2010.] Note, Reg. §404.1615(c) (3) and §416.1015(c)(3), authorizing disability determinations by the state disability examiner alone for claims adjudicated under QDD and CA expire on December 28, 2018 (81 *Fed. Reg.* 73027, October 24, 2016).

Quick Disability Determination Process: Under the Quick Disability Determination Process (QDD) process, a predictive model is used to identify claims where there is a high potential that the claimant is disabled and where the evidence of the claimant's allegations can be quickly and easily obtained. Those claims are then sent to a state agency where experienced disability examiners review the claims on an expedited basis. Development of the case must begin within one working day of receipt. [SSA POMS §DI 23022.040 (TN 1 10/08).] The agency is not required to issue a decision within a given time frame.

However, the notice of final rulemaking states that "State agencies should strive to adjudicate any claim referred under QDD within 20 days." If the quick disability determination examiner cannot make a determination that is fully favorable to the individual or if there is an unresolved disagreement between the disability examiner and the medical or psychological consultant, the state agency will adjudicate the claim using regular procedures. [72 *Fed. Reg.* 51173, Sept. 6, 2007, Regs. §404.1619, §404.1620, §416.1019, and §416.1020.]

Compassionate Allowances: Compassionate Allowances (CAL) is an expedited determination process that fast tracks applications for people with cancer and rare diseases. According to the press release announcing the program, decisions should take no more than six to eight days. However, the agency's internal operating manual, the POMS, states that compassionate allowance cases are not even limited to 20 days, although expedited processing procedures remain in effect for such cases. [SSA POMS §DI 23022.030 (TN 1 10/08).] In contrast to QDD cases, decisions as to which claims qualify for compassionate allowance processing are based solely on the claimant's allegations listed on Forms SSA-3368 or SSA-3820, disability report forms for adults and children, respectively. Unlike a QDD case, a claim can be fast tracked for compassionate allowance processing at any stage of the administrative determination process, but, as with the QDD case, development must begin within one working day of receipt. [SSA POMS §§DI 23022.017 and .040 (TN 1 10/08); SSA Press Release, October 27, 2008.]

Administrative guidelines for processing both Quick Disability Determination as well as Compassionate Allowance cases appear in the POMS at §DI 23022.000 *et. seq.* The initial list of qualifying conditions for Compassionate Allowance has been significantly expanded. [See *www.ssa.gov/compassionateallowances*.]

Diseases and Conditions Qualifying for Compassionate Allowance Determinations

1. Acute Leukemia
2. Adrenal Cancer - with distant metastases or inoperable, unresectable or recurrent
3. Adult Non-Hodgkin Lymphoma
4. Adult Onset Huntington Disease
5. Aicardi-Goutieres Syndrome
6. Alexander Disease (ALX) - Neonatal and Infantile
7. Allan-Herndon-Dudley Syndrome
8. Alobar Holoprosencephaly
9. Alpers Disease
10. Alpha Mannosidosis-Type II and III
11. Alstrom Syndrome
12. Alveolar Soft Part Sarcoma
13. Amegakaryocytic Thrombocytopenia
14. Amyotrophic Lateral Sclerosis (ALS)
15. Anaplastic Adrenal Cancer - with distant metastases or inoperable, unresectable or recurrent
16. Angelman Syndrome
17. Angiosarcoma
18. Aortic Atresia
19. Aplastic Anemia
20. Astrocytoma - Grade III and IV
21. Ataxia Telangiectasia
22. Atypical Teratoid/Rhabdoid Tumor
23. Batten Disease
24. Beta Thalassemia Major
25. Bilateral Optic Atrophy-Infantile
26. Bilateral Retinoblastoma
27. Bladder Cancer - with distant metastases or inoperable or unresectable
28. Breast Cancer - with distant metastases or inoperable or unresectable
28A. CACH—Vanishing White Matter Disease-Infantile and Childhood Onset Forms
28B. CDKL5 Deficiency Disorder
29. Canavan Disease (CD)
30. Carcionoma of Unknown Primary Site
31. Caudal Regression Syndrome-Types III and IV

32. Cerebro Oculo Facio Skeletal (COFS) Syndrome
33. Cerebrotendinous Xanthomatosis
34. Child Neuroblastoma-with distant metases or recurrent
35. Child Non-Hodgkin Lymphoma-recurrent
36. Child T-Cell Lympoblastic Lymphoma
37. Chondrosarcoma-with multimodal therapy
38. Chronic Idiopathic Intestinal Pseudo Obstruction
39. Chronic Myelogenous Leukemia (CML) - Blast Phase
40. Coffin-Lowry Syndrome
41. Congenital Lymphedema
41A. Congenital Myotonic Dystrophy
42. Cornelia de Lange Syndrome-Classic Form
43. Corticobasal Degeneration
44. Creutzfeldt-Jakob Disease (CJD) – Adult
45. Cri du Chat Syndrome
46. Degos Disease
47. DeSanctis Cacchione Syndrome
48. Dravet Syndrome
49. Early-Onset Alzheimer's Disease
50. Edwards Syndrome (Trisomy 18)
51. Eisenmenger Syndrome
52. Endometrial Stromal Sarcoma
53. Endomyocardial Fibrosis
54. Ependymoblastoma (Child Brain Tumor)
55. Erdheim Chester Disease
56. Esophageal Cancer
57. Esthesioneuroblastoma
58. Ewing Sarcoma
59. Farber's Disease (FD) – Infantile
60. Fatal Familial Insomnia
61. Fibrodysplasia Ossificans Progressiva
62. Follicular Dendtritic Cell Sarcoma-metastic or recurrent
62A. Fibrolamellar Cancer
63. Friedreichs Ataxia (FRDA)
64. Frontotemporal Dementia (FTD), Picks Disease - Type A – Adult
65. Fryns Syndrome
66. Fucosidosis-Type 1
67. Fukuyama Congenital Muscular Dystrophy
68. Fulminant Giant Cell Myocarditis
69. Galactosialidosis-Early and Late Infantile Types
70. Gallbladder Cancer
71. Gaucher Disease (GD) - Type 2
72. Giant Axonal Neuropathy
73. Glioblastoma Multiforme (Brain Tumor)
74. Glioma Grade III and IV
75. Glutaric Acidemia-Type II
76. Head and Neck Cancers - with distant metastasis or inoperable or uresectable
77. Heart Transplant Graft Failure
78. Heart Transplant Wait List – 1A/1B
79. Hemophagocytic Lymphohistiocytosis (HLH), Familial Type
80. Hepatoblastoma
81. Hepatopulmonary Syndrome
82. Hepatorenal Syndrome
83. Histiocytosis Syndromes
84. Hoyeaal-Hreidarsson Syndrome
85. Hutchinson-Gilford Progeria Syndrome
86. Hydraencephaly
87. Hypocomplementemic Urticarial Vasculitis Syndrome
88. Hypophosphatasia Perintal (Lethal) and Infantile Onset Types
89. Hypoplastic Left Heart Syndrome
90. I Cell disease
91. Idiopathic Pulmonary Fibrosis
92. Infantile Neuroaxonal Dystrophy (INAD)
93. Infantile Neuronal Ceroid Lipofuscinoses
94. Inflammatory Breast Cancer (IBC)
95. Intracranial Hemangiopericytoma
96.. Jervell and Lange-Nielsen Syndrome
97. Joubert Syndrome
98. Junctional Epidermolysis Bullosa, Lethal Type
99. Juvenile Huntington Disease (Note, Adult Huntington Disease is to be listed as a Compassionate Allowance (SSA Press Release, July 13, 2012)
100. Kidney Cancer - inoperable or unresectable
100A. Kleefstra Syndrome
101. Krabbe Disease (KD) – Infantile
102. Kufs Disease Type A and B
103. Large Intestine Cancer - with distantmetastasis or inoperable, unresectable or recurrent
104. Late Infantile Neuronal Ceroid Lipofuscinoses
105. Left Ventricular Assist Device Recipient
106. Leigh's Disease
107. Leiomyosarcoma
108. Leptomeningeal Carcinomatosis
109. Lesch-Nyhan Syndrome (LNS)
110. Lewy Body Dementia
111. Liposarcoma—metastatic or recurrent
112. Lissencephaly
113. Liver Cancer
114. Lowe Syndrome
115. Lymphomatoid Granulomatosis-Grade III
116. Malignant Brain Stem Gliomas-Childhood
117. Malignant Ectomesenchymoma
118. Malignant Gastrointestinal Stromal Tumor
119. Malignant Germ Cell Tumor
120. Malignant Melanoma-with metastases
121. Malignant Multiple Sclerosis
122. Malignant Renal Rhabdoid Tumor
123. Mantle Cell Lymphoma (MCL)
124. Maple Syrup Urine Disease
125. Marshall-Smith Syndrome
126. Mastocytosis Type IV
127. MECP 2 Duplication Syndrome
128. Medulloblastoma-with metastases
128A. Megacystis Microcolon Intestinal Hypoperistalsis Syndrome (MMIHS)
128B. Megalencephaly Capillary Malformation Syndrome (MCAP)
129. Menkes Disease-Classic or Infantile Onset Form
130. Merkel Cell Carcinoma-with metastases
131. Merosin Deficient Congenital Muscular Dystrophy
132. Metachromatic Leukodystrophy (MLD) - Late Infantile
133. Mitral Valve Atresia
134. Mixed Dementia
135. MPS I, formerly known as Hurler Syndrome
136. MPS II, formerly known as Hunter Syndrome
137. MPS III, formerly known as Sanfilippo Syndrome
138. Mucosal Malignant Melanoma
139. Multicentric Castleman Disease
140. Multiple System Atrophy

141. Myoclonic Epilepsy with Ragged Red Fibers Syndrome
142. Neonatal Adrenoleukodystrophy
143. Nephrogenic Systemic Fibrosis
144. Neurodegenration with Brain Iron Accumulation-Type 1 and 2
145. NFU -1 Mitochondiral Disease
146. Niemann-Pick Disease (NPD) - Type A
147. Niemann-Pick Type C
148. Non-Ketotic Hyperglycinemia
149. Non-Small Cell Lung Cancer - with metastases to or beyond the hilar nodes or inoperable, unresectable or recurrent
150. Obliterative Bronchiolitis
151. Ohtahara Syndrome
152. Oligodendroglioma Brain Tumor—Grade III
153. Ornithine Transcarbamylase (OTC) Deficiency
154. Orthochromatic Leukodystrophy with Pigmented Gila
155. Osteogenesis Imperfecta (OI) - Type II
156. Osteosarcoma (formerly know as Bone Cancer) with distant mesastases or inoperable or unresectable
157. Ovarian Cancer - with distant metastases or inoperable or unresectable
158. Pallister-Killian Syndrome
159. Pancreatic Cancer
160. Paraneoplastic Pemphigus
161. Patau Syndrome (Trisomy 13)
162. Pearson Syndrome
163. Pelizaeus-Merzbacher Disease Classic Form
164. Pelizaeus-Merzbacher Disease Connatal Form
165. Peripheral Nerve Cancer-metastatic or recurrent
166. Peritoneal Mesothelioma
167. Peritoneal Mucinous Carcinomatosis
168. Perry Syndrome
169. Phelan-McDermid Syndrome
169A. Pitt Hopkins Syndrome
170. Pleural Mesothelioma
171. Pompe Disease - Infantile
172. Primary Cardiac Amyloidosis
173. Primary Central Nervous System Lymphoma
174. Primary Effusion Lymphoma
174A. Primary Peritoneal Cancer
175. Primary Progressive Aphasia
176. Progressive Bulbar Palsy
177. Progressive Multifocal Leukoencephalopathy
178. Progressive Supranuclear Palsy
179. Prostate Cancer-Hormone Refractory Disease-or with visceral metastases
180. Pulmonary Atresia
181. Pulmonary Kaposi Sarcoma

182. Retinopathy of Prematurity-Stage V
183. Rett (RTT) Syndrome
184. Revesz Syndrome
185. Rhabdomyosarcoma
186. Rhizomelic Chondrodysplasia Punctata
186A. Richter Syndrome
187. Roberts Syndrome
188. Salivary Tumors
189. Sandhoff Disease
190. Schindler Disease Type 1
191. Seckel Syndrome
192. Severe Combined Immunodeficiency-Childhood
193. Single Ventricle
194. Sinonasal Cancer
195. Sjogren-Larsson Syndrome
196. Small Cell Cancer (of the Large Intestine, Ovary, Prostate, or Uterus)
197. Small Cell Cancer of the Thymus
198. Small Cell Lung Cancer
199. Small Intestine Cancer-with distant metastases or inoperable, unresectable or recurrent
200. Smith Lemli Opitz Syndrome
201. Soft Tissue Sarcoma-with distant metastases or recurrent
202. Spinal Muscular Atrophy (SMA) - Types 0 And 1
203. Spinal Nerve Root Cancer-metastatic or recurrent
204. Spinocerebellar Ataxia
205. Stiff Person Syndrome
206. Stomach Cancer - with distant metastases or inoperable, unresectable or recurrent
207. Subacute Sclerosis Panencephalitis
207A. Superficial Siderosis of the Central Nervous System
208. Tabes Dorsalis
209. Tay Sachs Disease
209A. Tetrasomy 18p
210. Thanatophoric Dysplasia, Type 1
211. The ALS/Parkinsonism Dementia Complex
212. Thyroid Cancer
213. Transplant Coronary Artery Vasculopathy
214. Tricuspid Atresia
215. Ullrich Congenital Muscular Dystrophy
216. Ureter Cancer - with distant metastases or inoperable, unresectable or recurrent
217. Usher Syndrome-Type I
218. Walker Warburg Syndrome
219. Wolman Disease
220. Xeroderma Pigmentosum
221. X-Linked Lymphoproliferative Disease
222. X-Linked Myotubular Myopathy
223. Zellweger Syndrome

Expedited disability claims for veterans. Note that, in 2014, Carolyn W. Colvin, Acting Commissioner of the SSA, along with Congressman John Sarbanes, D-MD, unveiled a new initiative to expedite disability claims by veterans with a Department of Veterans Affairs (VA) disability compensation rating of 100% Permanent & Total (P&T). Under the new process, the SSA will treat these veterans' applications as high priority and issue expedited decisions, similar to the way the agency currently handles disability claims from Wounded Warriors.

In order to receive expedited service, veterans must tell the SSA that they have a VA disability compensation rating of 100% P&T and show proof of their disability rating with their VA Notification Letter.

The VA rating only expedites Social Security disability claims processing and does not guarantee approval for Social Security disability benefits. The veterans still must meet the strict eligibility requirements for a disability allowance. See *www.socialsecurity.gov/pgm/disability-pt.htm.*

Payment for required medical evidence: The SSA will pay for the reasonable cost of medical evidence it requires and requests from any nonfederal hospital, clinic, laboratory, or other provider of medical services, or physician not employed by the federal government. [Soc. Sec. Act §223(d)(5).] The agency will also pay for consultative medical examinations arranged with its approval in those instances when the medical evidence is otherwise insufficient to assess the claim. [Reg. §404.1517.] The Listing of Impairments at 20 CFR 404, Subpart P, Appendix 1, may indicate, depending upon the medical condition, the circumstances under which a particular test may be ordered and paid for by the SSA.

Travel expenses: Reimbursement for the cost of travel by the most economical and expeditious means appropriate to the person's condition will be made to persons who incur travel expenses in connection with medical examinations requested by the Commissioner pursuant to a disability determination, and for payment to applicants, their representatives, and any reasonably necessary witnesses to attend reconsideration interviews and proceedings before Administrative Law Judges. However, travel expenses incurred in going to and from Social Security offices to file requests for reconsideration or to discuss the reconsideration decision are not covered. [Soc. Sec. Act §201(j).]

Reconsideration

A claimant may request reconsideration of an initial determination within 60 days after receipt of the notice of determination. The date of receipt of the notice is presumed to be five days after the date of the notice unless there is a reasonable showing to the contrary. [Reg. §404.910.]

Good cause for untimely request for reconsideration. If a claimant fails to submit a timely request for reconsideration, the SSA may allow an untimely filed request if good cause can be shown. Good cause includes, but is not limited to the following: (1) where the claimant is seriously ill, and was prevented from contacting the agency, (2) death or serious illness in the immediate family, (3) failure to know of the need to file for timely review due to physical, mental, educational, or linguistic limitations, (4) loss of important records, (5) failure to receive notice of the determination, or (6) submission of the request for reconsideration, in good faith, to wrong government agency within the time limit. [Regs. §§404.909, 404.911.]

Requests for reconsideration: All claimants representatives who request direct fee payment of authorized fees from benefits awarded to a claimant are required to file reconsideration requests electronically via the Internet. Representatives who fail to comply may be subject to sanction by the SSA, but appeals not in compliance with the rule will not be rejected, delayed or differently processed. The obligation is imposed on both attorneys as well as on non-attorney representatives. Claimants, even if they are represented, as well as representatives who are not eligible for or who do not request direct fee payment on a matter may continue to file all appeal requests either electronically or on paper. Note that the SSA issued a notice on April 18, 2016, providing advance notification of the requirement that for claims with certified electronic folders pending at the hearing or Appeals Council levels, an appointed representative must access and obtain a claimant's folder through Appointed Representative Services (ARS) in matters for which the representative requests direct fee payment (81 *Fed. Reg.* 22697). [Regs. §404.1713, §404.1740(b)(4), §416.1513, and §416.1540(b)(4) in conjunction with the announcement at 77 *Fed. Reg.* 4563, Jan. 31, 2012.]

To file an electronic appeal or request for hearing, a representative will need to access the appeals website at *https://secure.ssa.gov/apps6z/iAppeals/ap001.jsp*. According to a short video that provides some guidance for filing an electronic appeal, the online application (SSA i561) will require one hour of time: 20 minutes to complete the appeal request, and 40 minutes to provide an updated disability report [77 *Fed. Reg.* 4563, Jan. 31, 2012.]

Representatives who ignore the electronic filing requirement do so at their peril. The notice of establishing the electronic filing requirement warned that compliance will be monitored and that a representative who fails to use an electronic service when required to do so will be provided an opportunity for a hearing before an ALJ "who will decide whether to disqualify or suspend the representative." [76 *Fed. Reg.* 56107, Sept. 12, 2011.]

The reconsideration process is a thorough and independent review of the case based on the evidence submitted for the initial determination plus any further evidence that the claimant or another individual may submit in connection with the reconsideration. [Reg. §404.916.] At the reconsideration stage, a request may be made for a hearing before a disability hearing officer if the claimant had been receiving benefits based on disability and the determination was made that based on medical factors, the claimant is not now disabled. [Reg. §404.913.] See ¶520.5, below, regarding Continuing Disability Review.

Hearing before Administrative Law Judge

A request for review by an Administrative Law Judge (ALJ), Form HA 501, must be filed within 75 days after the date a claimant receives notice of the previous determination. As with requests for reconsideration, this time may be extended for good cause on the same basis as it is extended at the reconsideration stage. [Reg. §404.933.]

Note, the Ninth Circuit has ruled that, in the event a claimant cites the governing regulations in attempting to establish a good cause justification for an untimely request for a hearing, the ALJ must address each specific claim. Accordingly, a claimant was denied due process when an ALJ determined that lack of awareness of filing deadlines did not constitute good cause, but did not further consider whether the claimant's illness or the illness and death of her mother also justified the delayed filing. [*Dexter v. Commissioner*, No. 12-35074 (Ninth Cir. 2013).]

All claimants representatives who request direct fee payment of authorized fees from benefits awarded to a claimant are required to file hearing requests electronically via the Internet using form i501 (see above, under "Requests for reconsideration"). Evidence should be submitted with the request or within 10 days after filing the request. The submission should include evidence from attending and treating physicians. [Reg. §404.935.] Evidence should be submitted with a cover letter asking for a favorable decision on the record if the claim is particularly strong. However, a claimant or a designated representative has the right to appear personally before an ALJ. [Regs. §404.948 and §404.949.] Nearly one fourth of all claims are allowed at this level.

Time and place of hearing. The hearing usually is held in the area where the person requesting the hearing resides. The ALJ, however, effectively sets the time and place for the hearing. The Social Security Administration is authorized to set the time and place for a hearing, but only after consultation with the ALJ and the hearing office Chief ALJ. The SSA expects to use its authority only where an ALJ has been scheduling so few hearings as to "compromise [the agency's] efforts to make timely and accurate decisions." [Regs. §404.936 and §416.1436; 75 *Fed. Reg.* 39154, July 8, 2010.]

Note, the SSA has issued final rules that explain how a claimant may object to appearing at a hearing via video teleconferencing, or to the time and place of a hearing. The final rules adopt, with further clarification regarding the agency's good cause exception, the notice of proposed rulemaking (NPRM) that it published in the *Federal Register* on June 27, 2013). The SSA expects that the final rules will have a minimal impact on the public, help ensure the integrity of the agency's programs, and allow the SSA to administer its programs more efficiently (79 *Fed. Reg.* 35926, June 25, 2014).

Determination of how appearances are made. The SSA will consult with the ALJ to determine whether the appearance of a claimant or any other party to the hearing will be made in person or by video teleconference. The ALJ will schedule appearances by video teleconference, if warranted by concerns of efficiency and absent prohibitive circumstances. The claimant or any other party to the hearing may appear by telephone if the ALJ determines that extraordinary circumstances prevent the claimant or other party from appearing in person or by video teleconference. [Reg. §§404.936(c)(1); 404.315(c)(1); 416.1436(c)(1).]

The ALJ will also determine whether a person other than the claimant or other party to the hearing (e.g. medical expert or vocational expert) will appear in person, by video teleconferencing, or by telephone. A claimant or other party to the hearing may object to the appearance of another person by video teleconferencing or telephone. In addition, a federal court in Connecticut has further ruled that the SSA could not take a medical expert's testimony by telephone without prior notice to the claimant, and over the claimant's objection, absent regulatory authority allowing the witness to appear by telephone. [*Edwards v. Astrue*, No. 3:10cv1017 (DC CN 2011).] Addressing the issues raised in *Edwards*, the SSA amended the governing regulations to empower an ALJ to make the final determination of whether a party (other than the claimant or other party to the hearing), such as a medical expert, must appear in person, by video teleconferencing, or by telephone. [Reg. §§404.936(c)(2); 404.315(c)(2); 416.1436(c)(2).] The regulations generally require the ALJ to direct the third party to appear by telephone or video teleconferencing, if warranted by concerns of efficiency and not prohibited by circumstances.

Note that on December 18, 2019, the SSA published a final rule it proposed in November 2018 regarding setting the time, place, and manner of appearance for hearings at the administrative law judge (ALJ) level of the administrative review process, with modifications. The final rule states that the agency will determine how parties and witnesses will appear at a hearing before an ALJ, and that the SSA will set the time and place for the hearing accordingly. The agency will schedule the parties to a hearing to appear by video teleconference (VTC), in person, or, in limited circumstances, by telephone. Under the final rule, the SSA will decide how parties and witnesses will appear at a hearing based on several factors, but the parties to a hearing will continue to have the ability to opt out of appearing by VTC at the ALJ hearings level. The rule became effective on January 17, 2020 (84 *Fed. Reg.* 69298).

Hearing notice. Besides the changes the SSA finalized above, the agency also clarified its rule regarding the notice of hearing at the ALJ hearing level. Under current rule, the SSA sends a notice of hearing at least 75 days prior to the date of the scheduled hearing to all parties and their representative, if any. In addition to the time and place of a hearing, the notice has other information, including the issues to be decided, the right to representation, how to request a change in the time of the hearing, and how appearances will be made. The SSA now has clarified that when it sends an amended notice of hearing or notice of supplemental hearing, it would send the amended notice or notice of supplemental hearing at least 20 days prior to the hearing. If the agency needs to change the date of a hearing, the date it chooses will always be at least 75 days from the date the SSA first sent the claimant a notice of hearing, unless the claimant has waived his or her right to advance notice. [Reg. §§404.938(a); 416.1438(a).]

Right to appear and present evidence. Any party to a hearing has a right to appear before the ALJ in person, or by video teleconferencing or telephone, to present evidence. A party may also make an appearance through a designated representative, who may appear in person, or by video teleconferencing or telephone. [Reg. §§404.950(a); 416.1450(a).]

Witnesses. Witnesses may appear at the hearing in person, or by video teleconferencing or by telephone. [Reg. §§404.950(e); 4167.1450(e).]

Subpoenas. Witnesses may be subpoenaed at the SSA's cost and may be asked questions by the parties or their representatives and by the ALJ. A request for a subpoena must be filed in writing at least five days prior to the hearing date. [Reg. §§404.950(d); 416.1450(d).]

Prehearing case review: The SSA may conduct a prehearing case review under certain circumstances, such as where new evidence has been submitted or may be available, there is a change in the law, or there is an error in the file. If a fully favorable revised determination is issued after review, an ALJ will dismiss a request for hearing soon after the fully favorable determination is issued, rather than waiting 30 days before dismissing the hearing request. All parties will have 60 days after the notice is received to request that the ALJ vacate the dismissal. The request must state why the SSA's dismissal of the request for a hearing was erroneous. If a partially favorable determination is made during the prehearing case review process, a hearing will be held unless a written dismissal request is received. If the SSA receives a written statement agreeing to a dismissal before the ALJ mails the notice of his or her decision, the agency will dismiss the request for a hearing. [Regs. §404.941 and §416.1441.]

Attorney advisors: Prehearing proceedings (at the third level of review only) may be conducted by an attorney advisor if one of the following criteria is met: new and material evidence is submitted, there is an indication that additional evidence is available, there is a change in the law or regulations, or there is an error in the file or some other indication that a wholly favorable decision could be issued. Attorney advisors will have authority to issue fully favorable decisions and all decisions will be mailed to all parties. If an attorney advisor issues a fully favorable decision, the SSA will treat it as a hearing level decision and will not hold a hearing unless a party requests within 60 days after receiving notice of the decision that an ALJ reinstate the request for a hearing. The deadline may be extended upon a showing of good cause for missing the deadline. If the prehearing proceedings are not concluded before the hearing date, the case will be sent to the ALJ unless a decision wholly favorable to the claimant and all other parties is in process, or the claimant and all other parties to the hearing agree in writing to delay the hearing until the prehearing proceedings are completed. [78 *Fed. Reg. 45459,* July 29, 2013; 80 *Fed. Reg.* 31990, June 5, 2015; 82 *Fed.*

Reg. 34400, July 25, 2017; 83 *Fed. Reg.* 711, January 8, 2018; 83 *Fed. Reg.* 40451, August 15, 2018; Reg. §§404.942; §416.1442.]

Hearings: At the hearing, the claimant or the claimant's designated representative should deliver a short opening statement. Examination of the claimant should show the limitations caused by the impairments that form the basis of the claim. This examination should elicit testimony from the claimant of the pain being experienced, covering the type and degree of the pain, including its duration, causes, and consequences, such as loss of memory, concentration, and failure to complete tasks. Corroborating testimony from relatives and friends should also be provided. SSA experts, such as medical and vocational experts, should be cross-examined. A short closing statement may be submitted unless the ALJ indicates otherwise. Issues not previously considered may be raised after the request for hearing is submitted. If the ALJ decides to consider a new issue at any time prior to the issuance of the hearing decision, the ALJ must provide written notice to all parties. [Reg. §404.946.] The ALJ may receive evidence at the hearing even though the evidence would not be admissible in court. [Reg. §404.950.]

The ALJ's role: The ALJ acts neither as counsel for the claimant nor as an advocate for the government. Rather, the ALJ has a dual role as a nonpartisan decisionmaker and fact-gatherer, which has been held not to be contrary to due process. Exercise of this dual role includes advising an unrepresented claimant of his or her burden of proof and cross-examination of the claimant and witnesses, if necessary, in order to fully develop the case. The ALJ's decision must give findings of fact and reasons for the decision. [Soc. Sec. Act §205(b); Reg. §404.953.] In mental impairment cases, a standard document detailing findings and the degree of functional loss must be completed by the ALJ or a medical advisor unless the case is remanded to the state agency for completion of the document and a new determination. [Reg. §404.1520A.] Ultimately, a long line of cases has held that the decision must be based on all the evidence offered at the hearing or otherwise included in the record. The ALJ cannot pick and choose among the evidence in order to find support for his or her decision.

The decision of the ALJ is binding on all parties to the hearing and is not appealable to the courts unless a timely request for review by the Appeals Council is filed, the expedited appeals process is used, or the decision is reviewed or revised by the ALJ or the Appeals Council. [Reg. §404.955.]

Note, the SSA provides separate vehicles for addressing complaints of unfairness, prejudice, partiality, bias, misconduct, or discrimination by the ALJ. The Appeals Council of the Office of Disability Adjudication and Review (ODAR) addresses allegations in the context of claims adjudication. The ODAR's Division of Quality Services reviews and investigates those complaints outside of the claims adjudication process to determine whether any administrative or disciplinary action with respect to the ALJ is required.

The public may further submit complaints of discrimination based on race, sex, sexual orientation, age, or disability to the SSA. The SSA will also hear complaints charging retaliation for the prior filing of civil rights complaints with the agency. [SSR013-1p, 78 *Fed. Reg.* 6168, Jan. 29, 2013.]

Review by Appeals Council:

A review by the Appeals Council may be requested if a party to the hearing is not satisfied with the action of the Administrative Law Judge. The Council will grant, deny, or dismiss the request for review, or remand the matter to the ALJ. A request for review, Form HA 520, must be filed within 60 days after the date that notice of the hearing decision or dismissal is received, or within the extended time period. [Reg. §404.968.]

Note that the U.S. Court of Appeals for the Seventh Circuit in *Boley v. Colvin*, No. 13-1252 (2014), ruled that a "hearing" within the context of 42 U.S.C. §405(g), which authorizes review of the SSA's final decisions, means whatever process the SSA deems adequate to produce a final decision regardless of whether there was an oral presentation in the matter. The holding overrules a 34-year-old decision and finds the Seventh Circuit changing sides in an established conflict among the federal circuits. On March 14, 2016, the SSA issued AR 16-1(7), which explains how the agency will apply the holding in *Boley* as it conflicts with the SSA's interpretation of the law. In order for the AR to apply, a claimant must reside in Illinois, Indiana, or Wisconsin at the time he or she is denied review.

Although the Council must also initiate review action within 60 days and the Council may not review the ALJ's decision unless the claimant actually receives notice of review within the 60-day period, as a practical matter, much more time is available to the Appeals Council to revisit its decision. [Reg. §404.969.] If the Appeals Council is unable to decide within the applicable 60-day period whether to review a decision or dismissal, it may consider at a later time whether the decision or dismissal should be reopened and revised under Regs. §404.987, §404.988, §416.1487 or §416.1488. These sections, pertaining to reopening and revising decisions, generally provide that the Appeals Council may reopen a decision for any reason within 12 months of the date of the initial determination, or within four years of the date of the notice of the initial determination upon a showing of "good cause," and at any time under certain defined conditions, including fraud. The 60-day time limitation on the Council review on its own motion is imposed so that, if no appeal is taken by the claimant from the decision, the claimant may, in most circumstances, consider the matter settled and the decision of the ALJ final. [SSR 74-4.]

The Council's decision, or the decision of the ALJ if the request for review is denied, is binding unless the decision is revised or unless an action is filed in a federal district court within 60 days after the date of receipt of the notice of the Council's action. [Reg. §404.981.]

Appeal strategy:

A claimant may not have two claims for the same type of benefits administratively pending at the same time. Accordingly, under SSR 11-1p, 76 *Fed. Reg.* 45309, July 28, 2011, a claimant who has been denied benefits at a hearing must choose between pursuing his or her administrative review rights on the pending disability claim or decline to pursue further review and file a new application.

This ruling presents many claimants with a Hobson's choice: (a) delay filing a new claim until an appeal under the pending claim is exhausted, but lose the benefits that might have been received under the new claim for the period during which the earlier claim is pending and further delay what might have been a more compelling new claim, or (b) file the new claim, but potentially forego years of back benefits under the earlier claim that might have been allowed under appeal.

SSR 11-1p provides guidance for three scenarios in which new evidence is submitted.

1. If the claim is pending at the initial, reconsideration or hearing level, a claimant will continue to be able to submit evidence of a new medical condition or a worsening in existing conditions. That evidence then will be considered along with all other evidence in the file. See Regs. §404.900(b) and §416.1400(b).

2. If the claim is pending at the Appeals Council and new material evidence is submitted that relates to the period on or before the date of the hearing decision, the Appeals Council will consider it together with the entire record. If that evidence "shows a critical or disabling condition," the Appeals Council will expedite its review of the pending claim. [Regs. §404.970(b) and §416.1470(b).] This is not entirely clear however, since all disability claims, presumably, are filed with the intent of showing a disabling condition.

3. If the additional evidence does not relate to the period on or before the hearing decision, the evidence will be returned and an accompanying notice will explain why the Appeals Council did not accept it. Under this circumstance, the Appeals Council will consider the date of the request for Appeals Council review of the earlier claim as the filing date for a new claim. If the original and new claims are filed under Title II, a claimant will have six months from the date of the notice within which to file the new claim and preserve the date of filing for Appeals Council review as the filing date of the new claim. If original and pending claims are filed under Title XVI, a claimant has 60 days within which to file the new claim and preserve his or her rights. In either case, the Appeals Council may permit the filing of a new claim during the pendency of the original claim if the additional evidence shows a critical or disabling condition and the claimant informs the Appeals Council that he or she wishes to file a new claim.

If the new claim does not involve the same title or type of benefit, it will not be impacted by this ruling. If the subsequent claim under a different title or benefit type presents the same issue as the original claim, the SSA may choose to consolidate it with the pending claim if that claim is pending through the hearing level. If the original claim is pending at the Appeals Council, subsequent claims of a different title or benefit type will be processed in accordance with current procedures. [SSR 11-1p.]

Note that the SSA has revised its rules so that more of the agency's procedures at the hearing and Appeals Council levels of the administrative review process are consistent nationwide. The final rules became effective on January 17, 2017; compliance, however, was not required until May 1, 2017 (81 *Fed. Reg.* 90987, December 16, 2016).

The SSA also has finalized amendments to its regulations regarding the return of evidence at the Appeals Council level. Current rules state that the Council will return to the claimant additional evidence it receives when the Council finds the evidence does not relate to the period on or before the date of the ALJ's hearing decision. Now the Council has the discretion in returning additional evidence that it receives in such circumstances (81 *Fed. Reg.* 6170, February 4, 2016).

In addition, note that the Ninth Circuit, in a case of first impression, ruled that a claimant must first raise a challenge to the evidentiary basis of a vocational expert's job numbers during the administrative proceedings before the ALJ or the Appeals Council or such a challenge is waived on appeal to the federal district court (*Shaibi v. Commissioner*, No. 15-16849, August 22, 2017).

Alternative Disability Determination Procedures

In recent years the Social Security Administration has experimented with a number of alternative procedures to the four-part disability determination process outlined above (initial determination, reconsideration, hearing before ALJ, Appeals Council review) in an effort to both streamline the process and reduce the tremendous backlog in disability claims.

Disability Redesign Prototype/Single Decisionmaker Test:

The SSA ended the single decisionmaker test on October 1, 2018, in the 19 states and the territory of Guam that used this test. There were nine states and the territory of Guam that used single decisionmaker as a stand-alone test. The remaining 10 states used the single decisionmaker as part of a separate test that the SSA refers to as the "disability prototype."

One feature of the prototype test eliminates the reconsideration level of the administrative review process. The SSA is continuing to make decisions in these 10 states by maintaining the elimination of the reconsideration level, but as noted above, as of October 1, 2018, it has been making determinations by using medical consultants in those states with the prototype tests.

The SSA will begin phasing out the prototype test in January 2019 in the following five states: New Hampshire; New York; Louisiana; Colorado; and in the part of California where the prototype test is currently being conducted. This means that for the residents in these locations who apply for Social Security Disability Insurance Benefits or Supplemental Security Income, or both, and who receive an initial denial determination on or after January 1, 2019, the first step of the appeals process will be to request a reconsideration of that determination. If the agency denies an individual at the reconsideration step, he or she then may seek further review of the claim by requesting a hearing before an administrative law judge.

The SSA will eliminate the prototype test in the remaining five states (Pennsylvania; Alabama; Michigan; Missouri; and Alaska) by June 26, 2020, at which time the test will end. With the end of the prototype test, the SSA will return to a national, unified disability process that affords all disability claimants the same appeal rights in all states (83 *Fed. Reg.* 63965, December 12, 2018).

¶520.5 Continuing Disability Review

Once a claimant is found to be disabled, the Commissioner is required to re-evaluate the claimant's impairment(s) from time to time in order to determine whether he or she remains entitled to benefits. This process is referred to as a continuing disability review (CDR). The Commissioner may begin a continuing disability review for various reasons, but must first notify the claimant that his or her entitlement to benefits is being reviewed and give the reasons why review is being undertaken. In addition, the claimant must be informed that the medical improvement review standard will apply, that the review could result in the termination of benefits, and that the claimant has the right to submit medical and other evidence for consideration during the review process. If the review establishes that benefits should be terminated, then the claimant will be notified in writing and given an opportunity to appeal the decision. [Soc. Sec. Act §§221(i), 1631(d)(1), and 1633; Regs. §§404.1589, 416.989.]

Note that the SSA is *proposing* to revise its regulations regarding when and how often the agency conducts continuing disability reviews. New proposed rules would add a category to the existing medical diary categories that the SSA uses to schedule CDRs and revise the criteria for assigning each of the medical diary categories to cases. The proposed rules also would change the frequency with which the agency performs a CDR for claims with the medical diary category for permanent impairments. The revised changes would ensure that the SSA continues to maintain appropriate stewardship of the disability program and identify medical improvement (MI) at its earliest point.

The SSA also wants to have the flexibility to adjust the scheduling of CDRs when there have been advances in treatment for a person's impairment(s) that improve the ability to work or, for children receiving Title XVI payments, that improve overall health and functioning. Therefore, the agency is proposing to make three changes to its current rules on when and how often the agency conducts CDRs. First, the SSA proposes to add a fourth medical diary category. Next, it proposes to revise the criteria it follows to assign a medical diary to each case. Finally, the SSA proposes to retain the frequency for the MIE and MIP diary categories (6 to 18 months and 3 years, respectively), and revise the frequency with which it performs a CDR for the MINE diary category (84 *Fed. Reg.* 63588, November 18, 2019).

CDR "Triggers"

Some of the reasons that will trigger a CDR include: (1) a scheduled review based on designation of the case as a "medical improvement expected diary" (*i.e.,* a case that is scheduled for review at a later date because the individual's impairment(s) is expected to improve, generally within a period of not less than six months or more than 18 months); (2) scheduling of the case for a periodic review, *i.e.,* medical improvement is considered possible or medical improvement is not expected (in the case where medical improvement is considered possible, review will be undertaken at least once every three years, whereas in those cases where medical improvement is not expected, review will take place at least once every seven years but no more frequently than once every five years); (3) the need for a current medical or other report due to advances in medical technology that may affect the disability determination; (4) the claimant's return to work and successful completion of a period of trial work; (5) the reporting of substantial earnings; (6) evidence from other reliable sources, including a state vocational rehabilitation agency, that disability has ceased [Soc. Sec. Act §221(i); Reg. §§404.1588-.1590, 416.990], or (7) a childhood disability beneficiary under Title XVI reaching age 18 or, in the case of benefits being paid on the basis of low-birth weight, review is scheduled within one year of the beneficiary's birth. [P.L. 104-193, §212(b) and (c), amending Soc. Sec. Act §1614(a)(3)(H)(iii) and (iv), respectively.] At the time of a childhood disability beneficiary's review, the SSA requires the child's representative payee (see ¶571) to present evidence that the child is and has been receiving treatment considered medically necessary and available for his or her disabling condition. The SSA may waive this requirement if it determines that requiring such evidence would be inappropriate or unnecessary. [Reg. §416.994a.]

CDR Review Process

Generally, the SSA must determine if there has been any medical improvement in a disability beneficiary's impairment(s) and, if so, whether this medical improvement is related to the beneficiary's ability to work. An eight-step sequential evaluation process is used to determine if a beneficiary is still disabled under Title II of the Act, as follows:

1. Is the beneficiary engaging in substantial gainful activity? If so, and if any applicable trial-work period has ended, the disability will be found to have ended.

2. If not, does the beneficiary have an impairment or combination of impairments that meet or equal the severity of a listed impairment? If so, the disability will be found to be continuing.

3. If not, has there been medical improvement as shown by a decrease in the severity of the impairment(s)? If so, go to step 4; if not, go to step 5.

4. If there has been medical improvement, the SSA must determine whether it is related to a beneficiary's ability to do work. If medical improvement is not related to the beneficiary's ability to do work, go on to step 5. If medical improvement is related to the beneficiary's ability to do work, the SSA skips to step 6.

5. If the SSA finds at step 3 that there has been no medical improvement, or if it found at step 4 that the medical improvement is not related to the beneficiary's ability to work, it will consider whether one of the exceptions to medical improvement applies. If none of the exceptions to medical improvement applies, the SSA will find that the disability continues. However, if one of the exceptions applies, the SSA will find either that the disability has ended or that it will need to go on to step 6, depending on the exception that applies in the case.

6. If medical improvement is related to the beneficiary's ability to do work, or if any one of certain exceptions to medical improvement applies, the SSA will determine whether all of a beneficiary's current impairments in combination are "severe" (see Reg. §404.1521). If the beneficiary does not have a "severe" impairment(s), the SSA will find that the disability has ended.

7. If a beneficiary's impairment(s) is "severe," the SSA will assess the beneficiary's residual functional capacity based on all of the beneficiary's current impairments and consider whether the beneficiary can still do work the beneficiary has done in the past. If the beneficiary can do such work, the SSA will find that the disability has ended.

8. If the beneficiary is not able to do work performed in the past, the SSA will consider one final step. Given the residual functional capacity assessment and considering the beneficiary's age, education, and past work experience, can the beneficiary do other work? If so, the disability will be found to have ended. If not, the disability will be found to continue. [Reg. §404.1594(f).]

This same process is found in SSI cases except that step 1 does not apply since benefits are not terminated because of a work incentive provision for SSI recipients in which a beneficiary with a severe impairment, or combination of impairments, who engages in substantial gainful activity may continue to receive benefits. [SSA §1619; Regs. §§416.994(b)(5).]

¶520.5

Exceptions to CDR review process:

Individuals who have received Title II disability benefits for at least 24 months are entitled to a number of exceptions to the CDR process under Social Security Act §221(m), as follows:

- The SSA may not schedule a continuing disability review solely as a result of a beneficiary's work activity. [Soc. Sec. Act §221(m)(1)(A); Regs. §§404.1590(i) and 416.990(i).]

- The SSA may not use a beneficiary's work activity as evidence that the beneficiary is no longer disabled. [Soc. Sec. Act §221(m)(1)(B); Regs. §§404.1594(i)(2) and 416.994(b)(8)(ii).]

- The SSA may not presume that a beneficiary is unable to work merely because the beneficiary stopped working. [Soc. Sec. Act §221(m)(1)(C); Regs. §§404.1594(i)(2) and 416.994(b)(8)(ii).]

- A beneficiary is still subject to CDRs that are not triggered by work. [Soc. Sec. Act §221(m)(2)(A); Regs. §§404.1590(i)(3) and 416.990(i)(3).]

- Benefits may still be terminated if earnings exceed the level of earnings that represent substantial gainful activity. [Soc. Sec. Act §221(m)(2)(B); Regs. §§404.1574 and 404.1575.]

[Soc. Sec. Act §221(m), added by the Ticket to Work and Work Incentives Improvement Act of 1999, P.L. 106-170, §111(a); Conforming regulatory amendments added by 71 *Fed. Reg.* 66840, Nov. 17, 2006.]

These exceptions also will apply to CDRs under Title XVI for beneficiaries receiving disability benefits under both Titles II and XVI, except that, as mentioned earlier, the performance of substantial gainful activity is not a basis for determining that disability has ceased under the SSI program. The rules elaborate on how the 24-month period is counted in single and in dual entitlement cases. The months need not be consecutive, and may be counted even if a beneficiary was entitled to a benefit that was withheld in order to recover an overpayment. Note that CDRs may be started, even if a beneficiary has received benefits for at least 24 months, in cases where the CDR is started for reasons other than work activity, such as where the beneficiary has been routinely scheduled for a periodic review of the continuing disability or where the SSA receives evidence that raises a questions as to whether the disability continues. [Regs. §§404.1590(i)(2), (3) and 416.990(i)(2), (3).]

Compliance with Requests for a CDR

Social Security beneficiaries under Title II who fail to comply with a request for information in the course of a continuing disability review (CDR) will have their benefits suspended, rather than terminated.

The Social Security Administration will suspend an individual's Title II disability benefits during a CDR when he or she fails, without good cause, to comply with a written request for any necessary information. Once the SSA receives the information, it will reinstate benefits, including benefits for any prior months that were otherwise payable. The reinstatement will not be delayed until completion of the CDR process. [Regs. §§404.1587(b), 404.1596(d), and 416.1322.]

The Social Security Administration will terminate Title II benefits for noncompliance during a CDR only after 12 consecutive months of noncompliance, beginning with the 13th month after benefits were stopped. A terminated beneficiary will have the right to appeal the termination, but there will be no benefit continuation rights during the appeal. [Regs. §§404.1587(c), 404.1596(e), and 416.1335.]

¶520.6 Work Incentives—Rehabilitation Services— Trial-Work Periods

Recipients of disability benefits are encouraged to return to work. To achieve this goal, the Social Security Administration provides incentives that make it possible for recipients of disability benefits to work and still receive benefits. Among the many incentives are special rules for crediting earned income for substantial gainful activity determinations, the trial work period, the Ticket to Work program, and continued Medicare and Medicaid eligibility. Information on resources available to recipients of disability benefits is available online at *www.ssa.gov/work/index.html.* Included at the website is specific information about initiatives, activities, and programs to help people with disabilities who want to work (*www.ssa.gov/work/receivingbenefits.html*).

Vocational rehabilitation. In order to make vocational rehabilitation services more readily available to disabled individuals, state vocational rehabilitation agencies are reimbursed from Social Security trust funds for rehabilitation services rendered in cases where (1) the furnishing of the services results in the performance by the individuals of substantial gainful activity for a continuous period of nine months, (2) the individual is participating in an approved vocational rehabilitation program and completion of the program, or its continuation for a specified period of time, will increase the likelihood that the individual will be permanently removed from the disability benefit rolls, and (3) the individual, without good cause, refuses to continue to accept vocational rehabilitation services or fails to cooperate in a manner as to preclude his or her successful rehabilitation. [Soc. Sec. Act §222(d).]

Encouraging Return to Work

The SSA provides a series of rules that are designed to encourage disabled beneficiaries to return to work by allowing for the deduction of specified earnings for substantial gainful activity.

- *Impairment-related work expense:* The cost of certain items and services which a disabled beneficiary needs in order to work are deductible from earnings credited for SGA purposes even though these items or services are needed to carry out daily living functions unrelated to work. These include payments for attendant care services, medical devices such as wheelchairs, prosthetic devices, and work related equipment, residential modifications, drugs and medications, and certain transportation costs [Soc. Sec. Act §223(d)(4)(A); Reg. §404.1576];

- *Subsidies and special conditions* The value of subsidies and special conditions is deducted from earnings when determining SGA. Examples include situations where a beneficiary receives more supervision than other workers performing the same or similar job for the same pay, has fewer or simpler tasks to complete than other workers who are doing the same job for the same pay, or has a job coach or mentor who performs part or all of the individual's job duties. The SSA will only count earnings that are attributable to an individual's own productivity in applying the substantial gainful activity earnings guidelines [Reg. §404.1574(a)(2)]; and

- *Unincurred business expense:* The value of business support provided by a sponsoring agency or individual at no cost is deducted from net earnings from self-employment when determining SGA. The item or service must be that which the IRS would have allowed as a legitimate business expense had the disability benefit recipient paid for it, but is disallowed by the IRS only because the item or services was provided by another party. Examples of this type of expense include rent, utilities, equipment, and stock [Reg. §404.1575(c)].

Trial-Work Periods

A trial-work period is provided for persons who have been awarded childhood disability benefits, disability insurance benefits, or widow(er)'s or divorced spouse's benefits based on disability and who return to work, whether under approved plans of rehabilitation or otherwise, as an incentive for personal rehabilitation efforts. Individuals are allowed to work for as many as nine months during a 60-month period without affecting their right to cash benefits during this period, provided their disability does not cease during the nine-month period. [Soc. Sec. Act §222(c).]

Eligibility. Only one trial-work period is allowed in one period of disability. Individuals receiving disability benefits through "expedited reinstatement," i.e., individuals reentitled to benefits within 60 months of terminating a prior period of entitlement (see below, under "Expedited Reinstatement" in this section), must complete the "initial reentitlement period" of 24 months following reinstatement of benefits before becoming eligible for a new trial-work period. [SSA POMS §DI 13010.035C TN 30 12/09.]

The following individuals are not entitled to a trial-work period: any Title XVI-only recipient; beneficiaries who have already had a trial-work period during the same period of disability; certain statutorily blind beneficiaries, age 55 or older; and individuals receiving continued benefits on account of being engaged in a program of vocational rehabilitation even though the disability medically ceases. [SSA POMS §DI 13010.035C TN 30 12/09.]

Duration of trial-work period. The trial-work period begins with the month the beneficiary first becomes entitled to benefits, or (in the case of a disabled child) the month in which he or she attains age 18 or becomes entitled to such benefits, whichever is later. The nine months of trial work (whether or not consecutive) will be counted beginning with the first month within the trial period in which a beneficiary who is determined to still have a disabling impairment performs services. [Soc. Sec. Act §222(c).]

The trial-work period ends with the ninth month of work or, if earlier, with the month in which disability ceases, or upon death or attainment of full retirement age. A disability beneficiary's trial-work period will continue until he or she performs services in nine months of any period of 60 consecutive months. The provision gives beneficiaries the opportunity to test their ability to work over a sustained period of time before their benefits are cut off. [Soc. Sec. Act §222(c).]

In determining the number of months the person has worked in the trial-work period, only work that is (or normally would be) remunerative is counted, excluding work performed without remuneration, in therapy, training, routine duties at home, or self-care. In 2020, there must be earnings of at least $910 ($880 in 2019) for a month to count as a trial work month. This amount will increase in future years, based on increases in national average wages. Thresholds for the current and prior years are shown below:

Calendar Year	Threshold	Source	Calendar Year	Threshold	Source
1990–2000	200	Reg. §404.1592	2011	720	75 FR 74123
2001	530	Reg. §404.1592	2012	720	76 FR 66111
2002	560	66 FR 54047	2013	750	77 FR 65754
2003	570	67 FR 65620	2014	770	78 FR 66413
2004	580	68 FR 60437	2015	780	79 FR 64455
2005	590	69 FR 62497	2016	810	80 FR 66963
2006	620	70 FR 61677	2017	840	81 FR 74854
2007	640	71 FR 62636	2018	850	82 FR 59937
2008	670	72 FR 60703	2019	880	83 FR 53702
2009	700	73 FR 64651	2020	910	84 FR 56515
2010	720	74 FR 55614			

Any work done during these nine months, which need not be consecutive, is disregarded in determining whether disability has ceased during the trial-work period. However, work done in or after the trial-work period is considered in determining, once the trial-work period has ended, whether the disability has ceased. Benefits then continue for an additional three months, including the month of cessation, after the disability is determined to have ceased, in cases in which there were nine months of trial work. [Soc. Sec. Act §222(c); Reg. §404.1592; 71 *Fed. Reg.* 62636, Oct. 26, 2006.] Note that there is no entitlement to a trial-work period within the 12 months of the alleged onset of disability. [*Barnhart v. Walton*, 535 U.S. 212, 122 S. Ct. 1265, 152 L.Ed.2d 330 (2002).] See ¶520.1.

Fraudulent concealment of work activity:

An individual who is convicted of fraudulently concealing work activity during a trial work period will not be entitled to receive a disability benefit for trial work period months that occur prior to the conviction but within the same period of disability. If the individual has already been paid benefits for these months, he or she will be liable for repayment of these benefits, in addition to any restitution, penalties, fines, or assessments that are otherwise due. [Soc. Sec. Act §222(c), as amended by the Soc. Sec. Protection Act of 2004, P.L. 108-203 §208, Mar. 2, 2004; Regs. §§404.471 and 404.1592(f).]

Note that under the Social Security Benefit Protection and Opportunity Enhancement Act of 2015, individuals will be disqualified from receiving benefits during a trial work period if they are assessed a civil monetary penalty for fraudulently concealing work activity. [Soc. Sec. Act §208(a), as amended.]

Reentitlement period:

Individuals may be entitled to an effective extension of the trial-work period from 12 months (nine months plus three months), to 24 months. During the 36-month period immediately following the end of the trial-work period, an individual who was performing substantial gainful activity will not receive cash benefits while engaging in substantial work activity, but will receive the advantage of being automatically reinstated to active benefit status if earnings fall below the substantial gainful activity level. If a disability recipient's benefits are suspended on account of substantial gainful activity during the 36-month extended period of eligibility that follows a trial-work period, then the benefits of a secondary beneficiary on the same earnings record will also be suspended. [Soc. Sec. Act §§222(c), 223(a)(1)(D), 223(e); Reg. §404.1592; Reg. §404.1592a.]

When determining whether an individual's disability has ceased because of the performance of substantial gainful activity during and after a reentitlement period, earnings over continuous periods of work are averaged in the same way that earnings are averaged when a substantial gainful activity assessment is made on a disability claim. [Reg. §404.1592a.]

Ticket to Work and Work Incentives

The Ticket to Work and Work Incentives Improvement Act of 1999, P.L. 106-170, significantly changed how the Social Security Administration encourages a disabled individual to regain his or her ability to perform work. Prior to its enactment, individuals applying for disability benefits were promptly referred to state agencies or agencies administering state plans for rehabilitation services. In the case of a disabled worker entitled to disability insurance benefits, a disabled child beneficiary age 18 or over (see ¶524, below) or a disabled widow or widower (¶525.2) who had not attained age 60, benefits were denied for any month in which the individual refused, without good cause, to accept rehabilitation services available to him under a state plan approved under the Vocational Rehabilitation Act.

However, the Ticket to Work and Work Incentives Improvement Act repealed these provisions (former Soc. Sec. Act §§222(b) and 1615(c)) and expanded the scope of rehabilitation services. The Ticket to Work program rewards beneficiaries who work and progress towards self-sufficiency with continued suspension of continuing disability reviews (see below). On the other side, providers of services—either a state vocational rehabilitation agency or a private "employment network" (EN) receive payments based on their success in returning a disabled beneficiary to gainful employment. Since the suspension of these reviews means that some beneficiaries who no longer meet the definition of disability will continue to be eligible for benefits, the program is designed to ensure that the suspension of the reviews does not continue for "an undue length of time without a significant reduction in benefit payments due to earnings."[66 *Fed. Reg.* 67377, Dec. 28, 2001.]

Under the Ticket to Work program, which is voluntary, participating disability beneficiaries may receive a ticket that may be redeemed at a state rehabilitation agency or an employment network that will work with the individual to develop a vocational goal and provide services and supports necessary to accomplish that goal. Details on how the program works are located in 20 CFR Part 411 [66 *Fed. Reg.* 67370, Dec. 28, 2001; amended, 73 *Fed. Reg* 29324, May 20, 2008, eff. July 21, 2008], and at a webpage of the Social Security Administration: *http://www.socialsecurity.gov/work/aboutticket.html*.

There are four basic purposes to the program: (1) to reduce dependence on cash benefits by providing health care and employment preparation and placement services to disabled individuals; (2) to encourage states to allow disabled individuals to purchase Medicaid coverage that is necessary to allow such individuals to maintain employment; (3) to provide these individuals with the option of maintaining Medicare coverage while working; and (4) to establish a program that allows disabled individuals to seek the employment and vocational rehabilitation services needed to obtain and maintain the employment necessary to reduce their dependence on cash benefits. [P.L. 106-170, §2(b).]

Ticket use with a state vocational rehabilitation agency

If a state vocational rehabilitation (VR) agency elects to be paid under the cost reimbursement payment system for a given beneficiary, the beneficiary's ticket will no longer be assigned to that agency. In that situation, the beneficiary may assign the ticket to a different provider of services after the state vocational re-habilitation agency has closed his or her case. [Regs. §411.135 and §411.140.] However, if the beneficiary holds on to the ticket while receiving services from the state vocational rehabilitation agency that has elected the cost reimburse-ment option, the beneficiary will be considered to be "using a ticket," provided the beneficiary meets all of the related provisions in Subpart C regarding timely progress. [Reg. §411.170.]

For a beneficiary for whom the state VR agency has elected the VR cost re-imbursement option, whose ticket has not terminated and who continues to meet the timely progress requirements, the period of "using a ticket " will end with the close of the 90-day period following the date the state VR agency closes the beneficiary's VR case, unless the beneficiary assigns the ticket dur-ing this 90-day period. [Reg. §411.171.]

Concurrent payment may be made to an employment network under an employment network payment system and to a state VR agency under the VR cost reimbursement option with respect to the same beneficiary in certain circumstances. [Reg. 411.585.]

What is an "employment network" and how are they selected and reimbursed?

An employment network may include both state vocational rehabilitation agencies as well as private and other public providers, and is selected by the Commissioner based on the recruitment and recommendations of program managers who, themselves, are selected by the Commissioner through a com-petitive bidding process. The program managers also monitor all employment networks within the area covered by the program manager, ensure that benefi-ciaries are offered an adequate selection of services, assure that payment to an employment network is warranted, and ensure that sufficient employment net-works are available and that each beneficiary has reasonable access to services.

Outcome payment system: The Commissioner reimburses each employment network (or state vocational rehabilitation agency operating as an employ-ment network) through either an outcome-only payment or outcome-mile-stone payment system. Under the 2008 amendments, the payment is 67% of the national average monthly disability benefit and the number of months vary depending upon the type of benefit a ticket-holder receives: 36 months for beneficiaries receiving Title II disability benefits and 60 months for ben-eficiaries receiving Title XVI (SSI) benefits. [Soc. Sec. Act §1148, as enacted by The Ticket to Work and Work Incentives Improvement Act of 1999, P.L. 106-170, §101; Regs. §411.525(a)(1)(i) and §411.550.]

Outcome-milestone payment system: The outcome-milestone payment system is similar except that it provides for early payment(s) based on the achievement of one or more milestones directed towards the goal of permanent employment. Total potential payment under the outcome-milestone payment system is 90% of the total potential payment under the outcome-only payment system. In addition, milestone payments must occur before the beginning of the outcome period. Once the SSA begins making payments for a Title XVI beneficiary it will continue using the Title XVI payment rates even if the beneficiary later becomes eligible for disability insurance benefits under Title II. There is a two-phased milestone payment system and outcome payments parallel the steps beneficiaries take toward self-sufficiency. [Reg. §411.525 and §411.535.]

Phase 1 is modeled on the nine-month trial work period (TWP) provided for Title II beneficiaries. Four milestones at different points of employment retention will be paid when the beneficiary works for a period of time with gross earnings at or above the trial work earnings level. Phase 1 milestones are the only payments that will be the same for both Title II and Title XVI beneficiaries, and these payments will be 120% of the PCB or national average monthly disability benefit for Title II beneficiaries. The first milestone is met and payment is made to the employment network when the beneficiary who assigned a ticket to the employment network earns 50% of the trial work threshold amount in one month. The remaining milestone payments are met when the beneficiary has monthly earnings of at least the trial work threshold amount for the number of months indicated: second milestone—three months out of the last six; third milestone—six months out of the last 12; fourth milestone—nine months out of the last 18. Payment of the fourth milestone also requires substantial completion of services outlined in the beneficiary's Individualized Work Plan. [Regs. §411.525(a)(2)(i), §411.540; *http://www.socialsecurity.gov/work/documents/Chart_of_Key_Changes_to_Ticket_to_Work_Regulations_5292008.doc.*]

Note that work activity above the trial work earnings level ($910 month in 2020) in the 18 months prior to the first ticket assignment on each ticket may preclude the SSA from paying some or all of the Phase 1 milestones. [Reg. §411.535(a)(1)(ii).]

Phase 2 requires a substantial achievement on the path toward full self-sufficiency. The employment outcome triggering a Phase 2 milestone payment is a month where the beneficiary's gross earnings equal or exceed the substantial gainful activity earnings level (in calendar year 2020, $1,260 for non-blind individuals (see ¶520.1)). During Phase 2, the SSA will make a maximum of 11 monthly milestone payments with respect to a Title II beneficiary and a maximum of 18 monthly milestone payments with respect to a Title XVI beneficiary. Each payment is equal to 36% of the Title II or Title XVI PCB. [Regs. §411.525(a)(2)(i and ii); §411.540.]

The total value of the Title XVI milestones is 98 percent of the total value of the Title II milestones. The SSA anticipates that this will provide an additional incentive for ENs to accept tickets from Title XVI beneficiaries. [73 *Fed. Reg.* at 29326, May 20, 2008.]

The final phase is the outcome payment period, during which beneficiaries are not receiving Social Security disability benefits or federal SSI cash benefits because of work or earnings. Up to 36 payments equal to 36% of Title II PCB may be made to the employment network to which a Title II beneficiary assigned a ticket and up to 60 payments equal to 36% of Title XVI PCB may be made to the employment network to which an SSI beneficiary assigned a ticket. Consistent with the discussion above about milestones, the SSA is leaving the Title XVI outcome period at 60 outcome payment months in order to equalize the monetary value of the outcome payments and the total amount of all payments that potentially can be made to an employment network with respect to Title II and Title XVI beneficiaries. If the beneficiary does not achieve all the Phase 1 and Phase 2 milestones prior to the beginning of the beneficiary's outcome payment period, a "reconciliation payment," will be made equal to the total amount of unpaid Phase 1 and Phase 2 milestones that had been available at first ticket assignment. [Regs. §411.525(a)(2)(iv); §411.535(a)(3); and §411.545.]

A chart outlining key differences in the payment rules under the old and new regulations is available at the Social Security Administration's website: *https://www.ssa.gov/work/documents/Chart_of_Key_Changes_to_Ticket_to_Work_Regulations_5292008.doc.*

Who is eligible to receive a ticket?

In order to receive a ticket, a beneficiary under either Titles II or XVI must be age 18-64 and eligible for disability payments under the standard for adults, currently receiving benefits, and have a permanent impairment or a nonpermanent impairment (for which medical improvement is possible but cannot be predicted) or an impairment that is expected to improve and have undergone at least one continuing disability review. Beneficiaries not eligible for tickets are individuals who have not attained age 18 and individuals who received SSI payments prior to age 18, have now attained age 18, but who have not yet undergone a redetermination of their eligibility under the disability standard for adults. Individuals who have impairments that are expected to improve are not required to undergo a continuing disability review before participating in the program. [Reg. §411.125.]

Automatic mailings under Ticket to Work Program eliminated. Tickets are no longer sent automatically to newly eligible beneficiaries, regardless of the likelihood that the beneficiary will ever use the Ticket. The SSA *may* send a ticket to an eligible beneficiary. However, Ticket-eligible beneficiaries may receive a ticket upon request.

All newly eligible and current beneficiaries will be informed of the availability of the program through routine correspondence. To request a ticket, a beneficiary may contact the Ticket Call Center at 866-968-7842. In addition to informing newly eligible beneficiaries about the Ticket to Work program in their award notices and sending annual reminders in their annual Cost-of-Living Adjustment notices, the SSA also will be calling beneficiaries who are the most likely to return to work to tell them about the program. [Reg. §411.130, 78 *Fed Reg.* 45452, July 29, 2013.]

Before a ticket may be assigned, under Reg. §411.140 a beneficiary and employment network must agree to and sign an individual work plan or, in the case of a state vocational rehabilitation agency, an individualized plan for employment. A copy of the signed document must be submitted to and received by the program manager. [Reg. §411.150.] A beneficiary may take back a ticket after it has been assigned to an employment network or state agency [Reg. §411.145] and he or she may reassign it to another network or agency [Reg. §411.150]. If a beneficiary wishes to reassign the ticket to another network or agency, it must be done within 90 days after the ticket has been taken out of assignment. Otherwise, the beneficiary must re-satisfy all the requirements for issuance of a ticket. [Reg. §411.150(b)(3).]

When are continuing disability reviews suspended for program participants? When does a ticket terminate?

During any period in which a beneficiary is using a ticket under the Ticket to Work program, the Social Security Administration may not initiate a continuing disability review. [Soc. Sec. Act §1148(i).] The period of using a ticket begins when it is first assigned to an employment network or state vocational rehabilitation agency. [Regs. §§411.170.] The period of using a ticket ends when a beneficiary's eligibility for participation terminates or when the beneficiary is no longer making any progress towards self-support as described in the sections below. The ticket will also terminate as follows:

(1) the month after month in which an outcome payment period ends (for Title II beneficiaries: the 36th month, consecutive or otherwise, for which disability benefits are not payable because of substantial gainful activity or earnings from work activity; for Title XVI beneficiaries, the 60th month, consecutive or otherwise, for which SSI benefits are not payable because of earnings from work activity [Reg. §411.500(b)];

(2) the last day of the 90-day extension period, if the beneficiary has not reassigned the ticket within that period; and

(3) if the ticket was in cost reimbursement status, the 90th day following the

day the state vocational rehabilitation agency closes the case, unless the beneficiary assigns the ticket during the 90-day period.

[Reg. §411.155; Reg. §411.171.]

An individual may decide to place a ticket in inactive status if the individual is unable to participate in an employment plan for a significant period of time for any reason. However, since the ticket is not in use during this period, the beneficiary is subject to a continuing disability review should one become due. The months in which a ticket is in inactive status do not count toward the time limitations for making timely progress toward self-support. [Reg. §411.192.] If a beneficiary fails to make timely progress towards self-supporting employment, the program manager will find that the beneficiary is no longer using a ticket. The beneficiary may continue to participate in the Ticket to Work program but will be subject to a continuing disability review until he or she re-enters in-use status. [Reg. §411.210.]

How does a beneficiary make timely progress toward self-support?

A beneficiary using a ticket demonstrates timely progress towards self-supporting employment by engaging in increasing levels of employment over a six-year period as shown in the chart below. A beneficiary can also make timely progress through a combination of work and academic achievement if the combined proportional efforts relative to the annual requirement for each totals 100%. [Reg. §411.180(a).] In addition, the SSA has added a definition of "variance tolerance" in Reg. §411.166(h). Under the variance tolerance, the SSA will consider a beneficiary to have met the requirement for completing a specified amount of post-secondary credit hours in an educational degree or certification program or course requirements in a vocational or technical training program under Reg. §411.180 in the applicable progress certification period if the beneficiary's completion of credit hours or course requirements in that period is within 10 percent of the specified goal.

How Timely Progress Toward Self-Support Is Achieved

	Work	Academics
First 12 months	Three months of work with earnings in each month at or above the threshold amount for a trial work month ($910 in 2020)	One of the following: • Acquisition of high school diploma or GED certificate • Enrollment in 2 or 4-year degree or certification program and completion of 60% of credit hours required for a year of full-time study • Enrollment in a vocational or technical training program and completion of 60% of the course requirements that represent a year of full-time study

	Work	Academics
Second 12 months	Six months of work with earnings in each month at or above the threshold amount for a trial work month ($910 in 2020)	One of the following: • Enrollment in 2 or 4-year degree or certification program and completion of an additional 75% of credit hours required for a year of full-time study • Enrollment in a vocational or technical training program and completion of 75% of the course requirements that represent a year of full-time study
Third 12 months	Nine months of work with earnings in each month above the threshold amount for substantial gainful employment ($1,260 in 2020)	One of the following: • Completion of the course work and award of a degree or certificate from a 2-year degree or certification program • Enrollment in a 4-year degree or certification program and completion of additional credit hours required for a year of full-time study • Enrollment in a vocational or technical training program and completion of the course requirements by the end of the 12-month period
Fourth 12 months	Nine months of work with earnings in each month above the threshold amount for substantial gainful employment ($1,260 in 2020)	One of the following: • Enrollment in a 4-year degree or certification program and completion of additional credit hours required for a year of full-time study • Enrollment in a vocational or technical training program and completion of the course requirements by the end of the 12-month period
Fifth 12 months	Six months of work with earnings in each month that preclude payment of Title II disability payments or Title XVI benefits	Enrollment in a 4-year degree or certification program and • Completion of additional credit hours required for a year of full-time study, or • Completion of the course and award of a degree or certificate
Sixth 12 months	Six months of work with earnings in each month that preclude payment of Title II disability payments or Title XVI benefits	Completion of the course work and award of a degree or certificate from a 4-year degree or certification program
Seventh and subsequent 12-month periods	Six months of work with earnings in each month that preclude payment of Title II disability payments or Title XVI benefits	

[Reg. §411.180.]

When does a beneficiary's eligibility for participation terminate?

A ticket terminates the month in which entitlement to disability benefits ends for reasons other than the individual's work activity or earnings, the month in which a disabled widow(er) beneficiary attains full retirement age, or the month following the month in which a disabled or blind SSI beneficiary reaches age 65 and qualifies for SSI based on age. [Reg. §411.155.]

¶520.6

If a beneficiary's eligibility for disability benefits terminates on account of work or earnings then a ticket will terminate in any of the following months:

(1) the month the SSA makes a final determination or decision that an individual is not entitled to have Title II benefits based on disability reinstated within 60 months following termination of benefits on account of having performed substantial gainful activity;

(2) the month in which the SSA makes a final determination or decision that an individual is not entitled to Title II benefits based on disability or eligible for Title XVI benefits based on disability or blindness based on the filing of an application for benefits;

(3) the month in which a beneficiary reaches full retirement age;

(4) the month in which the beneficiary dies;

(5) the month in which a beneficiary becomes entitled to a Title II benefit that is not based on disability or eligible for a Title XVI benefit that is not based on disability or blindness; and

(6) the month in which the beneficiary again becomes entitled to Title II benefits based on disability, or eligible for Title XVI benefits based on disability or blindness, based on filing a new application.

[Reg. §411.155.]

Additional provisions of the regulations—

The rules also describe the use of one or more program managers to assist in administration of the program (Subpart D), the selection, responsibilities, evaluation and termination of employment networks (Subpart E), the participation of state vocational rehabilitation agencies (Subpart F), the requirements for individual work plans (Subpart G), procedures for the resolution of disputes that arise under the Ticket to Work program (Subpart I), and how implementation of the Ticket to Work Program affects the current alternate participant payment programs (Subpart J).

Participation and program operation—

The Ticket to Work program is available in all 50 states, the District of Columbia, as well as in American Samoa, Guam, the Northern Mariana Islands, Puerto Rico and the Virgin Islands.

Other laws designed to remove several disincentives for returning to work include the following:

(1) A continuing disability review (CDR) is no longer triggered by a return to work. CDR's for beneficiaries receiving benefits for at least 24 months are limited to periodic CDRs. This provision was effective starting in 2002. [Soc. Sec. Act §221(m) as enacted by P.L. 106-170, §111.]

¶520.6

(2) Individuals whose prior entitlement to disability and health care benefits have been terminated as a result of earnings from work activity, but who have become unable to continue working due to the medical condition for which benefits were originally awarded, may request reinstatement within 60 months of termination without filing a new application (see below).

Expedited Reinstatement

The expedited benefit reinstatement provisions relax the standard for benefit reinstatement for individuals whose prior entitlement to disability and health care benefits had been terminated as a result of earnings from work activity, but who must stop working because of their medical condition, by allowing them to have their benefits reinstated within 60 months of the prior benefit termination without having to submit a new application. The provisions also provide for provisional benefits while the claim for reinstatement is being determined. Reinstatement of previously awarded benefits is predicated upon a determination of disability based on the medical improvement review standard. The advantage of using this standard is that it places the burden on the SSA to prove that a beneficiary's impairment has so improved that the beneficiary is able to work as opposed to a claimant's burden of proving his or her inability to engage in any substantial gainful activity for at least 12 months on account of a disability. When reinstatement is requested, a claimant may be paid up to six months of provisional benefits and may be entitled to Medicare or Medicaid. If the request for reinstatement is denied, the SSA will generally not consider the provisional payments received to be an overpayment unless the individual knew or should have known that the requirements for reinstatement would not be met. [Soc. Sec. Act §223(i) as enacted by P.L. 106-170, §112.]

Expedited reinstatement is available to anyone; (1) who was previously entitled to disability benefits on their own earnings record or to benefits as a disabled widow or child (or who was entitled to Medicare based on disability and Medicare-qualified government employment) and (2) whose disability entitlement was terminated because of the performance of substantial gainful activity but, in the month a request for reinstatement is filed, is not able to perform substantial gainful activity on account of the medical condition that was the basis for the prior determination of disability. The individual must also be disabled under the medical improvement review standard, which places the burden of proof on the SSA. [Reg. §404.1592c(a) and 416.999a(a).]

Expedited reinstatement is also available to anyone who was previously entitled to spousal, divorced spousal, child's or parent's benefits on the account of an insured person who is or has been reinstated, and was entitled to benefits when the insured person's entitlement was terminated. To be reinstated, the previously entitled beneficiary must continue to meet the requirements for the previously received benefit. [Reg. §404.1592c(b) and 416.999a(b).]

Requests for reinstatement must be in writing and must be received within the 60-month period that begins with the month in which entitlement was terminated due to doing substantial gainful activity. The 60-month period may be extended if good cause can be established for failing to file within the 60-month period. [Regs. §404.1592d and §416.999b(d).]

Prior to April 17, 2017, entitlement to provisional benefits began with the month in which the request for provisional benefits is filed (Title II) or in the month after reinstatement is requested (Title XVI). After April 17, 2017, entitlement to provisional benefits begins with the month a request for reinstatement is filed if the individual does not perform substantial gainful activity in that month (Title II and Title XVI). The amount payable will be based on the monthly insurance benefit that was actually payable to the beneficiary at the time the prior entitlement had been terminated (Title II) or based on normal computational methods for an individual receiving SSI benefits with the same amounts and kind of income [Regs. §404.1592e(a) and §416.999c(a)]. Previous existing overpayments will not be recovered from provisional benefits [Regs. §404.1592e(g) and §416.999c(g)]. A determination regarding the right to receive provisional benefits will not be considered an initial determination and will therefore not be subject to administrative review [Regs. §404.903 and §416.1403].

Reinstated monthly benefits under Titles II or XVI will be paid under normal payment provisions of these titles; however, reinstated benefits for any given month will be offset by the amount of any provisional benefit already paid for that month [Regs. §404.1592f(c)(1) and §416.999d(b)]. Reinstated benefits are paid within a 24-month "initial reinstatement period" during which benefits may be terminated if the beneficiary engages in substantial gainful activity [Regs. §404.1592f(d) and §416.999d(c)]; and reinstated benefits end with the earliest month that precedes the third month following the month in which disability ceases, the month before eligibility is terminated for another reason or the month in which the beneficiary dies [Regs. §404.1592f(f) and §416.999d(d)].

Continuation of Medicare Coverage

Medicare protection is extended to disabled persons entitled to monthly benefits under the Social Security or railroad retirement programs. Those covered include disabled workers under age 65; disabled widows and widowers between the ages of 50 and 65; women age 50 or older entitled to mother's benefits who, for 24 months prior to the first month they would have been entitled to Medicare protection, met all the requirements for disabled widow's benefits except for the actual filing of a disability claim; people age 18 and over who receive Social Security benefits because they became disabled before reaching age 22; and disabled qualified railroad retirement annuitants. [Soc. Sec. Act §226(b); 42 CFR Reg. §406.12.] Disability beneficiaries who are not 65, and who are not entitled to benefits solely because of having earnings in excess of the amount permitted, may purchase Part A coverage under the voluntary enrollment provisions of the law. [Soc. Sec. Act §1818A; 42 CFR Reg. §406.20(c).]

¶520.7   Suspension or Termination of Benefits—Benefit Continuation—Subsequent Entitlement

Disability benefits may be terminated on grounds of cessation of disability only if substantial evidence demonstrates that there has been medical improvement in the individual's impairment or combination of impairments and the beneficiary is able to engage in substantial gainful activity or if one or more of the following is established: (1) new medical evidence and a new assessment of the beneficiary's condition demonstrate that he or she has benefited from advances in medical or vocational therapy or technology or has undergone successful vocational rehabilitation; or (2) new or improved diagnostic techniques indicate that the beneficiary's impairment is not as disabling as previously determined and that, therefore, the individual is able to engage in substantial gainful activity; or (3) substantial evidence reveals that a prior determination was in error. Termination would continue to be appropriate where the initial decision was clearly erroneous or was procured by fraud, or where the beneficiary is actually engaged in substantial gainful activity or refuses without good cause to follow prescribed treatment that would remedy the disabling condition. [Soc. Sec. Act §§216(i)(2)(D), 223(f).]

The Commissioner may also, on the basis of information obtained by or submitted to him, suspend the payment of benefits to an individual entitled to benefits who the Commissioner believes may have ceased to be under a disability. The individual's benefits will be suspended until the Commissioner can determine whether or not the individual's disability has ceased. [Soc. Sec. Act §225.] Under the continuing disability review

(CDR) program, disability benefits cannot be terminated until the SSA has notified the beneficiary, applied the proper standard of review, and allowed the beneficiary to provide medical evidence and other evidence for consideration during the review process (see further at ¶520.4). Disability beneficiaries may elect to have their disability and Medicare benefits continued through the hearing stage of an appeal in medical cessation cases. [Soc. Sec. Act §223(g).]

Note that disability benefits continue, even after medical recovery, if the individual is participating in a Ticket to Work Program under Soc. Sec. Act 1148 or, attending an approved state vocational rehabilitation plan or program and if the Commissioner of Social Security determines that continuing in the plan or program will increase the probability that the individual will go off the rolls permanently. Benefits may likewise be continued on the basis of participation in a private vocational rehabilitation program approved by the Commissioner and determined by the Commissioner to increase the likelihood that the individual will return to permanent work. [Soc. Sec. Act §225(b) and §1631(a)(6); Regs. §404.316(c) (1), §404.337(c)(1), §404.352(d)(1), §404.902(s), §404.1586(g)(1), §404.1596(c)(4), §404.1597(a), §416.1320(d)(1), §416.1331(a) and (b), §416.1338(a), and 416.1402(j).]

Students age 18 and over: Benefits may be continued for students, beginning at age 18, who are receiving services under Individualized Educational Programs when their disabilities cease as a result of continuing disability reviews or age 18 redeterminations. This is designed to encourage young people with disabilities to stay in school and complete their educational and vocational training. Benefits under this basis will continue through age 21. [Regs. §404.328(b) and §416.1338(e)(2).]

Benefit continuation for the blind: An individual whose eligibility for SSI benefits is based on blindness and whose blindness ends due to medical recovery while he or she is participating in a program of vocational rehabilitation services, employment services, or other support services may be eligible for continued benefits under §1631(a)(6) of the Act. [Regs. §416.1320(d), §416.1331(a) and (b), §416.1338(a), (b), and (e), and §416.1402(j).]

Beneficiaries for whom alcoholism or drug addiction was a contributing factor material to a determination of their disability prior to March 29, 1996, had their benefits terminated as of January 1997 under a provision of the Senior Citizens' Right to Work Act of 1996 [Title I of P.L. 104-121, §105(a) (4) and (5), repealing Soc. Sec. Act §225(c).]

Disability benefits may not be paid to a disabled inmate convicted of a criminal offense; however, the payment ban does not apply to beneficiaries entitled on the confined wage earner's account. Until recently, the payment suspension applied to crimes punishable by more than one year in prison. However, now benefits are suspended for any month during which an individual is confined because of a crime or a finding of not guilty by reason of insanity, so long as the period of confinement is for at least 30 days. [Soc. Sec. Act §202(x), as amended by P.L. 106-170, §402.]

Regarding events causing a loss of benefits, see ¶550 *et seq.*

Appeals of disability cessation determinations. When reviewing a medical disability cessation determination or decision, the SSA must consider whether the beneficiary was disabled at *any time* through the date of the adjudicator's final determination or decision. Thus, the SSA may not restrict the review to a determination of whether the individual's disability had ceased at the time of the initial cessation of determination. [*Difford v. Secretary of Health and Human Services*, 910 F 2d (Sixth Cir. 1990); SSR 13-3p, 78 *Fed. Reg.* 12130, Feb. 2, 2013.]

In the event a beneficiary's disability has medically ceased, the determination or decision must specifically address the initial cessation determination and the beneficiary's eligibility (or ineligibility) for a new period of disability, through the date on which the appeals determination or decision is being made, or, if earlier, through the date last insured.

Subsequent Entitlement to Benefits

When a worker who stops receiving disability benefits later becomes eligible to receive retirement or disability benefits, or has died, the primary insurance amount of the subsequent entitlement cannot be less than the primary insurance amount that was in effect in the last month of the insured individual's prior entitlement to disability benefits, increased under certain circumstances by any cost-of-living or general benefit increase since that time. This guarantee is also applicable to the maximum family benefit amount. [Reg. §§404.250–404.252, 404.403.]

¶520.8   Payment of Reduced Disability Benefits After Other Entitlement

If an individual becomes entitled to a disability insurance benefit after having been entitled to a reduced old-age insurance benefit, the disability insurance benefit is reduced by the amount by which the old-age insurance would have been reduced if the worker had reached full retirement age in the month in which he or she most recently became entitled to the disability insurance benefit. (See ¶535.1 for the reduction formula used.) [Soc. Sec. Act §202(q)(2).]

For example, if a person for whom full retirement is at age 65 became entitled at age 62 to a reduced old-age benefit of $80 (based on a primary insurance amount of $100) and then became entitled at age 63 to a disability insurance benefit of $100, the disability insurance benefit would be reduced by $6.60, the amount by which the old-age insurance benefit would have been reduced if the person had reached age 65 at the time when he or she became disabled. The effect of this provision is to reduce the disability insurance benefit to take account of the number of months for which the person actually got a reduced old-age insurance benefit before becoming disabled.

This rule is not absolute, however. In cases where an individual receives an early retirement benefit, but has already filed or will subsequently file a claim for disability benefits that results in an award of disability benefits that is retroactive to a date that is at or prior to the date of entitlement to retirement benefits, there will be no reduction of the disability benefit. This is because benefits are not subject to reduction for any month in which an individual is entitled to disability benefits. [Reg. §404.412(a)(6).]

¶520.9   Reduction of Disability Benefits on Account of Other Federal, State, and Local Disability Programs

The Social Security Act provides for the reduction, but not below zero, of Social Security disability benefits payable to individuals who are also receiving worker's compensation benefits under a state or federal program, if the total benefits payable to the worker or the worker's family exceed 80% of his or her prior average current earnings. An offset is imposed for other disability benefits provided by federal, state, and local governments, with the exception of needs-tested benefits, Veterans Administration disability benefits, benefits based on public employment covered by Social Security, and private insurance benefits. This rule is designed to eliminate duplicate benefits that overcompensate some disabled workers, thereby discouraging them from attempting to return to work. The offset applies to Social Security disability benefits paid to workers who have not attained full retirement age, and their families. The offset is made beginning with the first month in which concurrent receipt of disability insurance benefits and any other public disability benefit begins, rather than the month after the SSA is notified. [Soc. Sec. Act §224(a).] As discussed below at ¶559, amounts of Supplemental Security Income paid during the period that an individual is also entitled to retroactive OASDI benefits are offset against such retroactive OASDI benefits. SSI overpayments may also be recovered from current OASDI beneficiaries.

The reduction is made in the Social Security disability benefit (except where the alternate law or plan described above provides for an offset against Social Security disability benefits) in the event the total benefits paid under the two programs exceed 80% of the worker's average current earnings prior to the onset of disability. The worker's "average current earnings" are defined as the highest of (a) the "average monthly wage" as that term was used for purposes of computing Social Security benefits before 1979, (b) one-sixtieth of the total of the individual's wages and earnings from self-employment, computed without regard to the dollar limitations on "wages" for Social Security taxing and benefits purposes, during the five consecutive calendar years after 1950 for which the individual's wages and self-employment income were highest, or (c) one-twelfth of the total of the individual's wages and earnings from self-employment received during the individual's best year in the period consisting of the calendar year in which the disability began and the five years immediately preceding that year. In no event, however, are the total benefits payable with respect to a worker reduced below the amount of the unreduced monthly Social Security benefits. [Soc. Sec. Act §224(a); Reg. §404.408.]

The reduction is in the amount that the sum of the total of disability and dependents' benefits and other disability benefits provided and actually paid by federal, state, and local governments during the month exceeds the higher of 80% of the individual's "average current earnings" or the total of the disability insurance benefits for such month and of any monthly dependents' insurance benefits for the month based on the worker's wages and self-employment income, prior to reduction under these provisions. In no case may the reduction for any month after the first month for which this reduction is required reduce the total of disability and dependents' benefits to an amount that is less than the sum of the total of (a) disability and dependents' benefits after reduction under these provisions for the first month and (b) any increases in the benefits payable under this title effective after such first month with respect to the benefits payable to the disabled worker and the persons entitled to benefits on his or her wages and self-employment income in the month the subsequent reduction is made. [Soc. Sec. Act §224(a).]

Where a periodic federal, state, or local disability benefit is payable on other than a monthly basis (excluding a benefit payable as a lump sum except to the extent that it is a commutation of, or a substitute for, periodic benefits), the reduction is made at such times and in such amounts as the Commissioner determines will approximate as nearly as practicable the reduction discussed above. Since some workers incur medical, legal, or related expenses in connection with their workers' compensation claims, or in connection with the injuries they have suffered, and since the worker's compensation awards are generally understood to include compensation for these expenses (except to the extent that special provision is made in the award to cover them or they are provided without cost to the worker), the Commissioner would not, in computing the amount of the period benefit payable under a worker's compensation or other program, include any part of the lump sum or benefit that is equal to the amount of such expenses paid or incurred by the worker. [Soc. Sec. Act §224(b).]

Reduction of benefits under these provisions is made after reduction for the family maximum, but before deductions for failure to meet the retirement test (see ¶551) or the failure of a widow(er) or surviving divorced spouse to have a child in care (see ¶558), and before imposition of penalties for failure to report certain events to the Commissioner (see ¶552). This requirement is intended to assure consistency between the provisions for a reduction on account of receipt of federal, state, or local disability benefits and the provisions of the present law governing adjustments, actuarial reductions, and deductions (such as deductions on account of earnings), which are generally applied cumulatively. [Soc. Sec. Act §224(c).]

The Commissioner may require an individual entitled to Social Security disability benefits, and who also may be eligible for periodic federal, state, or local disability benefits, to certify whether he or she has or intends to file a claim for federal, state, or local disability benefits and, if so, whether there has been a decision on the claim. The Commissioner may rely upon the individual's statement that he or she has not filed and does not intend to file such a claim, or that a claim has been filed and no final decision thereon has been made, in certifying benefits for payment. [Soc. Sec. Act §224(e).]

In the second calendar year after the year in which reduction of a disabled worker's Social Security benefit (and those of any dependents) was first required, and in each third year thereafter, the Commissioner redetermines the amount of the benefits still subject to reduction; but the redetermination may not result in any decrease in the total amount of Social Security benefits payable on the basis of the individual's wages and self-employment income. The redetermination is made as of, and is effective with, the January following the year it was made. [Soc. Sec. Act §224(f)(1).]

In making this redetermination, the individual's "average current earnings" (as defined above) have been deemed to be the product of: (a) his or her "average current earnings" as initially determined (see above) and (b) the ratio of (i) the national average wage index (see ¶510) for the calendar year before the year in which such redetermination is made to (ii) the national average wage index for the calendar year before the year in which the reduction was first computed (but not counting any reduction made in benefits for a previous period of disability. Any amount so determined which is not a multiple of $1 is reduced to the next lower multiple of $1. [Soc. Sec. Act §224(f)(2).]

Whenever a reduction is made under this section in the total benefits based on an individual's wages and self-employment income, each benefit, except the disability benefit, is first proportionately decreased, and any excess of the reduction that is required for the month over the sum of all such benefits other than the disability benefits is then applied to such disability insurance benefit. [Soc. Sec. Act §224(g).]

FAMILY BENEFITS

¶521   In General—Simultaneous Entitlement to Benefits

In addition to providing monthly benefits for the retired or disabled worker, the old-age, survivors, and disability insurance system provides for the payment of monthly benefits to certain dependents of the retired or disabled worker, or to survivors in the event of death. Except in the case of some very elderly workers, monthly payments to members of a worker's family are equal to a certain part of the worker's primary insurance amount. [Soc. Sec. Act §202.]

A person may be entitled to more than one Social Security benefit at the same time. For example, a woman can be entitled to parent's benefits on her deceased child's Social Security account and wife's benefits on her husband's account. Generally, only the one with the highest benefit rate is payable (exceptions are discussed below). [Soc. Sec. Act §202(k)(2)(B).] In addition, the amount of benefits that may be paid to an individual on the basis of a single earnings record is limited (see discussion of "Maximum Family Benefits" at ¶538).

Note that the benefit with the lower rate (other than an old-age, disability insurance, or child's insurance benefit; see below) cannot be paid even if the one with the higher rate is *suspended* and therefore not payable for one or more months. However, if the benefit with the higher rate is *terminated*, the benefit with the lower rate will be automatically reinstated if the person is still entitled to that benefit. For example, assume that Alice is entitled to a wife's benefit of $102.10 and a parent's benefit of $94.40. Her wife's benefit is lost for several months because of her husband's excess earnings under the retirement test (see ¶551). Alice cannot be paid a parent's benefit for these months. However, if she divorces her husband and she does not meet the conditions of entitlement as a divorced spouse, her wife's benefits may be terminated. If she is still entitled to parent's benefits, these will be paid effective with the month her wife's benefits terminate. [*Soc. Sec. Handbook,* September 22, 2003, §733.]

A person who is entitled to both an old-age or a disability insurance benefit and a wife's or husband's benefit may not get both benefits in full. Individuals always receive the old-age insurance benefit they earn for themselves. In the event that benefit is higher than the benefit an individual is potentially eligible for as a wife or husband, the latter benefit is not payable. If the worker's old-age benefit is less than the wife's or husband's benefit payable on the spouse's earnings, the difference between the two benefits is paid as the wife's or husband's benefit. [Soc. Sec. Act §202(k)(3)(A).]

If a person is entitled to old-age or disability insurance benefits and to another higher benefit, he or she will receive the old-age or disability insurance benefit, plus the difference between this benefit and the higher one. Payment, however, may be made in a single benefit check. If one benefit is not payable for one or more months, the other benefit may be payable. For example, assume that Mary is entitled to old-age benefits of $130.50 and to wife's benefits of $142.10. The total benefit payable to her is $142.10, made up of an old-age insurance benefit of $130.50 and a wife's benefit of $11.60. If the wife's benefit is not payable for some months because of her husband's excess earnings under the retirement test (see ¶551), she will receive her own old-age benefit of $130.50. [Soc. Sec. Act §202(k)(3)(A).]

Note that while a person entitled to both old-age and disability benefits for any month is entitled to the larger of the benefits, the individual may elect the smaller benefit. [Soc. Sec. Act §202(k)(4).] This rule applies to the payment of disability benefits after entitlement to other monthly insurance benefits (see ¶520.7).

The following chart, summarizing the material in ¶522–¶528, shows how much of an insured wage earner's primary insurance amount (PIA) is payable as a benefit for each type of family benefit available under the Social Security Act. Note that this chart does not take into account any actuarial reduction unless otherwise indicated.

Amount of benefits payable based on family relationship

Type of Benefit	Percentage of Wage Earner's PIA Payable as a Benefit	Discussion
Husband's or Wife's Benefits	50%	¶522
Divorced Spouse	50%	¶522.5
Child's Insurance Benefits (living wage earner)	50%	¶524
Child's Insurance Benefits (deceased wage earner)	75%	¶524
Widow(er)'s Benefits	100%	¶525
Widow(er)'s Benefits for Surviving Divorced Spouse	100%	¶525.1
Widow(er)'s Benefits for Disabled Surviving Spouses and Disabled Surviving Divorced Spouses	71.5%	¶525.2
Mother's or Father's Benefits	75%	¶527
Mother's or Father's Benefits for a Surviving Divorced Spouse	75%	¶527.1
Parent's Benefits	82.5%	¶528
Parent's Benefits (where more than 1 parent is entitled to a benefit)	75%	¶528

* The amount is less if the decedent received reduced old-age benefits prior to death.

¶522   Husband's or Wife's Benefits

The husband or wife of an individual entitled to old-age or disability benefits may be entitled to a spouse's benefit if he or she (1) has filed an application; (2) either has attained age 62 or, in the case of a wife, has in her care at the time of filing a child entitled to child's benefits on the Social Security account of such individual or, in the case of a husband, has in his care at the time of filing a child entitled to child's benefits on the Social Security account of such individual (the special "in care" requirements are described at ¶558); and (3) is not entitled to benefits on his or her own account or to benefits based on a primary insurance amount that is less than half of the primary insurance amount of the insured spouse on whose account the benefits are claimed. [Soc. Sec. Act §202(b)(1), (c)(1); as amended by the Social Security Benefit Protection and Opportunity Enhancement Act of 2015, H.R. 1314, November 2, 2015.] See, below, for a discussion on "deeming filing."

Marital status is generally determined for Social Security purposes by the law of the state in which the insured party is living at the time of the application for benefits. Martial status, including the treatment of same sex spouses and common law spouses is discussed at ¶529.

Spouse defined. An applicant is deemed to be the spouse of an insured individual if (1) the applicant is the mother or father of the insured's child, or (2) he or she was married to the insured for at least one year preceding the day on which the application for benefits was filed, or (3) in the month before the month in which the applicant married the insured, the applicant was actually or potentially entitled (had the age and application requirements been met) to benefits as a spouse, surviving spouse, parent, or disabled child under the Social Security Act, or to benefits as a surviving spouse, parent, or child (age 18 or older) under the Railroad Retirement Act. [Soc. Sec. Act §216(b), (f).] As to whether an applicant is the spouse of an insured individual, see ¶529.

Amount of benefit. The full monthly benefit payable at retirement age to the husband or wife of an insured individual is equal to one half of the primary insurance amount of the insured spouse (absent delayed retirement credits earned by working past normal retirement age). Benefits paid to the spouse do not decrease the worker's benefits. [Soc. Sec. Act §202(b)(2), (c)(2).] However, remember that because benefits are based on an individual's own earnings first, a comparison of the respective monthly benefits based on the individual earnings of the spouses must be made (see ¶521).

Restricted applications. Under the formerly applicable "deemed filing" rules, individuals claiming benefits at age 62 were deemed to have applied for both spousal benefits and individual retirement benefits (Soc. Sec. Act Sec. 202(a), prior to amendment). The law, however, effectively allowed individuals eligible for both a spousal benefit and a retirement benefit based on their own work record to elect, when they attained full retirement age, to receive only the spousal benefit. Individuals electing such a "restricted application" strategy would ensure that their own retirement benefit grew (at 8% a year) until age 70, while relying on the spousal benefit.

The Social Security Benefit Protection and Opportunity Enhancement Act of 2015 foreclosed such restricted applications by extending the deemed filing rules to cover all benefits (i.e., not just early retirement benefits). Accordingly, an individual, regardless of age, will be deemed to have filed a claim for both spousal and individual retirement benefits. The individual would then receive the larger of the two benefits. [SSA 202(r)(1), as amended by H.R. 1314, November 2, 2015.]

Significantly, the modified deemed filing rules apply only to individuals who attain age 62 (and not full retirement age) in a calendar year after 2015. Restricted applications, thus, may continue to be filed by individuals born prior to 1954. [Soc. Sec. Act. §202(r), as amended by the Social Security Benefit Protection and Opportunity Enhancement Act of 2015, H. 13114, November 2, 2015.]

File and suspend. Married couples had also been able, under prior law, to pursue a "file and suspend" strategy that effectively enabled a higher earning employee to defer benefits while allowing his or her spouse access to one-half of the high earner's benefits. For example, if a spouse was at full retirement age, he or she could apply for retirement benefits and then request to have payments suspended. That way, the individual could receive spousal benefits (50% of a spouse's full benefit (excluding delayed retirement credit)) and the spouse could continue to earn delayed retirement credits until age 70. If the individual had reached full retirement age, and was eligible for a spouse's or ex-spouse's benefit and his or her own retirement benefit, the individual could choose to receive only spouse's benefits. If the individual did pursue this strategy, he or she could delay receiving his or her own retirement benefit until a later date to take advantage of delayed retirement credits to increase his or her own retirement benefit.

The file and suspend strategy not only enabled an individual to take advantage of the delayed retirement credit, but further enhanced his or her retirement savings by enabling the individual to maintain contributions to a 401(k) or other employer-sponsored retirement account.

The Social Security Benefit Protection and Opportunity Enhancement Act of 2015 eliminated the file and suspend strategy, stating that, if an individual requests a suspension of benefits: no retroactive benefits will be payable to the individual; no monthly benefit will be payable to any other individual on the basis of the individual's wages and self-employment income; and no monthly benefit will be payable to such individual on the basis of another individual's wages and self-employment income. [Soc. Sec. Act Sec. 202(z)(3)].

Note: An individual may still elect to suspend benefits. However, the election of a benefit suspension will suspend the spousal benefit and his or her individual retirement benefit, until reelected. Moreover, if the individual suspends the benefit, he or she will prevent a spouse from receiving benefits based on his or her earnings record during the period of suspension.

The restriction on the file and suspend strategy applied on an accelerated basis, affecting requests for benefits suspension submitted beginning at least 180 days after the November 2, 2015, enactment of the Social Security Protection and Opportunity Enhancement Act. Thus, beginning in May 2016, a request for a benefits suspension would effectively block spousal and retirement benefits.

Individuals who have attained full retirement age (or who will attain FRA) before the effective date of the restriction, were allowed to continue to follow an elected strategy until age 70.

Benefits subject to reduction. Unless the applicant has a minor or disabled child of the insured individual in his or her care, benefits will be subject to reduction if paid before full retirement age. Benefits likewise may be reduced if either spouse has excess earnings under the retirement test (see ¶551) or if the applicant for spouse's benefits is entitled to a public pension based on his or her own work in noncovered government employment (see ¶560). With regard to the reduction or suspension of spouse's benefits in cases where the spouse's disabled husband, wife, or child has incurred benefit losses because of a refusal to accept vocational rehabilitation services or because of the probability that the disability has ceased, see ¶520.5 and 520.6. Note that payment of a reduced spouse's benefit does not preclude eventual payment of a full widow(er)'s benefit (see ¶525).

When entitlement begins. Entitlement to husband's or wife's insurance benefits at full retirement age (see ¶518) begins with the first month in which the conditions of entitlement are met. Entitlement before full retirement age begins with the first month throughout all of which the conditions of entitlement are met. Accordingly, since any given age is *attained* on the day before the anniversary date of one's birth, a spouse is not entitled to benefits for the month of attainment of age 62 unless his or her birthday is on the second day of the month (see ¶535.1).

When do spouse's benefits end? The spouse's benefit will end in the month preceding the month in which: the recipient of the benefit dies; the worker dies; the spouse and the worker divorce; the spouse becomes entitled to retirement or disability benefits based on a PIA that is equal to or greater than 50%

of the PIA of the worker; or the spouse is under age 62 and the spouse's child is no longer in the care of the spouse [Soc. Sec. Act §202(b)(1) and (c)(1).]

However, a surviving divorced spouse of an insured worker may receive benefits if the individuals were married (or deemed married) for at least 10 years and the surviving divorced spouse was over age 62 and unmarried when the application was filed (see ¶522.5).

¶522.5 Benefits for a Divorced Spouse

The divorced husband or divorced wife of an individual entitled to old-age or disability benefits may be entitled to benefits as a divorced spouse if he or she was married to the insured for at least 10 years immediately before the divorce became final. In addition, the divorced spouse (1) must file an application, (2) must not be married, (3) must be at least 62 years old, and (4) must not be entitled to an old-age or disability benefit based on a primary insurance amount that is equal to or larger than one-half of the insured individual's primary insurance amount. [Soc. Sec. Act §§202(b)(1), (c)(1), 216(d).]

Deemed spouse. A deemed spouse (*i.e.*, one who married an insured individual in good faith without knowledge of a legal impediment to the validity of the marriage) is eligible for benefits as a divorced deemed spouse on the same basis as a divorced legal spouse (see ¶529).

Conditions for entitlement. The divorced spouse of an insured individual age 62 or over is eligible for benefits, whether or not the insured is entitled to old-age benefits. The wage earner need not have filed a claim for benefits. In addition to the usual conditions of entitlement for divorced spouses, the divorce must have been final for at least two years. The amount of benefits payable to the divorced spouse under this provision is based on the insured nonentitled individual's primary insurance amount as of the date the divorced spouse first became entitled to benefits. [Soc. Sec. Act §§202(b)(5)(A), (c)(5)(A).]

Because the law requires only that a divorced spouse be "unmarried," an applicant who divorced an insured spouse and then remarried may be entitled or reentitled on the insured former spouse's account if the subsequent marriage was terminated by death, divorce, or annulment and all other conditions of entitlement are met. [Soc. Sec. Act §§202(b)(1)(C), (c)(1)(C).] A legal spouse's entitlement ends, however, if the marriage to the insured is dissolved by an annulment, regardless of whether *ab initio* or prospective. [SSA POMS §RS 00202.010 (TN 16, 11/93).]

A distinction is made between the benefits payable to a divorced spouse, a surviving divorced spouse (¶525.1), and a surviving divorced mother or father (¶527.1). Note that the law does not provide benefits to a divorced spouse under age 62 with a child of the worker in his or her care, unless the worker is deceased.

Amount of benefits. The full monthly benefit payable to a divorced spouse, beginning at full retirement age, is equal to one-half of the primary insurance amount of the insured spouse or former spouse [Soc. Sec. Act 202(b)(2) and (c)(3).]

Reduction rules. The normal reduction rules apply with respect to the benefits of a divorced spouse (see ¶522.5). A divorced spouse's benefits are not subject to reduction on account of the insured's excess earnings (see ¶551) if the couple has been divorced for at least two years. However, this two-year waiting period is not required if the insured spouse was entitled to benefits before the divorce. Thus, for example, a spouse whose divorce took place after the couple had begun to receive retirement benefits, and whose former spouse (the insured worker) returned to work after the divorce, resulting in a suspension of the worker's benefits, would not lose benefits on which he or she had come to depend. [Soc. Sec. Act §§203(b)(2), (d)(1)(B).]

Payment of benefits to a divorced spouse does not reduce the benefits paid to any other person on the same Social Security account. Similarly, benefits payable to a divorced spouse are not reduced because some other person is being paid benefits on the same account. [Soc. Sec. Act §§203(a)(3)(C), (b)(2).]

Termination of entitlement to benefits. The entitlement of a divorced spouse (including an independently entitled divorced spouse) terminates the month before the month in which: (1) either the divorced spouse or the insured dies; (2) he or she marries someone other than the insured (except as noted below); (3) he or she becomes entitled to old age or disability benefits based on a PIA that equals or exceeds one-half of the insured's PIA; (4) the insured's disability benefits terminate and he or she does not become entitled to old age benefits (unless the divorced spouse meets the requirements for an independently entitled divorced spouse); or (5) for an independently entitled divorced spouse, the wage earner is no longer a fully insured individual or he or she marries the insured wage earner.

Effect of remarriage. Remarriage does not always result in the termination of benefits. A divorced spouse's benefit will not be terminated: (1) by marriage to an individual entitled to widow(er)'s, mother's, father's, or parent's monthly benefits; (2) by marriage to an individual entitled to childhood disability benefits, even if the insured's benefits are terminated due to the cessation of disability (see ¶525); or (3) by marriage to an individual entitled to divorced spouse's benefits. [Soc. Sec. Act §§202(b)(1), (b)(3)(B), (c)(1), (c)(4)(B).]

Separation is not divorce. "Divorce" refers to a divorce *a vinculo matrimonii*— *i.e.*, a total divorce of the husband and wife, by which the marriage tie is completely dissolved [Soc. Sec. Act §216(d)(8).] A separation is of no consequence for Social Security purposes.

A divorced spouse is considered unmarried throughout the month in which he or she becomes divorced. [Soc. Sec. Act §202(b), (c).]

¶524   Child's Benefits

Every unmarried child of an individual entitled to old-age or disability insurance benefits, or of an individual who died fully or currently insured, may be entitled to a monthly benefit equal to one-half of the individual's primary insurance amount if the individual is living, or to three-fourths of the primary insurance amount if he or she is dead. [Soc. Sec. Act §202(d)(1), (2).] The amount of the monthly benefit, however, may be reduced because of the limit on maximum family benefits (see ¶538). In addition, a child entitled to benefits on more than one individual's earnings record will generally receive only the benefit payable on the record with the highest PIA. [Soc. Sec. Act 202(d)(2); Reg. §404.3531.]

Note, a child's eligibility for benefits is determined under state intestacy law. Eligible children may include stepchildren, adopted children (see below), and posthumously conceived children (see ¶529).

Conditions of entitlement

In order to be entitled to child's benefits, an application for benefits must be filed. At the time the application is filed the child must be unmarried and under age 18, except that special rules may apply to students under age 19 (see "Child's Benefits for Students," below). Also, a child over age 18 may continue to meet the eligibility requirements if under a disability (see ¶520.1) that began before age 22. [Soc. Sec. Act §202(d)(1).]

An applicant for child's benefits on the account of an insured individual also must be able to meet certain dependency requirements. Generally, if the insured individual is living, the child must have been dependent on the insured at the time an application for child's benefits is filed; if the insured has died, the child must have been dependent on him or her at the time of death. If the insured individual had a period of disability that continued until entitlement to old-age or disability insurance benefits, or (if deceased) until the month of death, then the child can also establish dependency on the insured individual either at the beginning of the period of disability or at the time the individual became entitled to benefits. [Soc. Sec. Act §202(d)(1)(C).] See below with respect to children adopted after the adopting parent's entitlement to benefits, and as to the meaning of the word "dependent."

A child can qualify for benefits on the basis of either parent's Social Security credits (in some instances, a child can also qualify on the basis of a grandparent's wage record, as discussed below). However, a child will not be paid benefits based on the wage credits of both parents. A child who is entitled to child's benefits on the earnings record of more than one worker gets benefits based on the earnings record that will provide the highest benefit *amount*, provided that the payment does not thereby reduce the benefit of any other individual who is entitled to benefits based on that earnings record. [Soc. Sec. Act §202(k)(2)(A).]

Termination of entitlement

Entitlement to a child's benefit begins with the first month covered by the application in which all other applicable conditions are satisfied. Entitlement to child's benefits terminates with the month preceding whichever of the following first occurs [Soc. Sec. Act §202(d)(1)]:

(1) the month in which the child dies or marries (but see below regarding marriage of a childhood disability beneficiary);

(2) the month in which the child attains the age of 18 and is not under a disability (¶520.1) and does not meet the special rules applicable to full-time students during any part of such month (see below);

(3) if the child is not under a disability at the time he or she attained age 18, the earlier of (a) the first month during no part of which he or she was eligible as a full-time student, or (b) the month in which he or she reaches the age specified for termination of a student's benefits (see below), but only if he or she was not under a disability in that earlier month;

(4) if the child was under a disability at the time he or she reached age 18, or if not under a disability at such time but under a disability at or prior to the time he or she attained (or would attain) the age of 22, the termination month is the third month following the month in which disability ceases, unless the individual has engaged in trial work, in which case the termination month is the earlier of (a) the third month following the end of the period of trial work if the individual is determined to be no longer disabled, (b) the third month following the first month in which the individual engages or is able to engage in substantial gainful activity, except that the termination month will not be earlier than the first month occurring after the 36 months following the trial-work period in which the individual engages or is able to engage in substantial gainful activity, or (if later) the earlier of (c) the first month during no part of which he or she is a full-time student, or (d) the month in which the child reaches the age specified for termination of a student's benefits (see below), but only if he or she was not under a disability in that earlier month; or,

(5) in the case of benefits based on the work record of a stepparent, the month after the month of a divorce between the child's natural parent and the stepparent. [Soc. Sec. Act §202(d)(1)(H).] Benefits based on the work record of a stepparent will also terminate when there is a divorce between the stepparent and the parent of an adopted child. [Reg. §404.352(b)(7), as amended by 75 *Fed. Reg.* 52619, Aug. 27, 2010.]

If the child is entitled to benefits on the basis of the wages and self-employment income of an individual entitled to disability insurance benefits, entitlement ends with the month before the first month for which the individual is not entitled to disability benefits, unless the individual is, for the later month, entitled to old-age insurance benefits or dies in such month. [Soc. Sec. Act §202(d)(1).]

Disabled children:

"Child's" benefits may be paid to disabled persons of any age if they can meet the eligibility requirements described above. However, the law does contain the restriction that persons who meet the definition of "disability" only under the less-stringent requirements applicable to those who are age 55 or older and blind (see ¶520.1) may not receive child's benefits for any month in which they engage in substantial gainful activity. [Soc. Sec. Act §202(d)(1).] See the discussion on disability benefits for children at the end of ¶520.1.

A disabled child's benefits will not be terminated because of marriage if the disabled child marries a person entitled to old-age benefits, disability benefits, spouse's benefits, surviving spouse's benefits, mother's or father's benefits, parent's benefits, or, within the limitations discussed in the next paragraph, a person entitled to disabled child's benefits. [Soc. Sec. Act §202(d)(5).]

As noted above, a person with a childhood disability who is age 18 or over can continue to get benefits when he or she marries another beneficiary. It is also true that other kinds of beneficiaries can continue to get their benefits if they marry a person with a childhood disability. However, in order for continuation of benefits to be allowed in the event of such marriages, the "child" must, at the time of the marriage, be under a disability that began before he or she attained the prescribed age, or he or she must have been under the disability in the third month before the month in which the marriage occurred. [Soc. Sec. Act §202(s)(2), (3).]

Other special provisions apply in the case of marriage with a person entitled to benefits as a disabled child. For example, if a beneficiary receiving divorced spouse's, surviving spouse's, surviving divorced spouse's, mother's or father's, or parent's benefits marries an individual entitled to disabled child's benefits, the marriage will not terminate the beneficiary's previous entitlement to benefits, even if the spouse becomes ineligible for disabled child's or disability benefits. [Soc. Sec. Act §§202(b)(3), (c)(4), (e)(3), (f)(4), (g)(3), (h)(4).] Also, in the case of a child's insurance beneficiary's marriage to an individual entitled to disability benefits or disabled child's benefits, child's benefits will not terminate even if the spouse becomes ineligible for disabled child's or disability benefits. [Soc. Sec. Act §§202(d)(5), (s)(2).]

¶524

Reentitlement:

Reentitlement to child's insurance benefits is permitted for a person who had been entitled to child's insurance benefits on account of disability and who again becomes disabled within seven years after benefits were terminated because of medical recovery, or at any time if his or her previous entitlement to child's insurance benefits on account of disability was terminated because of the performance of substantial gainful activity. [Soc. Sec. Act §202(d)(6).]

A child whose benefits are terminated after attainment of age 18 and before attainment of age 19 may become reentitled to child's insurance benefits, on filing a new application, if he or she becomes a full-time student, as discussed below. Reentitlement ends in accordance with the regular termination provisions described above. [Soc. Sec. Act §202(d)(6).]

Child's Benefits for Students

Benefits for a nondisabled child who is a full-time elementary or secondary school student may continue until age 19. If the student has not completed school when he or she attains age 19, entitlement will end with the month in which the quarter or semester ends, unless the school does not have a quarter or semester system that requires enrollment, in which case benefits will end with the month in which the course is completed or, if earlier, the first day of the third month after attainment of age 19. [Soc. Sec. Act §202(d)(7)(D).]

Whether or not a student is in full-time attendance is determined by the Social Security Administration in light of the standards and practices of the school involved. Ordinarily, a student is in full-time attendance at an educational institution if he or she is enrolled in a non-correspondence course and carrying a subject load that is considered full time for day students under the institution's standards and practices. Specifically excluded from the definition of full-time student is a person who is paid by an employer while attending school at the request (or pursuant to a requirement) of the employer.

In the case of high schools and vocational schools (including technical, trade, business, and similar schools), a student is considered to be in "full-time attendance" if: (1) the student is enrolled for at least 20 hours of work per week; (2) the student is in a course of study which requires at least 13 school weeks; and (3) the school considers him or her a full-time student under its standards and practices. [Reg. §404.367.]

An individual will not be deemed a full-time student during any period of nonattendance if the nonattendance is due to expulsion or suspension, notwithstanding the fact that the individual intends to, or does, resume full-time attendance within four calendar months after the beginning of the period of nonattendance. [Reg. §404.368.]

An individual confined in a penal institution or correctional facility for having committed a felony is not eligible for student's benefits. [Soc. Sec. Act §202(d)(7)(A).]

A student may receive benefits for a month even though he or she attended school for only part of the month. In addition, an elementary or secondary school student is deemed to be in full-time attendance and benefits may be paid for a period of up to four months of nonattendance (for example, during a summer vacation period) if: (1) the student was in full-time attendance immediately before the period of nonattendance began; and (2) either (a) intends to return to full-time attendance immediately following the period of not more than four months, or (b) actually does return to full-time attendance in that time. [Reg. §§404.367, 404.368.]

Certification of full-time attendance by a school officer may provide the basis for payment of benefits to eligible students. Evidence required for proof of school attendance is discussed at ¶584.

"Child" Defined

The term "child" means: (1) the child or legally adopted child of an individual; (2) a stepchild who has been a stepchild for not less than one year immediately preceding the day on which application for child's benefits is filed or (if the insured individual is deceased) a stepchild who has been a stepchild for not less than nine months (except in special circumstances discussed below) immediately preceding the day on which such individual died; and (3) a person who is the grandchild or stepgrandchild of an individual or his or her spouse, but only under the circumstances described below. A child who was either living with or receiving one-half of his or her support from an insured individual who died before completing proceedings to adopt the child will be deemed to be the decedent's legally adopted child as of the date of death if the decedent's surviving spouse completed the adoption within two years. The dependency requirement was modified by a provision of the Omnibus Budget Reconciliation Act of 1990 (P.L. 101-508, §5104).

A child whose parent entered into a ceremonial marriage with an insured individual that was invalid by reason of a legal impediment of the type described at ¶529 will be treated as the stepchild of the insured individual. [Soc. Sec. Act §216(e).]

A child born out of wedlock will be deemed to be a "child" of the wage earner under the circumstances described at ¶529, below.

Nine-month relationship requirement for stepchildren. The stepchild of an insured individual is eligible for benefits if his or her natural or adopting parent married the insured party [Reg. §404.357.] The marriage must be valid under state law or be valid, but for a legal impediment (e.g., defect in procedure). As noted, in the event the insured is deceased, the claimant must have been his or her stepchild for at least nine months immediately preceding the date of death [Soc. Sec. Act §216(d)(2); Reg. §404.357.] However, the nine-month requirement need not be met if the marriage between the insured and the child's parent lasted less than nine months and the surviving parent is entitled to widow's or widower's benefits on the decedent's earnings record, or if the insured's death was accidental or occurred in the line of active military duty, unless the SSA determines that, at the time of marriage, the insured could not reasonably have expected to live for nine months [Soc. Sec. Act §216(k).]

The nine-month duration-of-relationship requirement is also waived in cases where the worker and the spouse were previously married, divorced, and then remarried; the relationship existed at the time of the worker's death; and the duration-of-relationship requirement would have been met if the worker had died on the date when he or she was divorced from the spouse. The requirement also will be deemed met if the insured had been married prior to the marriage to the surviving spouse; the prior spouse was institutionalized during the marriage to the insured due to mental incompetence or similar incapacity; the SSA determines, based on satisfactory evidence, that during this institutionalization the insured would have divorced the prior spouse and married the surviving spouse, but the divorce would have been unlawful in the state of the insured's domicile because of the institutionalization; the prior spouse remained institutionalized up until the time of his or her death; and the insured spouse married the surviving spouse within 60 days after the prior spouse's death. [Soc. Sec. Act §216(c), (g), and (k); Regs. §404.335 and §404.357.]

Note, the death of the stepparent does not end the entitlement to benefits of the child of the stepparent. However, the stepparent-stepchild relationship will end in the event the stepparent and the child's natural or adopting parent divorce, effective with the month in which the divorce becomes final [Soc. Sec. Act §202(d)(1)(H).]

Grandchildren and stepgrandchildren. The special circumstances under which an individual may be regarded as standing in the relationship of a "child," for Social Security purposes, to a grandparent or stepgrandparent are as follows: (1) the child's natural or adoptive parents were either not living or were disabled at the time the grandparent became entitled to old-age or disability insurance benefits or died, or, if the grandparent had a period of disability that continued until the grandparent became entitled to old-age or disability benefits or dies, at the time the period of disability began, or (2) the child was legally adopted after the death of the grandparent by the grandparent's surviving spouse in an adoption that was decreed in a court of competent jurisdiction within the United States and the child's natural or adopting parent or stepparent was not living in the grandparent's household and making regular contributions toward the child's support at the time the grandparent died. The grandchild of the worker-grandparent or spouse, in order to qualify for child's insurance benefits, is required to have been living with, and receiving at least half of his or her support from the worker for the year immediately before the worker became disabled, entitled to old-age or disability insurance benefits, or died. The child also must have been living with the worker-grandparent before attaining age 18. A child who was born in the one-year period during which he or she would otherwise be required to have been living with and receiving at least half of his or her support from the grandparent would be deemed to meet the requirement if the child was living with the grandparent in the United States and receiving at least half of his or her support for substantially all of the period occurring after birth. [Soc. Sec. Act §§202(d) (8), (9), 216(e).]

Adopted child: The SSA will determine an applicant's status as a legally adopted child by applying the adoption laws of the state or foreign country where the adoption took place. [Reg. §404.356.]

Dependency Status

A claimant's entitlement to child's benefits requires a showing of dependency. In the event the insured is living, the child must have been a dependent at the time the application for child's benefits was filed. If the insured is deceased, the child must have been dependent at the time of death. If the insured had a period of disability that continued until he or she became entitled to old age or disability insurance benefits, or if the insured has died, until the month of death, the child must establish that he or she was dependent on the insured, either at the beginning of the period of disability or at the time the insured became entitled to benefits [Soc. Sec. Act §202(d)(1)(c); Reg. §404.361-365.]

Deemed dependency. The evidence needed to prove dependency varies according to the claimant's relationship to the insured. Thus, a child's benefits claimant may be required to show that he or she lived with the insured at a specified time, the insured provided contributions for the child's support, or that the insured provided at least one-half of the child's support.

A child is deemed dependent upon the father or adopting father, or the mother or adopting mother, unless such individual is not living with or contributing to the support of the child and (a) the child is neither the legitimate nor adopted child of such individual, or (b) the child has been adopted by some other individual. However, there is an exception to (b): if the insured has a period of disability that lasts until the insured becomes entitled to disability or old-age benefits, or dies, a child is deemed dependent on the insured if the child is adopted by someone other than the insured after the insured's disability onset date. [Reg. §404.361.]

For the purposes of determining dependency status, a child deemed to be the child of an insured individual, even though the parent (mother or father) entered into a ceremonial marriage that was not valid because of a legal impediment of the type described at ¶529, or a child deemed to be the child of an individual even though he or she may not be a child of the individual under applicable state law (see ¶529), is also deemed to be the legitimate child of this individual. A child is deemed dependent upon his or her stepfather or stepmother if the child is receiving at least one-half of his or her support from the stepparent. [Soc. Sec. Act §202(d)(3); Reg. §404.363.] Note, however, according to one appellate court, the value of a deceased stepparent's homemaking may not be counted when determining if the stepparent provided at least one-half of the child's support. [*Reutter v. Barnhart*, 372 F.3d 946 (8th Cir. 2004).]

A child who is adopted by an old-age or disability insurance beneficiary after the latter becomes entitled to benefits is deemed not to be dependent on the beneficiary, as required under the law to be entitled to child's benefits, unless the child is the beneficiary's natural child or stepchild or unless the child was legally adopted by a beneficiary in an adoption decreed by a U.S. court of competent jurisdiction. In the case of an adopted child who had attained age 18 when the adoption proceedings began, the child must have been living with or receiving one-half of his or her support from the insured adoptive parent during the 12 months preceding the month in which the adoption was decreed. [Soc. Sec. Act §202(d)(8)(D).]

Note that if a child is entitled to benefits, the parent may qualify for benefits as a spouse, divorced spouse, mother or father, or surviving divorced spouse entitled to benefits. A child may lose all or part of the benefit for any month in which the child, or the person upon whose wage record the benefit is based, is charged with earnings in excess of those specified by the retirement test. See ¶551.

With respect to other events causing deductions or suspensions of the benefits of a (disabled) child, see ¶520.5, ¶520.6, ¶524.

¶525   Widow's or Widower's Benefits

To qualify for *full* benefits as a surviving spouse, the widow or widower (as defined below) of a worker who died fully insured must have attained full retirement age (see ¶518), must not be married (except as noted below), and must file an application for benefits. The filing of an application is not required, however, if he or she was entitled to spouse's benefits for the month preceding the month in which the worker died, or to mother's or father's benefits (¶527) for the month before the month in which he or she reached full retirement age. [Soc. Sec. Act §§202(e)(1), (f)(1).]

The full monthly benefit payable to the surviving spouse of a worker who died fully insured is generally equal to the benefit the decedent would receive if still living. The full benefit is payable to a widow or widower starting to receive benefits at full retirement age; a reduced benefit is payable if benefits begin between ages 60 and full retirement age, as discussed at ¶535.2, or, in some circumstances (see below), if the surviving spouse is receiving a government pension. [Soc. Sec. Act §§202(e)(2), (7), (f)(2), (3).]

Specifically, the widow or widower who first becomes entitled to benefits at or after full retirement age will be paid a benefit equal to 100% of the primary insurance amount of the deceased insured spouse, provided the insured did not receive reduced old-age benefits before death, in which case the surviving spouse's benefit may not exceed the amount the insured would be receiving if living, or 82½% of the insured's primary insurance amount, whichever is greater. [Soc. Sec. Act §§202(e)(2)(D), (f)(2)(D).]

The surviving spouse's benefit will be based on a specially computed primary insurance amount in the event that the insured dies before reaching age 62, but only if the special computation produces a primary insurance amount in excess of that computed under the regular provisions of the law. Instead of using the average indexed monthly earnings formula that would normally apply in the worker's eligibility year, benefits will be based on a "substitute year" formula applicable to workers who initially become eligible for old-age benefits in the second year following the earlier of (1) the year in which the deceased attained (or would have attained) age 60, or (2) the second year preceding the year in which the surviving spouse satisfies the age requirements of entitlement to widow's or widower's benefits or the second year preceding the year in which the insured worker died, whichever is later. Note that this "substitute year" will be used as the indexing year in determining the insured's average indexed monthly earnings and that cost-of-living increases in the primary insurance amount determined under these special provisions will begin with the second year after the substitute year. [Soc. Sec. Act §§202(e)(2)(B), (f)(2)(B).]

The delayed retirement credit extends to widow's and widower's benefits. Thus, the unreduced benefit for the surviving spouse of a deceased worker who was eligible for increased old-age benefits prior to his or her death will equal the deceased worker's old-age benefit increased as if he or she were still living, if (1) the worker was entitled to a benefit that was increased (or subject to increase) because of delayed retirement, and (b) the deceased worker's primary insurance amount is less than the increased benefit to which he or she was entitled in the month preceding death. [Soc. Sec. Act §§202(e)(2)(C), (f)(2)(C).]

Note that prior receipt of a reduced spouse's benefit will not cause a reduction of surviving spouse's benefits.

Duration of benefits. Widow's or widower's benefits (other than those based on disability; see ¶525.2) begin with the month in which all conditions of entitlement are met and end with the month preceding the first month in which the beneficiary (1) remarries before age 60 (but see the discussion at ¶525.3), (2) dies, (3) becomes entitled to an old-age benefit equal to or greater than the primary insurance amount of the deceased insured spouse, or (4) if entitlement began before age 60, the third month following the month of cessation of disability, unless the beneficiary attains full retirement age on or before the last day of such third month. Note that entitlement of a widow(er) who was validly married to the insured worker no longer precludes payments to a deemed widow(er) (see ¶529). [Soc. Sec. Act §§202(e)(1), (f)(1), 216(h)(1).]

Individuals are entitled to a survivor's benefit if they were married to their deceased spouse for at least 10 years (see ¶525.1). Note, the 10-year marriage requirement does not apply to individuals who were not divorced or who remained married at the time of their partner's death. Benefits for a disabled surviving spouse or disabled surviving divorced spouse are discussed at ¶525.2, below.

Remarriage often affects a surviving spouse's entitlement, as discussed at ¶525.3.

"Widow" and "Widower" Defined

The terms "widow" and "widower" have special definitions for Social Security purposes. "Widow" or "widower" means the surviving spouse of an insured individual, but only if she or he (1) is the mother or father of the insured's child, or (2) legally adopted the insured's child while they were married and while the child was under age 18, or (3) was married to the insured at the time both of them legally adopted a child under age 18, or (4) was married to the insured for not less than nine months (except in special circumstances described below) immediately prior to the day on which the insured died.

The term "widow" or "widower" also means the surviving spouse of an insured individual if (1) the insured legally adopted his or her son or daughter while they were married and while the son or daughter was under age 18, or (2) in the month before the month in which they married, he or she was actually or potentially entitled to a spouse's, surviving spouse's, parent's, or disabled child's benefit on another person's Social Security account, or (3) he or she was actually or potentially entitled to a surviving spouse's, child's (after age 18), or parent's annuity under Section 5 of the Railroad Retirement Act. [Soc. Sec. Act §216(c), (g).]

Waiver of 9-month marriage requirement. The nine-month duration-of-relationship requirement for the surviving spouse is waived in these special circumstances:

(1)   the insured's death is accidental or occurs in the line of duty as a member of a uniformed service serving on active duty unless the Commissioner determines that, at the time of the marriage involved, the insured could

not have reasonably been expected to live for nine months; "accidental death" means that the individual received bodily injuries solely through violent, external, and accidental means and, as a direct result of the bodily injuries and independently of all other causes, died not later than three months after the day on which he or she received the injuries [Soc. Sec. Act §216(k)(1); Reg. §404.335(a)(2)(i) and (ii)];

(2)   the worker and the spouse were previously married, divorced, and then remarried, where the relationship existed at the time of the worker's death, and where the requirement would have been met if the worker had died on the date of the divorce [Soc. Sec. Act §216(k)(2); Reg. §404.335(a)(2)(iii)]; or

(3)   the claimant and the deceased spouse would have been married for longer than nine months but for the fact that the deceased spouse was legally prohibited from divorcing a prior spouse who was in a mental institution, so long as the prior spouse continued to remain institutionalized up to the time of death and the individual married the surviving spouse within 60 days after the prior spouse's death [Soc. Sec. Act §216(c) and (g) as amended by the Soc. Sec. Protection Act of 2004, P.L. 108-203, §414; Reg. §404.335(a)(2)(iv)].

A widow or widower may be entitled to old-age benefits on the basis of her or his own record of covered employment, in which case these benefits will be paid instead if they equal or exceed the deceased spouse's primary insurance amount. [Soc. Sec. Act §202(e)(1), (f)(1).]

Benefits generally end with remarriage. A surviving spouse under age 60, who has in his or her care a nondisabled child who is under age 16 and entitled to child's benefits, may be entitled to a father's or mother's benefit; see ¶527. [Soc. Sec. Act §202(s)(1); Regs. §§404.348, 404.349.] A surviving spouse under full retirement age may lose all or part of his or her benefits on account of excess earnings under the retirement test (see ¶551). Note that "full retirement age" for purposes of the earnings test means the retirement age that would be applicable if the individual were receiving old-age benefits (see ¶518), regardless of the type of benefit that the individual is actually receiving. [Soc. Sec. §203(f)(9).] Benefits also may be reduced if the beneficiary is eligible to receive a public pension based on his or her own work in noncovered employment (see ¶560).

¶525.1   Widow's or Widower's Benefits for a Surviving Divorced Spouse

The divorced spouse of an individual who died fully insured may be entitled to widow's or widower's benefits as a surviving spouse if he or she is at least 60 years old or between age 50 and 60 and disabled. [Soc. Sec. Act §§202(e)(1), (f)(1).]

The full benefit payable to a surviving divorced spouse first becoming entitled at full retirement age or older is generally equal to the deceased former spouse's primary insurance amount (including a specially computed primary insurance amount (see ¶525)). If, however, the insured former spouse was at any time entitled to a reduced old-age benefit, the surviving divorced spouse's benefit will be reduced to either the benefit amount to which the insured former spouse would be entitled if still alive or 82½% of the insured's primary insurance amount, whichever is greater. [Soc. Sec. Act §§202(e)(2), (f)(3).] Benefits are subject to reduction if paid before full retirement age (*i.e.*, age 65–67, depending upon date of birth; see ¶518), as discussed at ¶535.2, or if the surviving spouse is entitled to a government pension based on his or her own work (see ¶560), or if the surviving spouse has excess earnings under the retirement test (see ¶551).

A man or woman is a "surviving divorced spouse" for Social Security purposes only if he or she was married to the deceased insured individual for a period of 10 years immediately before the effective date of the divorce. Ordinarily, an application for surviving spouse's benefits must be filed, although a separate application is not required if he or she was entitled to spouse's benefits on the insured's account for the month preceding the month in which the insured died, or if he or she was entitled to mother's or father's benefits on the insured's account for the month preceding the month of attainment of full retirement age. [Soc. Sec. Act §216(d)(2), (4).]

If a surviving divorced spouse is entitled to old-age benefits on the basis of his or her own Social Security record, his or her own benefits will be paid rather than a spouse's benefit if his or her old-age benefit equals or exceeds the deceased former spouse's primary insurance amount. [Soc. Sec. Act §§202(e)(1)(D), (f)(1)(D).]

A surviving divorced spouse's entitlement to benefits ends with the month in which he or she remarries prior to attainment of age 60 (age 50 if he or she is disabled; see ¶525.3), dies, or becomes entitled to an old-age benefit equal to or greater than the deceased former spouse's primary insurance amount, except that remarriage will not preclude continued entitlement if the remarriage is to someone entitled to benefits as a surviving spouse, parent, or disabled child over age 18. [Soc. Sec. Act §§202(e), (f), (s)(2).] Note that a divorced spouse who remarries an old-age beneficiary may become eligible for benefits on the new spouse's account (see ¶522). Remarriage at or after age 60 or, at or after age 50 by a divorced spouse who was disabled at the time of remarriage, will not preclude eligibility for benefits as a surviving divorced spouse. [Reg. §404.336(e).] See ¶525.2 and ¶525.3.

Regarding benefits for divorced spouses and surviving divorced mothers or fathers, see ¶522.5 and 527.1. Benefits for disabled and divorced disabled surviving spouses are discussed at ¶525.2.

¶525.2   Widow's and Widower's Benefits for Disabled Surviving Spouses and Disabled Surviving Divorced Spouses

The severely disabled surviving spouse or surviving divorced spouse of an insured worker may become entitled to a reduced widow's or widower's benefit after attainment of age 50. In order to qualify for this benefit, an applicant must meet the regular conditions of entitlement to benefits as a surviving spouse (see ¶525, 525.1) and, as discussed at ¶520.1, be disabled, *i.e.*, his or her physical or mental impairment(s) must be of a level of severity deemed by regulations prescribed by the Commissioner to be sufficient to preclude him or her from engaging in substantial gainful activity. In addition, the applicant must have become disabled either (1) before the death of the insured spouse, or (2) before his or her entitlement to father's or mother's benefits ceased, or (3) within seven years after either of these events, or (4) within seven years after a previous entitlement to disabled surviving spouse's benefits terminated because disability had ceased. [Soc. Sec. Act §§202(e)(1)(B)(ii), (f)(1)(B)(ii), 223(d).]

Waiting period. A waiting period must be served before benefits may begin. The waiting period is defined as the earliest five-month period, throughout which the applicant is under a disability, beginning not earlier than the later of (1) the first day of the 17th month before the month in which the application is filed, or (2) the first day of the fifth month before the month in which the requirements as to onset of disability are met. [Soc. Sec. Act §§202(e)(5), (f)(6).]

Benefits payable to currently and newly eligible disabled surviving spouses before age 60 are equal to the level payable to widows and widowers who became entitled at age 60 (*i.e.*, 71.5% of the insured's primary insurance amount). [Soc. Sec. Act §202(q)(6), (7).] Actuarial reduction of a disabled surviving spouse's benefits is discussed at ¶535.3.

Entitlement to benefits as a disabled (or disabled and divorced) widow or widower may begin with the month following the waiting period (which may be the month following the insured's death), or with the first month during all of which the applicant is disabled if he or she becomes reentitled because of a subsequent disability within a specified period (generally seven years) after termination of a previous entitlement to disabled widow's or widower's benefits. [Soc. Sec. Act §§202(e)(1)(F), (f)(1)(F).]

Entitlement ends with the month preceding the first month in which the beneficiary either (1) remarries before age 50 (see ¶525.3), (2) dies, (3) becomes entitled to an old-age benefit equal to or greater than the deceased insured worker's primary insurance amount, or (4) if the disabled surviving spouse became entitled to benefits prior to age 60, the third month following the month in which disability ceases (unless he or she reaches full retirement age on or before the last day of such third month). [Soc. Sec. Act §§202(e)(1), (f)(1).]

¶525.3   Remarriage

A claimant must be unmarried in order to satisfy the conditions of entitlement to widow(er)'s benefits, except that remarriage after attainment of age 60 will not preclude the entitlement of a widow(er) or surviving divorced spouse to benefits. In addition, remarriage after age 50 generally will not preclude entitlement to widow(er)'s benefits if the beneficiary was disabled at the time of the remarriage. [Soc. Sec. Act §§202(e)(3), (f)(4).]

The continued entitlement to widow's or widower's benefits upon remarriage may give rise to a dual entitlement combination where the individual is also eligible for wife's or husband's benefits. A determination of benefits arising from this dual entitlement is made as follows: the reduced wife's or husband's benefit is reduced, but not below zero, by an amount equal to the reduced widow(er)'s benefit. The difference, if any, between such wife's or husband's benefit and the widow's or widower's benefit is then payable as wife's or husband's benefits. [Soc. Sec. Act §202(k)(3)(B).] Note that if an individual is entitled to more than one widow's or widower's benefit, entitlement to which was not terminated as a result of marriage before the age of 60, then he or she will receive only the larger of such benefits. See, further, the general discussion of simultaneous entitlement to benefits at ¶521, and, in regard to situations where the new spouse works, ¶551.

Child's benefits. A beneficiary age 18 or older and entitled to benefits on the basis of childhood disability will not lose child's benefits if he or she marries an individual entitled to divorced child's, old age, divorced wife's, divorced husband's, widow's, widower's, divorced spouse's, mother's, father's, parent's or disability benefits.

¶527   Mother's or Father's Benefits

A mother's or father's benefit is payable to the surviving spouse of an individual who died fully or currently insured, provided the surviving spouse is not married; was married to the insured party for at least nine months before the insured died (with the exception of circumstances discussed at ¶525); is not entitled to a widow's or widower's benefit (¶525); is not entitled to old-age insurance benefits equal to or exceeding the amount of the unadjusted mother's or father's benefit after an increase in minimum sole survivor benefits; has filed an application for benefits (or was entitled to spouse's benefits on the insured's account for the month before the one in which the insured died); and at the time of filing the application, has "in care" (see ¶558) a child of the insured entitled to child's benefits, except a child getting benefits solely because he is a student— see ¶524). [Soc. Sec. Act §202(g)(1).] Note that an applicant need not be age 60, the minimum qualifying age for entitlement to widow's or widower's benefits, in order to be qualified for mother's or father's benefits.

For a discussion of entitlement to mother's or father's benefits in the case of a surviving divorced spouse, see ¶527.1, below.

Amount of benefits. A mother's or father's benefit is equal to three-fourths of the deceased worker's primary insurance amount. [Soc. Sec. Act §202(g)(2).] However, benefits may be reduced because of application of the family maximum limit (see ¶538) or the retirement earnings test (see ¶551); or because the father or mother is eligible for a government pension based on work in covered employment (see ¶560). Note, also, that if a surviving spouse is entitled to benefits based on his or her own Social Security record, these benefits will be paid if they equal or exceed the amount he or she would receive as father's or mother's benefits. [Soc. Sec. Act §202(g)(1)(C).]

Remarriage. A surviving spouse is not entitled to a mother's or father's benefit for a month in which she or he remarries or for months thereafter. However, such benefits will not be terminated by reason of remarriage if the remarriage is to someone entitled to old-age, disability, surviving spouse's, mother's or father's, parent's, or disabled child's benefits. [Soc. Sec. Act §202(g)(3).] See ¶524 regarding marriage to someone entitled to benefits as a disabled child.

Length of benefits. Entitlement to mother's or father's benefits ends with the month before the month in which the beneficiary dies, becomes entitled to widow's or widower's benefits, or does not have "in care" a child of the deceased worker entitled to child's benefits. [Soc. Sec. Act §202(g)(1).] Note that a nondisabled child age 16 or older, or a child entitled to benefits solely because he or she is a student, is deemed *not* entitled to benefits for purposes of continued entitlement of the surviving spouse to mother's or father's benefits, which means that entitlement to mother's or father's benefits would end if it depended solely on having such a child "in care." [Soc. Sec. Act §202(s)(1); Regs. §§404.348, 404.349.]

¶527.1   Mother's or Father's Benefits for a Surviving Divorced Spouse

A father's or mother's benefit, based on caring for a child of the deceased worker entitled to benefits, can be paid to the surviving divorced parent of a child of a deceased worker who died fully or currently insured, provided he or she is otherwise entitled to benefits and can meet the requirements outlined below. [Soc. Sec. Act §202(g)(1).]

A father's or mother's benefit is equal to three-fourths of the deceased worker's primary insurance amount, and can be paid to a mother or father at any age. However, if the surviving divorced parent is entitled to benefits based on his or her own Social Security record, those benefits will be paid instead if they equal or exceed the amount he or she would receive as father's or mother's benefits. [Soc. Sec. Act §202(g)(1), (2).]

In order to qualify for father's or mother's benefits, a surviving divorced spouse must have been validly married to the insured prior to divorce, not be currently married (see below), and have filed an application for benefits (unless he or she was entitled to spouse's benefits on the deceased former spouse's account for the month before the month in which he or she died). In addition, the claimant must have in his or her care at the time of filing a child of the deceased insured spouse who is entitled to child's benefits on the insured's account. Entitlement to mother's or father's benefits based on having a child of the wage earner "in care" terminates when the child attains age 16, unless the child is disabled. [Soc. Sec. Act §202(g)(1), (s)(1).]

The "child" on whom entitlement to benefits as a surviving divorced parent is based must be the insured's son, daughter, or legally adopted child. A "surviving divorced parent" is defined as a man or woman divorced from the deceased worker, but only if (a) he or she is the father or mother of the insured's child, (b) he or she, while married to the insured, legally adopted the insured's child (while the child was under age 18), or (c) the insured, while married to the parent, legally adopted his or her child (while the child was under age 18), or (d) they both, while married, legally adopted a child under age 18. [Soc. Sec. Act §§202(g)(1)(F)(i), 216(d).]

As has been indicated, payment of a father's or mother's benefit depends on the recipient having in his or her care a child (under age 16 or disabled) entitled to child's benefits. See, in this connection, ¶558. Child's benefits are discussed at ¶524. Note that a surviving divorced parent may not get father's or mother's benefits if the only child in his or her care is getting benefits solely because the child is a student. [Soc. Sec. Act §202(s)(1).]

Entitlement to father's or mother's benefits ends with the month before the month in which the beneficiary dies, remarries (except as noted below), becomes entitled to widow's or widower's benefits (see ¶525), becomes entitled to an old-age insurance benefit equal to or exceeding three-fourths of the primary insurance amount of the deceased individual, or there is no child of the deceased worker entitled to child's benefits. Entitlement also ends if no son, daughter, or legally adopted child is entitled to child's benefits on the basis of the deceased wage earner's Social Security record. [Soc. Sec. Act §202(g)(1).]

If the surviving divorced parent remarries, but the remarriage is to a person entitled to old-age, disability, widow's or widower's, parent's, or disabled child's benefits, benefits will not be terminated. [Soc. Sec. Act §202(g)(3).] See, further, ¶524 with respect to marriage to a person entitled to benefits as a disabled child.

A surviving divorced father or mother may lose all or part of his or her benefit if under full retirement age and charged with earnings in excess of those specified by the retirement test (¶551). Note that "full retirement age" for purposes of the earnings test means the retirement age that would be applicable if the individual were receiving old-age benefits (see ¶518), regardless of the type of benefit that the individual is actually receiving. [Soc. Sec. §203(f)(9).] A surviving divorced parent will not lose his or her benefit because his or her child is charged with excess earnings for failure to meet the retirement test [SSA POMS §RS 02501.095B 3 (TN 19 7/00)], but a surviving divorced parent's benefit may be reduced on account of eligibility for a government pension (see ¶560).

¶528   Parent's Benefits

A dependent parent of a son or daughter who dies fully insured is entitled to monthly benefits if such parent (1) has reached age 62, (2) was receiving one-half of his or her support from such individual, (3) filed an application for benefits, and (4) has not married since the worker's death.

Proof of support. The support requirement must be met at the time the worker died or, if the worker had a period of disability which did not end prior to death, either at the time this period began or at the time of death. Proof of support must be filed within two years after the period of disability began, or two years after the date of death, depending on the time as of which support is claimed. [Soc. Sec. Act §202(h)(1).]

Amount of benefit. A parent's insurance benefit will generally be 82.5% of the primary insurance amount of the deceased worker on whose wages and self-employment income the parent's benefit is based. [Soc. Sec. Act §202(h)(2)(A).] However, for any month for which more than one parent is entitled to parent's insurance benefits based on a deceased worker's earnings, the benefit for each parent will be 75% of the deceased worker's primary insurance amount. [Soc. Sec. Act §202(h)(2)(B).]

In the event one parent is entitled to parent's insurance benefits based on the earnings of a deceased worker for a month, and later, because of an application that is retroactively effective for the same month, another parent of the worker becomes entitled to parent's insurance benefits for that month based on this worker's earnings, the total of the parents' insurance benefits for any month in the period for which that application has retroactive effect is limited to 150% of the primary insurance amount. Since the parent who first became entitled to benefits will have been entitled to a benefit equal to 82.5% of the primary insurance amount for the month, the parent who later becomes entitled to benefits will get a benefit for that month equal to 67.5% of the primary insurance amount. For months beginning with the month in which the second parent filed an application for benefits, each parent's insurance benefit will be 75% of the primary insurance amount. [Soc. Sec. Act §202(h)(2)(C).]

Parent defined. The term "parent" means the mother or father of an individual, a stepparent of an individual by a marriage contracted before such individual attained the age of 16, or an adopting parent by whom an individual was adopted before reaching age 16. [Soc. Sec. Act §202(h)(3).] As to the law to be applied in determining whether a person is a parent of a deceased wage earner, see ¶529.

If a parent marries after the death of the individual upon whose wage record benefits are based, the parent's benefits are terminated. However, benefits will not be terminated because of remarriage if the remarriage is to a person entitled to wife's, husbands, widow's, widower's, mother's, father's, or parent's benefits, or, within the limitations discussed at ¶524, to a person entitled to disabled child's benefits. [Soc. Sec. Act §202(h)(4).]

A parent may be entitled to benefits based on his or her own Social Security record. The parent will receive these benefits instead if they equal or exceed 82.5% of the deceased worker's primary insurance amount, when entitlement of only one parent is at issue, or 75% of the primary insurance amount in other cases. [Soc. Sec. Act §202(h)(1)(D).]

A parent under full retirement age may lose all or part of his or her benefit if he or she is charged with earnings in excess of those specified by the retirement test for any month. See ¶551.

¶529   Determination of Family Status

Determination of Status as a Spouse or Surviving Spouse

For Social Security purposes, an applicant will be considered the wife, husband, widow, or widower of a fully or currently insured wage earner if the courts of the state in which the wage earner is domiciled at the time the application is filed (or the courts of the state in which a deceased wage earner was domiciled at the time of death) would find that the applicant and the wage earner were validly married at the time an application is filed or the wage earner died, whichever is applicable. If the wage earner was not domiciled in any state, the determination would be made by the courts in the District of Columbia.

In the event a state court determined that the applicant and the wage earner were not validly married, the applicant could nevertheless be deemed to be the wife, husband, widow, or widower of the wage earner, as the case may be, if the applicant would, under the laws applied by such courts in determining the devolution of intestate personal property, have the same status with respect to the taking of such property as a wife, husband, widow, or widower of the wage earner. [Soc. Sec. Act §216(h)(1)(A).]

Same sex spouses. The Defense of Marriage Act (DOMA) effectively denied the spousal benefits and rights available under the rules governing Social Security to same sex couples, even if they resided in a state that recognized same sex marriage.

In *United States v. Windsor,* U.S. Sup Ct (2013), 133 S Ct. 2675, however, the Supreme Court ruled that Sec. 3 of DOMA, as applied to persons of the same sex who had been legally married under state law, was a violation of their right to equal protection under the Fifth Amendment. Significantly, the Court's decision was restricted to same sex marriages that were legally performed in a state. The decision did not require states that had not recognized same sex marriage to do so. Nor did the decision nullify Sec. 2 of DOMA, which allows states to withhold recognition of same sex marriage performed in other states.

Subsequently, the IRS stated that, effective September 16, 2013, it would treat same sex couples who have been legally married in jurisdictions (including foreign countries) that recognize the marriage, as married for federal tax purposes. [Rev. Rul. 2013-17, I.R.B. 2013-85, 9-16-13.] Notably, the IRS will treat such couples as married even if they live in a jurisdiction that does not recognize same sex marriage.

However, the SSA also indicated that, after consultation with the Department of Justice, it would continue to follow the domicile rule. Therefore, legally married same-sex couples residing in a state that does not recognize same-sex marriage could be denied federal Social Security (and SSI) benefits.

The SSA position was rendered untenable in June 2015, when the Supreme Court ruled that states are prohibited under the 14th Amendment from refusing to either license same-sex marriages or recognize such unions performed in other states (*Obergefell, et. al. v.Hodges,* U.S. Sup Ct (2015), 135 S Ct. 2071). The decision effectively negated the power of the domicile rule to deny same-sex couples Social Security benefits.

The SSA is continuing to determine the effect of *Obergefell* on its programs. However, it has issued guidance governing the recognition of same-sex marriage in Title II survivor and lump-sum death benefit claims (SSA Emergency Measure, EM-15029). The guidance requires reference to the date on which same-sex marriages were authorized or recognized in a state. If a marriage occurred on or after the date on which same–sex marriage was permitted in a state (including the June 26, 2015, date of *Obergefell*), the marriage will be recognized as valid as of the date of celebration. By contrast, in the event a marriage occurred before the date the state or U.S territory permitted same sex marriage, a legal opinion must be requested of the SSA.

Accordingly, *Obergefell* will apply to same-sex couples who were legally married at the time of the benefits claim, irrespective of the laws in the state of domicile. The application of *Obergefell* to other claimants (i.e., individuals denied benefits because of residence in a state that prevented them from marrying) is still unclear. For further information, see *ssa.gov/people/same-sex couples.*

Invalid marriage may not preclude benefits. Note that an applicant may be entitled to benefits even if the marriage was not valid because of a legal impediment (e.g., a worker's failure to obtain a legal divorce from a prior spouse). However, the applicant and the insured must be living together at the time the applicant filed for benefits, or if the insured is deceased, at the time of the insured's death. [Soc. Sec. Act §216(h)(1)(B).]

Determination of Status as a Child

In determining whether an applicant is the child or parent of an insured individual for Social Security purposes, the SSA will determine a child's status by applying the state intestacy law that is in effect when the child's claim is adjudicated. [Soc Sec. Act §216(h)(2)(A).] If the child does not have inheritance rights under that version of state law, the SSA will apply the state law that was in effect when the insured died, or any version of state law in effect from the time the child first could be entitled to benefits based on his or her application until the time the SSA makes its final decision on the claim, whichever version is more beneficial to the child. In addition to the exception discussed in the next paragraph, a child is deemed to be the child of an individual if the child is the individual's son or daughter and the child's parents entered into a ceremonial marriage that, but for a legal impediment of the type described above, would have been valid. [Soc. Sec. Act §216(h)(2)(A), (B); Reg. §§404.354, 404.355.]

An applicant may be considered the child of the worker if the worker (1) has acknowledged in writing that he or she is the child's father or mother; (2) has been decreed by a court to be the child's father or mother; (3) has been ordered by a court to contribute to the support of the child because he or she is the child's father or mother; or (4) is shown by other evidence satisfactory to the Commissioner to be the child's father or mother and has been living with or contributing to the support of the child. In the case of a worker entitled to old-age insurance benefits (who was not, in the month preceding such entitlement, entitled to disability insurance benefits), the Act requires that such acknowledgment, court decree, or court order must have occurred not less than one year before the worker became entitled to benefits or attained full retirement age, whichever is earlier, or the worker must have been living with or contributing to the support of the child at the time the application for child's benefits is filed. [Soc. Sec. Act §216(h)(3)(A); Reg. §404.355.]

In the case of a worker who is entitled to disability insurance benefits (or was entitled to such benefits in the month preceding entitlement to old-age insurance benefits), the Act requires that such acknowledgment, court decree, or court order must have occurred before such insured individual's most recent period of disability, or the worker must have been living with or contributing to the support of the child at the time the disability began; however, because this requirement has been declared unconstitutional by the U.S. Supreme Court (*Jimenez v. Weinberger*, 417 US 628 (1974)), the regulations require that the worker must have been living with or contributing to the support of the child at the time the application for child's benefits was filed. [Soc. Sec. Act §216(h)(3)(B); Reg. §404.355.]

In the case of a deceased worker, such acknowledgment, court decree, or court order must have occurred before the worker's death, or the worker must have been living with or contributing to the support of the child at the time the worker died. [Soc. Sec. Act §216(h)(3)(C); Reg. §404.355.] Note that benefits payable as a result of these provisions may be severely reduced or eliminated entirely in the computation of the family maximum. See ¶538.

Posthumously conceived children. The eligibility of posthumously conceived children to receive child's insurance benefits on the account of an insured deceased parent has proven to be problematic. As noted, under Soc. Sec. Act §216(h)(2)(A), the SSA, in determining whether an applicant is the child or parent of an insured individual, is to apply the intestacy law of the insured individual's domiciliary state. However, many states do not treat children conceived (rather than born) posthumously (e.g., pursuant to in vitro fertilization) after the death of the insured worker as children entitled to benefits through intestate succession. Accordingly, even when parentage is not in dispute, children who were conceived after the death of the biological parent and, thus, ineligible to inherit personal property from the biological parent under state intestacy law, have been further denied child survivor benefits under Title II of the Social Security Act. By contrast a posthumously conceived child may be eligible for surviving child's benefits if the child is treated as a child of the insured under a state's intestacy law.

SSA position. The SSA has refused to extend benefits to posthumously conceived children (even when parentage is not at issue), reasoning that benefits should be limited to children who lost support after the unanticipated death of a parent. Children's survivor benefits, the SSA stresses, should not be provided to posthumously conceived children who could not have relied on the insured parent's wages prior to his or her death.

Split in federal courts. The federal courts had been split on the issue. The Fourth and Eighth Circuits supported the SSA position; the Third Circuit rejected the SSA position; and two panels of the Ninth Circuit issued divided opinions.

In *Gillett-Netting v. Barnhart*, the Ninth Circuit determined that the post-humously conceived children of an insured wage earner were eligible to receive child's insurance benefits under the Social Security Act. Because the children were the deceased wage earner's biological children, they were his children for purposes of the Act. And, because they were his legitimate children, as determined by state law, they were deemed to have been dependent under the Act and thus entitled to benefits. The court rejected an argument that the Commissioner was required by Soc. Sec. Act §216(h)(2) and (3) to apply state intestacy law in order to determine if a state court would have found each of the claimant children to be a "child" of the deceased wage earner. The court determined that these provisions were added to provide for entitlement in cases where the parents were not married or if paternity was in dispute, circumstances not present in the case under consideration. [*Gillett-Netting v. Barnhart*, 371 F.3d 593 (9th Cir. 2004).] Subsequently, on September 22, 2005, the SSA issued Acquiescence Ruling 05-1(9), deferring to the Ninth Circuit's ruling in *Gillett-Netting* (but, see below for further developments).

However, another panel of the Ninth Circuit held that a posthumously conceived child in California was not entitled to child's insurance benefits when there was no evidence that the deceased wage earner either consented to the conception or expressed willingness to support the child. According to the panel in *Vernoff, et al. v. Astrue*, 568 F3d 1102 (2009), the different outcomes between the two cases turned on differences in the deemed dependency requirements between the two states involved.

In *Gillett-Netting*, Arizona law governed, and a showing of consent was not required to establish deemed dependency for a posthumously conceived child, while in *Vernoff*, a showing of deemed dependency was based on California law, which requires consent or a willingness to support the child, conditions which were not present in the case.

In *Capato v. Commissioner*, 631 F.3d 626 (3rd Cir. 2011), *cert. granted*, 132 S.Ct. 576 (2011), the Third Circuit held that the posthumously conceived children were considered to be the wage earner's children under Act §216(e) and were not required to further prove under Act §216(h) their status as children under the applicable state's intestacy laws because they were the undisputed biological children of the deceased wage earner. The requirements of Soc. Sec. Act §216(h) apply only when parentage is disputed, the court explained.

By contrast the Fourth Circuit, in *Schafer v. Astrue*, 641 F3d 49 (4th Cir. 2011), and the Eighth Circuit, in *Beeler v. Astrue*, 651 F3d 954 (8th Cir. 2011), have sided with the position of the Social Security Administration on this matter and denied benefits to posthumously conceived children.

Supreme Court resolves issue. The United States Supreme Court resolved the issue on May 21, 2012, reversing the Third Circuit and ruling that post-humously conceived children could not inherit from their father through intestate succession because they were not conceived during the decedent's lifetime, as required under the law of Florida, the state in which the decedent resided at the time of his death. [*Astrue v. Capato,* U.S. Sup Ct (2012), 132 SCt 2021; See also, *Mattison v. Social Security Commissioner,* Mich Sup. Ct. (2012), No. 144385, applying Michigan intestacy law)]. Soc. Sec. Act 216(h) clearly requires reference to state intestacy law for purposes of determining a child's eligibility status for benefits. Reliance on state intestacy law for this purpose, the Court explained, further serves the Act's objective of providing dependent members of a wage earner's family with protection against the hardship occasioned by the loss of the insured's earnings. [*MacNeil v. Commissioner,* CA-2, No. 16-2180, August 24, 2017.]

Note, reflecting the Supreme Court's validation of the SSA's traditional position, the SSA in November 2012 rescinded Acquiescence Ruling 05-1(9), which was issued after the Ninth Circuit's holding in *Gillette-Netting.* [SSA Announcement (77 *Fed. Reg.* 67724, November 13, 2012).]

Non-biological children of same sex relationships: An individual may qualify as a child under the Social Security Act where the state recognizes a parent-child relationship outside of the context of marriage. Prior to *Windsor* (see above), the U.S. Attorney General had maintained that the Defense of Marriage Act did not bar the non-biological child of a partner in a Vermont civil union from receiving child's insurance benefits after the partner became eligible for disability benefits. [US AG Memorandum, October 16, 2007.]

Windsor would effectively allow the extension of this position to the non-biological children of legally married same-sex spouses. However, the general application of the position to the non-biological children of same sex couples who are in civil unions or residing in states that do not acknowledge same-sex marriage (under the surviving provisions of DOMA) is less certain.

Living in the Same Household

Whenever the applicant and the insured are required to have been living in the same household in order to establish a family relationship, an exception is allowed if the applicant or the insured is temporarily absent due to service in the armed forces, or absent less than six months on account of business, employment or confinement in a penal institution. An exception is also made for absences of any length of time due to a medically required confinement in a nursing home, hospital, or other medical institution. Other absences also

¶529

may be allowed if it can be shown that the applicant and insured reasonably could expect to live together in the near future. [Reg. §404.347.]

¶533   Lump-Sum Death Payments

A modest lump-sum death benefit of $255 is payable to the widow or widower of a deceased insured worker if he or she was living in the same household with the insured at the time of death. The temporary absence of one spouse does not preclude a finding that they were living in the same household. Absence because of military service will be considered temporary, as will certain absences of less than six months. [Reg. §404.347.] If there is no widow or widower who was living with the insured, the lump sum may be paid instead to a person eligible for widow's, widower's, mother's or father's benefits on the account of the insured worker in the month of his or her death. In the absence of such a beneficiary, the death benefit may be paid in equal shares to each surviving child eligible for child's benefits for the month in which the worker died. [Soc. Sec. Act §202(i).]

An application for the lump-sum death benefit must be filed within two years of the insured's death, except that no application is required in the case of a beneficiary who was entitled to wife's or husband's benefits on the insured's earnings record for the month prior to the death of the insured.

Lump-sum does not lower monthly benefits. The lump-sum payment is in addition to, and does not affect, monthly benefits to which the widow or widower may be entitled. [Soc. Sec. Act §202(i).]

GRATUITOUS WAGE CREDITS

¶534.1   Coverage of Veterans and Servicepersons

Members of the armed services are covered under Social Security on a contributory basis, like other employees, and credits are based on basic pay.

Wage credits in prior years: Originally, servicepersons were not covered under the Social Security system on a contributory basis, but they did receive gratuitous wage credits of $160 a month for each month of service prior to 1957. Beginning with 1957, servicepersons have been taxed under the Federal Insurance Contributions Act on a contributory basis just like other employees. [Soc. Sec. Act §§210(l)(1), 217(a), 229(a); IRC §3121(m).]

For each calendar quarter after 1956 and before 1978 in which a serviceperson was paid covered wages on a contributory basis for military service, he or she received noncontributory wage credits of $300. After 1977 and before 2002, a serviceperson who was paid wages for military service was deemed to have been paid additional wages of $100 for each $300 of wages received in a calendar year, up to a maximum of $1,200 in noncontributory wage credits for any calendar year. [Soc. Sec. Act §229(a); Reg. §404.1341.]

Congress eliminated the deemed military wage credit beginning in 2002, although the credits continue to be given for appropriate earnings in prior periods. [Social Security Legislative Bulletin 107-14; Department of Defense Appropriations Act FY2002, P.L. 107-117, §8134, enacted Jan. 10, 2002.]

Servicepersons. The term "serviceperson" refers to a member of a uniformed service on active duty or, beginning in 1988, inactive duty training (not including service performed while on leave without pay). A "uniformed service" may include the Army, Navy, Air Force, Marine Corps, or Coast Guard (including a reserve component) or the Coast and Geodetic Survey, the National Oceanic and Atmospheric Administration Corps, or the Regular or Reserve Corps of the Public Health Service. In addition, the term includes retired members of these services, members of the Fleet Reserve or Fleet Marine Corps Reserve, cadets and midshipmen in the service academies, certain members of the various branches of the ROTC, and persons ordered to report for induction. [Soc. Sec. Act §210(m); IRC §3121(n).]

Tax based on basic pay. The tax due and the amount of "wages" credited to the serviceperson's account for Social Security and hospital insurance purposes is based on the individual's "basic pay" as described in 37 USC §206(a) for members of the uniformed services engaged in inactive duty training and in 37 USC §1009 for active servicepersons, subject to the limitations imposed on wages generally (see ¶208 above) and, in the case of wage credits, subject to increase as a result of the additional amounts deemed to have been paid. [IRC §3121(i)(2).] What constitutes "active duty" and "inactive duty training" is defined in 38 USC §§101(21)–(23).

Basic determinations with respect to employment and wages in the case of members of the uniformed services are made by the Secretaries concerned and are accepted as final and conclusive by the Social Security Administration for old-age, survivors, and disability insurance purposes. [IRC §3122.]

¶534.2   Benefits for Veterans and Servicepersons

Old-age, survivors, and disability insurance benefits for servicepersons and their families are figured on the basis of their "basic pay," as is the case with other workers working for "wages" in "employment" covered under the system.

A member of a uniformed service who was still in active service after 1956 was permitted to count active military or naval service after 1950 for Social Security purposes if his or her only other federal retirement benefits based on the same service were payable by one of the uniformed services, the Coast and Geodetic Survey, or the Public Health Service. If a surviving spouse or child of a former serviceperson is entitled to a survivor's annuity under the Civil Service Retirement Act of May 29, 1930, and the serviceperson's military or naval service (performed after September 15, 1940, and before January 1, 1957) was included in the computation of such an annuity, the surviving spouse or child could have elected to have this military or naval service included after 1956 in the computation of monthly survivors benefits under the Social Security Act. This election was accomplished by irrevocably waiving any right to the civil service annuity. In the case of such a waiver, if the surviving spouse or child was already entitled to survivors benefits under the Social Security Act based on other employment or self-employment of the serviceperson, then the survivor could obtain a recomputation of the serviceperson's primary insurance amount to reflect the inclusion of this service. [Soc. Sec. Act §217(e), (f).]

Title VIII benefits. The Social Security Administration also administers a program under Title VIII of the Social Security Act to assure a basic level of income for certain veterans who are entitled to SSI and who want to leave the United States to live abroad. In order to qualify for benefits under Title VIII, an individual must have reached age 65 on or before December 14, 1999; be a WWII veteran; be eligible for Supplemental Security Income (SSI) under Title XVI for both December 1999 and the month an application for benefits under Title VIII is filed; and receive total monthly benefit income from other sources that is less than 75% of the federal benefit rate under SSI. [Soc. Sec. Act §802; Reg. §408.105.]

¶534.3   Wage Credits for World War II Internees

Special provisions of law protect the benefit rights of U.S. citizens of Japanese ancestry who were interned by the U.S. Government during the period December 7, 1941, through December 31, 1946. Noncontributory wage credits are provided for such persons who were age 18 or older during that period, so as to replace the wage credits they would have earned had they not been interned. Specifically, wages are deemed to have been paid at a weekly rate of basic pay that is (a) equal to 40 times the federal minimum wage prevailing at the time, if the individual had not been employed prior to the internment; or (b) equal to either 40 times the highest hourly rate received during employment prior to the internment, or, if larger, equal to 40 times the then-prevailing federal minimum wage. [Soc. Sec. Act §231.]

Noncontributory wage credits will be lost if a larger Social Security benefit would be payable without them. In addition, an internee generally will not be given such credits if he or she is receiving benefits under another law of the United States based on the period of internment. However, benefits received by an internee under another law of the United States may not result in a loss of noncontributory wage credits for the purpose of establishing a period of disability. [Soc. Sec. Act §231(b)(2).]

ACTUARIALLY REDUCED BENEFITS

¶535   Introduction

The law contains special reduction provisions applicable to old-age beneficiaries, wives, husbands, widows, widowers, surviving divorced spouses becoming entitled to benefits before reaching full retirement age (*i.e.,* age 65–67, depending upon year of birth and type of benefit—see ¶518 and ¶535.2), and severely disabled widows or widowers under age 60. A disability benefit, under certain circumstances (see ¶520.8, ¶520.9), may also be reduced. In each instance, the benefit is actuarially reduced to take into account the longer period over which it will normally be paid. [Soc. Sec. Act §202(q).]

In determining the amount by which benefits are to be reduced, the reduction amount is rounded up to an even multiple of 10 cents, if not already an even multiple of 10 cents. [Soc. Sec. Act §202(q)(8).]

¶535.1   Reduction of Old-Age Benefits

The old-age insurance benefit of a worker for any month before he or she attains full retirement age (see ¶518) is subject to reduction.

If you choose to retire at some point between 62 and full retirement age, the amount of your monthly benefit will be *permanently* reduced for each month for which benefits are paid prior to age 66. If you start receiving benefits at age 62, the earliest age you can qualify, the amount of reduction is 25.00% for most individuals. For each month after age 62 that you wait before applying for benefits, the reduction will be less.

The reduction amount for an individual reaching age 62 in 2020 depends upon when that person actually retires. For example, if you retire within 36 months of full retirement age, the reduction formula is the same as for those who reached age 62 prior to 2000—a reduction of 5/9 of 1% of the unreduced benefit for each month of retirement prior to the month in which you attain full retirement age. However, if you retire in the month you reach age 62, or in any of the eleven months that immediately follow, an additional 5/12 of 1% of the unreduced benefit for each month of retirement beyond 36 months is deducted from your primary insurance amount.

Because benefit payments do not commence until the first month throughout all of which a person is at retirement age, which, for most workers is the month *after* the month in which a worker reaches age 62, the maximum reduction period for most workers retiring at age 62 in 2020 will be 56 months. However, for Social Security purposes, an individual is deemed to have attained a given age on the first moment of the day *prior* to the anniversary date of birth. Thus, individuals born on the second day of any given month in 2020 and retiring on their 62nd birthday will have a 52-month reduction period, resulting in a slightly higher reduction amount and a correspondingly lower benefit, but also will be able to receive benefits for an additional month prior to reaching full retirement age. The reduction amount is:

$$\left(\left(\frac{5}{9}\times\frac{1}{100}\times\begin{array}{l}\text{no. of mos. before}\\\text{age 66 and eight mos.}\\\text{up to 36 mos.}\end{array}\right)+\left(\frac{5}{12}\times\frac{1}{100}\times\begin{array}{l}\text{no. of additional mos.}\\\text{before age 66 and}\\\text{eight mos.}\end{array}\right)\right)\times\begin{array}{l}\text{unreduced}\\\text{benefit}\end{array}$$

The spouse or divorced spouse of a worker who is getting benefits may also become entitled to benefits in a reduced amount on reaching age 62. In 2020, the benefit payable to a worker's spouse at age 62 is reduced by about 33.33% for most individuals. As with retiring workers, the actual reduction amount depends upon how soon prior to full retirement age the spouse retires. For the first 36 months prior to full retirement age that a spouse elects to receive a benefit, the formula is the same as for spouses who reached age 62 prior to 2000, but will increase by 5/12 of 1% for each additional month prior to the full retirement age of 66 and eight months. The formula is:

$$\left(\left(\frac{25}{36}\times\frac{1}{100}\times\begin{array}{l}\text{no. of mos. before}\\\text{age 66 and eight mos.}\\\text{up to 36 mos.}\end{array}\right)+\left(\frac{5}{12}\times\frac{1}{100}\times\begin{array}{l}\text{no. of additional mos.}\\\text{before age 66 and}\\\text{eight mos.}\end{array}\right)\right)\times\begin{array}{l}\text{unreduced}\\\text{benefit}\end{array}$$

¶535.2   Cost Analysis of Early vs. "Late" Retirement

Considering that benefits received by an individual at age 62 are reduced, is it more or less advantageous for an individual to wait until full retirement age before receiving a retirement benefit? This depends, in large measure, on an individual's health (especially for those working physically demanding jobs) and how long that person must wait before their accumulated unreduced benefits from retirement at full retirement age equals and then surpasses the accumulated reduced benefit they would have received had they begun receiving benefits at age 62 or some other age prior to full retirement age. This factor can be determined using the following formula, where "R" equals the number of months in the reduction period for the reduced benefit, "b_1" equals the amount of the reduced monthly benefit, "b_2" equals the amount of the full monthly benefit, and "A" equals the number of months beyond the reduction period at which point the cumulative reduced benefit equals the cumulative full benefit:

$$\frac{R \times b_1}{b_2 - b_2} = A$$

$$A + R \quad = \quad \text{total number of months required to reach point at which cumulative full benefit equals cumulative reduced benefit}$$

From a perspective that considers only the amount of benefits received, over the short run, the advantage goes to the age-62 retiree, who receives benefits for four years in which he otherwise still would be working. However, in the long run, the person who waits until age 66 before retiring will have the advantage, assuming the retiree lives more than 12 years beyond full retirement age, since the actuarial reduction (24.583% for individuals whose birthday falls on any day of the month other than the 2nd; 25% for individuals born on the second day of the month) is permanent. Further delaying retirement until age 70 will, of course, result in an increase in benefits of 8% per year (see "Delayed Retirement Credit" at ¶539).

Note: The preceding formula only allows for an approximation of the financial benefits of delayed retirement, as it cannot incorporate such variables as the precise date of a retiree's death. However, the formula does suggest the financial benefits possible with delayed retirement.

¶535.3   Reduction of Widow's or Widower's Benefits

The age of full retirement for recipients of the widow's or widower's benefit is also being gradually increased from 65 to 67. The first to be affected by this increase were individuals who attained age 60 in 2000: full retirement for these people was at age 65 and two months. For widow(er)s reaching age 60 in 2020, full retirement is at age 66 and eight months.

A widow's or widower's benefits are not reduced if the beneficiary has "in care" (see ¶558) a child of the insured spouse who is entitled to child's benefits on the insured spouse's account. [Soc. Sec. Act §202(q)(5)(D).]

At full retirement age, the reduction period will be adjusted to eliminate months in which benefits were not received for any of the reasons stated below (see "Recalculation" at ¶543).

Reduction period. For widows and widowers who have reached or will reach age 60 in years after 1999 and who thus will be affected by the increase in the retirement age (*i.e.*, the age of entitlement to unreduced benefit) under the 1983 Amendments (see ¶518), the benefit payable at age 60 will continue to be reduced by 28½%. However, the amount of the reduction for each month in the reduction period (or the adjusted reduction period) will range proportionately between 28½% at the month of attainment of age 60 and 0% at the month of attainment of full retirement age, with the reduction period gradually increasing, and the monthly reduction factor correspondingly decreasing, in future years. [Soc. Sec. Act §202(q)(9)(B).] The general reduction formula may be expressed as follows:

$$\frac{19}{40} \times \frac{1}{100} \times \frac{\text{no. of mos. from when benefits begin thru mo.}}{\text{total no. of mos. between age 60}} \times 60 \times \frac{\text{unreduced}}{\text{benefit}}$$

This formula yields the amount to be subtracted from the unreduced benefit in order to determine the final benefit amount. This formula may be reduced to a monthly reduction factor that is based on the year in which a widow or widower reaches age 60, as indicated in the table below. The reduction amount may be obtained by multiplying the full benefit by both the reduction factor and the number of months prior to full retirement age that a widow or widower elects to receive benefits.

Reduction table for widow(er)s and divorced widow(er)s

Date of birth *	Full benefit at age	Maximum reduction period	Monthly reduction factor
1/1/40 or earlier	65	60 months	$^{57}/_{12000}$
1940	65 + 2 months	62 months	$^{57}/_{12400}$
1941	65 + 4 months	64 months	$^{57}/_{12800}$
1942	65 + 6 months	66 months	$^{57}/_{13200}$
1943	65 + 8 months	68 months	$^{57}/_{13600}$
1944	65 + 10 months	70 months	$^{57}/_{14000}$
1945 through 1/1/57	66	72 months	$^{57}/_{14400}$
1957	66 + 2 months	74 months	$^{57}/_{14800}$
1958	66 + 4 months	76 months	$^{57}/_{15200}$
1959	66 + 6 months	78 months	$^{57}/_{15600}$
1960	66 + 8 months	80 months	$^{57}/_{16000}$
1961	66 + 10 months	82 months	$^{57}/_{16400}$
1962 or later	67	84 months	$^{57}/_{16800}$

* Month and date are January 2 unless otherwise shown.

Note that depending upon the benefit claimed, one could have a different early retirement age, and correspondingly, a different full retirement age and reduction period. "Early retirement age" means age 62 in the case of an old-age, wife's, or husband's insurance benefit, while it means age 60 in the case of a widow's or widower's insurance benefit. Because the scheduled increase in retirement age is defined in terms of when an individual attains "early retirement age" and because an individual's "early retirement age" is defined in terms of the type of benefit received, ultimately, an individual's full retirement age is dependent on what benefit is being claimed. [Soc. Sec. Act §216(l).]

¶535.4   Reduction of Disabled Widow's or Widower's Benefits

Benefits are payable to severely disabled widows and widowers at age 50 through 59. Current and newly eligible disabled widows and widowers will be eligible at ages 50 through 59 to a benefit equal to the widower's benefit at age 60 (i.e., 71.5 % of the worker's primary insurance amount) [Soc. Sec. Act §202(a)(6).]

Benefits payable to disabled widow(er)s at ages 50 through 59 (¶525.2) are no longer reduced on the basis of the number of entitlement months before age 60. The former reduction of 43/240 of one percent for months that the beneficiary is age 50 through 59 years and 11 months, was eliminated effective with respect to all benefits payable after 1983. A straight reduction of 28.5 percent is calculated for disabled widow(er)'s benefits first entitled after 1983. [Soc. Sec. Act §202(q)(6), (7); SSA POMS §RS 00615.310 (TN 24, 9/2002).]

¶535.5   Reduction of Wife's or Husband's Benefits

A reduction applies when entitlement to wife's or husband's benefits begins before full retirement age. As with the reduction for old-age benefits, the 1983 Amendments mandated an increase in full retirement age for spouses who reach age 62 after 1999. The age at which a spouse or divorced spouse is entitled to his or her full benefits is gradually increasing to 67 as shown in the table at ¶518. The reduction fraction for wife's or husband's benefits is 25/36 of 1%, in lieu of the 5/9 of 1% provided for old-age insurance benefits for the first 36 months of the reduction period, plus an additional 5/12 of 1% for each additional month in the reduction period [Soc. Sec. Act §202(q)(1)], as expressed in the following formula:

$$\left(\left(\frac{25}{36}\times\frac{1}{100}\times\begin{array}{c}\text{no. of mos. before}\\ \text{age 66 and 8 mos.}\\ \text{up to 36 mos.}\end{array}\right)+\left(\frac{5}{12}\times\frac{1}{100}\times\begin{array}{c}\text{no. of additional}\\ \text{mos. before}\\ \text{age 66 and 8 mos.}\end{array}\right)\right)\times\begin{array}{c}\text{unreduced}\\ \text{benefit}\end{array}$$

When an individual who receives early retirement benefits reaches full retirement age, the reduction period is adjusted to eliminate months in which benefits were not received for any of the reasons stated below (see "Recalculation" at ¶543).

A wife's or husband's benefits are not reduced if the beneficiary has "in care" (see ¶558) a child of the insured spouse who is entitled to child's benefits on the insured spouse's account. [Soc. Sec. Act §202(q)(5)(A).]

¶535.6 Separate Reduction Computation for Certain Increases in Benefits

If any benefit increase results from an increase in the primary insurance amount of the worker upon whose Social Security record a reduced benefit is based, the benefit will be further reduced, beginning in the first month for which it is effective, as though the increased primary insurance amount had been in effect beginning with the month in which the beneficiary first became entitled to the reduced benefit. [Soc. Sec. Act §202(q)(4).]

¶535.7 Reduction of Mother's, Father's, or Parent's Benefits

Mother's or father's insurance benefits are not subject to reduction on account of a beneficiary not yet having attained full retirement age. Rather, when a recipient of a mother's or father's benefit reaches early retirement age, the beneficiary becomes entitled to widow(er)'s or surviving divorced spouse's benefits, subject to reductions on account of early retirement. Once a beneficiary becomes entitled to widow(er)'s benefits, he or she may no longer receive a mother's or father's benefit. [Soc. Sec. Act §202(e)(1), 202(f)(1); 202(g)(1)(B).] However, in no event will the widow(er)'s or surviving divorced spouse's benefit be reduced, on account of early retirement, to an amount that is less than what the mother's or father's benefit would have been so long as the beneficiary continues to have in his or her care a child of the deceased wage earner entitled to child's benefits (except a child age 16 or older entitled solely because he or she is a student—see ¶527 and Soc. Sec. Act §202(s)(1)). [Soc. Sec. Act §202(q)(5)(D).] As previously discussed, a mother's or father's benefit may be reduced, however, in the event a beneficiary has earnings in excess of the amount allowed under the earnings test. [See ¶527.1 and ¶551.]

Parent's benefits [¶528] are also not subject to reduction on account of the beneficiary not yet having attained full retirement age. Reductions under the earnings test may occur if the beneficiary has not yet attained full retirement age as would be applicable were the beneficiary receiving an old-age benefit. [Soc. Sec. Act §§202(h), 203(f)(9).]

¶535.8   Special Rules for Spouses, Widow(er)s, or Surviving Divorced Spouses

A certificate of election to receive reduced spouse's benefits may be filed by a man or woman 62 or over who was receiving unreduced husband's or wife's benefits (based on having an entitled child of the insured spouse "in care"— see ¶522) that are suspended because the child is no longer in his or her care (see ¶558). The certificate of election is effective for any month in which the man or woman is between ages 62 and full retirement age, entitled to spouse's benefits, and does not have in care a child of his or her spouse entitled to child's benefits. (Note that in this case a child entitled to benefits solely because he or she is a student is deemed *not* entitled to benefits for purposes of determining the entitlement of a spouse to benefits; see ¶522.) The certificate of election may be retroactive for as many as 12 months before the month in which it is filed. Once reduced husband's or wife's benefits have been received, a reduced benefit rate will continue to be payable, even after full retirement age, for months in which he or she does not have an entitled child in care. [Soc. Sec. Act §202(q)(5), (6)(A)(ii).]

MINIMUM AND MAXIMUM BENEFITS

¶537 Minimum Benefits

Persons who became eligible for benefits before 1982 were guaranteed a minimum benefit amount, which was frozen at $122.00 for persons who first became eligible after 1978 and before 1982. Although the minimum has been eliminated for newly eligible individuals, the law still limits the amount of benefits that may be paid to the dependents or survivors of any one worker. For persons eligible for benefits before 1982 or whose benefits are based on another worker's eligibility or death before 1982, the minimum benefit provision assures retired or disabled workers of an unreduced monthly benefit of not less than $122.00 (after 1978), regardless of the amount payable on the basis of actual earnings. [Soc. Sec. Act §215(a)(1)(C)(i), prior to amendment by P.L. 97-35.]

¶538 Maximum Family Benefits

The law limits the total amount of monthly benefits payable to individuals entitled to benefits on the basis of the wages and self-employment income of an insured worker. Because of the "escalator" provisions of the law, it is no longer possible to state a fixed maximum benefit.

For persons using the old average monthly wage method of computing benefits (see ¶513), the benefit table that dictates the primary insurance amount includes a corresponding maximum family benefit.

The family maximum for 1979 and subsequent eligibility years is derived from a formula, rather than the benefit table, in those cases where the worker's primary insurance amount (PIA) is computed on the basis of indexed earnings or under the transitional guarantee applicable to workers reaching age 62 after 1978 and before 1984. The formula for determining the family maximum for eligibility year 1979 is [Soc. Sec. Act §203(a)(1)]:

150 percent of the first $230 of PIA, plus
272 percent of PIA's over $230 through $332, plus
134 percent of PIA's over $332 through $433, plus
175 percent of PIA's above $433.

While the percentages in the maximum family benefit formula remain constant, the dollar amounts—"bend points"—employed in the formula are subject to annual increases in correlation with increases in average wages in order to maintain the current relationship between maximum family benefits and primary insurance amounts. [Soc. Sec. Act §203(a)(2).]

The bend points in the maximum family benefit formula for each year since it first applied in 1979 are as follows:

1979	$ 230	$ 332	$ 433
1980	248	358	467
1981	270	390	508
1982	294	425	554
1983	324	468	610
1984	342	493	643
1985	358	517	675
1986	379	548	714
1987	396	571	745
1988	407	588	767
1989	433	626	816
1990	455	656	856
1991	473	682	890
1992	495	714	931
1993	513	740	966
1994	539	779	1,016
1995	544	785	1,024
1996	559	806	1,052
1997	581	839	1,094
1998	609	880	1,147
1999	645	931	1,214
2000	679	980	1,278
2001	717	1,034	1,349
2002	756	1,092	1,424
2003	774	1,118	1,458
2004	782	1,129	1,472
2005	801	1,156	1,508
2006	838	1,210	1,578
2007	869	1,255	1,636
2008	909	1,312	1,711
2009	950	1,372	1,789
2010	972	1,403	1,830
2011	957	1,382	1,803
2012	980	1,415	1,845
2013	1,011	1,459	1,903
2014	1,042	1,505	1,962
2015	1,056	1,524	1,987
2016	1,093	1,578	2,058
2017	1,131	1,633	2,130
2018	1,144	1,651	2,154
2019	1,184	1,708	2,228
2020	1,226	1,770	2,309

Accordingly, the formula for determining the maximum family benefit for eligibility year 2020 is:

If the primary insurance amount (PIA) is:	The family maximum will be:
Up through $1,226	150% of PIA
$1,226.01 to $1,770	$1,839 plus 272% of the excess PIA over $1,226
$1,770.01 to $2,309	$3,318.68 plus 134% of the excess PIA over $1,770
$2,309 or higher	$4,040.94 plus 175% of the excess PIA over $2,309

Disability. The formula in effect in a given year will not apply to a worker who becomes eligible for retirement or disability benefits or dies in that year if the worker was entitled to disability benefits for any month in the year before he or she reached age 62, had a new onset of disability, or died. In such cases, the year of eligibility will be the year of onset of the disability that resulted in his or her entitlement during the prior 12-month period. [Soc. Sec. Act §203(a)(2)(D).]

Family benefits based on a worker's disability are subject to a further limitation, under which disability insurance family benefits may not exceed the smaller of (a) 85 percent of the worker's average indexed monthly earnings (or 100 percent of the primary insurance amount, if larger) or (b) 150 percent of the worker's primary insurance amount. [Soc. Sec. Act §203(a)(6).]

Cost-of-living adjustments. Annual escalator increases (see ¶541) are added to family maximums. [Soc. Sec. Act §215(i)(2)(A)(ii).] For each calendar year, the bend points in the formula are subject to increase to maintain the same relationship between maximum family benefits and primary insurance amounts. [Soc. Sec. Act §203(a)(2).]

Super maximum benefits. If a child is entitled to benefits (but for the provisions limiting the payment of benefits to a child entitled to more than one benefit to the amount payable on the earnings record yielding the largest amount) on the basis of the earnings records of more than one insured worker, then the maximum amount of benefits payable to the family is the lesser of (a) the sum of each of the maximum family benefits, or (b) an amount equal to one and three-quarters of the highest primary insurance amount possible in the year, based on average indexed monthly earnings equal to one-twelfth of the contribution and benefit base for the year. Adjustments in this so-called "super maximum" can occur as a result of an increase in the tax and benefit base and also as a result of a cost-of-living increase. Any such adjustments are combined and made at the time of the annual cost-of-living increase. [Soc. Sec. Act §203(a)(3)(A).]

Benefits based on two PIAs. In any month after 1978 in which an individual is entitled to benefits based on two or more workers' primary insurance amounts, one having been computed before 1979, the other primary insurance amount having been determined under the revised benefit structure in effect after 1978, the total benefits payable to all individuals entitled to benefits on those workers' accounts will be reduced to an amount equal to 175 percent of the highest primary insurance amount possible in that month, based on average indexed monthly earnings equal to one-twelfth of the contribution and benefit base in effect for that year. [Soc. Sec. Act §203(a)(6).]

Reduction in benefits. When a reduction is necessary because of the family maximum, the insured person's benefit is not reduced. In the usual case, the equivalent of the insured person's primary insurance amount is subtracted from the applicable family maximum amount, and whatever is left over is divided equally among the other beneficiaries. However, if a family member's benefit is subject to reduction below the amount of that family member's proportionate share, the remaining unused amount is not divided among the other family members. [Soc. Sec. Act §§203(a), 215(g).]

Benefits paid to a divorced spouse or to a surviving divorced spouse will not be reduced because of the limit on total family benefits; and such benefits are not counted in figuring the total benefits payable to others on the basis of wages or self-employment income of the same individual. [Soc. Sec. Act §203(a)(3)(C).]

In cases involving benefits subject to reduction for both the family maximum and dual entitlement, the Social Security Administration considers only the amount of monthly dependent's or survivors benefits actually due or payable to a dually entitled person when determining how much to reduce the total monthly benefit because of the family maximum. In other words, in cases where a dually entitled person receives benefits, only those benefits that are actually paid to the dually entitled individual on the account of the other family member's earnings will count towards the family maximum. [Reg. §404.403(a)(5).]

Miscellaneous rules. Special provisions assure a benefit increase, when the benefit escalator raises benefits, to families whose benefits are already at or near the family maximum. [Soc. Sec. Act §203(a)(3).] Also, the law contains a permanent savings clause that prevents the decrease in total family benefits that might in some instances occur when there is an increase in the primary insurance amount. [Soc. Sec. Act §203(a)(5).]

The limits on the total benefits payable are applied after other deductions for failure to meet the retirement test (see ¶551, below), failure to have a child in care (see ¶558, below), penalties for failure to report certain events to the Social Security Administration (see ¶552, below), and refusal to accept rehabilitation services (see ¶520.6, above). [Soc. Sec. Act §203(a).] Thus, in some cases it would be possible for the family to receive maximum benefits even though one of the family members was regularly employed and failed to meet the retirement test.

Adjustments to benefits after change in family composition:

Benefit amounts received by auxiliary beneficiaries that are based on the same earnings account will be adjusted where there is an increase or decrease in the number of auxiliary beneficiaries eligible to receive benefits on that account. If there is a change in the family composition, such as where a minor child receiving child's insurance benefits reaches age 18 (and is not disabled), the family maximum will be reapportioned among those who remain entitled to benefits after the family composition changes. [SSA POMS §RS 00615.758 (TN 24 9/02).]

A change in the family composition will not change the entitlement of a family member to benefits since the requirements for entitlement are not dependent on the family maximum limitations found in the regulations. Accordingly, if there is a change in family composition such that a reduction under Reg. §404.403 is either changed or no longer required, Reg. §404.404 requires a proportional adjustment in the amount of benefits received by all beneficiaries on the same earnings account to the extent necessary to insure that the family maximum is not exceeded.

EVENTS CAUSING INCREASES IN BENEFITS

¶539   Delayed Retirement Credit

A worker may increase the amount of old-age benefits he or she eventually will receive by delaying retirement. For each month beyond the full retirement age (see ¶518) and until age 70, a delayed retirement credit will be applied for each month in which the worker is fully insured and eligible for, but does not receive, old-age benefits because he or she either is working or has not filed an application for benefits. The amount of the delayed retirement credit (DRC) depends on the year a worker first becomes eligible to receive a retirement benefit (whether or not applied for) and the number of months for which the credit was earned (increment months). Although delaying retirement until age 70 may not be an option for many employees, especially those working in physically demanding jobs, it can significantly increase benefits. For example, as illustrated below, an employee who would be entitled to 100% of his benefits upon retirement at age 66, would be entitled to 132% of his benefits at age 70.

Benefits may not be increased after age 70. Benefits should be paid at age 70, regardless of whether the worker retires, because there is no additional increase in the delayed retirement credit or benefits if the receipt of retirement benefits is delayed any further. [Soc. Sec. Act §202(w)(6)(D); Reg. §404.3(b)(4).] However, the "retirement test," pursuant to which benefits at age 70 were subject to deductions on account of earnings above certain thresholds, has long since ceased being applicable (see ¶551). [Soc. Sec. Act §202(w)(6)(C).]

Delayed retirement credit rates are summarized in the following chart.

Year of attainment of age 65	Monthly percentage	Annual percentage
Prior to 1982	$\frac{1}{12}$ of 1%	1.0%
1982—1989	$\frac{1}{4}$ of 1%	3.0%
1990—1991	$\frac{7}{24}$ of 1%	3.5%
1992—1993	$\frac{1}{3}$ of 1%	4.0%
1994—1995	$\frac{3}{8}$ of 1%	4.5%
1996—1997	$\frac{5}{12}$ of 1%	5.0%
1998—1999	$\frac{11}{24}$ of 1%	5.5%
2000—2001	$\frac{1}{2}$ of 1%	6.0%
2002—2003	$\frac{13}{24}$ of 1%	6.5%
2004—2005	$\frac{7}{12}$ of 1%	7.0%
2006—2007	$\frac{5}{8}$ of 1%	7.5%
2008 or later	$\frac{2}{3}$ of 1%	8.0%

Note, that the credit may not be paid until the individual reaches full retirement age. However, benefits may be paid at full retirement age, whether or not the worker retires, as that is the age at which the retirement test applies (see ¶551)

Application of increase. The worker's old-age benefit is increased by the product of the applicable percentage rate shown above times the number of increment months to which the credit applies (*i.e.*, months in which the worker was eligible for but did not receive old-age benefits), with the final product of the multiplication rounded down to the next-lower multiple of 10 cents if not already an even multiple. After addition of the DRC, the old-age benefit amount is reduced by the amount of the supplementary medical insurance (Part B) premium, if any, and the result rounded to the next-lower multiple of $1.00 if not already an even multiple. [Soc. Sec. Act §202(w)(1).]

Interaction of DRC and actuarially reduced benefit amounts: The following table shows the effect of early retirement vs. delayed retirement on the percentage of PIA received as a benefit. The chart also shows how these percentages differ as a result of the increase in full retirement age from age 65 to age 67.

Normal Retirement Age and Delayed Retirement Credits

Increases in Normal Retirement Age and Delayed Retirement Credits with Resulting Benefit as a Percentage of Primary Insurance Amount (PIA), Payable at Selected Ages for Persons Reaching Age 62 in Each Year From 1995 and Later

			Benefit, as a percentage of PIA, beginning at age—						
Year of birth	NRA[1]	Credit[2]	62	63	64	65	66	67	70
1933	65	5 1/2	80	86 2/3	93 1/3	100	105 1/2	111	127 1/2
1934	65	5 1/2	80	86 2/3	93 1/3	100	105 1/2	111	127 1/2
1935	65	6	80	86 2/3	93 1/3	100	106	112	130
1936	65	6	80	86 2/3	93 1/3	100	106	112	130
1937	65	6 1/2	80	86 2/3	93 1/3	100	106 1/2	113	132 1/2
1938	65, 2 mo.	6 1/2	79 1/6	85 5/9	92 2/9	98 8/9	105 5/12	111 11/12	131 5/12
1939	65, 4 mo.	7	78 1/3	84 4/9	91 1/9	97 7/9	104 2/3	111 2/3	132 2/3
1940	65, 6 mo.	7	77 1/2	83 1/3	90	96 2/3	103 1/2	110 1/2	131 1/2
1941	65, 8 mo.	7 1/2	76 2/3	82 2/9	88 8/9	95 5/9	102 1/2	110	132 1/2
1942	65, 10 mo.	7 1/2	75 5/6	81 1/9	87 7/9	94 4/9	101 1/4	108 3/4	131 1/4
1943-54	66	8	75	80	86 2/3	93 1/3	100	108	132
1955	66, 2 mo.	8	74 1/6	79 1/6	85 5/9	92 2/9	98 8/9	106 2/3	130 2/3
1956	66, 4 mo.	8	73 1/3	78 1/3	84 4/9	91 1/9	97 7/9	105 1/3	129 1/3
1957	66, 6 mo.	8	72 1/2	77 1/2	83 1/3	90	96 2/3	104	128
1958	66, 8 mo.	8	71 2/3	76 2/3	82 2/9	88 8/9	95 5/9	102 2/3	126 2/3
1959	66, 10 mo.	8	70 5/6	75 5/6	81 1/9	87 7/9	94 4/9	101 1/3	125 1/3
1960 & later	67	8	70	75	80	86 2/3	93 1/3	100	124

[1] Normal retirement age
[2] Credit for each year of delayed retirement after NRA (percent)

Increment months. Months for which delayed retirement credits are to be applied are called increment months. An increment month is any month after December 1970 in which the worker has attained full retirement age, is fully insured, and is not entitled to an old-age benefit, either because he or she has not applied or because the monthly benefit has been reduced to zero under the retirement test (see ¶551). The computation of a person's increment months is redetermined annually, and the increase is applicable beginning with the following calendar year. Thus, any increase in the monthly old-age benefit amount that is due to the delayed retirement increase is effective beginning with January of the year after the year in which the DRC is earned. However, in the case of a worker attaining age 70, the number of increment months is determined through the month before attainment of age 70 and is applied to benefits for the following months. [Soc. Sec. Act §202(w)(2).]

Widow(er)'s and other benefits. A worker's surviving spouse or surviving divorced spouse also may benefit from any DRC earned by the worker. The worker's primary insurance amount, increased by any DRCs accrued prior to death, is deemed to be the PIA on which the widow's or widower's or surviving divorced spouse's benefit is based. All DRCs earned prior to the month in which the insured worker died will be used in computing the surviving spouse's benefit. [Soc. Sec. Act §§202(e)(2)(C), (f)(3)(C), (w)(1).]

The DRC was extended to widow(er)'s benefits under a provision of the 1977 Amendments effective with respect to benefits payable for months after May 1978. The delayed retirement credit does not apply to benefits for other dependents or survivors. [Soc. Sec. Act §202(w)(1).]

Family maximum. Delayed retirement credits are added to the worker's old-age benefit after computation of the family maximum (see ¶538), but DRCs used to compute a surviving spouse's benefit are added to the spouse's benefit prior to reduction on account of the family maximum. [Soc. Sec. Act §§202(w)(4), 203.]

¶541   Automatic Cost-of-Living Increases

The law contains "escalator" provisions under which automatic cost-of-living increases in benefits are made whenever there has been an increase in the Consumer Price Index (CPI) between specified base periods. [Soc. Sec. Act §215(i).]

The following table shows the applicable increase percentage for each year that the escalator has applied:

Effective Date	Rate of Escalator Increase	Effective Date	Rate of Escalator Increase	Effective Date	Rate of Escalator Increase
June 1975	8.0%	December 1990	5.4%	December 2005	4.1%
June 1976	6.4%	December 1991	3.7%	December 2006	3.3%
June 1977	5.9%	December 1992	3.0%	December 2007	2.3%
June 1978	6.5%	December 1993	2.6%	December 2008	5.8%
June 1979	9.9%	December 1994	2.8%	December 2009	0.0%
June 1980	14.3%	December 1995	2.6%	December 2010	0.0%
June 1981	11.2%	December 1996	2.9%	December 2011	3.6%
June 1982	7.4%	December 1997	2.1%	December 2012	1.7%
December 1983	3.5%	December 1998	1.3%	December 2013	1.5%
December 1984	3.5%	December 1999	2.5%*	December 2014	1.7%
December 1985	3.1%	December 2000	3.5%	December 2015	0.0%
December 1986	1.3%	December 2001	2.6%	December 2016	0.3%
December 1987	4.2%	December 2002	1.4%	December 2017	2.0%
December 1988	4.0%	December 2003	2.1%	December 2018	2.8%
December 1989	4.7%	December 2004	2.7%	December 2019	1.6%

* A correction by the Bureau of Labor Statistics on September 28, 2000, resulted in an increase of the previously announced COLA for December 1999, 2.4%, by one tenth of one percent to 2.5%

Annual cost-of-living adjustments are ordinarily based on an increase in the CPI from the third quarter of the previous year to the third quarter of the current year. If the CPI has declined during that period, benefits are not reduced or subjected to a negative COLA; however, in subsequent years, the index first must make up for any decline and then rise above the previous high level in order to trigger a cost-of-living adjustment. The escalator applies to December benefits, so that cost-of-living increases first appear on checks for the following January.

Cost-of-living increases under the escalator apply to the primary insurance amounts of current beneficiaries (see ¶512), maximum family benefits (see ¶538), and the primary insurance amounts of people who become eligible for benefits or die before becoming eligible (although certain limitations apply to the automatic adjustment of the frozen minimum benefits, as described at ¶537). [Reg. §404.271.]

Applying cost-of-living adjustment. The actual monetary amount of an individual's cost-of-living benefit increase is determined by multiplying his or her monthly benefit by the applicable increase percentage (rounded to the nearest 0.1%) and rounding the product of this multiplication to the next-lower multiple of 10 cents, if not an even multiple of 10 cents. [Soc. Sec. Act §215(i)(2)(A)(ii).]

When the Commissioner determines that a base quarter is also a cost-of-living computation quarter (*i.e.*, a base quarter with a CPI higher than the CPI for the prior year's base quarter), the Commissioner is required to publish in the *Federal Register* within 45 days after the close of the cost-of-living computation quarter a determination that a benefit increase is required and the percentage of such increase. [Soc. Sec. Act §215(i)(2)(D).]

¶543 Recalculation

The actuarial reduction factor for persons electing to receive benefits "early" (see ¶535, et seq.) is designed to reflect the longer period during which such persons will, on the average, be receiving benefits. However, principally because of the operation of the retirement test, many beneficiaries will not, in fact, receive benefits for all of the months between the time of their election and the time they reach the specified age. Therefore, the law provides for a roundup recalculation at full retirement age. [Soc. Sec. Act §202(q)(1), (7).]

Following is a summary of the months that may be eliminated in computing the reduction period or additional reduction period in the case of old-age, wife's, husband's, widow's, or widower's benefits.

If the benefit being recomputed is an *old-age benefit,* eliminate from the reduction period any month for which benefits were subject to deductions under the retirement test, and any month in which the individual was entitled to a disability insurance benefit.

If the benefit being recomputed is a *wife's or husband's benefit,* eliminate from the reduction period any month for which benefits were subject to deductions under the retirement test; any month in which unreduced wife's, husband's, mother's, or father's benefits were payable because the individual had in his or her care a child entitled to child's benefits; and, if the individual's benefit is based on a disability benefit, any month for which benefits were withheld because of a refusal on the part of the worker to accept rehabilitation services or any month in which the benefit was withheld because the worker recovered from his or her disability.

If the benefit being recomputed is a *widow's or widower's benefit,* eliminate from the reduction period any month for which benefits were subject to deductions under the retirement test; any month for which unreduced benefits were payable because the widow(er) had in his or her care a child entitled to child's benefits; and any month prior to attainment of age 62; and also any later month before the month of attainment of full retirement age, for which the claimant was not entitled to a widow(er)'s benefit because of an event that terminated entitlement to such benefits. [Soc. Sec. Act §202(q)(7).]

Note, recalculation is distinct from the recomputation of benefits, which is discussed at ¶565.

EVENTS CAUSING LOSS OF BENEFITS

¶550   In General

After a retired worker and any dependents or survivors have established entitlement to benefits, the occurrence of certain events may cause loss of benefits. Paramount among these events is a "retirement test" applicable to working beneficiaries under full retirement age who are charged with earnings in excess of a specified amount; this test is discussed at ¶551. If a working beneficiary expects to have "excess earnings" under the retirement test, he or she must report to the Social Security Administration or risk penalties causing additional loss of benefits (see ¶552). Note, the earnings of workers at full retirement age are not limited and will not result in reduced benefits.

Reduction or loss of Social Security benefits also may be incurred by individuals whose entitlement was based on care of a child who is no longer in their care (see ¶558), recipients of a government pension (see ¶560), persons deported from the country (see ¶554), or, in certain cases, aliens living abroad for more than six consecutive months (see ¶555) or unlawfully residing in the United States (see ¶553). Benefits are also terminated upon conviction of certain crimes (see ¶556). Events causing reduction or loss of disability benefits (e.g., substantial gainful activity) are noted separately within the discussion of disability (see ¶520.6 *et seq.*) and the loss of benefits resulting from a stepparent's divorce when benefits are based on the stepparent's wage record is noted in the discussion of child's benefits (see ¶524).

¶551   The Retirement or Annual Earnings Test

The law provides for deductions from the benefits payable to a working beneficiary who is under full retirement age, and from the benefits of any dependents, if the worker is charged with earnings in excess of amounts specified by an annual earnings test, also called the retirement test. Dependents' benefits also are subject to deductions on the basis of the amount of wages and self-employment income they earn. [Soc. Sec. Act §203(f)(3), (5).] The test applies to the work of everyone who is entitled to Social Security benefits except individuals entitled on the basis of their disability, and individuals outside the U.S. whose work is not covered by the Social Security program. [Soc. Sec. Act §203(f)(1).]

Note: The SSA advises that benefits withheld while an individual continues to work are not "lost." Once the individual reaches full retirement age, the monthly benefit will be increased permanently to account for the months in which benefits were withheld.

Two tests: The test is applied differently depending upon whether the beneficiary has earnings prior to or during the year in which full retirement age is attained.

Excess earnings under the annual test are one-third ($1 of every $3) of earnings in excess of the annual exempt amount for the taxable year in the case of beneficiaries attaining full retirement age during the year, but only with respect to earnings for months prior to the attainment of full retirement age. (Earnings during or after the month in which full retirement age is attained will not reduce benefits).

During years prior to the year in which full retirement age is attained, excess earnings are one-half of earnings in excess of a lesser annual earnings limit.

Taxable year. Except in the year that full retirement age is attained, the individual's taxable year is normally 12 months, even if the individual is not entitled to benefits during all months of the taxable year. But it may be less when, for example, there is a change from a calendar to a fiscal year basis. Both the beginning and ending months of a short taxable year are counted, even if they are not full calendar months. The number of months in the taxable year is deemed to be 12 and the full annual exempt amount applies in the year of death. [Soc. Sec. Act §203(f)(3); Reg. §404.428.]

Exempt amounts prior to year full retirement age is attained: A beneficiary under full retirement age (varies depending upon date of birth; see table at ¶518) may earn as much as $18,240 ($1,520 per month) in 2020 without incurring a loss of benefits. In recent years the exempt amounts have been as follows:

Earnings Thresholds

	Age 62 Through Year Prior to Year Full Retirement Age is Attained
1996	$ 8,280 ($ 690 per month)
1997	$ 8,640 ($ 720 per month)
1998	$ 9,120 ($ 760 per month)
1999	$ 9,600 ($ 800 per month)
2000	$ 10,080 ($ 840 per month)
2001	$ 10,680 ($ 890 per month)
2002	$ 11,280 ($ 940 per month)
2003	$ 11,520 ($ 960 per month)
2004	$ 11,640 ($ 970 per month)
2005	$ 12,000 ($ 1,000 per month)
2006	$ 12,480 ($ 1,040 per month)
2007	$ 12,960 ($ 1,080 per month)
2008	$ 13,560 ($ 1,130 per month)
2009–2011	$ 14,160 ($ 1,180 per month)
2012	$ 14,640 ($ 1,220 per month)
2013	$ 15,120 ($ 1,260 per month)
2014	$15,480 ($1,290 per month)
2015–2016	$15,720 ($1,310 per month)
2017	$16,920 ($1,410 per month)
2018	$17,040 ($1,420 per month)
2019	$17,640 ($1,470 per month)
2020	$18,240 ($1,520 per month)

[Soc. Sec. Act §203(f)(3), (8).]

Note: Earnings in or after the month an individual reaches full retirement age will not be applied towards the retirement test.

In your first year of eligibility, a monthly test also applies if the beneficiary did not earn over the monthly limit **in or after** the month of entitlement to retirement benefits, regardless of yearly income. The retirement test threshold for the monthly test is one-twelfth of the annual amount in effect for the year ($18,240 for 2020). Thus, in 2020, a worker who becomes eligible for benefits and retires will be paid a full benefit for any month after retirement in which the worker neither earns more than $1,520 nor is substantially self-employed, regardless of total earnings.

Note: In the calendar year in which full retirement age is attained, a higher monthly exempt amount will apply to each month that precedes the attainment of full retirement age. In 2020 that higher threshold is $4,050.

The monthly test is available only once to each beneficiary. However, a person can ordinarily use it in the year entitlement to child's benefits ends, or in the year entitlement ends to wife's or widow's benefits that were based on having a child in care, and then use it again when retirement benefits begin.

Earnings threshold. The exempt amount in 2020, the full amount of which is applied to the months that precede the attainment of full retirement age, is

$48,600 ($4,050 per month). Exempt amounts in recent years are set forth below. [Senior Citizens' Right to Work Act of 1996 (Title I of the Contract with America Advancement Act), P.L. 104-121, §102, amending Soc. Sec. Act §203(f)(8)(D)]:

Earnings Thresholds

Applicable to Months Preceding Month In Year FRA is Attained	
1996	$12,500 ($1,461.66 per month)
1997	$13,500 ($1,125.00 per month)
1998	$14,500 ($1,208.33 per month)
1999	$15,500 ($1,291.66 per month)
2000	$17,000 ($1,416.66 per month)
2001	$25,000 ($2,083.33 per month)
2002	$30,000 ($2,500.00 per month)
2003	$30,720 ($2,560.00 per month)
2004	$31,080 ($2,590.00 per month)
2005	$31,800 ($2,650.00 per month)
2006	$33,240 ($2,770.00 per month)
2007	$34,440 ($2,870.00 per month)
2008	$36,120 ($3,010.00 per month)
2009–2011	$37,680 ($3,140.00 per month)
2012	$38,880 ($3,240.00 per month)
2013	$40,080 ($3,340.00 per month)
2014	$41,400 ($3,450.00 per month)
2015–2016	$41,880 ($3,490.00 per month)
2017	$44,880 ($3,740.00 per month)
2018	$45,360 ($3,780.00 per month)
2019	$46,920 ($3,910.00 per month)
2020	$48,600 ($4,050.00 per month)

[Soc. Sec. Act §203(f)(3), (8).]

New exempt amounts are published in the *Federal Register* on or before November 1 of the year preceding the calendar year in which they are to become effective. An increased exempt amount is effective with respect to each individual's taxable year that ends with the close of the calendar year in which the escalator benefit increase also takes effect. In the case of an individual who dies during the year in which the benefit increase takes effect, the new exempt amount takes effect with respect to the taxable year that ends at death or during that year. [Soc. Sec. Act §203(f)(8).]

Operation of Earnings Test

Regardless of total annual earnings, benefits are payable in full for any month in a "grace year" in which the beneficiary does not earn wages of more than the monthly exempt amount and does not perform substantial services in self-employment.

Use of the monthly earnings test is limited to a grace year, which can be: (1) an initial grace year; (2) a grace year following a break in entitlement; and (3) a termination grace year. Each beneficiary is entitled to use the monthly earnings test in at least one taxable year. If the beneficiary's taxable year is a calendar year, the initial grace year is the first calendar year in which a beneficiary has an entitlement month in which he or she does not earn wages over the monthly exempt amount and does not perform substantial services in self-employment. The termination grace year is the year that contains the month before the month the terminating event occurs. However, a termination grace year does not apply when entitlement ends by reason of death or because the beneficiary became entitled to another type of Social Security benefit without a break in entitlement. No "child in care" is a cause for suspension of benefits, *not* a termination event. Therefore, failure to have an entitled "child in care" does not qualify the parent for a termination grace year. [Soc. Sec. Act §203(f)(1); Reg. §404.435(c).]

Assessment of excess earnings. An individual's excess earnings are charged against monthly benefits beginning with the first entitled month of the taxable year and proceeding to the second and succeeding months until all the excess (not to exceed the amount of benefit available for charging) has been charged. Excess earnings from one taxable year that are not charged off are not carried over and charged off in succeeding taxable years. [Soc. Sec. Act §203(b), (f).]

If the taxable year is a calendar year, the first month charged is January. For fiscal years, the first month of the fiscal year is charged. However, the test corresponding with the end of the fiscal year is used. If a fiscal year runs from June 2019 through May 2020, for example, charging begins with June and the exempt amount to be applied is $18,240, if the individual is under full retirement age and will not attain full retirement age during the year, because $18,240 is the exempt amount for taxable years that end in 2020. [SSA POMS §RS 02501.025 (TN 19, 7/00).]

Excess earnings are not charged for any month in which the beneficiary who derived the earnings (1) was not entitled to benefits, (2) was in a "grace year" and neither worked for wages of more than the monthly exempt amount nor rendered substantial services in self-employment, (3) was age 70 or was at or above retirement age, or (4) was entitled to child's disability benefits, disabled widow's benefits, or disabled insurance benefits. [Soc. Sec. Act §203(f)(1).]

The amount of benefits subject to charging is the amount: (1) after any reduction for the maximum, (2) after any reduction for entitlement before full retirement age, (3) after any reduction because of an auxiliary's or survivor's entitlement to retirement or disability benefits, and (4) after the benefit amount is rounded to a multiple of 10 cents. [Reg. §404.437.]

Earnings from self-employment. Self-employment income of retired insurance agents, lawyers, farmers, accountants, etc., and other business owners is counted for retirement test purposes if it is based on service performed after benefit entitlement begins. "Service" in this context refers to any regular service performed in the ongoing operation or management of a trade, profession or business that can be related to the income received. The term will not encompass occasional, irregular, and insignificant services that have no bearing on the income realized. Mere ownership of a business or the sale of a crop already produced should not be considered a service. The intent of this rule is that self-employed persons not be penalized for the receipt of deferred income earned before the *year* of entitlement or for income received after the initial year of entitlement that primarily comes from ownership of a business or partnership share. Note, however, that the renewal commissions of an insurance agent on a policy that the agent sold while self-employed are counted in the year that the commission is received.

Counting excess earnings. In determining whether the amount specified in the annual earnings test has been exceeded, all wages are counted as earnings for the taxable year in which the services are rendered. At full retirement age or over, benefits are paid no matter how much wage income is earned. For purposes of the annual limit, a self-employed person will not be required to include earnings in or after the month in which full retirement age is attained.

Proration of earnings from self-employment. Net earnings (or net loss) from self-employment will be prorated equally over all months of the beneficiary's tax year to determine the excess earnings, even if the individual is not entitled to benefits for all months of the year. In the event the beneficiary was not engaged in self-employment in all months of the year, the earnings (or loss) are prorated over the months in which the beneficiary was self-employed.

Thus, if an individual reaches full retirement age in 2020, the earnings subject to the retirement test would be the annual earnings divided by 12, multiplied by the number of months prior to the month in which full retirement age is reached.

Engaged in self-employment. Note, as used with respect to net earnings, the term "engaged in self-employment" should not be equated with rendering "substantial services." "Engaged in self-employment" pertains to whether or not the beneficiary actually owns or operates a trade or business as opposed to just rendering services. Normally, a simple convincing explanation of the reason for being out of business will suffice to permit a prorating of net earnings or loss for a period other than the whole year. [Soc. Sec. Act §203(f)(4)(A); Reg. §404.429.]

Charging excess against family benefits. If both the insured individual and a person entitled (or deemed entitled) on the insured's earnings record have excess earnings, the insured individual's excess earnings are charged first against the total family benefits payable (or deemed payable). Next, the excess earnings of a person entitled on the insured individual's earnings record are charged against his or her own benefits, but *only* to the extent that the auxiliary benefits have not already been charged with the excess earnings of the insured individual. Nor are the excess earnings of auxiliary beneficiaries chargeable to the accounts of any other persons receiving benefits on the insured individual's account. Thus, for example, if, after charging excess earnings, an old-age beneficiary is entitled to $50 in a particular month, while the wife and child are each entitled to $25, the wife's own excess earnings of $125 are chargeable only against her own monthly benefit amount and not that of either her husband or her child, neither of whom has received any benefits on her account. [Soc. Sec. Act §203(b), (f)(1); Reg. §404.441.]

Excess not charged against benefits of divorced spouses. However, the wage earner's excess earnings are not chargeable against the benefits of the *divorced spouse* if their divorce has been final for at least two continuous years or if the wage earner had been entitled to benefits prior to the divorce. Note, also, that a divorced spouse of an eligible wage earner can be entitled to benefits even though the wage earner has not filed a claim for benefits. Since the wage earner is not entitled, his or her work will not cause a deduction from the independently entitled divorced spouse's benefit. Although the wage earner's earnings are not subject to work deductions, the divorced spouse entitled under this provision is subject to work deductions based upon the spouse's own work. [Soc. Sec. Act §203(b)(2), (d)(1)(B), (f)(7).]

In determining the months and the benefit amount against which excess earnings can be charged, the individual is subject to a *nonentitlement* month if a deduction applies for that month because of the foreign work test (discussed below) or a failure to have a child in care (where eligibility depends on having a child in care).

When an individual is deemed not entitled to benefits for a month because a deduction may apply under one of the above categories, or because of reduction to a zero benefit rate and the maximum is involved, the benefit rates of other beneficiaries in the same family unit should be readjusted for the maximum to allow for the deemed non-entitlement; the charging of excess earnings to the benefits of the other beneficiaries is then based on the new rates. [Soc. Sec. Act §§203(b), (c), (d).]

Apportionment of partial benefits. Partial benefits payable to the insured and to one or more auxiliaries entitled or deemed entitled on the earnings record are allocated between the insured and each of the auxiliaries in the proportion that the original entitlement rate of each bears to the sum of all their original entitlement rates. For the purpose of this apportionment, the original entitlement rate means the respective benefit rate as figured without adjustment for the family maximum, without any adjustment for entitlement before full retirement age, and without any reduction arising from an auxiliary's retirement or disability insurance benefits. [Soc. Sec. Act §203(f)(7); Reg. §404.439.]

Total Earnings Subject to Annual Earnings Test

An individual's total earnings for a taxable year, including all wages for services rendered for all months of the beneficiary's taxable year, as well as any net earnings or net loss from self-employment for the year, are used to determine total earnings and excess earnings, even though the individual may not be entitled to benefits during all months of the taxable year. Thus, any net loss from self-employment for the taxable year should be subtracted from any wages received by the individual for services rendered during the same year in arriving at the individual's total earnings for annual earnings test purposes. [Soc. Sec. Act §203(f)(5)(A).] In the case of beneficiaries who attain full retirement age during the taxable year, annual earnings include only earnings received during those months prior to that month in which the beneficiary attains full retirement age. [Soc. Sec. Act §203(f)(3).]

For deduction purposes, wages are counted for the period in which they are earned regardless of when paid. However, net earnings from self-employment are generally counted as earnings for the taxable year in which they are received, regardless of when they are earned. [Soc. Sec. Act §203(f)(6); Reg. §404.428.] Whether or not income may be deferred (*i.e.*, excluded from wages when earned) depends on whether the employee had an immediate right to possession of the compensation when earned.

Most earnings are subject to the annual retirement test, even earnings from work that is not covered by Social Security. The following is a generalized listing of exempt and nonexempt earnings, some of which are discussed in greater detail in subsequent paragraphs. [SSA POMS §RS 02505.240B (TN 12, 9/93 and subsequent transmittals).]

Exempt Earnings

Generally not counted as earnings for retirement test purposes are:

- Annuity payments that are exempt from income tax
- Back pay awards prior to 1984
- Capital gains
- Damages or legal penalty payments pursuant to a legal action for wages
- Deemed military wage credits
- Deferred compensation paid on account of retirement (but not excess "golden parachute payments")
- Dependent care payments by an employer
- Dividends and interest
- Economic assistance under federally sponsored programs (not wages for services)
- Farm rental income, if the recipient did not participate in producing the income
- Fiduciary fees (nonprofessional)
- Fringe benefits of generally low value, such as gift watches, pins, etc.
- Hobby income that is not from a trade or business
- Indian Council fees
- Insurance policy proceeds
- Investment income, such as rentals from real estate, interest from bonds, or dividends, where not attributable to performance of personal services
- IRA distributions and Keogh plan payments

¶551

- [ ] Jury duty pay
- [ ] Meals and lodging furnished on the business premises for the convenience of the employer as a condition of employment
- [ ] Military pay allowances for food, clothing, shelter, etc.; special or incentive pay, including combat pay
- [ ] Moving expenses (under certain conditions)
- [ ] Pensions and retirement pay
- [ ] Personal loans (not compensation for services)
- [ ] Prize winnings from contests (not part of a salesperson's wage structure)
- [ ] Relief payments (unemployment compensation, assistance to the needy)
- [ ] Rentals from real estate (unless derived from property held by a real estate dealer for sale, by a materially participating farmer, or by persons who furnish hotel-type services)
- [ ] Retirement payments from a partnership
- [ ] Royalties received after attaining full retirement age to the extent attributable to a copyright or patent received before attaining full retirement age
- [ ] Scholarship and fellowship grants for tuition and course-related expenses
- [ ] Sick payments made more than six calendar months after the employee's last month of employment
- [ ] Social Security benefits
- [ ] Strike benefits (not conditioned on service)
- [ ] Supplemental unemployment benefits
- [ ] Tips, if paid in a medium other than cash or if less than $20 per month
- [ ] Travel and business expenses specifically identified as such at time of payment
- [ ] Trust payments, if made under an employer's plan or system from or to a trust fund that is tax exempt
- [ ] Unemployment benefits
- [ ] Veterans' training pay and allowances
- [ ] Winnings other than those of professional gamblers, bookies, etc.
- [ ] Workers' compensation

Nonexempt Earnings

Examples of payments that must be counted under the retirement test include:

- [ ] Annuity payments under an employer's plan or system where plan does not qualify for an IRS tax exemption
- [ ] Back pay
- [ ] Bonuses and awards paid by employer
- [ ] Cash pay for work of any kind (except certain seasonal hand-harvest work)
- [ ] Commissions
- [ ] Director's fees
- [ ] Dismissal and severance pay (except payments on account of retirement)
- [ ] Educational assistance payments by an employer
- [ ] Election workers' payments
- [ ] Farm income to persons who participate in the farming
- [ ] Holiday pay
- [ ] Idle-time, standby, or nonwork payments
- [ ] Incentive awards
- [ ] Indian Council payments to employees
- [ ] IRA contributions deducted from wages and Keogh plan *contributions* are counted (payments *from* these plans are not)
- [ ] Loans repaid by work in employment relationship
- [ ] Military pay (excluding combat pay and other special or incentive pay)
- [ ] Moving expenses (under certain conditions)
- [ ] Net earnings from self-employment
- [ ] Royalties from patent or copyright obtained after attaining full retirement age
- [ ] Sick pay paid before the expiration of six months following the last month of work
- [ ] Stock bonuses (counted to the extent of their fair market value if not tax exempt)

- Stock option plans (count the difference between the fair market value of stock at the time the option is exercised and the option price, but count in the period the option was granted [SSA POMS §RS 02505.240B.72 (TN 12 9/93), citing IRS Revenue Ruling 56-452])
- Strike pay for performance of services to union
- Taxes owed by employee and deducted from wages
- Television residuals (counted in period within which services were provided)
- Tips, in cash, $20 or more per month
- Traveling and other business expenses if not specifically identified as such at the time of payment
- Trial-work period earnings
- Vacation pay and annual leave pay

Impact on Medicare benefits. Note, even though deductions are applied to an individual's benefits under the Social Security work test, the individuals' entitlement to Medicare benefits will not be affected.

Wages

Wages subject to the earnings test are determined without regard to the annual wage limitation, the $100-a-year test in effect with respect to casual labor not in the course of an employer's trade or business, the $150-a-year test in effect with respect to some agricultural labor, the $$1,900-a-year test in effect with respect to election workers, or the $2,200-a-year test in effect with respect to domestic service in the private home of an employer. All remuneration, whether cash or noncash, for work as a homeworker or for a nonprofit organization, is counted, whether or not the $100-a-year test is met. Note, however, noncash remuneration for casual labor and to an employee performing domestic service is not counted. [Soc. Sec. Act §§203(f)(5), 209(a)(6)(A).] In summary, if the payment otherwise meets the definition of wages, even though it is not in covered employment, it is earnings for deduction purposes. [Soc. Sec. Act §203(f)(5)(C).]

The following special income categories should be considered:

Advances or reimbursements for traveling or other deductible *expenses* incurred or reasonably expected to be incurred in the business of the employer are not wages if they are paid specifically for traveling or other deductible expenses, and they are identified as such at the time of payment. [Reg. §404.1045.]

IRA and 401(k) distributions generally are not counted for earnings test purposes. [Soc. Sec. Act §209(a)(4); Reg. §404.1049; SSA POMS §RS 01402.326 (TN 10, 9/90).] Employer contributions *to* such plans are also not counted. [Soc. Sec. Act §209(a)(4); SSA POMS §RS 02505.240B.39 (TN 12, 9/93).]

The value of certain *employer-furnished meals and lodging* is not wages and is not counted for purposes of the annual earnings test, regardless of when they were furnished, if they are furnished on the business premises of the employer for the convenience of the employer and the employee is required to accept such provision as a condition of employment. [SSA POMS §RS 01402.240 (TN 10, 9/90).]

The value of *employer-provided group-term life insurance premiums* will be treated as wages if includible in gross earnings for income tax purposes. [P.L. 100-203, §9003.]

The following *retirement payments* are excluded from the definition of "wages" for annual earnings test purposes: (1) payments made by an employer under a plan or system to an individual who has reached an age specified in the employer's plan or system and whose employment relationship has terminated because of retirement; (2) payments made "on account of retirement," *i.e.,* to an employee as additional compensation for services performed prior to retirement from regular employment, whether or not such payments are under an employer's plan or system; and (3) amounts paid by an employer for insurance or annuities or into a fund to provide for a payment upon or after "retirement."[Soc. Sec. Act §203(f)(5)(C).]

Sickness or accident disability payments (including payments for related medical or hospitalization expenses under an employer's approved plan) made to or on behalf of an employee or his dependents more than six consecutive calendar months after the last calendar month in which the employee worked are excluded from wages. (Payments made during the six consecutive months are included as wages.) The exclusion also applies to payments made by a third party (*e.g.*, an insurance company); however, if an employee contributed to a company sick pay plan, that portion of the third-party payments attributable to the employee's contribution is not wages. Also excluded are payments to employees under a workers' compensation law. [Reg. §404.1051.]

Self-Employment Earnings

Net earnings from *self-employment* and net losses from self-employment generally have the same definition for earnings test purposes as for coverage purposes. However, while there is a $400 threshold for crediting self-employment income for coverage purposes, earnings for deduction purposes include all net earnings from self-employment, including any amount either under $400 or over the maximum limitation for self-employment tax. [Reg. §404.429.]

Under the self-employment income exclusion rule, except for income from royalties, all or any part of the income from self-employment received in a taxable year after the initial year of entitlement to Title II benefits (other than disability or childhood disability benefits) that is not attributable to services performed after the initial month of entitlement may be excluded from gross earnings for such taxable year. The exclusion of certain self-employment income is for earnings test purposes only, *i.e.*, for use in determining work deductions

¶551

and suspensions. It does not apply for coverage or tax liability purposes. Therefore, the amount of earnings used for deduction and suspension purposes may be different from the earnings shown on the beneficiary's self-employment tax return. The intent of the income exclusion provision is that self-employed persons not be penalized for the receipt of deferred income earned before entitlement to benefits or for income received after the initial year of entitlement to such benefits (grace year) that is derived mainly from the ownership of a business or partnership share. [Soc. Sec. Act §203(f)(5)(D)(ii).]

"Services" for the self-employment income exclusion provision has a meaning completely different from "substantial services" for purposes of applying deductions under the earnings test. For purposes of this provision, "services" means any regular services performed in the ongoing operation or management of a trade, profession, or business that can be related to the income received. It does not include occasional, irregular, and insignificant services that have no bearing on the income realized, *i.e.*, the income the beneficiary receives remains the same whether or not the beneficiary performs "services." Mere ownership of a business or the sale of a crop already produced should not be considered as "services." [SSA POMS §RS 02505.135 (TN 9, 5/90).]

There is no single rule for determining whether a person is performing substantial services in self-employment, and decisions are based on the particular facts in each case, including the amount of time worked, the amount of capital invested, the nature of the services rendered, and the presence or absence of an adequately qualified paid manager. [Reg. §404.446.] Regarding "substantial services," see ¶420.1.

Each month is considered separately. Although months may be grouped for the purposes of a determination where a person's activities over a series of months are substantially uniform, the determination must be valid with respect to each month to which it relates. [SSA POMS §RS 02505.065C (TN 11 9/92).]

Generally, the rules discussed at ¶404 *et seq.* are followed, except that the performance of the functions of a public office is not excluded from the term "trade or business" and ministers, certain members of religious orders, and Christian Science practitioners must count their self-employment earnings even though (except in the case of public officials) the individuals may not be covered. [Soc. Sec. Act §203(f)(5)(B); Reg. §404.429.]

Corporate directors' earnings are treated as received when services are performed, regardless of when actually paid (unless paid or received in a prior year), for purposes of the Social Security earnings test. [Soc. Sec. Act §203(f)(5)(E).]

Any royalties received in or after the year in which a beneficiary has attained full retirement age (varies, depending upon date of birth; see chart at ¶518) are excluded from gross income for retirement test purposes to the extent that: (1) the royalties are attributable to a copyright or patent that was obtained before the taxable year in which the beneficiary attained full retirement age and (2) the property to which the copyright or patent relates was created by the beneficiary's personal efforts. Royalties attributable to a copyright or patent obtained in or after the taxable year in which an individual attained full retirement age are included in gross income from self-employment for deduction purposes. For deduction purposes, the date of the filing of an application for a patent is the date the patent is considered to be obtained. The date of copyright is when a work is reduced to a fixed, tangible form. [Soc. Sec. Act §203(f)(5)(D)(i).]

Noncovered Work Outside the United States

A separate monthly retirement test applies to any person working outside the United States. Since the primary purpose of retirement/survivor benefits is the partial replacement of earnings lost by the retirement or death of the wage earner, deductions are required if the beneficiary engages in employment or self-employment beyond a certain limit. Differences in the values of foreign currencies make it administratively impractical to apply a test based on the dollar amount of earnings to noncovered work outside the U.S. The foreign-work test, therefore, provides for a deduction from the benefits (other than disability benefits) of beneficiaries who engage in noncovered remunerative activity outside the U.S. for more than 45 hours in a month before the month in which they attain full retirement age. [Soc. Sec. Act §§203(c), (d).]

An individual is engaged in noncovered remunerative activity outside the U.S. if employed outside the U.S. in a job not covered by U.S. Social Security or self-employed outside the U.S. in a trade or business. Generally, "outside the United States" means outside the territorial boundaries of the 50 states, the District of Columbia, the Virgin Islands, Puerto Rico, Guam, the Northern Mariana Islands, and American Samoa. [Soc. Sec. Act §210(i); Reg. §404.2.]

If a retirement insurance beneficiary works and loses benefits for one or more months, family benefits are also withheld for the same months, with the exception of the benefits of a divorced spouse who has been divorced at least two years. Even if the spouse has not been divorced for at least two years, his or her benefits will not be withheld under the foreign-work test so long as the retirement insurance beneficiary became entitled to benefits prior to the date of the divorce. [Soc. Sec. Act §203(d); Reg. §404.417.] Family benefits will also not be withheld if the retirement insurance beneficiary who loses benefits under the foreign-work test has been deported or if that beneficiary lost benefits under the alien nonpayment provision. See ¶554 and ¶555. [SSA POMS §RS 02605.005A.1.c (TN 12 12/04).]

Net earnings from self-employment abroad are to be computed without regard to any foreign earned income exclusions under the income tax provisions. It is not necessary that a self-employed person be making a profit to be subject to the foreign-work test. However, mere ownership of a business will not trigger foreign-work deductions. A self-employed individual must actually work or be available to work for more than 45 hours in a month in a functioning business before the deduction can be applied. [SSA POMS §RS 02605.005 (TN 12 12/04).]

Both work tests apply if a beneficiary is engaged in two or more distinct activities, one covered and subject to the earnings test, and the other a noncovered remunerative activity and subject to the foreign-work test. In these cases, deductions are first assessed under the foreign-work test with respect to any noncovered remunerative activities, and then the earnings test is applied with respect to all earnings subject to that test. [SSA POMS §RS 02605.020F (TN 12 12/04).] However, neither the foreign-work test nor the earnings test applies to activity that would, if carried on in the U.S., result only in income that is specifically excepted from coverage, such as rentals from real estate, capital gains, dividends or interest, retirement pay to partners who rendered no services, or limited partnership income. [SSA POMS §RS 02605.001C (TN 12 12/04).]

Effect of Earnings Test on Retroactive Entitlement

Benefits can, in a proper case and where all other conditions of entitlement have been met, be paid retroactively for a period of up to six months (see ¶575). In such a case, however, the provisions of the retirement test apply to the retroactive period and, accordingly, benefits paid for the retroactive period may be subject to deductions. For this reason, a claimant may restrict his or her retroactive right to benefits by making a request in writing at the time an application is filed (see ¶575). In considering when to make an application effective, the effect of the retirement test should be carefully considered. [Soc. Sec. Act §202(j)(1)(B).]

Note that if an individual expects to receive earnings in excess of the annual exempt amount, the anticipated earnings should be promptly reported to the Social Security Administration so that benefits can be withheld. Any benefits that were incorrectly paid may have to be repaid. Concerning the annual reporting requirements, see ¶552.

¶552   Annual Report of Earnings

If a beneficiary subject to the retirement test expects total earnings from employment and self-employment for a year to exceed the applicable annual exempt amount for the taxable year (in the case of a short taxable year, the monthly exempt amount times the number of months in the short year), this fact must be reported to the Social Security Administration. This report must be filed with the SSA on or before the 15th day of the fourth month following the close of the taxable year (an extension of as much as four months is provided if there is a valid reason for delay). Note, however, the W-2 report filed by the employer with the SSA and/or the self-employment tax return filed by the beneficiary with the Internal Revenue Service can be used as the report of earnings, thus eliminating the need for most beneficiaries to file a separate annual report.

Because earnings for income tax purposes and earnings for annual earnings test purposes are not always equivalent, some beneficiaries still will need to file additional information with the Social Security Administration. Under the earnings test, wages are counted for the year in which services are performed, while under IRS regulations, wages are reported on forms W-2 for the year in which they are paid. Thus, if the W-2 or self-employment income tax form shows wages or earnings that were earned in a year prior to the year for which the form is filed, *e.g.*, deferred compensation, a beneficiary will need to report to the SSA the correct amount of earnings for the year for which the report is made in order to insure that the correct amount of earnings is recorded for that year. An official form for these reports no longer exists; however, the report may be made to the SSA in person, by telephone, in writing, or online.

Other circumstances where a beneficiary still may need to provide the SSA with additional information include the following:

- the year in which the monthly earnings test applies (frequently the year of retirement), monthly earnings information will need to be provided;
- the beneficiary earned wages above the exempt amount and also had a net loss from self-employment;
- wages are reported on a W-2 that are also included on a self-employment tax return (*e.g.* members of the clergy and certain employees of religious institutions);
- earnings are reported on a fiscal year basis which is not the calendar year;
- the beneficiary had federal agricultural program payments or income from carry-over crops that is included on the self-employment tax return; and
- the beneficiary estimated earnings over the exempt amount and some benefits were withheld, but there were no earnings for the year, *i.e.*, no wages reported, no self-employment.

A beneficiary who does not separately notify the SSA and report the correct amount of earnings when one or more of these circumstances is present may risk an erroneous reduction in benefits under the earnings test.

Because the deadline for filing W-2 forms is well within the time frame for the required annual reports, the SSA will assume that posted earnings are based on timely filed reports. However, if a beneficiary requests an extension of time from the IRS for filing a self-employment tax return, the beneficiary must either file a timely report with the SSA or request from the agency an extension of time. [Reg. §404.452; 62 *Fed. Reg.* 15607 (Apr. 2, 1997).]

The SSA is authorized to request declarations of estimated earnings from beneficiaries in certain high-risk categories so that overpayments may be avoided. If the individual fails to file such a report, additional benefit deductions may result. The Commissioner also is entitled to suspend benefit payments if he or she has evidence that a beneficiary will fail to meet the retirement test. [Soc. Sec. Act §203(h).]

If a beneficiary has had benefits suspended under the retirement test for all months of a taxable year, an annual report of earnings does not have to be filed for that year. [Soc. Sec. Act §203(h)(1)(A).]

An individual who receives benefits that are subject to deduction on account of noncovered work outside the United States (see ¶551) must report his or her liability for such deductions prior to the receipt and acceptance of an insurance benefit for the second month following the month in which the work occurred. The penalty for the first failure to report the occurrence is equal to one month's benefit; for the second failure, two months' benefits; for a third or subsequent failure, three months' benefits. In no case, however, will the amount of the penalty exceed the total amount of the benefit withheld. [Soc. Sec. Act §203(g).]

¶553   Ineligibility of Aliens Not Lawfully Present in the U.S.

Retirement, survivors, and disability benefits under Title II are not payable to aliens who are not lawfully present in the United States. [Soc. Sec. Act §202(y), as added by the Illegal Immigration Reform and Immigrant Responsibility Act of 1996 (Div. D of P.L. 104-208), §503; Reg. §404.464.]

Supplemental Security Income (Title XVI) benefits may nevertheless be available to such aliens if they were receiving such benefits on August 22, 1996, or to certain "qualified" aliens. Qualified aliens include, among others, aliens granted asylum under the Immigration and Naturalization Act (INA), §208; refugees under INA §207; aliens paroled into the United States under INA §212(d)(5) for at least one year; certain aliens whose deportation is being withheld; aliens whose entry into the U.S. was conditional under INA §203(a)(7) as in effect prior to April 1, 1980; certain Cubans and Haitians; a U.S. citizen's alien spouse who has been battered or subject to extreme cruelty by certain family members; certain alien children who have been battered or subject to extreme cruelty and the parents of such children. [Personal Responsibility and Work Opportunity Reconciliation Act of 1996, P.L. 104-193, §§401-403 and 431, as amended by the Noncitizen Benefit Clarification and Other Technical Amendments of 1998, P.L. 105-306, §2.]

¶553.1   Ineligibility of Aliens Not Entitled to Work in the U.S.

Retirement, survivors, and disability benefits under Title II are not payable to any person who was not legally permitted to engage in employment in the United States prior to or during the time he or she applies for Title II benefits. This provision applies only to benefit applications based on Social Security account numbers issued on or after January 1, 2004. [Soc. Sec. Act §214 and §223(a)(1), as amended by the Social Security Protection Act of 2004, P.L. 108-203, §211.]

Some individuals who are issued a non-work SSN may later become U.S. citizens or receive authorization to work. However, unless such individuals report these changes to the SSA, the agency will not be aware of them and will deny benefits unless the individual maintained records to document the change. Note that individuals who begin working illegally and later obtain legal status could still use their illegal earnings to qualify for Social Security benefits. [Senate Report 108-176, Oct. 29, 2003.]

¶554   Termination of Benefits upon Removal (Deportation)

No benefits are payable to an individual for any month after the month in which the SSA is notified by the Attorney General of the United States that the individual has been deported under sections 212(a)(6)(A) or 237(a) of the Immigration and Nationality Act (other than under paragraph (1) (C)—relating to a failure to maintain status under which the individual was admitted to the United States), nor will any benefits be paid before the month in which he or she is thereafter lawfully readmitted to the U.S. for permanent residence. Under these provisions of the Immigration and Nationality Act, aliens are deportable if they were inadmissible at the time of entry, violate certain laws of the United States (including crimes of moral turpitude, aggravated felonies, certain firearms offenses and drug laws, domestic violence, stalking or abuse, and document fraud), terminate conditional permanent residence, engage in the smuggling of aliens, procure a visa through a sham marriage, or participated in Nazi persecution or genocide. The dependents and survivors of an individual so deported and not lawfully readmitted may not receive benefits for any month in which they are neither inside the U.S. nor citizens of the U.S. This applies also to a lump-sum death payment based on the deported individual's earnings. However, the earnings of the deported individual while abroad may not deprive any survivors and dependents of other benefits to which they are otherwise entitled. [Soc. Sec. Act §202(n), as amended by P.L. 108-203, §412; Reg. §404.464.]

¶555   Suspension of Benefits of Aliens Outside the U.S.

There are a number of restrictions on the payment of benefits to persons outside the U.S. who are not citizens or nationals of the U.S. Generally, benefits are not payable to aliens living outside the U.S. for six months or more, unless one of a number of conditions (outlined below) is met (i.e., "lawful presence" test). This restriction on the payment of benefits applies to an insured worker who is an alien, as well as to any dependents or survivors who are aliens. However, if the dependents continue to live in the United States, there will be no suspension of their benefits, even if the worker's benefits are suspended because he or she is outside the U.S. [Soc. Sec. Act §202(t)(1); Reg. §404.460(a).]

Exception to lawful presence test. A noncitizen who is entitled to benefits, but cannot meet the lawful presence test, may receive benefits outside of the United States if:

- The alien is a citizen of a country that has a social insurance or pension system that pays benefits to eligible U.S. citizens residing outside that country;

- The alien is a citizen of a country that has a totalization agreement (see ¶330) with the United States;

In addition to the above, alien dependents and survivors must have lived (legally or illegally) in the United States for at least five years previously and the family relationship to the worker must have existed during that time.

Six-month period of absence. When it is determined that a person is subject to these "alien nonpayment" provisions, the test operates as follows: when the individual has been outside the U.S. for 30 consecutive calendar days, the period of absence is considered to continue unbroken until he or she returns to the U.S. and remains for 30 consecutive calendar days. Thus, when the individual leaves the U.S. and fails to return, the first day of the month following the month of departure is the starting point for the six-month period after which benefits are suspended. The running of the six-month period will be interrupted only if the beneficiary returns to the U.S. and remains for 30 full consecutive days. Furthermore, once the individual has been outside the U.S. for six full calendar months, benefits can be reinstated only after he or she has returned to the U.S. and remained for a full calendar month. [Soc. Sec. Act §202(t)(1).]

The test is applied on the basis of the individual's physical presence, not the legal residence. [SSA POMS §RS 026010.020C (TN 15 5/08).]

"Outside the U.S." means, generally, outside the territorial boundaries of the 50 states, the District of Columbia, the Virgin Islands, Puerto Rico,

Guam, the Northern Mariana Islands, and American Samoa. [Soc. Sec. Act §210(i); Reg. §404.460(a)(1).]

Countries without social insurance. An alien beneficiary can continue to receive benefits while outside the U.S. if he or she satisfies the terms of any one of a list of exceptions to the nonpayment provisions. Thus, if the beneficiary has a total of at least 40 quarters of Social Security coverage, or has resided in the U.S. for a period or periods totaling 10 years or more, benefits can sometimes continue even while he or she remains outside the U.S. [Soc. Sec. Act §202(t) (4).] However, if the beneficiary is a citizen of a country that does have a social insurance or pension system of general application, but does not provide for full payment to eligible U.S. citizens who are outside of that country; is a citizen of a country that has no social insurance or pension system of general application; or lives in a country to which Treasury Department or Social Security Administration regulations prohibit the payment of a check (indicated by an asterisk: *), the nonpayment provisions will apply regardless of his or her 40 quarters of coverage or 10-year residence in the United States. The countries include:

Algeria	Iran	Qatar
Andorra	Iraq	Romania
Angola	Kazakhstan	Russia
Armenia	Kiribati	Rwanda
Azerbaijan	Kosovo	Sao Tome and Principe
Bahrain	Kuwait	Saudi Arabia
Belarus	Kyrgyzstan	Seychelles (Republic of)
Benin	Libya	Suriname
Brunai	Maldive Islands	Syria
Cambodia	Moldova	Tajikistan
Comoros	Mongolia	Timor-Leste
Congo (Democratic Republic of)	Mozambique	Turkmenistan
Cuba*	Namibia	Tuvalu
Djibouti	Nauru	Ukraine
Egypt	New Zealand	United Arab Emirates
Equatorial Guinea	Niger	Uzbekistan
Estonia	North Korea*	Vanuatu
Georgia	Oman	Vietnam
Guinea	Papua-New Guinea	Zambia
Guinea-Bissau	Paraguay	Zimbabwe

[Soc. Sec. Act §202(t)(4); Reg. §404.460(c)(3); 31 CFR §211.1; SSA POMS §RS 02610.015 (TN 15 5/2008); SSA Notice (78 Fed. Reg. 28698), May 15, 2013.]

If a United States citizen is unable to receive payments on account of physical presence in a country to which payments may not be sent on account of Treasury Department regulatory restrictions, the SSA will forward the withheld payments to the beneficiary once the beneficiary leaves the restricted country and goes to a country to which payments may be made. This does not apply to beneficiaries who are not United States citizens. Exceptions can be made for certain eligible beneficiaries in countries with Social Security restrictions in place. To qualify for an exception, one must agree to the conditions of payment, which includes the beneficiary appearing in person at the U.S. Embassy every six months to receive payment. [SSA Publication No. 05-10137, July 2017, *http://www.ssa.gov/pubs/10137.html#countries.*]

Restrictions limited to foreign citizens. The fact that a beneficiary, whether the insured worker or any other person, is an alien living outside the U.S. does not in itself affect the benefits of any other person entitled to benefits on the same Social Security earnings record. Also, the restrictions based on foreign citizenship affect only benefits payable to the foreign citizen, and not payment to other beneficiaries on the same earnings record. [Reg. §404.460(a).]

Countries with social insurance. An alien who is a citizen of a foreign country that has been found to have a social insurance system that is of general application in that country, under which periodic benefits are payable because of old age, retirement, or death, and under which benefits are payable without restriction to eligible citizens of the U.S. who are not citizens of that country (regardless of whether or not, and for how long, the U.S. citizen is outside that country), may receive benefits without regard to the six-month test. [Soc. Sec. Act §202(t)(2).] Note that non-U.S. citizen dependent and survivor beneficiaries who are eligible for Social Security benefits must have resided in the U.S. for at least five years as the spouse, widow/widower, child, or parent of the worker on whose earnings record benefits are paid in order to receive benefits. [SSA §202(t)(11); SSA POMS §RS 02610.025 (TN 15 5/08).] The countries to which the social insurance exception applies are as follows:

Albania (eff 10/93)
Anguilla (see United Kingdom)
Antigua and Barbuda (eff. 11/81)
Argentina (eff. 7/68)
Ascension Island (see United Kingdom)
Australia (eff. 9/01)
Austria
Bahamas (eff. 10/74
Barbados (eff. 7/68)
Belgium (eff. 7/68)
Belize (eff. 9/81)
Bermuda (see United Kingdom)
Bolivia
Bosnia-Herzegovina (eff. 2/95)
Brazil
British Virgin Islands (see United Kingdom)
Bulgaria (eff. 1/2000)
Burkina Faso
Canada (eff. 1/66)
Cayman Islands (see United Kingdom)
Channel Islands (see United Kingdom)
Chile

Colombia (eff. 1/67)
Costa Rica (5/62)
Cote d'Ivoire
Croatia (eff. 4/92)
Cyprus (eff. 10/64)
Czech Republic (eff. 1/93)
Czechoslovakia (See Czech Republic or Slovak Republic for months after 12 /92) (eff. 7/68)
Denmark (eff. 4/64)
Dominica (eff. 11/78)
Dominican Republic (eff. 11/84)
Ecuador
El Salvador (eff. 1/69)
Falkland Islands (see United Kingdom)
Faroe Islands (see Denmark)
Finland (eff. 5/68)
France (eff. 6/68)
French Guinea (see France)
French Polynesia (see France)
Gabon (eff. 6/64)
Gibraltar (see United Kingdom)
Greenland (see Denmark)

Grenada (eff. 4/83)
Guadeloupe (see France)
Guatemala (eff. 10/78)
Guyana (eff. 9/69)
Hungary (eff. 9/16)
Iceland (eff. 12/80)
Jamaica (eff. 7/68)
Jordan (eff. 5/80)
Korea, South (eff. 1/88)
Latvia (see RS 02650.100B.2. for months before 10/92) (eff. 10/92)
Liechtenstein (eff. 7.68)
Lithuania (eff. 1/03)
Luxembourg
Macao (see Portugal)
Malta (eff. 9/64)
Isle of Man (see United Kingdom)
Marshall Islands
Martinique (see France)
Mexico (eff. 3/68)
Micronesia, Federated States of
Monaco
Montserrat (see United Kingdom)
The Netherlands (eff. 7/68)
Netherlands Antilles (see Netherlands)
New Caledonia (see France)
Nicaragua (eff. 5/86)
Northern Ireland (see United Kingdom)
Norway (eff. 6/68)
Palau
Panama
Peru (eff. 2/69)

Philippines (eff. 6/60)
Pitcairn Island (see United Kingdom)
Poland (eff. 3/57)
Portugal (eff. 5/68)
Reunion (see France)
Ryukyu Islands (see Japan, below table)
St. Kitts and Nevis (eff 9/83)
St. Lucia (eff. 8/84)
St. Pierre and Miquelon (see France)
St. Vincent and the Grenadines (eff. 12/09)
Samoa (formerly Western Samoa)
San Marino (eff. 1/65)
Serbia and Montenegro (See Yugoslavia, Federal Republic of, for months prior to 02/03) (eff. 2/03)
Slovakia (eff. 1/93)
Slovenia (eff. 4/92)
Spain (eff. 5/66)
Sweden (eff. 7/66)
Switzerland (eff 7/68)
Trinidad-Tobago (eff. 7/75)
Tristan de Cunha (see United Kingdom)
Trust Territory of the Pacific Islands (eff. 7/76)
Turkey
Turks and Caicos Island (see United Kingdom)
United Kingdom
Uruguay (eff. 7/93)
Venezuela (eff. 1/78)
Wallis and Futana (see France)
Yugoslavia, Federal Republic of (formerly Serbia-Montenegro) (eff. 4/17/92 - 01/03)
Yugoslavia (ended 1/91)

[SSA POMS §RS 02610.015 (TN 15 5/08).]

Alien beneficiaries who are citizens of Germany, Greece, Ireland, Israel, Italy, Japan, and the Netherlands (survivor beneficiaries only) are protected by treaty from application of the alien nonpayment provisions, and thus will not be denied benefits, regardless of the duration of their absence from the United States. [Soc. Sec. Act §202(t)(3), Reg. §404.463(b).]

Military service exemption. Remaining outside the U.S. for six months or more in the active military or naval service of the U.S. does not cause cessation of benefits under these provisions. Nor does cessation apply in some miscellaneous circumstances involving death while in military service or credits for railroad employment. [Soc. Sec. Act §202(t)(5), (6).]

Restriction on lump-sum payment. If an alien worker is outside of the United States when he or she dies, and if no benefit may be paid for the month preceding the month of death either because he or she had been outside the United States for six full consecutive calendar months or more, or because of the ban on payments to certain Communist-controlled countries, no lump-sum death payment may be made on the basis of that individual's wages and self-employment income. [Soc. Sec. Act §202(t)(6).]

Residency requirements for dependents and survivors. Dependents and survivors must satisfy residency requirements in order to be exempted from the alien nonpayment provisions outlined above. Nonresident aliens claiming benefits as a spouse, parent, or natural child of an insured individual will not be entitled to benefits unless they lived in the United States for a total of at least five years during which their relationship with the insured was the same as the relationship upon which eligibility for benefits is based (*e.g.*, spouse, parent, or child). Natural children will be deemed to meet the residency requirement if their parents resided in the U.S. for at least five years or if the insured parent died while residing in the U.S.

Special provisions apply to adopted children. An adopted child will be entitled to benefits as a nonresident alien only if he or she was adopted by the insured within the U.S. and lived in the U.S. with the insured and received at least one-half of his or her support from the insured during the year immediately preceding the insured's eligibility for benefits or onset of disability. [Soc. Sec. Act §202(t)(11).] Note, however, that a foreign adopted child under the age of 18 and lawfully admitted into the United States for permanent residence automatically acquires United States citizenship, as long as at least one parent is a United States citizen. [The Child Citizenship Act of 2000 (P.L. 106-395).]

Individuals who become United States citizens subsequent to their receipt of a Social Security Number while residing in the United States as a permanent resident alien must notify the SSA of their changed status in order for their citizenship to be properly reflected in Social Security records. Otherwise, the individual could improperly be subjected to residency requirements for aliens.

¶556   Convicts, Fugitives, and Parole/Probation Violators

Benefits may be suspended or terminated where an insured beneficiary is convicted of certain crimes, is fleeing prosecution or confinement, is confined to a penal institution, or is violating probation or parole.

Conviction for certain crimes: The courts may, at their discretion, as an additional penalty, terminate an individual's benefit rights, based on earnings before his or her conviction, for crimes such as espionage, sabotage, treason, sedition, or other subversive activities. The benefit rights of members of the convicted individual's family are not affected. Thus, for example, the wife of a convicted individual continues to have benefit rights based on his entire earnings record, even though the convicted worker's rights can be based only on any earnings he might have after conviction. [Soc. Sec. Act §202(u)(1) and §202(x)(2).]

Any survivor who is found to have intentionally caused the death of an insured individual may not become entitled to, or continue to receive, benefits based on the earnings record of the deceased insured individual. [Reg. §§404.305, 404.468.]

Confinement following conviction: Retirement, survivor's, or disability benefits may not be paid to any individual during his or her incarceration for an offense punishable by imprisonment for more than 30 days, regardless of the actual sentence imposed. However, an exemption applies to those confined to their home by court order.

Note that individuals confined to institutions by court order pursuant to a verdict of guilty but insane, a verdict of not guilty by reason of insanity, a finding of incompetence to stand trial, or a similar verdict or finding are subject to benefit suspension. [Soc. Sec. Act §202(x).]

Fugitives, parole, and probation violators: Monthly Title II retirement, survivor's, or disability benefits may not be paid to any individual fleeing prosecution or confinement after conviction of an act or attempted act that constitutes a felony, or, in jurisdictions that do not define crimes as felonies, is punishable by death or imprisonment for a term exceeding one year, regardless of the actual sentence imposed. In order for an individual to be considered "fleeing," law enforcement must be pursuing the individual. [Senate Report 108-176, p.15, on H.R. 743, October 29, 2003.] Thus, benefits under Title II or Title XVI will be withheld or suspended only in those cases in which the relevant law enforcement agency notifies the SSA that it intends to pursue the individual by seeking arrest, extradition, prosecution, or the revocation of probation or parole. In turn, the Commissioner is required to furnish any law enforcement officer with personal information about any beneficiary, upon request, if: (1) the beneficiary is fleeing prosecution or confinement, or violating a condition of probation or parole; and (2) the location or apprehension of the beneficiary is within the officer's official duties. [Soc. Sec. Act §202(x)(3)(C).] Additionally, benefits may not be paid to those violating probation or parole under federal or state law. [Soc. Sec. Act §202(x)(1)(A)(v).]

The Commissioner may pay benefits withheld under these provisions for good cause shown if the offense or probation or parole violation was nonviolent and not drug-related. These benefits must be paid in the event of an acquittal, dismissal of charges, a vacation of an arrest warrant, or erroneous implication in connection with the criminal offense by reason of identity fraud. [Soc. Sec. Act §202(x), as amended by the Soc. Sec. Protection Act of 2004, P.L. 108-203, §203.]

Non-payment of retroactive benefits: In addition to the ban on monthly benefit payments described above, retroactive payments under Title II or Title

XVI may not be made to individuals while they are in prison, are in violation of the conditions of their parole or probation, or are fleeing to avoid prosecution for a felony or a crime punishable by a sentence of more than one year. The SSA will not pay these retroactive benefits until the beneficiary is no longer a prisoner, on probation, a parole violator, or a fugitive felon. [SSA §204(a)(1)(B), §1631(b), as amended by the No Social Security Benefits for Prisoners Act of 2009, P.L. 111-115.]

¶557 Penalties for Nondisclosure, Fraud, and Interference

False, Misleading and Withheld Statements

Individuals who knowingly make false or misleading statements or omit a material fact in connection with a claim for benefits under Titles II, VIII or Title XVI are subject to administrative penalties under the Social Security Act as described below.

Affirmative Duty to Disclose

The Social Security Protection Act of 2004 (P.L. 108-203) significantly expanded the anti-fraud provisions of the Social Security Act by also providing that the same civil monetary penalties, assessments, and sanctions imposed for fraudulent and misleading statements will also be imposed for the failure to come forward and notify the SSA of changed circumstances that affect eligibility or benefit amount when the person knows, or should know, that the failure to come forward is misleading.

The amended statute imposes penalties for any person or organization that "withholds disclosure of, a fact which the person knows or should know is material to the determination of any initial or continuing right to or the amount of monthly benefits under Title II or payments under Title VIII or XVI, if the person knows, or should know ... that the withholding of such disclosure is misleading." [Soc. Sec. Act §1129, as amended by P.L. 108-203, §201; Regs. §404.459 and §416.1340.] The SSA has implemented a centralized computer file that records the date on which a disabled beneficiary reports a change in work or earnings status.

The enhanced disclosure requirement is not intended to "include those individuals whose failure to come forward to notify the SSA was not done for the purpose of improperly obtaining or continuing to receive benefits." Thus, the legislation was not "to be used against individuals who do not have the capacity to understand that their failure to come forward is misleading." The expanded duty to disclose, however, is designed to include situations where: (1) an individual who has a joint bank account with a beneficiary in which the SSA direct deposits the beneficiary's Social Security checks and, upon the death of the beneficiary, the individual fails to advise the SSA of the beneficiary's death, and instead spends the proceeds from the deceased beneficiary's checks; and (2) an individual who is receiving benefits under one Social Security number while working under another Social Security number. [Senate Report 108-176, p. 14, Oct. 29, 2003.]

Penalties Under Section 1129

Any person, agency, or organization that makes false or misleading statements that are material to a determination of initial or continuing benefit eligibility or withholds disclosure of facts that are material to such determination is subject to a civil monetary penalty of $8,606, effective January 15, 2020, for such statement or representation or each receipt of benefits or payments while withholding disclosure of such facts. Note that in the case of a person who receives a fee or other income for services performed in connection with any determination (including a claimant representative, translator, or current or former employee of the SSA) or who is a physician or other health care provider who submits, or causes the submission of, medical or other evidence in connection with any determination, the amount of the penalty will not be more than $8,116. [Social Security Benefit Protection and Opportunity Enhancement Act of 2015, H.R. 1314, November 2, 2015; Soc. Sec. Act §1129(a); Regs. §§498.102–498.104.]

The Commissioner also may impose an assessment of not more than twice the amount of benefits or payments paid as a result of such statement, representation or nondisclosure. The Commissioner also may recommend to the Secretary of Health and Human Services that medical providers or physicians who violate these provisions be barred from participation in the Medicare program under Title XVIII. These penalties are in addition to any other civil or criminal penalty that may be imposed by law. [Soc. Sec. Act §1129(a); Regs. §§498.102–498.104.]

If the Commissioner has reason to believe that any person has engaged, is engaging, or is about to engage in any activity which would make the person subject to a civil monetary penalty under Section 1129, the Commissioner also may bring an action in the appropriate U.S. district court to enjoin such activity and/or to protect assets that may be required to pay any penalties that might be imposed. [Soc. Sec. Act §1129(i).]

The Commissioner may initiate and conduct a proceeding to determine whether to impose a penalty or assessment. However, any proceeding to recommend that a medical provider or physician be barred from participation in the Medicare program must be authorized by the Attorney General pursuant to procedures agreed upon by the Commissioner of Social Security and the Attorney General. Any action initiated under Section 1129 must be brought within six years after the date the violation was committed. [Soc. Sec. Act §1129(b)(1).]

Procedure: No adverse determination with respect to any person may be made under Section 1129 without first providing such person with written notice and an opportunity for the determination to be made on the record at a hearing. The person charged with a violation is entitled to representation by counsel, and may present witnesses and cross-examine adverse witnesses. The hearing officer may impose a broad range of sanctions, up to and including default judgment, against any party or attorney who fails to comply with an order, fails to defend an action, or engages in other misconduct. [Soc. Sec. Act §1129(b)(2); Regs. §§404.459, 416.1340, 498.109–498.114.]

Individuals upon whom an adverse determination is imposed may appeal the determination to the U.S. Court of Appeals for the circuit in which the person resides or in which the false or misrepresented statement was made. The individual must file the appeal within 60 days following the date he or she was notified of the Commissioner's determination. The circuit court may affirm, modify, remand, or set aside the determination. The Commissioner's findings of fact are conclusive if supported by substantial evidence on the record. [Soc. Sec. Act §1129(d); Reg. §498.127.]

Recovery of penalties imposed: The Commissioner has a number of options through which to recover any penalty imposed under Section 1129. These include civil action in U.S. district court; reduction of tax refunds; decrease in benefit payments under Titles II, VIII, or XVI; suit under the Debt Collection Act of 1982; offset against any other payment owed by the United States to the person subject to the assessment; or any combination of these. [Soc. Sec. Act §1129(e); Regs. §§498.128–498.132.]

Penalties Under Section 1129A

In addition to the penalties imposed under Section 1129, individuals who knowingly make false or misleading statements or omit a material fact in connection with a claim for benefits under Title II or Title XVI are subject to administrative penalties under the Social Security Act. The penalty will be nonpayment of benefits for a six, 12, or 24-month period for a first, second or third and successive offense, respectively. These penalties may be in addition to any other penalties, including criminal penalties, allowed by law. Imposition of the penalty alone will not affect an individual's eligibility for Medicare or Medicaid benefits, and benefits will continue to be payable to other beneficiaries on the same earnings record. [Soc. Sec. Act §1129A, added by the Foster Care Independence Act of 1999 (P.L. 106-169).] However, if the benefits of other family members are limited by the family maximum, their benefits will not be increased when imposition of a penalty has temporarily stopped benefit payments to one of the family members on the same wage earning account. [Reg. §404.459.]

Just as with Section 1129, the Social Security Protection Act of 2004 added a provision that imposes these penalties upon any person who withholds disclosure of a fact that the person knows or should know is material to the determination of any initial or continuing right to benefits under Title II or Title XVI.

Individuals upon whom a penalty is imposed will be given an opportunity to object and present evidence in an administrative appeal procedure that follows the same path as appeals for denial of benefits: reconsideration, hearing before an Administrative Law Judge, Appeals Council review, and appeal to a U.S. District Court. The penalty will begin the first day of the month for which the beneficiary would otherwise receive payment of benefits were it not for imposition of the penalty. Once a sanction begins, it will run continuously even if payments are intermittent. If more than one penalty is imposed, they will not run concurrently. [Regs. §404.459, §416.1340.]

Note, also, the SSA has imposed an affirmative duty upon beneficiaries of disability benefits under Title II to disclose any improvement in medical condition, as well as a return to work, or any increase in earnings or in the amount of work. A more expanded disclosure rule exists for recipients of SSI benefits. [Regs. §§404.1588 and 416.708.]

Obstruction of SSA Activity

Social Security Administration employees have the same protections against interference with the performance of official duties that have been provided to employees of the Internal Revenue Service. Anyone who by force or threat of force attempts to intimidate or impede any SSA officer, employee, or contractor while carrying out their official activities is subject to a fine of not more than $5,000, imprisonment of not more than three years, or both. However, for mere threats, the maximum penalty is $3,000 and/or no more than one year in prison.

¶558   Failure to Have Child "In Care"

Having "in care" a child of the insured worker who is entitled to child's benefits on the insured's account is a condition of entitlement to monthly benefits for a wife or husband under age 62 or a widow or widower (or surviving divorced spouse) receiving mother's or father's benefits. In these cases, monthly benefits are not payable to the claimant for any month in which he or she does not have "in care" a child, including a stepchild or adopted child of the worker, entitled to child's benefits. [Soc. Sec. Act §203(c); Reg. §§404.348-404.349.] "In care" is defined below. Note, however, that although benefits may be suspended for failure to have a child "in care," entitlement to benefits is not terminated unless there is no child entitled to benefits on the insured's earnings record who is under age 16 or disabled. [Reg. §§404.332(b)(4) and 404.341(b)(2).]

Upon attainment of age 16, a nondisabled child is deemed *not* entitled to benefits on the insured worker's account. A child's attainment of age 16 thus precludes payment of spouse's and mother's or father's benefits on the basis of having a child "in care." [Soc. Sec. Act §203(c); Reg. §404.348.]

Where a wife or husband is concerned, the child must be entitled on the same worker's Social Security account. Where a surviving divorced mother or father is concerned, the child also must be her or his natural or legally adopted child and the child's insurance benefit must be payable on the same worker's account. In the case of a divorced spouse, a widow(er), a surviving divorced spouse, or a widow(er) receiving mother's (or father's) benefits, the child may be entitled to child's benefits on any Social Security record. [*Soc. Sec. Handbook,* Sept. 1, 2009, §1829.]

For an individual to have a child "in care" for Social Security purposes, he or she must (1) exercise parental control and responsibility for the welfare and care of a child under age 16, or of a child age 16 or over who is mentally incompetent, or (2) perform personal services for a mentally competent but physically disabled child 16 years of age or over. The mother or father may be exercising parental responsibility or performing personal services alone or jointly with another parent. [Regs. §§404.348–.349.]

Report failure to have child in care to SSA. Failure to have a child in care must be reported to the Social Security Administration by any claimant whose right to benefits is based on having a child in care. The claimant must report this fact before receiving and accepting benefits for the second month following the one in which he or she first did not have the child in care. For the first time the claimant fails to report within the time limit that the child is not in care, one month's benefit is withheld. The penalty for the second failure to report is equal to two months' benefits, and the penalty for the third or a subsequent failure to report is equal to three months' benefits. In no case, however, will the amount of the penalty exceed the total amount of benefits withheld. The withholding of benefits for failure to report is in addition to the withholding of benefits because the claimant does not have a child in care. [Soc. Sec. Act §203(g); Reg §§404.450–.451.]

¶559   Cross-Program Recovery of Benefit Overpayments

Cross-program recovery under the Social Security Act allows the SSA to recover incorrectly paid amounts under one Social Security program from benefits being paid under another Social Security program. Specifically, notwithstanding the anti-assignment provision of the Social Security Act (see ¶568), the SSA may now recover overpayments paid under Title II, Title VIII, or Title XVI from the benefits paid under any of these programs even when the overpayment is not due to simultaneous entitlement under the same program. The Social Security Protection Act of 2004 expanded the cross-program recovery provisions of the Social Security Act. Previously, recovery efforts could be blocked when eligibility changed from one program to another. Additionally, the SSA had authority to collect prior SSI overpayments from amounts payable under Title II or Title VIII, but this authority was limited to 10% of the benefits paid. However, effective March 2, 2004, with respect to overpayments that are outstanding on or after that date, while any recovery under Title II or Title VIII continues to be limited to 10% of any monthly payment, recovery under Title XVI is limited to the lesser of 100% of the monthly benefit or 10% of the individual's total monthly income. [Soc. Sec. Act §1147, as amended by P.L. 108-203, §210; Regs. §404.530, §404.535(b)(1), §408.930, §408.931(b)(1), §416.572, and §416.573(b)(1).] The Social Security Administration may also entirely withhold *past-due* benefits in one program in order to recover an overpayment paid under another program. [Regs. §404.535(a), §408.931(a), and §416.573(a).]

¶560   Government Pension Offset

Monthly Social Security benefits payable to a spouse, divorced spouse, surviving spouse or surviving divorced spouse (including those entitled to benefits on the basis of having a child of the insured in their care) will generally be reduced if he or she receives any public pension based on his or her own noncovered employment with a federal, state, or local government agency. The benefit reduction is equal to two-thirds of the government pension. If the government pension is not paid monthly or is paid in a lump sum, it will be allocated proportionately as if it were paid monthly. [Soc. Sec. Act §202(k)(5); Reg. §404.408a(a).]

The purpose of the offset is to ensure that spouses who receive federal, state, or local government pensions based on their own non-covered earnings receive no more in combined pension/Social Security benefits than spouses who are receiving Social Security benefits both on their own record and on their spouse's record. Public pension offset provisions reduce—to zero, if necessary—the benefits of a spouse, widow(er), divorced spouse, surviving divorced spouse, mother or father, on account of such individual's receipt of any government pension based on his or her own noncovered employment with a federal, state, or local government agency. The public pension offset does not apply to persons entitled only to old-age or disability benefits, or to child or parent beneficiaries. [SSA POMS §GN 02608.100 (TN 15, 11/93).] However, a similar provision, the Windfall Elimination Provision—WEP, applies to them. See ¶512.

Government pension offset does not apply if a local, state, or federal employee worked in federal employment that is covered under Social Security for 60 months or more during the relevant period and ending with the first month of entitlement to spouse's benefits or if the governmental pension is based wholly on service performed as a member of the uniformed services, whether on active or inactive duty. The 60 months do not have to be consecutive. [SSA POMS §GN 02608.102 (TN 24 8/10) and GN 02608.103 (TN 25 1/11).] The public pension offset also does not apply to Social Security beneficiaries receiving government pensions based on employment with an interstate instrumentality. [Reg. §404.408a(b)(1).]

Note that the government pension offset is applied after reduction on account of age and/or simultaneous entitlement to other Social Security benefits. [Reg. §404.408a(d).]

MISCELLANEOUS PROVISIONS

¶565   Recomputation of Benefits

An automatic recomputation of benefits is made to take account of any earnings a beneficiary might have after he or she comes on the benefit rolls that would increase the benefit amount. These provisions apply for each year during any part of which the individual is entitled to retirement or disability benefits and has wages or self-employment income. [Soc. Sec. Act §215(f)(2).]

The recomputation for a living beneficiary will take effect beginning in January of the year following the year in which the earnings were received. The recomputed benefit of a beneficiary's survivor will take effect from the month of the beneficiary's death.

Recomputation requires that the actual dollar amounts in the SSA's records for the entitlement year and each subsequent year be compared on an annual basis with the earnings from the base year that were used in the last computation. Higher earnings from years that were not used in the last computation will be substituted for lower earnings for years that were previously used.

The PIA then will be recomputed using the same bend points (i.e., the dollar amounts used to compute average indexed monthly earnings) and indexing year (the second year before the earliest of the year the individual attains age 62, becomes disabled, or dies before age 62) that applied when current eligibility was established.

Recomputation does not decrease benefits. A recomputation never decreases primary insurance amounts or benefits, but an automatic recomputation will increase benefits generally, only if earnings in the additional base year considered are higher than earnings in the lowest computation year actually used in the worker's last previous computation or recomputation. A recomputation also will be disregarded if it increases the primary insurance amount by less than $1.00. [Soc. Sec. Act §215(f)(4).]

¶567   Overpayments and Underpayments

Beneficiaries will be compensated for underpayments of benefits. However, the government may recover overpayments made to a beneficiary or reduce future benefits.

Underpayment of benefits. An underpayment means a benefit or a part of a benefit (including a lump-sum death payment) to which a person was found to be entitled but which was not paid. If a person is paid less than the correct amount, the Commissioner pays the balance due to the underpaid person. If the underpaid person dies before receiving the full amount due, or after receiving but before negotiating checks representing the correct payments, the balance of the amount due, or the amount for which checks were properly issued but not negotiated, are paid pursuant to a designated order of priority. [Soc. Sec. Act §204(a)(1)(B); Reg. §404.503.]

Cash benefits (including unnegotiated checks) due a beneficiary at the time of death are paid in the following order of priority: (1) to the surviving spouse who was either living with the deceased beneficiary at the time of death or entitled to benefits on the same earnings record; (2) to the child or children entitled to benefits on the same earnings record as the deceased beneficiary; (3) to the parent or parents entitled to benefits on the same earnings record as the deceased; (4) to the surviving spouse who was neither living with the deceased beneficiary nor entitled to benefits on the same earnings record; (5) to the child or children not entitled to benefits on the same earnings record as the deceased; (6) to the parent or parents not entitled to benefits on the same earnings record as the deceased beneficiary; or (7) to the legal representative of the deceased beneficiary's estate, if any. [Soc. Sec. Act §204(d).]

Overpayment of benefits. An overpayment may be either a payment in a higher amount than was due or a payment made when none was due. Erroneous payments can be recovered from any person liable for the overpayment. [Soc. Sec. Act §204(a)(1).] Relief from making repayments can be granted in certain cases, however, as explained below.

Adjustment of an overpayment may be accomplished by requiring the overpaid person or his or her estate to make a refund, or by decreasing any Social Security benefits payable to the overpaid person or to any other person on the earnings record that served as the basis of the benefit payments to the overpaid person. However, where payment has been made on the basis of an erroneous report by the Department of Defense of the death of an individual in the line of duty while a member of the uniformed services on active duty, the payment is considered a correct payment. [Soc. Sec. Act §204(a)(1)(A).]

Note that if a beneficiary has died, and a benefit overpayment is made by direct deposit to a joint account that the deceased held with another person who is either entitled to benefits or is the deceased's benefit-eligible surviving spouse, the overpayment will be treated as an overpayment to the survivor. [Soc. Sec. Act §204(a)(2).]

Offsetting overpayments against underpayments: The Social Security Administration offsets underpayments due an individual against amounts that were overpaid to the individual, but only with respect to payments under Title II and Title XVI. [Reg. §416.543.] The offset will be applied unless the SSA has waived recovery. [Reg. §404.503.]

Waiver of recovery: The Commissioner may waive adjustment or recovery of an overpayment from any person who is without fault, even where that person is not the overpaid person and the overpaid person is at fault, if adjustment or recovery would defeat the purpose of the law or if it would be against equity and good conscience. [Soc. Sec. Act §204(b); Regs. §§404.506–404.512, 416.550–416.556.]

Administrative Wage Garnishment

The Social Security Administration may use administrative wage garnishment (AWG) to collect past due overpayments and administrative debts under Titles II and XVI. Under 31 U.S.C. §3720D, all employers are required by law to comply with an administrative wage garnishment order. [See 68 *Fed. Reg.* 74177, December 23, 2003, adding Subpart E to Part 422 of 20 CFR, Regs. §422.401–422.445, effective Jan. 22, 2004.] Administrative wage garnishment applies to non-federal employees. Federal salary offset applicable to federal government employees is discussed below.

The Social Security Administration will not attempt to recover the overpayment by adjusting benefits payable to an individual other than the debtor [Reg. §422.402(c)(6) and (d)(7)]. The SSA will implement AWG only if a debtor:

- Is not currently receiving benefits under the program under which the overpayment occurred [Reg. §422.403(c)(1) and (d)(1)];

- Has already received overpayment, reminder and past-due notices [Reg. §422.402(c)(2) and (d)(3)];

- Has no installment payment arrangement with the government for repayment of the overpayment or has failed to make payments under such an arrangement for two consecutive months [Reg. §422.402(c)(3) and (d)(4)];

¶567

- Has not requested waiver of the overpayment or, if waiver was requested, the SSA determined that it would not waive the overpayment [Reg. §422.402(c)(4) and (d)(5)]; and

- Has not requested reconsideration of the initial overpayment determination or, if the debtor has requested reconsideration, the SSA affirmed the initial determination in whole or part [Reg. §422.402(c)(5) and (d)(6)].

A debtor must receive notice of the Social Security Administration's intention to implement AWG [Reg. §422.405] 60 days prior to the time the process begins. Moreover, garnishment could be tolled after receipt of such a notice if review of the overpayment is requested [Reg. §422.425] or if the debtor sets up a written agreement for repayment of the debt [Reg. §422.415].

The SSA will not use AWG to recover debt if an individual's Title II benefits are stopped during a reentitlement period [Reg. §422.403(b)(3)], if Medicare entitlement is continued because a beneficiary is deemed entitled to Title II disability benefits [Reg. §422.403(b)(4)], or if a beneficiary is participating in the Ticket to Work and Self-Sufficiency Program [Reg. §422.403(b)(5)].

Garnishment does not justify dismissal An employer may not use a garnishment order as the basis for discharging an employee from employment or taking disciplinary action. If the employer violates this prohibition, the employee may file a civil action against the employer in a federal or state court of competent jurisdiction. [Reg. §422.440.]

Federal Salary Offset

Analogous to Administrative Wage Garnishment for non-federal employees, is Federal Salary Offset (FSO) for federal government workers. Under FSO, the salary-paying agency withholds and pays to the Social Security Administration up to 15 percent of the debtor's disposable pay until the debt has been repaid. [Soc. Sec. Act §204(f), as amended by P.L. 103-387, §5 and P.L. 104-134, §31001(z)(2); Soc. Sec. Act §1631(b), as amended by P.L. 106-169, §203. Both amendments authorized the use of FSO set forth in 5 USC §5514 and in 31 USC §3716. 71 *Fed. Reg.* 38066, July 5, 2006.]

¶568   Assignment of Benefits: Offset Against Federal Debts

Social Security Act §207 bars the assignment or attachment of Title II benefits through execution, levy, attachment, garnishment or any other legal process. The provision may not be superseded by any other federal law except by direct reference. Thus, Social Security benefits are generally not transferable or assignable. Until passage of the Debt Collection Improvement Act of 1996 (Omnibus Consolidated Rescissions and Appropriations Act of 1996,

Ch. 10, P.L. 104-134), the only exceptions to Section 207 were provisions allowing for tax collection (IRC §6334(c)) and for the withholding of benefits for payment of alimony or child support (Soc. Sec. Act §459).

The Debt Collection Improvement Act did not amend Soc. Sec. Act §207, but did reference that section, thus allowing for a third exception to the bar against legal process: the collection of any federal non-tax debt. The SSA uses computer matching programs to earnestly collect both federal tax and non-tax debts against other federal payments, including Social Security benefits under Title II. However, SSI payments under Title XVI are not covered by the program.

Garnishment of Bank Accounts

The anti-assignment provisions of Social Security Act §207 protect Social Security benefits from garnishment. Accordingly, pursuant to interim final rules effective May 1, 2011, banks and other financial institutions may not automatically freeze an account upon receipt of a garnishment order. The rules establish procedures that financial institutions must follow when a garnishment order is received for an account into which federal benefit payments have been directly deposited. Up to two months' worth of benefits may be protected from garnishment unless the garnishment order is obtained by the United States or by a state child support enforcement agency. [Regs. §404.1821, §416.534, and 31 CFR Part 212 as added by 76 *Fed. Reg.* 9939, Feb. 23, 2011.]

¶569   Expedited Benefit Payments

Individuals may file a special request for the expedited payment of retirement or survivors' benefits that are due but have not been paid. The prescribed method is designed to avoid situations in which delays may occur because the SSA is seeking definitive evidence of eligibility even though there is a prima facie case that a benefit is due the individual. [Soc. Sec. Act §205(q).]

In cases involving entitlement to monthly retirement and survivors insurance benefits or the resumption of benefits that have been suspended, a written request for expedited payment may be filed after 90 days have elapsed from the date when the claimant submitted the last of the evidence requested to show that a payment was due. In a case involving an initially unexplained interruption in benefit payments, or the transition from one type of benefit to another (from wife's to widow's benefits, for example), a written request for expedited payment may be filed after 30 days have elapsed after the 15th of the month in which the benefit payment was due. If payments are found to be due, they will begin within 15 days after the date of the request for special payment. [Soc. Sec. Act §205(q)(2).]

Preliminary payment. In any case in which the Commissioner determines that there is some evidence (although additional evidence might be required for a final decision) that a monthly benefit under this title is due the person for a particular month but was not paid, payments must be made on a preliminary basis even though the 30- or 90-day period has not elapsed. [Soc. Sec. Act §205(q)(3).]

¶570   Benefit Checks—Direct Deposit

All new recipients of Social Security benefits have been required to receive their benefit payments by direct electronic deposit. The direct deposit requirement was further extended to existing check recipients. [31 CFR §208.3 and §208.4] Payments can be made to a bank or credit union account. In the event an individual does not have a bank or credit union account, a pre-paid debit card option is provided. Limited exceptions apply.

Note: It should be noted that if a beneficiary has any federal debts, state or local government tax debts, or unpaid child support obligations, the requirement to receive benefit payments by direct deposit will expose these payments for debt collection through garnishment since these debts are not barred from collection as are other types of debts under Social Security Act §207. See ¶568 and 31 CFR §212.4.

Direct deposit procedures. People newly applying for federal benefits must choose an electronic payment option at the time they sign up for their benefits. If they wish to direct their money into a bank or credit union account, they will need to have the following information on hand at the time they apply for their benefits: the financial institution's routing number, the account type (checking or savings), and an account number. People who do not have an account at a financial institution or prefer receiving their payments on a prepaid debit card can receive a Direct Express debit card.

Automated enrollment process. Beneficiaries/recipients can ask their financial institutions to send direct deposit information electronically to the SSA through the "automated enrollment" process. This service allows financial institutions to transmit direct deposit signup information to the SSA electronically, thereby avoiding the need to contact the toll free 800 number staff or field offices. Participation in the automated enrollment process is voluntary on the part of financial institutions. [SSA POMS §GN02402.025 (TN 41 10/11).]

Prepaid Debit Card

If direct deposit into a bank or credit union account is not a viable option, a prepaid debit card can be used as an alternative to paper checks for benefit payments.

Direct Express Debit Card. The Direct Express debit card is recommended by the U.S. Department of the Treasury and the Social Security Administration. Cardholders can make purchases, pay bills, and get cash at thousands of locations nationwide. Cardholders have access to one free cash withdrawal with each deposit to the Direct Express card account. For cash withdrawals at ATMs outside the Direct Express ATM network, the ATM owner may charge a surcharge fee. There are no sign-up fees, monthly fees or overdraft charges. Some fees for optional services may apply. Money is immediately available on payment day. [75 *Fed. Reg.* 80315, Dec. 22, 2010; 31 CFR §208.6.]

To sign up for the card, or to learn more about its features and fees, individuals can visit www.USDirectExpress.com, call 1-800-333-1795 or ask their local Social Security, VA, or other federal benefit agency office.

Waivers and Exceptions

Excluded from the direct deposit requirement are lump-sum death payments, underpayments paid after the deaths of beneficiaries, claims for which no payment is possible because of government pension offset, and payments to beneficiaries residing outside of the U.S. in a country where direct deposit is not yet available. [SSA POMS §GN 02402.001 (TN 12 5/00) and .005 (TN 31 1/08).]

For beneficiaries residing in many other countries, funds can be deposited into a U.S. bank. They would then be available for withdrawal using an ATM. [SSA POMS §GN 02402.200 (TN 38 9/09).]

Cancellation of direct deposit. Direct deposit is canceled when the beneficiary or representative payee dies, or the beneficiary requests that it be canceled, or the financial institution cancels its agreement to receive the direct deposit payment, or the financial institution chooses not to accept the initial direct deposit payment. The financial institution may cancel its agreement by notifying the beneficiary, not the SSA, 30 days in advance of the cancellation date and advising the beneficiary to contact the SSA immediately to make other arrangements for delivery of payments. [SSA POMS §GN 02402.090 (TN 40 4/11).]

¶571 Representative Payees

It is the basic policy of the SSA with respect to the appointment of a representative payee (that is, a person selected to receive cash benefit payments on behalf of a beneficiary) that every adult is entitled to receive his or her own cash benefit payments unless determined to be incapable of doing so. Where it appears that the interest of a beneficiary would be better served, the Social Security Act provides, however, that payment may be made for his or her use and benefit to a relative or some other person, regardless of the legal competency or incompetency of the beneficiary. [Soc. Sec. Act §205(j); *Soc. Sec. Handbook,* Nov. 16, 2010, §§1600, 1601.]

Basis for appointment of a representative payee: There must be convincing evidence of an adult beneficiary's incapability of managing the funds before it will be found to be in his or her best interest to designate a representative payee. The evidence may include medical or legal findings of incompetence or other acceptable evidence, such as signed statements from people (such as relatives, close friends, neighbors or landlords) who are in a position to know of the beneficiary's ability to manage his or her funds. Disability benefits to alcoholics and other drug addicts are paid to representative payees to ensure that the benefits are not used to support addictions. [Soc. Sec. Act §205(j)(1), (2), (4); *Soc. Sec. Handbook*, Nov. 16, 2010, §§1601, 1604-1607.]

A minor child (a child under 18 years of age) is ordinarily considered incapable of managing benefit payments and a representative payee will be selected to receive payment on the child's behalf. However, payment may be made directly to a minor child age 15 or over if the minor does not have a legal guardian, and is (1) receiving disability insurance benefits on his or her own Social Security earnings record; (2) serving in the military services; (3) self-supporting and living away from home; (4) a parent filing for Social Security benefits for the parent and/or a child, who has experience in handling his or her own finances; (5) capable of using the benefits to provide for current needs and no qualified payee is available; or (6) within seven months of attaining age 18 and is filing an initial application for benefits. Additionally, if a minor beneficiary has the status of an adult under state law, the Social Security Administration also may make direct payment [*Soc. Sec. Handbook*, Nov. 16, 2010, §1602.]

Preferences for selecting a representative payee (minor child). For a minor child, representative payees are selected in the following order of preference: (1) a natural or adoptive parent who has custody of the beneficiary, or a court-appointed legal guardian; (2) a natural or adoptive parent who does not have custody of the beneficiary but who demonstrates strong concern for the beneficiary's well-being; (3) a relative or stepparent who has custody of the beneficiary; or (4) any one of the following: a friend with custody who provides for the beneficiary's needs; a relative or close friend who does not have custody of the beneficiary but who demonstrates concern for the child's well-being; or an authorized social agency or custodial institution. [*Soc. Sec. Handbook*, Nov. 16, 2010, §1609.]

Preferences for selecting a representative payee (adult). For adult beneficiaries, the selection of a representative payee follows this order of preference: (1) a spouse, parent, or other relative who has custody of the beneficiary, or who shows a strong concern for the personal welfare of the beneficiary; (2) a legal guardian or conservator who has custody of the beneficiary, or who shows strong concern for the welfare of the beneficiary; (3) a friend who has custody of the beneficiary; (4) a public or nonprofit agency or institution; (5) a federal or state institution; (6) a statutory guardian; (7)a voluntary conservator; (8) a private institution operated for profit and licensed under state law that has custody of the beneficiary; (9) a friend without custody but who demonstrates a strong concern for the personal welfare of the beneficiary, including persons with a power of attorney; (10) people other than the above who can carry out the responsibilities of a payee and who are able and willing to serve, without reimbursement for services, as a payee for a beneficiary; *e.g.*, members of community groups or organizations who volunteer to serve as a payee for a beneficiary; and (11) an organization that charges a fee for its services. Note, however, if a disabled beneficiary has a substance abuse issue, preference is usually given to organizations, rather than family members or friends unless the Commissioner of Social Security determines that a family member is appropriate. [Soc. Sec. Act §205(j)(2)(C)(v); *Soc. Sec. Handbook,* Aug. 1, 2011, §1610.]

A beneficiary may appeal the Commissioner's determination of the need for a representative payee or the designation of a particular person to serve as payee. A person who has been convicted of a Social Security felony is precluded from serving as a representative payee, as is an individual with a record of misusing a beneficiary's funds while serving as payee.

Advance designation. The Strengthening Protections for Social Security Beneficiaries Act of 2018 [P.L. 115-165] allows beneficiaries to designate an individual to serve as payee in advance of the Commissioner determining the a representative payee is necessary, and requires the SSA to select the designated individual with certain exceptions. [Soc. Sec. Act. Sec. 205(j)(1).]

On November 26, 2019, the SSA proposed new rules that would specify the information Social Security beneficiaries and applicants must provide in order to designate a representative payee in advance (84 *Fed. Reg.* 65040).

Disqualified individuals. Individuals convicted of fraud under the Social Security Act are disqualified from serving as representative payees. In addition, any individual who (1) has been convicted of any offense resulting in imprisonment for more than one year; (2) is fleeing to avoid prosecution, or custody or confinement after conviction; or (3) violated a condition of probation or parole is disqualified from serving as a representative payee. An exception applies if the Commissioner of Social Security determines that a person who has been convicted of any offense resulting in imprisonment for more than one year would, notwithstanding such conviction, be an appropriate representative payee. [Soc. Sec. Act §205(j)(2)(C)(i)(IV) and (V) and (j)(2)(C)(ii), as added by P.L. 108-203, §103(a)(4); Regs. §§404.2022 and 416.622.]

Where the Commissioner is unable to find a representative payee and determines that direct payment would cause substantial harm to the beneficiary, payment may be withheld for up to one month. Thereafter, the beneficiary must be paid directly unless he or she is under age 15, legally incompetent, or eligible to receive disability benefits in whole, or in part, due to alcoholism or drug addition. [Soc. Sec. Act §205(j)(2)(D).]

¶571

Public Law 115-165, signed on April 13, 2018, allows the SSA to disqualify current or prospective payees who do not consent to background checks, effective January 1, 2019. [Soc. Sec. Act 205(j)(2).]

On March 18, 2019, the SSA finalized rules on conducting background checks to prohibit persons convicted of certain crimes from serving as representative payees (84 *Fed. Reg.* 4323, February 15, 2019).

Duties of representative payee. The duties of a representative payee are: (1) to determine the beneficiary's current and future needs and to use the benefits in the best interests of the beneficiary, conforming to SSA regulations and policies; (2) to apply the benefit payments only for the beneficiary's use and welfare; (3) to maintain a continuing awareness of the beneficiary's needs and condition (if the beneficiary is not living with the representative payee, this interest should be shown by contact, by visiting the beneficiary and consulting with the beneficiary's custodians concerning the beneficiary's condition and needs); (4) to notify the SSA of any change in circumstances that would indicate he or she is no longer suitable to serve as payee or would affect the payee's performance; (5) to report to the SSA the occurrence of any event affecting the beneficiary's right to receive Social Security payments; (6) to maintain a written record of all payments received from the SSA along with receipts to show how funds were spent and/or saved on behalf of the beneficiary; (7) to give the SSA annual written reports accounting for the use of benefits; and (8) to return conserved funds to the SSA when no longer serving as the beneficiary's representative payee and return any payments not due when a beneficiary has died. Annual reports must be provided more frequently, if requested. The representative payee should keep records as to how benefits were used in order to make the accounting reports and must make those records available to the Social Security Administration upon request. [Regs. §§404.2035, 404.2065, 416.635, and 416.665; *Soc. Sec. Handbook,* Nov. 16, 2010, §1616.]

The addresses and Social Security numbers (or employer identification numbers) of all representative payees, and the addresses and Social Security numbers of all beneficiaries to whom representative payees are assigned, will be maintained in a centralized file retrievable by all local Social Security offices. Also, the Commissioner must (1) cease payments to a representative payee when the payee has misused benefit payments, (2) keep lists of payees who stopped receiving payments on account of misuse and/or who were convicted of Social Security felonies, and (3) give such lists to local field offices. [Soc. Sec. Act §205(j)(2)(B)(ii).]

Transfer of Representation

If a representative payee is no longer going to serve in that capacity, the payee must return conserved funds to the Social Security Administration or transfer them to a successor payee, as specified by the SSA. [Regs. §404.2060 and §416.660.]

Misuse of Funds

Representative payees who violate their responsibilities are subject to penalty. Beneficiaries who suffer any loss as a result of fund misuse by representative payees are entitled to reimbursement.

Civil monetary penalties: Representative payees who misuse Title II, VIII, or XVI benefits are liable for a penalty of up to $8,116 and double the amount of misused benefits for each violation [Soc. Sec. Act §1129(a), as amended by P.L. 108-203, §111; as amended by the Social Security Benefit Protection and Opportunity Enhancement Act of 2015, H. 1314, November 2, 2015.]

Fee forfeiture. Representative payees must forfeit their fee for those months during which they misused funds, as determined by the Commissioner of Social Security or a court of competent jurisdiction (For 2020, the fee is limited to the lesser of (1) 10% of the monthly benefit involved, or (2) $44 per month ($83 per month for individuals entitled to disability benefits who have alcoholism or drug addiction conditions and cannot manage their benefits). [Soc. Sec. Act §205(j)(4)(A)(i) and §1631(a)(2)(D)(i), as amended by P.L. 108-203, §104; as amended by the Social Security Benefit Protection and Opportunity Enhancement Act of 2015, H. 1314, November 2, 2015.]

Treatment as overpayment. Benefits misused by a non-governmental representative payee (including all individual representative payees) are treated as overpayments to the representative payee, rather than the beneficiary, thus subjecting the representative payee to current overpayment recovery authorities. Any recovered benefits not already reissued to the beneficiary must be reissued to either the beneficiary or their alternate representative payee, up to the total amount misused. [Soc. Sec. Act §205(j)(7), §807(l), and §1631(a)(2)(H), as amended by P.L. 108-203, §105.]

Reimbursement. The Commissioner is required to reissue benefits under Titles II, VIII and XVI in any case in which a beneficiary's funds are misused by an organizational payee or an individual payee representing 15 or more beneficiaries. Misuse is defined as any case in which a representative payee converts the benefits entrusted to his or her care for purposes other than the "use and benefit" of the beneficiary. [Soc. Sec. Act §205(j), §807(i), and §1631(a)(2)(E), as amended by P.L. 108-203, §101; Reg. §404.2041.] In expanding upon the meaning of "use and benefit," the Social Security Administration has stated that it considers "funds to have been used for the use and benefit of the beneficiary if they are used for the beneficiary's current care and maintenance. Any remaining funds should be conserved or invested for the beneficiary pursuant to §404.2045." [69 *Fed. Reg.* 60224, Oct. 7, 2004.]

CLAIMS FOR BENEFITS AND APPEALS

¶575   How and When to File Claims

Social Security benefits are generally paid only if applied for by the person entitled to receive them. Benefits are not paid automatically. The applicant must fill out an application and furnish proof of the statements as to age and certain other facts needed to establish the claim. Applications for retirement, disability, and spousal benefits also are available and may be filed online at the Social Security Administration's website, *http://www.socialsecurity.gov/ onlineservices/#apply* (scroll down to "Apply for benefits"). The online application site also lists what additional information, forms, and supporting documents will be required, depending upon what benefit is being claimed. Many of these forms are also available online. [Reg. §422.505.]

How to File

The Social Security Administration no longer requires a pen-and-ink signature on benefit applications. An application for benefits may be filed with the Social Security Administration online, as mentioned above, or on an official SSA form, obtained at a Social Security office or downloaded from the SSA's website, and signed or attested by the applicant or a proper person. The person claiming benefits must execute the application if he or she is at least 18 years old, mentally competent, and physically capable of executing the form. A claimant who is between 16 and 18 years old may sign or attest his or her own application unless he or she is mentally incompetent, has a court-appointed representative, or is in someone's care. In all other situations, an application may be filed on behalf of the claimant by a legal guardian or other legal representative or, in some cases, by the person (including appropriate personnel of an institution) responsible for the care of the claimant. [Reg. §404.612.]

Attestation: For claims filed at a Social Security office, the applicant must establish an intent to file a claim and also must be provided with the penalty clause that explains the consequence for providing false information to the agency. The Social Security Administration employee will ask the applicant to confirm the correctness of the application data and the applicant's intent to submit the application. The employee then will attest by annotating the applicant's affirmation in the electronic claim record. This annotation will document the affirmation and will be the equivalent of a pen-and-ink signature on a paper application. For applications submitted via the Internet, the individual will be asked to confirm that he or she is filing for benefits, the truthfulness of the information on his or her application, and agree to sign the electronic application by pressing a "sign now" button on the screen. The individual will also be required to verify his or her identity. [SSR 04-1p, May 4, 2004.]

Disability Claims: Because the conditions of entitlement to disability benefits are generally more complex than those applicable to benefits based on old age, dependency, or survivorship, applications for disability benefits take longer to process than other types of claims. The Social Security Administration advises that individuals can expedite their claims if they have the following in writing when they apply for disability benefits:

- The Social Security numbers of the disabled worker, his or her spouse, and dependents.

- The date the condition began.

- A concise statement of why the impairment(s) prevents him or her from working.

- The date he or she stopped working.

- Information concerning current job, if any, including the date of return to work and the name of the employer.

- A complete list of names, addresses (including zip codes), and phone numbers of all doctors, hospitals, or other medical facilities from which he or she received treatment or tests related to the disabling condition.

- Hospital, clinic, and/or Medicaid identification numbers.

- The claim number for any other disability benefits he or she has applied for or receives.

- A list of medicines now taken, including names and dosages.

- Any restrictions his or her doctor has placed on the disabled individual.

- Work history and daily activities.

Disability claimants must complete a Disability Report Form for Adults (SSA 3368) and an Authorization to Release Information form (SSA 827). The SSA will help claimants complete these forms which are also available online.

Even if a person files an application after he or she is no longer eligible for benefits, benefits may sometimes be paid. As discussed at ¶520.3, an application for disability benefits may be accepted up to 12 months after the disability has ceased. If a delay in filing an application is attributable to the applicant's physical or mental condition, an application will be accepted even if 36 months have elapsed between the time the disability ended and the time the application is filed, if the applicant is still alive. [Soc. Sec. Act §216(i)(2).]

When to File

Workers who are approaching retirement should contact their local SSA office in advance to discuss their options regarding the date of filing an application for old-age benefits, particularly if there is a likelihood that the applicant will continue to work and have earnings in excess of the amounts permitted under the retirement test (see ¶551) after he or she begins to draw old-age benefits. Note that individuals who are not working or who plan to stop working when they file for benefits are advised to contact their local SSA office or apply online one to three months before they expect to begin receiving benefits. Those who are unsure of their retirement plans, who are self-employed, or who intend to continue to work and earn more than the retirement test exempt amount for any month during the year in which they expect to file for old-age benefits should contact the SSA during the year before they would like to begin receiving benefits. Workers who plan to continue working beyond full retirement age should contact the SSA one to three months before reaching full retirement age to discuss applying for Medicare, assuming they have not already applied for Medicare or Social Security benefits. [SSA Program Circular No. 02-92-ORSI.]

Lump-sum benefits. A claim for the lump-sum death benefit generally must be filed within two years after the worker's death. [Soc. Sec. Act §202(i).]

Monthly benefits. An application for any monthly benefits filed *before* the first month in which the applicant satisfies the conditions of entitlement is deemed valid only if the conditions are satisfied before the administrative decision is issued. Benefits may be paid from the first month in which the conditions are satisfied. A new application is required if the conditions of entitlement are eventually satisfied after a claim has been denied. [Soc. Sec. Act §§202(j)(2), 223(b); Reg. §404.620.]

Protective filing: An individual who can demonstrate that failure to file or a delay in filing for Social Security benefits resulted from misinformation provided by the Social Security Administration will be deemed to have applied on either (1) the date the incorrect information was provided, or (2) the date the claimant met all the conditions of entitlement (other than the requirement of filing an application), whichever is later. [Soc. Sec. Act §202(j)(5).] If all of the requirements for a protective filing date for a benefit application are otherwise met, an applicant's initial contact with the SSA will be considered to be the filing date of the application. Thus, if an applicant contacts the SSA by telephone to inquire about filing an application for benefits and if a completed application is ultimately timely filed, the date of the initial telephone contact will be considered the date of the application.

The rule also applies to applications made via the Internet. Thus, the SSA will use as the protective filing date for such applications, the date it receives the Personal Identification Information (PIN) data on the Internet Social Security Benefit Application (ISBA), which is usually the date that the ISBA is started. [Regs. §404.630 and §404.633, 71 *Fed. Reg.* 24812, Apr. 27, 2006.]

If an individual who could have received benefits on the basis of a deemed filing date dies before the application is filed, the application may be filed by a person who would be qualified to receive any benefits due the deceased person. [Reg. §404.615(d).]

Retroactive Benefits

If all other conditions of entitlement are met for months prior to the month in which an application for benefits is filed, benefits may be paid retroactively for as many as six or 12 months, depending on the type of benefit. The retroactive period for benefits based on disability is generally 12 months, whereas the retroactive period is generally limited to six months for benefits unrelated to disability. This is so even where the claim is for benefits based on a child's or adult child's disability. This is because such claims are filed under the Child Insurance Benefit provisions of the Social Security Act. See ¶520.1 regarding disabled child's benefits. [Soc. Sec. Act §202(d) and (j).]

A claimant who files an application for disability benefits, widow(er)'s benefits based on disability, or wife's, husband's, or child's benefits on the account of an individual who is entitled to disability benefits may receive benefits for a retroactive period of up to 12 months immediately before the month in which the application is filed, if the claimant met the other conditions of entitlement throughout the period. Retroactive payments may not be made, however, to a wife or husband whose benefits are subject to actuarial reduction on account of age. [Soc. Sec. Act §202(j)(1)(A).]

A claimant who files an application for old-age, dependent's, or survivor's benefits on the earnings record of a disabled worker, as well as claimants who apply for mother's, father's, or parent's benefits, may receive benefits for as many as six months prior to the month in which the application is filed if all other conditions of entitlement were met throughout the retroactive period. [Soc. Sec. Act §202(j)(1)(B).]

If the payment of benefits for months prior to the month in which the application is filed would, because of the age of the applicant, cause an actuarial reduction in the monthly benefit amount, the applicant generally would not be entitled to benefits for prior months. [Soc. Sec. Act §202(j)(4)(A).]

There are two qualifications to the general ban on retroactive payments where an actuarial reduction would apply. Actuarial reduction of benefits will not preclude payment of: (1) retroactive benefits if the applicant is a disabled surviving spouse (or disabled surviving divorced spouse) who could be entitled to retroactive benefits for months before attainment of age 60, or (2) widow(er)'s benefits for the month in which the wage earner died if the application is filed in the following month. [Soc. Sec. Act §202(j)(4)(B)(i), (ii).]

Note that the SSA is required to reduce a retroactive monthly Social Security benefit under certain conditions if the individual received supplemental security income payments for the retroactive period. The amount of the reduction is equal to the amount of the SSI payment that would not have been paid had the monthly Social Security benefits been paid when they were regularly due, rather than retroactively. [Soc. Sec. Act §204(e); Reg. §§404.408b, 404.501, 404.902.]

Withdrawal of Application

Current rules limit the time period under which beneficiaries may withdraw an application for retirement benefits to within 12 months of the first month of entitlement and to one withdrawal per lifetime. [Regs. §404.313 and §404.640, 75 *Fed. Reg.* 76256, Dec. 8, 2010.]

¶576   Application Blanks

In filling out an application for benefits, the claimant should write or print clearly. If the claimant does not know the answer to a question, he or she should write in the word "unknown." If the claimant does not answer a question material to benefit entitlement, an award cannot be made. The application should be signed by the claimant, preferably in ink. If he or she cannot write, the name should be written in on the signature line and the claimant should make a mark. Signature by mark must be witnessed as indicated on the application form. [*Soc. Sec. Handbook,* Sept. 1, 2009, §1511.] Teleclaims and in-person claims can provide an alternative to the traditional pen-and-ink signature through electronic signatures and verbal affirmation, respectively [*Soc. Sec. Handbook,* April 12, 2010, §1500.2.]

¶577   Proofs Required

Each claimant must prove his or her identity and that he or she has met all the conditions of entitlement to the benefit claimed. For example, in connection with a claim for child's benefits, proof may be required of age, the parent-child relationship, dependency or support; and, in survivor claims, of the death of the worker. The district office will advise each claimant of what evidence should be submitted. [*Soc. Sec. Handbook,* March 2001 and later, §1700 *et seq.*] Information submitted in connection with a person's claim cannot be disclosed to any other person, except for very limited purposes. [Soc. Sec. Act §1106.]

¶578   How to File Proofs

Generally, a copy of the document or record, properly certified by the custodian, should be submitted as evidence. Documents in foreign languages may be acceptable and can be translated by government translators. Ordinarily, any documents submitted will be returned upon request. If a photocopy of a document is submitted as evidence, the original document also must be submitted to the Social Security Administration for comparison and return unless the photocopy has been certified by the official custodian of the original document to be an exact copy of the original. Statements submitted as evidence must be signed, but need not be notarized. [*Soc. Sec. Handbook,* Aug. 9, 2005, §1702.]

Any false statement made by a claimant in an attempt to obtain benefits to which the claimant or another person is not entitled is criminally punishable under the Social Security Act by a fine of up to $5,000, or imprisonment for up to five years, or both. [Soc. Sec. Act §208(a)(7), (8).] Penalties for false statements by individuals in positions of trust can be as high as $8,116, with imprisonment of up to 10 years. [Social Security Act §1129(a), as amended by the Social Security Benefit Protection and Opportunity Enhancement Act of 2015, H. 1314, November 2, 2015.] Other federal laws may provide more severe penalties. For further information regarding civil penalties under Soc. Sec. Act §1129 and §1129A, see ¶557.

Electronic Records Express

Electronic Records Express is an initiative by the SSA and state Disability Determination Services (DDS) to offer electronic options for submitting health and school records related to disability claims.

When a representative receives a request for health or school records or other information about a person who has applied for Social Security disability benefits, the representative can choose the method of sending the information that works best for him or her:

- Online to the SSA's secure website; or

- By fax to the state DDS or to the SSA.

The records one sends are automatically associated with the applicant's unique disability claim folder.

The website has restricted access. Only authorized users can access the secure website by using their assigned user ID and password.

To get started one must call the Social Security Electronic Records Express Help Desk at 1-866-691-3061 or send them an email at *electronic-records-express@ssa.gov* for additional information. [*http://www.ssa.gov/ere/.*]

¶579   Proof of Age

A claimant must file supporting evidence showing the date of birth if age is a condition of entitlement or is otherwise relevant to the payment of benefits. Generally, the highest probative value will be accorded a public record of birth or a church record of birth or baptism established or recorded before age five. When such preferred evidence is not available, other documents may be submitted, such as a school record, census record, Bible or other family record, church record of confirmation or baptism in youth or early adult life, insurance policy, marriage record, passport, employment record, military record, delayed birth certificate, birth certificate of a child of the applicant, labor union record, fraternal organization record, voting record, vaccination record, or a physician's or midwife's record of birth. For a foreign-born individual, the record of arrival or a naturalization record may be the earliest established available domestic record of the individual's date of birth. [Reg. §404.716.]

¶580   Proof of Death

Proof of the worker's death is required to be submitted with all claims for survivor's insurance benefits, or for a lump-sum death payment. The best evidence of a person's death is: (1) a certified copy or extract from the public record of death, coroner's report of death, or verdict of a coroner's jury; or a certificate by the custodian of the public record of death; (2) a statement of the funeral director, attending physician, or intern of the institution where death occurred; (3) a certified copy of, or extract from, an official report or finding of death made by an agency or department of the United States; or (4) if death occurred outside the United States, an official report of death by a United States Consul or other employee of the State Department; or a copy of the public record of death in the foreign country. [Reg. §404.720(b).]

If the claimant cannot obtain the preferred evidence of a person's death, he or she will be asked to explain why and to give other convincing evidence, such as the signed statements of two or more persons who have personal knowledge of the death, giving the place, date, and cause of death. [Reg. §404.720(c).]

An individual who has been unexplainably absent from his or her residence and unheard of for a period of seven years may be deemed by the SSA to have died. In the absence of evidence establishing a later date, the missing date is deemed the date of death for purposes of benefit payments. [Reg. §404.721.]

¶581   Proof of Marriage

Upon request, a person who applies for monthly benefits or the lump-sum death payment on the basis of a marriage relationship is required to submit supporting evidence of the marriage, the time and place of marriage, and the termination of any former marriage. This requirement is not limited to spouses. For example, a stepchild must furnish proof of the marriage of a natural parent to a stepparent. [Reg. §§404.723, 404.732.]

In determining the validity of an insured individual's marriage, the law of the state in which the insured had his or her permanent home when the claim was filed or, if earlier, when he or she died, will be applied. The evidence to be submitted in connection with such a determination depends upon whether the insured's marriage was a ceremonial marriage, a common-law marriage, or a "deemed valid" marriage. [Reg. §404.723.] See ¶230.1 and ¶529 for discussion of the treatment of same-sex spouses.

A valid ceremonial marriage is one that follows procedures set by law in the state or foreign country where it takes place. Preferred evidence of a ceremonial marriage includes signed statements from the applicant and the insured (if living) about when and where the marriage took place, a copy of the public record of marriage or a certified statement as to the marriage, a copy of the religious record of marriage or a certified statement as to what the record shows, or the original marriage certificate. [Reg. §404.725.]

In states that recognize common-law marriages, a valid marriage relationship may exist between two persons free to marry, who consider themselves married, live together as spouses, and, in some states, meet certain other requirements. Preferred evidence of a common-law marriage includes the signed statements of the husband and/or wife and those of two blood relatives, or the signed statements of one blood relative of each spouse, if both the husband and wife are dead. [Reg. §404.726.]

A "deemed valid marriage" is a ceremonial marriage that is considered valid for Social Security purposes even though the correct procedures set by state law were not strictly followed or a former marriage was not legally terminated. [Reg. §404.727.]

Evidence of the termination of a marriage may be required if the claimant's right to benefits depends on the validity of a subsequent marriage. A valid ceremonial or common-law marriage can end only by death, divorce, or annulment. The termination of a marriage may be established by a certified copy of the divorce decree, a certified copy of the annulment decree, or a certified copy of a death certificate (or other proof of death). If none of these is obtainable, any other evidence of probative value may be submitted. [Reg. §404.728.]

¶582   Parent-Child Relationship

Where the existence of a parent-child relationship affects eligibility for benefits, an applicant must file appropriate evidence of the relationship. [Reg. §404.730.]

Evidence of a natural parent-child relationship may include: (1) a copy of the insured's public or religious birth record made before age five, if the applicant is the insured's natural parent or natural child; (2) evidence of relevant marriage relationships, if needed to dispel any reasonable doubt about family ties; (3) evidence that the applicant would be able to inherit personal property from the insured under the laws of the state in which the insured had a permanent home; and (4) the insured's signed statement that the applicant is his or her natural child, or a copy of any court order showing the insured to be the applicant's natural parent or requiring the insured to contribute to the applicant's support because the applicant is the insured's son or daughter. [Reg. §404.731.]

Proof of adoption. Where parent-child relationships are created by adoption, the following evidence will be required: (1) a copy of the birth certificate made following the adoption, if available, or other evidence of the adoption and, if needed, evidence of the date of adoption; (2) if the widow or widower adopted the child after the death of the insured, the evidence described in the preceding paragraph; the applicant's written statement whether the insured was living in the same household with the child at the time of death; what support the child was receiving from any other person or organization; and, if the widow or widower had a deemed valid marriage with the insured, evidence of that marriage (see ¶581); and (3) if the applicant is the insured's stepchild, grandchild, or stepgrandchild as well as his or her adopted child, evidence of the applicant's relationship to the insured prior to the adoption may also be required. [Reg. §404.733.]

Equitable adoption. In states that recognize equitable adoption, the law will treat someone as the child of another if he or she agreed to adopt the child, the natural parents or guardian agreed, he or she and the child then lived together as parent and child, and certain other requirements of state law were met. An applicant who was equitably adopted will be asked for evidence of the adoption agreement and for written statements of the natural and adopting parents and other evidence of the applicant's relationship to the adopting parents. [Reg. §404.734.]

¶583   Proof of Dependency or Support

In the case of applications for child's benefits, evidence that the applicant was dependent on the insured (whether his or her parent, adopting parent, stepparent, grandparent or stepgrandparent) at a specific time—usually the time the application was filed or the time the insured died or became disabled—may be required. The evidence generally will consist of a signed statement by someone in a position to know sufficient facts confirming a dependency relationship, including when and where the parties lived together (or why they may have lived apart) and the nature and extent of contributions for support during the relevant periods of time. [Reg. §§404.736, 404.750.]

An application for parent's benefits will require proof that the applicant received at least one-half of his or her support from the insured during the one-year period before the insured died or became disabled (see ¶528). [Reg. §404.750.]

¶584   School Attendance

An applicant for child's benefits as a student may be asked to submit (a) a signed statement that he or she is attending school full-time and is not being paid by an employer to do so, and (b) if applying before the school year has started and the school is not a high school, a letter of acceptance from the school, a receipted bill, or other evidence showing that he or she has enrolled or has been accepted at the school (see ¶524) [Reg. 404.745.]

A claimant may not be considered in full-time school attendance for Social Security purposes while imprisoned for conviction of a felony. [Soc. Sec. Act §202(d)(7).]

¶584.5   Affidavits by SSA Personnel

Requests for testimony by an SSA employee must be sent to the SSA's Office of the General Counsel, Office of General Law, P.O. Box 17788, Baltimore, MD 21235-7788. The request should be marked "Attn: Touhy Officer." [Reg. §403.120.] Any request for testimony by an employee of the Office of the Inspector General should be sent to the address specified in Reg. §403.125.

¶586   Review and Appeal of Administrative Decisions

All claims and all questions relating to benefits are first acted upon by the Social Security Administration, which makes an initial determination (in the case of disability determinations, after a determination as to the disability by the appropriate state agency—see ¶520.4). In each case the persons concerned are notified in writing of the decision. [Reg. §§404.902–404.905.] If they are dissatisfied with the SSA's findings, they may pursue the following sequence: (1) reconsideration by the Social Security Administration, (2) hearing before an Administrative Law Judge or Hearing Examiner, (3) review by an Appeals Council established within the Social Security Administration at Washington, and (4) a civil suit in the federal courts. [Reg. §§404.907, 404.929, 404.967; Soc. Sec. Act §205(g).]

On December 18, 2019, the SSA published a final rule regarding setting the time, place, and manner of appearance for hearings at the ALJ level. The agency is retaining the existing option for a party to opt out of appearing via video teleconference (84 *Fed. Reg.* 69298).

Requests for reconsideration must be filed within 60 days after notice of the decision is received. [Soc. Sec. Act §205(b).]

SSR 19-3p explains the two options available to claimants appealing the SSA's determinations that they are not disabled based on medical factors (84 *Fed. Reg.* 40467, August 14, 2019).

On December 20, 2019, the SSA issued a proposed rule to clarify when and how Administrative Appeals Judges (AAJs) on the Appeals Council may hold hearings and issue decisions (84 *Fed. Reg.* 70080).

Service of process. Summonses and complaints in transcript litigation cases must be mailed directly to the Office of the General Counsel's office that is responsible for the processing and handling of litigation in the particular jurisdiction in which the complaint has been filed. A list of all regional chief counsel's offices, their addresses, and the courts for which they have jurisdiction was published in the October 28, 2019, *Federal Register* (84 *Fed. Reg.* 57799), and is available online at *http://www.gpoaccess.gov/fr/index.html*. A list of all hearing offices, by region is available at the website of the Office of Disability Adjudication and Review (ODAR) at *http://www.socialsecurity.gov/appeals/ho_locator.html.*

No telephonic request for review. SSA , because of security concerns, doe not allow for telephonic request for review of initial decisions.

Representatives and attorneys. Any person having dealings with the Social Security Administration may appoint someone to represent his or her interests. The representative must be designated in a signed statement that will be acknowledged by the representative, if the representative is not an attorney, and filed at an SSA office or with the Administrative Law Judge or the Appeals Council. Union officials, employers, or other qualified persons may act as representatives. A party appointing a representative may at any time revoke the appointment. [Soc. Sec. Act §206(a); Regs. §§404.1705, 404.1707.]

The Commissioner may refuse to recognize as a representative, or disqualify as a representative, an attorney who has been disbarred or suspended from any court or bar, or who has been disqualified from participating in or appearing before any federal program or agency. Due process (*i.e.,* notice and an opportunity for a hearing) would be required before taking such action. Also, if a representative has been disqualified or suspended as a result of collecting an unauthorized fee, full restitution is required before reinstatement can be considered. [Soc. Sec. Act §206(a)(1), as amended by P.L. 108-203, §205.]

The SSA is required to maintain up-to-date computerized records of the identities of legal representatives of all Social Security claimants. The law also requires that Social Security benefit denial notices include information on obtaining legal representation before the agency, including the availability of legal service organizations that provide assistance without charge. [Soc. Sec. Act §206.]

¶587   Attorneys' Fees

A "reasonable fee" to compensate an attorney for his or her services may be fixed by the Commissioner in any claim for benefits before the Commissioner in which the determination was favorable to the claimant. The amount of the fee that may be charged for representing a Social Security claimant must be approved independently by either the SSA or the court. [Soc. Sec. Act §206(a) and (b).]

Fees are generally charged on a contingency basis, but are subject to a limit of the lesser of 25% of back due benefits or $6,000 (subject to adjustments for inflation). Note that in *Lasley v. Commr.*, No. 14-3044, November 4,

2014, the 6th Circuit affirmed a district court's order awarding reduced attorney fees because the attorney failed to demonstrate that the 25% contingency fee agreed to by his client was reasonable and not a "windfall."

The law also allows for the payment of appellate attorneys' fees and for the direct payment of fees to non-attorney representatives.

Under the streamlined process, representatives must have a written agreement with the claimant that the representative will accept as a fee the lesser of 25% of past due benefits or a prescribed dollar amount that does not exceed an allowable maximum. Attorneys representing claimants may charge fees higher than the maximum amount, so long as the amount does not exceed 25% of the past-due benefits. However, the fee request is then subject to review by the Administrative Law Judge (ALJ) or other adjudicator who allowed the benefits claim. Under the streamlined process, the fee is not subject to review so long as there is a written fee agreement, as mentioned above, and the claimant or ALJ has not submitted to the Commissioner of Social Security within 15 days after receipt of the notice of a favorable determination on the benefit claim a request to reduce the fee.

Fee arrangements will not be approved if a claimant appoints more than one representative from the same firm and not all of the representatives sign the same contract, or if a claimant retains more than one representative from different firms. In addition, the arrangement will be rejected if the representative withdraws before the SSA makes a decision with respect to benefits or a federal court reverses the SSA's denial of benefits and awards [POMS GN 03940.001.]

Registration Requirement for Direct Payment of Fees

Attorneys and non-attorneys who represent claimants before the SSA must submit their Social Security Numbers (SSN) in order for the SSA to directly pay a fee or a portion of the fee to the representative from a claimant's past-due benefits. IRS regulations further require anyone engaged in a trade or business that pays in one year aggregated fees of $600 or more to a professional to file an information return with the IRS. [IRC §6041(a); 26 CFR 1.6041-1.] To meet this requirement, anyone who is appointed by a claimant to represent him or her before the SSA, who is otherwise eligible for direct fee payment, and an attorney for whom a federal court has approved a fee will be required to provide the SSA with his or her Social Security Number as a prerequisite for direct fee payment.

In the event the SSA makes a direct fee payment, it charges an assessment to cover administrative costs, which is deducted from the amount payable to a representative.

User Fees

In the event the SSA makes a direct fee payment, it will assess a charge to cover administrative costs. The service charge will be deducted from the amount payable to the representative. The representative cannot charge or collect the expense from the claimants.

Cap on service charge. The service charge is capped at the lower of either a flat dollar rate or 6.3% of the amount withheld for direct payment to attorneys. The flat dollar rate cap is adjusted periodically based on the cost-of-living. For direct payments made to representatives, the service charge is capped in 2020 at a flat dollar rate of $95. [84 *Fed. Reg.* 67987, Oct. 24, 2019.]

Attorney waiver of fee. In the event that the Social Security Administration directly pays a fee to an attorney and deducts the 6.3% user fee even though the attorney waived direct payment of the fee, the SSA will refund *to the client* the amount of the assessment. The attorney must contact the SSA about the erroneous payment. Also, the SSA must have received a waiver statement from the attorney prior to the date it received the fee petition, the date the SSA decision-maker approved the fee, or the date a court's order awarded fees. [SSA POMS §GN 03920.051 (TN 13 2/05).]

Direct Payment of Fees to Non-Attorney Representatives

The SSA authorizes the direct payment of fees to non-attorney representatives. [Social Security Disability Applicants' Access to Professional Representation Act of 2010 (P.L. 111-142).] Social Security Act §206(e), which was added by P.L. 111-142, sets forth prerequisites that non-attorney representatives must satisfy in order to receive direct payment of fees. Non-attorney representatives must possess a bachelor's degree or equivalent qualifications, pass a written examination administered by the Social Security Administration, secure professional liability insurance or the equivalent, undergo a criminal background check, and complete continuing education courses.

Application fee: Non-attorneys applying to be a non-attorney representative must pay a $1,000 application fee. Refunds will be made only if (1) the SSA fails to administer a scheduled examination and an applicant is unable to take a rescheduled examination, and (2) the SSA agrees that "circumstances beyond the applicant's control that could not have been reasonably anticipated and planned for prevented the applicant from taking a scheduled examination." The agency will not apply the fee to a future application. Additionally, the SSA will not apply "principles of fairness and sound management" to determine when to refund an application fee. Rather, it will "consider an applicant's individual circumstances." Applicants will have 10 days to correct problems in the application.

Ineligibility and protest procedures: The SSA may find a representative is ineligible to receive direct fee payment if he or she: (1) Provided false or misleading information about his or her bachelor's degree or equivalent qualifications; (2) would fail a criminal background check if conducted today; (3) has not provided sufficient proof of maintaining continuous liability insurance; or (4) has not completed or provided documentation of the required continuing education courses. Failure under the first two items will result in permanent ineligibility to receive a direct fee. Failure in the latter two items will result in a six-month suspension of eligibility. In all cases, a representative will have notice and opportunity to protest an adverse finding. The representative must submit his or her protest in writing, and all protests must be submitted within 10 calendar days from the date the representative receives notice of the action finding him or her ineligible. The SSA's action in response to a protest will be final and will not be subject to further review. [Regs. §404.903, §404.1717(d) and (e), §416.1403 and 416.1517(d) and (e).]

Licensed attorneys or suspended or disbarred attorneys may not become eligible as non-attorney representatives. [Amended Regs. §404.1711 and §416.1517.]

Electronic Appeal Requirements for Direct Pay Representatives

All claimants representatives who request direct fee payment of authorized fees from benefits awarded to a claimant must file certain appeals electronically via the Internet. The requirement had been limited to the filing of a request for reconsideration or for a hearing before an Administrative Law Judge (ALJ) for disability claims under Titles II or XVI of the Social Security Act that were denied for medical reasons. Subsequently, the SSA clarified that representatives also must electronically file the Disability Report-Appeal. Representatives must satisfy the electronic filing requirement by using the SSA's web portal at www.socialsecurity.gov. [77 *Fed Reg.* 13968, March 8, 2012.]

Representatives who fail to comply may be subject to sanctions by the SSA, but appeals not in compliance with the rule will not be rejected, delayed or differently processed. The obligation is imposed on both attorneys as well as on non-attorney representatives. The requirement, as set forth in Regs. §404.1713, §404.1740, §416.1513, and §416.1540, is open ended, in that a representative who requests direct fee payment is required to conduct business electronically, in the "manner" that the SSA "prescribes," without further specification. [77 *Fed. Reg.* 4653, Jan. 31, 2012].

To file an electronic appeal or request for hearing, a representative must access the appeals website at *https://secure.ssa.gov/apps6z/iAppeals/ap001.jsp.*

Fee Payment by Third Parties

Representatives may be paid fees by a third party, such as an insurance company, for representation of a claimant before the SSA without obtaining approval from the SSA for the fee that is charged. SSA approval is not required so long as the claimant is free from any liability for the fee and the representative waives the right to charge and collect one. The SSA's approval of the fee request also will not be necessary where a court has already authorized the fee in cases where legal guardians or court-appointed representatives provide representational services in claims before the agency.

Third parties include "any business, firm, or other association, including but not limited to partnerships, corporations, for-profit organizations, and not-for-profit organizations." Additionally, the SSA does not need to authorize a fee if "a federal, state, county, or city government agency uses its funds to pay the representative fees and expenses" and certain other criteria are met. [Regs. §404.1703, §404.1720, §416.1503, §416.1520.]

Equal Access to Justice Act

Reasonable attorneys' fees and/or expenses also may be awarded under the Equal Access to Justice Act (EAJA) to parties that successfully challenge an administrative denial of benefits in federal court, unless the position of the government was "substantially justified" throughout the proceeding, or special circumstances render an award unjust. The court will set the amount of expenses to be reimbursed to the claimant and will order the SSA to pay such amount to the claimant. The EAJA was intended to reduce any deterrent to litigation caused by the disparity of resources and expertise between individual parties and their government. [5 U.S.C. §504; 28 U.S.C. §2412.]

"Substantially justified" government position. The government has the burden of establishing that its position was substantially justified. The Ninth Circuit has further explained that, in determining substantial justification, the government position in the litigation *and* in the underling agency action must be considered. Thus, where the ALJ's decision in an underlying action was not supported by substantial evidence, the position of the government was not substantially justified for EAJA fee purposes. The government, the court stressed, must establish that both the underlying position and the litigation position were substantially justified in order to avoid an EAJA fee award [*Meier v. Colvin*, No. 11-35736 (9th Cir. 2013)].

Maximum fee. The maximum fee under the EAJA is $125 per hour. The Act does not authorize fee awards at market rate. However, fees may be increased above the statutory maximum if warranted by a rise in the cost-of-living or other special factors, and a claimant would be denied legal representation without such an adjustment [*Mathews-Sheet v. Astrue*, 653 F. 3d 560 (7th Cir. 2011.]

File petition for fees within 30 days. Petitions for fees under the EAJA must be submitted within 30 days of a final favorable judgment. However, only a final judgment by a court of law will trigger the 30-day period for filing an EAJA petition. The 30-day period begins to run after expiration of the 60-day period in which the judgment may be appealed. [*Melkonyan v. Heckler*, 111 SCt 2157 (1991.] Note that the U.S. Supreme Court has held that if the EAJA fee petition fails to allege a lack of substantial justification, it may be amended after the 30-day period has run in order to cure the defect, so long as the original petition was otherwise timely filed. [*Scarborough v. Principi*, 124 SCt 1856 (2004).]

Concurrent awards under the SSA and EAJA: Fees awarded under Social Security Act §406(a) for work performed at the administrative level are not subject to offset when the claimant also receives an award under the EAJA since the latter pays only for work performed at the judicial level [*Kellems v. Astrue*, 628 F3d 215 (5th Cir. 2010).]

¶588 Recognition, Disqualification, and Reinstatement of Representatives

The Social Security Act, in Section 206(a), provides that attorneys and non-attorneys may represent claimants. The Social Security Administration, after notice and opportunity to be heard, may refuse to recognize as a representative, or may disqualify a representative who is already recognized, any attorney who has been disbarred or suspended from practice by any court, bar or federal program or agency. Additionally, the SSA also may take the same action with respect to non-attorney representatives who are attorneys that were disbarred or suspended from any court or bar to which they were previously admitted to practice. The Social Security Act also bars the reinstatement of any representative who was disqualified or suspended from appearing before the SSA as a result of collecting or receiving an excess fee until full restitution is made to the claimant, and then only under such rules as the SSA may impose. [Soc. Sec. Act §206(a).] The SSA has clarified existing policy that it may refuse to recognize an individual as a representative if he or she does not meet agency requirements. If the SSA decides not to recognize an individual as a representative, it will notify the claimant as well as the individual the claimant chose to provide representation of its decision [Reg. §404.1705(c); §416.1505].

The basis upon which the SSA may file charges against a representative or an individual applying to become a representative now includes: disbarment or suspension from any court or bar to which he or she was previously admitted to practice, or disqualification from participating in or appearing before any federal program. [Reg. §404.1745.]

Note that the basis upon which the SSA may file charges against a nonattorney includes removal from practice or suspension by a professional licensing authority for reasons that reflect on the individual's character, integrity, judgment, reliability, or fitness to serve as a fiduciary.

Disqualification is the sole sanction available if the charges against a representative are sustained because the representative has been, by reasons of misconduct, disbarred or suspended from any court or bar to which he or she was previously admitted to practice or disqualified from participating in or appearing before any federal program or agency. It is also the sole sanction in situations where the representative has collected or received, and retains, a fee for services in excess of the amount authorized. [Reg. §404.1770.] This is intended to ensure that such a representative is barred from appearing before the SSA until full restitution has been made.

Note that "administrative disbarments" will not trigger disqualification. The regulatory amendments narrow the circumstances under which the SSA will disqualify a representative of those disbarments, suspensions or disqualifications that were based on misconduct. Thus, if the sanction was taken for reasons unrelated to misconduct, such as for failure to pay dues or complete continuing legal education requirements, the SSA will not disqualify the individual from acting as a representative. Although the agency will look to the reasons for disciplinary sanction, it will not reexamine or revise the factual or legal conclusions that led to the disbarment, suspension or disqualification. [Reg. §404.1770.]

Charges and Hearing

The General Counsel, or his or her designee, is the official who decides whether or not to initiate a representative sanction proceeding and is also the official who may withdraw charges against a representative. Representatives must file their answer to a notice of charges at the address specified in the notice within 14 days from the date of the notice or from the date it was personally delivered. The General Counsel or his or her designee may extend the 14-day period for good cause. A representative who does not timely file an answer will forfeit the right to present evidence on his or her behalf. If the General Counsel does not withdraw the charges within 15 days after an answer is filed, a hearing will be held for which notice will be given at least 14 days prior to the hearing date. Subpoenas may be issued, witnesses may be called, and the representative may be represented by counsel. [Regs. §404.1750, §404.1755, §404.1765, §416.1550, §416.1555, and §416.1565.]

¶588

If the hearing officer sustains the charges, he or she will either suspend the representative from practice before the SSA from one to five years or disqualify the representative from acting as a representative before the SSA until reinstated [Reg. §404.1770; 416.1570]. Either party may ask the Appeals Council, in writing, to review the decision within 14 days after the hearing officer mailed the decision. [Reg. Sec. 404.1775.]

The Appeals Council may affirm, reverse, or modify the hearing officer's decision [Regs. §404.1790; §416.1590].

Refusing to recognize, disqualifying or suspending a person from acting as a representative is not an "initial determination" for purposes of the Social Security Act and is therefore not subject to judicial review [Regs. §404.903; §1403].

Reinstatement

A suspended representative is automatically reinstated at the end of the period of suspension. [Regs. §404.1797 and §416.1597.] However, if an individual has been disqualified, reinstatement can occur only if the individual asks the Appeals Council of the Office of Hearings and Appeals for permission to serve as a representative again and the Appeals Council decides that it is reasonable to expect that the individual will, in the future, act in accordance with the provisions of §206(a) of the Act and the SSA's rules and regulations. [Regs. §404.1797 and §416.1597.]

If the representative has been disqualified because he or she was disbarred or suspended from a court or bar, the Appeals Council will grant reinstatement to the individual as a representative only if the individual not only satisfies the Council with respect to the required expectation of future behavior, but also shows that he or she has been admitted (or readmitted) to and is in good standing with the court or bar from which he or she had been disbarred or suspended. The rules are similar for the reinstatement of a representative who has been disqualified because he or she was disqualified from participating in or appearing before any federal program or agency. This rule provides that such an individual must not only satisfy the Appeals Council with respect to the required expectation of future behavior, but also show that he or she is once again qualified to participate in or appear before that federal program or agency. [Regs. §404.1799 and §416.1599.]

Table of Cases

References are to paragraph (¶) numbers

Topical Index

References are to paragraph (¶) numbers.

Deposit of taxes ... 223.1, 223.2

Determinations and appeals ... 575- 586

Differential pay ... 316

Direct deposit ... 570

Direct sellers ... 401.5

Directors of corporations ... 302.2, 401.2

Disability
. after entitlement to other benefits ... 520.2, 520.8
. applications ... 520.2, 520.3, 576
. blindness ... 505.5, 520.1
. children... 520.1
. chronic fatigue syndrome...520.1
. Compassionate Allowances...520.4
. defined ... 520.1
. degree of severity necessary to qualify ... 520.1
. determination by state agencies ... 520.4
. evaluation process ... 520.1
. evidence ... 520.1
. fibromyalgia...520.1
. freeze ... 520.3
. generally ... 520
. insured-status requirement ... 502, 505.5
. intellectual disability ... 520.1
. mental disorders...520.1
. obesity...........................520.1
. offset ... 520.9
. pay as wages ... 211, 212
. payments after ... 222.1
. period of, defined ... 520.3
. periodic review ... 520.5
. primary insurance amount ... 511
. psychiatric review technique...520.1
. reductions in benefits ... 520.8, 520.9
. residual functional capacity........520.1
. rehabilitation ... 520.6
. retroactive applications ... 520.2
. substantial gainful activity ... 520.1
. surviving divorced spouses ... 525.2
. suspension of benefits ... 520.7
. Ticket to Work ... 520.6
. trial-work periods ... 520.6
. visual disorders.......520.1
. waiting period ... 520.2, 525.2
. widow(er)'s ... 525

Disability Redesign Prototype ... 520.4

Disaster relief payments ... 211.1

Discounts on purchases ... 218

Dismissal pay ... 220

Disregarded entities ... 227.2

District of Columbia ... 305, 314.1

Dividends ... 410

Divorced mother's or father's benefits ... 502, 527, 527.1

Divorced spouse's benefits ... 502, 522.5, 525.1

Doctors, coverage of ... 401.3

Domestic service
. coverage of ... 209.2, 307, 309, 310
. defined ... 309
. family employment ... 310
. farm ... 307, 309
. tax returns ... 223.3
. withholding of tax ... 204

Drivers, agent or commission ... 303, 303.1

Drug addiction and alcoholism
. representative payees ... 571
. treatment as condition for entitlement ... 520.1, 520.7

Due dates
. deposits ... 223.1
. domestic workers, returns for ... 223.3
. employees' receipts ... 205
. employer returns ... 223, 223.2, 223.3
. self-employment taxes ... 224

Duration-of-relationship ... 522- 525

E

Early retirement ... 535.2

Earnings
. amount subject to tax ... 508
. annual report...............552
. Average Indexed Monthly Earnings Computation...............510
. averaging earnings ... 507, 509, 510
. creditable earnings ... 508
. earnings after age 62 ... 508.1
. excess earnings ... 551
. exempt from retirement test....551
. indexed earnings ... 510
. maximum taxable earnings ... 510
. nonexempt from retirement test...5551
. statement of earnings (earnings record) ... 585

Educational assistance ... 216.2

Educational institution ... 321.3, 524

Elapsed years ... 507.3

Election of coverage
. clergymen ... 401.1
. foreign subsidiaries of domestic corporations ... 321.1
. generally ... 321
. ministers ... 321.3, 401.1
. nonprofit organizations ... 321.3
. policemen and firemen ... 321.2
. state and local governments ... 321.2
. U.S. citizens working abroad ... 321.1

Election workers ... 321.2

Electronic filing and payment ... 104, 205, 223, 223.1

Eligibility for benefits ... 504, et seq.